Less managing. More teaching. Greater learning.

INSTRUCTORS...

Would you like your **students** to show up for class **more prepared**?
(Let's face it, class is much more fun if everyone is engaged and prepared...)

Want an **easy way to assign** homework online and track student **progress**?
(Less time grading means more time teaching...)

Want an **instant view** of student or class performance?
(No more wondering if students understand...)

Need to **collect data and generate reports** required for administration or accreditation?
(Say goodbye to manually tracking student learning outcomes...)

Want to **record and post your lectures** for students to view online?
(The more students can see, hear, and experience class resources, the better they learn...)

With **McGraw-Hill's** *Connect,*™

INSTRUCTORS GET:

- Simple **assignment management**, allowing you to spend more time teaching.
- **Auto-graded** assignments, quizzes, and tests.
- **Detailed visual reporting** where student and section results can be viewed and analyzed.
- Sophisticated **online testing** capability.
- A **filtering and reporting** function that allows you to easily assign and report on materials that are correlated to learning objectives and Bloom's taxonomy.
- An easy-to-use **lecture capture** tool.
- The option to **upload course documents** for student access.

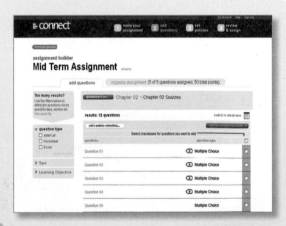

Get more from
The Core.

the core

MARKETING

THIRD CANADIAN EDITION

ROGER A. KERIN
Southern Methodist University

STEVEN W. HARTLEY
University of Denver

WILLIAM RUDELIUS
University of Minnesota

CHRISTINA CLEMENTS
Humber College Institute of Technology & Advanced Learning

HARVEY SKOLNICK
Sheridan Institute of Technology and Advanced Learning

McGraw-Hill Ryerson

Connect. Learn. Succeed.

Marketing: The Core
Third Canadian Edition

ISBN-13: 978-0-07-038565-8
ISBN-10: 0-07-038565-3

1 2 3 4 5 6 7 8 9 10 TCP 1 9 8 7 6 5 4 3 2

Printed and bound in Canada.

Care has been taken to trace ownership of copyright material contained in this text; however, the publisher will welcome any information that enables them to rectify any reference or credit for subsequent editions.

Publisher: Leanna MacLean
Executive Marketing Manager: Joy Armitage Taylor
Senior Developmental Editor: Jennifer Cressman
Senior Editorial Associate: Stephanie Giles
Editorial Associate: Erin Catto
Supervising Editor: Jessica Barnoski and Stephanie Gay
Photo/Permissions Research: Tracy Leonard
Copy Editor: Michael Kelly
Production Coordinator: Lena Keating
Cover Design: Valid Design and Layout/Dave Murphy and Valerie Bateman
Cover Image: Used by permission of Suunto Canada
Interior Design: Valid Design and Layout/Dave Murphy
Page Layout: Valid Design and Layout/Dave Murphy
Printer: Transcontinental Printing Group

Library and Archives Canada Cataloguing in Publication

Marketing : the core / Roger A. Kerin ... [et al.]. — 3rd Canadian ed.

Includes bibliographical references and index.
ISBN 978-0-07-038565-8

1. Marketing—Textbooks. I. Kerin, Roger A.

HF5415.M374 2012   658.8   C2011-907228-9

Author Profiles

Roger A. Kerin is the Harold C. Simmons Distinguished Professor of Marketing at the Edwin L. Cox School of Business, Southern Methodist University in Dallas, Texas. Professor Kerin holds a B.A. (magna cum laude), M.B.A., and Ph.D. from the University of Minnesota. His teaching and research interests lie in marketing planning and strategy, product management, financial aspects of marketing, and marketing research. Professor Kerin is a frequent participant in executive development programs and is also an active consultant on matters of marketing planning and strategy. Professor Kerin has published and authored several texts and many articles on marketing. He also serves on numerous journal editorial review boards and is currently a member of the Board of Governors of the Academy of Marketing Science.

Steven W. Hartley is Professor of Marketing in the Daniels College of Business at the University of Denver. He holds Bachelor of Mechanical Engineering, M.B.A., and Ph.D. degrees from the University of Minnesota. Dr. Hartley was formerly the chair of the Department of Marketing at the University of Denver, and has taught at the University of Colorado, the University of Minnesota, and in several executive development programs. His teaching interests include principles of marketing, marketing research, and marketing planning. Dr. Hartley's research has appeared in many leading marketing publications. He is an active consultant to several prominent U.S. corporations and is active in many professional organizations including the American Marketing Association, the Academy of Marketing Science, and the Marketing Educators' Association.

William Rudelius holds the Endowed Chair in Global Marketing at the Graduate School of Business of the University of St. Thomas in Minnesota. He holds a B.S. degree in Mechanical Engineering from the University of Wisconsin and an M.B.A. in Marketing and Ph.D. in Applied Economics from the Wharton School of the University of Pennsylvania. Professor Rudelius has co-authored other marketing textbooks. His articles have appeared in leading academic journals. During the past ten years, he has taught extensively in Europe; he serves on the board of directors for several business and not-for-profit organizations.

Christina Clements is an award-winning professor from the Business School at Humber College Institute of Technology & Advanced Learning in Ontario. She is renowned for the creativity and knowledge she brings to the field of marketing education. She is a recipient of the Leadership in Faculty Teaching Award, honouring Ontario's best university and college faculty, from the Ministry of Training, Colleges and Universities, and the Distinguished Faculty award from the Humber Institute of Technology & Advanced Learning. She holds an M.B.A. from the Bradford University Management Centre in the U.K. and recently completed a Master Certificate in Internet Marketing from the University of San Francisco. She has a wealth of experience in marketing and advertising from both client and agency perspectives. Her experience spans two continents and covers a variety of industries including consumer packaged goods, cosmetics, food service, and personal care. She now channels her practical experience, knowledge, and creativity into the field of education, by teaching, managing social media sites, and developing written materials, online resources, and educational tools that bring the subject of marketing alive. Her passion lies in teaching marketing communication and Internet marketing courses. She is frequently called upon to mentor others in the field of education.

Harvey Skolnick is a marketing professor in the School of Business at the Sheridan Institute of Technology and Advanced Learning. He is the author of many articles that have appeared in *Marketing* magazine and other business publications. He holds an M.B.A. from the University of Toronto, specializing in marketing, and a B.Sc. from McGill University, specializing in psychology. Professor Skolnick's teaching interests include principles of marketing, consumer behaviour, integrated marketing communications, and marketing management. He has also previously taught at York University and the University of Toronto.

Brief Contents

Contents

Preface

Welcome to the exciting, dynamic, and challenging field of marketing! Each day brings new products, services, technologies, and ideas to the marketplace. You've probably observed the growing interest in social networking, environmental sustainability, mobile technologies, YouTube, iPhones, blogs, interactive advertising, social responsibility, and many other new aspects of business. Tomorrow will most certainly add to the list!

Our popular magazine-style format returns in the third Canadian edition of *Marketing: The Core* and continues to engage students with its visual appeal and direct writing style. It weaves together current marketing approaches and active-learning techniques to challenge students to learn and enjoy learning about marketing. We incorporate many current examples using products and services that students will recognize and may have purchased as consumers. Our in-chapter study aids and design elements—such as **Ask Yourself** concept checks and easy-to-read figures—were developed to match the learning styles of today's students.

Text Organization and Content

Marketing: The Core, Third Canadian Edition, is divided into four parts. Part 1, "Understanding Marketing," looks first at what marketing is and how it creates customer value and customer relationships (Chapter 1). Chapter 2 analyzes the major environmental factors in our changing marketing environment.

Part 2, "Understanding Markets and Their Behaviour," first describes, in Chapter 3, how individual consumers reach buying decisions. Chapter 4 examines the marketing research function and how information about prospective consumers is linked to marketing strategy and decisions. Chapter 5 looks at industrial and organizational buyers and how they make

purchase decisions. The process of segmenting and targeting markets and positioning products appears in Chapter 6.

Part 3, "Designing Marketing Strategies and Marketing Mix Elements," covers the four Ps of marketing: product, price, placement, and promotion. The product element is divided into two chapters. Chapter 7 looks at the way existing products, services, and brands are managed. Chapter 8 discusses the development of new products and the product life cycle. Pricing is discussed, focusing on the way organizations set prices (Chapter 9). Two chapters address the place aspects of marketing: "Distribution and Supply Chain" (Chapter 10) and "Retailing and Wholesaling" (Chapter 11). Chapter 12 discusses marketing communications from an online and offline perspective, including integrated approaches. Chapter 13, "Customer Relationship Management," examines the three stages of CRM: customer acquisition, customer retention, and customer reacquisition.

Part 4, "Putting It All Together," provides an overview of the strategic marketing process that occurs in an organization.

Finally, Appendix A in the **connect** Library provides a guide to preparing a marketing plan.

New to the Third Canadian Edition

This fresh new edition of *Marketing: The Core* builds on the strengths of the previous edition, and adds new and exciting features that make the material even more interactive and engaging. The authors have gone to extreme lengths to include fresh, current Canadian content that reflects reality—no easy feat in an environment where technological changes quickly render products and marketing approaches obsolete! The authors also turned to the teaching environment to capture approaches within the book that help students learn and help faculty teach. The freshness of the third Canadian edition is reflected as follows:

- **New Critical Thinking and Problem Solving Features:** New to the third Canadian edition are **Reality Check** and **Hands on...Apply Your Knowledge** sections, designed to enhance critical thinking and problem solving. At the end of each opening vignette, Reality Check questions ask students to think about marketing concepts in relation to the vignette as they read the chapter that follows. Later in the chapter, students are reminded to revisit the Reality Check questions and answer them by applying the knowledge they gained from reading the chapter. At the end of each chapter, a Hands On...Apply Your Knowledge activity directs students back to the opening vignette with a practical marketing scenario that needs to be assessed and solved.

    Other new critical thinking features include discussion questions at the end of each **Marketing NewsFlash** and **Focus on Ethics** box. These questions encourage students to apply marketing concepts and critically assess marketing situations.

    These new critical thinking and problem solving features are designed for lively in-class discussions or as practical assignments for the home or classroom setting.

- **New Videos:** A series of 14 videos (11 of them new for this edition) has been carefully selected to enhance the teaching and learning of marketing concepts. Each video relates to a particular chapter and is accompanied by a written case and relevant questions and worksheets. Videos focus on marketing programs from brands such as Baskin–Robbins Canada, Pizza Hut, Prince Sports, Advertising Week Canada, YAK Communications, and Tourism Queensland, just to name a few.

- **New Content:** The third Canadian edition has been fully revised to reflect the digital reality that permeates marketing in Canada—no quick update here. Current online and offline examples are used in every chapter in order to reflect a marketing reality that increasingly uses the online environment to reach its market. This approach is reflected in new examples and new sections within the chapters.

    A bold new marketing communications chapter (Chapter 12) has evolved to fully integrate content on this topic. It reflects the new marketing reality where online communications are often front and centre in communication programs. This new chapter replaces two chapters on this topic from the previous edition, adding in new online marketing communications content and integrated approaches. This avoids repetition and accurately reflects the industry as it stands today.

Chapter-Specific Content Changes

In addition to new opening vignettes, Marketing NewsFlashes, Focus on Ethics boxes, data boxes, and digital content that appear in each chapter, the following new content is included:

Chapter 1: Marketing Fundamentals

- Digital marketing
- Partnership marketing
- Metrics
- Social media
- Strategic alliances

Chapter 2: The Marketing Environment

- Aging international markets
- Canadian media usage trends
- Contest regulations
- Consumers' use of technology
- Generation Z
- Privacy issues
- Spam issues
- Expanded content on:
    - Advertising Standards Canada regulations
    - CRTC regulations
    - Canadian Marketing Association regulations
    - Competition Bureau regulations

Chapter 3: Consumer Behaviour

- Effects of technology on purchase behaviour
- Expanded content on:
    - Evaluation of alternatives: assessing value
    - Post-purchase behaviour: value in consumption or use
    - Limited problem solving
    - Attitude change

Chapter 4: Market Research

- Advantages and disadvantages of survey techniques
- Clarification of exploratory research
- Online research studies
- Omnibus surveys
- Online secondary data sources
- Online research bulletin boards
- Online research communities
- Privacy issues
- Simulated test markets
- Social listening
- Survey panels
- Syndicated studies

Chapter 5: B2B Marketing

- The role of fear in B2B buyer behaviour
- B2B market segmentation
- Expanded content on:
  - People in the buying centre
  - E-marketplaces: virtual organizational markets

Chapter 6: Segmentation, Targeting, and Positioning

- Product positioning factors
- Revised section on the steps in market segmentation

Chapter 7: Products and Brands

- Brand extensions
- Global brands
- Labelling
- Perishability
- Virtual services

Chapter 8: New Product Development

- Greenwashing
- Line extensions

Chapter 9: Pricing

- Expanded content on:
  - Market share
  - Competitors' prices
  - One-price policy
  - Loss leader pricing
  - Price fixing
  - Deceptive pricing

Chapter 10: Distribution and Supply Chain

- Factors affecting channel choice
- Key logistics functions in a supply chain
- Cross-channel shoppers
- Expanded content on conflict in marketing channels

Chapter 11: Retailing and Wholesaling

- Target market selection and positioning
- Planograms
- Store atmosphere
- Retailer usage of the mobile channel
- Expanded content on online retailing
- Revised section on retailing mix

Chapter 12: Marketing Communications

This chapter streamlines chapters 12 and 13 from the previous edition and adds fresh new content to accurately reflect the marketing communication industry today. Offline and online approaches are reviewed, and the following new areas have been added:

- Advergaming
- Affiliate marketing
- Augmented reality
- Branded entertainment
- Consumers, the media and technology
- Customer advocacy funnel
- Earned media, owned media, and paid media

- E-mail marketing
- Marketing communication agencies, associations, and research companies
- Mobile marketing
- Online display advertising
- Online video advertising
- Outbound and inbound marketing communications
- Product placement
- Regulations
- Retargeted ads
- Search advertising
- Search engine marketing
- Search engine optimization
- Social media
- Social media releases
- Social network marketing
- User-generated content
- Webisodes
- Word-of-mouth marketing

Chapter 13: Customer Relationship Management

- Customer experience management (CEM)
- Social media and CRM
- Airlines and social media
- Credibility issues of social media

Chapter 14: Marketing and Strategic Planning

This chapter on strategic marketing planning has been placed at the end of the text so that students can gain a greater understanding of marketing before embarking on this more complex topic. The following new content has been included:

- Dashboards and metrics
- Tracking strategic performance with marketing dashboards
- Planning, implementation, and evaluation phases of the marketing plan
- Expanded content on market-product analysis

A Student's Guide to *Marketing: The Core*

Marketing: The Core offers an array of features to help you learn and apply marketing concepts.

Each chapter opens with a **vignette** on a Canadian marketing situation or program. No revamp of an article here—only current facts, real approaches, and tangible examples from one-on-one interviews with marketers in Canada. Clear and precise **Learning Objectives** help students preview chapter content and study effectively. New **Reality Check questions** appear at the end of each vignette.

chapter 7

Products *and* Brands

Meeting customer needs is central to successfully marketing a product, whether it is a good, a service, or an idea. In this chapter we explore products and brands more thoroughly to understand how they are marketed. Creating a strong brand is no easy task, and marketers work to build brand images that are meaningful and real. Peter Furnish, director of retail experience at Virgin Mobile, takes us inside Virgin Mobile to explain how this brand, launched

in Canada as recently as 2005, is now touted as one of Canada's "Superbrands." "Virgin Mobile is a cheeky, youthful brand that is different, fun, and exciting. We're lucky to have Sir Richard Branson, a flamboyant personification of the brand, to flaunt Virgin Mobile and draw attention to the brand," states Furnish, who goes on to explain how Virgin Mobile in Canada has evolved from a virtual unknown to now being highly recognized as a fun, irreverent, and trusted brand champion. Let's look at how this brand evolved.

Launch year. In 2005 Virgin Mobile launched with a publicity stunt designed to get attention. Rebel billionaire Sir Richard Branson zip-lined into Dundas Square in Toronto; crushed three cars—inscribed with "High Rates," "Completely Confusing Mobile Service Contract," and "Hidden Fees"—with a monster Virgin Mobile truck; and freed three female models from the shackles of long-term contracts. The publicity stunt worked; Virgin Mobile

was portrayed in the media as the new and cheeky cellphone carrier with attitude! Despite the fun stunts, Furnish points out there are important core values that permeate Virgin businesses. Although these businesses may seem diverse, they are joined by these shared values. In Canada, Virgin lends its name to Virgin Mobile, Virgin Radio, Virgin Games (online gaming), and Virgin Money (credit cards). These core brand values are as follows:

- **Fun:** a youthful, energetic, and positive brand that people enjoy
- **Innovative:** a brand willing to incorporate proven changes that consumers embrace
- **High quality:** a brand associated with high quality, which is the entry price in the wireless category
- **Good value:** a brand that provides good value but is never positioned as the cheapest
- **Champion of customer service:** a brand that excels in customer service
- **Consumer advocate:** a brand that challenges big business practices for consumers

Launch year focused on communicating these core values and establishing strong retail distribution. Virgin Mobile was launched as the irreverent brand with no contracts, no hidden fees, and no complicated plans. It opened four Virgin Mobile stores and its salespeople, Mobile Mavericks, obtained distribution at over 1,500 Future Shop, Best Buy, Walmart, and Tbooth stores. Customer service was front and centre of empowered employees who quickly solved [...] including the CEO, work

As you read Chapter 7, refer back to this Virgin Mobile vignette to answer the following questions:

- What type of brand is Virgin Mobile: a manufacturer's brand, a private label brand, or a generic brand?

- Review the elements of a good brand name and discuss the strength of the Virgin Mobile brand name in the cellphone category.

- How does the Virgin Mobile brand distinguish itself from competitors in the cellphone category?

L1 Distinguish between goods and services

L2 Describe and apply the total product concept

L3 Differentiate between products, product lines, and product mixes

L4 Identify the ways consumer and business goods and services are classified

L5 Explain the elements of branding and how these can be protected

L6 Distinguish between the different types of brands that exist in the market

L7 Apply product and brand knowledge to ongoing marketing strategies

Real metrics are used to emphasize points within the text through stand-alone Marketing Meters and data boxes that bring attention to the importance of metrics in marketing. **Data boxes** present tangible facts and numerical examples of elements discussed in the text, and serve as important examples of how metrics are used by the industry. **Marketing Meters** highlight unique and relevant, facts that are often surprising and interesting.

Top Ten Global Brands

Ranking	Brand	Value ($ millions)
1	Coca-Cola	70,452
2	IBM	64,727
3	Microsoft	60,895
4	Google	43,557
5	GE	42,808
6	McDonald's	33,578
7	Intel	32,015
8	Nokia	29,495
9	Disney	28,731
10	Hewlett-Packard	26,867

Source: "Best Global Brands 2010," Interbrand, accessed January 2011, at www.interbrand.com/en/best-global-brands/Best-Global-Brands-2010.aspx.

The Popularity of Private Label Brands

Canadian grocery shoppers who purchase private label brands such as President's Choice **80%**

Frequent private label buyers who say that the products are comparable, or better, in quality than national brand names **48%**

Private label buyers for whom the most popular category of food is canned **71%**

marketing meter

Source: "Private label brands transforming how Canadians shop," CNW Group, accessed at www.newswire.ca/en/releases/archive/July2010/07/c2795.html.

Marketing Tips showcase valuable thoughts from real-world marketers that are relevant to the topics discussed in each vignette.

Marketing ▶ tip

"The consumer of today has more choices than ever before. Retailer customers have a bigger say in what products get sold. The regulatory environment is also more complicated than ever. Great marketing plans give deep consideration to these external environments."

Andrew Pollock, senior VP marketing, Canada Bread

Marketing NewsFlashes provide exciting, current examples of marketing in action, making the material relevant and memorable. **Focus on Ethics** boxes focus on current topics of ethical and social concern. New for the third Canadian edition, discussion questions at the end of each box encourage students to apply marketing concepts and critically assess marketing situations.

focus on *Ethics* — The Power of Word of Mouth

One of the most powerful forms of marketing is the result of one of the most natural activities: talking. Word-of-mouth marketing is an extraordinary tool for marketers to use as they spread their brands, as it is the most effective form of marketing available—and the simplest. The Word of Mouth Marketing Association (WOMMA) is the official trade association for word-of-mouth marketers and is a coalition comprised of top marketers who are interested in learning how to encourage and utilize word of mouth while respecting and protecting its integrity.

WOMMA aids its members with the implementation of word of mouth using training, best practices, standards and metrics, and mainstreaming. WOMMA provides outreach and education, aids marketers in creating sustainable word-of-mouth programs, creates accountability for practices, and works at bringing word of mouth into the centre of the marketing world. WOMMA's mission is to improve word-of-mouth marketing by "Promoting 'best practices' to ensure more effective marketing; protecting consumers and the industry with strong ethical guidelines; evangelizing word of mouth as an effective marketing tool; and setting standards to encourage its use."

Recently, WOMMA developed a code of ethics for word-of-mouth marketing. These guidelines are meant to protect the consumer during the use of and participation in word-of-mouth marketing. The code focuses on openness between consumers, advocates, and marketers; advocates are encouraged to be open with consumers about their relationship with the marketers. Advocates are also encouraged to be honest with their opinions about the products that they are marketing and to disclose their identity to the consumers. WOMMA created the code of ethics in order to help marketers see what practices they should be supporting and to allow the word-of-mouth industry to set clear standards for itself.[30] ●

Questions

1. Imagine that you are paid by [...] to promote one of Molson's brands by talking to customers in a bar. WOMMA's code of ethics says that you should [...] are being paid to promote the brand. Would you do that or would you not disclose your [...]

2. When you consider buying [...] research yourself on the pro[...]

marketing *NewsFlash* — Research Reveals Value of a Facebook Fan

Online research experts from Syncapse Corp. and Hotspex teamed up to quantify the value of a Facebook fan for marketers. While it is nice for a brand to have numerous fans on Facebook, its value has long been debated in the hallways of major corporations. Michael Scissons, president and CEO of Syncapse Corp., stated in a recent press release that research findings support the value of Facebook. Syncapse Corp., with offices in Toronto, New York, London, and Portland (Oregon), works with Fortune 500 companies and global media agencies on social media initiatives. Hotspex Market Research is a global expert in online research.

The 2010 quantitative study collected data from Hotspex' online panel of 4,000 North American respondents with a 25-minute survey that focused on Facebook's top 20 consumer brands: Nokia, BlackBerry, Motorola, Secret, Gillette, Axe, Dove, Victoria's Secret, Adidas, Nike, Coca-Cola, Oreo, Skittles, Nutella, Red Bull, Pringles, PlayStation, Xbox, Starbucks, and McDonald's. Respondents were asked to identify the brands they had "fanned" or "liked" on Facebook and to project future behaviour, attitudes, and feelings toward them. Data was analyzed, comparing reactions of fans versus non-fans over a two-year period.

The study analyzed the value of a Facebook fan on five parameters: (1) product spending, (2) brand loyalty, (3) propensity to recommend, (4) brand affinity, and (5) earned media value. The key findings indicated that Facebook fans spent an average $71.84 more on a brand than non-fans. These fans were also 28 percent more likely to continue to use the brand than non-fans and 41 percent more likely to recommend the brand to others. In addition, 81 percent of fans felt connected to the brand versus 39 percent for non-fans.

When reviewing all factors, the study concluded that the value of a Facebook fan to an organization over two years averages $136.38. This value can vary considerably among brands. The study cites McDonald's as an example of a brand with a high Facebook average fan value of $259.82 over two years, versus Oreo with a low Facebook average fan value of $60.60.

The study points to the fact that as consumers increasingly use social networks, marketers are tasked to engage them on these platforms to drive brand loyalty and revenue growth. Marketers need to create specific approaches to nurture their Facebook fans, which can help drive business and brand advocacy.[4] ●

Questions

1. Consider a brand you have "fanned" or "liked" on Facebook and discuss how it has tried to engage its fans.

2. Discuss creative ways this brand could drive brand advocacy.

Ask Yourself checkpoints, found near the end of major sections in each chapter, allow students to test their comprehension of the chapter material before moving on.

ask yourself

1. What are the four stages in the product life cycle? How do they differ in terms of sales and profits?

2. How do high-learning and low-learning products differ?

3. What is the shape of the product life cycle for a cellphone in today's marketplace?

[adAlyze]

© 2009 Porsche Cars Canada Ltd. Porsche recommends seatbelt usage and observance of all traffic laws at all times.

What demographic profile is this ad targeting?

What psychographic interests can you determine about the target market from this ad?

For more information visit www.porsche.ca

Hopefully, you'll run into your ex.

The new Boxster is here.

What behavioural insight can you determine about the target market from this ad?

PORSCHE

160 | PART 3 DESIGNING MARKETING STRATEGIES AND MARKETING MIX ELEMENTS

AdAlyze features give students the opportunity to critically evaluate and dissect the message of an actual print advertisement, helping them understand real-world application.

At the end of each chapter, the **Summary** and list of **Key Terms** help students review the chapter's most important concepts. New **Hands On...Apply Your Knowledge assignments** direct students back to the beginning of the chapter to solve a practical marketing scenario related to topics in the opening vignette. Video cases, comprehension and discussion questions, and additional resources are available within **connect**.

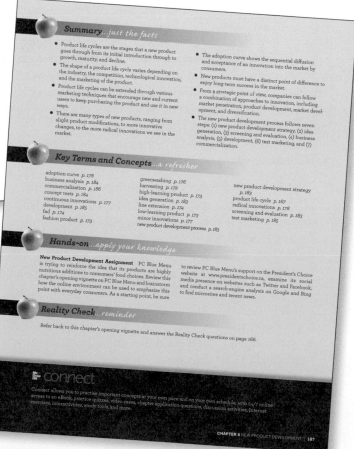

Summary...just the facts

- Product life cycles are the stages that a new product goes through from its initial introduction through to growth, maturity, and decline.
- The shape of a product life cycle varies depending on the industry, the competition, technological innovation, and the marketing of the product.
- Product life cycles can be extended through various marketing techniques that encourage new and current users to keep purchasing the product and use it in new ways.
- There are many types of new products, ranging from slight product modifications, to more innovative changes, to the more radical innovations we see in the market.
- The adoption curve shows the sequential diffusion and acceptance of an innovation into the market by consumers.
- New products must have a distinct point of difference to enjoy long-term success in the market.
- From a strategic point of view, companies can follow a combination of approaches to innovation, including market penetration, product development, market development, and diversification.
- The new product development process follows seven steps: (1) new product development strategy, (2) idea generation, (3) screening and evaluation, (4) business analysis, (5) development, (6) test marketing, and (7) commercialization.

Key Terms and Concepts...a refresher

adoption curve p. 178
business analysis p. 184
commercialization p. 186
concept tests p. 184
continuous innovations p. 177
development p. 185
fad p. 174
fashion product p. 173

greenwashing p. 176
harvesting p. 172
high-learning product p. 173
idea generation p. 183
line extension p. 174
low-learning product p. 173
minor innovations p. 177
new product development process p. 183

new product development strategy p. 183
product life cycle p. 167
radical innovations p. 178
screening and evaluation p. 183
test marketing p. 185

Hands-on...apply your knowledge

New Product Development Assignment PC Blue Menu is trying to reinforce the idea that its products are highly nutritious additions to consumers' food choices. Review this chapter's opening vignette on PC Blue Menu and brainstorm how the online environment can be used to emphasize this point with everyday consumers. As a starting point, be sure to review PC Blue Menu's support on the President's Choice website at www.presidentschoice.ca, examine its social media presence on websites such as Twitter and Facebook, and conduct a search-engine analysis on Google and Bing to find microsites and recent news.

Reality Check...reminder

Refer back to this chapter's opening vignette and answer the Reality Check questions on page 166.

connect

Connect allows you to practise important concepts at your own pace and on your own schedule, with 24/7 online access to an eBook, practice quizzes, video cases, chapter application questions, discussion activities, Internet exercises, interactivities, study tools, and more.

CHAPTER 8 NEW PRODUCT DEVELOPMENT | 187

Supplements Guide to *Marketing: The Core*

To help instructors and students meet today's teaching and learning challenges, *Marketing: The Core*, Third Canadian Edition, offers a complete, integrated supplements package.

 For Instructors

Mc Graw Hill connect

McGraw-Hill Connect™ is a web-based assignment and assessment platform that gives students the means to better connect with their coursework, with their instructors, and with the important concepts that they will need to know for success now and in the future.

With Connect, instructors can deliver assignments, quizzes, and tests online. Instructors can edit existing questions and author entirely new problems. Track individual student performance—by question, by assignment, or in relation to the class overall—with detailed grade reports, integrate grade reports easily with Learning Management Systems (LMS) such as WebCT and Blackboard, and much more!

The Connect™ Instructor Library provides all the critical resources instructors will need to build their courses:

- **Test Bank:** More than 1,400 multiple-choice, true-false, and short answer questions, each categorized according to learning objective, topic, level of difficulty, level of Bloom's taxonomy, text page reference, and correct answer.

    The test bank is available through EZ Test Online, a flexible and easy-to-use electronic testing program that allows instructors to create tests from book-specific items. EZ Test accommodates a wide range of question types and allows instructors to add their own questions. For secure online testing, exams created in EZ Test can be exported to WebCT and Blackboard. EZ Test Online is supported at www.mhhe.com/eztest where users can download a Quick Start Guide, access FAQs, or log

a ticket for help with specific issues. Test items are also available in Word format (rich text format).

- **Instructor's Manual:** The highly-rated Instructor's Manual returns with lecture notes and answers to Ask Yourself, adAlyze, Reality Check, and Hands On...Apply Your Knowledge questions. The popular "Bring It to Life" section contains new metrics assignments and new worksheets and handouts for video cases, News-Flashes, Focus on Ethics boxes, and in-class activities.

- **PowerPoint® Presentations:** Two versions of ready-made presentations are available: lecture style, which are heavier on text than visuals; and magazine style, which incorporate high-quality images, including figure slides, product shots, and advertisements. As an aid for instructors who wish to create their own presentations, an **Image Library** containing all visual elements from the text is also available.

- **Video Case Studies:** A unique series of 14 contemporary marketing video cases is available. Each video corresponds with chapter-specific topics, a written case, and helpful teaching notes. This series is also available on DVD.

- **Alternate Cases:** Marketing Advisor cases and Marketing Metrics cases provide even more opportunities to bring course content to life for students. Cases are accompanied by teaching notes, which contain helpful teaching suggestions and solutions to questions posed in these cases.

- **Brief Video Clips and Discussion Questions:** This new resource is perfect for instructors who lack the time to play a longer video or Video Case in class. Recommendations are given for short (2-5 minute), engaging, and current video clips, as well as suggestions for encouraging class discussion around each clip.

- **Newsletters:** Posted to Connect quarterly each year, these newsletters help provide instructors with innovative teaching resources to improve student learning, offer timely marketing examples, and make class preparation time easier.

By choosing Connect, instructors are providing their students with a powerful tool for improving academic performance and truly mastering course material. Connect allows students to practise important skills at their own pace and on their own schedule. Importantly, students' assessment results and instructors' feedback are all saved online so that students can continually review their progress and plot their course to success.

Connect also provides 24/7 online access to an eBook—an online edition of the text—to aid them in successfully completing their work, wherever and whenever they choose.

Superior Service

Integrated Learning Your Integrated Learning Sales Specialist is a McGraw-Hill Ryerson representative who has the experience, product knowledge, training, and support to help you assess and integrate any of our products, technology, and services into your course for optimum teaching and learning performance. Whether it's helping your students improve their grades, or putting your entire course online, your *iLearning* Sales Specialist is there to help you do it. Contact your *iLearning* Sales Specialist today to learn how to maximize all of McGraw-Hill Ryerson's resources!

Course Management McGraw-Hill Ryerson offers a range of flexible integration solutions for Blackboard, WebCT, Desire2Learn, Moodle, and other leading learning management platforms. Please contact your local McGraw-Hill Ryerson *iLearning* Sales Specialist for details.

Tegrity is a service that makes class time available all the time by automatically capturing every lecture in a searchable format for students to review when they study and complete assignments. With a simple one-click start-and-stop process, you capture all computer screens and corresponding audio. Students can replay any part of any class with easy-to-use browser-based viewing on a PC or Mac. Educators know that the more students can see, hear, and experience class resources, the better they learn. With Tegrity, students quickly recall key moments by using Tegrity's unique search feature. This search tool helps students efficiently find what they need, when they need it across an entire semester of class recordings. Help turn all your students' study time into learning moments immediately supported by your lecture. To learn more about Tegrity, watch a two-minute Flash demo at http://tegritycampus.mhhe.com, and speak with your local iLearning sales specialist.

CourseSmart brings together thousands of textbooks across hundreds of courses in an eTextbook format providing unique benefits to students and faculty. By purchasing an eTextbook, students can save up to 50 percent off the cost of a print textbook, reduce their impact on the environment, and gain access to powerful Web tools for learning, including full text search, notes and highlighting, and e-mail tools for sharing notes between classmates. For faculty, CourseSmart provides instant access to review and compare textbooks and course materials in their discipline area without the time, cost, and environmental impact of mailing print examination copies. For further details, contact your *iLearning* Sales Specialist or go to www.coursesmart.com.

McGraw-Hill Ryerson's Create Online gives you access to the most abundant resource at your fingertips—literally. With a few mouse clicks, you can create customized learning tools simply and affordably. McGraw-Hill Ryerson has included many of our market-leading textbooks within Create Online for eBook and print customization as well as many licensed readings and cases. For more information, go to www.mcgrawhillcreate.ca.

McGraw-Hill Connect allows students to practise important skills at their own pace and on their own schedule. Importantly, students' assessment results and instructors' feedback are all saved online so that students can continually review their progress and plot their course to success. Connect also provides 24/7 online access to an eBook to aid students in successfully completing their work, wherever and whenever they choose.

Connect offers practice quizzes as well as other study tools and resources:

- *Applying Marketing Concepts and Perspectives* questions allow you to assess your comprehension of chapter material

- *Discussion Forum* questions present a thought-provoking scenario for you to discuss with other students.

- *Internet Exercises* ask you to think critically about a specific company's use of the Internet—helping you apply your knowledge of key chapter concepts, terms, and topics, as well as evaluate the success or failure of the company's efforts.

- *Video Case Studies* provide an up-close look at a company example—reinforcing the chapter content, while bringing the material to life.

- The *Creating a Successful Marketing Plan* Appendix can be used in a number of ways, throughout your use of this text and beyond. This guide to planning, researching, and writing a winning marketing plan incorporates the marketing plan rationale, detailed plan contents, and effective design and execution of the plan, as well as checklists for implementing and evaluating the marketing plan.

- Interactive figures, flash cards, vocabulary quizzes, and study cards.

Acknowledgements

We appreciate the time and effort spent by individual marketers that are profiled or involved in chapter opening vignettes, Marketing NewsFlash boxes, or videos. You have helped make a difference in marketing education in Canada. Your efforts make the chapters vibrant and dynamic, culminating in a book that is fresh, spirited, and real. Thank you:

Alex Barseghaian, *Samba Days*
Julia Bossis, *Buzz Creation*
Lucy Brun, *Agnew Peckham*
Ashley Caristena, *Rexall Pharma Plus*
Karen Charness, *ZenithOptimedia*
Matthew Corrin, *Freshii*
Emma Croft, *Queensland Tourism*
Molly Fuchs, *Agnew Peckham*
Peter Furnish, *Virgin Mobile*
Paula Gignac, *Interactive Advertising Bureau of Canada (IAB)*
Ian Gordon, *Loblaw Companies*
Gillian Graham, *Institute of Communication Agencies (ICA)*
Livia Grujich, *On Q Communications*
Paul Heinrich, *Georgian Bay General Hospital*
Ruth Klostermann, *ZenithOptimedia*
Mary Lye, *Childhood Cancer Foundation Canada*
Brandy Martin, *Scotts Miracle-Gro Company*
Kyle McCarthy, *Atomic Skis Canada*
Jackie McLaughlin, *Georgian Bay General Hospital*
Will Mlacak, *Humber College*
Rob Morash, *Suunto Canada*
Randy Pilon, *Virox Technologies Inc.*
Andrew Pollock, *Canada Bread*
Tina Powell, *Big Fat Pen Publishing Inc.*
Isadore Sharp, *Four Seasons Hotels and Resorts*
Luke Sklar, *Sklar, Wilton and Associates*
Gene Swinton, *Baskin Robbins*
Ron White, *Ron White Shoes*
Gordon Woit, *MapArt*

To all the companies that have provided us with images to include in the book, we thank you.

In addition, we extend our appreciation to the reviewers who helped steer the development of this new edition with their comments, feedback, and suggestions:

Tom Arhontoudis, *George Brown College*
Marc Boivin, *University of Calgary*
Sammy Bonsu, *York University*
Ingrid Brand, *Durham College*
Brian Broadway, *Seneca College*
John Brown, *Georgian College*
Sergio Carvalho, *University of Manitoba*
John Dickason, *Humber College*
George Dracopoulos, *Vanier College*
Bob Graves, *Grant MacEwan University*
Jim Higginson, *University of Guelph-Humber*
Marion Hill, *SAIT Polytechnic*
Richard Hill, *Capilano University*
Steve Janisse, *St. Clair College*
Vern Kennedy, *Centennial College*
Ed McHugh, *Nova Scotia Community College*
Megan Mills, *Okanagan College*
David Moulton, *Douglas College*
Margaret O'Brien, *Algonquin College*
Christine Oldfield, *Centennial College*
Beth Pett, *Niagara College*
Allen Richert, *Confederation College*
Micki Rivers, *Seneca College*
Diana Serafini, *Dawson College*
Les Smith, *Sir Sandford Fleming College*
Robert Soroka, *Dawson College*
Carolyn Sterenberg, *Mount Royal University*
Diane Wolf, *Trent University*

We also extend our gratitude to the people at McGraw-Hill Ryerson for their professionalism, namely Leanna MacLean, publisher, and Jennifer Cressman, senior developmental editor, who managed to cheerfully keep the process moving forward. Jessica Barnoski and Stephanie Gay (supervising editors) and Mike Kelly (copy editor) were invaluable in their attention to detail and ability to juggle so many elements. Thank you also to the design team at Valid Design.

Finally, we would like to thank our families for their enthusiasm and patient support.

Christina Clements and Harvey Skolnick

chapter 1

Marketing Fundamentals

Marketing in the fast-paced business world centres on understanding consumers—how they think, what drives purchases, and what does not. Marketers use this knowledge to craft marketing programs that encourage purchases and translate into company profits. In today's digital world, marketers compete with global and local brands in an online and offline environment, resulting in a more complex competitive space. In Canada, today's marketers need to understand not only what drives consumers but also how to navigate this digital landscape to meet consumers in their worlds and on their terms.

The digital world of the Internet has resulted in an abundance of product choices, a variety of price points, easy-to-access information, and a 24/7 hub for entertainment, communication, information-gathering, and purchasing. Consumers purchase products online and offline, accessing information through websites, apps, and online comparison-shopping guides to help steer choices. Witness the free downloadable Snaptell[1] app for iPhones or Android smartphones that uses image recognition technology to provide updated information on books, DVDs, CDs, and video games. Once the app is downloaded, the user can snap a photo of the item and instantly receive information on product ratings, retail prices, retail locations, and relevant links to Google and YouTube sites, and then be able to immediately purchase the product online. These developments put marketers on alert, prompting them to be knowledgeable about technology and how it impacts businesses and consumers.

Rob Morash, managing director at Suunto Canada, takes us into the world of sports training devices, an evolution of the sports watch. He refers to these devices as "sports laboratories on your wrist" and explains how online and offline marketing is used to reach consumers. Rob Morash is a seasoned sports marketer with experience at Atomic Skis, Nike, and Bauer. He tells us that understanding consumer trigger points is vital to marketing success. Marketers need to stay on top of new technology, understand how it is used, and integrate it into products and marketing programs. "Suunto products are on the leading edge of technology and in Canada our challenge is to bring this technology to committed athletes who embrace technology and use it to support their sport."

Suunto is a top-quality, Finnish brand of digital sports training devices sold in over 100 countries through a network of local companies. Suunto Canada drives sales and profits with marketing initiatives that build brand awareness, sales, and profits. We look to their t-Series Training Packs to get a practical view of marketing at work.

The t-Series Training Pack is a line of products for athletes and fitness enthusiasts who want the most from their training. Specifically, the target market (the group to which marketing is directed) for the t-Series Training Pack consists of committed, digitally savvy, elite, aspiring, or recreational athletes. These athletes use measurement and analysis to improve performance and tend to be male, higher income, and between 25 and 45 years old. They are sports enthusiasts who take their sport seriously and travel extensively to compete or follow sporting endeavours.

Suunto Canada manages the marketing mix (product, price, place, and promotion) for the t-Series Training Pack, designing each element to meet target market needs and ultimately make a profit. Let's look at this marketing mix in detail:

Product: The t-Series Training Pack centres on a watch, a comfort belt strap, and a POD that captures data, wirelessly sending it to the watch. The comfort belt straps around a user's chest to monitor heart rate while the POD attaches to an athletic shoe, bike wheel, or arm to monitor speed, distance, cadence, position, or location. The features vary, depending on the sport, but all devices come with a computer attachment so that once training is complete, athletes can upload training data from the devices to an online location to track and share data with coaches.

Four specialty categories exist in the t-Series Training Pack line: (1) the Triathlon Pack for competitive triathletes, (2) the Cycling Pack for active cyclists, (3) the Running Pack for competitive or avid runners, and (4) the GPS Pack for ski or water-sport athletes. All watches have stopwatch features, show time and date, have two-year warranties, and capture metrics for specific sports. Watches, PODs, and comfort belts are also sold separately.

Price: Prices vary, depending on product complexity. Individual watch-devices start at $99, climbing to $499. Prices are based on an analysis of product costs, profit targets, what consumers are willing to pay, and competitive price points.

Place: Suunto sells the t-Series Training Pack at locations that reflect its premium image and where top athletes and training enthusiasts purchase equipment. Products can be found at outdoor sporting goods stores (e.g., Mountain Equipment Co-op and Atmosphere), general sporting goods stores (e.g., SportChek, Sport Mart, and Fitness Depot), and independent sporting goods stores (e.g., Skiis and Biikes, Sporting Life, and Running Room). Consumers can also purchase Suunto products online, often on large e-commerce sites where competitive products can be compared.

In the offline retail environment, Suunto provides stores with point-of-sale material to reflect its top-quality image. Large posters are created for pillars and back walls, while display units and pamphlets are placed on countertops.

Promotion: A mass media approach does not effectively reach Suunto's target group. Instead, Suunto uses event sponsorship and brand ambassadors to reach its specialized target market. It sponsors international and Canadian sporting events while providing products to top athletes.

- **Sponsorship:** Suunto is the official timekeeper and data-partner for the World Championship Series of the International Triathlon Union. These events are broadcast around the world to an audience of over 176 million people. Here Suunto is profiled as top in precision timing and training devices with its brand highly visible at events, as well as online on event websites. Its logo often appears on event banners and is placed on athlete apparel, and its data is streamed live during TV broadcasts from athletes wearing its devices. In Canada, Suunto sponsors events such as the 5 Peaks Trail Running Series as its official timekeeper and training partner.

- **Brand ambassadors:** Top athletes are given Suunto training devices to wear. This creates strong word-of-mouth and exposure during sporting events. These ambassadors are profiled on the Suunto website.

- **Digital marketing:** Suunto uses e-mail marketing, social media, and company websites to communicate to its target market. Athletes can like its Facebook page, follow the company on Twitter, and watch athlete videos at www.suunto.tv.

In 2010 Suunto launched its own social network and web portal, www.movescount.com, where Suunto users can download software and personal training data, search for competition information, enter contests, follow top athletes, update profiles, join/share training programs, and post links to other social networks.

Newsletters are e-mailed monthly to Suunto's database of subscribers, often pointing to its corporate website at http://suunto.com for further details on Suunto products, training videos, elite events, and brand ambassadors.

The marketing of Suunto training devices requires each element of the marketing mix to meet target market needs and to present a consistent image to consumers. Suunto creates top-quality, high-tech *products* that are easy to use; its *pricing* is premium to reflect this top-quality image; its products are sold at *places* where top athletes purchase sporting goods; and it is *promoted* online and offline through top athletes and elite sporting events.

Rob Morash explains that the marketing of sporting goods is both exhilarating and complex. He wants students to realize that marketing has a purpose and it is not just about fancy ads, sponsoring events, and hanging out with athletes. "Yes, this may be part of the business," he explains, "But ultimately the purpose of marketing is to drive sales and profits. At the end of the day, this is what counts and marketers must always keep this in sight." Be sure to visit the Suunto websites at http://suunto.com and www. movescount.com to see more of Suunto's marketing efforts.[2] 🍎

As you read Chapter 1, refer back to the Suunto t-Series Training Pack vignette to answer the following questions:

- Are the t-Series Training Packs goods, services, or ideas?

- Who is the target market for the t-Series Training Pack?

- What tools is Suunto using with its t-Series Training Packs that provide added value to consumers?

reality CHECK

The Essence of Marketing

LO ① The Suunto Canada vignette demonstrates a marketing reality—marketing success is rooted in focusing on customers and providing value through goods and services designed to meet customer needs. The challenge, as we saw with the t-Series Training Pack, is to stay relevant to changing consumer expectations, to craft marketing programs that meet target market needs, and to distinguish products in the marketplace. Marketers are challenged to stay current to ensure that products and marketing approaches are contemporary and meaningful. Suunto met this challenge by introducing technologically advanced products and using new social media initiatives to add value to its products. It understood that in this competitive market, if it does not provide relevant added-value elements, then competitors will do so.

Often, students believe marketing revolves around slick commercials and fancy promotions. In fact, marketers' ultimate objectives are to drive profits for a company, or if working in the non-profit sector, to generate revenue and support to fund programs and run operations. Only one aspect of marketing revolves around promotion, with all other elements required to drive profitability or revenue generation for an organization.

This chapter works to explain the fundamental principles that guide marketing, dispelling the myth that promotion and marketing are one and the same. In this introductory chapter, we emphasize the basic marketing principles of meeting customer needs and providing customer value, while also providing background on the evolution of business approaches. We explain the marketing process, the concept of target markets, and the importance of integrating each element of the marketing mix into a marketing program that focuses on consumer needs. We also emphasize new and evolving marketing approaches such as digital marketing, social media, experiential marketing, customer relationship management, corporate social responsibility, partnership marketing, and the increased importance of metrics. Finally, we lead students into a discussion on careers in the marketing industry.

The chapters in this textbook are carefully sequenced to maximize student learning. Marketing fundamentals are introduced in Chapter 1 and then revisited in more detail in subsequent chapters. The book leads students from marketing fundamentals into an understanding of consumer behaviour, market research, and business markets. It then launches into the more complex areas of market segmentation and marketing mix strategies, followed by a chapter on strategic planning, a topic that requires a solid understanding of marketing to be meaningful and clearly understood.

Focusing on Customer Needs

The essence of successful marketing is focusing on customer needs and developing programs that delight consumers and encourage customer loyalty. Frequently, the challenge is to clearly determine these needs and to understand how they can best be met. Marketers often turn to research to provide clarity; however, consumers do not always know what they want and may not want (or be able) to articulate feelings and opinions. In certain categories, such as fragrances or luxury cars, choices are not entirely rational, but partly based on self-image and emotional attachment to a brand, which are difficult to articulate. In other situations where children

The Core: Chapter 1

The focus of marketing is satisfying consumers' needs.

Target Customers

In marketing, consumer needs are front and centre.

customer value
The unique combination of benefits received by targeted buyers that includes quality, price, convenience, delivery, and both before-sale and after-sale service

or professionals are involved, a child may be unable to express ideas while professionals may not have the time to participate in research. Sometimes marketers may not be asking the right questions.

The digital world adds another level of complexity to market research. On the one hand it facilitates the online gathering of information, while on the other hand it introduces new communication platforms that challenge marketers to understand the biases that may exist in this new environment.

There are some general insights about consumer needs in the online environment that marketers need to consider when developing marketing programs. First, the initial point of contact for consumers with a brand is often online on a company website—consumers expect this platform to be available to check product offerings and company information. Marketers must therefore ensure they have top-quality websites that accurately reflect products and quickly engage consumers. Second, consumers must be able to quickly find a website through search engines such as Google or Bing. Websites must therefore be written so that search engines find them when consumers conduct online searches. Third, consumers are impatient in the online environment—websites must therefore load quickly and be designed to provide content within two to three clicks. Lastly, consumers are widening their online search to include social networks, blogs, product review sites, and personal contacts. Having a positive presence on social media sites is therefore an important communications tool for marketers who increasingly engage through social media. The *Global Social Media Check-Up 2011* research report from Burson-Marsteller noted that 84 percent of Fortune 100 companies now post Facebook status updates, an increase of 25 percentage points versus the previous year.[3]

The travel industry is an example of where marketers spent time to understand consumers' online needs and developed new approaches to remain relevant in the online environment. Consider a person booking a trip to Banff, Alberta; the first point of contact is no longer a travel agent and a brochure, but instead an online travel website such as www.itravel2000.com

> *The essence of marketing is focusing on the consumer.*

where travel options, hotel prices, and flight information are easily accessible. The second point of contact may be www.tripadvisor.com, a social media product review site, to read customer reviews on hotels and airlines. Finally, the traveller may navigate to a short list of hotel websites to review additional offers before returning to the online travel site to book the trip. At some point in this process the traveller may have reached out on a social network to get advice from friends/followers. In this online environment there was no need to visit a travel agent, speak to an airline, or make inquiries at the hotel!

Travel websites, hotels, and airlines now all consider the online needs and expectations of travellers, including how they search online to gather information and use customer-review websites for product ratings and price comparisons. Travel websites, recognizing these needs, often provide these tools within their websites.

Creating Customer Value

Developing customer loyalty is prompting many firms to provide customer value in two ways. First, companies create products that provide customers with goods and services that have added value versus competitive offerings. Second, they reward customers for their loyalty through marketing programs that focus on repeat purchases and incentives to encourage future purchases. For our purposes, **customer value** is the unique combination of benefits received by targeted consumers that includes quality, price, convenience, delivery, and both before-sale and after-sale service. Marketers work diligently to deliver this value by carefully managing each element of the marketing mix (product, price, place, and promotion) so that this value is evident to consumers who in turn purchase or use the products. Ongoing marketing programs then come into play, encouraging these consumers to become long-term loyal customers and spread the word to others. Creating products with added value is often achieved through a combination of (1) product design, (2) pricing strategies, and (3) service elements. Retailers such as Walmart focus on the lowest price; Mountain Equipment Co-op claims to provide the best products; and companies such as Pizza Pizza highlight their fast delivery service as a point of difference. Let's examine two online brands to find out how they balance product design, pricing, and service levels to create meaningful products with added value.

Google is an online brand designed to deliver highly accurate data with a product that is easy to use and fast, and that provides exceptional value. The product is provided free to users and has become the gold standard in the search industry with a 64 percent market share of the search market, followed by Yahoo! at 18 percent, and Microsoft at 12 percent.[4] Its branded platform has been extended into other areas such as Google Maps, Gmail, and Google Analytics, all providing the same value proposition that balances product design, pricing, and service to deliver value. Google encourages customer loyalty by keeping customers informed on its latest products and providing incentives to use its related products that may not be free of charge, such as Google AdWords, an online advertising platform. In a recent promotion, Google used direct mail to provide added value to its customers by sending them $100 gift cards to try its paid AdWords product.

Google adds exceptional value to the world on another level, through its humanitarian efforts. For example, during the 2011 earthquake and tsunami disaster in Japan, Google immediately launched its "Person Finder: 2011 Japan Earthquake" application to help find displaced persons. It provided an open-access searchable database in Japanese and English for people to post queries and updates on loved ones. After a single day, the site tracked 51,000 records, climbing to over 107,000 within two days.

Amazon.com is another online brand that presents customers with outstanding value through a searchable database of well-priced products that are peer-rated and reviewed. It also recommends related products and tracks delivery dates through timely e-mails—design, price, and service all rolled into one. E-mail blasts to its database of customers encourage loyalty through special offers, featured gifts, and the announcement of new releases. Amazon.com dominates online retailing, accounting for 57 percent of web-only merchant sales.[5]

Appealing to Target Markets

In a competitive marketplace, companies cannot satisfy everyone's needs with a single product, and so products are designed to appeal to specific groups of consumers. Marketing follows the principle that, with limited funds, it is better to channel resources toward consumers who are most interested in purchasing a product, rather than target everyone and squander funds on those who have little interest. This approach results in marketers tailoring products to meet the specific needs of different target markets. A **target market** can be formally defined as the specific group of existing and potential consumers to which marketers direct their marketing efforts. Marketing efforts are geared to appeal to a product's specific target market, ensuring that each element of the marketing mix appeals to the characteristics of the target group.

Coordinating the Marketing Mix

The elements of the **marketing mix**—known as the 4 Ps, product, price, place, and promotion—need to be carefully managed by marketers to ensure that they are well coordinated and that each appeals to the distinct characteristics of

target market
The specific group of existing and potential consumers to which marketers direct their marketing efforts

marketing mix
The 4 Ps—product, price, place, and promotion

the target market. There is no point in having an amazing product if consumers cannot find it at the retail stores they frequent or online through a search. If the product is priced too high for the target market, it will be unaffordable; if it's priced too low, it will simply portray the wrong image. If marketers promote a product on TV but the target market rarely watches TV, instead spending time online, then the message will not be received. In all instances, marketers need to understand what makes their consumers tick: what delights them, what does not, and how to best send communications. This information is often clarified by market research and metrics on consumer behaviour to help determine how marketing efforts can be designed or modified to meet consumer needs and deliver profits or support for the company. Marketers use this information to improve marketing programs and coordinate each element of the marketing mix to meet specific target market needs. These elements are all included in a brand's annual marketing plan where details for each element of the marketing mix are outlined, together with the required budgets and profit and loss statements for the brand. Chapter 14 provides more details on this area.

The elements of the marketing mix in either an online or offline environment can be simply described as follows:

1. **Product:** All the attributes that make up a good, a service, or an idea, including product design,

Retail merchandising is an important part of the marketing mix for Suunto Canada.

features, colour, packaging, warranty, and service levels.

2. **Price:** The expected regular retail or sale price for a product.

3. **Place:** The distribution channels, retail formats, and merchandising used to sell a product.

4. **Promotion:** The communication tools needed to inform consumers about a product, including advertising, public relations, sales promotion, public relations, direct response, event marketing and sponsorship, and personal selling.

We look at two Nestlé products, Smarties and After Eight Straws, to review how marketers at this company carefully craft each element of the marketing mix to appeal to two distinct target groups. Smarties, targeting youth aged 13 to 17, are brightly coloured, candy-coated chocolates that come in bright blue packages. The product comes in round bite-sized pieces that are fun, colourful, and easy to share. It is relatively inexpensive, selling for approximately $1.09 for 50 grams, making it an affordable treat. It is merchandised at retail in supermarkets, convenience stores, and drug stores, often close to cash registers to stand as a visual reminder of this treat and to prompt impulse purchases. The product continues its appeal to youth with both online and offline marketing campaigns; TV spots airing around youth programming such as the MuchMusic Video Awards (MMVAs) announce that "Blue Is Back," referring to the return of blue-coloured Smarties. Online communications at www.smarties.ca and on Facebook integrate

> **MARKETERS NEED TO UNDERSTAND WHAT MAKES THEIR CONSUMERS TICK: WHAT DELIGHTS THEM, WHAT DOES NOT.**

with offline messaging and emphasize that Smarties are free from artificial colours, that blue Smarties are back, and that consumers can enter a contest to win an Apple computer. The MMVA website celebrates the return of blue Smarties by transforming the event's green celebrity rooms into blue rooms and posting images, blogs, and contest details. Consumers are also pointed to the Smarties' Facebook page where they can post comments and receive or respond to offers.

On the other hand, After Eight Straws, targeting adults, are dark-chocolate mints designed to be sleek, stylish, and classy. The product comes in an upscale dark-green cylinder that contains 20 thin After Eight Straws that are filled with a delicate mint-cream filling. The product combines bitter, dark chocolate with a minty flavour that appeals to adults. The product is sold at a premium price of $3.99 for a 90-gram package, reflecting its high-quality image and adult target market. Typically, this product is not merchandised at cash registers, but instead on the shelves of many grocery stores and drug retailers. It enjoys more-prominent seasonal displays during the winter holidays when the product is popular for entertaining. After Eight Straws are promoted online within the Nestlé website as a stylish accompaniment to a dinner party with tips on adult entertaining and suggestions on how to dress up an after-dinner beverage. In previous years, the product has been promoted at the Toronto Symphony Orchestra, reflecting its image as a product for adult entertaining.

In both instances, Nestlé moulded each element of the marketing mix to appeal to its specific target group. Neither product is geared to appeal to everyone. Instead, Smarties targets youth, and After Eight Straws targets adults. It is important to note that, over time, marketers gather extensive information on their target markets, being able to identify purchase motivation

that goes beyond age and gender into behavioural and psychological motivation, which is an important determinant in many purchases. In this way, marketers define their target markets in more-complex terms, including elements such as likes, dislikes, motivation, interests, and concerns.

The digital reality has prompted many new marketing approaches that make the marketing mix more complex. Marketers realize that each element now has many layers that need to be managed, no easy task in the online environment. A product, for example, now has many faces; offline in stores and online on corporate websites and microsites where marketers can control its image. It also appears on social networks such as Facebook and Twitter, an environment that cannot be controlled by marketers. Instead, marketers carefully monitor this environment and politely engage with consumers to help create a positive space for their products.

Later in this chapter we review some of the latest marketing approaches that are used to connect with consumers in this multi-tiered marketing environment. These approaches harness the power of corporate social responsibility, customer relationship management, experiential marketing, and partnership marketing to drive the marketing mix and establish long-term relationships with consumers.

The Marketing Process

The marketing process is a continuous one that requires marketers to pay attention to detail and apply strategic, analytical, and creative-thinking skills. In short, the **marketing process** involves (1) identifying consumer needs, (2) managing the marketing mix to meet these needs, and (3) realizing profits, or in the case of non-profits, secure revenues or provide services to those in need (see Figure 1–1). Throughout the cycle, marketers constantly evaluate program success, implementing and recommending

ask yourself

1. What is the essence of marketing?
2. What is a target market?
3. What is the marketing mix?

marketing process
The process of (1) identifying consumer needs, (2) managing the marketing mix to meet these needs, and (3) realizing profits

marketing
The process of planning and managing goods, services, or ideas to meet consumer needs and organizational objectives. It includes the conception of these products and the pricing, promotion, and distribution programs designed to make a profit and generate revenue or support for an organization

exchange
The trade of things of value between buyers and sellers so that each benefits

product
A good, service, or idea

good
A product you can touch and own

Figure 1–1
The marketing process

| Identify consumer needs | Manage the marketing mix to meet consumer needs | Realize profits for a company (or objectives for non-profit organizations) |

A logical process that focuses on consumer needs

future changes to strengthen efforts. We look to the non-profit Google product mentioned earlier, "Person Finder: 2011 Japan Earthquake," to see how this works. Google identified a need: people desperately wanting to locate loved ones in Japan but unable to do so since telecommunications was sparse and disaster relief stretched. Google created a marketing mix to meet this need. The *product* was an online searchable database, easily accessed by individuals and disaster relief organizations that were looking for missing persons or had information on their situations. The *price* was free to ensure maximum utility. The *place* was online to maximize global reach and to circumvent traditional telecommunications services that were not accessible. *Promotion* was through the news media, directly to disaster relief organizations, and through the Google website. In terms of profit, Google was not looking to make a profit with this product. The service was managed through its Google Crisis Response humanitarian arm, which facilitates critical information dissemination during times of crisis. It managed similar efforts during natural disasters in Haiti, New Zealand, Chile, and China in 2010 and 2011.

It is imperative to understand that marketers are ultimately responsible for generating company profits (or revenues and support for non-profit organizations), and that marketing programs are designed with this end in mind. On occasion, students have the misconception that marketing is all about advertising or selling, when in fact it is about managing *all* the elements of the marketing mix and using research to help generate profits or revenues and support for an organization. Formally, **marketing** is described as the process of planning and managing goods, services, or ideas to meet consumer needs and organizational objectives. It includes the conception of these products, and the pricing, promotion, and distribution programs designed to make a profit and generate revenue

or support for an organization.[6] The objectives of both buyers and sellers must be met for exchanges to occur and for profits to be realized.

Exchange is the trade of things of value between buyers and sellers so that each benefits. In simple terms, the trade is money for a product or service. However, there is more to exchange than just money—customers may provide referrals to a tutoring service or to a fitness club in return for discounts or additional services. A consumer may volunteer time with a non-profit organization such as the Heart and Stroke Foundation, which in return may satisfy the consumer's need to support the cause. In the online environment, exchange is often more complex. In many instances, websites may not be selling a product at all but instead providing free information or a service that drives traffic to their website where advertising is served to help pay for the service. The numbers of unique visitors to the website and metrics on their demographics are used to sell this advertising space and generate revenue for the website. This results in a three-way exchange between the website provider, the visitor to the website, and the advertiser. Many news websites, such as www.ctv.ca, www.theglobeandmail.com, or www.macleans.ca, and web portals, such as Yahoo! Canada and Canada.com, fall into this category.

What Can Be Marketed?

L3 In marketing, the term **product** encompasses goods, services, and ideas. These can all be marketed to encourage people to buy something or, as in the case of ideas, to encourage support.

A **good** is a product you can touch and own. Examples are a pair of Adidas running shoes or a can of Red Bull energy drink. Red Bull energy drink is a tangible product that is marketed in four varieties, sold at a premium price, merchandised in-store, promoted with humorous ads, and publicized through the sponsorship of extreme sporting events. Red Bull streams highlights from its action, motor sports, and

Annually on the last Saturday of March, at 8:30 p.m. local time, the lights go out across Canada and in many countries around the world to send a strong message that people can make a difference in the efforts to reduce climate change. People marvel and cheer as lights dim on modern office towers, ancient sites, shops, and individual homes to mark this annual event. This is not a blackout, but a successful marketing campaign for Earth Hour, an event created by the World Wildlife Fund (WWF) to put a spotlight on global warming and to raise awareness of climate change.

Earth Hour is a largely grassroots effort that highlights how people can show their support against climate change by turning off their lights for one hour on the last Saturday of March. Earth Hour was first celebrated in Sydney, Australia, in 2007, with over 2 million people participating. In 2008 participation spread to

35 countries and by 2010 over 126 countries participated, impacting over 1 billion people. By 2011 Earth Hour reached record participation with 134 countries, including new participants such as Lebanon, Jamaica, Iran, Uganda, Swaziland, Tajikistan, Chad, Azerbaijan, Gibraltar, Palestine, Suriname, Uzbekistan, and Lesotho.

Millions of Canadians take part in this annual event with over 400 cities and towns turning off their lights for an hour. Restaurants offer candlelight dining and people get together to celebrate the event, or take the time to absorb the moment. Landmarks such as Toronto's City Hall and CN Tower, the clock on Parliament's Peace Tower in Ottawa, and the Lions Gate Bridge in Vancouver are all dimmed as Canada marks its participation.

Earth Hour uses digital marketing tools to communicate with participants. It uses a website, blog,

YouTube channel, Facebook page, Flickr stream, Myspace account, BlackBerry app, Twitter account, and LinkedIn group to communicate with supporters and post inspiring stories, photos, and videos. In Canada, people are encouraged to use these social media tools to share stories and to highlight neighbourhood events.

Earth Hour now spreads across the globe, starting in New Zealand and rolling through more than 14 time zones before ending on North America's West Coast. The Sydney Opera House, the Acropolis in Athens, and Coke's billboard in Times Square, as well as other famous landmarks and individual homes around the world, are plunged into darkness to show their support for environmental awareness. Earth Hour is an example of marketing an idea.[7]

Questions

1. What *idea* is being marketed by Earth Hour?

2. What benefits are being exchanged by Earth Hour participants and the WWF?

---

music events online on its Web TV channel designed to appeal to its target market that engages with online content.

A **service** is an intangible product you cannot touch. It does not result in something you take home. A physiotherapy session, a holiday, or going to a movie are examples of services. When you watch a movie at Cineplex, marketers have worked to ensure that your experience encourages you to return. Movie selection, theatre layout, seating, and concession items have all been carefully selected with the comfort and needs of the target market in mind. The Cineplex-Scotiabank

Marketing ideas can encourage people to support causes.

SCENE loyalty rewards program has been designed to encourage customers to return to Cineplex movie theatres time after time to collect points and receive benefits such as discounted concession items, free movies, or discounted DVDs.[8]

Ideas can also be marketed. An **idea** is a concept that typically looks for support. An example is the Earth Hour campaign from the World Wildlife Fund (WWF), which encourages people around the world to show their support to reduce climate change by turning

service
A product that is intangible, that you cannot touch

idea
A concept that typically looks for support

off their lights for one hour on the last Saturday of March. This campaign has been tremendously successful with the latest results showing over one billion people supported the cause in over 134 countries and 4,000 cities and towns. The WWF successfully marketed the idea and garnered support for the cause.[9] (See the Marketing NewsFlash on page 11.)

Many successful marketers today launch products with layers of goods, services, and ideas to connect with consumers. For example, Smart cars, a division of Mercedes-Benz, staggered the launch of its new electric vehicle, Smart fortwo Electric Drive, over the 2010 to 2012 period, as a zero-emissions car (*product*) that can run 135 km on a single battery charge. During the testing phase, Smart Canada worked with Toronto Hydro to provide battery charging stations in testers' garages. Smart Canada also provided auxiliary services such as battery charging stations, winter tire packages, and 24-hour roadside assistance (*services*). Promotional programs such as the Smart Electric Lounge at the 2011 International Auto Show also pointed to the importance of using electric power to support the environment (*idea*). See the Marketing NewsFlash on page 13.

What Is a Market?

The term **market** is used in marketing to describe potential consumers who have both the *willingness* and *ability* to buy a product. Importantly, just being

willing to buy a product does not constitute a market. For example, Fisher Price's iXL learning tablet was introduced in 2010 to rave reviews as an interactive hand-held gadget for children three to six years old. Kids could interactively read, draw, look at pictures, and play video games using the product's six programs, which are accessed through touchscreen technology. Programs included a story book, game player, notebook, photo album, art studio, and music player—learning and fun all rolled into one. Although the product was designed for young children, these children are not considered the market because they do not have the money or the physical means to buy the product. The market consists of parents with young children ages three to six years.

This product touches on an interesting marketing issue: Sometimes the market, target market, and consumers are different groups of people, and marketers need to decide on a balance of who should be targeted with their programs. While the *market* for Fisher Price's iXL is parents with children three to six years old, the marketing also needs to focus on the children, who may exert some influence over their parents. Therefore, we see the *target market* for the product includes both children and parents. Finally, the *consumers* of the product, in this case the users, are the children, not the parents, and marketers need to ensure that the product is designed with their abilities and interests in mind, without overlooking the parents who are the main decision-makers in the purchase process.

ask yourself

1. What steps are involved in the marketing process?

2. What are the differences between goods, services, and ideas?

3. Are credit cards goods, services, or ideas?

Smart fortwo Electric Drive Car

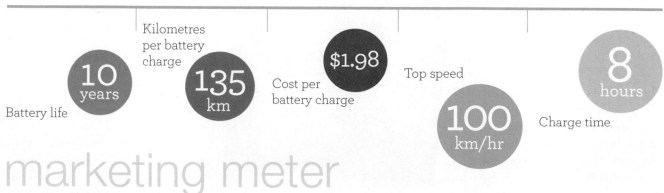

10 years — Battery life

135 km — Kilometres per battery charge

$1.98 — Cost per battery charge

Top speed

100 km/hr

8 hours — Charge time

marketing meter

Source: Smart Canada, "smart fortwo electric drive," accessed May 2011 at www.thesmart.ca.

The Evolution of Business Philosophies

L4 Marketing was not always the driving force in business philosophy. Up until the 1930s, businesses were in the **production orientation** stage. This stage focused on manufacturing, which until the industrial revolution was not a widespread phenomenon. Manufactured goods tended to sell, regardless of their quality, because they were in short supply. Consumer needs were not a priority. The second stage, from the 1930s to the 1960s, was the **sales orientation** stage. This stage focused on selling as many

marketing *NewsFlash*

Smart Marketing Launches Electric Car

So your product meets consumer trends but requires a radical shift in consumer behaviour for success—what do you do? This was the question facing marketers of the new electric-powered Smart car, a small, fun, peppy brand owned by Mercedes-Benz. It was the first publically available electric car brought to market by a major manufacturer in Canada. It faced many hurdles.

It was no easy task being the first to market a fully electric car in a country where public electric recharging stations were non-existent and where consumers were comfortable with gasoline cars. Marketers carefully staggered the Smart fortwo Electric Drive launch to ensure success.

In late 2010 it launched a small advocacy program in conjunction with Toronto Hydro that asked electric car supporters to register to become one of 15 brand ambassadors to receive the new electric Smart car. The 15 recipients signed four-year leases and were given free home-based charging stations, complementary winter tires, free roadside assistance, and car maintenance packages. Each car was completely electric and ran on a rechargeable battery with zero emissions. Its features included a 10-year battery life, top speeds of 100 km/hr, and a driving range of 135 km on a single charge. Each car came with distinct government-issued green licence plates that allowed for unrestricted driving in carpool lanes.

There was no big splash for this below-the-radar soft launch that was really revving up for a full public unleashing in mid-2012. Meanwhile, it was important to establish a presence and a foothold in the market, using a select Toronto sample as a testing ground to determine the full public offering.

The 2010 soft launch carefully used public relations, corporate websites, social media, and experiential marketing to profile this new urban vehicle without creating a backlash from consumers who could not purchase the car. Press releases, announcing the first electric car recipient, were picked up by the news media, with information also spreading to car blogs and online auto sites. Marketing communications used the Smart car's corporate website (www.smartcar.ca) and its online club (www.clubsmartcar.ca) to include new tabs and links on the new electric car. Social media programs used Twitter and Facebook to provide timely updates on contests such as free passes to the 2011 International Auto Show and test-drive opportunities. Video links were also posted to CityTV's *Breakfast Television* coverage of the new electric car at the Auto Show. Experiential marketing involved the creation of the Smart Electric Lounge at the Auto Show where visitors could relax, enter contests, charge cellphones, try out the new electric vehicle, and enjoy a free cup of coffee. It also used brightly painted white cement mixers, printed with images of the new electric Smart car, to create buzz as they drove around the city.

Toronto Hydro was involved with the soft launch, partnering to study the car's associated driving patterns, battery-charging habits, and the potential impact of electric cars on the hydro grid. Its microsite, the "Toronto Hydro Smart Experience" at www.smartexperience.ca provided details on the car, the brand ambassador program, and Toronto Hydro's involvement in the free home-based electric charging stations.

Marketers for Smart cars are well known for their creative marketing programs, such as placing huge over-sized bicycle locks around Smart cars to humorously draw attention to its small size and placing giant shoehorns behind tightly parked Smart cars to create buzz on blogs and social media sites. Expect more of this creativity with the 2012 full-scale launch of its Smart fortwo Electric Drive car.[10]

Questions

1. What experiential marketing tools did Smart use for the soft launch of its electric car?

2. What role did social media play in this soft launch?

products as possible. The market had become more competitive, production had become more efficient, and products were in abundance. Companies started to hard-sell to make a profit, and consumer needs were still not a major consideration. As the marketplace became more competitive, businesses developed more-sophisticated approaches, and the basic marketing stage evolved in the 1960s. At this point, consumer needs became paramount, and the marketing concept became the focus of businesses. The **marketing orientation** stage focuses on the idea that an organization should strive to satisfy the needs of consumers while also trying to achieve an organization's goals. The **marketing concept** follows this idea. An organization that has a marketing orientation focuses its efforts on continuously collecting information about customers' needs, sharing this information across departments, and using it to create customer value.[11]

In the last decade, marketing has evolved from a discipline with a short-term focus on transactions to one that now also focuses on building long-term customer relationships. This relationship marketing stage sees organizations considering the lifetime value of their customers and striving to offer better services, higher-quality products, and meaningful long-term relationships. Over the last few years, relationship marketing has included a greater use of social media, and an increased focus on customer relationship management and corporate social responsibility

to create meaningful relationships. These approaches emphasize customer retention and ongoing customer satisfaction rather than short-term transactions. It carefully uses information on customer interests to develop relationships with customers and retain their loyalty. Businesses recognize that improved customer relationships can result in increased customer loyalty, improved customer retention levels, and greater profits for an organization. Formally, the concept of **relationship marketing** is when organizations create long-term links with their customers, employees, suppliers, and other partners to increase loyalty and customer retention. (Figure 1–2 summarizes this evolution of business philosophies.)

It is important to understand that relationship marketing involves a personal, ongoing relationship between an organization and its customers that often starts before a sale occurs and lasts well beyond the point when a sale has concluded. The automobile industry has used this approach for many years, seeing the value of a satisfied customer play out in future purchases. It is common practice for car dealerships to regularly phone customers with invitations to events, send out mailings with car maintenance information, and even distribute branded magazines for customers to enjoy. Car manufacturers are also developing online relationship marketing tools. For example, Smart Canada has created online opportunities to make connections with its consumers and build lasting customer relationships. Owners of Smart cars can join an online club (www.clubsmartcar.ca) to access forums, post

Figure 1-2
The evolution of business philosophies

Production orientation | 1930s | Sales orientation | 1960s | Marketing orientation | 1990s | Relationship marketing orientation

articles, and view updates. Consumers can also access the Smart Canada website to view product information and subscribe to newsletters, while the Smart Canada Facebook page posts promotional offers and timely responses to questions. Additional information on its electric vehicles can also be found on the Toronto Hydro Smart Experience website.

Internet technology is fuelling the growth of relationship marketing as a business approach. Social media, database technology, and the increased importance of corporate social responsibility are all pointing toward creating meaningful relationships with customers to drive business success. Let's look at these three elements of relationship marketing in more detail.

Social media, with its ability to interact with consumers, often in real time, through social networks such as Facebook, Twitter, MySpace, YouTube, and blogs, has added a new dimension to relationship marketing, making it more immediate and interactive. Social media provides consumers with the ability to interact with marketing messages by posting comments that are visible to all. This open environment encourages companies to be more transparent and interactive in their communications. **Social media** is formally defined as a form of online media that allows members to create their own network of friends and contacts to share comments, videos, and images as a form of self-expression.

Social media can be used in four ways. First, marketers use social media to engage and connect with consumers. Special offers such as coupons may be sent out through Twitter or Facebook, while YouTube and promotional microsites can provide visual interest and further information. Second, marketers use social media to monitor real-time consumer engagement and brand buzz and to provide customer service. Social media metrics can be found on Twitter and Facebook with additional online metrics available to monitor consumer comments and allow marketers to respond in real time to customer queries. Third, marketers can use social media to measure the impact of specific promotional programs. Fourth, marketers can use social media to identify informal brand advocates that can spread positive messages about a brand. Typically, marketers seek brand fans with influential social networks and send them brand updates and information they

Suunto's social networking site creates an online community with a common passion for elite-level sports.

customer relationship management (CRM)
The overall process of building and maintaining profitable customer relationships by delivering superior customer value and satisfaction

corporate social responsibility (CSR)
When organizations voluntarily consider the well-being of society by taking responsibility for how their businesses impact consumers, customers, suppliers, employees, shareholders, communities, the environment, and society in general

may find useful. You may remember from this chapter's opening vignette that Suunto created its own social networking and web portal site, www.movescount.com, to create an online hub for its athletes and product users. Social media is discussed at length in Chapter 12.

Database technology has surfaced as a tool that facilitates relationship marketing by putting a focus on **customer relationship management (CRM)** for the marketing industry. This approach is rooted in the knowledge that it is less expensive to service and maintain current customers than to obtain new ones. CRM identifies a firm's most-valued customers and builds loyalty programs to appeal to their needs. It systematically identifies what leads to customer satisfaction and profitable brand loyalty. It is often facilitated by CRM software. Formally, CRM is defined as the overall process of building and maintaining profitable customer relationships by delivering superior customer value and satisfaction.[12]

We look to the Canadian retail industry to better understand CRM and to find out how it is applied. In its simplest form, CRM involves the occasional customer phone call on upcoming events such as an open house at a fitness club. In a more advanced state, it includes sophisticated customer loyalty programs that reward continued purchases and usage. Air Miles is an example of a widely recognized and sophisticated CRM program that partners with brands to provide members with travel rewards.

Retailers use CRM loyalty programs to help secure a greater *share-of-wallet* (dollars purchased) from their customers. They use loyalty cards to track individual purchases and then correlate the data with offers and incentives to determine what works best. Offers are then customized to meet the purchase habits of people with similar buying preferences. HBC with its HBC Rewards Card and Shoppers Drug Mart with its Optimum Card are pioneers of CRM in Canada.

Advanced CRM considers the value of specific customers over their lifetime and what offers are most suited to their stage in life. Let's look at a simple example. If a pregnant woman buys prenatal vitamins at a store that uses CRM tracking software, such as loyalty cards, in time she may start receiving coupons for diapers, baby food, and tips on infant nutrition; her prenatal purchase has triggered sophisticated computer

programs to recognize her eventual need for baby products. As this woman's needs evolve, and as the children get older, the offers may change to include over-the counter medications for toddlers or school supplies for youths. This is one of the ways that companies can use CRM to encourage customer loyalty.

Another simple example of how CRM can be applied at retail is in the area of store design. Retailers can use customer purchase data to analyze departmental purchases to improve store design and maximize profitability. If, for instance, CRM identifies organic foods as a highly purchased product for a store's catchment area, when the store is refurbished, the section for these products may be expanded and given more prominence. CRM is covered in more detail in Chapter 13.

Corporate social responsibility (CSR) has become an important part of the relationship marketing stage with companies realizing that consumers want to be associated with companies that share their values and interests. In this manner, CSR programs become part of a brand's fabric and help to build long-term relationships and solidify brand connections with consumers. CSR is an approach where companies consider the well-being of society as part of their business approach, with companies such as the Bank of Montreal reducing its greenhouse gas emissions by 5 percent over a three-year period.[13] CSR is a concept where organizations voluntarily consider the well-being of society by taking responsibility for how their businesses impact consumers, customers, suppliers, employees, shareholders, communities, the environment, and society in general.

Many organizations now include CSR components in their business plans, and since 2009, *Maclean's* magazine has published an annual corporate social responsibility report detailing Canada's "Top 50 Socially Responsible Corporations." Recent highlights include the Bank of Montreal focusing on clean air directives, Loblaw piloting a project that uses rooftop solar panels to generate electricity, and the ING Group linking executive compensation to CSR programs.[13]

CSR initiatives can range from the simple to the complex, and typically include one of three approaches. In its simplest forms, CSR can involve (1) the sponsorship and/or spearheading of community programs, and (2) the sponsorship and/or involvement in fundraising initiatives for charitable organizations. In its most advanced form, CSR is used (3) as a business philosophy that permeates an organization that implements socially responsible business practices to positively impact the community at large. At its most sophisticated level, executive compensation is linked in part to CSR results. Here are some outstanding examples that we see in Canada today.

- Tim Hortons is passionate about community involvement and the environment, and stands behind its CSR efforts to the extent that it has branded and trademarked its efforts under the heading "Making a True Difference."™ In 2011 it began publishing an annual sustainability and responsibility report. Tim Hortons has a long tradition of community involvement—in 1974 it established the Tim Horton Children's Foundation to honour the memory of Tim Horton, his love of children, and his desire to help the less fortunate. Annually, the foundation provides economically disadvantaged children with a fun-filled camp experience, with participation of 17,000 children as a targeted goal for 2013. Tim Hortons also sponsors local children's house leagues for hockey, soccer, lacrosse, T-ball, and baseball with over 275,000 children participating in the Timbits Minor Sports programs. Its long-term store directives focus on reducing the company's carbon footprint through recycling, and energy reduction programs.[14] Visit www.timhortons.com to read about their other CSR programs.

- CIBC is a Canadian financial institution that implements CSR by supporting major charitable

Tim Hortons CSR Directives

Kids sent to camps	17,000
Local community initiatives	$15 million in funding
Timbits Minor Sports programs	275,000 participants
Overseas coffee partnerships	2,500 small farmers

Source: "Tim Hortons Sustainability and Responsibility Summary," accessed May 2011 at www.timhortons.com/ca/pdf/2009CSR.pdf.

institutions such as its CIBC Children's Foundation, the United Way, and the Canadian Breast Cancer Foundation. The CIBC has supported breast cancer research, education, and awareness for over 15 years as the lead sponsor of the annual CIBC Run for the Cure fundraiser. In 2010, this charitable event involved over 170,000 participants and raised more than $33 million for the cause. Team CIBC alone included 13,000 participants that contributed over $3 million through the sale of pink merchandise, employee fundraising events, and the collection of pledges.[15] Visit www.cibc.com to see the results of its latest fundraiser for the Canadian Breast Cancer Foundation.

- HBC (The Bay, Home Outfitters, and Fields stores) uses CSR as a philosophy of doing business, with its efforts focused on reporting, measuring, and delivering on its promises to support the well-being of society. HBC's CSR efforts focus on four key areas: the environment, wellness, community investment, and ethical sourcing. The result has been very positive, with HBC responding to the 2010 Haitian earthquake disaster with a $360,000 donation to the Canadian Red Cross Haiti Earthquake fund and continuing to retrofit its stores with energy-control systems to regulate and monitor electricity usage. In 2007 HBC was applauded as the first Canadian head-office tower to be certified zero waste, and in 2008 it launched the first fully environmentally friendly Bay store in Conestoga, Ontario, boasting a 120,000-square-foot building supported by solar panels, energy-efficient lighting, recyclable carpet, thermal-reduction roofing, waterless urinals, touchless water faucets, touchless toilets, and an automated energy-management sys-

societal marketing concept

Marketing programs that focus on the consumer *and* the well-being of society

tem to reduce energy consumption. Today, all new HBC stores are built with energy-efficient lighting and energy-control systems.[16]

The marketing community is also putting an increased focus on the well-being of society and the environment. It is commonplace to now see marketing programs include a component that addresses these needs, an approach described as the **societal marketing concept**. An example is the Cadbury Bicycle Factory project where Cadbury pointed consumers to a microsite to enter UPC codes from its chocolate and confectionary products in an effort to collect bicycles for Ghana. Five thousand bicycles were sent to Ghana in three consecutive years to help provide transportation for families in need. (See the Marketing NewsFlash on page 23.)

Another example of the societal marketing concept is the Pepsi Refresh project that asks individuals, businesses, and non-profits to submit ideas on how to make the world a better place. This successful project launched in Canada in 2010, with Pepsi awarding grants based on the highest number of online votes. Projects need to positively impact communities, be achievable within 12 months, and be measurable. Pepsi accepted ideas for different projects categorized under arts and culture, food and shelter, the planet, education, health, or neighbourhoods. Pepsi Refresh grants are awarded at $5,000, $10,000, $25,000, or $100,000 levels. Recently, the project awarded $100,000 to the Lions Camp Dorset group to help people on dialysis take a family vacation. The funds helped purchase dialysis machines for the Lions Camp Dorset in Muskoka.[17]

New and Evolving Marketing Practices

L5 Marketing thinking has progressed over the years in response to changes in consumer expectations, societal pressures, technological changes, and the philosophy of doing business. Marketing today focuses not only on meeting short-term consumer needs and generating immediate company profits but also on the long-term viability of its business and the meaningful customer relationships and community initiatives it develops. Some of the most recent areas of focus include customer relationship management and corporate social

responsibility (as previously discussed), with additional emphasis placed on (1) digital marketing, (2) experiential marketing, (3) partnership marketing, and (4) metrics.

Digital Marketing

The widespread use of digital technology in Canada is the most important trend impacting how marketers go to business. Digital technology drives how consumers gather information, want to be entertained, and purchase products. When consumers first look for product information, a website is often their first point of contact with a company, followed by an online search to reveal further information. Social media sites such as Twitter, Facebook, YouTube, and blogs often appear in search results, putting a spotlight on personal experiences and positive or negative ratings. Poor service, substandard products, or unethical practices can quickly surface in a search and negatively impact product sales. The fact that marketers and companies are now held accountable in this digital arena, and that consumers are increasingly spending time online, is driving marketers to use digital marketing to communicate with consumers. It is worth pausing to note that consumers between the ages of 18 and 34 spend most of their media time on the Internet (39 percent) versus other forms of media such as TV or radio, with other age groups also increasingly using this format.[18]

ComScore, a highly respected online-research company, recently released statistics on Canada's use of digital media. Its *Canada Digital Year in Review 2010* highlights fourth-quarter data and states that people in Canada spend more time online that any other country. Standing at 44 hours per month, this is almost twice the worldwide average of 23 hours. Canada ranks top in the number of website visits per month at 95 per person, far outpacing the U.S. and U.K. at 81 visits and 69 visits, respectively. Canada's high usage rate is no surprise, related in part to its 95 percent high-speed Internet penetration rate and the fact that free public Internet hotspots exist throughout the country.

Drilling down into the data reveals some interesting trends. The younger demographic (2–17 years) is spending less time on the Internet than in previous years (down 4 percent), possibly attributable to the popularity of cellphone text messaging, which takes less Internet time. Conversely, people over 55 years are spending more time on the Internet than in previous years (up 12 percent), judged to be partly attributable to Internet familiarity and people taking their Internet habits with them as they age. This older age group frequently visits social networks with the 55-to-64 age-band increasing social network visits by 48 percent. Blog visits saw substantial growth, with people in Canada spending more time on these sites than in previous years.

While social network usage increased in total by 13 percent, e-mail usage declined by 28 percent. This is judged to be partly due to the popularity of text messaging, but also to Facebook's new messaging platform and the popularity of Skype and Apple's iChat (face-time video platforms). In line with these trends, marketers shifted online advertising dollars away from e-mail and business and finance sites onto social networks. Online video gained popularity in all age groups.

Looking to the future, consumers are expected to continue their love affair with mobile devices (cellphones and tablet computers) and increasingly use them to access online content, communicate with others, and make shopping decisions. Mobile apps that allow shoppers to easily interact with brands and check prices will push marketing dollars into the mobile marketing arena.[19]

This increased Internet usage is prompting marketers to use digital marketing to engage and communicate with consumers. Digital marketing includes many stellar online tools such as display advertising, affiliate marketing, search engine marketing, search engine optimizations, pay-per-click advertising, mobile marketing, e-mail marketing, and social media. These elements are discussed in detail in Chapter 12.

An example of digital marketing can be seen with the online retailer www.amazon.ca, which provides affiliates with display ads to place on their websites, sends e-mail alerts with special offers to its database of customers, uses pay-per-click advertising when various book terms are entered into a search engine, and carefully manages its website for optimization so that search queries deliver its website at the top of search rankings.

Offline products, such as the Smart car mentioned earlier in this chapter, also use digital marketing practices such as search engine optimization, display ads, e-mail newsletters, and social media to engage with consumers. At Smart Canada, they combine these online approaches with offline tools such as event marketing, public relations campaigns, and brochures and dealership signage to drive automobile sales.

Today's successful marketers go to business armed with strategies and approaches that meet consumer needs in both the online and offline environment. Marketers must have a clear understanding of how consumers navigate this digital world and how it relates to their non-digital offline interactions and behaviour.

Experiential Marketing

Experiential marketing is an approach where marketers create opportunities for consumers to interact directly with a brand. Instead of relying on mass media, a brand creates an occasion for a few consumers to interact personally with it and then spread the word to others. This builds awareness and generates word-of-mouth buzz and other forms of publicity for the brand. The brand goes from being passive to actively interacting with the target market. A brand can follow a number of approaches, often using a combination of public relations, event marketing, and promotions to break

Internet Usage Rankings, by Country

Average monthly data per visitor (rounded)

Rank	Country	Website Visits/ Month	Hours per Visitor/ Month
1.	Canada	95	44
2.	U.S.	80	35
3.	U.K.	69	32
4.	France	69	27
5.	Germany	60	24
6.	Brazil	57	26

Source: ComScore Inc. Media Metrix, World Media Metrix, All Locations, Persons: 15+, 3 MO.AVG Q4 2010. comScore, *The 2010 Canada Digital Year in Review*, March 2011, accessed at www.comscore.com/Press_Events/Presentations_Whitepapers/2011/2010_Canada_Digital_Year_in_Review.

> *Today's successful marketers go to business armed with strategies and approaches that meet consumer needs in both the online and offline environment.*

through the clutter of competing marketing messages. A recent example of experiential marketing in Canada relates to a relatively new shopping centre, the Shops at Don Mills, Ontario's first outdoor lifestyle centre, which offers best-in-class stores, restaurants, and services, as well as a skating rink and town square, in a European high-street setting. In order for people to live within the brand and experience the lifestyle centre firsthand, the shopping centre hosts a number of events, including concerts by celebrity music artists such as Jesse Cook, children's scavenger hunts, educational birds of prey demonstrations, and firework displays. Other mini-events are scheduled throughout the year such as a jazz festival, an exotic petting zoo, and a Movie Night in the Square.[20]

The hair-care brand John Frieda also recently launched an experiential marketing campaign to promote its Sheer Blonde product. A Facebook event invited blondes to attend a special hair-care function in Toronto, the Sheer Blonde Experience, to learn from its top stylists and to enter a draw to win a VIP trip for two to New York. Online ads and shout-outs on Facebook spread the word, while street teams created additional buzz by inviting blondes spotted in the city to the event. Over 330 people attended the event, enjoyed complementary hair consultations, and had the opportunity to participate in a photo shoot. All participants received complementary gift bags of beauty items including John Frieda beauty products.[21]

Partnership Marketing

Partnership marketing has gained momentum over the last few years with companies providing customers with added value through complementary promotional offers. The intent of **partnership marketing** is to create formal associations between brands that will result in incremental business for both brands that could not have been achieved separately. The purpose of partnership marketing is to drive incremental business and a strong return on investment (ROI). It is rooted in the idea that brands with similar customers but different distribution channels can combine marketing expertise and use each other's strengths to build brand awareness and incremental revenue

A strategic alliance between Scotiabank and Cineplex created the SCENE loyalty card.

streams. The challenge lies in finding appropriate partners, setting realistic goals, tracking results, and aligning partnership goals with business objectives.[22]

Examples of companies that practise partnership marketing are Shoppers Drug Mart, Yahoo!, Sears, Coca-Cola, and the Ontario Science Centre. When Shoppers Drug Mart selects a certain day to provide customers with $20 Esso gift cards for in-store purchases over $75, this is an example of partnership marketing. Shoppers Drug Mart and Esso teamed up to drive increased distribution to their retail outlets and provide exceptional customer value.

Partnership marketing takes many forms, permeates different platforms, and exists online or offline. Partnerships can be simple **promotional partnerships** and involve short-term offers between brands such as Shoppers Drug Mart and Esso. Coca-Cola also uses promotional partnerships with its iCoke.ca loyalty program where members enter pin numbers located under bottle caps of Coca-Cola, Diet Coke, Coke Zero, and Sprite to collect iCoke reward points. Consumers collect these points to enter contests or redeem them for products that

> *Brands with similar customers but different distribution channels can combine marketing expertise and use each other's strengths.*

are part of this program, such as Pizza Pizza (win a Pizza Pizza party), McDonald's (redeem points for a gift card), Canada's Wonderland (redeem points for passes), and the Calgary Stampede (redeem points for free kid's admissions).

Another form of partnership marketing, with a longer-term focus, is the **strategic alliance**. This involves long-term arrangements between companies with similar values and objectives that extend beyond short-term promotional offers into long-term business agreements. An example of a strategic alliance exists with the SCENE loyalty movie rewards program where Cineplex and Scotiabank formed a long-term arrangement to benefit both companies. SCENE members collect points when purchasing Cineplex movie tickets or concession items. Points can be redeemed for free movies or discounted DVDs. Scotiabank Visa credit card holders earn additional points when paying with their Scotiabank Visa card. In its first 14 months, the SCENE loyalty program built a database of a million customers, with Scotiabank adding 100,000 new bank accounts, many from the 18-to-34 demographic it was targeting with this program.[23]

Partnership marketing does not just involve the use of loyalty cards. The Ontario Science Centre uses partnership marketing to add value to its educational programs and to offset costs. It looks for partners with similar marketing objectives and parallel values. One of its valued partners, Telus, shares similar interests in education, youth, science, and technology. This resulted in a 15-year partnership that saw the creation of the Teluscape outdoor learning space as well as the Telus Rain Forest exhibit. Annually, Telus and the Ontario Science Centre review joint promotional opportunities that can benefit each organization.[24]

Metrics

The Canadian business world is a performance-based culture that uses metrics to improve programs and deliver better results. **Metrics** are an important area that measures and monitors business performance. It includes the collection and usage of data to evaluate programs and to recommend changes.

Metrics can take many forms and are generally classified as either *routine metrics* or *program-specific*

metrics. Routine metrics are measured against marketing plan targets and look at elements such as sales, market share, profit margins, and profit levels. Program-specific metrics analyze specific marketing programs and measure performance against benchmarks and targets. Theses metrics can include elements such as return on investment (ROI), awareness levels, ad recall, sales conversions, coupon redemption rates, contest entries, or media mentions, depending on the task at hand.

Digital marketing has increased the emphasis on metrics, which are quick, easy, and affordable in the online environment. Digital technology allows marketers to measure online sales and drill down to the origin of the sale and when consumers may have opted in or opted out of the purchase funnel. Online measurement tools also allow marketers to measure website interactions such as unique visitors, time on site, page views, returning visitors, newsletter signups, digital downloads, online buzz, or online purchases. This data can be meshed with cost information to deliver actionable analyses on costs-per-click, costs-per-conversion, and program-specific goals. Changes to website design and other forms of online communications such as display ads, landing pages, social media outreach, and e-mail blasts can then be made to optimize programs. Marketers are challenged to sift through the deluge of online metrics and to use the information to understand how to build better relationships with consumers.

A Focus on Ethics

Companies and marketers focus more and more on the well-being of society and the environment, realizing they can make a difference. However, not all organizations and marketers are interested in CSR or the societal marketing concept. This orientation requires a long-term financial investment from an organization and a genuine commitment from its employees. In Canada, regulations are put in place to safeguard people, communities, and the environment from businesses

that may not have their well-being in mind (see Chapter 2). These regulations can take many forms, such as pollution-emission thresholds, food and safety regulations, advertising standards, telemarketing regulations, and water safety guidelines, just to name a few. A recent example relates to the 2010 draft federal copyright legislation, designed to protect digital copyright holders from content being unlawfully downloaded, sold, or shared on the Internet. The *Copyright Modernization Act*, Bill C-32, proposes that consumers be permitted to make one copy per device of a digital download such as a music track, movie, or TV program, making it illegal to download copyrighted materials that have been digitally locked by the owner. Breaking these locks could result in $20,000 fines. Readers are advised to access final updates to this bill which at press time had not yet been passed by the government.[25]

Consumer groups also exert pressure on government bodies to protect society. This was seen in 2010 when Toyota's ethics came into question regarding its delayed response to necessary product recalls. This prompted consumer advocates to demand stricter government regulations, which expedited a federal bill that now allows the government to directly recall dangerous products, rather than rely on voluntary manufacturer recalls.[26]

In addition to government regulations, many companies, industries, and professional associations have guidelines and codes of ethics that provide direction to employees and members on areas that are considered unacceptable. The Canadian Marketing Association (CMA) is the professional body for the marketing industry. It responds to legislative issues and sets guidelines on areas such as responsible business practices, ethics, and privacy policy. The CMA has dealt with policy issues concerning telemarketing fraud, electronic commerce,

and privacy. It has over 800 corporate members from major financial institutions, insurance companies, manufacturers, publishers, retailers, charitable organizations, agencies, relationship marketers, and those involved in e-business and Internet marketing.

The CMA has a code of ethics with which all members must comply. Its purpose is to encourage ethical and legal marketing. It covers topics such as accurate representations, truthfulness in marketing communications, price claims, fulfillment practices, privacy policy, marketing to children, and direct marketing approaches. The CMA's website contains a wealth of information for marketers, including its code of ethics, marketing tips, case studies, news releases, educational courses, and job postings. Visit www.the-cma.org to become familiar with this important marketing association.

Marketing Careers

L⑥ Many students wonder whether there are jobs in the marketing field. As in any business, it is somewhat dependent on the strength of the economy, and entry-level jobs exist for college and university graduates. The starting point is to get an education and, while studying, to create a network of business professionals to contact upon graduation. Creating this network can be done through summer jobs and volunteering in areas that might be of interest. Networking with guest speakers who may visit your institution is also an important avenue to pursue. These strategies are a wonderful way to gain exposure to the marketing discipline. Be sure to bookmark Canadian marketing job-search websites and to track job postings. Examples of sites that have job postings include www.iabcanada.com, www.marketingmag.ca, www.strategymag.com, www.the-cma.org, and www.mediajobsearchcanada.com.

Entry-level positions exist in sales, marketing, and promotions in a variety of fields. Job titles vary from company to company, but typical jobs include marketing coordinators, marketing analysts, marketing assistants, sales representatives, and account coordinators. These entry-level jobs usually include

"JOBS EXIST FOR COLLEGE AND UNIVERSITY GRADUATES."

on-the-job training, the creation of analytical reports, liaison with other departments within the company, exposure to marketing program development, and the potential to move up within the organization. Areas of growth are in promotions and Internet service businesses. Opportunities exist in small, medium, and large organizations, and can be found in the private sector, in the non-profit sector, and in the government. In the private sector, marketers are required in consumer marketing and in the business-to-business market. For students who have the advantage of a foreign language, this language can be leveraged with companies dealing in foreign markets, or in Canada with multicultural target groups. Companies are often looking for employees with language skills.

Students wanting to get into the marketing field need to be analytical, to be able to work with others, to be capable of working in teams, and to have strong communication skills in both written and verbal contexts. As a marketer, you need to keep your finger on the pulse of the consumer. This requires you to stay current, to be intellectually curious, and to be involved in the conversation of life. Marketers need to read newspapers, magazines, and blogs; attend conferences and webinars; surf the Internet, watch TV, and listen to the radio; and absorb the trends that are evolving in society and around the world. Publications such as *Marketing* magazine, *Strategy* magazine, *Canadian Business*, and *Maclean's* magazine are highly recommended as well as subscribing to the *Mashable* blog and *eMarketer* online newsletter.

marketing *NewsFlash* | Cadbury Sends Bikes to Africa

Cadbury Canada was recently applauded for delivering 5,000 bicycles to Ghana as part of its Bicycle Factory program. This successful program, running in 2011 for a third year, is part of Cadbury's focus on community well-being and helping disadvantaged communities in Africa. Cadbury has been involved in community programs in Ghana for over 100 years and saw an opportunity to help communities in the region. In a recent press release, Luisa Cirotto, vice president corporate affairs, Cadbury North America, tells us about the importance of bicycles to these communities, "In Africa, a bicycle can mean access to clean water, medical care, and education. Through the Bicycle Factory program we can improve overall mobility and therefore livelihood and we know Canadians will be empowered to help us realize our goal."

The Bicycle Factory initially used traditional TV ads to point consumers to its microsite at www.thebicyclefactory.ca. Here consumers entered UPC codes from Cadbury products such as Caramilk, Dairy Milk, Trident gum, Dentyne gum, Maynards Wine Gums, and Sour Patch Kids to help build bicycles. Each code represented one part of a bicycle, with 100 parts needed to build a bike. In Ghana, where a farmer may make only $1 per day, a bicycle costing over $90 is considered a luxury. The Bicycle Factory program was designed to give more families access to bicycles and to therefore improve their quality of life. The campaign's impactful TV spot showed the multiple uses of a bicycle in Ghana ranging from a delivery truck, to an ambulance, to a school bus, showing that bicycles in Ghana are more

than just a mode of transportation; they represent hope, survival, and freedom. In 2011 Cadbury supplemented its campaign with a Facebook page that asked consumers to trades LIKES for BIKES.

In Ghana, although school is free, many children have to walk over two hours to attend school. This results in children not attending school or being too tired to participate after the long walk. According to the United Nations, 40 million children in Africa do not attend school due to access issues—a bicycle can give these children easy access to education.[27]

Questions

1. What added value is Cadbury providing to its brand with the Bicycle Factory program?

2. Is the Bicycle Factory initiative part of the societal marketing concept or a CRS initiative or both?

Marketers often spend part of their careers working in a sales or promotional role, and moving into marketing with this relevant and valuable experience. We look to two recent marketing graduates, Brandy Cremascoli and Ashley Caristena, to get a glimpse into the types of jobs available for marketing graduates. Brandy Cremascoli entered the marketing field while still completing her full-time studies, working part-time for an Internet marketing company where she evaluated pay-per-click advertising campaigns. Upon graduation, Brandy found her passion working as an insight analyst with Cadbury Adams, moving on to become a go-to-market coordinator, a position where she liaised with the marketing and sales departments. "Working at Cadbury Adams was the best possible experience for me," explains Brandy. "I learned how sales and marketing departments function and that these areas make for rewarding career choices!" Now Brandy Cremascoli is at the world's leading marketer of branded consumer lawn and garden products, the Scotts Miracle-Gro Company as a program coordinator working in expanded roles within both the sales and marketing departments. "My job is insanely busy," explains Brandy, who juggles marketing projects such as catalogue development and the creation of online video news-clips in her sales-support role. She provides product training to corporate employees at Lowe's, Canadian Tire, Home Depot, RONA, and Home Hardware. She also develops in-store support

materials and plays a key role in many high-profile trade shows. A recent highlight was the creation of Scotts eLearning Solutions Centre, complete with online audio-visual materials that explain the usage and benefits of Scotts' products. "This tool allows retailers living in remote regions to learn about our products, a difficult task when sales calls are infrequent. This system allows us to track retailer involvement in the site and then work with them to make improvements," explains Brandy.

Ashley Caristena, also a marketing graduate, entered the marketing field at a digital advertising agency where she worked on client projects. "This was a great entry-level job for me," explains Ashley, "But I learned that client-side work was what I really wanted to do, so I moved on to the Katz Group where I work with the corporate stores, Rexall Pharma Plus. As a marketing coordinator I realized marketing was the area for me!" Ashley managed Rexall's sports sponsorships, the Rexall Edmonton Indy race car championship and the Rogers Cup international tennis tournament held at the Rexall Centre in Toronto. She recently moved into the increasingly important CRM area as a loyalty marketing coordinator. In this new role, Ashley helps to create loyalty programs focused on acquiring customers and building long-term relationships that drive business. "Retail marketing is a fascinating area where everyday holds something new. The challenge lies in staying on top of trends and understanding how to build relationships with customers," states Ashley.

Both graduates pass along their insights into what it takes to work in marketing and how to get a job in the field. Brandy tells us, "Networking really is the key! Meet as many people as possible, stay in touch, and never burn a bridge." Ashley echoes this same sentiment, pointing students toward the business network LinkedIn to create a professional profile and a solid network of contacts. She also emphasizes the value of college and university career centres for job leads.

As for what it takes to work in marketing, these marketing graduates emphasize the importance of having a passion for what you do, thriving in a fast-paced environment, having strong communications skills, and a solid understanding of current trends; being analytical, creative, and hard-working are also on top of Ashley's lists. Brandy mentions that once you are established within a company, volunteering for increased responsibilities can expose you to new areas.

Marketing is an exciting area where change is the norm and being able to rise to the challenge is imperative. Learn the fundamentals through education and apply your knowledge by working in the industry. Good luck, Brandy Cremascoli and Ashley Caristena!

[adAlyze]

Who is the target market?

Is this advertising a good, a service, or an idea?

What gets your attention in this ad?

porter
flying refined

Breeze into the Windy City.
Only Porter offers up to 6 daily non-stops between Toronto City Airport and Chicago's downtown Midway Airport.

Book online, call 1-888-619-8622 or contact your travel agent.

Sign up for VIPorter frequent flyer program
www.flyporter.com

Summary...*just the facts*

- The essence of marketing is to focus on consumer needs and to generate revenue, profits, or support for an organization.

- The marketing process follows three main steps: (1) identifying consumer needs, (2) managing the marketing mix to meet consumer needs, and (3) realizing revenues or profits.

- The marketing mix, also known as the 4 Ps, consists of product, price, place, and promotion.

- Product refers to all the attributes that make up a good, a service, or an idea. Product elements include areas such as product design, product features, colour, packaging, warranty, and service levels.

- Price refers to the retail shelf price and sale price of a product.

- Place refers to the distribution channels and retailers required to sell the product.

- Promotion refers to the communication tools needed to communicate to consumers, such as advertising, sales promotion, public relations, direct marketing, and personal selling.

- Marketers are responsible for bringing profits and revenues into the company.

- The evolution of marketing has progressed from a production orientation stage, to a sales orientation stage, to a marketing orientation stage, and finally to a relationship marketing stage.

- Important areas of the relationship marketing stage are customer relationship management (CRM) and corporate social responsibility (CSR).

- New and evolving marketing practices have surfaced in the areas of digital marketing, partnership marketing, experiential marketing, and metrics.

- The Canadian Marketing Association (CMA) is the professional body for the marketing industry that responds to legislative issues and sets guidelines on responsible business practices.

- The starting point to a career in marketing is to get an education and, while studying, to create a network of business professionals to contact upon graduation.

Key Terms and Concepts...*a refresher*

corporate social responsibility (CSR) p. 16
customer relationship management (CRM) p. 16
customer value p. 6
exchange p. 10
experiential marketing p. 19
good p. 10
idea p. 11
market p. 12

marketing p. 10
marketing concept p. 14
marketing mix p. 7
marketing orientation p. 14
marketing process p. 9
metrics p. 21
partnership marketing p. 20
place p. 8
price p. 8
product pp. 8, 10

production orientation p. 13
promotion p. 8
promotional partnerships p. 20
relationship marketing p. 14
sales orientation p. 13
service p. 11
social media p. 15
societal marketing concept p. 18
strategic alliances p. 21
target market p. 7

Hands-on...*apply your knowledge*

Marketing Mix Assignment Suunto has created a new sports training device for professional hockey teams where coaches can measure, monitor, and compare athlete performance during practices. Review the opening vignette on Suunto and then brainstorm on the marketing mix required to market this new product to professional hockey teams. Outline the marketing mix under the headings *Product, Price, Place,* and *Promotion*.

Reality Check...*reminder*

Refer back to this chapter's opening vignette and answer the Reality Check questions on page 4.

 connect

Connect allows you to practise important concepts at your own pace and on your own schedule, with 24/7 online access to an eBook, practice quizzes, video cases, chapter application questions, discussion activities, Internet exercises, interactivities, study tools, and more..

Visit
www.mhconnect.ca
to learn more.

the marketing environment

In marketing, staying abreast of consumer trends is important and marketers work to understand consumer concerns and motivations and adjust products and programs to meet evolving needs. In Chapter 2 we focus on the *marketing environment*—the factors that marketers monitor to stay current and informed—and explain how these factors impact marketing decisions. We start by looking at Dempster's breads and speak to Andrew Pollock, senior vice president of marketing at Canada Bread, to understand how

Dempster's reviews these *marketing environmental factors* to develop relevant and compelling marketing programs that meet changing consumer needs. "We try to make our brands stand out in today's supermarket," he tells us. "Dempster's competes with in-store bakeries that offer freshly baked breads as well as pre-packaged loaves that appear side-by-side on supermarket shelves. We must deliver the very best quality to really stand out in the marketplace." He goes on to explain that the marketing of bread has its challenges. Canada Bread keeps a close eye on the marketing environment to overcome these challenges.

Dempster's was started by the James Dempster bakery in the early 1900s and later purchased by Canada Bread and Maple Leaf Foods. The brand prides itself on creating high-quality nutritious breads that taste great. Its line includes whole-grain and white breads as well as specialty products such as flatbreads, English muffins, and OvenFresh par-baked baguettes and rolls for freshness. Andrew Pollock points us toward Dempster's Smart bread, a highly successful brand developed to meet changing consumer needs. "Smart bread is a success story that shows how staying on top of consumer trends and understanding what affects consumer decision-making can result in a very viable brand," explains Pollock. "In five years, Smart bread has become an $80 million business for Canada Bread, and Dempster's Smart bread is now #1 in the category." Let's look at the marketing of Smart bread in more detail and focus on the marketing environment to see how Canada Bread used this information to launch a successful new brand.

The marketing environment looks at demographic trends, socio-cultural changes, the economic environment, the use of technology, the competitive nature of the market, and regulatory forces. Canada Bread considered the latest trends and concerns in these areas as it moved toward developing new products for the market. Specifically, Canada Bread noted the following:

- **Socio-cultural factors:** Canada Bread wanted to understand consumers' food interests to determine whether new product and marketing opportunities existed. Canada Bread noted that families were experimenting with new food choices and enjoying a wider assortment of multicultural dishes and ethnic foods. Society was also becoming more aware of the relationship between food, nutrition, and health and looking for nutritious, easy, meal-time solutions. Nutrition and the environment were top concerns with people wanting to make choices that benefited their families and the environment but they were not always willing to pay a premium for these benefits. Canada Bread saw an opportunity in the health and nutrition area, particularly with products directed toward families with children.

- **Demographic factors:** Canada Bread reviewed demographic information and saw continued increases in single-parent families, time-starved parents, and an aging population that was educated and knowledgeable. Dempster's realized there was an opportunity to help busy families make informed decisions on nutritious food choices and to make meal-planning easier. Dempster's reviewed its target market information to see where the greatest potential existed. Its target market consisted of four main groups: (1) *dual-income soccer moms*, which are time-starved parents looking for ideas on quick and nutritious tasty meals; (2) *no-frills families*, people who watch their pennies and want affordable nutritious foods; (3) *healthy foodies*, adults who

love food and are focused on health and nutrition; and (4) *private-label pensioners,* older adults who are price-sensitive and see bread as a functional food. A demographic and socio-cultural review of these target groups revealed that dual-income soccer moms and no-frills families had the strongest business potential for a healthier white bread.

- **Economic factors:** A review of economic factors confirmed that bread is recession-proof and that during uncertain economic times people buy bread more than ever and choose to bring sandwiches to work and eat meals at home or at their desks. Dempster's understood that the demand for quality breads was strong in the current economic climate.
- **Technological factors:** Canada Bread wanted to understand how consumers used new technology and how this affected its marketing practices. Its review highlighted that its target markets were at ease with the Internet and that Dempster's should continue to integrate online approaches into communication programs.
- **Competitive factors:** Canada Bread confirmed that Dempster's has strong branded presence in the retail industry and that Dempster's is seen as a top-quality brand competing head-on with brands such as Wonder Bread and D'Italiano. These competitive brands have guaranteed distribution through Loblaw Company stores, which are owned by the same parent company, George Weston Limited.
- **Regulatory factors:** A thorough review of this area highlighted Canada Bread functions in a highly regulated environment, with Health Canada and the Canadian Food Inspection Agency monitoring and regulating product claims, product names, and manufacturing processes to ensure that all products meet government guidelines for health and safety. Health claims cannot be made unless they are supported by rigorous clinical studies and then approved by Health Canada. Even product names are scrutinized for making health associations. The Canadian Food Inspection Agency adds another level of complexity, vetoing the use of certain ingredients and manufacturing practices unless they fall within approved guidelines. Dempster's realized that working within these regulations is a necessary but a time-consuming challenge.

Canada Bread looked at these areas of the marketing environment and saw substantial business opportunities in a soft-textured, more-nutritious white bread. Research indicated almost a third of current white bread purchasers would buy such a product as long as it had the same soft texture and appearance as their regular white bread. Canada Bread created product prototypes and fielded consumer research to select a winning formulation. A blend of whole grain and white flour was selected and a unique name chosen to launch the product as Smart bread under the Dempster's brand umbrella. Dempster's knew it could not make overt health claims and relied on the product name and subtle claims that the product had the goodness of whole grains.

Canada Bread positioned Smart bread to appeal to consumer needs for a soft-textured, nutritious family bread that is fun for kids (influencers in the category). The name, Dempster's Smart bread, cleverly emphasized the product benefits. Canada Bread did not stop here. "We knew we had to do something more to differentiate Smart bread," explains Pollock. "So we created a superhero mascot, Smartman, to make the product fun and to shout out its benefits. A mascot was unheard of in the category but one of our talented marketers with insights into the cold cereal business understood that a mascot could distinguish the brand and make emotional connections with kids. To this day we get letters asking whether Smartman can make appearances at kid's birthday parties!"

The Smartman mascot was placed front and centre on all Smart bread marketing materials, including the packaging. This differentiated the brand and made a bold statement in the category. The Smartman mascot makes appearances at store openings and during in-store promotional events. It is also the focus of a fun microsite at www.smartman.ca where children can play online games and parents can find quick and nutritious meal ideas and enter contests. Over time, hamburger buns, hot dog buns, tortillas, English muffins, and 100% whole-grain bread were introduced under the Dempster's Smart bread line. Visit www.smartman.ca and www.dempsters.ca to see Canada Bread's latest marketing initiatives.[1] 🍎

---

reality **CHECK**

As you read Chapter 2, refer back to the Smart bread vignette to answer the following questions:

- What changes do you see in the current marketing environment that may influence Smart bread's product development?
- What other marketing communication tools could Smart bread integrate into its marketing mix?
- If the Smart bread brand wanted to increase its strength in ethnic communities in Canada, what should it do?

> *Marketers constantly monitor the marketing environment with a view to capitalizing on new opportunities and curtailing potential threats.*

The Marketing Environment

L○₁ Chapter 2 focuses on understanding the marketing environment and how it provides marketers with direction on how to best market products to meet changing consumer needs. Marketers and consumers do not function in a vacuum and marketers understand that successful marketing programs must reach out and address changes in the marketplace while also touching areas of increasing interest. In the example noted in this chapter's opening vignette, Canada Bread recognized consumers were demanding more nutritious products and that its efforts needed to mesh with today's busy lifestyles. Product development considered industry regulations and reviewed competitive offerings to determine whether new business opportunities existed and whether there was room to improve marketing approaches. An opportunity to reach consumers on an emotional level with a line of more-nutritious products surfaced and helped create the successful Smart bread product line.

Marketers take this approach and scan the elements of the marketing environment to identify business opportunities. After conducting further analysis and research, marketers integrate sound business ideas into marketing plans that provide direction for the business. Businesses and non-profit organizations use this approach to stay appraised of changes that affect their target markets. Marketers constantly monitor the marketing environment with a view to capitalizing on new opportunities and curtailing potential threats that may challenge their businesses. In short, marketers scan the marketing environment and review six key areas of focus: (1) demographic forces, (2) socio-cultural forces, (3) economic forces, (4) technological forces, (5) competitive forces, and (6) regulatory forces. This chapter looks at developments in these areas, providing a variety of examples that demonstrate how heeding and responding to these changes can result in more-effective marketing programs.

Dempster's creates new products to meet changing consumer needs.

The Core: Chapter 2

A marketing environmental scan helps marketers identify what changes affect their consumers.

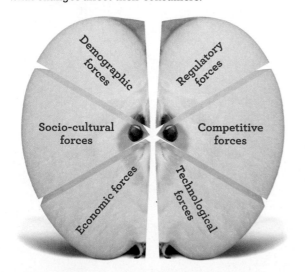

A marketer looks at opportunities and threats that stem from the world around the consumer.

A Marketing Environmental Scan

L○₂ A **marketing environmental scan** is the process of continually acquiring information on events occurring outside an organization to identify trends and pinpoint opportunities and threats to a business. Marketers use this knowledge to ensure that their goods, services, and ideas are relevant and meaningful, often using a marketing environmental scan as a steppingstone to conducting a more extensive SWOT analysis. A **SWOT analysis** (**S**trengths, **W**eakness, **O**pportunities, and **T**hreats) is discussed in more detail in Chapters 6 and 14, but in simple terms, it involves assessing how well a company is faring in servicing its businesses and target consumers by assessing an organization's internal strengths and weaknesses, as well as its external opportunities and threats. It looks at this in relation to the industry, its competitors, and trends identified in an environmental scan. This information is then used to set the future direction for the business and lay the groundwork for competitive marketing programs that can bring revenue into an organization. A marketing environmental scan looks at the forces identified in "The Core" image (page 31), namely demographic forces, socio-cultural forces, economic forces, technological forces, competitive forces, and regulatory forces.

Demographic Forces

L3 The statistical study of populations is referred to as **demographics**. It looks at characteristics such as gender, age, ethnicity, income, education, and occupation of a group of people. Marketers can access demographic information through Statistics

Who's Who in Canada?

	Population
Baby boomers	9.6 million
Generation X	3.9 million
Generation Y*	8.7 million

*Also known as the millennials

Source: Statistics Canada, 2006 Census of Population, Statistics Canada catalogue no. 97-551-XCB2006009.

Figure 2–1
Foreign-born populations in Canada

Foreign-Born Population (by census divisions

- 0.3% – 3.4%
- 3.5% – 7.7%
- 7.8% – 14.9%
- 15.0% – 30.7%
- 30.8% – 50%
- Non-ecumene population (sparsely populated area

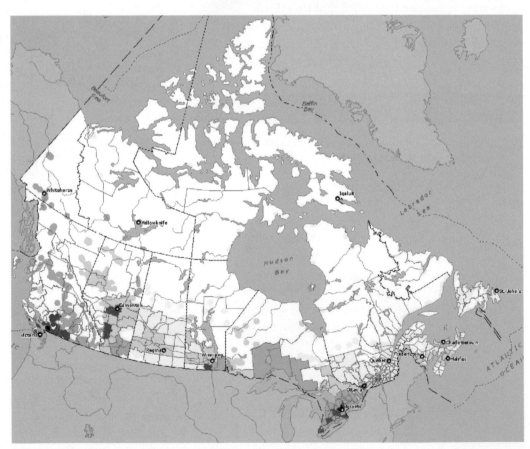

Source: Natural Resources Canada, "Foreign-born Population, 2006." Accessed at http://atlas.nrcan.gc.ca/site/english/maps/peopleandsociety/immigration/FB.

Canada or through their own surveys and databases of information. It is important for marketers to clearly understand changes that are occurring in the demographic arena to ensure that marketing efforts are well placed and opportunities are not over-looked.

Statistics Canada provides demographic data through its census information. The Census of Canada, which occurs every five years, just occurred in 2011, and data will be published in batches over the subsequent two years. Currently available data (2006) shows that the Canadian population is growing older, contains diverse generations, is settling in the suburbs of large cities, is becoming more ethnically mixed (see Figure 2–1), and is increasingly living in non-traditional families.[2] We look at these trends and identify their impact on marketing efforts.

An Aging Population The 2006 Census of Canada shows that Canada is populated by approximately 31.6 million people, of which 3.7 million, or 11.7 percent, are between the ages of 55 and 64, an all-time high.[3] The percentage of the population over the age of 65 also continues to increase due to low birth rates and better health care, which extends people's lifespans. This age group now represents 13.7 percent of the population (see Figure 2–2), resulting in a higher proportion of seniors who require different goods and services. Marketers are also noting an important fact: People over the age of 50 control 75 percent of the net worth of Canadian households,[4] flagging this as an opportunity for business growth. Figure 2–3 (page 36) tracks the increasing number of people in Canada over the age of 65 from 1956 until the latest 2006 census information, showing an increase of 6 percentage points.

Marketers are rising to the occasion and addressing this greying market with new products and services geared to this target group. The cosmetics and hair-care industry is awash in products that meet the aging population's demand for products that address aging skin-care and hair-care needs. Face creams focus on reducing the signs of aging, while the hair-care industry increasingly launches new products for men and women that cover grey hair. In addition, research indicates that the greying population in Canada is more likely to spend its resources on travel and electronics and channels funds toward health-related products. On the health care front, Tylenol is an example of a health care brand specifically addressing the aging population. Noting that arthritis is

becoming more prevalent due to the aging population, it developed Tylenol Arthritis Pain to help relieve pain symptoms. Tylenol advertises this product in magazines such as *CAA Magazine*, which focuses on older Canadians who travel.

Diverse Generations Marketers note four main generational groups of consumers: baby boomers, Generation X, Generation Y (also known as Millennials), and Generation Z (the Net Generation). **Baby boomers** are the main reason for the greying of North America. During the baby boom (people born between 1946 and 1964), families had an average of 4 children versus the current average of 1.54.[5] This group now accounts for approximately 60 percent of expenditures on consumer goods and services, and will continue to be a key force as it moves into its senior years.[6] Baby boomers are currently redefining the concept of aging with a keen interest in health, self-image, and retirement. Marketers have noted these interests and are developing products to address these needs. Examples that we noted earlier were for the host of anti-wrinkle creams and grey-hair products that have saturated the personal care arena, but we also see an increase in other items, such as luxury educational vacations for the aging boomers with high levels of disposable income. Baby boomers are increasingly using digital technology to communicate with others and research products. While not at the forefront of social media usage during its early days, in 2010 eMarketer reported a surge in baby boomers' social media usage—a jump of 15 percent from the previous year, resulting in 46 percent of baby boomers now maintaining a profile on social networks such as Facebook, MySpace, Twitter, or LinkedIn.

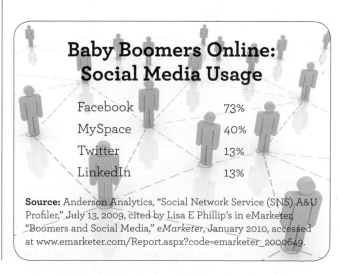

Baby Boomers Online: Social Media Usage

Facebook	73%
MySpace	40%
Twitter	13%
LinkedIn	13%

Source: Anderson Analytics, "Social Network Service (SNS) A&U Profiler," July 13, 2009, cited by Lisa E Phillip's in eMarketer "Boomers and Social Media," *eMarketer*, January 2010, accessed at www.emarketer.com/Report.aspx?code=emarketer_2000649.

Figure 2–2
Percentage of people over 65 years of age

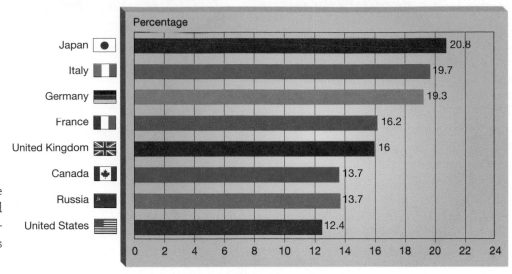

Country	Percentage
Japan	20.8
Italy	19.7
Germany	19.3
France	16.2
United Kingdom	16
Canada	13.7
Russia	13.7
United States	12.4

The aging population is a trend shared by many countries.

Sources: Statistics Canada, 2006 Census, accessed at http://www12.statcan.ca/census-recensement/2006/as-sa/97-551/figures/c4-eng.cfm.

Marketers take note of these changes and adjust their communication platforms accordingly.[7]

Generation X is the group of people born after the baby boomers, between 1965 and 1974. In Canada, this generation numbers 3.9 million, accounting for 12 percent of the population.[8] These consumers differ from baby boomers in that they are not as brand loyal and tend to be more self-reliant, entrepreneurial, and better educated. They are less prone to materialism and extravagance than the baby boomers. Generation X is becoming a key influence in the market.[9]

Generation Y is the group of people born between 1975 and 1991.[10] These are mostly children of baby boomers, and are also referred to as the *echo boom* or *millennials*. They number 8.7 million and account for 27.5 percent of the Canadian population.[11] Music, video games, sports, and computer purchases are key products developed to meet the needs of this demographic group. In time, this generation is expected to become as influential as their baby-boom parents.

Generation Z is the group of people born between 1992 and 2010. They have grown up with the Internet, and as pioneers of social media are considered the most disruptive of the generations. Otherwise known as the *net generation*, they are avid users of social media, very objective in their purchases, and not very brand loyal. They are discoverers and creators of content that they readily critique and share with others.

Each of these four generations has very different tastes, consumption patterns, and attitudes. For each generation, marketers need to develop distinct marketing programs, products, and services. For example,

Smart bread creates recipe booklets for in-store retail displays.

Baby Boomers Flock to Social Media

Marketers take note! Baby boomers, once considered uncomfortable in the online environment, are using the Internet to gather information and communicate with others. An Anderson Analytics Usage and Attitude study highlights that boomers are comfortable in the online environment and use social networks to connect with others—46 percent of baby boomers have a profile on a social network, the most popular being Facebook, once considered the bastion of Generations X and Y. Among the online socially connected boomers, 73 percent are reported to use Facebook, followed by a distant 40 percent for MySpace, 13 percent for Twitter, and 13 percent for LinkedIn. Almost half of baby boomers claim their purchase decisions are influenced by a brand's online presence and yet they do not readily befriend brands on social networks.

Once engaged online by a brand, baby boomers can become vocal about either positive or negative experiences with a brand and can be nurtured by marketers to help informally spread positive brand messages in the online environment. Generations X and Y are more apt to use a social network than baby boomers, with 77 percent of young people between the ages of 14 and 28 using social networks.

Baby boomers have the money—they want to spend it—and marketers are increasingly taking note. In terms of sheer population, baby boomers are the spine of Canadian consumer culture. Those born in the years following World War II—1946 through 1964—represent the bulk of the country's money and buying power. Canadians aged 44 years and older control more than 77 percent of the country's wealth. According to Statistics Canada, 73 percent have a household income over $100,000, with 83 percent having securities surpassing $500,000.[12]

Questions

1. Why are baby boomers now flocking to social networks?

2. Why do you think Facebook is more popular in Canada than micro-blogging sites such as Twitter?

---

each of these generations uses the media quite differently, and marketers have to carefully select which communication tools should be used. Smart bread, discussed earlier in this chapter's opening vignette, provides an example of how marketers adjust their media platforms to meet the evolving habits of their target markets. To engage with children, Smart bread uses an interactive website with educational games, fun graphics, and contests; to connect with parents, Smart bread posts information on the brand's website and also uses e-mail blasts and TV spots to communicate the product's nutritional goodness. In addition, still focusing on parents, Smart bread drops coupons within newspaper flyers and uses in-store displays to disseminate recipes, consumer contests, and draw attention to the brand.

Big City Dwelling
Canada is one of the most urbanized nations in the world. In 2006, more than 80 percent of Canadians lived in urban areas or their suburbs. Statistics indicate that cities are growing much faster than rural areas, which lag behind the rest of the country in growth rates. Comparing the latest census information, between 2001 and 2006, the overall population of Canada grew by 5.4 percent compared to rural areas, which only grew by 1.0 percent.[13]

Canadian cities are not the vast metropolitan areas we see in many other countries. There are only six urban areas in Canada with populations over one million people: Toronto, Montreal, Vancouver, Ottawa-Gatineau, Calgary, and Edmonton. Interestingly, in the biggest cities, the city centres are growing more slowly than the suburbs. Over the five-year period from 2001 to 2006, the cities with the highest growth rates were Barrie, Ontario, at 19.2 percent, and Calgary, Alberta, at 13.4 percent. Population declines were seen in Saint John, New Brunswick, and Saguenay, Quebec.[14]

Ethnic Diversity
Canada prides itself on being a multicultural country (see Figure 2–1 on page 32). The latest census shows that two-thirds of the nation's growth between 2001 and 2006 was due to immigration, with most new immigrants coming from Asia (58 percent). In 2006, there were 6.2 million foreign-born people living in Canada (the highest level in 75 years), with one in five people citing their mother tongue as neither English nor French.[15] Other than English or French, the

Figure 2–3
Canada's population over 65 years of age
Canada has an aging population.

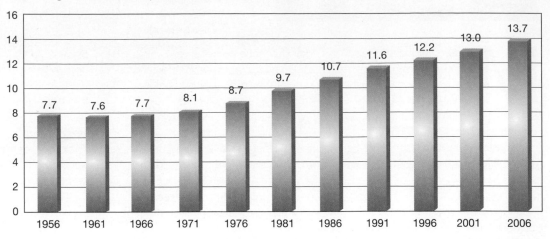

Percentage of Canada's Population over 65 Years of Age

Year	Value
1956	7.7
1961	7.6
1966	7.7
1971	8.1
1976	8.7
1981	9.7
1986	10.7
1991	11.6
1996	12.2
2001	13.0
2006	13.7

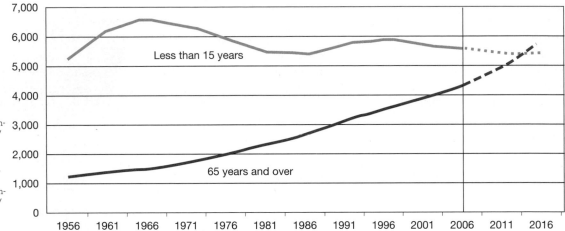

Actual and Projected Population in Canada over 65 Years of Age

Less than 15 years

65 years and over

Sources: Figure 2–3a: Statistics Canada, 2006 Census, accessed at www12.statcan.ca/census-recensement/2006/as-sa/97-551/figures/c2-eng.cfm. Figure 2–3b: Statistics Canada, 2006 Census, accessed at www12.statcan.ca/census-recensement/2006/as-sa/97-551/figures/c1-eng.cfm.

top two languages used at home were the Chinese languages and Punjabi. Visible minorities now make up 50 percent of the population in large urban areas.

This multicultural mix creates an interesting array of opportunities for marketers. These specific ethnic groups have their own particular interests and habits, which can be addressed in unique ways. Companies such as Rogers Communications have risen to this challenge, offering a diverse list of foreign-based TV stations to people in Canada. A person can watch Greek TV stations, Korean TV programs, and movies from India, just to mention a few.

World Markets   The world population is showing growth in underdeveloped areas such as Africa, Asia, and India.[16] China and India alone are home to 2.5 billion people, 38 percent of the world's population. These areas represent future opportunities for marketers seeking to expand into foreign markets. The sheer size of

these countries presents an opportunity to sell products and services, which is becoming increasingly easy due to the global appeal of the Internet, which allows companies to target foreign markets through online communication tools.

Non-Traditional Families   The traditional nuclear family of two parents and two children has changed over time. Family size has decreased with

> ## ETHNIC GROUPS HAVE THEIR OWN PARTICULAR INTERESTS AND HABITS, WHICH CAN BE ADDRESSED IN UNIQUE WAYS.

families having one or two children versus three or four (or more) in previous generations. The structure of the family has also changed with evidence of more common-law relationships, single-parent families, and blended families. Over the last few years, same-sex marriages have also surfaced.

This change in family structure impacts marketers who need to determine whether these new trends will affect their markets. An interesting example is DeBeers Canada, which took these societal changes and used them as an opportunity to develop products that address evolving needs. DeBeers continued to market its diamond engagement rings to traditional groups, but also expanded into diamond pendants and anniversary bands, and also developed a celebratory three-stone ring to symbolize the past, the present, and the future for less traditional target groups.

Socio-Cultural Forces

L③ Socio-cultural trends are more difficult to pinpoint than demographic changes. It is not easy to identify societal and cultural shifts in attitudes, or to track newly evolving trends. Socio-cultural changes tend to be gradual, over a prolonged period of time, and sometimes very subtle. Statistical data is not as readily available in these areas, but marketers are able to observe changes in society and identify evolving trends and opportunities. Sometimes, identifying these trends involves consumer research; other times it involves a keen eye and good intuition.

When we discuss **socio-cultural forces**, we are referring to cultural values, ideas, and attitudes that are learned and shared among a group of people. It also includes society's morals and beliefs and is demonstrated through behaviour common among a socio-cultural group. Canadians are known to be trustworthy, family oriented, worldly, organized, reliable, socially conscious, and conservative. Canadian society is tolerant of different cultural beliefs; welcomes new ideas and perspectives; and values honesty, integrity, fairness, and hard work. Marketers monitor changes

in these areas in order to capitalize on new opportunities with their marketing programs. Most recently, marketers are responding to socio-cultural changes as they relate to media usage, food consumption, health and fitness, the environment, and the modification of gender roles in society.

Media Usage The widespread use of the Internet and people's increased reliance on social media to communicate and search for information is changing how consumers interact and communicate with each other and organizations. Marketers note that consumers have taken the reins of the communication channel, choosing how, if, and when to listen to marketing messages. The media landscape is blurring, making marketing communications more complex and challenging. Magazines and newspapers now use websites to stream video clips online, while TV news programs have their own websites that post written articles.

The Internet and portable devices such as cellphones, laptops, and computer tablets are impacting Canada's socio-cultural fabric by influencing how consumers interact with each other, gather information, and stay informed. These devices are making the media accessible at all times whether this is at home, in the workplace, or out-of-home. As seen with the broadcast of the 2010 Olympic Winter Games, the media is adapting to how consumers access content by making it available across multiple platforms, including regular TV stations, dedicated TV channels, on-demand channels, movie theatres, smartphones, and websites with live content, streaming video, and social media interactivity. Online content at www.ctvolympics.ca included hundreds of articles, photos, and videos, as well as areas to post comments and social media buttons for

Top Five Population Hot Spots

1.	China	1,330,141,295
2.	India	1,173,108,018
3.	United States	308,282,053
4.	Indonesia	242,968,342
5.	Brazil	201,103,330

Source: U.S. Census Bureau, International Data Base, 2010, accessed at www.census.gov/population/international/data/idb/rank.php.

easy sharing on Facebook, Twitter, and MySpace, just to name a few options. A Facebook page boasting over a million fans was created and a Twitter profile was used to keep followers up-to-date.[17]

This multiplatform media landscape is resulting in socio-cultural changes that see consumers in control of a diverse set of tools to access the media and communicate with each other. This leaves a fragmented media landscape for marketers who find that consumers, spread across multiple platforms and media outlets, are more elusive and difficult to reach. Marketers respond with integrated marketing communications approaches that use a wider array of communication tools to engage target markets. Where once marketing communications might have relied on a mass market TV or print campaign, marketers now reach beyond these forms of media into other channels to match the current media habits of target markets.

In most instances, online platforms have become one of the building blocks of communication campaigns using carefully designed microsites, online ads, and creative social media tactics to engage consumers. E-mail blasts to databases of interested consumers may also be part of the mix, used to communicate one-on-one with consumers and point toward websites or retail outlets for special offers. Traditional media is not ignored in this mix but finds its place carefully integrated into campaigns to help drive messaging.

The widespread use of social media is impacting the socio-cultural environment in Canada and providing new communication platforms for marketers. Social media has given consumers an easy-to-use public voice that keeps organizations on alert. Consumers now intuitively use social media to interact with organizations and vocally express opinions for all to see. Consumers post comments on websites, create YouTube videos to express ideas, share opinions through social networks, and upload content to personal websites or

blogs. Social media has given rise to micro-journalists, video-bloggers, and social media pundits who readily create and engage online with others. Marketers realize these consumers can influence how products and marketing approaches are received and therefore target messages toward these influential social media advocates. Creativity has become a prime ingredient in the social media space used by marketers to captivate individuals and engage in conversations that help build business.

Food Consumption The government study *Canadian Food Trends to 2020*[18] outlines food consumption trends over the next few years, highlighting that people will continue to demand high-quality foods that balance good taste with nutrition and convenience. Consumers will also demand fresh and nutritious foods that offer good value and choice. Ethnic foods will continue to infiltrate the Canadian palate with Asian and South American influences giving rise to blended cuisines, new dishes, novel ingredients, and unexpected food presentations.

When it comes to ethnic foods, consumers in Canada are exposed to a wide variety of international meals from friends, families, restaurants, and multicultural communities. This variety trickles down to the foods people enjoy and wish to purchase. Marketers note these trends and develop products geared to evolving palates. Examples are Patak's, which markets a full line of Indian sauces in mainstream supermarkets, and Club House with their spice line, Seasoning Blends, that includes Thai, Greek, Cajun, and Indian Masala spices. Dempster's, in the bread category, launched a line of ethnic breads consisting of tortillas, naans, and pitas to meet this ethnic food trend.

Cultural diversity stimulates the creation of new products.

Canada's aging population, shrinking household size, and high incidence of dual-income parents that balance work and family is impacting food consumption patterns. People are shifting food expenditures away from raw ingredients toward pre-prepared foods that are purchased at supermarkets or food-service establishments. People are also replacing traditional mealtimes with snacking occasions and consuming more and more meals on-the-go. An example of how marketers meet these changing needs can be seen with SupperWorks, an interesting new food concept prompted by changing food consumption trends.

SupperWorks is a retail food concept with a number of retail locations in Canada. It provides consumers with the convenience of preparing home-cooked meals out of the house without the fuss and bother of purchasing ingredients and chopping or measuring items. There is no cleanup required at SupperWorks where recipe ingredients have already been purchased, washed, chopped, and measured for patrons to include in recipes featured each month. Consumers come to SupperWorks to assemble ingredients into meals that are then taken home and frozen for easy thawing and cooking at a later date. Its latest venture sees the overlay of a delivery service for these prepared meals.[19]

A growing trend also lies with meatless meals, organic offerings, local produce, and small indulgent gourmet brands that are expected to exhibit slight increases over the next few years. Food safety and health-related food issues are expected to pepper the media from time to time, focusing consumers on this all-important area. The study, *Canadian Food Trends to 2020*, points food marketers toward a continued interest in trans fats, low sodium/sugar products, healthy carbohydrates, high-fibre offerings, allergy identification, and foods that help prevent disease.

Health and Fitness   There is an increased focus on healthy living with Canadian government agencies, the medical profession, the media, and educational institutions all encouraging people to be active and fit and to make healthier choices in their lives. Companies recognize this shift in socio-cultural focus and are responding with healthier products and new ideas that address concerns around obesity and its associated medical conditions—diabetes and cardiovascular disease. This interest in healthy living extends into a variety of avenues, such as the food industry, pharmaceutical business, fitness industry, entertainment world, and toy market. These sectors are developing new products and applications to address this societal trend.

Looking toward the food industry, this health and fitness orientation is resulting in a host of healthier food choices. For example, Starbucks recently introduced a Tazo full-leaf tea made from natural botanicals and spices, Aquafina Plus introduced a bottled water

Dawn focuses on environmental awareness.

line that is fortified with vitamins, and Fontaine Santé is selling dips such as hummus, bruschetta, and spinach in mainstream supermarkets with products that are 100 percent natural, are good sources of omega 3s, and contain no trans fats or preservatives. Even well-established products with less healthy images such as chocolate bars, chips, and carbonated beverages are addressing health concerns by introducing smaller portion sizes and lower calorie offerings. Frito-Lay, for example, now offers consumers an alternative to its large packs of chips and popcorn with a line of small 100-calorie snack-packs, sub-branded Mini Bites, for products such as SunChips, Smartfood popcorn, and Doritos chips.

One of the most significant changes stemming from increased socio-cultural interest in health, fitness, and nutrition is the Canadian Children's Food and Beverage Advertising Initiative (CAI). Introduced in 2007, this directive is gaining momentum today with expanded core principles that were added in 2010. This directive was voluntarily created by 19 of Canada's largest food and beverage companies to restrict children's

> *"There is an increased focus on healthy living"*

advertising messages to healthy choices. In 2010, all participants agreed to either eliminate all advertising to children under the age of 12, or to restrict it to better-for-you products.

It is hoped that this initiative will steer children away from junk-food products and help them make healthier food choices. (See the Marketing NewsFlash on page 49 for further details.)

Environmental Awareness Global warming has received enormous attention in the press, rallying Canadians around the cause to reduce pollution and save the environment. Canadians are showing a keen interest in being less wasteful, recycling, and making choices that do not negatively impact the environment. Many companies are rallying around the cause, genuinely managing business practices to reduce waste and provide customers with environmentally friendly products. Canadian Tire has its Smart Energy Solutions program focused on helping homeowners save electricity and reduce pollution. Other companies focus on recycling, packaging reduction, environmentally friendly components, and conservation efforts. Sunlight has plant-based detergents, SunChips have biodegradable chip bags, Chevy Volt has an electric car, and electricity companies market off-peak energy-saving rates and tips to encourage reduced energy consumption.

From a consumer perspective, attitudes to green products waver over time and can vary from being highly engaged to being moderately interested. While people may support actions against global warming, paying extra for products that are green is not always the case. Marketers monitor consumers' attitudes to this green trend and carefully measure reactions to green initiatives. Recent research published in the *Journal of Personality and Social Psychology* indicates that consumers often balance green living with more wasteful purchases and buy high-profile green products such as hybrid or electric cars to make public statements about their beliefs, purchasing less environmentally friendly products in less public circumstances.[20]

While many organizations have a genuine interest and concern for the environment, others are criticized for *green-washing*, a term used to describe those that paint themselves and their products as "environmentally friendly," purely to market more products and to gain positive publicity. Oil companies and a number of product manufacturers have been tarred with this green-washing brush, while others such as RBC with its Blue Water Project have been lauded for its corporate social responsibility (CSR) programs that weave green initiatives into its corporate fabric and positively impact the environment. RBC's Blue Water Project is a 10-year global directive that has already pledged over $28 million to protect, revive, and improve the world's freshwater. (See the Marketing NewsFlash on page 41.)

Evolving Gender Roles Over the past 30 years, one of the most notable socio-cultural changes in Canada is the evolving roles of women and men in society. Increasingly, women are working full-time and men are becoming more involved in household duties. This has resulted in dual-income families that are time-starved. Marketers and companies have identified an opportunity to address this issue with more convenience products and better services to help busy families. Increasingly, we see companies offering flexible hours for employees and the continued growth of the home office. Supermarkets cater to this same socio-cultural change by offering prepared foods and expanded areas that merchandise these items. Many restaurants also address these needs by delivering food to help time-starved families. Many public schools have responded to this societal change by providing daycare centres and before- and after-school programs to assist working parents.

Recession Impact—Automobile Sales in Canada

Total new car sales -15%

Chrysler -27%

General Motors -29%

Ford +7%

marketing meter

Source: DesRosiers Automotive Consultants Inc, reported in Paul Brent, "Changing Lanes," *CAA Magazine*, Spring 2010, pp. 28–29.

Economic Forces

L○4 The **economy** is another area in a marketing environmental scan that marketers need to note. The economic ability of a consumer to purchase a product is what interests marketers. If there is a significant change in the economy, this will impact on a household's income and ability to purchase. If people become unemployed, they will likely defer the purchase of a new car and concentrate their purchases on life's necessities. When the economy slows down and people do not feel secure in their jobs, many higher-priced purchases are delayed. In an economic downturn, the automotive sector is one of the first industries to suffer. The recession of 2009 saw new car purchases in Canada fall by 15 percent versus the previous year

economy
The collective income, expenditures, and resources that affect the cost of running a business or a household

---

RBC's Blue Water Project Makes Waves

Did you know Canada had a rain forest? Visit RBC's Blue Water Project website or its YouTube channel to watch stunning short documentaries on projects funded by RBC around the world to help conserve, maintain, and improve the world's freshwater. The RBC Blue Water Project is a ten-year initiative that channels $50 million to non-profit organizations that apply and qualify to protect bodies of freshwater. It funds educational projects, awareness programs, and cooperative and collaborative efforts between people, companies, and organizations to help protect the world's water. Recent projects include the protection of wetlands, shoreline recovery, and the restoration of rivers and lakes.

RBC is recognized as a front runner on the world stage for social and environmental issues and has been named one of Canada's Greenest Employers and one of Canada's 50 Most Socially Responsible Corporations. Its approach to environmental issues is a good example of how companies are increasingly supporting environmental issues.

Project 13-Tides Canada is an example of a Blue Water Project funded by RBC. It protects the Canadian Great Bear Rainforest in British Columbia. This temperate rain forest covers 21 million acres of land and contains over 100 unspoiled watersheds. It is home to the white Spirit Bear and many rare plants. The Great Bear Rainforest accounts for 25 percent of the world's current ancient coastal temperate rain forests and is an economic and cultural resource for B.C.'s First Nations communities. The Blue Water Project protects five million acres of this rain forest from logging and channels $500,000 into conservation programs and sustainable economic development projects for the community.

Project 20-National Geographic is another RBC Blue Water Project. It raises awareness of water conservation issues in the U.S., putting a spotlight on water depletion at its largest water reservoir, Lake Mead. This reservoir supplies water to Las Vegas, Los Angeles, as well as farms in Arizona and California. Over the last few years, increased water usage in the area has resulted in a drop in water levels by over 100 feet, giving rise to potential water distribution issues. RBC is helping to raise awareness of this issue and is encouraging individuals to reduce water consumption.

RBC's Blue Water Project covers a 10-year period and extends to many parts of the world. Since its start in 2007, RBC has pledged over $28 million to more than 380 organizations

The Great Bear Rainforest in British Columbia is benefiting from RBC's Blue Water Project.

with $50 million earmarked for its projects. Four years after launch, RBC is telling the world about the Blue Water Project through a series of short documentaries that profile select projects as well as a full-length documentary that highlights freshwater conservation, preservation, and maintenance.

The Blue Water Project is communicated by RBC through TV ads, movie theatre commercials, and online display ads that point viewers to a microsite to soak up footage on the projects. Social media overlays include a branded YouTube channel and a Facebook page that reached over 10,000 members in its first few days. Introductory TV spots ran on the Discovery Channel and Global TV and were scheduled to coincide with programs focused on water.[21] ●

Questions

1. What objectives is RBC trying to achieve with its Blue Water Project?

2. Does the RBC Blue Water Project change how you feel about RBC as a financial institution?

macroeconomic forces

The state of a country's economy as a whole as indicated by its growth rates, inflation rates, unemployment rates, and consumer confidence indexes

inflation

A period when the cost to produce and buy products and services gets higher as prices rise

recession

A time of slow economic activity with two consecutive periods of negative growth

microeconomic forces

The supply and demand of goods and services and how this is impacted by individual, household, and company decisions to purchase

with people moving to used car sales to save money. In the U.S., where the 2009 recession was more severe, new car sales for this same period dropped 30 percent, pushing the industry into government-supported bankruptcy protection.[22]

Marketers need to recognize how the economy affects the purchase behaviour of their specific target groups. Some products, such as flour, do better in a poor economy with consumers making their own cookies and muffins rather than spending the extra money to buy more expensive ready-to-eat items. However, as noted earlier, the purchase of automobiles tends to suffer in a worsening economy.

The economy consists of macroeconomic forces and microeconomic forces. **Macroeconomic forces** refer to the state of a country's economy as a whole. Indicators of strength and weakness should be on a marketer's radar screen so that they can react quickly to changes that affect their consumers. A country's key economic indicators are its inflation rate, its unemployment rate, and its economic growth rate. Consumer confidence is also an important indicator of the economy's health, showing how people feel about their long-term economic prospects.

A key economic indicator is **inflation**, a period when the cost to produce and buy products and services gets higher as prices rise. From a marketing standpoint, if prices rise faster than consumer income, consumer purchasing power decreases.

A **recession** is a time of slow economic activity with two consecutive periods of negative growth. During recessions, production levels decline, unemployment levels rise, and many consumers have less money to spend. At these times,

consumers tend to focus their spending on life's necessities.

A country's business cycle fluctuates between different levels of growth depending on the state of the economy, international economic factors, and global pressures. Canada's growth is described by the Organisation for Economic Co-operation and Development (OECD) as relatively strong due to its strength in productivity, investment levels, the Canadian dollar, and technological advances. Canada's economy outperformed most nations during the 2009 recession and 2010 recovery.[23]

Marketers keep appraised of a country's key economic indicators—inflation rate, unemployment rate, and economic growth rate—to have a clear understanding of whether to expect a downturn or upswing in the economy. Marketers then couple this information with anticipated business performance during the expected economic climate and adjust marketing programs to maximize business results—no easy task given the uncertainty of economic forecasts and the unpredictability of consumer reactions.

Microeconomic forces directly refer to the supply and demand of goods and services and how

ask yourself

1. What do we mean by time-starved?

2. What are the marketing implications of ethnic diversity in Canada?

3. How are important values such as health and fitness reflected in the marketplace today?

Figure 2–4
Three levels of consumer income

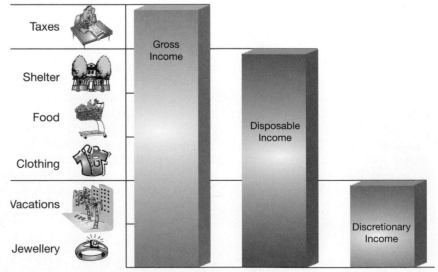

Taxes

Shelter

Food

Clothing

Vacations

Jewellery

Gross Income

Disposable Income

Discretionary Income

this is impacted by individual, household, and company decisions to purchase. A marketer needs to be alerted as to how these areas affect consumer buying power. Here are some terms you need to know (see Figure 2–4):

- **Gross income:** This is the total amount of money made in one year by a person, household, or family unit including taxes.

- **Disposable income:** This is the after-tax income that consumers have left for spending and savings. Typical purchases are for rent, clothing, and transportation. If taxes rise at a faster rate than income, consumers have less disposable income with which to pay the bills.

- **Discretionary income:** This is the after-tax income a consumer has left after paying for necessities such as food, shelter, and clothing. This income is used for discretionary purchases that are not deemed a necessity. Examples include going to a movie, eating at a restaurant, or going on a vacation.

Technological Forces

L⑤ Changes in how consumers use technology must be understood by marketers. This is another area in a marketing environmental scan that must be noted or the results can be problematic. Marketers need to know not only what new inventions are coming on the scene but also how consumers are integrating technology into their daily lives. An example lies with Canada Bread that recognized the popularity of Wii computer games with its target market (families with young children) and created a promotion for consumers to win Wii fitness-related games and hardware. This also aligned with consumers' interest in family health and fitness.

Technological forces refer to inventions or innovations that stem from scientific or engineering research. Each new wave of technology can replace existing products, and companies need to be aware of technological changes to ensure that their products do not become obsolete. The latest research on Canadians' use of technology shows the following:

- **Canadians are very comfortable with the latest communication technology.** The 2010 Bensimon Byrne Consumerology Report, *Technology and Canadian Consumers*, tracks how consumers use and integrate technology into their lives.[24] It tells us that 40 percent of Canadians are comfortable with the latest technology with only 10 percent feeling very lost. No surprise, young adults are more comfortable with new technology and spend more time online than their parents. Young adults in Canada view the Internet as source of exploration, gaming, and entertainment while older adults seem to miss the entertainment factor, instead perceiving the Internet as a new way of doing old things such as shopping, talking, learning, and banking.

- **Computers and the Internet are essential tools today.** The study explains that 74 percent of respondents consider desktop computers essential with

gross income
Total amount of money made in one year by a person, household, or family unit, including taxes

disposable income
Balance of income left after paying taxes; income that is used for spending and savings

discretionary income
Money that consumers have left after paying taxes and buying necessities

technological forces
Inventions from science or engineering research

Smart bread promotions tap into health and fitness trends and consumers' use of technology.

83 percent seeing high-speed Internet as a necessity. The newer communication platforms such as instant messaging and social networks are readily accepted and used daily by half the population. People are multitasking with technology—62 percent of people in Canada are on a computer or smartphone while watching TV.

- **Computers are the screen of choice for going online.** In order of popularity, the most popular online activities are checking the news, going on Facebook, and reading printed news. Computers and cellphones are both used for instant messaging with a small portion of the population going online via smartphone.

Looking to future technological trends, a 2011 comScore study points out that Canadians lead the world in the use of tablet computers,[25] and it is worth noting that people in Canada are expected to continue to be captivated by mobile devices such as iPhones, BlackBerrys, and iPads and to increasingly use eReaders, mobile Internet devices, social media platforms, and cloud computing. Cloud computing refers to the ability to access and use programs on the Internet without owning the software. Examples of cloud computing are Google Docs for word processing, Blogger for blog creation, Google Analytics for online measurement, and Facebook, YouTube, and Twitter to share videos, photos, or links. The increased popularity of cloud computing will raise issues related to website reliability, security, privacy, and content ownership. Free Internet content will evolve with premium media brands charging for online content in an effort to generate revenue.[26]

Some of the most recent technological advances that have changed how consumers conduct their daily lives are noted below:

- The Internet and search engines are replacing bricks-and-mortar libraries as instant sources of information.

- E-mail, text messaging, and instant messaging are reducing the need for traditional mail delivery systems.

- Social networking sites such as Facebook, Twitter, and MySpace are surfacing as new virtual meeting places.

- Video-sharing sites such as YouTube and Vimeo are allowing people to create and share their own video content.

- Music and video download sites such as iTunes are replacing traditional music and DVD retailers.

- Blogs are allowing people to create their own content and voice opinions.

- High-speed Internet connections are facilitating the viewing of TV/video online.

- Cellphones are replacing land-line phones.

- Computer tablets and eReaders such as iPads and Kindles are encouraging consumers to read books, magazines, and newspapers online rather than in hard copy.

"Changes in how consumers use technology must be understood by marketers."

Figure 2–5
Types of competitions

Monopoly
One firm
Example: regional electricity companies

Oligopoly
Few firms
Example: airlines

Monopolistic Competition
Many firms, similar products
Example: electricity companies

Perfect Competition
Many firms, identical products
Example: apple farmers

Competitive Forces

L⑥ Another important element in the marketing environmental scan is the competition. This puts a focus on **competitive forces** that present alternative products to satisfy a need. There are various types of competition and each company must consider its present and potential competitors when designing its marketing strategy. Determining a product's main competitors can be done in a number of ways and this varies depending upon the product and category, and whether the product exists online, offline, or in both environments. Large organizations often purchase research data from companies such as the Nielsen Company to obtain competitive market share data and to identify general industry trends or market growth patterns. Smaller companies may prefer to reduce their expenditures in this area, instead relying on competitive information gleaned from salespeople, suppliers, retailers, and online research. Gathering consumer insights on new competitive products is also a useful tool to add to the mix.

One of a marketer's primary concerns is to monitor the competitive activity of products that compete head-to-head with its brands. Any changes made by a major competitor in areas of product, price, place, and promotion are routinely noted and detailed analyses conducted to determine the impact on business results. These head-to-head competitors are called **direct competitors** and refer to very similar products sold in the same category. An example is Coke versus Pepsi in the cola category.

Marketers also understand that consumers do not function in a vacuum and often make choices between products that do not directly compete in the same category. Marketers therefore also look (a little less intently) at **indirect competitors**, those products that compete for the same buying dollar but in a slightly different category. Consider, for example, Pizza Hut. If Pizza Hut wants to review its direct competitors, it may focus on Domino's and Pizza Pizza. However, an indirect competitor such as Swiss Chalet should not be ignored because this competitor also competes for consumers wanting to purchase fast food for home delivery. Pizza Hut must also consider other indirect competitors found in the freezer

Direct and indirect competitors must be considered in the pizza category.

sections of supermarkets, such as Kraft's Delissio pizza and the many varieties of McCain frozen pizzas. When it comes to pizza, a consumer can order a pizza online or on the phone, go to a pizza parlour, take one out of the freezer, make one from scratch, or buy something altogether different. All these variables need to be considered.

Marketers need to be intimately familiar with competitive products and try to anticipate competitive moves in the marketplace. This will help avoid the pitfalls that can surface from underestimating the competition. When analyzing the competitive environment, a marketer needs to review all major competitors, taking its direction from the choices consumers make between brands and products in the category. More attention is given to those that can directly impact a marketer's business.

Apart from intimately understanding direct and indirect competitors, marketers need to have a clear understanding of the competitive nature of the industry in which they function and factor this into a marketing environmental scan. If for instance there are very few competitors, a marketer will consider changes among competitors to be significant, while in a situation where numerous competitors and undifferentiated products exist, changes may be viewed differently. Figure 2–5 shows the four basic types of competition as identified by economists.

At one end of the competition spectrum is a **monopoly**. A monopoly exists when there is only one company selling in the market. Monopolies are legal in Canada but they are carefully monitored by the Competition Bureau to ensure

that consumers are not charged excessive prices. Governments do not like to see unregulated monopolies and actively seek to reduce their control of the market through regulation and by encouraging competition. Examples of monopolies in Canada are regional electricity companies.

The second point in the continuum is an **oligopoly**, which occurs when a few companies control a market. In Canada, this situation exists with oil companies that control the gasoline industry. Companies such as Shell, Petro Canada, Husky, and Esso dominate the market. Because there is limited competition, these companies can easily control prices and are often criticized for price collusion (fixing prices among competitors). This has yet to be proven in the oil industry. Marketers who function in an oligopoly need to be acutely aware of competitive moves and particularly changes in price. An unnecessary price cut that is followed by the entire industry may result in profits being taken out of the category for everyone.

The third type of competition is **monopolistic competition**. This is when a large number of sellers compete with each other, offering customers similar or substitute products. Marketers need to know that in this instance branding plays an important role, as does product differentiation and added-value activities to draw consumers to the product. Being in touch with consumer needs and adjusting the marketing mix to meet these needs is crucial for long-term survival. The market for jeans is a good example. This market is dominated by major brands such as Levi's and Calvin Klein, but there are also many premium specialty brands such as Seven, Guess, and Diesel, as well as many lower-priced offerings that marketers need to keep in mind when marketing their products.

The fourth type of competition is **perfect competition** when there

ask yourself

1. What is the difference between a consumer's disposable and discretionary income?

2. What is the most common form of competition?

3. What are the indirect competitors to a bag of Doritos chips?

are many sellers with nearly identical products and little differentiation. Companies that deal in commodities, that is, products such as grains, vegetables, or coal, often function in an environment where perfect competition exists. In this instance, marketers need to know that pricing plays a key role in securing business, and that the focus will be on cost reduction in every element of the business.

Regulatory Forces

The final area involved in a marketing environmental scan relates to **regulations**, which are restrictions placed on marketing practices by different levels of government and industry associations. These regulations are put in place to protect consumers from unscrupulous business practices, to set acceptable standards of practice, and to encourage fair competition. Marketers need to clearly understand all legal and ethical guidelines that affect their business practices and to retain legal guidance as needed to ensure that its practices are legal. Ethical business practices should also be followed to avoid consumer backlash and negative publicity.

The key groups that regulate marketing practices in Canada are the Competition Bureau, Advertising Standards Canada (ASC), the Canadian Radio-television and Telecommunications Commission (CRTC), the Better Business Bureau (BBB), and the Canadian Marketing Association (CMA). In addition to these general regulatory bodies, marketers need to review other regulatory bodies and associations specific to their industry, as well as those that have jurisdiction in other countries, provinces, or states where they conduct business.

The **Competition Bureau** is responsible for the administration and enforcement of the *Competition Act*, the *Consumer Packaging and Labelling Act*, the *Textile Labelling Act*, and the *Precious Metals Marking Act*, just to name a few areas of responsibility. The bureau's role is to promote and maintain fair competition and to curtail false and misleading representations to sell products. In this manner, people in Canada can benefit from lower prices, increased product choice, and high-quality services. Prohibited business practices include, among others, price fixing among competitors, predatory pricing by large competitors to run small companies out of business, and bid-rigging among competitors to inflate prices on government contracts. Prohibited practices to lure consumers include bait-and-switch advertising, fraudulent advertising claims, and misleading pricing practices such as double ticketing. Bait-and-switch advertising refers to the practice of advertising a low-priced product (bait) to lure consumers into a store and then, because the product is not made available in large quantities, selling these consumers higher-priced products (switch).

Failure to abide by Competition Bureau rules can result in fines and jail time. False and/or misleading representations to sell products can result in orders by the Competition Bureau for companies to publish corrective notices, stop the prohibited practice, pay administrative costs, and pay restitution to purchasers. In addition, the Competition Bureau has the legal clout to levy hefty fines on individuals and/or companies. Guidelines for fines reach as high as $1 million for individuals and $15 million for corporations. A landmark case worth noting occurred in December 2009 when the Competition Bureau slapped a record $15 million fine on DataCom Marketing Inc. for fraudulently selling business directories. In addition, the company's founder was sentenced to two years in jail, three years probation, and tasked with a ten-year ban on conducting any form of telemarketing.

Figure 2–6
Advertising Standards Canada—The *Code*

Advertising Standards Canada (ASC) encourages truth in advertising through a *Code* that provides guidelines under these areas:

- Accuracy and clarity
- Disguised advertising techniques
- Price claims
- Bait and switch
- Guarantees
- Comparative advertising
- Testimonials
- Professional or scientific claims
- Imitation
- Safety
- Superstition and fears
- Advertising to children
- Advertising to minors
- Unacceptable depictions and portrayal

Details can be found on the ASC website at www.adstandards.com.

Another senior manager received a two-year conditional sentence.[27] To find out more about the Competition Bureau, and to see a complete list of its regulations and examples of recent rulings, visit its website at http://competitionbureau.gc.ca.

Advertising Standards Canada (ASC) is a self-regulatory non-government association run by advertising, media, and marketing professionals with the purpose of setting and regulating standards of professional practice in the advertising industry. The industry has agreed to abide by its leadership, code, process, and rulings. Advertising Standards Canada sets and regulates advertising guidelines, monitored through a consumer complaint process. A single complaint will trigger a review of advertising placed in the Canadian media, with the eventual withdrawal of the ad if changes are required and not made. The ASC also provides advice and pre-clearance services for advertisers.

ASC's jurisdiction does not carry over into the legal arena. It does not levy fines or engage in legal proceedings. Instead, it relies on industry compliance to ensure that ads contravening its guidelines, the *Canadian Code of Advertising Standards* (or the *Code*) cease to air. Deceptive and fraudulent advertising, although covered under the *Code*, is also scrutinized by the Competition Bureau, which can levy fines and take legal action if necessary.

The *Code* has a strict set of guidelines designed to encourage truthful, fair, and accurate marketing communications. It covers 14 areas, as shown in Figure 2–6, that address issues such as comparative advertising, accuracy, safety, decency, and advertising to children. These guidelines are updated as required with a detailed list of guidelines available at www.adstandards.com.

The **Canadian Radio-television and Telecommunications Commission (CRTC)** is another government agency that sets guidelines and enforces a clear set of regulations on Canadian businesses. It

> *"The Canadian Marketing Association (CMA) is the backbone of the marketing industry"*

administers the *Broadcasting Act* and *Telecommunications Act*, among others, setting guidelines for broadcast standards. It also adjudicates on the ownership of media companies to ensure that monopolies do not exist and approves broadcast licences for TV and radio stations. It also sets guidelines on the broadcast of Canadian content and sets the number of minutes of advertising permitted hourly on TV. While it does not directly regulate the content of ads, primarily an ASC concern, it does oversee the advertising of alcohol beverages and works with the ASC on issues related to advertising to children. The CRTC regulates the amount of advertising permitted in the Canadian broadcast media.

The CRTC also has jurisdiction over the telemarketing national **Do Not Call List (DNCL)**. The DNCL gives consumers the ability to not receive telemarketing calls on cellphones, landline phones, and fax machines by registering the numbers of their communication devices. Registration keeps these numbers in the DNCL for five years, after which consumers must re-register. Telemarketers are required by law to subscribe to the DNCL and to not call the numbers in its database.

There are five exemptions to the DNCL: registered charities, newspaper subscriptions, political parties/candidates, market-research companies, and companies with which business has been conducted in the last 18 months. Failure to comply with this DNCL can result in fines of up to $1,500 for an individual and up to $15,000 for a corporation for each violation. In December 2010, Bell Canada was fined $1.3 million for violating the DNCL through third-party independent telemarketers who contacted people on the DNCL to promote Bell Canada's TV, telephone, wireless, and Internet services.[28]

In terms of the amount of advertising that can be broadcast, the CRTC currently restricts TV advertising to the following:[29]

- 12 minutes per hour on specialty channels
- No advertising on pay-television, pay-per-view, and video-on-demand channels
- No limits on AM and FM radio stations
- No limits on regular TV stations
- No advertising on CBC radio networks except for programs that are available only on a sponsored basis

In all instances, advertising messages need to be legal and ethical, and abide by industry guidelines. It is wise to *always* obtain legal counsel before launching a campaign to ensure that it is ethical and does not contravene any laws, including criminal ones that may not be mentioned above. You can find out more about the CRTC at www.crtc.gc.ca.

The **Better Business Bureau (BBB)** is a voluntary alliance of businesses whose members are committed to being fair and honest in their dealings, to promoting self-regulatory practices, and to collecting and dispensing information to help businesses and consumers make sound decisions. It provides businesses with guidelines for building trust in the marketplace. It advises organizations to establish and build a positive reputation in the market by honestly representing products. Organizations are advised to be transparent, honour promises, and quickly respond to disputes in a professional manner and in good faith. Privacy data needs to be protected. Information on the BBB can be found at www.bbb.org/canada.

The **Canadian Marketing Association (CMA)** is the backbone of the marketing industry in Canada. It provides guidelines for its members through its *Code of Ethics and Standards of Practice*. It is mandatory for

Advertising Junk Food to Kids: The Children's Advertising Initiative

focus on **Ethics**

In response to community concerns about childhood obesity and the health of children in Canada, 19 of Canada's prominent food and beverage manufacturers created a voluntary association to help promote healthy eating among children in Canada. The Canadian Children's Food and Beverage Advertising Initiative promotes healthy lifestyle and dietary choices for children under 12 years of age by shifting advertising dollars away from unhealthy products and toward more-nutritious products that meet governmental nutrition guidelines.

Ten of the participating companies have changed their advertising practices to children less than 12 years of age to promote only healthy choices. These companies are Burger King, Campbell's, General Mills, Kellogg's, Kraft, McDonald's, Nestlé, Parmalat,

Post, and Weston Bakeries. The other nine companies involved in the initiative, Cadbury Adams, Coca-Cola, Ferrero, Hershey, Janes Family Foods, Mars, McCain, PepsiCo, and Unilever, have committed to not advertising their products to children under 12 years.

This children's advertising directive covers not only online and offline advertising directed to children but also was expanded in 2010 to include word-of-mouth buzz and company-owned websites directed at children, as well as ads on video/computer games, DVDs, smartphones, and those placed in elementary schools. This initiative is monitored by Advertising Standards Canada, which publishes an annual compliance report. Whether this move will actually change children's

eating habits remains to be seen, but companies seem committed to supporting healthier food choices for children.[30]

Questions

1. Do you think the Children's Advertising Initiative will change the amount of junk food consumed by youngsters in Canada?

2. What other marketing changes do you think food and beverage companies should consider to help children and their parents make healthier food choices?

all members to abide by these policies, which are clearly outlined on the CMA website at www.the-cma.org. This website provides marketers with numerous practical guides on topics such as telemarketing, e-mail marketing, Internet marketing, privacy compliance, promotional contests, fundraising, database marketing, and marketing to children and teenagers. Its latest guides provide information on video marketing and using mobile apps to reach consumers.

Marketers are advised to become familiar with the guidelines and restrictions that regulate the marketing industry in Canada and also to look further afield to the other countries where they conduct business. Legal advice is prudent.

The following sections focus on three important regulatory areas that are highlighted by the CMA: privacy, spam, and contests.

Privacy

In 2004, privacy laws came into place across Canada in the form of the *Personal Information Protection and Electronic Documents Act* (PIPEDA), which in 2010/2011 is being updated to ensure that it adequately protects individuals' right to privacy. PIPEDA provides businesses and individuals with guidelines on what information can be collected, shared, and distributed. PIPEDA protects personal information such as name, address, purchase habits, age, and gender, and requires businesses to regularly review their privacy policies, appoint a privacy policy officer, and collect only necessary information. PIPEDA also stipulates that consent is needed for the collection, use, and disclosure of information and that that information must be safely stored. Security breaches must be communicated to consumers.

In the online environment, privacy policies must be clearly posted on all websites and detail what personal information is collected, how it is collected, how it is used and protected, whether information is disclosed to outside parties, and whether the company complies with Canadian privacy legislation and anti-spam laws. The policy needs to be

honest, clear, and regularly reviewed. More details on privacy guidelines can be found on the *CMA Privacy Compliance Guide* at www.the-cma.org.[31]

Spam

Spam refers to the dissemination of unsolicited electronic messages to recipients. Canada's anti-spam legislation is being amended in 2010/2011 to reduce the amount of spam that clogs the Internet. The legislation requires senders to identify themselves and the organization they represent and to send information only to those who have requested it. Recipients need to be able to easily unsubscribe from e-mail updates and be sent only accurate information. The revised legislation is expected to make electronic spam software illegal.

Contests

Promotional contests are widely used in Canada to encourage consumers to purchase products. They are governed by laws that protect consumers from unscrupulous marketing practices. Marketers obtain legal advice and often use professional contest administrators when conducting contests to ensure that they comply with the law. These laws fall under the criminal code, the *Competition Act*, the common law of contracts, and Quebec's Act respecting lotteries, alcohol, publicity contests, and amusement machines.

Specifically, the following highlights important areas that need to be noted, with further details available in the *Canadian Marketing Association Guide to Promotional Contests*, which can be found on its website at www.the-cma.org.[32]

- Quebec's *Consumer Protection Act* prohibits advertising to children under the age of 13 in Quebec, other than on in-store displays, packaging, or in child-specific magazines.

- The *Criminal Code* states that "illegal lotteries," where the winnings are based purely on chance, are prohibited unless for a government lottery or conducted under a charitable gaming licence.

  - Contests that require a mix of chance and skill are legal, as well as pure skill-based contests.

    - Penalties for contests contravening the *Criminal Code* include imprisonment for up to two years and a fine of up to $25,000.

      - The *Competition Act* prohibits lotteries, contests, and games of chance unless there is adequate and fair disclosure of the rules, prizes, odds of winning, and allocation of prizes. All contest terms and conditions must be clear, visible, easy to read, easy to find, and easy to understand. They must include details on how to enter, age restrictions, contest entry limitations, contact information, geographic prize allocation, the odds of winning, the value and number of each prize, prize description, contest closing date, and clarification that no purchase is necessary

- The online environment complicates the administration of contests with the need to abide by privacy laws, security issues, and the possibility of technical glitches. Contests directed at children must adhere to further restrictions that are detailed in the *CMA Guide to Promotional Contests.*

ask yourself

1. What role does the Canadian Radio-television and Telecommunications Commission (CRTC) play in Canadian marketing regulations?

2. Do you think the Canadian Children's Food and Beverage Advertising Initiative will have any impact on advertising messages?

3. Does self-regulation work? Why or why not?

A Marketing Environmental Scan in Practice

The launch of the iPad in 2010 and its potential to drastically impact the sale of eReaders such as the Kindle and the Kobo, prompted a group of students in late 2010 to review the Kindle eReader, marketed by Amazon.com. The students conducted a marketing environmental scan to identify how the Kindle could best compete against other eReaders and the iPad tablet device, which also supports electronic reading with its iBooks app and bookstore. At that time, most eReaders lagged behind the iPad in their lack of touch technology, colour images, and full browsing capacity.

The ideas generated during the student marketing environmental scan are particularly interesting in light of the new Kindle Fire, a tablet device launched by Amazon in November 2011 in the U.S., less than two years after

the iPad was first announced. This new Kindle product not only addresses the more obvious weaknesses that were pointed out by the students, such as touch technology and colour images, but also provides users with the ability to access music, movies, TV shows, and gaming apps, as well as books, magazines, and newspapers. The Kindle Fire has a 7-inch screen and weighs less than 15 ounces, making it easy to slip into a purse, briefcase, or knapsack for easy access on the go. It also allows users to surf the Internet with a new fast browser from Amazon, taking the product into areas that were not considered by the students. At $199, its price point interestingly addresses students concerns about value in comparison to the iPad.

Let's review the student marketing environmental scan, shown in Figure 2–7: After gathering competitive data on the Kobo, Sony Reader, and iPad, the students identified that the Kindle was a thin paperback-sized electronic device used to download, store, and read electronic books on a small six-inch black-and-white screen. The basic model weighed only 8.7 ounces, was 1/3-inch thin, and easily fit into a purse or bag. Its battery life ranged from two weeks to one month depending on model

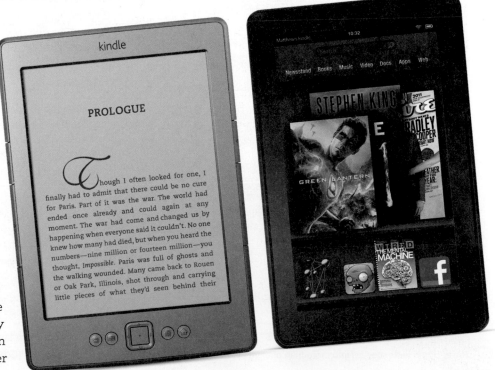

and usage. It had the capacity to store 3,500 books, and users had access to over 630,000 books from the Kindle library at Amazon.com. An additional 1.8 million pre-1923 books were also available at no cost to the Kindle user. Books listed on the New York Times bestseller list were available on the device for $11.99 in Canada. In 2010, the device was priced at $139, $189, or $379, depending on size, features, and whether it used 3G technology. Its pricing was comparable to other eReaders but lower than the iPad, which started at about $500.

The students added this information to facts on demographics, regulations, socio-cultural factors, economic trends, and technology usage. They then finalized the marketing environmental scan captured in Figure 2–7 to identify marketing ideas they considered important for the Kindle to remain competitive in the market, as well as some interesting promotional opportunities for the Canadian market. These ideas demonstrate the usefulness of a marketing environmental scan and how it can be used to build business.

Figure 2–7
Marketing environmental scan: 2010 Kindle eReader

EXAMPLE MARKETING ENVIRONMENTAL SCAN – KINDLE eREADER		
	FACTS	**MARKETING IDEAS**
Demographic factors	• Aging population • Baby boomers have more leisure time • Time-starved parents • Multicultural families • Shrinking family size • Increase in non-traditional families • Big city dwelling • Focus on education	• Create eReader packs for traveling baby boomers focused on different interests—i.e., best-sellers, classics, gardening, politics, current affairs, etc. • Create language options that provide books in more than one language • Create homework packs for textbook reading on the go
Socio-cultural factors	• Focus on health and fitness • Interest in the environment • Concerns with childhood obesity • Internet-savvy families • Changing gender roles • Multicultural influences	• Create multicultural downloads for new Canadians in their native languages that highlight support services and cultural aspects of Canada as well as leisure reading material • Highlight the environmental benefits of eReaders • Market the Kindle as a portable textbook device for school-aged children and post-secondary students • Ensure that Kindles continue to be compatible with PC- and Apple-based software so that eBooks can be transferred from one to the other
Economic factors	• Concerns about the economy • Concerns about unemployment	• Ensure that Kindle's pricing is competitive and provides value versus computer tablet options
Technological factors	• People comfortable with digital technology • People spending more time on the Internet	• Ensure that the value proposition, ease of portability, outdoor usage, and battery life are emphasized in marketing materials • Create alliances with computer giants to ensure compatibility
Competitive factors	• Major computer companies have tablet-computers. • Tablet-computers use colour, graphics, apps, and touch technology.	• Upgrade Kindle software to ensure colour capability • Research the importance of touch technology with consumers • Create a strong competitive proposition that includes good value and benefits such as outdoor usage and battery life versus computer tablets
Regulatory factors	• Increased awareness of green-washing and truthful marketing communications	• Ensure that marketing claims are accurate, ethical, and comply with all regulations

Note: Some facts may fall into more than one area in a marketing environmental scan. These should be repeated as necessary to avoid omission.

Summary...*just the facts*

- A marketing environmental scan is the process of continually acquiring information on events outside an organization to identify trends, opportunities, and threats.
- Demographics are the statistical study of populations, looking at characteristics such as gender, age, ethnicity, income, education, and occupation.
- Socio-cultural forces look at cultural values, ideas, and attitudes as they relate to society's trends and beliefs.
- Economic forces are important in terms of a target market's disposable income, and the general health of the economy including consumer confidence.

- Technological forces relate to scientific inventions and innovations that may impact the running of a business and influence consumer behaviour and interactions.
- Competitive forces refer to direct and indirect competitors as well as the competitive nature of the market in which they function.
- Regulatory forces are the restrictions placed on a business, product, or service by the government or industry association.

Key Terms and Concepts...*a refresher*

Hands-on...*apply your knowledge*

Marketing Environmental Scan Assignment Assume that Canada Bread wants to refresh its marketing efforts for its Smart bread product line with a focus on revitalizing the product and its marketing efforts.

Review this chapter's opening vignette on Smart bread and then navigate to the Smartman website at www.smartman.ca to review product and marketing details. Conduct a marketing environmental scan with a view to outlining the facts and marketing ideas that should be considered in the future. Outline the marketing environmental scan in the format outlined in Figure 2–7.

Reality Check...*reminder*

Refer back to this chapter's opening vignette and answer the Reality Check questions on page 30.

Mc Graw Hill connect *Practise and learn online with Connect.*

Connect allows you to practise important concepts at your own pace and on your own schedule, with 24/7 online access to an eBook, practice quizzes, video cases, chapter application questions, discussion activities, Internet exercises, interactivities, study tools, and more.

3

consumer
behaviour

MapArt is one of North America's leading developers of accurate and user-friendly maps. They are easily recognizable in stores by their yellow covers. MapArt has the largest market share in Canada with a wide variety of road atlases, street guides, and fold maps. The MapArt team is comprised of some of the best cartographers and graphic designers in the industry. MapArt boasts a library of maps covering every Canadian city or town with a population over 5,000. Its *Toronto & Area* book alone sells approximately 120,000 copies every year.

Gordon Woit is the financial and marketing director of MapArt. When asked about the effect of Google Maps and MapQuest on his business, Gord had this to say: "In the recent past, online maps made consumers more aware of using maps, and ironically, this resulted in increased sales of MapArt printed maps. From the years 2000 to 2008, sales of MapArt books increased exponentially every year. However, from the year 2008 onward, sales of MapArt printed maps have been declining slightly every year."[1]

Gord describes changes in consumer behaviour by using the example of a Generation Y person travelling by car for the first time to a friend who had recently moved to a new subdivision. Woit says that this person will not use a printed map, but a GPS instead. Research shows that this person is lost without the GPS. If asked to describe roughly the route to his friend's house, he has no idea. Contrast this with a baby boomer or a Generation X person, who use a printed map. These two demographic groups would have an idea of the location even if the map was removed because they see the big picture. Gord says that a person's brain is engaged when using a map, but disengages when relying totally on the GPS. Another difference between the Generation Y person and both Generation Xers and baby boomers is that the older demographic may also currently be using a GPS, but they do have the MapArt map available as a backup.

Gord keeps his pulse on trends in the consumer market by constantly doing market research. His research has uncovered that the yellow cover of the MapArt book is not perceived as modern or hip as a blue cover, for example. As a result of this research, Gord is looking at marketing a new line of maps with a blue cover, which will be branded as Mapmobility. The blue cover will also have pictures of people on it instead of a photo of a map on the current yellow covers. In this way, the current MapArt maps will still available for purchase by people who are comfortable with the yellow cover, and the new Mapmobility maps will be available for the purchaser who wants a more modern-looking product.

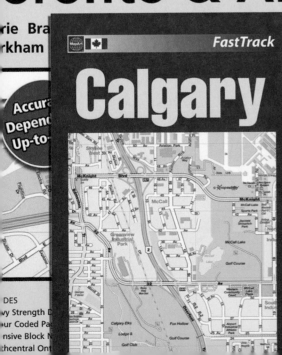

Gord's research also found that consumers want a fold map that is laminated and easier to fold. Gord is responding to this observation by providing consumers with an easier-to-fold laminated map.

The above vignette shows how consumer behaviour is changing due to GPS technology. In Chapter 2, we learned about the effect of technology on marketing. This chapter focuses on consumer behaviour, from a psychological and socio-cultural point of view, and specifically how technology is changing the behaviour of consumers. **Consumer behaviour** is defined as the actions a person takes when purchasing and using products and services.

Step 2 of the marketing plans described in Chapter 14 deals with market-product focus, which includes market segmentation. Consumer behaviour plays a big part in market segmentation. Market segmentation involves aggregating buyers into groups that have common needs and who are similar in terms of their consumer behaviour. 🍎

As you read Chapter 3, refer back to the MapArt vignette to answer the following questions:

- Describe each step of the consumer purchase decision process as it relates to the purchase of a street guide map book.
- After reading the section "Effects of Technology on Purchase Behaviour," explain how consumer behaviour is being changed by GPS technology.

reality **CHECK**

Consumer Purchase Decision Process

LO 1 Behind the visible act of making a purchase lies an important decision process. The stages that a consumer passes through when making choices about which products and services to buy is the **purchase decision process**. This process has the five stages, as shown in Figure 3–1: problem recognition, information search, alternative evaluation, purchase decision, and post-purchase behaviour. The Internet is changing how consumers are obtaining information and how they are making a purchase decision.

We should note that businesses also go through a purchase decision process when considering products and services from suppliers. Business-to-business (B2B) marketing requires a slightly different approach than consumer marketing. Chapter 5 looks at (B2B) marketing in detail.

Problem Recognition: Perceiving a Need

Problem recognition, the initial step in the purchase decision, occurs when a person realizes that the difference between what he or she has and what he or she would like to have is big enough to actually do something about it.[2] The process may be triggered by a situation as simple as finding an empty milk carton in the refrigerator; noting, as a first-year college or university student, that your high school clothes are not in the style that other students are wearing; or realizing that your laptop computer may not be working properly.

In marketing, advertisements or salespeople can activate a consumer's decision process by showing the shortcomings of a consumer's cellphone and the advantages of owning a smartphone.

Information Search: Seeking Value

After recognizing a problem, consumers begin to search for information about what product or service

The Core: Chapter 3

Marketers understand what influences consumers' purchase decisions.

Psychological influences

Socio-cultural influences

Effective marketers keep an eye on their target market, and work to understand them and satisfy consumers' wants and needs.

Figure 3–1
Purchase decision process

| Problem recognition: Perceiving a need | → | Information search: Seeking value | → | Evaluation of alternatives: Assessing value | → | Purchase decision: Buying value | → | Post-purchase behaviour: Value in consumption or use |

might satisfy the newly discovered need. First, they may scan their memory for knowledge of or previous experiences with products or brands.[3] This action is called *internal search*. For frequently purchased products such as shampoo and conditioner, this may be enough. Or a consumer may undertake an *external search* for information.[4] This is especially needed when one does not have much past experience or knowledge, the risk of making a bad decision is high, and the level of interest in the product is high. The primary sources of external information are *personal sources*, such as relatives and friends who the consumer trusts; *public sources*, such as Google searches on the Internet, including various product-rating organizations such as *Consumer Reports* or government agencies; and *marketer-dominated sources*, such as information from sellers that include advertising, company websites, salespeople, and point-of-purchase displays in stores.

Suppose you consider buying your first smartphone. You will probably tap several of these information sources: friends and relatives, advertisements for smartphones, brand and company websites, and stores carrying smartphones (for demonstrations). You might also study comparable evaluation of various smartphones as found in *Consumer Reports*, either published in hard copy or found

online. In fact, online information search has become very popular, with recent research indicating that the Internet is one of the primary information-gathering and search tools used by Canadian consumers. Also, consumers are relying on social media for information on products and are paying very close attention to what others are saying about various brands on these social media sites.

Evaluation of Alternatives: Assessing Value

The information search stage clarifies the problem for the consumer by suggesting criteria, or points to consider, for the purchase; providing brand names that might meet the criteria; and developing consumer value perceptions. What selection criteria would you use in buying a smartphone? Would you use price, features, or some other combination?

Consider all the factors you may consider when evaluating smartphones. These factors are a consumer's *evaluative criteria*, which represent both the objective attributes of a brand (such as the number of applications available on the iPhone versus the BlackBerry) and the subjective ones (such as the status of a business executive owning a BlackBerry) you use to compare different products and brands.[5] Firms try to identify and make the most of both types of evaluative criteria to create the best value for consumers. These criteria are often emphasized in advertisements.

For a product like a smartphone, the information search process would probably involve visiting wireless providers such as Rogers and Telus, checking out these providers' websites, and talking to friends who own smartphones. Consumers often have several criteria for comparing products. For example, among the evaluative criteria you might think of, suppose that you focus on two that are crucial for you, namely a superior and reliable e-mail program, and the ease of use of a QWERTY keyboard versus a touch screen. These criteria determine the brands in your *evoked set*—the group of brands that a consumer would consider acceptable from among all the brands in the product class of which he or she is aware.[6] Your two evaluative criteria may result in two brands (BlackBerry and iPhone) in your evoked set.

Purchase Decision: Buying Value

Having examined the alternatives in the evoked set, you are almost ready to make a purchase decision. Three choices remain: the chosen brand, from whom to buy, and when to buy. The choice of which wireless provider to buy from will depend on such considerations as the provider's location, your past experience buying from the provider, and the return policy.

Deciding when to buy is frequently determined by a number of factors. For instance, you might buy sooner if one of your preferred brands is on sale or its manufacturer offers a rebate. Other factors such as the store atmosphere, pleasantness of the shopping experience, salesperson persuasiveness, time pressure, and financial circumstances could also affect whether a purchase decision is made or postponed. If your decision is the BlackBerry, you may decide to buy it from Telus because it offers unlimited local calling for six months as an added incentive.

Use of the Internet to gather information, evaluate alternatives, and make buying decisions adds a technological dimension to the consumer purchase decision process and can accelerate the process because it puts information at consumers' fingertips.

Effects of Technology on Purchase Behaviour
The Internet is making it much more convenient to purchase certain products and services. For example, purchasing vacations is done more often these days on the Internet than visiting a travel agent. Expedia.ca's website, for example, allows consumers to plan their vacation by date, by price, and by activity. Travellers can now book flights, hotel accommodations, car rentals, cruises, and vacation packages, all at the click of a mouse.

Advances in technology are changing behaviour in everyday living. For example, many consumers are viewing movies on their cable channels instead of running to the video store to rent movies. This has led to the demise or decrease in the numbers of corner video stores.

Amount of Time It Took Apple to Sell One Million Units	
iPhone	74 days
iPad	28 days

Source: "Apple Sells a Million iPads in One Month," *Telecommunications Industry News*, accessed at www.teleclick.ca/2010/05/apple-sells-a-million-ipads-in-one-month.

With the advent of e-readers such as the Kindle and iPad, some consumers are switching to e-reading as opposed to purchasing physical books. Although e-reading is still a niche market, it may become more mainstream in time.

Post-Purchase Behaviour: Value in Consumption or Use

After buying a product, the consumer compares it with his or her expectations and is either satisfied or dissatisfied. A company's sensitivity to a customer's consumption experience strongly affects the value a customer perceives after the purchase. Studies show that satisfaction or dissatisfaction affects consumer communications and repeat-purchase behaviour. Satisfied buyers tell three other people about their experience. Dissatisfied buyers complain to nine

Travellers can now book flights, hotel accommodations, car rentals, cruises, and vacation packages at the click of a mouse.

> *Some companies are hiring employees to exclusively monitor sites such as Twitter and interact with unsatisfied customers right on the site.*

people![7] The Internet has allowed buyers to complain and be heard by potentially thousands of people.

Consumers who are not finding satisfaction when a problem occurs are starting to take things into their own hands, thanks to the Internet. If a company were to Google its name followed by the word "sucks," it will find a large number of hits that consist of negative stories about consumers' experiences with their products. Other consumers are venting their frustrations on Twitter and Facebook. Smart companies are looking at these complaints as an opportunity to link up with these disgruntled customers and resolve the problems. Some companies are hiring employees to exclusively monitor sites such as Twitter and interact with unsatisfied customers right on the site. They are beginning to realize that the voice of the consumer on the web is very powerful.

Often, a consumer is faced with two or more highly attractive alternatives, such as choosing between an iPhone and a BlackBerry. If you choose the BlackBerry, you may think, "Should I have purchased the iPhone?" This feeling of post-purchase psychological tension or anxiety is called *cognitive dissonance*. To alleviate it, consumers often attempt to applaud themselves for making the right choice. So, after purchase, you may seek information to confirm your choice by asking friends questions like, "What do you think of my new BlackBerry?" or by reading ads of the brand you chose. You might even look for negative features about the brand you didn't buy. Firms often use ads or follow-up calls from salespeople in this post-purchase stage to assure buyers that they made the right decision.

Involvement and Problem-Solving Variations

LO2 Sometimes consumers don't engage in the five-step purchase decision process. Instead, they skip or minimize one or more steps depending on the level of involvement. The level of **involvement** that a consumer has in a particular purchase depends on the personal, social, and economic consequences of that purchase to the consumer.[8] Items such as soft drinks or toothpaste may have such a low level of involvement for consumers that they may skip or minimize one or more steps in the process. But they may do just the opposite for a high-involvement purchase like a computer or an automobile.

High-involvement purchase occasions typically have at least one of three characteristics: The item to be purchased is expensive; it is bought infrequently; or it could reflect on one's social image. For these occasions, consumers engage in extensive information search, consider many product attributes and brands, form attitudes, and participate in word-of-mouth communication. Marketers who sell high-involvement products such as cars, homes, and computers must understand the information-gathering and evaluation process of consumers. Researchers have identified three general variations in the consumer purchase process based on consumer involvement and product knowledge. Figure 3-2 summarizes some of the important differences between the three problem-solving variations.[9]

Figure 3–2
Comparison of problem-solving variations

CHARACTERISTICS OF PURCHASE DECISION PROCESS	LOW ◄ CONSUMER INVOLVEMENT ► HIGH		
	ROUTINE PROBLEM SOLVING	LIMITED PROBLEM SOLVING	EXTENDED PROBLEM SOLVING
Number of brands examined	One	Several	Many
Number of sellers considered	Few	Several	Many
Number of product attributes evaluated	One	Moderate	Many
Number of external information sources used	None	Few	Many
Time spent searching	Minimal	Little	Considerable

Marketers know that a logo encapsulates consumers' feelings about the company that are formed over time. The sentimental brand association of a logo can be so powerful that it inspires consumers to take actions they might not have otherwise intended to take. According to a new University of Toronto study, even a glimpse of a fast-food logo can make a person more impatient and impulsive with money. "The logo activates associations with the brand," explains study co-author Chen-Bo Zhong, professor of organizational behaviour and human resource management at the university.

In one part of the study, the fast-food group saw logos of McDonald's and KFC; the control group instead viewed pictures of two generic low-priced dinners. Afterward, they were all asked if they would like to receive a higher amount of money in one week or a lower amount of money immediately. Those exposed to the fast-food logos were much more likely to want the money immediately. "Fast food seemed to have made people impatient in a manner that could put their economic interest at risk," the study concludes.

A 2008 Duke University study found people who looked at the Apple logo scored higher on a creativity test than those who had looked at an IBM logo—presumably because they were reflecting the differing brand traits they associated with those logos. The stronger the brand "personality," the stronger the association, Mr. Zhong said. In the case of fast food, logos from popular chains such as McDonald's promote associations with fast food, namely relating to immediate gratification and saving time.

Recent research from the University of Michigan found children as young as three can recognize brand logos and products. Children viewed logos of 50 brands across 16 product categories including fast food, toys, electronics, and apparel, and were asked questions about the brands. The results showed that a majority of the children recognized logos of fast-food restaurants.[10] ●

Questions

1. When you think of the Apple logo, what associations come to mind?

2. Give some examples of logos that elicit positive associations and those that elicit negative associations.

Routine Problem Solving For products such as table salt and milk, consumers recognize a problem, make a decision, and spend little effort seeking external information and evaluating alternatives. The purchase process for such items is virtually a habit and typifies low-involvement decision-making. Routine problem solving is typically the case for low-priced, frequently purchased products. An example is a consumer who stops by Tim Hortons on his way to work and purchases a coffee and a bagel. He doesn't ponder the potential benefits of going to a Second Cup or Starbucks even though they are all on his way to work. Marketers strive to attract and maintain habitual buying behaviour by creating strong brand relationships with the consumer.

Limited Problem Solving Limited problem solving is characterized by low consumer involvement but significant perceived differences among brands. For example, a consumer loves Activia yogourt but switches to BioBest yogourt, not out of dissatisfaction but just out of a desire to try something new. The consumer may have spent a moderate amount of time evaluating the available brands in the store before selecting BioBest. With limited problem-solving behaviour, consumers rely on past experience more than external information but they may pay attention to new varieties shown in advertising and point-of-purchase displays. Marketers of leading brands should focus on getting consumers to shift to routine problem-solving behaviour

by dominating shelf space and running advertisements that remind consumers of the benefits of their brands. Consumers might use limited problem solving when choosing a pair of jeans, deciding on a restaurant for dinner, and making other purchase situations in which they have little time or effort to spend researching options.

Extended Problem Solving In extended problem solving, each of the five stages of the consumer purchase decision process is used in the purchase, including considerable time and effort on external information search and identifying and evaluating alternatives. Several brands are in the evoked set, and these are evaluated on many attributes. Extended problem solving exists in high-involvement purchase situations for items such as automobiles, houses, and financial investments.

Figure 3–3 shows the many influences that affect the consumer purchase decision process. The decision to buy a product also involves important situational, psychological, and socio-cultural influences, the topics discussed during the remainder of this chapter. Marketing mix influences are described later, in Part 3 of the book.

Figure 3–3
Influences on the consumer purchase decision process

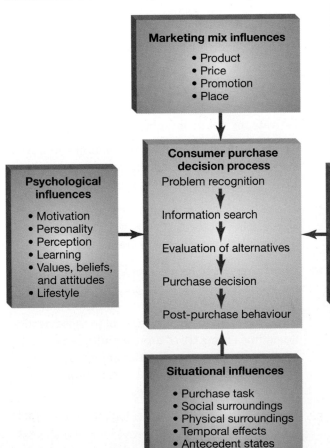

ask yourself

1. What is the first stage in the consumer purchase decision process?

2. The grouping of brands that a consumer considers buying out of the set of brands in a product class is called the _____.

3. What is the term for post-purchase anxiety?

Situational Influences

LO 3 Often the purchase situation will affect the purchase decision process. Five *situational influences* have an impact on your purchase decision process: the purchase task, social surroundings, physical surroundings, temporal effects, and antecedent states.[11]

1. The *purchase task* is the reason for engaging in the decision in the first place. Information searching and evaluating alternatives may differ depending on whether the purchase is a gift, which often involves social visibility, or for the buyer's own use. For example, some consumers may be frugal shoppers when it comes to purchasing products for themselves, but may spend lavishly if the product is a gift for a friend.

2. *Social surroundings*, including the other people present when a purchase decision is made, may also affect what is purchased. For example, Paco Underhill, a behavioural research consultant has shown that when two women shop together, they spend more time in the store shopping than they would if they were alone.[12]

3. *Physical surroundings* such as decor, music, and crowding in retail stores may alter how purchase decisions are made. Crowding, for example is a two-edged sword. When consumers see a throng of people in the Apple Store, they may be eager

to enter the store to be part of the experience. On the other hand, some people may be turned off because they don't like shopping in a crowded environment.

4. *Temporal effects,* such as time of day or the amount of time available, will influence where consumers have breakfast and lunch and what is ordered.

5. Finally, *antecedent states,* which include the consumer's mood or the amount of cash on hand, can influence purchase behaviour and choice. For example, a consumer who procrastinates buying a gift may choose one in a hurried state but may regret the purchase. If that consumer did not wait to the last moment, a more satisfying product may have been purchased instead.

Psychological Influences on Consumer Behaviour

L④ Psychology helps marketers understand why and how consumers behave as they do. In particular, concepts such as motivation and personality; perception; learning; values, beliefs, and attitudes; and lifestyle are useful for interpreting buying processes and directing marketing efforts.

Figure 3–4
Maslow's hierarchy of needs

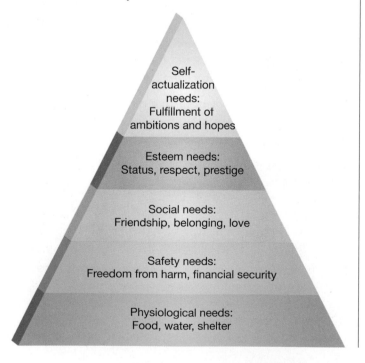

Self-actualization needs:
Fulfillment of ambitions and hopes

Esteem needs:
Status, respect, prestige

Social needs:
Friendship, belonging, love

Safety needs:
Freedom from harm, financial security

Physiological needs:
Food, water, shelter

Motivation and Personality

Motivation and personality are two familiar psychological concepts that have specific meanings and marketing implications. They are both used frequently to describe why people do some things and not others.

Motivation **Motivation** is the energizing force that stimulates behaviour to satisfy a need. Because consumer needs are the focus of the marketing concept, marketers try to arouse these needs.

An individual's needs are boundless. People have physiological needs for basics such as water, food, and shelter. They also have learned needs, including esteem, achievement, and affection. The late psychologist Abraham Maslow developed a theory that characterized needs and arranged them into a hierarchy. He argued that people take care of their lower-level needs first and then are motivated to satisfy their higher-level needs. Figure 3–4 shows Maslow's hierarchy of needs, which contains the following five need classes:[13]

1. *Physiological needs* are basic to survival and must be satisfied first. A Burger King advertisement featuring a juicy hamburger attempts to activate the need for food.

2. *Safety needs* involve self-preservation and physical well-being. Smoke detector and burglar alarm manufacturers focus on these needs.

3. *Social needs* are concerned with love and friendship. Dating services such as eHarmony and fragrance companies try to arouse these needs.

4. *Esteem needs* are represented by the need for achievement, status, prestige, and self-respect. Using the American Express Gold Card and shopping at Holt Renfrew appeal to these needs. Sometimes firms try to arouse multiple needs to stimulate problem recognition. Michelin combines security with parental love to promote tire replacement for automobiles.

5. *Self-actualization needs* involve personal fulfillment. For example, travel providers offer specialized educational and exotic trips.

personality
A person's character traits that influence behavioural responses

perception
Process by which someone selects, organizes, and interprets information to create a meaningful picture of the world

Personality **Personality** refers to a person's character traits that influence behavioural responses. Although numerous personality theories exist, most identify key traits such as assertiveness, extraversion, compliance, dominance, and aggression, among others. Research suggests that compliant people prefer known brand names and use more mouthwash and toilet soaps. In contrast, aggressive types use razors, not electric shavers; apply more cologne and aftershave lotions; and purchase signature goods such as Gucci, Yves St. Laurent, and Donna Karan as an indicator of status.[14]

Personality characteristics are often revealed in a person's *self-concept*, which is the way people see themselves and the way they believe others see them. Marketers recognize that people have an actual self-concept and an ideal self-concept. The actual self refers to how people actually see themselves. The ideal self describes how people would like to see themselves. Marketers appeal to these two self-images in the products and brands a person buys, including automobiles, home appliances and furnishings, magazines, clothing, grooming products, and leisure products, and in the stores where a person shops. The use of attractive models in ads for grooming products appeals to

> # RESEARCH SUGGESTS THAT COMPLIANT PEOPLE PREFER KNOWN BRAND NAMES AND USE MORE MOUTHWASH AND TOILET SOAPS.

a person's ideal self-concept. Men are becoming more concerned about their self-concept when it comes to body image and grooming. Unilever has responded to this trend by introducing a line of grooming products for men called Dove Men+Care.

Perception

One person sees a Porsche as a mark of achievement; another sees it as showing off. This is the result of **perception**—the process by which an individual selects, organizes, and interprets information to create a meaningful picture of the world.

Selective Perception The average consumer operates in a complex, information-rich environment. The human brain organizes and interprets all this information with a process called *selective perception*, which filters the information so that only some of it is understood or remembered or even available to the conscious mind. *Selective exposure* occurs when people pay attention to messages that are consistent with their attitudes and beliefs and ignore messages that are inconsistent. Selective exposure often occurs in the post-purchase stage of the consumer decision process, when consumers read advertisements for the brand they just bought. It also occurs when a need exists—you are more likely to "see" a McDonald's advertisement when you are hungry rather than after you have eaten a pizza.

Selective comprehension involves interpreting information so that it is consistent with your attitudes and beliefs. A marketer's failure to

understand this can have disastrous results. For example, Toro introduced a small, lightweight snow-blower called the Snow Pup. Even though the product worked, sales failed to meet expectations. Why? Toro later found out that consumers perceived the name to mean that Snow Pup was a toy or too light to do any serious snow removal. When the product was renamed Snow Master, sales increased sharply.[15]

Selective retention means that consumers do not remember all the information they see, read, or hear, even minutes after exposure to it. This affects the internal and external information search stage of the purchase decision process. This is why furniture and automobile retailers often give consumers product brochures to take home after they leave the showroom.

Perceived Risk Consumers' beliefs about the potential negative consequences of a product or service strongly affect their purchasing decisions. **Perceived risk** represents the anxieties felt because the consumer cannot anticipate the outcomes of a purchase but believes that there may be negative consequences. Examples of possible negative consequences concerning snowboarding are the price of the product (Can I afford $400 for a snowboard?) and the risk of physical harm (Is snowboarding more dangerous than alpine skiing?). Some products such as hair colouring lend themselves to perceived risk. There is always the fear that the hair colouring may not turn out to the consumer's satisfaction. Perceived risk affects the information search step of the purchase decision process: The greater the perceived risk, the more extensive the external search is likely to be.

Recognizing the importance of perceived risk, smart marketers develop strategies to make consumers feel more at ease about their purchases. Strategies and examples of firms using them include the following:

- **Obtaining seals of approval:** The Good Housekeeping seal that appears on many brands
- **Securing endorsements from influential people:** Reebok's products endorsed by Sidney Crosby
- **Providing free trials of the product:** Samples of perfume offered at The Bay

- **Providing illustrations:** Photos of different colours and hairstyles on Clairol Canada's website
- **Providing warranties and guarantees:** BMW's two-year, unlimited-mileage warranty on all of their automobiles[16]

Learning

Why do consumers behave in the marketplace as they do? Over consumers' lifetimes, they learn behaviours, and they also learn responses to those behaviours—this learning is a continual process. Consumers learn which sources to use for information about products and services, which evaluative criteria to use when assessing alternatives, and how to make purchase decisions. **Learning** refers to those behaviours that result from repeated experience and reasoning.

Behavioural Learning *Behavioural learning* is the process of developing automatic responses to a type of situation built up through repeated exposure to it. Four variables are central to how one learns from repeated experience: drive, cue, response, and reinforcement. A *drive* is a need, such as hunger, that moves an individual to action. A *cue* is a stimulus or symbol that one perceives. A *response* is the action taken to satisfy the drive, and a *reinforcement* is the reward. Being hungry (a drive), a consumer sees a cue (a billboard), takes action (buys a hamburger), and receives a reward (it tastes great!). If what the consumer experiences upon responding to a stimulus is not pleasant (I feel sick now!), then *negative reinforcement* has occurred. Behavioural learning plays a major role in consumer decision-making—in this case, causing the consumer to avoid the behavioural response rather than repeat it.

Marketers use two concepts from behavioural learning theory. *Stimulus generalization* occurs when a response brought about by one stimulus (cue) is generalized to another stimulus. Using the same brand name to launch new products is one common

> **brand loyalty**
> Favourable attitude toward and consistent purchase of a single brand over time

> **attitude**
> Tendency to respond to something in a consistently favourable or unfavourable way

> **beliefs**
> Consumer's perceptions of how a product or brand performs

> *Consumers familiar with one product will often transfer their feelings to others that seem similar—whether the similarity is in a brand name or in the shape and colour of the packaging.*

application of this concept, as when the makers of Tylenol followed up their original pain reliever with Tylenol Cold, Tylenol Flu, Tylenol Sinus, and others. Consumers familiar with one product will often transfer their feelings to others that seem similar—whether the similarity is in a brand name or in the shape and colour of the packaging. Are you familiar with President's Choice Cola or Costco's Simply Soda? They use red cans, similar in colour to Coca-Cola cans—this is stimulus generalization in action!

Stimulus discrimination refers to one's ability to perceive differences among similar products. Consumers may do this easily with some groups of products, such as automobiles. But in many cases, such as low-involvement purchases, advertisers work to point out the differences. For example, consumers' tendency to perceive all light beers as being alike led to Budweiser Light commercials that distinguished between many types of lights and Bud Light.

Cognitive Learning Consumers also learn without direct experience—through thinking, reasoning, and mental problem solving. This type of learning, called *cognitive learning*, involves making connections between two or more ideas or simply observing the outcomes of others' behaviours and adjusting your own accordingly. Firms also influence this type of learning. Through repetition in advertising, messages such as "Advil is a headache remedy" attempt to link a brand (Advil) and an idea (headache remedy) by showing someone using the brand and finding relief.

Brand Loyalty Learning is also important to marketers because it relates to habit formation. Developing habits means that a consumer is solving problems (such as what to do when she's hungry) routinely and consistently, without much thought. Not surprisingly, there is a close link between habits and **brand loyalty**, which is a favourable attitude toward and consistent purchase of a single brand over time. Brand loyalty results from positive reinforcement. If a consumer is satisfied with a product, he reduces his risk and saves time by consistently purchasing that same brand.

Values, Beliefs, and Attitudes

Values, beliefs, and attitudes play a central role in consumer decision-making.

Attitude Formation An **attitude** is a "learned predisposition to respond to an object or class of objects in a consistently favourable or unfavourable way."[17] Attitudes are shaped by our values and beliefs, which we develop in the process of growing up. For example, we speak of core values, including material well-being and humanitarianism. We also have personal values, such as thriftiness and ambition. Marketers are concerned with both, but focus mostly on personal values. Personal values affect attitudes by influencing the importance assigned to specific product attributes, or features. Suppose thriftiness is one of your personal values. When you evaluate cars, fuel economy (a product attribute) becomes important. If you believe a specific car has this attribute, you are likely to have a favourable attitude toward it.

Beliefs also play a part in attitude formation. In consumer terms, **beliefs** are one's perception of how a product or brand performs on different attributes. Beliefs are based on personal experience, advertising, and discussions with other people. Beliefs about product attributes are important because, along with personal values, they create the favourable or unfavourable attitude the consumer has toward certain products and services.

Attitude Change Marketers use three approaches to try to change consumer attitudes toward products and brands, as shown in the following examples.[18]

1. *Changing beliefs about the extent to which a brand has certain attributes.* To reduce consumer concern that Aspirin use causes an upset stomach, Bayer Corporation successfully promoted the gentleness of its Extra Strength Bayer Plus Aspirin.

2. *Changing the perceived importance of attributes.* Consumers up to now were divided on the number of hours of sleep required for good health. Recent articles in the media are changing consumers' perceived importance of required hours. The Mayo Clinic, for example, recommends seven to nine hours of sleep for adults.[19] Sleep Country Canada emphasizes in its commercials the importance of getting a good night's rest and how Sleep Country can help the situation by providing a mattress that can improve the quality of sleep.

3. *Adding new attributes to the product.* Most consumers know that eating foods with antioxidants is a great way to protect themselves from damaging free radicals and help support their bodies' defences. But most people don't know that coffee contains naturally occurring antioxidants. Nescafé, for example, promotes this fact on its website and in its advertising.

Lifestyle

Lifestyle is a way of living that is identified by how people spend their time and resources (activities), what they consider important in their environment (interests), and what they think of themselves and the world around them (opinions). The analysis of consumer lifestyles, called

psychographics, has produced many insights into consumer behaviour. For example, lifestyle analysis has proven useful in segmenting and targeting consumers for new and existing products.

One of the most popular examples of psychographic analysis is the VALS™ Program developed by SRI International.[20] The VALS Program identifies eight interconnected categories of adult lifestyles based on a person's self-orientation and resources. Self-orientation describes the patterns of attitudes and activities that help a person reinforce his or her social self-image. Three patterns have been uncovered, which are oriented toward principles, status, and action. A person's resources range from minimal to abundant and include income, education, self-confidence, health, eagerness to buy, intelligence, and energy level. Each of these categories exhibits different buying behaviour and media preferences.

VALS is an American-based system, and the psychographics of Americans differ significantly from those of Canadians. When some market researchers have tried to use American values and lifestyles to describe Canadians, they have not succeeded. The firm Millward Brown Goldfarb created psychographic

Figure 3–5

Goldfarb psychographic market segments for Canada

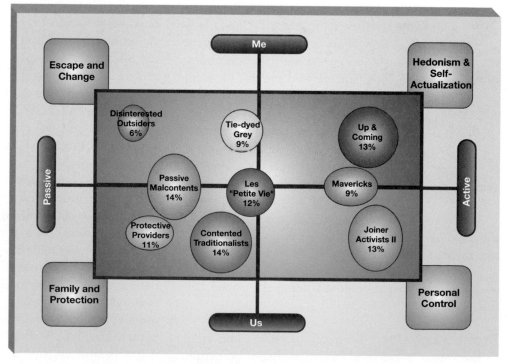

Source: Consumer TrendZ Report, Millward Brown Goldfarb

groups based on an extensive survey of Canadian values, ethics, opinions and interests over a three-year period. Figure 3–5 shows their nine segments and the percentage of the Canadian adult population that matches the characteristics of each group. The axes of the chart show orientations toward key traits; for example, a "Tie-dyed Grey"

is more oriented toward individuals, while a "Contented Traditionalist" considers family or other close group as more important.

Figure 3–6 summarizes the nine lifestyle types and highlights selected behavioural characteristics of each and their implications for marketers, who can use this information in a variety of ways.

Figure 3–6
Goldfarb psychographic market segments for Canada

SEGMENT	PERCENTAGE OF CANADIAN POPULATION	DESCRIPTION	MARKETING IMPLICATIONS
Disinterested Outsiders	6%	Materialistic, price conscious, willing to bend rules, younger, fewer married, lower education, lack respect for authority, not intellectually curious, less into technology, dislike change	Materialistic yet price conscious, low income (offer financing, incentives, and discounts), need to know immediate benefits, like Irreverent tone of communications, want non-mainstream items, TV is a good way to reach them
Tie-Dyed Grey	9%	Older, lower income, more unmarried (single, divorced), urban dwellers, few with children, open minded, environmentally conscious, slightly uncomfortable with technology, like cultural events, independent	Do not respond well to family focus or romantic appeals, big readers (like newspapers, TV, magazines, current affairs shows), natural market for travel/holiday packages, marketing should have little jargon and technospeak, like personal touch in services
Passive Malcontents	14%	Older, maybe ethnic, patriotic, lack self-confidence, trusting, not too health conscious, participate in on-line chat	Unhappy (may respond well to products that improve), full-service offerings, health concerns, stress "made in Canada," respectful of authority figures, enjoy reading (magazine & newspaper ads appeal to them), very loyal
Protective Providers	11%	Hard-working, personal initiative, committed to family, financial pressures, distrustful, dislike change, enjoy outdoor activities, married with children, patriotic and proud, not highly educated	Very price conscious, looking for best value and incentives, home improvement and children's products appeal to them, brand names important, respond to respectful promotion, reinforce ideas of safety and security for family to attract them, use TV
Contented Traditionalists	12%	Older, married, religious focus, family oriented, conservative, ethical, respectful of authority, organized, brand loyal, not materialistic	Products/brands with a clean image, tone not irreverent or disrespectful, appreciate products that promote healthy living and family togetherness, like full service offerings, like to take care of future, need reassurance
Up & Comers	12%	Younger, many visible minorities or foreign-born, materialistic, outgoing, looking for quick gratification, optimistic, value friendships	Latest trends and gadgets, entertainment and sports-related products, brand names important, conservative advertising tastes, reach through TV and cinema ads, not newspapers/magazines
Mavericks	9%	Higher household income, solid employment, natural leaders, enjoy challenge, seek wealth, conservative views on family issues	Early adopters, voracious consumers, willing to pay, time poor, like to see benefits emphasized, technology is important to them and high-tech items, make them feel in control and empowered
Joiner Activists II	13%	Married, younger, higher income, optimistic, financially sound, non-religious, environmentalists, health conscious, like cultural activities, comfortable with online purchases	Crave information, like details, interested in new experiences/products, good quality and unique, upscale products, expect intelligent and sophisticated promotions, socially responsible companies attract them, early adopters
Les "Petite Vie"	12%	Friends and family very important, relaxed life, not leaders, respect business leaders, support government, open-minded, many French-speaking, low university attendance	Watch lots of TV, do not trust outsiders, not materialistic, believe spokespeople or experts, brand names are important, do not respond well to "new and improved" (instead they like tried and true)

Source: Consumer TrendZ Report, Millward Brown Goldfarb

Socio-Cultural Influences on Consumer Behaviour

L⑤ Socio-cultural influences, which evolve from a consumer's formal and informal relationships with other people, also have an impact on consumer behaviour. These include personal influence, reference groups, family, culture, and subculture.

Personal Influence

A consumer's purchases are often influenced by the views, opinions, or behaviours of others. Two aspects of personal influence are important to marketing: opinion leadership and word-of-mouth activity.

Opinion Leadership
Individuals who have social influence over others are called **opinion leaders**. Opinion leaders are more likely to be important for products that provide a form of self-expression. Automobiles, clothing, and club memberships are products affected by opinion leaders, but appliances usually are not.[21]

A small percentage of adults—from influential community leaders and business executives to movie stars—are opinion leaders. Identifying, reaching, and influencing opinion leaders is a major challenge for companies. Some firms use sports figures or celebrities as spokespersons to represent their products, such as Sidney Crosby for Reebok, in the hope that they are opinion leaders.

Word of Mouth
People influencing each other during conversations is called **word of mouth**. Word of mouth is perhaps the most powerful information source for consumers, because it typically involves friends or family who are viewed as trustworthy.

The power of personal influence has prompted firms to make efforts to increase positive and decrease negative word of mouth.[22] For instance, "teaser" advertising campaigns are run in advance of new-product introductions to stimulate conversations. Other techniques such as advertising slogans, music, and humour also heighten positive word of mouth. On the other hand, rumours about McDonald's (worms in hamburgers) and Corona Extra beer (contaminated beer) have resulted in negative word of mouth, none of which was based on fact. Overcoming negative word of mouth is difficult and costly. Firms have found that supplying factual information, providing toll-free numbers for consumers to call the company, and giving appropriate product demonstrations also have been helpful.

The term *buzz marketing* refers to a brand becoming popular as a result of people talking about it to friends and neighbours. Another way that a company can create buzz is by hiring an outside agency. Word-of-mouth agencies such as Matchstick specialize in product seeding programs. Product seeding consists of hiring people to talk up a brand to others. The Word of Mouth Marketing Association (WOMMA) has issued ethical guidelines on product seeding, including the guideline that brand representatives must always disclose their relationship to the brand when promoting it to others.

The power of word of mouth has been magnified by the Internet. The online version of word of mouth is called *viral marketing*. This includes the use of messages that consumers pass along to others through online forums, social networks such as Facebook and Twitter, chat rooms, bulletin boards, blogs, and e-mails. These messages can be positive or negative. Companies are now recognizing the value of social media platforms such as Twitter and Facebook, and are monitoring messages so that they can respond to consumers quickly. Chapter 13, which covers customer relationship management, focuses in more detail on the importance of social media.

Reference Groups

A **reference group** is a group of people who influence a person's attitudes, values, and behaviour. For example, you might consider your family or the other students in your school as a reference group. Other examples of reference groups are movie stars and sport celebrities. Reference groups affect consumer purchases because they influence the information, attitudes, and aspiration levels that help set a consumer's standards. Reference groups have an important influence on the purchase of luxury products but not of necessities—reference groups exert a strong influence on the brand chosen when its use or consumption is highly visible to others.[23]

Consumers have many reference groups, but three groups have clear marketing implications.

- **Membership group:** One to which a person actually belongs, including fraternities and sororities, social clubs, and the family. Such groups are easily identifiable and are targeted by firms selling insurance, insignia products, and vacation packages.

"Product seeding consists of hiring people to talk up a brand to others."

- **Aspiration group:** One that a person wishes to be a member of or wishes to be identified with. An example is a person whose dream it is to play in the NHL. Brands such as Gatorade and Nike frequently rely on spokespeople or settings associated with their target market's aspiration group in their advertising.

- **Dissociative group:** One that a person wishes to maintain a distance from because of differences in values or behaviours.

Family Influence

Family influences on consumer behaviour result from three sources: consumer socialization, passage through the family life cycle, and decision making within the family or household.

Consumer Socialization   The process by which people acquire the skills, knowledge, and attitudes necessary to function as consumers is *consumer socialization*.[24] Children learn how to purchase by interacting with adults in purchase situations and through their own purchasing and product usage experiences. Research demonstrates that children show signs of brand preferences as early as age two, and these preferences often last a lifetime. This knowledge prompted Time Inc. to launch *Sports Illustrated for Kids*. The brand of toothpaste, laundry detergent, or soft drink used in your home will very likely influence your brand choice when you purchase these items for yourself.

Family Life Cycle   Consumers act and purchase differently as they go through life. The **family life cycle** concept describes the distinct phases that a family progresses through from formation to retirement, each phase bringing with it identifiable purchasing behaviours.[25] Today, the traditional family—married couples with children younger than 25 years—constitute just over 41 percent of all Canadian households. Nearly 40 percent are households without children. Common-law couples with children account for 8 percent of all households and those without children account for 10 percent.[26]

Young single consumers' buying preferences are for non-durable items, including prepared foods, clothing, personal care products, and entertainment. They represent a significant target market for recreational travel, automobile, and consumer electronics

firms. Young married couples without children are typically more affluent than young singles because usually both spouses are employed. These couples exhibit preferences for furniture, housewares, and gift items for each other. Young marrieds with children are driven by the needs of their children. These families make up a sizable market for life insurance, various children's products, and home furnishings. Single parents with children are the least financially secure type of households. Their buying preferences are usually affected by a limited economic status and tend toward convenience foods, child care services, and personal care items.

Middle-aged married couples with children are typically better off financially than their younger counterparts. They are a significant market for leisure products and home improvement items. Middle-aged couples without children typically have a large amount of discretionary income. These couples buy better home furnishings, status automobiles, and financial services. Persons in the last two phases—older married and older unmarried—make up a sizable market for prescription drugs, medical services, vacation trips, and gifts for younger relatives.

Family Decision-Making   A third family-based influence on consumer decision-making occurs in the context of the relationship dynamics of the household. Two decision-making styles exist: spouse-dominant and joint decision-making. With a joint decision-making style, most decisions are made by both husband and wife. Spouse-dominant decisions are those for which either the husband or the wife has more influence in the purchase decision. Research indicates that wives tend to have the most say when purchasing groceries, children's toys, clothing, and medicines. Husbands tend to be more influential in home and car maintenance purchases. Joint decision-making is common for cars, vacations, houses, home appliances and electronics, medical care, and long-distance telephone services. As a rule, joint decision-making increases with the education of the spouses.[27]

Roles of individual family members in the purchase process are another element of family decision-making. Five roles

> **family life cycle**
> A family's progression from formation to retirement, with each phase bringing distinct needs and purchasing behaviours

The late Steve Jobs, the visionary in the black turtleneck, co-founded Apple, built it into the world's leading tech company, and led a mobile computing revolution with wildly popular devices such as the iPod, iPhone, and iPad.

exist: information gatherer, influencer, decision maker, purchaser, and user. Family members assume different roles for different products and services.[28] For example, 89 percent of wives either influence or make outright purchases of men's clothing. Knowing this, Haggar Clothing, a menswear marketer, advertises in women's magazines such as *Chatelaine* and *Redbook*. Even though women are often the grocery decision makers, they are not necessarily the purchaser. Husbands do about one-half of food shopping. Increasingly, preteens and teenagers are the information gatherers, influencers, decision makers, and purchasers of products and services items for the family, given the prevalence of working parents and single-parent households. Children and teenagers directly influence billions of dollars in annual family purchases. These figures help explain why, for example, Johnson & Johnson, Apple, Kellogg, P&G, Sony, and Oscar Mayer, among countless other companies, spend billions annually in media that reach preteens and teens.[29]

Culture and Subculture

Culture refers to the set of values, ideas, and attitudes that are learned and shared among the members of a group. Thus we often refer to Canadian culture, American culture, or Japanese culture.

> "*Even though women are often the grocery decision makers, they are not necessarily the purchaser. Husbands do about one-half of food shopping.*"

focus on **Ethics**   The Power of Word of Mouth

One of the most powerful forms of marketing is the result of one of the most natural activities: talking. Word-of-mouth marketing is an extraordinary tool for marketers to use as they spread their brands, as it is the most effective form of marketing available—and the simplest. The Word of Mouth Marketing Association (WOMMA) is the official trade association for word-of-mouth marketers and is a coalition comprised of top marketers who are interested in learning how to encourage and utilize word of mouth while respecting and protecting its integrity.

WOMMA aids its members with the implementation of word of mouth using training, best practices, standards and metrics, and mainstreaming. WOMMA provides outreach and education, aids marketers in creating sustainable word-of-mouth programs, creates accountability for practices, and works at bringing word of mouth into the centre of the marketing world. WOMMA's mission is to improve word-of-mouth marketing by "Promoting 'best practices' to ensure more effective marketing; protecting consumers and the industry with strong ethical guidelines; evangelizing word of mouth as an effective marketing tool; and setting standards to encourage its use."

Recently, WOMMA developed a code of ethics for word-of-mouth marketing. These guidelines are meant to protect the consumer during the use of and participation in word-of-mouth marketing. The code focuses on openness between consumers, advocates, and marketers; advocates are encouraged to be open with consumers about their relationship with the marketers. Advocates are also encouraged to be honest with their opinions about the products that they are marketing and to disclose their identity to the consumers. WOMMA created the code of ethics in order to help marketers see what practices they should be supporting and to allow the word-of-mouth industry to set clear standards for itself.[30] ●

Questions

1. Imagine that you are paid by an agency to promote one of Molson's brands by talking to customers in a bar. WOMMA's code of ethics says that you should disclose to the consumer that you are being paid to promote the brand. Would you do that or would you not disclose your relationship with Molson? Why or why not?

2. When you consider buying a large ticket item, how much do you rely on word of mouth from family, friends, etc., versus doing research yourself on the product that you want to buy?

Subgroups within the larger, or national, culture with unique values, ideas, and attitudes are referred to as **subcultures**. Subcultures can be defined by regions, by demographic groups, or by values. The most prominent types of subcultures are racial and ethnic, and many of these exist within the Canadian mosaic of people. French, German, Italian, Chinese, and Ukrainian subcultures are the ones we see most in Canada, and they make up nearly 40 percent of the Canadian population. Each one exhibits unique buying patterns and socio-cultural behaviours.

Canada's outlook on ethnicity is that cultural and ethnic groups are welcome to continue with their traditions, languages, and values. Canada is a nation of many faces, and people have been immigrating here continually over many decades. A person may regard herself as Italian, yet never have been to Italy—her grandparents may have immigrated here many years ago. If Italian customs have been maintained by the family, she may behave much like a recently arrived Italian. Some countries encourage immigrants to join the mainstream national culture, while diversity is encouraged in Canada.

Our ethnic composition, and the philosophy that we take toward it, has led to the creation of many ethnic neighbourhoods in our cities. As our population becomes more diverse, people immigrating here bring foods from their native lands. Canadians do not have a lot of native food and preparation styles, so the country has been particularly welcoming of cuisine from around the world. Immigration has had a major influence on Canada's food market, both in the many restaurants and in the food items available from all corners of the globe. Not only food consumption is affected by immigration but also many cultural events have become mainstream, and many local happenings are the result of a tradition or celebration brought here by some new Canadians.

French-Canadian Subculture There are more than 9 million French-speaking Canadians in this country, about 30 percent of the population.[31] By far the largest majority of them live in the province of Quebec. Research shows that French-speaking Quebecers do exhibit different consumption behaviour than the rest of Canada.[32] For example, when asked what is important to them, Quebecers are more likely than other Canadians to say "enjoying life" and "seeking happiness." French Canadians, more so than English Canadians, are more likely to believe that everybody should be free to do their own thing. Quebecers are also more willing to pay higher prices for convenience and premium brands.

French Quebecers are cautious about new products and often postpone trying something new until they see that the product has proven itself. They exhibit brand loyalty, but they will switch brands if offered a special. French Quebecers are less likely to buy grocery items on impulse, and are increasingly calculating in their food purchases. Some grocery chains have responded to this characteristic by offering more discount coupons, weekly specials, and money-saving tips. Quebecers like things that please the senses. For example, they like fine restaurants and fine wines. Quebecois women are also very fashion-conscious, and upscale brands such as Prada and Lancome sell well in Quebec. This desire for beauty helps explain why

In the female the ability to match colors comes at an early age.

In the male it comes when he marries a female.

The City Casuals three-button, crepe jacket. 100% cotton, French-yarn shirt, Bedford cord pants, and a touch of color.

HAGGAR
Stuff you can work with

The Haggar Clothing Co. recognizes the important role women play in the choice of men's clothing. The company directs a large portion of its advertising toward women because they influence and purchase men's clothing.

Ethnic Groups in Canada

British descent	28%
French descent	23%
Other European descent	15%
Native descent	2%
Other	6%
Mixed descent	26%

Source: "Canada," Central Intelligence Agency, The World Factbook website, accessed at https://www.cia.gov/library/publications/the-world-factbook/geos/ca.html.

Chinese New Year celebrations take place in Vancouver each year and have become an integral part of the city's cultural fabric.

campaigns for anti-wrinkle products are even more successful in Quebec than in the rest of Canada.[33]

While the province of Quebec has the highest percentage of alcohol drinkers and the most relaxed drinking laws in Canada, it also has the lowest percentage of excessive drinkers and the fewest alcohol-related problems. French Quebecers are big buyers of lottery tickets and more likely to subscribe to book clubs, but they make fewer long-distance phone calls. They travel less, whether for business or pleasure. More French Quebec adults hold life insurance policies, but they are less likely to have a credit card. They also tend to use the services of credit unions (*caisses populaires*) rather than banks.

Some people feel that French Quebec can be characterized by a set of values that are traditional, consistent, and relatively static, but changes are evident. While values are still strong regarding family life and having children in a marriage, the use of birth control is rising, and the marriage rate is below the national average.

Marketers must realize that certain products and other elements of the marketing mix may have to be modified in order to be successful in French Quebec. In addition to cultural differences, there are other issues that marketers must address. Commercial advertising to children is prohibited and greater restrictions exist for alcohol advertising. Provincial regulations also require that labels and packages must be both English and French, while storefront signage must be in French, not English. Good investigation and analysis of this market is a requirement for all companies wishing to do business in this province.

Chinese-Canadian Subculture

This group is one of the largest and fastest-growing visible minorities. In fact, 3.74 percent of Canada's population is Chinese, with 40 percent residing in Toronto and 31 percent in Vancouver. The average Chinese household spends $63,500 each year, slightly higher than the Canadian average of $58,500. In general, these consumers are relatively young, educated, and affluent. They tend to spend their money on home furnishings, automobiles, kids' education, high-tech gadgets, travelling, and gifts. They like to do business within their own communities and prefer media in their own languages. They have strong allegiance to brands and are very family-oriented. Because they live in close-knit communities, word of mouth is very important to them.[34]

Chinese-Canadians have a preference for luxury vehicles, and many car dealerships see them as good potential customers for new cars. In general, they tend to eat out at restaurants more than the average Canadian, and there has been significant growth in the

Attitudes of Quebec Women versus Women in the Rest of Canada

Quebec women who admit to being high maintenance **75%**

Women in the rest of Canada who admit to being high maintenance **38%**

Quebec women who say they will do anything to look 10 years younger **36%**

Women in the rest of Canada who say they will do anything to look 10 years younger **19%**

marketing meter

Source: "Crunch," *Marketing Magazine*, October 27, 2008.

number of Chinese restaurants in Canada, and particularly in Vancouver and Toronto, over the past 10 years. For these, and a number of other factors, many marketers cater to the Chinese market as they see them as being good prospective customers.

Global Cultural Diversity

Canada has become increasingly multiethnic and multicultural, making it one of the most diverse countries in the world. Different countries take different approaches to admitting immigrants and integrating them into society. Canada's approach is often referred to as a mosaic, meaning that people who come to the country from another are welcome to maintain their cultural identities and customs—the belief is that this will create a situation where all Canadians can learn from the rich variety of over 200 cultures that make up the citizenry of the country. This environment works to increase Canadian companies' sensitivity and orientation toward other cultures, so the transition to global activities and relationships is facilitated.

Just as marketers must be sensitive to subcultures in Canada, they must appreciate the cultural differences

marketing NewsFlash Toyota's Fall from Grace

One of the fundamental principles at Toyota is *genchi genbutsu*, or "mutual ownership of problems." This principle mirrors the Japanese people valuing the group over the individual. The other, more famous principle is *Kaisen*, "continuous improvement," a method by which all workers are motivated to compete with their own previous achievements to make the company ever better. So how do you explain Toyota's accelerator pedal problems as well as other quality issues?

Toyota was a *Common Purpose* organization, meaning that everybody around the world seemed to know what the company stood for, which, in turn, helped them understand how to do their jobs better. For example, everyone knew that quality was more important than profits, that part of everyone's job was to fix something that went wrong, and that if they had a concern about a product or process they would be heard. They also knew that selling a second car to a customer was more important than the first. Loyalty counted for a lot. Back then, in all likelihood, someone would have spotted and fixed a problem with an accelerator pedal or

braking system immediately, not after two years and not after it affected more than two million cars. Someone would have pulled the cord.

Some people feel that Toyota's rush to become the world's biggest carmaker in 2008 may have resulted in them cutting corners as opposed to dealing with the problems. Others have pointed fingers at the company's suppliers. But Toyota has always been the least vertically integrated of the automobile companies. It was a networked company of autonomous and semi-autonomous suppliers as far back as the 1950s; some have worked with Toyota since its inception. Its managers were adept at managing supplier relationships to make certain everyone understood the company's goals. It's unlikely that Toyota's managers simply forgot what had been widely hailed as one of the company's most important attributes.

Others have suggested Toyota's problems are a result of its size. As the world's largest automobile company, it has grown too big to manage. This is also not likely the case. Toyota did not grow through mergers or acquisitions, but did so organically. This meant that there was nothing new to integrate into the

Toyota system and that there were no clashes of corporate cultures. In addition, Toyota became number one not because of a growth spurt, but because its main rivals fell.

It seems as if there is no one definitive reason that accounts for the quality problems. What seems more likely is that Toyota's brand equity may have been slightly damaged, but consumers' positive associations with Toyota over the years remain strong.

As a footnote to the above, a report conducted by NASA and the National Highway Traffic Safety Administration in the U.S. vindicated Toyota with respect to the recalls involving "sudden acceleration." One investigator said most of the cases involved "pedal misapplication," that is, "the driver stepped on the gas rather than the brake or in addition to the brake."[35]

Questions

1. Describe two Japanese cultural traits that are exemplified by Toyota?

2. Do you feel that Toyota's vindication will positively affect consumers' negative perceptions of Toyota? Why or why not?

of people in other countries if they want to market products and services to them. A necessary step in this process is **cross-cultural analysis**, which involves the study of similarities and differences among consumers in two or more nations or societies.[36] A thorough cross-cultural analysis involves an understanding of and an appreciation for the values, customs, symbols, and language of other societies.

Values
A society's **values** represent socially preferable modes of conduct or states of existence that tend to persist over time. Understanding and working with these aspects of a society are important factors in global marketing. For example, consider the following:[37]

- McDonald's does not sell hamburgers in its restaurants in India because the cow is considered sacred by almost 85 percent of the population. Instead, McDonald's sells the McMaharajah: two all-mutton patties, special sauce, lettuce, cheese, pickles, onions on a sesame-seed bun.

- Germans have not been overly receptive to the use of credit cards such as Visa or MasterCard, nor to the idea of borrowing to purchase goods and services. The German word for "debt," *Schuld*, is the same as the German word for "guilt."

Customs
Customs are what is considered normal and expected about the way people do things in a specific country or culture. Clearly, customs can vary significantly from country to country. Some customs may seem unusual to Canadians. Consider, for example, that in France men wear more than twice the number of cosmetics that women do, and that the Japanese consider slurping their food to be a sign of approval and appreciation to the chef.

The custom of giving token business gifts is popular in many countries where they are expected and accepted. However, bribes, kickbacks, and payoffs offered to entice someone to commit an illegal or improper act on behalf of the giver for economic gain is considered corrupt in most cultures. The widespread use of bribery in global marketing has led to an agreement among the world's major exporting

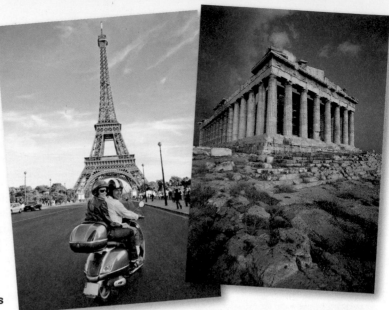

What cultural lesson did Coca-Cola executives learn when they used the Eiffel Tower and the Parthenon in a recent global advertising campaign? Read the text for the answer.

nations to make bribery of foreign government officials a criminal offence.

The Organisation for Economic Co-operation and Development (OECD) is an international body whose goal is to foster democratic government and a market-driven economy. With its global reach, OECD addresses issues of general interest to its members and affiliates. Corruption has become an issue of major importance in the past decade, and the OECD has taken action to set guidelines and procedures for preventing international bribery and corruption. Canada has adopted the OECD's anti-corruption convention and has made bribery of foreign public officials a criminal offence.[38]

Bribery paid to foreign companies is another matter. In France and Greece, bribes paid to foreign companies are a tax-deductible expense!

Cultural Symbols
Cultural symbols are objects, ideas, or processes that represent a particular group of people or society. Symbols and symbolism play an important role in cross-cultural analysis because different cultures attach different meanings to things. By cleverly using cultural symbols, global marketers can tie positive symbolism to their products and services to enhance their attractiveness to consumers. However, improper use of symbols can spell disaster. A culturally sensitive global marketer will know the following:[39]

- North Americans are superstitious about the number 13, and Japanese feel the same way about the number 4. Shi, the Japanese word for "four," is also the word for "death." Knowing this, Tiffany &

Company sells its fine glassware and china in sets of five, not four, in Japan.

- "Thumbs-up" is a positive sign in Canada. However, in Russia and Poland, this gesture has an offensive meaning when the palm of the hand is shown, as AT&T learned. The company reversed the gesture depicted in ads, showing the back of the hand, not the palm.

Cultural symbols stir up deep feelings. Consider how executives at Coca-Cola's Italian office learned this lesson. In a series of advertisements directed at Italian vacationers, the Eiffel Tower, Empire State Building, and the Tower of Pisa were turned into the familiar Coca-Cola bottle. However, when the white marble columns in the Parthenon that crown Athens's Acropolis were turned into Coca-Cola bottles, the Greeks were outraged. Greeks refer to the Acropolis as the "holy rock," and a government official said the Parthenon is an "international symbol of excellence" and that "whoever insults the Parthenon insults international culture." Coca-Cola apologized for the ad.[40]

Language Global marketers should know not only the basics of the native tongues of countries in which they market their products and services but also the subtleties and unique expressions of the language. For example, Pepsi found that Spanish-speaking people in Argentina tend to pronounce the soft drink as Pecsi rather than Pepsi. Pepsi responded by launching a successful marketing campaign that temporarily used the spelling Pecsi rather than Pepsi on billboards in Argentina. The brand name Pepsi was never really legally changed, but humorously altered for the period of the campaign.[41]

About 100 official languages exist in the world, but anthropologists estimate that at least 3,000 different languages are actually spoken. There are 11 official languages spoken in the European Union, and Canada has two official languages (English and French). Seventeen major languages are spoken in India alone.

English, French, and Spanish are the principal languages used in global diplomacy and commerce. However, the best language with which to communicate with consumers is their own, as any seasoned global marketer will agree. Language usage and

TOMÁS PEPSI, TAMBIÉN.

Pepsi, in a humorous marketing campaign in Argentina, had billboards refer to Pepsi as Pecsi. Read the text for the whole story.

ask yourself

1. What are the two primary forms of personal influence?

2. What challenges do marketers face when marketing to ethnic subcultural groups?

translation can present challenges. Unintended meanings of brand names and messages have ranged from the absurd to the obscene, as in the following examples:

- When the advertising agency responsible for launching Procter & Gamble's successful Pert shampoo in Canada realized that the name means "lost" in French, it substituted the brand name Pret, which means "ready."

- The Vicks brand name common in North America is German slang for sexual intimacy; therefore, Vicks is called Wicks in Germany.

Experienced global marketers use **back translation**, where a translated word or phrase is retranslated back into the original language by a different interpreter to catch errors.[42] IBM's first Japanese translation of its "Solution for a small planet" advertising message yielded "Answers that make people smaller." The error was caught by back translation and corrected. Sometimes, unintended translations can produce favourable results. Consider Kit Kat bars marketed by Nestlé worldwide. Kit Kat is pronounced "kitto katsu" in Japanese, which roughly translates to "I will win." Japanese teens eat Kit Kat bars for good luck, particularly when taking crucial school exams.[43]

back translation
Retranslating a word or phrase back into the original language by a different interpreter to catch errors

What does the Nestlé Kit Kat bar have in common with academic achievement in Japan? Read the text to find out.

[*adAlyze*]

Does this ad get your attention?

Do you feel that the number of words in the ad is just right or perhaps too many?

What are some of the benefits of using this brand of toothbrush?

1. Are you brushing too hard?
2. How do you remove the most plaque?
3. How do you reverse gingivitis?
4. How long should you brush?
5. When should you replace your brush head?
6. When should you shift quadrants?
7. What's a quadrant?

**Don't know the answers?
This toothbrush does.**

Oral-B Triumph with SmartGuide is the most intelligent brush on earth. Its wireless guidance system even tells you when you're brushing too hard. And its FlossAction head cleans deep – between teeth and along the gumline – to reverse gingivitis. Any questions?

www.oralb.com

Oral-B
TRIUMPH SMART GUIDE

Brush like a Dentist

Summary...*just the facts*

- When a consumer buys a product, it is not an act but a process. There are five stages in the purchase decision process: problem recognition, information search, alternative evaluation, purchase decision, and post-purchase behaviour.

- Consumers evaluate alternatives on the basis of attributes. Identifying which attributes are most important to consumers, along with understanding consumer beliefs about how a brand performs on those attributes, can make the difference between successful and unsuccessful products.

- Consumer involvement with what is bought affects whether the purchase decision process involves routine, limited, or extended problem solving. Situational influences also affect the process.

- Perception is important to marketers because of the selectivity of what a consumer sees or hears, comprehends, and retains.

- Much of the behaviour that consumers exhibit is learned. Consumers learn from repeated experience and reasoning. Brand loyalty is a result of learning.

- Attitudes are learned predispositions to respond to an object or class of objects in a consistently favourable or unfavourable way. Attitudes are based on a person's values and beliefs concerning the attributes of products or services.

- Personal influence takes two forms: opinion leadership and word-of-mouth activity. A specific type of personal influence exists in the form of reference groups.

- Family influences on consumer behaviour result from two sources: family life cycle and decision making within the household.

- Within Canada there are subcultures that affect consumer values and behaviour. Marketers must be sensitive to these influences when developing a marketing mix.

Key Terms and Concepts...*a refresher*

attitude *p. 65*
back translation *p. 75*
beliefs *p. 65*
brand loyalty *p. 65*
consumer behaviour *p. 56*
cross-cultural analysis *p. 74*
cultural symbols *p. 74*
culture *p. 70*

customs *p. 74*
family life cycle *p. 69*
involvement *p. 59*
learning *p. 64*
motivation *p. 62*
opinion leaders *p. 68*
perceived risk *p. 64*
perception *p. 63*

personality *p. 63*
purchase decision process *p. 56*
reference group *p. 68*
subcultures *p. 71*
values *p. 74*
word of mouth *p. 68*

Hands-on...*apply your knowledge*

Effects of Technology on Purchase Behaviour Assignment
The opening vignette on MapArt describes the negative effects of GPS products on the sales of printed map books. Two examples of the effects of technology on purchase behaviour are physical books, which are threatened by e-readers, and watch sales, which are decreasing because consumers, especially younger ones, are turning to their cellphones or smartphones if they want to know the time.

Imagine that you are the marketing manager of the Timex brand of watches. Brainstorm some ideas to elevate the sales of Timex watches, especially to the younger demographic.

Reality Check...*reminder*

Refer back to this chapter's opening vignette and answer the Reality Check questions on page 56.

connect *Practise and learn online with Connect*

Connect allows you to practise important concepts at your own pace and on your own schedule, with 24/7 online access to an eBook, practice quizzes, video cases, chapter application questions, discussion activities, Internet exercises, interactivities, study tools, and more.

market Research

Market research is an area used by marketers to reduce the risk of making poor business decisions and to drive decision making by using clear, accurate, and actionable insights. Often marketers are looking for glimpses into the lives of target consumers, searching for insights that lead to new opportunities or data that solves problems. This chapter focuses on market research, explaining its role, its uses, and its strengths and limitations, as well as how it has evolved during this digital era to encompass new Internet-based tools. The Internet, with its ability to make research faster, cheaper, but not necessarily better, has made the role of the market researcher even more crucial. Marker researchers help marketers navigate through a sea of information, which may or may not be relevant and actionable, to provide clarity on the issues at hand. In this digital era, while many new research tools are available, the basic building blocks of market research, which couple scientific approaches with strategic vision, are still intact, ensuring rigorous, meaningful, and actionable results.

We spoke with Luke Sklar, partner and founder of the market research company Sklar Wilton & Associates (SW&A), to understand how the Internet is now used for market research purposes and to gain a practical perspective on market research. SW&A, founded in 1986, has grown to include four main partners and thirty-five associates. Its clients are some of the most respected organizations in Canada, including, among others, Mars, Cara, J.M. Smuckers, Molson, HMV, and Rogers. Heinz, its first client in 1986, continues to work closely with SW&A today. SW&A works in partnership with its clients to bring a fact-based approach to marketing decision-making. The firm facilitates marketing decision-making by fusing marketing, market research information, strategy, and innovative thinking into the services it provides its clients. Although market research is its passion and focal point, SW&A also helps companies make sound decisions in the areas of strategy development, branding, and innovation. SW&A is passionate about its clients' businesses and prides itself on delivering market research that makes a difference.

SW&A's attitude to market research places front and centre its belief that research for the sake of research is an expensive proposition that does not yield results. Sklar explains, "If the research we commission does not drive a decision or avoid a mistake, then our job is not done. Research that confirms or denies smart ideas is worth more than the research that searches aimlessly for insights." Sklar emphasizes that research needs to be evaluated on the basis of the value it brings to an organization and that it should be treated with the same rigour and return-on-investment criteria as any other investment decision.

In today's digital world, Sklar explains that the need for reliable market research is intensified by a sea of information that is flooding the Internet, challenging

LEARNING OBJECTIVES

LO1 Explain the use and benefits of a marketing information system and market research

LO2 Outline the importance and challenges of market research to companies

LO3 Differentiate between exploratory, descriptive, and causal research

LO4 Identify the step-by-step market research approach

LO5 List and describe the primary research tools available to marketers

LO6 Describe the advantages and disadvantages of primary research tools

marketers, more than ever, to discern what is real, clear, and insightful. The importance of making the right marketing decision is heightened by the realities of social media where social networks mercilessly take marketers to task for mistakes they may have made. The Internet also has its advantages, providing marketers with quick and well-priced research tools (discussed later in this chapter), such as online communities, bulletin boards, publicly available syndicated studies, social listening, and online surveys that can replace or supplement traditional focus groups or telephone surveys.

Mistakes are not completely avoidable in the marketing world. SW&A acknowledges that market research has its limitations. First, researchers do not always ask the right questions, and second, respondents do not have all the answers. Marketers can provide leadership and direction for a business while respondents can provide insights as to what is important to consumers, provided they are asked the right questions. Sklar points to a well-known market research gaffe by Coca-Cola to demonstrate the limitations of market research and the importance of asking the right questions. Coca-Cola introduced New Coke in April 1985 in Canada and the U.S. as a new and improved version of the traditional Coca-Cola beverage. It was touted as a sweeter Coke that people preferred to their traditional Coca-Cola, and even liked better than Pepsi. The product was launched with a media frenzy that had people heading to the stores to try the new product. This positive exposure soon backfired with consumers voicing complaints that their regular Coca-Cola had been replaced by this New Coke. Consumers were in an uproar over the disappearance of their beloved Coca-Cola and started hoarding the old beverage. The old Coca-Cola even surfaced on the black market and the company was barraged with complaints about the new product. In a little over two months, bowing to public pressure, Coca-Cola pulled New Coke off the shelves and replaced it with the old formula. Why the mistake? Coca-Cola did its homework, asked its consumers about the new product, and conducted extensive market research for over two years. The answer is that researchers forgot to ask one key question: *Can we replace your current Coca-Cola with this new beverage?* It's all about asking the right questions.

The automotive industry is another example cited by Luke Sklar to demonstrate how marketers cannot expect consumers to provide business leadership and how researchers need to ask the right questions. The automobile industry, facing an economic crisis that led up to the recession of 2009, was challenged over the years to do business differently to avoid the disruption of not meeting changing consumer needs. Consumers were showing an interest in greener technologies and products that could better meet their needs in an economically challenged world. However, the industry failed to acknowledge these consumer insights and did not have the vision and leadership to navigate this new reality. Sklar observes that the car manufacturers did not ask the right questions or look beyond their standard customer service surveys that had acceptable results. They failed to recognize the disruption that was occurring and the need to develop products with added value such as better mileage, greener technologies, and small amenities that can make a tremendous difference. Finally, managers missed the critical role that women play in the purchase decision and failed to fully respect their product and service needs. Again, it is all about creative minds asking the right questions.

Luke Sklar cites these examples to remind us that market research is about staying ahead of consumers and inventing on their behalf. It filters out useless information and identifies and differentiates fads versus trends, as well as insights from *nice-to-know* nuggets of information. It looks beyond the numbers and statistics to discern insights that are disruptive and actionable. Sklar reminds us that successful research needs vision, hypotheses, instincts, and energy. He emphasizes that to get this successful blend, the best researchers have diverse backgrounds, rooted in areas other than research, that help develop the mental agility and creative thinking that can capture insights, opportunities, and recommendations for clients.[1]

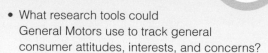

As you read through Chapter 4, refer back to this opening vignette on SW&A and answer the following questions:

- What research tools could General Motors use to track general consumer attitudes, interests, and concerns?

- What research tools could General Motors use to research current consumer motor vehicle needs?

Marketing Information Systems and Market Research

Companies constantly require information. They need to understand how elements may impact their businesses, and they need to be able to use information to anticipate competitive moves and predict customers' wants, needs, and preferences. Information can be an important competitive advantage for firms, as well as a key marketing tool that can help develop compelling marketing programs that boost business and reduce the risk of making poor decisions.

Today, marketers are flooded with an abundance of information, and the challenge is to determine which information is the most reliable, accurate, and relevant. The Internet with its wealth of information is making data more easily available to marketers. Businesses, service experts, and the media often use their websites to release research data. Research companies and marketing associations also post highlights of their market research as a way to draw attention to their expertise. Such companies include Léger Marketing, Ipsos Canada, Nielsen, Solutions Research Group, comScore, Forrester Research, and the Interactive Advertising Bureau of Canada (IAB Canada). Léger Marketing posts research data on demographic trends and voting

intentions; Ipsos Canada posts research highlights on economic, social, lifestyle, and political studies; Nielsen posts research updates on Canadian consumer insights; Solutions Research Group focuses on digital consumer behaviour; comScore provides updates on digital marketing trends; Forrester Research specializes in business and technology; and IAB Canada publishes at least two reliable research reports on digital marketing every month. IAB Canada's website is a one-stop destination for research studies and updates on digital marketing. (See the Marketing NewsFlash on page 97 for recent IAB highlights.)

The wealth of market research information available on the Internet is demonstrated by two examples. A recent study, *Women and Digital Life*, from the Solutions Research Group outlined the differences between the online behaviour of Canadian women and their American counterparts. The study interviewed over 3,500 women in the U.S. and 1,000 women in Canada and posted its main conclusions on the research company's blog. The Bensimon Byrne Consumerology Report also routinely researches up to 1,500 consumers, posting its entire quarterly report on its website for public access. Its 2011 Consumerology report, *Segmentation*, detailed important marketing insights on attitude segments in Canada, resulting in a new typology for marketers. The study suggests consumers be grouped by their attitudes into three basic segments: *runners*, *walkers*, and *spectators*. *Runners* represent 29 percent of Canadian consumers. They are anxious but optimistic achievers with high ambitions and expectations. They purchase branded items

IAB Canada updates the industry with at least two reputable research studies every month.

The Core: Chapter 4

Consumer insights can stimulate new marketing programs.

Market research

Market research helps marketers understand their consumers and make fact-based decisions.

as a form of self-expression. *Walkers* represent 47 percent of Canadian consumers. They are positive and contented family-oriented people, concerned about society. They tend to be older females who purchase brands for functionality rather than fashion. *Spectators* represent 24 percent of Canadian consumers. They are primarily males who are either younger or older and not very optimistic. They enjoy spending time alone and purchase items out of necessity. Few brands are seen as relevant.[2]

Information presents itself to companies in two ways: (1) a marketing information system and (2) market research studies. Many companies have a **marketing information system (MIS)**, which is a set of procedures and processes for collecting, sorting, analyzing, and summarizing information on an ongoing basis. An MIS collects information on elements such as market conditions, competitive marketing actions, and local sales figures, and then analyzes it to provide a current market assessment. This information may come from internal reporting systems and/or from external sources such as research companies that track competitive behaviour. Many publicly available reports, such as those cited earlier, may also become part of an MIS, or used as a starting point for a research study.

Separate from an MIS, companies often require proprietary research studies to answer questions that cannot be answered through an MIS. This chapter focuses on these studies and describes the tools used to gather accurate and reliable information. In addition, this chapter explains the methodical steps followed in market research studies to reduce the cost and to expedite the delivery of actionable results.

What Is Market Research?

LO 2 **Market research** is formally defined as the process of planning, collecting, and analyzing information in order to recommend actions to improve marketing activities.[3] Although market research is not perfect at predicting consumer

behaviour, it can reduce the risk and uncertainty of making poor decisions. It provides managers with facts that can be used to make sound decisions. Solid marketing decisions are often the result of managers using vision, knowledge, and experience, together with clear market research information.

Market research is not an easy undertaking. Gleaning accurate information from consumers can be difficult. If a researcher asks the wrong questions, or fails to investigate an important insight, the research will be inaccurate. Sometimes the topic being researched is personal, which can result in respondents being unwilling to impart their private information. Other times, consumers are not necessarily truthful about their choices; when market researchers ask respondents about different pricing options, inevitably respondents will suggest a lower price; or in the instance when market researchers ask respondents about new products they have never seen, inevitably respondents are unable to clearly conceptualize them.

The task of market research is to overcome these challenges and to obtain accurate information that marketers can use to make sound decisions. Market researchers use methodical approaches to ensure that research results are as accurate and cost efficient as possible. Questions are planned and scripted to ensure that insights are not missed and consumers are not confused. This all occurs within mathematical frameworks to ensure that the data is accurate and reliable.

The following sections look at the different types of market research and how market research is collected.

> ## INFORMATION CAN BE AN IMPORTANT COMPETITIVE ADVANTAGE FOR FIRMS, AS WELL AS A KEY MARKETING TOOL.

Research Classifications

L[3] Market research provides marketers with information that can be used in different ways. It can help identify consumer needs, assess future opportunities, evaluate new ideas, and determine purchase intent. Market research can also shed light on the relative success of current and competitive marketing practices and troubleshoot problems. Market research is a tool that clarifies marketing problems and opportunities and provides information for marketing decision-making. Market research can be classified into three basic areas: (1) exploratory research, (2) descriptive research, and (3) causal research. Each area serves a different function, uses different techniques, and can be used in conjunction to better solve a research problem.

Exploratory Research Preliminary research that clarifies the scope and nature of a marketing problem is referred to as **exploratory research**. It generally provides researchers with a better understanding of the dimensions of the marketing problem before focusing on areas that require further research. Marketers who are well-versed in their businesses may be quick to assume general conclusions about their research needs and prone to avoiding the exploratory research step. However, exploratory research provides research projects with clear direction and identifies where business problems and opportunities may lie. Marketers understand that avoiding exploratory research comes with the risk of heading down the wrong path and missing potential opportunities or issues.

Exploratory research is often conducted with the expectation that subsequent and more conclusive research will follow. For example, the Dairy Farmers of Canada, an association representing dairy producers in the country, wanted to discover why milk consumption was declining in Canada. They conducted a search of existing literature on milk consumption, talked to experts in the field, and even conducted preliminary interviews with consumers about why they were drinking less milk. This exploratory research helped the association crystallize the issues and identified areas that required more detailed follow-up.

Another example of exploratory research relates to the value of a Facebook fan. Marketing companies teamed up to determine the value of a Facebook fan for businesses. The research was able to compare engagement levels of fans versus non-fans for 20 top brands, extrapolating a monetary value for marketers and pointing to the need for marketers to engage their fans on this platform. (See the Marketing NewsFlash on page 84.)

(See the Marketing NewsFlash on page 84.)

Descriptive Research Research designed to describe the basic characteristics of a given population or to clarify its usage and attitudes is known as **descriptive research**. Unlike exploratory research, with descriptive research the researcher has a general understanding of the marketing problem and is seeking more conclusive data that answers particular questions. Examples of descriptive research include providing more detailed profiles of product purchasers (e.g., the characteristics of the Canadian health food shopper), describing the size and characteristics of markets (e.g., the types of products sold in Canadian pizza restaurants), detailing product usage patterns (e.g., how frequently people use bank machines), or outlining consumer attitudes toward particular brands (e.g., Canadian attitudes toward store brands). Magazines, radio stations, and television stations almost always conduct descriptive research to identify the characteristics of their audiences in order to present it to prospective advertisers. As a follow-up to its exploratory research, the Dairy Farmers of Canada conducted descriptive research to determine the demographic characteristics of milk consumers, their current usage patterns, and their attitudes toward milk consumption.

exploratory research
Preliminary research conducted to clarify the scope and nature of a marketing problem

descriptive research
Research designed to describe basic characteristics of a given population or to clarify its usage and attitudes

Causal Research Research designed to identify cause-and-effect relationships among variables is termed **causal research**. In general, exploratory and descriptive research precedes causal research. With causal research there is usually an expectation about the relationship to be explained, such as predicting the influence of a price change on product demand.

Typical causal research studies examine elements such as the effect of advertising on sales, the relationship between price and perceived product quality, and the impact of package design on sales. When the

Dairy Farmers of Canada conducted their descriptive research on milk consumers, they discovered that many people believed milk was fattening and high in cholesterol. The association felt that these beliefs factored in to the decline in milk consumption. To test this assumption, it conducted causal research that included running a TV campaign stating that milk was healthy and essential to a healthy diet. The causal research found that the TV campaign changed consumer attitudes toward milk and helped improve milk consumption.

Procter & Gamble (P&G) is a company that believes in using causal market research to improve business results. Specifically it often uses causal research to

marketing NewsFlash

Research Reveals Value of a Facebook Fan

Online research experts from Syncapse Corp. and Hotspex teamed up to quantify the value of a Facebook fan for marketers. While it is nice for a brand to have numerous fans on Facebook, its value has long been debated in the hallways of major corporations. Michael Scissons, president and CEO of Syncapse Corp., stated in a recent press release that research findings support the value of Facebook. Syncapse Corp., with offices in Toronto, New York, London, and Portland (Oregon), works with Fortune 500 companies and global media agencies on social media initiatives. Hotspex Market Research is a global expert in online research.

The 2010 quantitative study collected data from Hotspex' online panel of 4,000 North American respondents with a 25-minute survey that focused on Facebook's top 20 consumer brands: Nokia, BlackBerry, Motorola,

Secret, Gillette, Axe, Dove, Victoria's Secret, Adidas, Nike, Coca-Cola, Oreo, Skittles, Nutella, Red Bull, Pringles, PlayStation, Xbox, Starbucks, and McDonald's. Respondents were asked to identify the brands they had "fanned" or "liked" on Facebook and to project future behaviour, attitudes, and feelings toward them. Data was analyzed, comparing reactions of fans versus non-fans over a two-year period.

The study analyzed the value of a Facebook fan on five parameters: (1) product spending, (2) brand loyalty, (3) propensity to recommend, (4) brand affinity, and (5) earned media value. The key findings indicated that Facebook fans spent an average $71.84 more on a brand than non-fans. These fans were also 28 percent more likely to continue to use the brand than non-fans and 41 percent more likely to recommend the brand to others. In addition, 81 percent of fans

felt connected to the brand versus 39 percent for non-fans.

When reviewing all factors, the study concluded that the value of a Facebook fan to an organization over two years averages $136.38. This value can vary considerably among brands. The study cites McDonald's as an example of a brand with a high Facebook average fan value of $259.82 over two years, versus Oreo with a low Facebook average fan value of $60.60.

The study points to the fact that as consumers increasingly use social networks, marketers are tasked to engage them on these platforms to drive brand loyalty and revenue growth. Marketers need to create specific approaches to nurture their Facebook fans, which can help drive business and brand advocacy.[4]

Questions

1. Consider a brand you have "fanned" or "liked" on Facebook and discuss how it has tried to engage its fans.

2. Discuss creative ways this brand could drive brand advocacy.

*vs. the next leading regular liquid detergent.   ©2009 P&G

Marketers use carefully researched facts in ads.

objectives
Specific, measurable goals

studies. It is worth noting that not all research projects require quantitative studies (step 4). In many instances qualitative research can suffice, while in others quantitative studies are required for greater certainty.

1. Define the problem/issue/ opportunity.
2. Design the research plan.
3. Conduct exploratory and qualitative research.
4. Collect quantitative primary research.
5. Compile, analyze, and interpret data.
6. Generate reports and recommendations.

assess the effectiveness of its advertising campaigns. When creating new ads, P&G routinely looks to the advertising research it has conducted over the years. It also tests its new creative ideas to ensure that they are clear and compelling. Its recent print ad for 2X Ultra Tide liquid laundry detergent is a typical example of how P&G uses research in its advertising campaigns. Typically its ads in this category cite market research data to support competitive claims of product superiority. This data is then used visually to portray its products as superior. Over the years P&G's advertising research indicates that this advertising approach yields results. It is worth noting at this point that P&G could not make these competitive advertising claims unless its claims were accurate and the facts supported by data.

The Six-Step Market Research Approach

L④ Effective market research is not left to chance. A systematic approach ensures that research is done thoroughly, all elements are considered, and results are accurate. Here is a basic six-step approach that is used to conduct market research

Figure 4–1 shows this sequence of steps, and in the next few pages we will discuss these steps in detail.

Step 1: Define the Problem/Issue/ Opportunity

The first step in the market research process is to clearly define the problem, issue, or opportunity, and to clarify the objectives. This is often posed as a question that needs to be answered. Most market researchers would agree with the saying that "a problem well-defined is half-solved," but defining a problem is a difficult task. Most market research issues stem from poorly defined problems and objectives that are vague and unclear: If objectives are too broad, the problem may not be tangible; if the objectives are too narrow, the value of the research may be questionable. Market researchers spend considerable time precisely defining marketing problems and clarifying research objectives in formal proposals that clearly describe the research task and its approach. **Objectives** are specific, measurable goals that the decision maker seeks to achieve. Common research objectives are to discover consumer needs and wants, and to determine why a product is not selling.

ask yourself

1. What are the three research classifications?
2. What steps are included in the six-step market research process?

Figure 4–1
The basic market research process

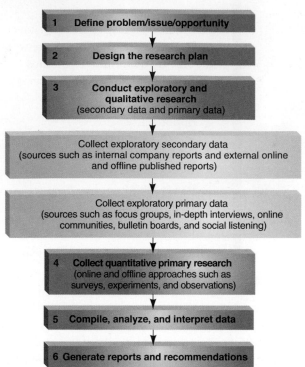

1. Define problem/issue/opportunity
2. Design the research plan
3. Conduct exploratory and qualitative research (secondary data and primary data)

Collect exploratory secondary data (sources such as internal company reports and external online and offline published reports)

Collect exploratory primary data (sources such as focus groups, in-depth interviews, online communities, bulletin boards, and social listening)

4. Collect quantitative primary research (online and offline approaches such as surveys, experiments, and observations)
5. Compile, analyze, and interpret data
6. Generate reports and recommendations

Let's look at the Insurance Corporation of British Columbia (ICBC) as an example. This Crown corporation is responsible for providing auto insurance and administering driver licensing and vehicle registration for drivers in British Columbia. It is committed to reducing injuries and fatalities, and has spent millions on advertising to encourage British Columbians to drive more safely. Looking at the large amount of money spent on advertising, ICBC realized it needed to know whether its anti-speeding ads were working. Did the ads change the speeders' behaviour? This was the basis of the problem and its research objectives.

Step 2: Design the Research Plan

The second step in the market research process is to identify which approach will be taken to complete the project. This includes identifying what information is needed, how it will be collected, and whether a sampling plan is needed. Let's look at these three areas:

Information Requirements   Often, market research studies collect data that is interesting but not relevant to the task at hand. Marketers need to avoid this situation because it is time consuming, confusing, and costly. In ICBC's situation, the researchers may have been curious about which cars were most likely to speed, but this information is not relevant to the research objectives—understanding whether anti-

speeding advertisements worked. One of the research study's first tasks was to determine how to best collect this information affordably. Clearly, speeders could tell the ICBC what it needed to know, but how are speeders defined and how can they be contacted? Is a speeder a driver who has received a speeding ticket in the past two years, or is it a driver with three or more speeding tickets in the past twelve months? Perhaps the research study should consider drivers who had never received a speeding ticket but nonetheless drive over the speed limit? ICBC had to determine its approach.

Collection Methods   In order to collect data in an organized fashion, it is important to have a data collection plan. There are mathematical considerations and operational issues that the researcher must consider. Determining *how* to collect the data is often as important as actually collecting the data. Researchers can purchase data from a pre-existing study, or conduct their own research using a variety of data-collection methods such as in-depth personal interviews, focus groups, telephone surveys, central location surveys, personal questionnaires, or mail surveys. The Internet also provides numerous online tools that facilitate the gathering of information. Surveys can be easily completed online, and online communities and online bulletin boards can also be used to provide additional data (see page 91).

To ensure accurate answers are obtained, researchers carefully select research methodologies that encourage

---

The Value of a Facebook Fan

Research shows that Facebook fans add the following value to a business over a two-year period:

Product spending: Fans spend $71.84 more on a brand.

Brand loyalty: Fans are 28% more likely to use the brand.

Recommendations: Fans are 41% more likely to recommend a brand.

Brand affinity: Fans feel more connected to the brand.

Average value: Fans add an average of $136.38 to a corporation.

Source: Syncapse Corp, "Powerful New Research Reveals Value of Facebook for Marketers," Marketwire, June 11, 2010, accessed at www.marketwire.com/press-release/Powerful-New-Research-Reveals-Value-of-Facebook-for-Marketers-1274905.htm.

honesty. The method chosen is critical to obtaining accurate results. In the case of the ICBC, it may be more helpful to conduct focus groups or personal interviews, rather than telephone interviews or online surveys where the responses may be questionable and not easily probed.

Canadian market researchers rely on their training, expertise, and judgment to make appropriate methodology decisions. They can also turn to their professional association, the Professional Marketing Research Society, for resources and training.

Sampling

Sampling is another important factor in research design. A researcher's sampling plan identifies who is to be sampled, how large the sample should be, and how the sample will be selected. Rarely does a research project involve a complete census of every person in the research population because this is time-consuming and costly. Therefore, market researchers use smaller samples that are representative of the population being surveyed. **Sampling** is the process of gathering data from a subset of the total population, rather than from all members of that particular group.

A properly selected sample should be representative of the population being researched; however, sampling errors can occur, and thus the reliability of the data is sometimes an issue. Savvy researchers know that the first and most-critical sampling question for researchers is: *Who is to be sampled?* Another key question concerns sample size: *How big should the sample be?* The final question relates to selection: *How should the sample be selected?*

Currently, a number of market researchers are debating the validity of online market research studies, questioning whether online samples are valid because they exclude respondents that are not online. Luke Sklar from SW&A advises us to consider the reality that each methodology has its limitations

> **"*Rarely does a research project involve a complete census of every person in the research population, because it is time-consuming and costly.*"**

and that while online market research may overlook certain respondents, it is not unlike telephone or mail surveys, which also exclude certain groups. Market researchers always need to understand the limitations of the methodology they select.

There are two basic sampling techniques: probability and non-probability sampling. **Probability sampling** involves precise rules to select the sample so that each element of the population has a specific known chance of being selected. For example, if your university wants to know how last year's 1,000 graduates are doing, it can put their names into a bowl and randomly select 100 names to contact. The chance of being selected (100 out of 1,000, or 1 in 10) is known in advance, and all graduates have an equal chance of being contacted. This procedure helps to select a sample (100 graduates) that should be representative of the entire population (the 1,000 graduates), and allows conclusions to be drawn about the population being researched.

Non-probability sampling involves the use of arbitrary judgment by the market researcher to select a sample so that the chance of selecting a particular element of the population is either unknown or zero. If your university decided to talk to 100 of last year's graduates, but only selected those who lived closest, many graduates would be excluded. This would introduce a bias, tainting the representativeness of the sample and its ability to draw accurate conclusions.

It is worth noting at this point that the researcher may decide to follow this non-probability sampling approach in the interest of time and to maintain costs. In fact, non-probability samples are often used when time and budgets are limited,

sampling
The process of gathering data from a subset of the total population rather than from all members of that particular group

probability sampling
Selecting a sample so that each element of a population has a specific known chance of being selected

non-probability sampling
Selecting a sample so that the chance of selecting a particular element of a population is either unknown or zero

or for exploratory research purposes when conclusions are mostly directional and may require further research. In general, market researchers use data from such non-probability samples with caution. The data can provide valuable information, but the results need to be viewed carefully as they may not accurately represent the population being researched.

Step 3: Conduct Exploratory and Qualitative Research

Exploratory research is preliminary research conducted to clarify the scope and nature of a marketing problem. It is done to ensure that researchers have not overlooked key insights that are important to the study. Exploratory research is often conducted with the expectation that subsequent and more-conclusive quantitative research may follow.

If researchers decide to conduct exploratory research, they have two avenues from which to glean data. The first avenue is to collect exploratory *secondary data*, which is already available through internal company documents or external online and offline published reports. A second avenue involves researchers creating their own data, exploratory *primary data*, through options such as focus groups, in-depth interviews, online communities, online bulletin boards, and social listening research. Let's look at these approaches in more detail.

Focus group research, in-depth interviews, online communities, online bulletin boards, and social listening

are forms of research called **qualitative research**. This research provides insightful and directional information to the researcher, with the understanding that although the data is not gleaned from a large consumer base, it provides useful direction to the research study and may in fact thoroughly answer the questions at hand. In this manner it may allow marketers to avoid costly quantitative research studies. In other instances, qualitative research may not be enough to draw firm conclusions and will be used instead to provide insights and direction for a more detailed quantitative research study.

Quantitative research, discussed later in this chapter, is statistically reliable information that uses observational techniques and/or questioning methods such as surveys or experiments to deliver statistically significant results.

Let's take a hypothetical example to demonstrate this point. The marketing manager for cranberry juice at Ocean Spray is considering an opportunity to export cranberry juice to Asian markets. He needs to determine whether this is a viable opportunity but is concerned that these consumers may not be interested in cranberries because they are virtually unknown in Asia. This may, however, present an opportunity to sell something unique in the market. One of the major stumbling blocks is that the word "cranberry" does not exist in any of the Asian languages. Exploratory research would be advisable in this situation, starting with secondary research to find out whether any information is available on beverage consumption in

Asia. This may be followed up by focus groups or research with online communities and bulletin boards to probe attitudes and opportunities in this area.

Secondary Data Exploratory research can include the gathering of **secondary data**. This data comes in two forms; external data and internal data; 1) *Internal data* exists within a company and includes data such as sales reports, profitability data, and costing information. 2) *External data* comes from published sources outside the organization, such as Nielsen, which can track what consumers watch on television, mobile devices, or online, as well as what they buy from online or offline retails. As a form of self-promotion, many research companies now publish top-line research data on their websites for public viewing. A list of company websites worth checking for their latest research reports is identified on page 91 later in this chapter. These reports can provide valuable information for marketers at no cost, with access to full reports sometimes requiring additional payment.

Statistics Canada, the federal government's statistical agency, publishes a wide variety of useful reports, such as census data that includes information on the number of people per household and their age, gender, ethnic background, income, occupation, and education. Statistics Canada also publishes a wide range of other statistical

The $78 Billion* Question

What's in your basket?

Nielsen has the solutions to help you understand what's in your shopper's basket - so you can influence their behaviour.

In order to grow, you need to know.

www.nielsen.com

Just ask **nielsen**

*Nielsen Total Retail Sales, Canada All Channels 52 Weeks to March 13, 2010

Secondary data on retail purchases can be purchased from companies such as Nielsen.

reports that are used by businesses across the country. These reports include information on the following:

- Economic indicators
- International trade
- Culture and leisure
- Agriculture
- Tourism and travel
- Manufacturing
- Government
- Environment
- Justice and crime
- Health

There are many other sources of secondary information used by the marketing industry. These sources are often posted online. Marketers can read interesting articles, view short snapshots of research projects, download full reports, or read synopses of research studies. Examples include third-party organizations that audit magazine and newspaper circulation or the popularity of TV shows. Often, a portion of this information is provided at no charge, with full report coverage provided for a price. Similarly, competitive market-share data is available for marketers to purchase to help track competitive activity. Check our list of top online resources that are used by marketers in Canada and visit their websites to gain an understanding of the available information (see Figure 4–3 on page 91).

Figure 4–2
Information sources

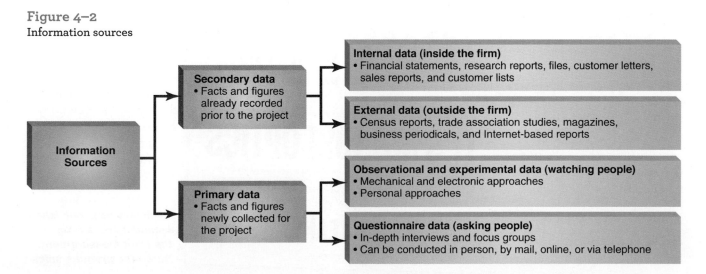

Information Sources

Secondary data
- Facts and figures already recorded prior to the project

Primary data
- Facts and figures newly collected for the project

Internal data (inside the firm)
- Financial statements, research reports, files, customer letters, sales reports, and customer lists

External data (outside the firm)
- Census reports, trade association studies, magazines, business periodicals, and Internet-based reports

Observational and experimental data (watching people)
- Mechanical and electronic approaches
- Personal approaches

Questionnaire data (asking people)
- In-depth interviews and focus groups
- Can be conducted in person, by mail, online, or via telephone

Primary Data In a research project, a general rule is to first obtain secondary data followed by detailed, proprietary primary data. **Primary data** is data that is original and specifically collected for the project at hand. This sequencing is due to the fact that secondary data is lower in cost and easier to obtain than primary data. Secondary data can also help illuminate further data requirements. These advantages of secondary data must be weighed against its disadvantages, namely that (1) the secondary data may be out of date, (2) the definitions or categories may not be right for the project, and (3) the data may not be accurate or specific enough for the study. Let's review the primary sources of information.

Focus Groups A popular exploratory research technique is the focus group. A **focus group** is an informal interview session in which six to ten people are brought together in a room with a moderator to discuss topics surrounding the market research problem. The moderator poses questions and encourages individuals to discuss the issues. Often, focus-group sessions are watched by observers and the sessions are videotaped. Participants are always informed that they are being observed and/or taped and asked for permission to do so.

The ICBC research study discussed earlier in this chapter included focus groups where participants were shown anti-speeding ads and probed on their attitudes and responses to these messages. The focus groups suggested an association between personality and speeding. This exploratory research stage was followed up by quantitative research with a larger number of people to confirm the personality/speeding linkage and to further understand the effectiveness of the ICBC advertising campaign.

In-Depth Interviews Another exploratory research technique

PMB Research Data – Top 3 Saturday Newspapers

The Print Measurement Bureau (PMB) provides online secondary data on the readership and circulation of newspapers and magazines in Canada.

Newspaper	Circulation
1. *Toronto Star*	557,000
2. *The Globe and Mail*	377,000
3. *National Post*	151,000

Source: *2011 PMB Topline Report*, Canadian Print Measurement Bureau, accessed at www.pmb.ca/public/e/pmb2011_fall/overview.shtml.

used to obtain primary data involves the use of in-depth interviews. **In-depth interviews** are detailed individual interviews where the researcher discusses topics with an individual at length in a free-flowing conversation in order to discover information that may help solve a marketing problem. Sometimes these interviews can take a few hours, and they are often recorded with respondents' consent.

General Mills, a major food manufacturer of brands such as Betty Crocker, Yoplait, Haagen-Dazs, and Cheerios, used in-depth interviews to better market its Hamburger Helper product. When the product was first introduced, sales were not brisk. Initial instructions called for cooking half a pound of hamburger separately from the noodles, and later adding it to the noodles. In-depth interviews revealed that consumers did not think the recipe called for enough meat and that they did not want the hassle of cooking in two pots. As a result, the recipe for Hamburger Helper was changed to include a full pound of meat with all the ingredients cooked in one pot.[5]

Maclean's uses published secondary data from the Print Measurement Bureau to promote sales.

Figure 4–3
Online sources of secondary data

- Audit Bureau of Circulations: www.accessabc.com
- BBM Canada: www.bbm.ca
- Bensimon Byrne Consumerology Report: www.consumerology.ca
- Canadian Marketing Association: www.the-cma.org
- Communispace: www.communispace.com
- comScore: www.comscore.com
- Forrester Research: www.forrester.com
- Government of Canada: www.canada.gc.ca
- Industry Canada: www.ic.gc.ca
- Interactive Advertising Bureau of Canada: www.iabcanada.com
- Ipsos Canada: www.ipsos.ca
- Léger Marketing: www.legermarketing.com
- Media Digest: www.cmdc.ca
- Newspaper Audience Databank: www.nadbank.com
- Nielsen Canada: www.ca.nielsen.com
- Print Measurement Bureau: www.pmb.ca
- SEDAR: www.sedar.com
- Solutions Research Group: www.srgnet.com/canada
- Statistics Canada: www.statcan.gc.ca
- Television Bureau of Canada: www.tvb.ca

Worth Noting

Your library may have access to various online business databases that can assist with research projects. Examples of these databases are *Business Periodicals Index, Canadian Business Index, Canadian News Index, Canadian Periodical Index, Canadian Statistics Index, Canadian Trade Index, Dun & Bradstreet Canada, Gale, Scott's Directories, Standard Periodical Directory,* and *Ulrich's International Periodicals Directory.*

> *"A popular exploratory research technique is the focus group."*

online research communities The use of consumer groups, brought together privately in an online environment, to answer questions, respond to ideas, and collaborate with researchers in real time

online research bulletin boards Private online static forums, without real-time dialogue and engaging conversations, where respondents can post their responses to questions posed by researchers

Typically, this approach invites consumers to join an online community on a specific topic in return for interesting, lively debate, thought-provoking ideas, and a small stipend for their time. An online community is managed by a research company to ensure that the community is engaged and continues to be interested in the topic. Participants can be gathered from a variety of sources such as website visitors, consumer lists, or company databases. The community usually exists for one year, involves regular two-way communication visible to all within the community, is managed by a researcher, and can involve 200 to 300 people depending on the need. Multinational brands often maintain large global communities to help answer their marketing questions.

A research company considered best-in-class for online community research is Communispace, which can be found online at www.communispace.com. This company is used by many companies around the world and by top researchers in Canada such as SW&A to help provide real-time feedback for its clients.

Online Research Communities A new qualitative research tool used by marketers to gain feedback on marketing approaches is the online research community. **Online research communities** involve the use of consumer groups, brought together privately in an online environment, to answer questions, respond to ideas, and collaborate with researchers in real time. This approach uses vocal consumers, often in high-involvement categories such as sports and entertainment, or other areas where consumers are passionate about their products such as chocolate and baby food. These consumers provide feedback to researchers in a private online environment where only the marketers, researchers, and respondents are privy to the conversations.

Online Research Bulletin Boards Another new research tool available to researchers is the online research bulletin board. **Online research bulletin boards** are private online forums where respondents can post their

---

Secondary Research—BBM Top TV Programs **English Canada** March 14–20, 2011 (millions of viewers)

American Idol performance show

2.78

American Idol results show

2.70

The Amazing Race

2.44

2.36

Survivor: Redemption Island

Criminal Minds: Suspect Behavior

2.26

marketing meter

Source: BBM Top 30 TV Programs accessed at http://bbm.ca/index.php?option=com_content&task=view&id=87&Itemid=70; BBM Top Programs – Total Canada (English) March 14–20, 2011, accessed at http://bbm.ca/_documents/top_30_tv_programs_english/2011/nat03142011.pdf

social listening
Research that monitors public online consumer conversations on social media sites such as social networks, blogs, and forums

responses to questions. Unlike online communities, online bulletin boards do not engage respondents through dialogue. Instead they are static website locations where questions are posted online and respondents are asked to comment on ideas. Only those with access to the bulletin board are privy to the posted questions and responses. While online bulletin boards may not provide researchers with the depth of information available through an online community, they are easier to manage and administer.

Social Listening The growth in social media and its ability to influence consumers has given rise to a new exploratory research technique, **social listening**, which monitors public online consumer conversations on social media sites such as social networks, blogs, and forums. The metrics derived from social listening can measure positive and negative sentiments, popularity scores, and message reach, as well as the levels of conversation and buzz. Social listening research can take the form of qualitative or quantitative information depending on the parameters of the study. Well-respected research companies such as Forrester Research and Nielsen both emphasize that the benefits of social listening research extend beyond measuring brand mentions into gaining insights that can lead to new ideas and opportunities. Nielsen notes Kraft as an example of a food company that used social listening to better understand product trends and consumer profiles. Kraft used social listening to determine market segmentation profiles for people that eat hamburgers at home. This is useful information for companies that sell products in this category. (See the Focus on Ethics on page 93 for more about Kraft's social listening approach.)

Social listening raises an important ethical issue: While participants

ask yourself

1. Why do researchers use exploratory research?

2. What are some of the new online tools available to market researchers?

3. What are the advantages and disadvantages of secondary data?

Figure 4–4
Quantitative research: Comparing techniques

TECHNIQUE	EXAMPLES	ADVANTAGES	DISADVANTAGES
Observations	• Portable People Meters • Google Analytics • Personal observations of consumer interactions • Social listening • Store scanner information	• Reflect actual behaviour • Highly accurate when collected by machines • Mechanical observations reduce interviewer bias • Appropriate when respondents cannot clearly articulate opinions	• Do not indicate why consumers behave as they do • Do not provide data on attitudes and opinions • Different researchers may interpret behaviour differently • May require further explanation • Ethical questions exist around privacy issues
Surveys	• Personal interviews • Central location interviews such as mall-intercepts • Mail questionnaires • Telephone interviews • Internet surveys	• Can ask numerous questions • Questions are standardized • Interviewers can often probe for in-depth answers • Questions can be administered via e-mail, mail, telephone, the Internet, or in person	• Results can be biased by the methodology • Results can be influenced by the interviewer • Can be expensive and time-consuming
Experiments	• Test markets • Simulated test markets • Lab experiments	• Researchers can change key variables and measure results in a controlled setting • Can avoid costly failures by allowing marketers to modify marketing programs prior to full launch • Can provide a more accurate reflection and predictor of consumer behaviour than other forms of research	• Can be expensive and time-consuming • Results can be difficult to interpret • Actual test markets may be visible to the competition • Difficult to find a representative sample

in social networks realize many of their comments are publicly posted, they may not be aware that their conversations may be monitored and used for research purposes. Social networks are required to have privacy policies that protect consumer data from being kept and misused by third parties, and marketers need to abide by these laws.

A term worth noting at this point is *netnography*. This academic term refers to the online market research tools previously mentioned.

Step 4: Collect Quantitative Primary Research

L₆ Further research can be conducted using quantitative research through observational and/or questioning techniques. The main advantage of **quantitative research** is that it is designed to be statistically accurate and it is less open to interpretation. The main disadvantage of quantitative

quantitative research
Statistically reliable information that uses observational and/or questioning techniques such as observations, surveys, and experiments

focus on **Ethics** — Social Listening Gathers Insights

Social listening on the Internet has become a standard practice for many companies, but research giant Nielsen points out that it is often not used to discover the passions that drive consumers.

Food chatter on the Internet accounts for approximately 10 percent of conversations, and therefore social listening on this topic requires a methodical approach so that time and money is not wasted. In order to gather solid insights into online chatter on food passions, trends, and insights, Kraft followed Nielsen's social listening framework, looking for insights into the hamburger and mini-hamburger market. A framework was designed to gather useful data that was then analyzed to deliver actionable information.

The first step determined the areas of interest and pinpointed the online social conversation themes that were occurring in these areas. The second step quantified the online buzz in this area and then analyzed the data to determine conversation drivers, passions, and topics of significant interest. Significant topics were then identified for further in-depth analysis.

Forward-thinking researchers emphasize that this is where the

research must not stop; it must be given further context so that real business opportunities can be identified. The last step therefore involves combining the social listening information with other metrics such as search engine volume, keyword search terms, and trend data such as market size, growth, and sales levels within a category to determine the parameters of the opportunity.

Nielsen's social media framework helped Kraft gain insight into the passion points for mini-hamburgers (referred to as sliders) and helped identify the following four distinct segments for at-home hamburger eaters:

Aficionados: People who create gourmet hamburgers for their spouses, friends, and sometimes children. This group is found online on personal blogs and foodie community websites.

Dieters: People who purchase premade hamburgers, turkey burgers, and veggie burgers and cook them on an electric grill or in the microwave. These people are found online on personal blogs and on weight-loss community websites.

Moms and Household Chefs: People who cook basic hamburgers or turkey burgers for family dinners and weekend cookouts with their

spouses and children. This target market can be found online on personal blogs, recipe-sharing websites, and mom websites.

Entertainers: People who cook hamburgers or turkey burgers on an outdoor grill in a fun casual atmosphere on weekends, holidays, and during warm-weather days with friends and extended family.

Listening to the conversations around mini-hamburgers also helped Kraft understand the popularity of sliders. Social conversations pointed out that sliders are flexible items that can be served as appetizers, as snacks, or as main meals for different target groups. They are often available at adult social functions, can be served as a fun treat for kids, and are used as late night snacks by students.[6] ●

Questions

1. Some people question the ethics of social listening to public "conversations" on social networks. What ethical issue(s) does the practice of social listening raise?

2. Would social listening be a useful approach in gleaning new ideas for Kraft Dinner?

> # MARKET RESEARCHERS HAVE TO MAKE IMPORTANT TRADEOFFS TO BALANCE COSTS AGAINST THE EXPECTED QUALITY OF INFORMATION.

research is that it is far more costly and time-consuming to collect than exploratory research. The primary quantitative research techniques include (1) observations, (2) surveys, and (3) experiments (see Figure 4–4 on page 92).

Observational Research

Observational research is obtained by watching how people behave either in person or by using a machine to record events. National TV ratings, such as those provided by BBM Nielsen Media Research Inc., is an example of electronic observational data collected by a Portable People Meter (PPM). The PPM is a pager-like device worn by participants to monitor their TV-viewing and radio-listening habits. The device automatically detects and logs audio signals into a database, which is then uploaded to a central site together with information from other participants.[7] Other examples of observational research can be in the form of store scanner information, which captures data on consumer purchases; the social listening research mentioned earlier; or web-tracking software such as Google Analytics that measures website traffic, unique visitors, page views, time on site, and referring sites. Observational research can also be in person with researchers observing elements such as children's play patterns to determine the potential for new toys.

Observational research tools are both useful and flexible, but they can be costly and unreliable when dependent upon human observations, which can at times report different conclusions after watching the same event.

Surveys

Surveys are also used to gather quantitative information. Survey questions can be standardized in the form of a **questionnaire** and asked to a large representative sample to obtain accurate data. These surveys can be conducted in person, through the mail, on the telephone, or through the Internet, with each method having limitations.

In choosing between these alternatives, market researchers have to make important tradeoffs to balance costs against the expected quality of information. Personal interviews have the major advantage of enabling interviewers to ask probing questions and get reactions to visual materials. However, this approach is very costly. Mail surveys are less costly but have low response rates and are usually biased because those most likely to respond have had positive or negative experiences. Telephone interviews allow respondents to be probed but they are increasingly difficult to complete due to call-display features and respondents' reluctance to participate. Internet surveys are restricted to respondents that have the technology but this approach is becoming an increasingly popular method of gathering information. Figure 4–5 summarizes the advantages and disadvantages of different survey approaches.

Researchers can reduce the costs of proprietary questionnaires by joining established syndicated studies that are conducted by well-respected research conglomerates. **Syndicated studies** are a hybrid of primary and secondary research conducted by a research company, spreading the cost across many clients to reduce the price. These studies are routinely conducted with extensive panels of consumers to determine trends. TSN Canadian Facts conducts individual *panel* surveys and *omnibus* surveys on topics such as financial products and services, health care practices, family opinions, and teenage attitudes. Depending on the panel, questions are administered online, through the mail, or on the telephone.

Formally, a survey **panel** includes a large sample of respondents that voluntarily completes questionnaires on a regular basis so that researchers can assess

changes in behaviour and attitudes. An **omnibus survey** also includes the voluntary participation of respondents in routine surveys, allowing individual marketers to add a small number of questions to an existing survey to receive cost-effective data on their questions.

Experiments Experiments are the third quantitative research approach used in market research. It involves measuring changes in consumer behaviour over time to determine reactions to new-product introductions or new promotional offers. A marketing **experiment** involves changing a variable involved in a purchase to find out what happens. Ideally, the researcher changes just one element, usually one of the factors in the marketing mix, and keeps the other variables constant.

Experiments can be conducted either in contrived environments that mimic real-life situations, known as *simulated* test markets, or *in-market* through real-time in-field tests where the product/promotion is actually sold in a limited location and monitored for success during a specific time period. Contrived, simulated experiments use computer simulations to predict consumer behaviour. Marketers typically input marketing mix variables and rely on complex forecasting programs to determine potential success levels. Formally, a **test market** is an in-market localized regional approach, or short-term online destination, used to test the success of promotional offers, new services, or new-product launches.

Test markets can provide a more realistic evaluation of product or promotional success than other research options. However, test markets are time-consuming, costly, and visible to the competition. In terms of promotional offers, Internet marketers routinely test pay-per-click advertising campaigns, alternative online consumer offers, and the design of various website landing pages. For new products, large companies often use test markets to determine whether consumers will buy new products or brands, or shop at a new store concept. The fast

omnibus survey
The voluntary participation of respondents in routine research surveys that allow marketers to add a small number of questions to an existing survey to receive cost-effective data

experiment
In marketing, changing a variable involved in a customer purchase to find out what happens

test market
An in-market localized regional approach, or short-term online destination, used to test the success of promotional offers, new services, or new-product launches

Figure 4–5
Advantages and disadvantages of survey techniques

SURVEY TECHNIQUE	ADVANTAGES	DISADVANTAGES
Personal interview	• Can probe for detailed responses • Can demonstrate marketing programs • Can result in high levels of accuracy	• Time-consuming • Expensive • Interviewers can bias responses
Telephone survey	• Can be conducted quickly and cheaply • Computerized techniques allow for randomized calling • Appropriate when data is needed quickly	• People are reluctant to participate • Low response rates • Call-display features screen-out calls • Increasing number of people with no home phone • Interviews are limited to 5–10 minutes • Interviewers can bias responses • Questionable representativeness of samples
Mail survey	• No interviewer bias • Useful for national surveys • If using a panel, can track changes over time • Can be affordable if part of a syndicated or omnibus survey	• Lengthy time-lag for data collection • Low response rates • Questionable data accuracy • Inability to probe respondents
Internet survey	• No interviewer bias • Can be conducted quickly and cheaply • Efficient for electronic data collection • High Internet penetration can lead to good sampling • Can easily target customer databases • Useful for national surveys • If using a panel, can track changes over time • Can be affordable if part of a syndicated or omnibus survey	• Difficult to verify respondents' identity • Questionable data accuracy due to anonymity • Inability to probe respondents • Difficult to provide incentives for completion • Some debate over sample representativeness

food industry is a well-known user of test markets. In the U.S., McDonald's recently tested a Snack and Wrap Mac, a new product, consisting of a small beef patty wrapped in a flour tortilla.

Step 5: Compile, Analyze, and Interpret Data

After data has been collected, it has to be compiled, analyzed, and summarized so that it can be turned into actionable information. The researcher must know how to analyze the data and what tools to use. There are many statistical packages that can make this task easier. Market researchers face the challenge of synthesizing and simplifying pages of data into clear charts with relevant observations and conclusions that can help marketers address business problems, challenges, and opportunities.

Step 6: Generate Reports and Recommendations

Once the data has been analyzed, the researcher will discuss the results with a marketing manager and prepare reports to communicate the research findings. The report will include recommendations that address the marketing problem and research objectives. It is important to understand that marketing data and information have little value unless they are translated into findings and recommendations that lead to marketing action. Managers generally prefer clear, concise reports with the key findings highlighted, including relevant charts, graphs, and tables of data.

ask yourself

1. Which survey approach provides the greatest flexibility for asking probing questions: mail, telephone, Internet, or personal interview?

2. What is the difference between an online bulletin board and an online community?

In our example of the ICBC, the corporation's final research report pointed out that the people who like speeding resisted the ads. The research told the ICBC that its advertising dollars were not well spent and recommended changes.[8]

The Future of Market Research

Today's marketer has extensive sources of information available on the competition, the market, and the consumer. This information can come from secondary sources or primary sources to help marketers make fact-based decisions. Technology is facilitating the gathering of this information with more and more individuals having easy access to the Internet and researchers increasingly using this approach to gather information. Léger Marketing tells us that 20 percent of research surveys in Canada are already online,[9] and we learned from Luke Sklar at SW&A that online market research is the way of the future.

The wealth of research information now available to marketers presents its own challenges. Marketers find they need to adopt strategies and approaches to filter out unreliable and useless information from critical and actionable facts. In all instances, marketers need to remember that market research should be actionable and that decisions to purchase a study, or embark upon a market research project, should be evaluated as any investment decision. A marketer must weigh the costs of conducting the research against the expected results and actions that can evolve. Marketers need to work with market researchers as a team that evaluates the value of a research study, ensuring objectives are clear, the process efficient, and the study is actionable and cost-effective.

Marketers and market research practitioners need to keep consumers' privacy top-of-mind. Privacy laws in Canada require businesses to comply with the *Personal Information Protection and Electronic Documents Act* (PIPEDA), which was first introduced in 2001, updated in 2004, and with further modifications expected in 2011/2012. The law attempts to balance organizational needs to collect information with an individual's right to privacy. Violations can result in fines of up to $100,000. PIPEDA limits an organization's collection of personal information to specific short-term projects. It also demands that information is securely stored and collected only with the consent of respondents. Organizations are required to obtain separate permissions for using an individual's information in three areas: (1) service renewal, (2) marketing purposes, and (3) the use of personal sensitive data. Marketers are well advised to check the latest on privacy legislation at www.priv.gc.ca to ensure compliance with the latest legal requirements. Lawyers should be consulted for advice.

marketing NewsFlash

IAB Canada – New Digital Research

Are you looking for the latest on digital marketing research? Look no further than IABCanada.com, the website of the Interactive Advertising Bureau of Canada. On the site you'll find valuable research studies in the Insights + Research section, which includes releases from the *Faces Of IAB Canada* and *Hump Day Bump Of Research* studies.

A recent *Faces* release featured Carat and Microsoft's *New Shopper Journeys*, which highlights how consumer shopping behaviour has changed due to economic pressures and digital technology. It details how offline, online, and in-store media now shape purchase decisions in the apparel, quick-service restaurant, grocery, and home electronics markets. Price is seen as more important than ever, with more time spent researching and looking for special promotions. Consumers not only visit more retailers to find the best deals but also turn to online forums, websites, and social networks to make decisions. Purchases are now made through an expanded array of outlets including bricks-and-mortar stores as well as e-commerce sites and online auctions.

A new monthly feature by IAB Canada is the *Hump Day Bump Of Research*, which issues new research

studies from across the globe. "The goal of IAB Canada is simple," states Paula Gignac, president of IAB Canada, "To provide time-stressed marketers (and students) with at least two pieces of credible digital advertising research every month that is reliable and easily accessible. It also profiles our members' expertise in all things digital."

One of its latest studies features a social media survey from Delvinia and Environics, *AskingCanadians™ Social Media PRIZMC2-Link*. It looks at social media habits, pointing to three broad categories: (1) content creators, (2) social media followers, and (3) non-users of social networks. The study reveals that about a third of Canadians use social networks to stay in touch with family members in Canada and abroad. It also shows that people who create social media are not the same as those who follow it. Creators tend to be young, upwardly mobile immigrants that live in cities, while followers tend to be affluent, middle-aged people with older families that live in the suburbs. Social media non-users are often older, risk-averse private people who do not live in urban areas.

"Trust and reliability are key attributes we look for when

sourcing industry research," says Karl Flanders, VP, media director, Saatchi & Saatchi. "IAB Canada has a proven track record of supplying us with leading-edge articles, facts, and insights that help us help our clients, so we're excited to know that we'll be hearing about new member and non-member research finds in a more regular manner as a result of this program."

IAB Canada also highlights the latest industry trends in its September and March MIXX Canada Conference + Roadshow Series. See the latest MIXX Canada lineup at www.mixx-canada.com.[10] ●

Questions

1. What issue is IAB Canada addressing by regularly posting research studies?

2. Check the IAB Canada website at www.iabcanada.com and review one of its latest research studies. What interesting facts are revealed by the study and what areas you think require further research?

Summary...*just the facts*

- Market research is the process of defining a marketing problem or opportunity, systematically collecting and analyzing information, and recommending actions to improve an organization's marketing activities.

- Market research can be classified as exploratory, descriptive, or causal research.

- Secondary research data consists of internal company reports and external online and offline published studies.

- The first step in the research process describes the problem, issue, or opportunity and establishes the research objectives.

- The second step involves designing the research plan and identifying the methodology required to gather the information.

- During the third step, exploratory and qualitative research is conducted.

- The fourth step involves collecting quantitative research information.

- The fifth step is when the data is analyzed and interpreted.

- The final step is when the information is translated into reports that include research highlights, necessary details, and recommendations for future actions.

- Primary research data consists of qualitative or quantitative studies. Qualitative studies include focus groups, in-depth interviews, online communities/bulletin boards, and social listening. Quantitative studies include surveys, experiments, and observations.

- Privacy policies need to be instituted by marketers and research companies to protect consumer information and to adhere to legal privacy legislation.

Key Terms and Concepts...*a refresher*

causal research *p. 84*
descriptive research *p. 83*
experiment *p. 95*
exploratory research *p. 83*
focus group *p. 90*
in-depth interview *p. 90*
marketing information system (MIS) *p. 82*
market research *p. 82*

non-probability sampling *p. 87*
objectives *p. 85*
observational research *p. 94*
omnibus survey *p. 95*
online research bulletin boards *p. 91*
online research communities *p. 91*
panel *p. 94*
primary data *p. 90*
probability sampling *p. 87*

qualitative research *p. 88*
quantitative research *p. 93*
questionnaire *p. 94*
sampling *p. 87*
secondary data *p. 89*
social listening *p. 92*
syndicated studies *p. 94*
test market *p. 95*

Hands-on...*apply your knowledge*

Market Research Assignment The course you are completing may require you to submit a report on the marketing of a product. Navigate your way to the online sources identified on page 91 to review and collect secondary data available on your product or its target market. Write a list of bullet points for each secondary source to summarize your findings. Be sure to attach a list of the sources to your information and bookmark the information for future reference.

Reality Check...*reminder*

Refer back to this chapter's opening vignette and answer the Reality Check questions on page 80.

McGraw Hill connect *Practise and learn online with Connect.*

Connect allows you to practise important concepts at your own pace and on your own schedule, with 24/7 online access to an eBook, practice quizzes, video cases, chapter application questions, discussion activities, Internet exercises, interactivities, study tools, and more.

This is your brain

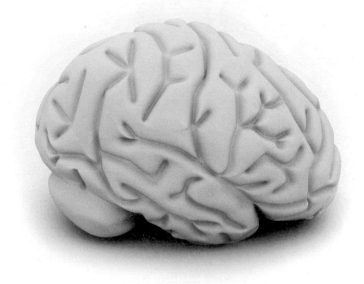

This is your brain on

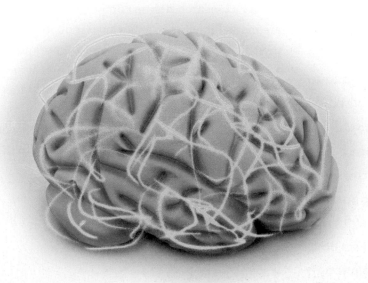

5

B2B
marketing

The mission of Virox Technologies Inc., located in Oakville, Ontario, is to equip the entire spectrum of global markets that are concerned with infection control with state-of-the-art chemical-based antimicrobial technology in the war against germs. In 1998, Virox found a novel way to harness the cleaning and disinfecting power of hydrogen peroxide for the first time. It had long been known that hydrogen peroxide could kill germs without being harmful to the user. However, up to now, this remarkable chemical had not been considered stable enough to be practical as the foundation for a system of commercial disinfectant cleaners. Virox Technologies Inc. changed all that by developing a technology known as Accelerated Hydrogen Peroxide (AHP) that has now five issued patents and six pending that attest to the uniqueness of formulations. Virox has pioneered the broader acceptance of hydrogen peroxide as an active ingredient by creating superior disinfectant formulations that are recognized by the science community.

Virox sells its technology, Accelerated Hydrogen Peroxide (AHP), under licence to leading infection control companies around the world. For example, in the veterinary market, Bayer represents AHP in Canada under the brand name Peroxigard. The AHP logo and words "Accelerated Hydrogen Peroxide is a trademark of Virox used under license by Bayer Inc." appear on every Peroxigard label and associated marketing support material. The AHP logo is prominently displayed on all of Bayer's products that use this technology. The AHP logo on Bayer's products builds brand equity and customer confidence for the technology owned by Virox. The AHP logo is fast becoming synonymous with a new standard in cleaning and disinfection.

As a research-driven company, Virox partners with companies that are market leaders in an array of industries, all of whom have validated the scientific claims and market acceptance of AHP technology. Just as computer companies have the "Intel Inside" logo prominently displayed on each computer, Virox similarly has its AHP logo displayed on all products that its partners produce.

Virox's partners represent their products with the Virox AHP formulation to markets including but not limited to the following:

- Industrial and institutional market, such as hospitals and public buildings, including school boards
- Medical device reprocessing market
- Hand hygiene market
- Dental market
- Dairy market
- Veterinary market

Randy Pilon, the president, CEO, and founder of Virox, says that companies that purchase disinfectant products have four criteria that they look for from a potential supplier: (1) cleaning efficacy, (2) speed and range of pathogens it kills, (3) user and occupant safety, and (4) environmental impact.

Virox is in an enviable position because its AHP formulations are designed with these criteria in mind. Its products perform extremely well on each of the criteria. Virox's products clean better than competitors, work faster, and are safer by being non-toxic, non-irritating, non-corrosive, and safe for the environment.

Randy mentions that the criteria that companies consider when purchasing disinfectants are virtually the same for every company, but the weight that each company places on each criterion can vary. For example,

LEARNING OBJECTIVES

LO 1 Identify the distinguishing characteristics of industrial, reseller, government, and non-profit markets

LO 2 Understand how to measure industrial, reseller, government, and non-profit markets

LO 3 Explain which key characteristics of organizational buying make the process different from consumer buying

LO 4 Describe how buying centres and buying situations influence organizational purchasing

LO 5 Outline the process of business segmentation

LO 6 Explain the growing importance of and the approaches to online buying for industrial, reseller, and government markets

if the president of a company is very concerned about the environment, that could be the criterion that has the most weight in the purchase decision.

The employees who influence the purchase of Virox's products can place different emphasis on each of the criteria. For example, the head of infection prevention at a health care facility is concerned with the effectiveness of the product, how quickly it works, and the spectrum of pathogens it will terminate. On the other hand, the occupational health and safety person at the same facility may be concerned with the safety of the product for employees as well as its effects on the environment. The purchasing manager, who is another influencer, may focus more on the product cost to determine whether the company has the budget to support the product. Ultimately, it is a collaborative effort that gets synthesized into one purchasing decision, but knowing there are several criteria to consider, means that the salesperson must have comprehensive product knowledge.

When asked about the criterion of cost as a factor in the business-to-business (B2B) purchase of disinfectants, Randy has this to say: "We're in the prevention business. Companies have to look at the cost of preventing an illness through purchasing a superior disinfectant product and following effective use protocols versus the cost of curing those who contract a pathogen that could have been prevented in the first place."

Randy gives an example of the cost of prevention versus cost of cure with the SARS outbreak in 2003. Virox Technologies received panicked calls from hospitals for the firm's disinfecting wipes that contained the AHP technology and thus became a must-have product in hospitals. Demand was significant as a result of this deadly new strain of pneumonia. Randy says that the cost of curing people who contract SARS is far more expensive than preventing it in the first place, not to mention to possibility of loss of life and the risk to the organization's reputation. He goes on to say, "New drugs and vaccines have traditionally enjoyed the medical limelight while prevention has played the ugly duckling. But that's changing. Indeed, scientists have watched aghast for over a decade as bacteria and viruses develop which are resistant to drugs."

When asked about the effects of the Internet on his B2B business, Randy says that his website is set up so that companies who want further information about the superiority of AHP technology can find it very easily. Other influencers, who want to read research papers touting the effectiveness of AHP, can also find it on the website. Randy says that Virox is involved in social media with employees taking part in many blogs on the Internet. The blogs link back to the Virox website so that a connection is made between social media and the website.

Randy explains that another way that the Internet is changing how business is done is by collaboration. Websites such as Yet2.com are set up to bring customer and supplier together. This is an emerging trend called "Open Innovation." A company that is in need of a formulation, for example, can list its needs on the site and a company that can provide the formulation also lists itself on the site and thus customer and provider get together in this way. This may result in the provider obtaining a licensing agreement from the customer.

Another trend that Randy shares is that the Internet has levelled the playing field for small companies. Ten years ago, a small company would not have a chance to do business with a large company due to the "not invented here" attitude that pre-existed. But now sites such as Yet2.com are bringing buyer and seller together, no matter what their size. Research and development (R&D) departments of large companies are beginning to be receptive to dealing with "outsiders" as long as the latter has solutions to their needs. At some companies, the R&D employees are asked to allocate 20 to 30 percent of their time scouring sites such as Yet2.com for technology that they would like to purchase. This phenomenon is aptly called "search and development" as opposed to the traditional research and development. This encourages employees to search for outside help, which lowers the "not invented here" barrier and the world becomes the company's laboratory. Randy concludes by saying, "The B2B strategies that companies can employ are varied and many and evolutionary. I suspect you will continue to see dynamic change in this important mode of commerce." 🍎

reality CHECK

As you read Chapter 5, refer back to the Virox vignette to answer the following questions:

- Businesses use organizational buying criteria when purchasing a product. What buying criteria do companies purchasing disinfectant products use?

- There are five possible roles that an individual can play in the buying centre. Identify the role that each of the following persons in a health care facility would play: (a) head of infection, (b) occupational health and safety person, and (c) purchasing manager.

Business marketers recognize that their customers require specialized needs.

B2B marketing

Effective marketers provide business solutions to customers in order to secure their business.

Just as Chapter 3 focuses on consumer behaviour, Chapter 5 focuses on the organizational consumer. Marketers identify, analyze, and seek to satisfy their organizational target markets.

The Nature and Size of Organizational Markets

L **1** Understanding organizational markets and buying behaviour is necessary for effective business marketing. **Business marketing** is the marketing of products to companies, governments, or non-profit organizations for use in the creation of goods and services that they then produce and market to others.[1] It is also referred to as business-to-business (B2B) marketing. So many firms engage in business marketing that it is important to understand the characteristics of organizational buyers and their buying behaviour, as they differ from consumer buying behaviour. Marketing plans are important as road maps for firms selling industrial products just as they are for companies that sell consumer products. Chapter 14 describes marketing plans in greater detail.

Organizational buyers are those manufacturers, wholesalers, retailers, and government agencies that buy goods and services for their own use or for resale. For example, these organizations buy computers and

smartphones such as the BlackBerry for their own use. Manufacturers buy raw materials and parts that they reprocess into the finished goods they sell, and wholesalers and retailers resell the goods they buy without reprocessing them. Organizational buyers include all buyers in a nation except ultimate consumers. These organizational buyers purchase and lease large volumes of equipment, raw materials, manufactured parts, supplies, and business services. They often buy raw materials and parts, process them, and sell them. This upgraded product may pass through several different organizations (as it is bought and resold by different levels of manufacturers, distributors, wholesalers, and retailers) before it is purchased by the final organizational buyer or final consumer. So the total purchases of organizational buyers in a year are far greater than those of ultimate consumers.

Organizational buyers are divided into three different markets: industrial, reseller, and government markets (see Figure 5–1).[2]

business marketing
Marketing to firms, governments, or non-profit organizations

organizational buyers
Manufacturers, wholesalers, retailers, and government agencies that buy goods and services for their own use or for resale

Industrial Markets

There are over 1.6 million firms in the industrial, or business, market in Canada. These *industrial firms* in some way reprocess a product or service they buy before selling it again to the next buyer. For example, there are many suppliers that sell to car companies. Although the consumer purchases one consumer product, i.e., the car, the automobile company purchases parts from many suppliers just to make that one car. There are suppliers for such parts as steering wheels, brakes, doors, tires, seats, etc. The business market involves more purchases and dollars than the consumer market.

The importance of services in Canada today is emphasized by the composition of the industrial markets shown in Figure 5–1. Primary industries (agriculture, fishing, mining, and forestry), utilities, manufacturers, and construction firms sell physical products and represent 33 percent of all of the industrial firms, or about 546,000. The service market sells diverse services such as legal advice, auto repair, and dry cleaning. Along with finance, insurance, and real estate businesses; transportation, communication, and public utility firms; and non-profit associations, these service firms represent about 67 percent of all industrial firms, or about 1.1 million.

Marketing tip

"We're in the prevention business. Companies have to look at the cost of preventing an illness through purchasing a superior disinfectant product and following effective use protocols versus the cost of curing those who contract a pathogen that could have been prevented in the first place."

- Randy Pilon, president and CEO, Virox Technologies Inc.

Reseller Markets

Wholesalers and retailers that buy physical products and sell them again without any reprocessing are *resellers*. In Canada, there are over 200,000 retailers and over 65,000 wholesalers. Some of the largest Canadian-owned retailers in Canada include Loblaw, Alimentation Couche-Tard, Empire Company Limited (Sobeys), Metro, Shoppers Drug Mart, and Canadian Tire.

In this chapter, we look at these resellers mainly as organizational buyers in terms of how they make their own buying decisions and which products they choose to carry.

Figure 5–1
Type and number of organizational customers, as reported by Statistics Canada

BUSINESS MARKETS IN CANADA

KIND OF BUSINESS MARKET	TYPE OF ORGANIZATION	NUMBER OF FIRMS IN CANADA
All industries		2,024,508
Industrial markets: 1,641,170	Primary industries (agriculture, fishing, mining, forestry)	209,657
	Utilities	4,926
	Manufacturers	105,256
	Construction	225,837
	Services	691,779
	Transportation, storage, and communications	102,168
	Finance, insurance, and real estate	301,547
Reseller markets: 375,538	Wholesale trade	132,666
	Retail trade	242,872
Government markets: 7,800	Public administration (federal, provincial, municipal, regional)	7,800

Source: Statistics Canada (www.statcan.ca/english/Pgdb/econ18.htm).

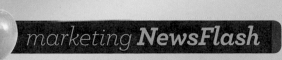

marketing *NewsFlash*

B2B Marketers Must Keep Pace with Social Media

Social media has become the go-to resource for B2B customers, both to share feedback about companies they are doing business with as well as to monitor discussions about products and services they are considering. The control of a B2B company's brand is rapidly changing from corporate marketing departments to the customer-to-customer conversations taking place in social media networks. Just as shared positive experiences can drive new prospects to a business, unmanaged negative comments can spread like wildfire, incinerating the organization's hard-earned reputation. Not surprisingly, customers recognize their growing influence and realize the impact of their praise or, more importantly, their criticism on a company.

Businesses of all sizes are learning the importance of listening, rather than preaching, in order to acquire and retain their customers. Customers using social media are not interested in vague and impersonalized advertising and sales pitches. They are socially savvy and know how to connect with one another (more than half of active Twitter users follow at least one company, brand, or product) and possess little desire to maintain loyalty for a company that does not care for and accommodate their needs.

This new environment creates big challenges but also incredible opportunities for B2B sales. Sales professionals can no longer completely rely on traditional e-mail and cold-calling campaigns. The good news is that social media is levelling the playing field for selling to customers. Sales professionals can now gain timely and relevant insights about their customers as well as engage at a very deep and personal level—two huge boons to the B2B sales process. Thanks to social media monitoring and conversation, individuals within the organization have the ability of championing the identity of their corporate brand.[3] ●

Questions

1. If you are a new, small B2B company with limited resources, what can you learn from the above article?

2. How has social media levelled the playing field between business marketers and their customers?

Government Markets

Government units are the federal, provincial, regional, and municipal agencies that buy goods and services for the constituents that they serve. With a spending budget of close to $180 billion

annually, the federal government is a major customer, possibly the largest in Canada.[4] In addition to specialized purchases for the military, government agencies also buy almost everything that regular consumers buy, from toilet paper to chewing gum to cars for federal prisons, hospitals, and schools. At the federal government level, the bulk of the purchasing is done by Public Works and Government Services Canada. Provincial and municipal governments typically have government departments that do the buying for them. In addition, hundreds of government departments, agencies, and Crown corporations (owned by the government on behalf of the people of Canada) such as CBC, VIA Rail, and the Royal Canadian Mint purchase supplies and services to operate. An example of a very successful Canadian company is Bombardier. Over the years, it has produced regional aircraft, business jets, mass transportation equipment such as subways and passenger rail vehicles, and recreational equipment. Many of its sales are to governments.

Non-Profit Organizations

Organizations that operate without having financial profit as a goal, and which seek to provide goods and services for the good of society, are called *non-profit organizations*. They are also known as charitable organizations, and some 83,000 of them are registered with Canada Revenue Agency.[5] Tax advantages make it beneficial for this type of organization to register with the federal government.

You are probably familiar with many non-profit organizations. Were you a member of the Boy Scouts or Girl Guides? Have you participated in a Canadian Cancer Society run or marathon? Have you been asked for a donation to the United Way? Hospitals, arts organizations, cultural groups, and some research institutes can be classified as non-profit organizations. In your school, you may have a foundation office that raises money for student awards and aid; this too is a non-profit organization. In the past, marketing in these organizations has been limited, but increasingly they are adopting the same types of marketing techniques that other business firms employ, and with good success. As purchasers, this sector of business buys a wide array of goods and services to conduct their operations.

World's Largest Exporters

Canada is the 12th largest exporter.

1. China
2. Germany
3. United States
4. Japan
5. Netherlands
6. France
7. Italy
8. Belgium
9. Republic of Korea
10. United Kingdom

Source: "International Trade Statistics" World Trade Organization, press release, March 26, 2010 (www.wto.org/english/news_e/pres10_e/pr598_e.htm).

Measuring Industrial, Reseller, Government, and Non-Profit Markets

LO2 The measurement of industrial, reseller, government, and non-profit markets is an important first step for a firm interested in determining the size of one, two, or all of these markets in Canada and around the world. This task has been made easier with the **North American Industry Classification System (NAICS)**.[6] The NAICS provides common industry definitions for Canada, Mexico, and the United States, which facilitate the measurement of economic activity in the three member countries of the North American Free Trade Agreement (NAFTA). The NAICS replaced the Standard Industrial Classification (SIC) system, a version of which had been in place for more than 50

Figure 5–2
NAICS breakdown for the Arts, Entertainment, and Recreation sector: NAICS code 71 (abbreviated)

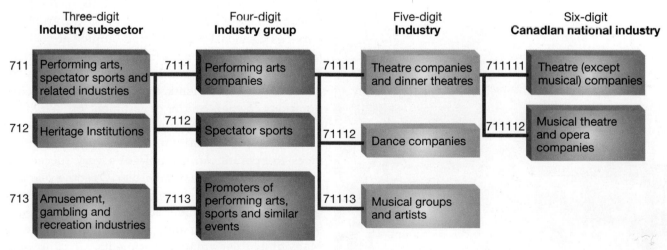

Three-digit **Industry subsector**	Four-digit **Industry group**	Five-digit **Industry**	Six-digit **Canadian national industry**
711 Performing arts, spectator sports and related industries	7111 Performing arts companies	71111 Theatre companies and dinner theatres	711111 Theatre (except musical) companies
712 Heritage Institutions	7112 Spectator sports	71112 Dance companies	711112 Musical theatre and opera companies
713 Amusement, gambling and recreation industries	7113 Promoters of performing arts, sports and similar events	71113 Musical groups and artists	

Source: Statistics Canada.

derived demand
Demand for industrial products and services driven by demand for consumer products and services

years in the three NAFTA member countries. The SIC neither permitted comparability across countries nor accurately measured new or emerging industries. Furthermore, the NAICS is consistent with the *International Standard Industrial Classification of All Economic Activities*, published by the United Nations, to help measure global economic activity.

The NAICS groups economic activity to permit studies of market share, demand for goods and services, competition from imports in domestic markets, and similar studies. The NAICS designates industries with a numerical code in a defined structure. A six-digit coding system is used. The first two digits designate a sector of the economy, the third digit designates a subsector, and the fourth digit represents an industry group. The fifth digit designates a specific industry and is the most detailed level at which comparable data is available for Canada, Mexico, and the United States. The sixth digit designates individual country-level national industries. Figure 5–2 presents an abbreviated breakdown within the Arts, Entertainment, and Recreation sector (code 71) to illustrate the classification scheme.

The NAICS permits a firm to find the NAICS codes of its present customers and then obtain NAICS-coded lists of similar firms. Also, it is possible to monitor NAICS categories to determine the growth in various sectors and industries to identify promising marketing opportunities. However, NAICS codes, like the earlier SIC codes, have important limitations. The NAICS assigns only one code to each organization based on its major economic activity, but large firms that engage in many different activities are still given only one NAICS code. A second limitation is that five-digit national industry codes are not available for all three countries because the respective governments will not reveal data when too few organizations exist in a category. Despite these limitations, the NAICS represents yet another effort toward economic integration in North America and the world.

Characteristics of Organizational Buying

L○3 Organizations are different from individuals in the way they purchase goods and services, so buying for an organization is different from buying for yourself and your family. In both cases the objective in making the purchase is to solve the buyer's problem—to satisfy a need or want. Unique objectives and policies of an organization put special constraints on how it makes buying decisions. Understanding the characteristics of organizational buying is essential in designing effective marketing programs to reach these buyers. Key characteristics of organizational buying are listed in Figure 5–3 and discussed next.[7]

Derived Demand

Consumer demand for products and services is affected by their price and availability and by consumers' personal tastes and discretionary income. By comparison, industrial demand is derived. **Derived demand** means that the demand for industrial products and services is driven by, or derived from, demand for consumer products and services, as demonstrated in Figure 5–4. For example, the demand for Weyerhaeuser's pulp and paper products is based on consumer demand for newspapers, Domino's "keep warm" pizza-to-go boxes, FedEx packages, and disposable diapers. Derived demand is often based on expectations of future consumer demand. For instance, Whirlpool purchases parts for its washers and dryers in anticipation of consumer demand, which is affected by the replacement cycle for these products and by consumer income. Another example of derived demand is the car industry. Demand for auto parts is driven by new car sales. Magna International Inc., a Canadian company based in Aurora, Ontario, is Canada's largest automobile parts manufacturer, and one of the country's largest companies.

ask yourself

1. Organizational buyers are divided into three different markets. What are they?

2. What is the North American Industry Classification System (NAICS)?

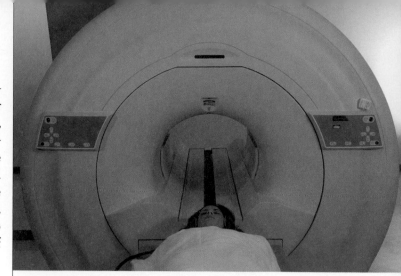

Inelastic Demand

Inelastic demand means that regardless of whether there is an increase or decrease of the price of a B2B product, customers will buy the same quantity. For example, if the price of brake pads goes up, a car manufacturer will still order the same quantity. A single business product, such as a brake pad, is only one of many parts that go into making the final product, and is only a minor portion of the price of the car.

Fluctuating Demand

Small changes in demand for consumer products can result in large increases or decreases in demand for the facilities and equipment needed to make the consumer product. This is referred to as **fluctuating demand**. A product's life expectancy also has a bearing in this type of demand. For example, business products such as large machinery are purchased infrequently. Demand for such products can be high one year when they are wearing out but low in the following year if the old machinery is operating satisfactorily.

Size of the Order or Purchase

The size of the purchase involved in organizational buying is typically much larger than that in consumer buying. The dollar value of a single purchase made by an organization often runs into the millions of dollars. For example, Bombardier is selling 180 new subway cars to the Toronto Transit Commission (TTC) for a value of $390 million.[8]

With so much money at stake, most organizations place constraints on their buyers in the form of purchasing policies or procedures. Buyers must often get

Figure 5–3
Key characteristics of organizational buying behaviour

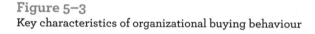

CHARACTERISTICS	DIMENSIONS
Market characteristics	• Demand for industrial products and services is derived. • The number of business customers is typically small, and their purchase orders are typically large.
Product or service characteristics	• Products or services are technical in nature and purchased on the basis of specifications. • Many goods purchased are raw or semifinished. • Heavy emphasis is placed on delivery time, technical assistance, and postsale service.
Buying process characteristics	• Technically qualified and professional buyers follow established purchasing policies and procedures. • Buying objectives and criteria are typically spelled out, as are procedures for evaluating sellers and their products or services. • There are multiple buying influences, and multiple parties participate in purchase decisions. • There are reciprocal arrangements, and negotiation between buyers and sellers is commonplace. • Online buying over the Internet is widespread.
Marketing mix characteristics	• Personal selling to organizational buyers is used extensively, and distribution is very important. • Advertising and other forms of promotion are technical in nature. • Price is often negotiated, evaluated as part of broader seller and product or service qualities, and frequently affected by quantity discounts.

Figure 5–4
Direct versus derived demand

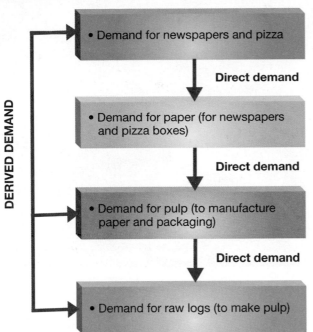

competitive bids from at least three prospective suppliers when the order is above a specific amount, such as $5,000. When the order is above an even higher amount, such as $50,000, it may require the review and approval of a vice president or even the president of the company. Knowing how the size of the order affects buying practices is important in determining who participates in the purchase decision and makes the final decision and also the length of time required to arrive at a purchase agreement.

Number of Potential Buyers

Firms selling consumer products or services often try to reach thousands or millions of individuals or households. For example, your local supermarket or bank probably serves thousands of people, and Kellogg tries to reach millions of Canadian households with its breakfast cereals and probably succeeds in selling to a third or half of these in any given year. In contrast, firms selling to organizations are often restricted to far fewer buyers. Bombardier Aerospace can sell its Challenger business jets to a few thousand organizations throughout the world, and B. F. Goodrich sells its original equipment tires to fewer than 10 car manufacturers.

Organizational Buying Objectives

Organizations buy products and services for one main reason: to help them achieve their objectives. For business firms, the buying objective is usually to increase profits through reducing costs or increasing sales. 7-Eleven buys automated inventory systems to increase the number of products that can be sold through its convenience stores and to keep them fresh. Nissan Motor Company switched its advertising agency because it expects the new agency to devise a more effective ad campaign to help it sell more cars and increase sales. To improve executive decision-making, many firms buy advanced computer systems to process data.

The objectives of non-profit firms and government agencies are usually to meet the needs of the groups they serve. Thus, a hospital buys a high-technology diagnostic device to serve its patients better. Understanding buying objectives is a necessary first step in marketing to organizations.

Organizational Buying Criteria

In Chapter 3, we discussed the criteria that consumers use when purchasing a product. Businesses also use criteria in their purchasing: They specify *organizational buying criteria*, which are detailed specifications

Understanding buying objectives is a necessary first step in marketing to organizations.

for the products and services they want to buy and the characteristics of the suppliers that will supply them. When suppliers are selected, their products and their firm's characteristics are evaluated using these criteria. The following lists some of the most commonly used criteria:

- Price
- Ability to meet the quality specifications required
- Ability to meet the required delivery schedules
- Technical capability
- Warranties and claim policies
- Past performance on previous contracts
- Production facilities and capacity

In the opening vignette on Virox, Randy Pilon, the president, CEO, and founder of Virox, says that for his particular business, companies that purchase disinfectant products have four criteria that they look for from a potential supplier. The criteria are listed in the vignette. Suppliers that meet or exceed the criteria create customer value for the business doing the purchasing.

Many organizational buyers today are transforming their buying criteria into specific requirements that are communicated to suppliers. This practice, called *reverse marketing*, means that organizational buyers are attempting to work with suppliers to make their products, services, and capabilities fit the buyer's needs. Working closely and collaboratively like this with suppliers also helps build buyer–seller relationships and leads to supply partnerships.

The Role of Fear in B2B Buyer Behaviour

It's important at this point to examine the role of emotion in the B2B buying process. Emotions drive human behaviour and are the engines that propel people forward to reach their goals.

According to one author, B2B buying decisions are usually driven by one emotion—fear. Specifically, B2B buying is all about minimizing fear by eliminating risk. There are two distinct types of risk. There is organizational risk, typically formalized and dealt with in the buying process, and then there is personal risk, which is unstated but remains a huge influencing factor in organizational buying. For example, a buyer who chooses to deal with the same trusted supplier for many years is minimizing fear by eliminating organizational risk. Personal

risk is explained by the buyer who chooses not to work with a new supplier even if that potential supplier's products offer better value. The buyer may fear that the latter may not produce a quality product, for example, and the buyer fears being reprimanded and thus may fear working with new suppliers to avert any risk. Humans do not always make rational decisions. In fact, some decisions are made irrationally. People use shortcuts, gut feel, emotions, beliefs, instincts, and habits to reach decisions. Consumer research found this out long ago, but for some reason, many people refuse to accept that the same mechanisms are at play in the business world.[9]

Buyer–Seller Relationships and Supply Partnerships

Another distinction between organizational and consumer buying behaviour lies in the nature of the relationship between organizational buyers and suppliers. Specifically, organizational buying is more likely to involve complex and lengthy negotiations concerning delivery schedules, price, technical specifications, warranties, and claim policies. These negotiations can last for more than a year.

Reciprocal arrangements also exist in organizational buying. Reciprocity is an industrial buying practice in which two organizations agree to purchase each other's products and services. Governments frown on reciprocal buying because it restricts the normal operation of the free market. However, the practice exists and can limit the flexibility of organizational buyers in choosing alternative suppliers.

RIM Voted Highest in Innovation

RIM (Research in Motion) is a successful B2B company by just about any metric. The maker of the BlackBerry scored well in many aspects of the Reputation Institute's study on corporate brands. The Reputation Institute measures both the emotional appeal of a brand along with a handful of so-called rational attributes, such as how consumers perceive the quality of products and services offered by a company. Canadian consumers ranked RIM as the most innovative company in the study, and rated it first in terms of its work environment, leadership qualities, and financial performance. As an example of RIM's work environment, employees of RIM were loaded onto a bus for a very special evening. The Waterloo-based tech giant had rented out the

Rogers Centre in Toronto and brought in U2 to play a private concert for its employees.

RIM lagged in one key area relative to its high marks elsewhere: emotional appeal. Canadians know in their heads that RIM is a well-run company, but it does not set their hearts atwitter. Tim Hortons, on the other hand, came first as having the best corporate reputation in the country because of a high score received for its emotional appeal.

Referring to RIM, Rob Jekielek, a principal consultant with the Reputation Institute, says, "You really get the feeling that if they were able to create the right emotional appeal in addition to all the things they do well rationally, they could improve their reputation even more. The attitude Canadians have toward RIM illustrates a

fundamental truth about consumers in this country. Like others around the world, they are primarily emotional beings. That means a corporation will find it difficult to build a good reputation if it fails to connect on an emotional level."[10]

Questions

1. Why do you think that RIM scores lower on emotional appeal than Tim Hortons?

2. Can you think of another Canadian company that you think should score high in emotional appeal?

In some cases, buyer–seller relationships develop into supply partnerships.[11] A **supply partnership** exists when a buyer and its supplier adopt mutually beneficial objectives, policies, and procedures for the purpose of lowering the cost or increasing the value of products and services delivered to the ultimate consumer. For example, Virox, featured in the opening vignette, partners with companies that are market leaders in an array of industries, all of whom have validated the scientific claims and market acceptance of Virox's AHP technology.

Just as computer companies have the "Intel Inside" logo prominently displayed on each computer, Virox similarly has its AHP logo displayed on all products that its partners produce. Virox sells its technology, Accelerated Hydrogen Peroxide (AHP), under licence to leading infection control companies around the world. The AHP logo is fast becoming synonymous with a new standard in cleaning and disinfection.

ask yourself

1. What is derived demand?

2. A supply partnership exists when _____.

supply partnership
Relationship between a buyer and supplier that adopt mutually beneficial objectives, policies, and procedures

ACCELERATED®
HYDROGEN PEROXIDE

The Organizational Buying Process and the Buying Centre

L ⊕ Organizational buyers, like consumers, engage in a decision process when selecting products and services. **Organizational buying behaviour** is the decision-making process that organizations use to establish the need for products and services and identify, evaluate, and choose among alternative brands and suppliers. There are important similarities and differences between the two decision-making processes. To better understand the nature of organizational buying behaviour, we first compare it with consumer buying behaviour. We then describe a unique feature of organizational buying: the buying centre.

Stages in the Organizational Buying Process

As shown in Figure 5–5, the five stages that a student might use in buying a smartphone also apply to organizational purchases. However, comparing the two right-hand columns in Figure 5–5 reveals some key differences. For example, when a smartphone manufacturer buys digital cameras for its smartphones, more individuals are involved, supplier capability becomes more important, and the post-purchase evaluation behaviour is more formal. The buying decision process of an organization purchasing cameras for smartphones is typical of the steps made by organizational buyers.

The Buying Centre: A Cross-Functional Group

For routine purchases with a small dollar value, a single buyer or purchasing manager often makes the purchase decision alone. In many instances, however, several

Figure 5–5

Comparing the stages in a consumer and organizational purchase decision process reveals subtle differences

STAGE IN THE BUYING DECISION PROCESS	CONSUMER PURCHASE: SMARTPHONE FOR A STUDENT	ORGANIZATIONAL PURCHASE: CAMERA FOR A SMARTPHONE
Problem recognition	Student doesn't like the features of the cellphone now owned as compared to the features of a smartphone and desires to purchase one.	Marketing research and sales departments observe that competitors are improving the quality of cameras that are contained in a smartphone. The firm decides to improve the cameras on their new models, which will be purchased from an outside supplier.
Information search	Student uses past experience, that of friends, ads, the Internet, and magazines to collect information and uncover alternatives.	Design and production engineers draft specifications for the camera. The purchasing department identifies suppliers of cameras.
Evaluation of alternatives	Alternative smartphones are evaluated on the basis of important attributes desired in a smartphone, and several stores are visited.	Purchasing and engineering personnel visit with suppliers and assess facilities, capacity, quality control, and financial status. They drop any suppliers not satisfactory on these factors.
Purchase decision	A specific brand of smartphone is selected, the price is paid, and the student leaves the store.	They use quality, price, delivery, and technical capability as key buying criteria to select a supplier. Then they negotiate terms and award a contract.
Post-purchase behaviour	Student re-evaluates the purchase decision, and may return the smartphone to the store if it is unsatisfactory.	They evaluate the supplier using a formal vendor rating system and notify the supplier if camera does not meet their quality standard. If the problem is not corrected, they drop the firm as a future supplier.

people in the organization participate in the buying process. The individuals in this group, called a **buying centre**, share common goals, risks, and knowledge important to purchase decisions. For most large multi-store chain resellers, such as Sears, 7-Eleven convenience stores, or Safeway, the buying centre is very formal and is called a *buying committee*. However, most industrial firms or government units use informal groups of people or call meetings to arrive at buying decisions.

A firm marketing to industrial firms and government units must understand the structure, technical and business functions represented, and the behaviour of the buying centre. One researcher has suggested four questions to provide guidance in understanding the buying centre in these organizations:[12]

- Which individuals are in the buying centre for the product or service?
- What is the relative influence of each member of the group?
- What are the buying criteria of each member?
- How does each member of the group perceive the potential supplier, its products and services, and its salespeople?

People in the Buying Centre   Who makes up the buying centre in a given organization depends on the specific item being bought. Although a buyer or purchasing manager is almost always a member of the buying centre, individuals from other functional areas are included, depending on what is to be purchased.

buying centre
Group of people in an organization who participate in the buying process

For example, in the opening vignette, we learned that the employees who influence the purchase of Virox's products can put different emphasis on each of the criteria. Randy Pilon gives the example of a health care facility where there are three distinct types of employees who have purchasing criteria that differ from one another. See the chapter-opening vignette for a discussion of these criteria.

In buying a million-dollar machine tool, the president (because of the size of the purchase) and the production vice president would probably be members. For key components to be included in a final manufactured product, a cross-functional group of individuals from research and development (R&D), engineering, and quality control are likely to be added. For new word-processing software, experienced office staff who will use the equipment would be members. Still, a major question in understanding the buying centre is finding and reaching the people who will initiate, influence, and actually make the buying decision.

Roles in the Buying Centre   Researchers have identified five specific roles that an individual in a buying centre can play (see Figure 5–6).[13] In some purchases, the same person may perform two or more of these roles.

Five Reasons to Own a Smartphone

1. You will look more professional.
2. Smartphones make it easier to organize your life.
3. Smartphones are a breeze when it comes to synchronizing them with a PC.
4. You will have more ways to get in touch.
5. You will have more ways to have fun when you have spare time.

Source: "5 Reasons To Own A Smartphone," accessed at http://www.istudioweb.com/5-reasons-to-own-a-smartphone-2009-01-19/

> STILL, A MAJOR QUESTION IN UNDERSTANDING THE BUYING CENTRE IS FINDING AND REACHING THE PEOPLE WHO WILL INITIATE, INFLUENCE, AND ACTUALLY MAKE THE BUYING DECISION.

Figure 5–6
Roles in the buying centre

- *Users* are the people in the organization who actually use the product or service, such as office staff who will use new word-processing software.

- *Influencers* affect the buying decision, usually by helping define the specifications for what is bought. They usually have specialized knowledge. The information systems manager would be a key influencer in the purchase of a new computer network.

- *Buyers* have formal authority and responsibility to select the supplier and negotiate the terms of the contract. The purchasing manager probably would perform this role in the purchase of a computer network.

- *Deciders* have the formal or informal power to select or approve the supplier that receives the contract. Whereas in routine orders the decider is usually the buyer or purchasing manager, in important technical purchases it is more likely to be someone from R&D, engineering, or quality control. The decider for a key component being included in a final manufactured product might be any of these three people.

- *Gatekeepers* control the flow of information in the buying centre. Purchasing personnel, technical experts, and office staff can all help or prevent salespeople (or information) from reaching people performing the other four roles.

Buying Situations and the Buying Centre

The number of people in the buying centre largely depends on the specific buying situation. Researchers who have studied organizational buying identify three types of buying situations, called **buy classes**. These buy classes vary from the routine reorder, or *straight rebuy*, to the completely new purchase, termed *new buy*. In between these extremes is the *modified rebuy*. Some examples will clarify the differences.[14]

- **Straight rebuy:** Here the buyer or purchasing manager reorders an existing product or service from the list of acceptable suppliers, probably without even checking with users or influencers from the engineering, production, or quality control departments. Office supplies and maintenance services are usually obtained as straight rebuys.

- **Modified rebuy:** In this buying situation, the company is purchasing a product that it has experience purchasing, such as new laptops for salespeople, but it wants to change the product specifications, price, delivery schedule, or supplier. The changes usually mean involving users, influencers, and/or deciders in the buying decision—more input than would be necessary for a straight rebuy.

- **New buy:** In this situation, the company is buying the product or service for the first time. This purchase involves greater potential risk and is more complex than other buying situations. The buying centre is larger, comprised of people representing those parts of the organization having a stake in the new buy. Procter & Gamble's purchase of a multimillion-dollar fibre-optic network from Corning, Inc., linking its corporate offices, represented a new buy.[15]

Figure 5–7 summarizes how buy classes affect buying centre tendencies in different ways.[16]

B2B Market Segmentation

L⑤ Chapter 6, "Segmentation, Targeting, and Positioning," focuses primarily on the consumer market. Here we focus on the business market. Consumer market segmentation groups consumers into groups that have common needs and respond similarly to marketing programs. The process of segmenting business markets divides markets based on type of customer, size, buying situation, customer location, and benefits sought. By applying market segmentation concepts to groups of business customers, a marketer can develop a strategy that best suits a particular segment's needs.

Type of Customer

The NAICS codes discussed earlier provide a useful tool for identifying business target markets. For example, Steelcase, a major producer of office furniture, segments its customers into ten industries including banking, higher education, hospitality, and health care.

Size of Customer

Many B2B marketers divide their potential market into large and small accounts, using separate distribution channels to reach each segment. For example,

ask yourself

1. What one department is almost always represented by a person in the buying centre?

2. What are the three types of buying situations or buy classes?

marketers may develop one strategy to reach Fortune 500 corporations, which have complex purchasing procedures, and another strategy for small firms where decisions are made by one or two people. For example, American Express provides information and assistance for small business owners with its Small Business Services unit, which is dedicated exclusively to the success of small business owners and their companies.

Type of Buying Situation

B2B marketers can divide their potential market by the three types of buy classes: new buy, modified rebuy, and straight rebuy. We recognized in that discussion above that a new buy is significantly different from a straight rebuy in several important respects. Consequently, a business seller might well segment its market into the three buy-class categories.

Customer Location

The product manager might segment on the basis of region or actual location of the potential customer. Firms located in a metropolitan area might receive a personal sales call, whereas those outside this area might be contacted by telephone.

Benefits Sought

The market may also be segmented on the basis of benefits sought. Xerox may decide to focus on firms looking for quality products and good customer service as opposed to those looking simply for lower prices.

Figure 5–7
How the buying situation affects buying centre behaviour

BUYING CENTRE DIMENSION	Buy-Class Situation		
	STRAIGHT REBUY	MODIFIED REBUY	NEW BUY
People involved	1	2–3	Many
Decision time	Short	Short	Long
Problem definition	Well-defined	Minor modifications	Uncertain
Buying objective	Low-priced supplier	Low-priced supplier	Good solution
Suppliers considered	Present	Present	New/present
Buying influence	Purchasing agent	Purchasing agent and others	Technical/operating personnel

Online Buying in Organizational Markets

"At General Electric, online buying has cut the cost of a transaction from $50 to $100 per purchase to about $5."

Organizational buying behaviour and business marketing continue to change with the use of the Internet and e-commerce. Organizations vastly outnumber consumers both in terms of online transactions made and purchase volume.[17] In fact, organizational buyers account for about 80 percent of the total worldwide dollar value of all online transactions. Online organizational buyers around the world purchased between $8 and $10 trillion worth of products in 2010. Organizational buyers in North America will account for about 60 percent of these purchases.

Online buying can assume many forms. Organizational buyers can purchase directly from suppliers. For instance, a buyer might acquire a dozen desktop photocopiers from Xerox.ca. This same buyer might purchase office furniture and supplies online through a reseller, such as Staples at staples.ca. Increasingly, organizational buyers and business marketers are using e-marketplaces and online auctions to purchase and sell products and services.

Prominence of Online Buying in Organizational Markets

Online buying in organizational markets is prominent for three major reasons.[18] First, organizational buyers depend heavily on timely supplier information that describes product availability, technical specifications, application uses, price, and delivery schedules. This information can be conveyed quickly online. The Internet has altered one aspect of B2B purchasing: Buyers have much more knowledge at their fingertips about the seller's product than in the past. Second, web-based technology has been shown to substantially reduce buyer order-processing costs. At General Electric, online buying has cut the cost of a transaction from $50 to $100 per purchase to about $5. Third, business marketers have found that web-based technology can reduce marketing costs, particularly sales and advertising expense, and broaden their potential customer base for many types of products and services. For these reasons, online buying is popular in all three kinds of organizational markets. For example, airlines order over $400 million in spare parts from the Boeing Company website each year.

E-Marketplaces: Virtual Organizational Markets

A significant development in organizational buying has been the creation and growth of online trading communities, called **e-marketplaces**, that bring together buyers and supplier organizations.[19] These online communities go by a variety of names, including portals, exchanges, and e-hubs, and make possible the real-time exchange of information, money, products, and services. Globally, the number of e-marketplaces for businesses is extensive.

E-marketplaces can be independent trading communities or private exchanges. Independent e-marketplaces typically focus on a specific product or service, or serve a particular industry. They act as a neutral third party and provide an online trading platform and a centralized market that enable exchanges between buyers and sellers. Independent e-marketplaces charge a fee for their services and exist in settings that have one or more of the following features:

- Thousands of geographically dispersed buyers and sellers

B2B Attitudes Toward Social Media

The number of B2B marketers who participate in microblogging (e.g., Twitter)  75%

The number of B2B marketers who monitor company-related mentions on social media sites 73%

The number of B2B marketers who have at least two part-time staff dedicated to social media  42%

marketing meter

Source: "B2B Marketers Gain Ground with Social," eMarketer, May 27, 2010, accessed at www.emarketer.com/Article.aspx?R=1007717; "Is B2B on Board with Social?" eMarketer, May 13, 2010, accessed at www.emarketer.com/mobile/article_m.aspx?R=1007688; "Social initiatives: B2B versus B2C," eMarketer, December 4, 2009, accessed at www.emarketer.com/Article.aspx?R=1007404.

There is a heightened sense of formality in Japanese interaction. When doing business in Japan, your suitability in respect to conducting business will be assessed during a first meeting, so always maintain a sense of professionalism.

The bow is an integral part of Japanese society. It is used when meeting, getting attention, to show gratitude, to express sympathy, or as an apology. When doing business in Japan as a Westerner, you would not be expected to bow. You will most likely be greeted with a handshake combined with a slight nod of the head. Introduce yourself with your full name followed by your company name. It is important to use proper titles when addressing someone, so always establish the position of the other person.

The exchanging of business cards when doing business in Japan involves a degree of ceremony. The card is seen to represent the individual, so it should be treated with respect. Before travelling to Japan, ensure you have ample cards and have one side translated into Japanese. Include your position within the company on it. Invest in a carry case to store cards and keep this in an easy-to-access location. When exchanging cards, offer your card with both hands with the Japanese side up. Ensure that there is no barrier between you and the recipient, such as a table, chair, or plant. When accepting a card, always use two hands as this shows deference. For Japanese people, as elsewhere in the Asia-Pacific region, exchanging cards is like shaking hands. If you are in a formal situation,

it is proper to place the card face up on the table in front of you and refer to it when necessary.

The Japanese like dealing with quiet, sincere, and compromising individuals. Extroverts are seen as brash and arrogant. Early on in negotiations, remain humble, indirect, and non-threatening. Silence is considered a virtue. If things go quiet when doing business in a meeting, don't panic. Reflection is taking place. Silence may be also be accompanied by the closing of the eyes. Never interrupt or break the silence.[20] ●

Question

1. Can you think of other customs that a businessperson should be aware of in doing business in other foreign countries?

● Frequently changing prices caused by demand and supply fluctuations

● Time sensitivity due to perishable offerings and changing technologies

● Easily comparable offerings between a variety of suppliers

Well-known independent e-marketplaces include PaperExchange (paper products), PlasticsNet (plastics), Altra Energy (electricity, natural gas, and crude oil), and XSAg.com (agricultural products). Small business buyers and sellers, in particular, benefit from independent e-marketplaces. These e-marketplaces offer suppliers an economical way to expand their customer base and reduce the cost of purchased products and services.

Large companies tend to favour private exchanges that link them with their network of qualified suppliers and customers. Private exchanges

focus on streamlining a company's purchase transactions with its suppliers and customers. Like independent e-marketplaces, they provide a technology trading platform and central market for buyer–seller interactions.

Large firms such as IBM, General Motors, and Toyota have formed private exchanges. Some, such as IBM and GE, have mandated that their suppliers must deal with them primarily through online exchanges. These private exchanges provide tremendous cost savings through the elimination of periodic negotiations and routine paperwork.

Quadrem is an e-marketplace that connects more than 60,000 suppliers and 1,500 buyers. It handles more than $20 billion in orders annually. Quadrem's global membership includes buyers and suppliers from a variety of industries. It was originally set up by 14 of the world's most prominent mining, minerals, and metals companies "as a one-stop solution to specifically meet the e-procurement needs of the

Figure 5–8
This diagram from Quadrem's website shows the efficiency of e-marketplaces

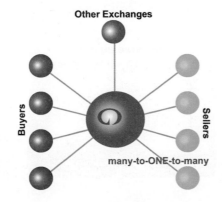

natural resource industry."[21] Figure 5–8 diagrams how Quadrem facilitates its e-marketplace.

Online Auctions in Organizational Markets

Online auctions have grown in popularity among organizational buyers and business marketers. Many e-marketplaces offer this service. Two general types of auctions are common: a traditional auction and a reverse auction.[22] Figure 5–9 shows how buyer and seller participants and price behaviour differ by type of auction. Let's look at each auction type more closely to understand the implications of each for buyers and sellers.

In a **traditional auction**, a seller puts an item up for sale and would-be buyers are invited to bid in competition with each other. As more would-be buyers become involved, there is an upward pressure on bid prices. Why? Bidding is sequential—that is, bidders bid in order, one at a time. Prospective buyers observe the bids of others and decide whether to increase the bid price. The auction ends when a single bidder remains and "wins" the item with its highest price. Traditional auctions are frequently used to dispose of excess merchandise. For example, Dell Computer sells surplus, refurbished, or closeout computer merchandise at its dellauction.com website.

A reverse auction works in the opposite direction from a traditional auction. In a **reverse auction**, a buyer communicates a need for a product or service and would-be suppliers are invited to bid in competition with each other. As more would-be suppliers become involved, there is a downward pressure on bid prices for the buyer's business. Why? Like traditional auctions, bidding is sequential and prospective suppliers observe the bids of others and decide whether to decrease the bid price. The auction ends when a single bidder remains and "wins" the business with its lowest price. Reverse auctions benefit organizational buyers by reducing the cost of their purchases. As an example, General Electric, one of the world's largest companies, has its own Global eXchange Services unit, which runs online reverse auctions for the company. It claims that it saved $780 million on the purchase of $6 billion worth of products and services.[23]

Clearly, buyers welcome the lower prices generated by reverse auctions. Some suppliers also favour the reverse auction process because it gives them a chance to capture business that they might not have otherwise had because of a long-standing purchase relationship between the buyer and another supplier. On the other hand, suppliers argue that reverse auctions put too much emphasis on prices, discourage consideration of other important buying criteria, and threaten supply partnership opportunities.[24]

ask yourself

1. What are e-marketplaces?

2. How do traditional auctions and reverse auctions affect bid prices?

Figure 5–9

How buyer and seller participants and price behaviour differ by type of online auction

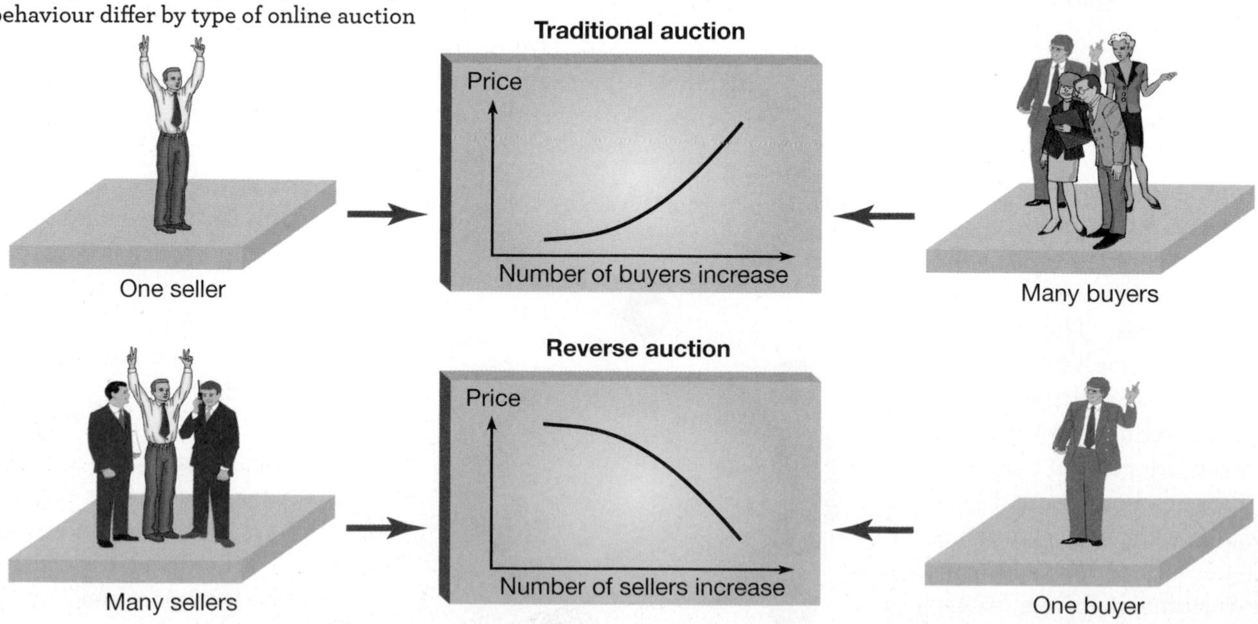

Traditional auction

Price | Number of buyers increase

One seller

Many buyers

Reverse auction

Price | Number of sellers increase

Many sellers

One buyer

Summary...*just the facts*

- Organizational buyers are divided into four different markets: industrial, reseller, government, and non-profit. There are about 1.6 million industrial firms, 376,000 resellers, 7,800 government units, and 83,000 non-profit (charitable) organizations in Canada.

- Measuring industrial, reseller, government, and non-profit markets is an important first step for firms interested in determining the size of markets. The North American Industry Classification System (NAICS) is a convenient starting point to begin this process.

- Many aspects of organizational buying behaviour are different from consumer buying behaviour. Some key differences between the two include demand characteristics, number of potential buyers, buying objectives, buying criteria, size of the order or purchase, buyer–seller relationships and partnerships, and multiple buying influences within companies.

- The three types of buying situations, or buy classes, are the straight rebuy, the modified rebuy, and the new buy. These range from a routine reorder to a totally new purchase.

- The stages in an organizational buying decision are the same as those for consumer buying decisions: problem recognition, information search, evaluation of alternatives, purchase decision, and post-purchase behaviour.

- The buying centre concept is central to understanding organizational buying behaviour. Knowing who makes up the buying centre and the roles they play in making purchase decisions is important in marketing to organizations. The buying centre usually includes a person from the purchasing department and possibly representatives from R&D, engineering, and production, depending on what is being purchased. These people can play one or more of five roles in a purchase decision: user, influencer, buyer, decider, or gatekeeper.

- The process of segmenting business markets divides markets based on type of customer, size, buying situation, customer location, and benefits sought. By applying market segmentation concepts to groups of business customers, a marketer can develop a strategy that best suits a particular segment's needs.

- Online buying is prevalent in industrial, reseller, and government markets. Globally, the number of e-marketplaces for businesses is extensive. Online auctions are commonly used by organizational buyers and business marketers.

Key Terms and Concepts...*a refresher*

business marketing *p. 103*
buy classes *p. 114*
buying centre *p. 113*
derived demand *p. 107*
e-marketplaces *p. 116*

fluctuating demand *p. 108*
inelastic demand *p. 108*
North American Industry Classification System (NAICS). *p. 106*
organizational buyers *p. 103*

organizational buying behaviour *p. 112*
reverse auction *p. 118*
supply partnership *p. 111*
traditional auction *p. 118*

Hands-on...*apply your knowledge*

B2B Marketing Assignment Review the opening vignette on Virox. If you were giving your friend, who is thinking of starting a B2B business, some advice, what points from the Virox vignette can help your friend understand the factors that must be considered in a B2B business?

Reality Check...*reminder*

Refer back to this chapter's opening vignette and answer the Reality Check questions on page 102.

McGraw Hill connect™ *Practise and learn online with Connect.*

Connect allows you to practise important concepts at your own pace and on your own schedule, with 24/7 online access to an eBook, practice quizzes, video cases, chapter application questions, discussion activities, Internet exercises, interactivities, study tools, and more.

segmentation, targeting, and positioning

Target marketing, market segmentation, and product positioning are basic driving forces in the world of marketing, and accurately using these concepts is critical to business success. We take a glimpse inside the world of sports marketing at Atomic Skis Canada to learn how it approaches this area, and we see that by using these concepts, it took a fresh look at its business, more clearly understood what its consumers needed, and created better products and marketing programs to target consumers.

Seasoned marketers understand that strong marketing programs are grounded in gaining insights into what drives consumers to purchase particular products. Having clarity on consumer trigger-points is crucial to accurately positioning products and driving business results. Kyle McCarthy, director at Atomic Skis Canada, takes us into the ski world to explain how Atomic Skis uses *authenticity*, a real look at the market, its consumers, and its products, to create outstanding products and marketing programs.

"Being authentic is the foundation of our business at Atomic Skis," explains Kyle McCarthy. "A few years ago our business needed a boost. Atomic, the number one name in skis, was not delivering the products that consumers wanted, in ways they had come to expect. We had stopped listening to our consumers and lost sight of the fact that Atomic, a company rooted in a tiny village in the Austrian Alps, stood for trust and authenticity. Skiers trusted us to deliver technologically advanced ski equipment and this is what we had to do." So Atomic went back to its roots, spoke to its consumers, and created products that were true to its skiing heritage. They call this *authenticity*.

Atomic Skis analyzed the market in detail and looked at consumer needs in each of its market segments. Multiple focus groups were held with high-profile athletes, local ski superstars, buyers at ski stores, and top coaches to determine the real needs of skiers in each segment. An analysis showed there were four basic segments, each with different needs and common characteristics from a psychographic (lifestyle and interests) and behavioural (product usage and benefit) perspective. Atomic Skis asked consumers two basic questions, "Where do you ski?" and "How do you ski?" This provided insight into target group aspirations and what drives skiing decision-making and product selection. Atomic Skis needed to understand skiers' product needs for groomed runs versus deep powdered snow, and for multiple terrains versus the backcountry. Atomic Skis also needed to understand the punishment that ski equipment undergoes so that it could create authentic equipment that meets consumer needs and expectations.

Atomic Skis segmented the ski market into four basic categories: (1) free-skiers, (2) recreational all-mountain skiers, (3) women, and (4) high-performance racers. Let's look at these segments in more detail to find out how they differ.

- **Free-skiers:** This market consists of people who live for the sport. They are passionate skiers who search for adventure in their sport and know exactly what they need in a ski. They ski on runs that are not groomed and enjoy skiing in the backcountry with ski-lift access. These skiers are 15 to 35 years old, well-informed about their sport, and moderately brand loyal. Performance of a ski is the most important buying variable. Graphic design plays a less important role, but it is still important, and manufacturers need to incorporate graphics that are youthful, modern, and edgy.
- **Recreational all-mountain skiers:** This segment consists of casual skiers who are less knowledgeable about ski products. They tend to be recreational skiers with purchase decisions rooted in the *appearance* of the ski rather than its *performance*. They want a ski that expresses a youthful attitude that is tempered by age. These skiers are somewhat conservative, in the 35-to-50-year age bracket, and design conscious. They prefer safe, appealing graphics and are moderately brand loyal.
- **Women:** The women's market is the fastest-growing segment in the ski business and has evolved from recreational skiers looking for fashionable skis, to a segment that includes women with a wide range of abilities. Women in this segment include recreational skiers through to advanced athletes—all of whom have specific ski needs. Body shape, size, and strength all dictate different ski construction relative to products used by male skiers. Female skiers are also more design-oriented and tend to select skis based on trends and graphic design rather than performance. They have little brand loyalty.
- **Racers:** These are the high-performance athletes, men and women, looking for reliable, leading-edge equipment that delivers results. Their focus is on training, and product performance is critical to their decision making. Graphics need to be minimized, be very conservative, and heavily emphasize brand names and logos. These skiers are highly brand loyal.

For each of these segments Atomic Skis develops specific products and crafts marketing programs that meet the expectations of each target group. Let's look in detail at the free-skiing segment to understand how Atomic Skis caters to this specific target group and builds authenticity into its business.

LEARNING OBJECTIVES

L1 Explain market segmentation and its relevance to marketing

L2 Describe and differentiate among the different forms of market segmentation

L3 Outline the steps involved in segmenting a market

L4 Create a target market profile

L5 Position a product in the market and develop a positioning map

The free-skiing segment consists of people who intimately understand their equipment needs. This group felt Atomic Skis was missing the mark with its products and it wanted a product that really delivered. Atomic Skis realized new product development was crucial to business success and made this its priority and starting point. The company signed top North American skier Chris Benchetler to work with its research and development team on the structure, design, and construction of a new ski that would carry his name. After countless months, the Bent Chetler ski was created to deliver high-performance skiing on both firm snow and powdery terrains. The ski was specially constructed with technical expertise to be durable, impact resistant, and fun for aggressive skiers who wanted

Chris Benchetler in action with the new Atomic Bent Chetler ski.

high-end performance and to get the most out of their mountain experience. Loud and funky graphics were created to house the ski and appeal to this target group, who wanted edginess in design.

Looking to emphasize the authenticity, Chris Benchetler was also asked to design the graphics for this new ski and worked with Atomic Skis to ensure that graphic designs met technical requirements. "Social media has put marketing on alert," states Kyle McCarthy. "If our skis do not deliver, or we just slap an athlete's name on a product that does not meet the mark, it will be all over Twitter and Facebook in days. We have to stay true to our consumers and to our brand, and deliver *authentic* products that are top quality, technically advanced, and visually pleasing. The Bent Chetler ski is authentic from the very start to the finish; it was created, designed, and envisioned by Chris for our consumers, making sure it met requirements for free-skiing experts."

Looking at the marketing mix for the Bent Chetler ski, this product is priced in the $900 range, in line with competitive products and with what these passionate skiers are willing to pay for high-performance skis. It is sold nationally at sporting goods retailers, independent ski stores, and ski resorts. When it comes to promotion, it is promoted through the sponsorship of free-skiing athletes such as Chris Benchetler and other top athletes

who race in competitions such as the X Games, which provide high levels of TV exposure for Atomic Skis. The skis are also featured in quality ski films that feature ski footage from these top athletes and are watched by avid ski fans. These ski films are released on DVDs, sold at ski shops, premiered at ski film festivals in Montreal and Calgary, and shown at a number of universities and high-profile venues across Canada. These films also have strong online presence at related websites where Atomic Skis has strong presence. Atomic Skis has moved its focus away from using magazine-based print ads that have limited exposure, to using tools that maximize its messaging on the slopes, at events, online, and in high-profile ski films.

The marketing program for the Bent Chetler ski is indeed authentic from the start to the finish. Atomic Skis took a real look at this market segment and designed a product and other elements of the marketing mix to deliver outstanding value and true communications to knowledgeable free-skiers. Having worked for over 20 years in the ski business, in roles ranging from racer to coach to sports psychologist to technical rep, Kyle McCarthy understands that working with top athletes to design products and other marketing elements adds a new level of authenticity to Atomic Skis' products. McCarthy combines his industry knowledge with his business acumen and passion for the sport to drive growth for Atomic Skis on its new authenticity platform. You can find out more about Atomic Skis at www.atomicsnow.com.[1] 🍎

As you read Chapter 6, refer back to the Atomic Skis vignette to answer the following questions:

- What form of market segmentation is Atomic Skis using: mass marketing, segment marketing, niche marketing, or individualized marketing?

- What is the demographic profile of Atomic's free-skier segment?

- What is the behavioural profile of Atomic's free-skier segment?

Market Segmentation

The essence of market segmentation, target markets, and product positioning is based on three important facts. First, consumers have diverse needs, and a single product cannot satisfy everyone. Second, companies have finite amounts of money and it needs to be spent efficiently and effectively on consumers who are most likely to purchase the product. Marketers do not want to waste their resources by focusing on all consumers with the hope that someone may be interested in their product. The market is too competitive for this to work, and there is an abundance of information on consumers that can help effectively channel resources. Third, as demonstrated in the vignette on Atomic Skis, marketers need to have clear consumer insights on their target markets in terms of product needs, price expectations, purchase habits, and the communication tools used to gather information, stay informed, and be entertained.

In simple terms, a market segment means a piece of the market. In the marketing world there are two main market segments: the consumer market and the business market. The **consumer market** consists of goods, services, and ideas that a person can purchase or support for his or her own personal use. The **business market** involves products that are purchased either to run a business or to be used as a component in another good or service. How a product is classified depends on its usage. Let's look at some examples to clarify this point. A person buys a new computer in order to e-mail friends, surf the Internet, and download music for entertainment. A company buys new computers to upgrade technology in the office and ensure that its business runs efficiently. The products are exactly the same. In the first instance, the computer is a consumer product for personal use; in the second instance, the computer is a business product for the office. There are many other similar examples, but it is important to understand that many products are tailored specifically for one market or the other, and not necessarily both. Heavy machinery used for landscaping is not a consumer product, and a comic book is not a business product.

Formally, **market segmentation** involves aggregating prospective buyers into groups that have common needs and respond similarly to marketing programs. These groups are relatively homogeneous and consist of people who are fairly similar in terms of their consumption behaviour, attitudes, and target market profiles.

There is normally more than one firm vying for the attention of prospective buyers in a market. This results in marketers following a strategy of **product differentiation** to position their products apart from the competition in the eyes of consumers. It is important to note that product differentiation does not mean a product has to be better than the competition. Marketers position their products as best they can to meet the needs of their target consumers. Sometimes this may mean adding a unique feature; other times it may mean minimizing all costs to provide a cheaper alternative to the market.

Forms of Market Segmentation

There are a number of different approaches companies can take to segment the market. Whether a company is in the business-to-business market or the consumer market, it can follow one of these four approaches: mass marketing, segmented marketing, niche marketing, or individualized marketing.

In simple terms, a market segment means a piece of the market.

consumer market
Consists of products, ideas, and services that a person can purchase or support for personal use

business market
Products that are purchased either to run a business or to be used as a component in another product or service

market segmentation
The aggregation of prospective buyers into groups that have common needs and respond similarly to marketing programs

product differentiation
Involves positioning a product apart from the competition in the eyes of consumers

The Core: Chapter 6

Market segmentation, target marketing, and product positioning are interdependent.

Market Segmentation → Product Positioning ← Target Market Profile

Mass Marketing This approach exists in a limited capacity today due to the competitiveness of the market and the need for marketers to specifically address consumer needs with their offerings. **Mass marketing** involves a product being marketed to the entire market with no differentiation at all. Examples can be found in the utilities area with items such as natural gas being marketed with no differentiation from either a product or marketing perspective. Propane for gas barbecues also follows this approach to segmentation in both the business and consumer markets. In the consumer market, one can buy small propane gas tanks for outdoor barbecues; in the business-to-business market, companies such as Superior Propane sell bulk propane to businesses, filling super-sized, permanent tanks with propane.

Segment Marketing

This form of market segmentation is the most common form of segmentation followed by large companies. **Segment marketing** involves designing specific products and services to meet the needs of different target groups. Examples of this approach can be seen in the breakfast cereal category with companies such as General Mills and Kellogg's, or in the beverage industry with organizations such as Coca-Cola and PepsiCo. This approach was also followed by Atomic Skis with its ski equipment.

Let's examine the Kellogg's brand approach to market segmentation. Kellogg's has a host of breakfast cereals that appeal to different market segments. If we look at the cereal market in general there are products that appeal to different demographic and psychographic groups. For example, there are adult-oriented, healthy cereals; fun,

> "A SEGMENTED APPROACH IS ALSO FOLLOWED BY COMPANIES IN THE BUSINESS-TO-BUSINESS MARKET."

pre-sweetened children's cereals; and wholesome family cereals that are neither too healthy nor too sweet. In 1906, Kellogg's started the cereal business as the Battle Creek Toasted Corn Flake Company with only one product, Kellogg's Corn Flakes. This product was marketed to everyone, and Kellogg's followed a mass-marketing approach. Now, generations later, Kellogg's is a company with multiple cereal products and brands that appeal to different market segments. It now follows a segment-marketing approach, using different products to meet the needs of different target groups. For example, for the mainstream health-oriented adult, Kellogg's has All Bran, Special K, and Muslix. For families who demand fun, pre-sweetened cereals, Kellogg's offers Froot Loops, Mini-Wheats, and Frosted Flakes. For wholesome family goodness, consumers can choose from Rice Krispies, Corn Flakes, and Corn Pops.

Each product not only caters to the specific product needs of individual target markets but also has its own marketing programs to ensure that each target group's needs are properly met. If you look at the packages for these products, they reflect the different target market interests and needs. Mini-Wheats, for example, has a fun package that uses bright colours and a cartoon-type character to appeal to young families. All Bran, targeting an older, more serious group, has more subdued graphics, muted tones, and a clear focus on dietary needs.

Similarly, each product's promotional programs are designed to speak to each target group in a different manner. All Bran ads are serious in tone, focus on nutrition, and are placed in consumer magazines geared to older adults, such as *Canadian Gardening*. Mini-Wheats, on the other hand, is geared to young families and uses catchy TV ads with jingles and fun graphics placed around family-oriented programming to appeal to parents with young families.

A segmented approach is also followed by companies in the business-to-business market. This is evident in the food-service industry where companies create specific products to meet the needs of their large customers. A product such as Bick's pickles may be created for a large fast-food chain, designed to meet this key account's specifications. The product would be sliced in a particular fashion to meet the specific requirements of this chain; it would be flavoured to meet its specifications, and it may be packaged in plastic packaging to fit the equipment needs of the fast-food outlet. Bick's pickles may also create a customized pickle product for another key account. This time the product may be packed in small glass jars, with a particular spice for a retail food chain, and packaged under the retailer's brand name. In both these business-to-business instances, customized products

marketing NewsFlash

Koodo Targets Youth Segment

In 2008 Koodo Mobile set tongues wagging with its in-your-face launch platform of neon, spandex-clad Koodo-cizers plastered on billboards, transit shelters, and posters in the streets of Vancouver, Edmonton, Calgary, Toronto, and Montreal. Its campaign of "fat-free mobility" sent street teams of exercisers into the city inviting consumers to take part in the fun. TV ads spoofed exercise infomercials and spread the word of the new discount cellphone, Koodo, targeted at 18- to 25-year-olds. Koodo was a no-frills cellphone alternative of per-second billing with simple talk-and-text plans for consumers not wanting long-term contracts and Internet access. In year one, Koodo attained an outstanding 89 percent brand recognition level.

Three years later, Koodo continues to surprise with innovative marketing that flaunts its positioning as a fun, value-conscious brand for youth. The constant? Its cheeky, irreverent tone, bright neon colours, and use of outdoor media make a splash in the market, breaking through the clutter of competing messages. Creative online promotions bring additional focus to the brand and raise awareness among its target group. 2009

saw the introduction of Koodo's Sugar Streak interactive game on YouTube where players interacted with a virtual gingerbread man as he raced through city streets—the game had over a million views on YouTube. 2010 saw the introduction of the Build-a-Bash virtual all-ages party game on the BuildaBash.ca microsite where players searched for codes, played word games, and voted to win a dream party valued at $50,000. The El Tabador game was later uploaded to Koodo's YouTube channel for players to interact with a virtual boxing ring game to fight Bloatimus Contractimus.

One of its most successful promotions was Last Mask Standing, a partnership between Koodo and MuchMusic/MusiquePlus. Using the insight that its target market loves music, reality shows, and social networking, the promotion asked viewers to wear a Koodo-style mask and upload photos, videos, or documents to a microsite, explaining why they should be a finalist in the Last Mask Standing contest. Four finalists were selected on the basis of creativity, humour, originality, and relevance, and they were asked to compete

for the final prize of a March Break trip for four to Mexico. Finalists were flown to Toronto where they competed in silly activities such as slathering unknown persons with suntan lotion until the Last Mask Standing was selected based on accumulated points. Meanwhile, finalists spread the word through social networks, encouraging people to enter a separate contest to win a trip to Mexico. Media supporting the event included TV spots on MuchMusic/MusiquePlus, online Internet ads, social media blasts on Facebook and Twitter, and a MuchMusic-Koodo branded microsite.[2] ●

Questions

1. How does Koodo differentiate itself in the competitive cellphone market?

2. What form of market segmentation is Koodo following?

are being created for the company's key accounts. The business-to-business market is often segmented by the needs of key accounts.

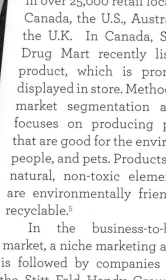

Niche Marketing   The type of market segmentation that allows a company to focus its efforts on a limited segment in the market is called **niche marketing**. Staying with the cereal market, the Kashi brand was launched by a small company with a niche-marketing approach that concentrated its efforts on cereals with all-natural ingredients. The Kashi brand does not try to sell to all market segments like the Kellogg's brand, but instead sells a line geared to health enthusiasts. Kashi's product line includes whole-grain varieties, high-fibre options, and organic varieties. Interestingly, Kashi's successful niche-marketing approach prompted its eventual acquisition by Kellogg's, which now carefully markets the brand separately from its Kellogg's products under its natural and functional foods division.[3] Understanding that the Kashi name is associated with purity and good health,[4] and that its niche market image led to its success among health enthusiasts, Kellogg's keeps the two brands totally separate.

On a similar note, Koodo (see the Marketing NewsFlash on page 125) markets to a young crowd of 18- to 25-year-olds who want only to talk, text, and use social media on their phones. One might consider this a niche market segmentation approach, but once we understand that Koodo is in fact owned by Telus Communications and marketed separately as its budget brand, we wonder whether this is really a segmented marketing approach. What do you think?

Smaller firms often adopt niche-marketing approaches to compete with large corporations that dominate categories. This can be seen with Method laundry detergent, which has gone up against P&G and Unilever head-on with its super-concentrated, non-toxic, biodegradable detergent that accurately dispenses the fluid with a pump rather than a pour-cap. The product is eight times more concentrated than conventional detergents and requires consumers to use 75 percent less detergent than the leading

Kashi launched with a niche market segmentation approach.

national brand. The carbon footprint of Method is 35 percent lower than standard double-concentrated detergents due its lower requirements for water, plastic, energy, and oil. Method laundry detergent was created in the year 2000 in a small apartment in San Francisco by two friends, Adam Lowry and Eric Ryan, and is now sold in over 25,000 retail locations in Canada, the U.S., Australia, and the U.K. In Canada, Shoppers Drug Mart recently listed the product, which is prominently displayed in store. Method's niche market segmentation approach focuses on producing products that are good for the environment, people, and pets. Products contain natural, non-toxic elements that are environmentally friendly and recyclable.[5]

In the business-to-business market, a niche marketing approach is followed by companies such as the Stitt Feld Handy Group, which provides services in training, negotiation, mediation, arbitration, and dispute resolution to corporations, government bodies, and their agencies. Stitt Feld Handy provides specialized services that assist in dispute resolution and conflict management. Its marketing efforts, directed specifically at this group, include targeted e-mail and mail campaigns, radio ads on 680 NEWS in Toronto, and newspaper ads in publications such as the *Toronto Star*. It also markets through specialized publications, association newsletters, and events. From an online perspective, it uses Facebook, YouTube, and pay-per-click advertising, and ensures that its website at www.sfhgroup.com is optimized for the search engines.

STITT FELD HANDY GROUP

EXPECT SUCCESS

Individualized Marketing New technology has boosted **individualized marketing** as a segmentation option for marketers. The Internet allows marketers to use database technology to track consumer purchases and predict interests and future purchases. This enables marketers to customize offers and, in some cases, products to fit individual needs.

Marketers are rediscovering today what previous generations knew running a general store a century ago. Every customer is unique, has particular wants and needs, and requires special care from the seller. Efficiencies in manufacturing and marketing during the past century made mass-produced goods so affordable that most customers were willing to compromise their individual tastes and settle for standardized products. Today's Internet ordering and flexible manufacturing and marketing approaches have facilitated individualized market segmentation by making it easier to tailor goods and services to suit individual customer needs.

Dell uses this approach in marketing its technology products to both the consumer and business markets. In the consumer market, it allows consumers to customize their purchases to meet individual needs. Dell's three-day deliveries, from time of order placement, are made possible by restricting its computer line to only a few basic models and stocking a variety of each. This gives customers a good choice with quick delivery. In the business-to-business market, Dell also offers a customized approach to its customers, providing the same custom-order approach, with the addition of leasing arrangements if requested.

Some companies in the service industry follow similar approaches by tracking individual preferences and sending offers that meet individual consumer requirements. If you use the same travel agent, visit the same restaurant, or buy concert tickets from the same online services, over time these companies will recognize and predict your needs, sending you information, offers, or special services that meet your requirements. For example, if you purchase vintage DVDs from Amazon.ca, the site may start sending you product alerts when similar products enter their portfolio.

The key to successful product differentiation and market segmentation strategies lies in finding the ideal balance between satisfying a customer's individual wants and being able to do this profitably. A company will go to the trouble and expense of segmenting its markets when it expects this will ultimately increase its sales, profits, and return on investment.

individualized marketing
Involves customizing offers and, in some cases, products to fit individual needs

ask yourself

1. What are the advantages of a segment-marketing approach to market segmentation?

2. Does Kashi still use a niche market segmentation approach?

3. What are the disadvantages of individualized market segmentation?

Steps in Market Segmentation

L③ Segmenting a market requires a number of skills. A marketer needs to combine strong analytical skills, sound strategic thinking, an understanding of the consumer, a vision on where the market is heading, and how this all fits with the company's direction. The process of segmenting a market for both the consumer and business-to-business market is divided into ten steps, which can be seen in Figure 6–1.

1. *Review strategic company objectives.* Objectives need to be clear and quantifiable. They should include sales, revenue, and profit targets, but also qualitative elements such as corporate social responsibility initiatives and new business direction for its divisions.

2. *Identify specific business unit objectives.* These objectives need to be in

Niche marketing can be used to compete with large established businesses.

line with a company's strategic direction and outline the specific sales, market share, and profit targets for the business unit.

3. *Identify consumer/customer needs and common characteristics in the market.* This should be done from a consumer/customer perspective, looking at what drives the category and what future trends are evolving. Marketers should be able to easily identify common interests and evolving trends by analyzing what products currently exist in the category, which areas of the market are expanding and shrinking, and where consumer/customer interests lie. Looking to other countries sometimes provides interesting ideas on where potential future interests may lie.

4. *Cluster common consumer/customer variables to create meaningful market segments.* A marketer needs to stand back from the market and look for clusters of products and gaps in the market that point to common consumer/customer interests, usage patterns, and prevailing attitudes. New areas of interest should not be overlooked as these may point to evolving segments. These clusters will identify the segments that exist in the market. Sometimes there is overlap between segments, and other times the segments are not well-defined, but this is generally a reflection of the consumers/customers who can be fickle and non-committal.

It is very important during this step to review the market from a consumer/customer perspective and not from a product perspective. For example, if we continue to review the cereal market, we may group products into those that contain whole grains and establish this as a segment. However, if we look at this category from a consumer perspective, we would see whole-grain products as only one of many appealing to health-conscious, adult consumers. The segment is in fact better defined, and more meaningful to marketers, when identified as appealing to health-conscious adults.

Groups of students were asked to review the cold-cereal market, to cluster consumer needs into possible market segments, and to give product examples for each segment. They came up with four main clusters that addressed the market's needs for health, taste, and nutrition, which are shown in Figure 6–2.

5. *Conduct SWOT analyses on the segments to determine strengths, weaknesses, opportunities, and threats.* A **SWOT analysis** can be conducted on many different areas in marketing. It is very

Figure 6–1
The ten-step process for segmenting a market

STEPS IN MARKET SEGMENTATION

1. Review strategic company objectives.
2. Identify specific business unit objectives.
3. Identify consumer/customer needs and common characteristics in the market.
4. Cluster common consumer/customer variables to create meaningful market segments.
5. Conduct SWOT analyses on the segments to determine strengths, weaknesses, opportunities, and threats.
6. Identify the segment that best meets strategic company objectives.
7. Identify marketing programs and budget requirements needed for this segment.
8. Create a sales forecast for this segment.
9. Conduct a profit-and-loss financial analysis for this segment.
10. Check financial forecasts against specific business unit objectives.

useful when analyzing a market as it can identify opportunities and whether a company has the strength to compete in a segment that may already be well-served by the competition. SWOT stands for *strengths*, *weaknesses*, *opportunities*, and *threats*. The strengths and weaknesses refer to the internal areas of a company or a product/brand. Examples may be the product image, its quality, or lack of advertising spending. The opportunities and threats look to areas outside the company, product, or brand, such as the competition, consumer trends, or technology. It is important to involve a number of people when conducting a SWOT analysis so that different perspectives and ideas are captured. A SWOT analysis is discussed more fully in Chapter 14.

6. *Identify the segment that best meets strategic company objectives.* At this point in the process, a marketer sifts through the facts and ideas that have surfaced during the SWOT analysis and generally assesses the opportunities and threats in relation to a company's strategic direction. A market segment may surface as particularly interesting at this point.

7. *Identify marketing programs and budget requirements needed for this segment.* If a particular segment has surfaced as an area of interest, it will require further investigation. This will include a full financial evaluation of the market to assess the costs of doing business and identify what programs are required to support an initiative. It also highlights what resources are needed to adequately compete in this segment.

> *SWOT stands for strengths, weaknesses, opportunities, and threats.*

Figure 6–2
Identifying consumer clusters

CONSUMER CLUSTERS EXAMPLE: COLD CEREALS		
CONSUMER CLUSTER	**CLUSTER ATTITUDES**	**PRODUCT EXAMPLES**
Adults with dietary needs	Feeling healthy Taste is secondary	All Bran Fibre First
Adults focused on taste and nutrition	Nutrition is key Taste is important Not health fanatics	Oatmeal Crisp Muslix
Families looking for fun and taste	Family-oriented Want kids to eat breakfast Taste is important Nutrition is not as important as taste	Froot Loops Nesquik
Families focused on wholesome goodness	Taste and nutrition are both important Good family health is key	Cheerios Rice Krispies

8. *Create a sales forecast for this segment.* Once a thorough market assessment has been conducted, a marketer is tasked with forecasting the sales potential for this segment, which should also consider anticipated competitive reactions.

9. *Conduct a profit-and-loss financial analysis for this segment.* The marketing programs, budget requirements, and sales forecasts are put together with projected costs to determine what level of profits can be achieved in this market segment. A projected profit-and-loss statement is created to assess the financial viability of doing business in this market segment. Marketers often work with financial analysts to determine these costs.

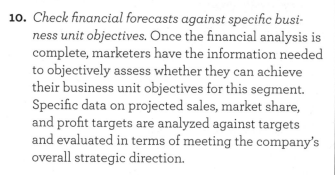

Who is the target market for the Smart car?

10. *Check financial forecasts against specific business unit objectives.* Once the financial analysis is complete, marketers have the information needed to objectively assess whether they can achieve their business unit objectives for this segment. Specific data on projected sales, market share, and profit targets are analyzed against targets and evaluated in terms of meeting the company's overall strategic direction.

Target Market Profiles

L❹ Marketers need to have a clear understanding of what drives their consumers, what delights them, and what does not. This helps marketers develop meaningful consumer products, design programs that meet consumer needs, and communicate to consumers in the manner in which they are accustomed. Developing an accurate target market profile is crucial to the success of all marketing initiatives as it drives all elements of the marketing mix. This profile is created by marketers, updated periodically as new information surfaces, and included in an area dedicated to ensuring that this information is readily available to marketers as they work on the business. Target market profiles are usually included in annual marketing plans and in strategic documents that relate to a specific product.

Marketers define their target markets by looking at four main variables: (1) geographics, (2) demographics, (3) psychographics, and (4) behaviouristics. In marketing, all these variables are identified to clearly describe a target market so that when a marketer develops programs to meet this target group's needs, there is no confusion as to what drives this target market. Figure 6–3 on page 132 clearly outlines these four variables.

Geographics

A **geographic** descriptor of a target market looks at where a target market lives using variables such as country, region, province, city size, and type of location such as urban, suburban, or rural. Marketers often find that Canadians differ in terms of needs or preferences based on where they live. An example is found in the flour industry: Consumers in Western Canada tend to buy larger packages than in Ontario and Quebec due to a greater incidence in baking. Another example is a product such as the Smart car, which is small and compact and geared toward urban dwellers. The target market for this car mainly resides in city centres.

Demographics

One of the easiest factors to determine is the **demographic** profile of a target market. This includes identifying ranges for age, gender, family life cycle, income, occupation, education, ethnic background, and home ownership for the main target market. This information can be identified through a company's market research information and other secondary data sources such as Statistics Canada. An example of where demographics play a leading role in a target market profile is with the Centrum vitamin brand. Centrum markets many of its products based on age and gender requirements. Centrum Select 50+ is formulated for adults over 50 years of age; Centrum Materna is a pre-natal vitamin created for pregnant women; and Centrum Junior is geared to children between the ages of 2 and 12.

Other examples of demographic descriptors

of target markets can be seen with the *Canadian Business* magazine and the MSN.ca website. *Canadian Business*, with over a million readers, identifies the demographic profile of its readers as being primarily male with an average age of 43 and an average annual household income over $95,000. MSN.ca has a variety of demographic profiles depending on the pages being visited within the web portal. MSN.ca is organized by channels of interest such as automobiles, astrology, shopping, music, money, news, sports, and travel. One of its latest web channels is Delish, an online destination for aspiring cooks that provides its mainly female target market with recipes, downloadable grocery lists, cooking videos, and the ability to interact with other food enthusiasts. In contrast, the MSN.ca Sports web channel is directed mainly to men and provides sports news, scores, analysis, quizzes, and blogs for sports enthusiasts.

Psychographics

Psychographics is one of the most difficult variables to identify for marketers. It involves understanding consumers' attitudes to life, their personalities, general interests, opinions, and activities. This information is generally based on the primary research that marketers have conducted to gather insights on their consumers. Psychographic variables are central to

understanding the delight points of consumers and what gives them that extra spark. Image-based products gear much of their marketing efforts around these psychographic variables.

The fragrance industry, for example, relies heavily on psychographics, as do many soft drink companies. Reflect for a minute on Coca-Cola, positioned as a traditional, refreshing soft drink rooted in old-fashioned Americana. Now think of Pepsi-Cola, marketed as the energetic cola for those with a youthful attitude to life. The products may vary only slightly in taste, but their target markets differ considerably in attitudes, interests, and opinions. Coca-Cola and Pepsi-Cola use psychographics as main variables in their marketing efforts.

Koodo, discussed in the Marketing NewsFlash on page 125, targets a young demographic of people between the ages of 18 and 25 years. When designing a marketing communications program to communicate with this target group, Koodo needed to understand the psychographic profile of this target market. It determined this included a love of social media, computer games, YouTube, and spending time on the Internet. Using this information it created Facebook pages, YouTube channels, and interactive online games to engage with its audience.

The Bent Chetler ski, discussed in this chapter's opening vignette and shown here, was designed by the athlete specifically to appeal to the psychographic profile of the product's target market. Looking at this ad, the graphics of the ski, and the information provided in the opening vignette, what psychographic information can you glean about the target market?

THE NEW ATOMIC BENT CHETLER

CHRIS BENCHETLER HAS BUILT YOU A SKI

What is the psychographic profile of the Bent Chetler ski?

Behaviouristics

Behaviouristics directly refers to how consumers use the product. It looks at why consumers buy a product, the product benefit, how the product is used, and whether consumers are brand loyal in their purchase behaviour. Usage rate also plays a role in this information. The cellphone industry often uses behaviouristics to market to its customers, focusing on the key benefits that consumers require in a cellphone. Koodo, for example, markets basic cellphone services to young adults who want cheap, no contract, talk, text, and social media plans. Rogers, on the other hand, frequently targets customers that require data plans to conveniently access the Internet on their smartphones. Its customers value long-term contracts in exchange for high-tech communication devices.

Figure 6–3
Segmentation variables and breakdowns for Canadian consumer markets

TARGET MARKET PROFILES		
CATEGORIES	**VARIABLES**	**TYPICAL BREAKDOWNS**
Geographics	Region	Atlantic; Quebec; Ontario; Prairies; British Columbia
	City or census metropolitan area (CMA) size	Under 5,000; 5,000–19,999; 20,000–49,000; 50,000–99,999; 100,000–249,000; 250,000–499,999; 500,000–999,000; 1,000,000–3,999,999; 4,000,000+
	Density	Urban; suburban; rural
	Climate	Cold; warm
Demographics	Age	Infant; under 6; 6–11; 12–17; 18–24; 25–34; 35–49; 50–64; 65+
	Gender	Male; female
	Family size	1–2; 3–4; 5+
	Stage in family life cycle	Teenager; young single adult; young married, no children; young married, youngest child under 6; young married, youngest child 6 or older; older married, with children; older married, no children under 18; older single; other older married
	Income	Under $10,000; $10,000–19,999; $20,000–29,999; $30,000–39,999; $40,000–54,999; $55,000–74,999; $75,000+
	Occupation	Professional; managerial; clerical; sales; labourer; student; retired; housewife; unemployed
	Education	Grade school or less; some high school; high school graduate; some college; college graduate
	Ethnic background	Country of origin
	Home ownership	Own home; rent home
Psychographics	Personality	Gregarious; compulsive; extroverted; introverted
	Lifestyle	Structured; discontented; fearful; assured; resentful; caring
Behaviouristics	Benefits sought	Nutrition; entertainment; status
	Usage rate	Light user; medium user; heavy user
	User status	Non-user; ex-user; prospect; first-time user; regular user
	Loyalty status	None; some; medium; strong

Canada.com Site – Statistics and Demographic Profile

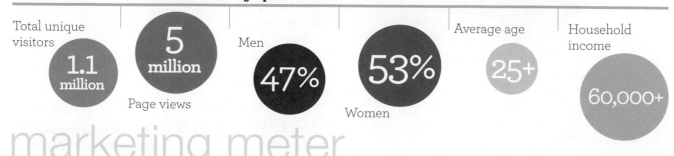

Total unique visitors 1.1 million

5 million Page views

Men 47%

Women 53%

Average age 25+

Household income 60,000+

marketing meter

Psychographic Interests of Generation Y

- Visiting Facebook and YouTube websites
- Spending 10 hours per week on the Internet
- Watching TV programs on the Internet
- Multitasking while watching TV
- Recording TV or time-shifting
- Spending 11 hours per week watching regular TV

Source: "TV Still Tops with Gen Y... For Now," *Marketing* magazine, November 12, 2008, accessed September 2010, at http://www.marketingmag.ca/news/marketer-news/tv-still-tops-with-gen-y-for-now-18427.

An example of how usage rate plays a role in marketing can be seen with the fast-food industry. Research indicates that for every $1 spent by a light user in a fast-food restaurant, a heavy user spends over $5.[6] Marketers may focus on the heavy user in this market to yield a greater return on investment.

Often students wonder why it is important to identify all these variables when describing a target market. If someone is buying chewing gum, what is the relevance of their income level, or where they live? In fact, usually only a few elements in a target market profile are the main determinants in why a consumer purchases a product. Nonetheless, all variables need to be included in the target market profile as this profile is used extensively in other marketing areas. If elements are missing, crucial errors could be made. For example, a target market profile is used extensively when creating advertising programs. The consumer insights are used to help develop campaigns that talk to the target group and media is bought against this target market profile.

Let's assume we are marketing a video on hockey heroes and are considering an online campaign to market to consumers. The MSN.ca website is suggested as an option for running banner ads on its sports page. If we navigate to the advertising area of the MSN site and look at its sports section, it provides us with demographic information on the target market of this site. If the target market profile for the hockey video matches all these variables, then this site would be an appropriate advertising option. However, if the marketers failed to provide enough information, marketers may not know whether this website is appropriate to market the product.

Target Market Profile
Canadian Business Magazine

Gender	Men/women	66%/34%
Age	Average	43 years
Occupation	Managers/owners/professionals	33%
Income	Average household income	$95,956
Reading time	Per issue	37 minutes

Source: *Canadian Business Media Kit 2010*, page 7.

ask yourself

1. What are the steps involved in market segmentation?
2. What elements are included in demographics?
3. What is the difference between psychographics and behaviouristics?

Product Positioning

One of the central elements in marketing is product positioning. Marketers position products in the market to appeal to certain target groups and to present a particular impression relative to the competition. **Product positioning** refers to the impression of the product you want to establish in consumers' minds relative to their needs and also in contrast to the competition. Companies generally use a combination of factors to position their products, always leading with the elements that are real, differentiate the product, and create long-term, memorable impressions with consumers. In this way there are three basic factors, or combination of factors, that tend to surface in product positioning:

1. *Image*: Products are often positioned as leaders, contenders, or rebels in the market, also taking on characteristics such as trusted, prestigious, or thrifty. Koodo, for instance, positions itself as the thrifty, fun, humorous alternative in the cellphone carrier market, sparring with established players on elements such as long-term contracts and price. Bell, on the other hand, positions itself as a trusted leader in this category with claims such as "the best network" and "the best mobile screen."

2. *Product attribute:* Products with features that differentiate them from the competition are often positioned on this platform, bringing product claims to the forefront. The retailer Danier, for example, positions itself as the premier leather retailer in Canada, providing quality leather and suede for men and women. Its brand is synonymous with luxury, style, and value—a positioning that combines image, product attribute, and price. Danier uses its stylish, contemporary designs and collections to support this positioning.

3. *Price:* Products with brand parity and little product differentiation may position themselves on a price platform. Retailers such as Walmart position themselves as offering the lowest retail prices to support its image in the market.

Marketers create **positioning statements** to clearly and simply outline the positioning of a product in the market. These statements are used to crystallize the image for marketers so that they can design a marketing mix that aligns with the product's positioning. This is very important; otherwise the product may present a confusing image to consumers who will refrain from buying it. Similar to a target market profile, a positioning statement is generally included in an annual marketing plan and in relevant strategic documents.

Positioning statements are simple, clear, and focused. They identify the main reasons the target market buys the product and what sets it apart in the market. It is important to understand that a product's positioning is reflected in all areas of the marketing mix and one needs to look at each element of the marketing mix to accurately determine its positioning in the market. Positioning statements identify two

> ## "Positioning statements are simple, clear, and focused."

key areas: (1) how the product meets consumer needs, and (2) how the product is differentiated in the market versus the competition.

Students were asked to identify a positioning statement for the Kashi cereal brand. Their starting point was to research the cereal by visiting the company's website, seeing it in a store setting, sampling the product, examining its packaging, and reviewing its print ads. The students came up with the following positioning statement, which clearly and simply expresses the possible positioning of this product: *"Kashi cereal is positioned in the cold-cereal market as a great-tasting, all-natural, whole-grain cereal, perfect for people who want to lead healthy lives. It focuses on all-natural ingredients."* For the product's competitive stance the students mentioned that the cereal was positioned as being healthier and more natural than competing brands, making it a good choice for health enthusiasts.

Positioning statements are this clear and focused. They average a short paragraph and identify four elements: (1) the product name, (2) the category in which the product competes, (3) one or two main reasons that the target market buys the product (product benefits), and (4) what sets the product apart from the competition.

Joe Fresh Style, highlighted in the Marketing NewsFlash opposite, directly competes with George fashions from Walmart and Attitude garments from Sears. Write a positioning statement that clearly outlines Joe Fresh Style's positioning in the market and identifies its positioning versus the competition.

Breakfast is a new focus for McDonald's.

Joe Fresh Style, Loblaw's budget fashion brand, set the Canadian fashion industry on fire in 2006 when it launched a collection of trendy, value-priced clothing across Canada in anticipation of Walmart entering the Canadian food industry and impacting profits. Originally designated for Loblaw Superstores, Joe Fresh Style is now conveniently sold at approximately 350 Loblaw-owned supermarkets across Canada including Loblaw, Fortinos, and the Real Canadian Superstore. Its target market of fashionable, thrifty shoppers, soccer moms, and young working adults do not blink at placing a fashionable sweater in among the vegetables in their grocery carts.

Five years later, Joe Fresh Style is the second-largest clothing label in Canada, is the top-selling children's brand in the country, and is positioned to hit its all-time sales' target of $1 billion. The appeal: trendy, stylish, and affordable products are in line with the food retailer's image, which is indeed trendy and affordable.

The competition is fierce in the affordable clothing segment with major retailers such as Sears and Walmart competing for the same consumer dollar. Multinational clothing retailers, such as H&M from Sweden, Zara and Mango from Spain, and Forever 21 from the U.S., also enjoy successful footholds in this market with fast-fashion that places fashionable items in stores within six weeks. However, Loblaw, no slouch at marketing, realizes its competitive advantage lies not only in its trendy, affordable styles but also with the daily foot traffic generated by its loyal grocery shoppers.

Competitive reaction to Joe Fresh Style has heated up with Walmart and Sears revamping their product lines and launching or re-staging brands and collections to compete head-on with Canada's new fashion brand. In 2010 Walmart revamped and re-launched its George line of budget clothing, eliminating its other private-label clothing lines and retro fitting 319 stores to showcase George within stores. 2009 also saw Sears launch its value-priced Attitude brand of clothing in 100 department stores to attract modern shoppers in their 40s who may not consider Sears for purchasing clothes.

Nonetheless, Loblaw seems to be one step ahead. To solidify its positioning as the new stylish affordable clothing brand, in late 2009, it rolled out Joe Fresh Beauty and Joe Fresh Bath, lines of beauty and bath products that, true to the brand, offer consumers quality products that are fashionable and affordable. Joe Fresh expanded its brand positioning so that its customers can feel stylish from head to toe at affordable prices, including cosmetics and skincare.

In 2010 and 2011, combating increased marketing efforts from Walmart and Sears, Joe Fresh stepped up its marketing programs. High-profile TV, print, and billboard campaigns ran while it continued its customer relationship marketing (CRM) efforts at joe.ca and maintained its associations with Toronto Fashion Week and the Rethink Breast Cancer Foundation. Joe Fresh also started opening standalone stores in popular shopping destinations such as its new flagship Joe Fresh stores in Vancouver and Toronto and an international flagship store on New York City's Fifth Avenue. To learn more about Joe Fresh, visit its website at joe.ca.[7]

Questions

1. What factor, or combination of factors, is Joe Fresh Style considering in its positioning: image, product attribute, or price?

2. Who is the target market for Joe Fresh? Describe it in terms of (1) geographics, (2) demographics, (3) psychographics, and (4) behaviouristics.

Repositioning

Companies rarely change a product's positioning but do so when long-term changes in consumer attitudes require a shift to more accurately reflect consumer needs. **Repositioning** is often done with a refresh of a product and the various elements of its marketing mix. McDonald's is a recent example of a repositioning effort that includes interior and exterior store design, healthier menu choices, product ingredient changes, new website components, and focused advertising messages. We see trans fats being eliminated from McDonald's products, healthy choices included on the menu, nutrition calculators appearing on its website, and the store ambience modified to be more comfortable and inviting. McDonald's is repositioning itself as a more engaging fast-food restaurant, offering not only the healthier food choices consumers are demanding but also an

repositioning
A revamping of a product and its marketing mix to more accurately meet consumer needs

environment where a more comfortable setting is available for consuming products at all times of day. Its most recent focus on breakfast foods and breakfast beverages fits into this repositioning and is successfully driving traffic in store during the morning—a traditional slow time for McDonald's. See the Marketing NewsFlash opposite.

Positioning Maps

Positioning maps, also known as perceptual maps, are visual representations of how products or product groups are positioned within a category to consumers/customers. Positioning maps can visually represent categories within a market, or more specifically, product and brand offerings within a segment. Positioning maps are useful tools for marketers as they can reveal gaps in the market where consumers may be underserved, while also highlighting the competitive nature of the category.

Positioning maps need to clearly identify the two most important attributes that drive purchases in a category, whether this is in the business-to-business or the consumer market. One must be able to assess these attributes objectively from a consumer perspective. One might rush to immediately identify price as a key variable, but often, this is a less important feature, evaluated by consumers once a short list of attributes on which they initially evaluate a purchase are identified. Let's make this clearer with two

How is this beverage positioned in the market?

examples. First, in the cereal market, nutrition and sweetness might be key attributes used by parents of young children to evaluate product offerings. (Price would come into play later in the purchase decision.) These factors of nutrition and sweetness can be objectively used to evaluate products in the category and identify how one product is positioned against another. In a second example, if one is looking at this category from the perspective of very health-oriented consumers, one might set different parameters to evaluate the product offerings. Natural ingredients and fibre content may instead play a central role in the consumer's decision to purchase a cereal, and these variables would be used by marketers for a positioning map.

The variables will change depending on what is important to a specific target group and in all instances the variables will need to be objective and measurable for marketers to use. Looking at the affordable fashion business where price is a key purchase variable for consumers, a positioning map in this instance will indeed include *price* and another variable such as *fashionable designs*. In this way, while Joe Fresh Style from Loblaw and George from Walmart may compete at the lower end of the scale against retailers such as H&M and Zara, other higher quality retailers may occupy other quadrants in the positioning map. Create your own positioning map for these and other brands in this market.

Figure 6–4 on page 138 shows a positioning map for the beverage industry using the measurable variables of nutrition and age. The positioning map shows

McDonald's repositioning is reflected in its new store designs.

milk, tea, sports drinks, fruit juices, and soft drinks rated relative to each other on these key elements. We can see diet drinks are geared to adults, while milkshakes appeal to teenagers.

Positioning maps can identify opportunities to launch new product offerings in the market. Staying with the beverage industry, in 2009, PepsiCo Canada introduced Aquafina Plus Vitamins 10 Cal beverage, a vitamin-enhanced water that contains PureVia™, an all-natural sweetener with less calories than sugar. The beverage contains 10 calories, comes in five varieties—Strawberry Lemonade, Black and Blue Berry, Fuji Apple Pear, Acai Fruit Punch, and Yumberry Pomegranate—is fortified with vitamins C, E, and B; and has no artificial flavours or preservatives.[8] What gap in the market

What gap in the market does this product fill?

did PepsiCo identify before it created this product? Where would you place this type of product on the beverage positioning map?

Similarly, Starbucks introduced a high-quality instant coffee, Starbucks VIA® Ready Brew, available in its cafes and in grocery stores in Canada. The product comes in multipacks of single-serve sachets that instantly dissolve in a cup of hot water, a departure from their fresh-brewed coffee served in their coffee shops. It is available in many varieties, including Colombia, Italian Roast, and Vanilla. What opportunity did Starbucks recognize in the market? Create your own positioning map for Aquafina Plus Vitamins 10 Cal and Starbucks Via Ready Brew in the beverage market.[9]

---

marketing **NewsFlash**   McDonald's Breakfast Success

McDonald's continues to refresh its image from that of a pure fast-food restaurant to one where you can also sit, relax, and enjoy a cup of coffee in comfortable leather chairs while those in a rush can grab a quick burger on-the-go. Keeping abreast of consumer trends, McDonald's is transforming the decor and menu of its Canadian fast-food outlets to also compete with coffee shops such as Starbucks and Tim Hortons. A new coffee culture in Canada sees consumers flocking to Starbucks and Tim Hortons for a morning cup of coffee, and research showed that coffee was the number one breakfast item purchased. The destination of choice was not McDonald's, which lacked a quality image in this area, seen instead as a lunchtime destination.

Rising to the challenge, many McDonald's fast-food outlets have been redesigned to include fireplaces, leather chairs, and plasma-screen televisions for the coffee-loving crowd. McDonald's also put a renewed focus on its breakfast fare, energizing its offerings with both new food and beverage choices. Premium roast coffee was made available in regular and decaf varieties, as well as high-quality teas such as Earl Grey, Orange Pekoe, Peppermint, and Green Tea. Fresh Canadian eggs became the centrepiece of Egg McMuffin ads, followed by a free coffee promotion that gave away

small coffees during breakfast hours. This culminated with a campaign spotlighting McDonald's Breakfast Burritos, McGriddles, and McMuffins, all supported with TV spots, radio ads, billboards, microsites, and social networking campaigns. The free coffee event used a giant steaming coffee cup on high-profile city streets in Toronto, Montreal, Vancouver, and Calgary to draw attention to its new coffees.

The results speak for themselves: Over a one-year period, morning restaurant traffic at McDonald's increased 18 percent, coffee sales grew 28 percent, and breakfast sales were up 9 percent.[10]

Questions

1. List the consumer trends being addressed by McDonald's with its food and beverage breakfast initiative.

2. What variables are important to consumers purchasing fast food? Consider these variables and then review McDonald's competitors to create a positioning map that positions McDonald's in relation to other fast-food outlets, such as Harvey's, Burger King, Wendy's, and KFC.

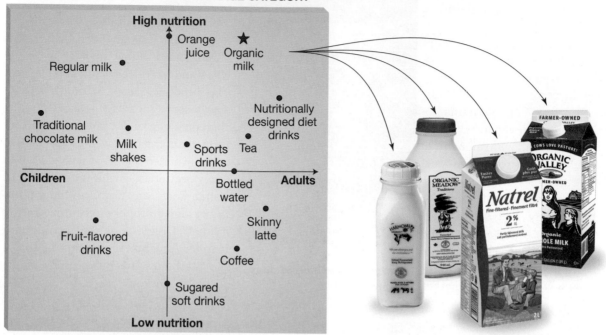

POSITIONING MAP FOR THE BEVERAGE CATEGORY

Market Segmentation, Target Markets, and Product Positioning in Practice

Segmentation, target markets, and positioning are fundamental concepts central to how marketers run their businesses. When creating marketing plans and developing marketing ideas to increase sales, marketers immediately look to how their products are positioned in the market, consult with positioning statements, and then use the target market profiles to ensure that all elements are true to the image of their products. A mistake in this area could mean losing your consumers and clouding the image of your product in the market. Marketers are careful to ensure that all elements of the marketing mix are well-coordinated to meet the product's positioning and target market expectations.

Market segmentation helps marketers place their product offerings in the context of a competitive market. It allows them to see the bigger picture from a consumer perspective, and to focus on how competitors are servicing consumer needs. A market segmentation analysis also allows a marketer to identify gaps in the market and determine where future opportunities may lie.

Marketers such as Kyle McCarthy at Atomic Skis use these approaches to ensure that their product offerings and marketing programs are fresh, relevant, and focused. This approach helps maintain a competitive edge in the market and helps marketers to stay in touch with the latest trends. Market segmentation, target markets, and positioning are key factors in the world of marketing.

ask yourself

1. What is product positioning?

2. What is the purpose of a positioning statement?

3. Why do marketers use positioning maps?

> " A MARKET SEGMENTATION ANALYSIS ALSO ALLOWS A MARKETER TO IDENTIFY GAPS IN THE MARKET AND DETERMINE WHERE FUTURE OPPORTUNITIES MAY LIE. "

[*adAlyze*]

What demographic profile is this ad targeting?

What psychographic interests can you determine about the target market from this ad?

For more information visit www.porsche.ca

Hopefully, you'll run into your ex.

The new Boxster is here.

What behavioural insight can you determine about the target market from this ad?

Summary...*just the facts*

- Market segmentation involves aggregating prospective buyers into groups that have common needs and who respond similarly to marketing programs.
- In the marketing world there are two main market segments: (1) the consumer market and (2) the business market.
- Companies segment the market using the following four approaches: mass marketing, segmented marketing, niche marketing, and individualized marketing.
- Segmenting the market involves ten steps that require analytical skills, strategic thinking, an understanding of the consumer, a vision of where the market is heading, and how this fits with company objectives.
- Marketers define their target markets by looking at four main variables: (1) geographics, (2) demographics, (3) psychographics, and (4) behaviouristics.
- Geographics looks at where a target market lives using variables such as country, region, province, city size, and types of location such as urban, suburban, or rural.
- Demographics includes identifying ranges for age, gender, family life cycle, income, occupation, education, ethnic background, and home ownership.

- Psychographics involves understanding consumer attitudes to life, their personalities, general interests, opinions, and activities.
- Behaviouristics looks at why consumers buy a product, the product benefit, how the product is used, and whether consumers are brand loyal in their purchase behaviour. Usage rate also plays a role in this information.
- Product positioning refers to the image of the product in consumers' minds relative to the competition.
- Marketers create positioning statements to clearly and simply outline the positioning of a product.
- Repositioning includes a shifting of the product image and adjusting its marketing mix to more accurately meet consumer needs.
- Positioning maps are otherwise known as perceptual maps. They visually represent how products or product groups are positioned within a category to consumers.

Key Terms and Concepts...*a refresher*

behaviouristics *p. 132*
business market *p. 123*
consumer market *p. 123*
demographics *p. 130*
geographics *p. 130*
individualized marketing *p. 127*

market segmentation *p. 123*
mass marketing *p. 124*
niche marketing *p. 126*
positioning maps *p. 136*
positioning statement *p. 134*
product differentiation *p. 123*

product positioning *p. 133*
psychographics *p. 131*
repositioning *p. 135*
segment marketing *p. 124*
SWOT analysis *p. 128*

Hands-on...*apply your knowledge*

Positioning Assignment Atomic Skis markets its products to four distinct market segments: free-skiers, recreational all-mountain skiers, women, and racers. Review the opening vignette for Atomic Skis, taking note of the interests of the target markets, and determine which variables you think should be used for the two axes in a positioning map for this category. Create the positioning map and plot these categories on the map. Separately, review the opening vignette for information on the Bent Chetler ski and create a positioning statement for this product, ensuring that it (1) reflects the needs of the target market and (2) sets the product apart from the competition.

Reality Check...*reminder*

Refer back to this chapter's opening vignette and answer the Reality Check questions on page 122.

McGraw-Hill Ryerson
Connect. Learn. Succeed.

Get Connected.

Stay Connected.

Visit
www.mhconnect.ca
to learn more.

McGraw-Hill Ryerson

chapter 7

Products *and* Brands

Meeting customer needs is central to successfully marketing a product, whether it is a good, a service, or an idea. In this chapter we explore products and brands more thoroughly to understand how they are marketed. Creating a strong brand is no easy task, and marketers work to build brand images that are meaningful and real. Peter Furnish, director of retail experience at Virgin Mobile, takes us inside Virgin Mobile to explain how this brand, launched in Canada as recently as 2005, is now touted as one of Canada's "Superbrands."[1] "Virgin Mobile is a cheeky, youthful brand that is different, fun, and exciting. We're lucky to have Sir Richard Branson, a flamboyant personification of the brand, to flaunt Virgin Mobile and draw attention to the brand," states Furnish, who goes on to explain how Virgin Mobile in Canada has evolved from a virtual unknown to now being highly recognized as a fun, irreverent, and trusted brand champion. Let's look at how this brand evolved.

Launch year. In 2005 Virgin Mobile launched with a publicity stunt designed to get attention. Rebel billionaire Sir Richard Branson zip-lined into Dundas Square in Toronto; crushed three cars—inscribed with "High Rates," "Completely Confusing Mobile Service Contract," and "Hidden Fees"—with a monster Virgin Mobile truck; and freed three female models from the shackles of long-term contracts. The publicity stunt worked; Virgin Mobile

LEARNING OBJECTIVES

LO ① Distinguish between goods and services

LO ② Describe and apply the total product concept

LO ③ Differentiate between products, product lines, and product mixes

LO ④ Identify the ways consumer and business goods and services are classified

LO ⑤ Explain the elements of branding and how these can be protected

LO ⑥ Distinguish between the different types of brands that exist in the market

LO ⑦ Apply product and brand knowledge to ongoing marketing strategies

was portrayed in the media as the new and cheeky cellphone carrier with attitude! Despite the fun stunts, Furnish points out there are important core values that permeate Virgin businesses. Although these businesses may seem diverse, they are joined by these shared values. In Canada, Virgin lends its name to Virgin Mobile, Virgin Radio, Virgin Games (online gaming), and Virgin Money (credit cards). These core brand values are as follows:

- **Fun:** a youthful, energetic, and positive brand that people enjoy
- **Innovative:** a brand willing to incorporate proven changes that consumers embrace
- **High quality:** a brand associated with high quality, which is the entry price in the wireless category
- **Good value:** a brand that provides good value but is never positioned as the cheapest
- **Champion of customer service:** a brand that excels in customer service
- **Consumer advocate:** a brand that challenges big business practices for consumers

Launch year focused on communicating these core values and establishing strong retail distribution. Virgin Mobile was launched as the irreverent brand with *no* contracts, *no* hidden fees, and *no* complicated plans. It opened four Virgin Mobile stores and its salespeople, Mobile Mavericks, obtained distribution at over 1,500 Future Shop, Best Buy, Walmart, and Tbooth stores. Customer service was front and centre with a unique call centre of empowered employees who quickly solved problems without scripted messages. All employees, including the CEO, work in the call centre once a month to fully understand customer issues.

Year 2. The second year started with a major win: Business was strong and Virgin Mobile was honoured in its first year with the coveted J.D. Power and Associates Service Award™ for excellent customer service. (Virgin has been honoured with these awards for five consecutive years.) On the branding front, there were lessons learned. Brand awareness was growing, but Virgin Mobile needed to showcase its core values and concentrate on what it was rather than what it was *not*. The Virgin Mobile brand was perceived as a lightweight option rather than a new, high-quality, fun, and reliable alternative. Virgin tweaked its image to highlight its core values and introduced higher quality phones and a package redesign that improved its image. Packaging components were also reworked to be biodegradable. Classy black pamphlets replaced faded red graphics and point-of-sale material mirrored this higher quality image. Retail kiosks were rolled out into malls. The brand leveraged its British heritage with the launch of a Virgin music festival that flaunted Virgin as a hip brand with roots.

Year 3. Two years after launch, Virgin's brand values shone through. The brand was perceived as a high-quality, credible contender in the cellphone market and it continued to win customer service awards. Its focus was to solidify its position in the market. Virgin adjusted its programs and, staying true to its image as a consumer advocate, challenged big business on two fronts. First, Virgin Mobile offered a rate plan that gave consumers the ability to select their free-minute time block, and second, it challenged the industry to introduce wireless number portability between carriers. From a branding perspective, Virgin Mobile continued to upgrade its retail signage and leveraged its British heritage—this time launching a gala event for the global Virgin Unite charity in Canada, which raised over $2 million to help tackle youth homelessness and health issues in South Africa.

Year 4. After three successful years, Virgin Mobile earned the trust of Canadians and established itself as a legitimate player that offered value, quality, and fun to consumers. Its core values shone through but Virgin Mobile did not stand still. It leveraged its unique image to differentiate the brand from other carriers by using social media such as blogs, Twitter, Facebook, and YouTube to build emotional connections with consumers and portray Virgin as the fun mobile carrier with heart. Virgin Radio was also launched this year (licensed to a separate company),

with the same core values. Its constant on-air brand mentions benefited Virgin Mobile as it appealed to the same target audience.

Year 5. In its fifth year, Virgin Mobile expanded product offerings and solidified its image as the brand with heart. "Building a brand is a continuous process," explains Peter Furnish, who helped launch Virgin Mobile in Canada. "Great brands stand the test of time because they evolve, connect, and develop personalities that emotionally connect with people. Virgin is one of those brands that we constantly nurture to stay true to its core values and make meaningful connections with consumers." In year 5, Virgin Mobile added the latest smartphones, such as iPhones, BlackBerrys, and Androids, to its product line. It also focused on a membership program that offered Virgin Mobile users exclusive offers from Virgin America and Virgin Money, as well as unique access to concerts, music festivals, and sporting events. It also continued to support Virgin Unite fundraisers.

Today, Virgin Mobile Canada continues to emphasize that it is a brand with heart. Its new RE*Generation program encourages Virgin Mobile subscribers to volunteer their time for at-risk youth in exchange for Virgin rewards such as concert tickets and access to entertainment events across Canada.[2]

In a few short years, Virgin Mobile has created a strong brand in Canada and established itself as the fun, high-quality/good-value brand with heart. It is a fun, innovative brand that offers excellent customer service and additional benefits through its membership program. Its fun platform and image as the champion of local causes and worldwide issues helps separate it from other cellphone carriers and positions it as a brand with heart. In Canada, Virgin Mobile products are now sold in over 2,000 retail outlets, including over 250 Virgin Mobile stores, and it has over 1 million members. Check out its website at www.virginmobile.ca.[3] 🍎

As you read Chapter 7, refer back to this Virgin Mobile vignette to answer the following questions:

- What type of brand is Virgin Mobile: a manufacturer's brand, a private label brand, or a generic brand?

- Review the elements of a good brand name and discuss the strength of the Virgin Mobile brand name in the cellphone category.

- How does the Virgin Mobile brand distinguish itself from competitors in the cellphone category?

Marketing ▶ tip

Types of Products

L1 The essence of marketing lies in managing and developing products and brands such as Virgin Mobile that meet the needs of their target markets. In marketing, a **product** is a good, a service, or an idea, consisting of a bundle of tangible and intangible attributes. Tangible attributes include physical characteristics such as colour or sweetness, and intangible attributes include those aspects of a product that can't be "touched," such as how being a member of the Virgin Mobile club may make you feel.

Products can include a variety of things in either the online or offline environment. In the offline environment, examples of products are breakfast cereals, cars, or the emergency services provided by a hospital. In the online world, examples are search engines such as Google, micro-blogging sites such as Twitter, online gaming websites, and software websites such as McAfee, which sells downloadable software to protect computers from viruses and spyware. It is important to realize that with the widespread use of the Internet today, even offline products such as Virgin Mobile develop a strong web presence, realizing that the first point of contact with consumers is often online at a company website or on its Facebook page. Virgin Mobile creates synergy between its offline and online retail presence with an informative website, an interactive Facebook page, and a Twitter account that answers questions and sends out membership offers.

Products are divided into three main categories: (1) non-durable goods, (2) durable goods, and (3) services. **Non-durable goods** are items that do not last and that are consumed only once, or for a limited number of times. Examples of non-durable goods are food products and fuel. A **durable good** is a product that lasts for an extended period of time and encompasses items such as appliances, automobiles, and stereo equipment. **Services** are defined as intangible activities, benefits, or satisfactions such as banking, conducting an online search, visiting a doctor, taking a vacation, going to a movie, or taking an online course.

In the service industry, it is useful to distinguish between a company's primary service and its supplementary services. A bank's primary service may be providing bank accounts, but it also offers supplementary services such as parking, ABMs, foreign exchange transactions, and monthly statements. Supplementary services often allow products to differentiate their offerings from the competition while also adding value to consumers. Common supplementary services can include product updates, free delivery, complimentary consultations, order-taking, billing, and payment terms. Companies also offer free trials, online support services, complimentary webinars, or free subscriptions as added-value services to its customers. Virgin Mobile's supplementary services include a free membership rewards program that provides access to music events, contests, and special offers. Canada has a strong service-based economy, which makes up approximately 72 to 75 percent of its gross domestic product (GDP).[4]

It is important to realize that most products cannot be defined as "pure goods" or "pure services." In fact, in today's marketplace, firms often combine goods and services to offer a more competitive product to consumers.

product
A good, a service, or an idea consisting of tangible and intangible features

non-durable good
An item that does not last and is consumed only once, or for a limited number of times

durable good
An item that lasts over an extended number of uses

services
Intangible activities, benefits, or satisfactions

The Core: Chapter 7

There are many levels of product.

Core product

Actual product

Augmented product

It is important to manage all levels of a product to be competitive.

Many goods are augmented with intangible services such as warranties, websites, and online support. Services also use goods to ensure a more complete offering to consumers. A college or university, for example, provides educational services, but it also provides graduates with hard-copy diplomas and transcripts. Importantly, the online environment is giving rise to new **virtual services** that exist *only* online and have no form of person-to-person interaction or tangible component. Social media sites, online gaming sites, and online analytics are examples of virtual services.

As companies look at what they bring to market, there is a range from the tangible to the intangible, or goods-dominant to service-dominant. This is defined as the **service continuum** and is demonstrated in Figure 7–1 where the services continuum for a number of products is shown. Online analytics, nursing, and going to the theatre are examples of intangible, service-dominant activities, while salt, neckties, and dog food are goods-dominant. Fast-food restaurants are in the middle of the service continuum, offering a combination of both tangible and intangible goods and services; the food is the tangible good, while the courtesy, cleanliness, speed, and convenience are the intangible services they provide.

The Uniqueness of Services

There are four unique elements to services: intangibility, inconsistency, inseparability, and inventory. These four elements are referred to as the *four Is of services*.

Figure 7–1
The service continuum

What type of product is being marketed by the Royal Ontario Museum?

Intangibility Services are intangible; that is, for the most part, they cannot be held, touched, or seen before a purchase. In contrast, before purchasing a physical good, a consumer can touch a box of laundry detergent, kick a car tire, or sample a new beverage. Services tend to be more performance-oriented and, as experiences, cannot be tried before purchase. To help consumers assess and compare services, it is important for marketers to demonstrate the benefits of using the service. Techniques that are frequently used are online video testimonials or demonstrations that show the quality of a service. Online services often provide potential customers with free limited online trials or time-sensitive downloads as a means of testing out the service. A new successful approach that is prompting consumers to try new services (and goods) are the local "deal-of-the-day" e-mail campaigns from e-mail discount marketers such as Groupon, LivingSocial, or Dealicious.ca. Dealicious.ca is a Canadian venture started in 2010 that sends out daily e-mail blasts with local deals that are customized to 30 cities across Canada.

Inconsistency Developing, pricing, promoting, and delivering services is challenging because the quality of a service

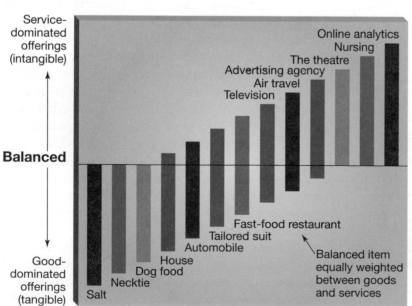

perishability
When products cannot be stored for long periods of time to use at a later date

idle production capacity
When the supply of a service exceeds its demand

> *In today's marketplace, firms often combine goods and services to offer a more competitive product to consumers.*

is dependent on the people who provide it and it can therefore vary in consistency. Quality can vary with each person's capabilities, experience, motivation, and even personality. One day the Toronto Blue Jays baseball team may have a great game, and then the next day it may have a very disappointing showing. Similarly, you may have a very successful stay at one location of a Travelodge hotel, but then have a terrible experience at another due to the varying standards of the staff at its locations. Companies try to overcome the inconsistent delivery of services by training employees on how to deliver a consistent quality experience. Virgin Mobile, discussed in the opening vignette of this chapter, is a recipient of the J.D. Power and Associates Service Award™ and prides itself on providing customers with exceptional customer service through training programs that empower each employee to solve customer inquiries quickly. Each employee spends time working the phones in the call centre to more fully understand customer needs.

Online products are often able to overcome issues of inconsistency through standardized software, consistent website interfaces, and reliable Internet servers that limit service disruptions. However, when new online services are launched, they often cannot keep up with demand and therefore provide subpar services to users. This was the case with the micro-blogging site Twitter, which was often overcapacity during its early days.

Inseparability A third difference between services and goods, and related to problems of consistency, is inseparability. In most cases, the consumer cannot (and does not) separate the deliverer of the service from the service itself. For example, in the non-profit industry, the quality of an educational institution may be high, but if a student has difficulty interacting with certain instructors, the student may not be satisfied with the educational experience. Similarly, if a surgeon has a poor bedside manner, this immediately reflects poorly on the hospital, which may in fact be excellent.

Inventory The inventory of services is more complex than that of goods due to the nature of services. Inventory problems exist because services cannot necessarily be stored and accessed when in demand.

This is complicated by the fact that sales forecasts may be inaccurate, warehousing of related items can be expensive, and some services may be perishable. **Perishability** arises when products cannot be stored for long periods of time for use at a later date, as in the instance of concerts where unsold tickets become lost revenue forever. As with goods, not all services are perishable. Online services can often be stored and accessed at a later date, as evident with online virus scans that can be run as needed. Similarly, online movies are often configured to be conveniently viewed on demand to suit viewers.

In the service industry, issues arise due to fluctuating demand throughout the day and the difficulty in assessing the manpower needed to service these needs. Idle production capacity is expensive and arises when a service is available when there is little demand. **Idle production capacity** is formally defined as a situation when the supply of a service exceeds its demand. To deal with this issue, the service industry often uses part-time employees who are paid an hourly wage and are scheduled to work shifts. This is clearly demonstrated in a grocery store setting where the number of cashiers varies depending on the time of day and day of the week. The number of cashiers at 2.30 p.m. during the week will be far less than the number of cashiers available at noon on a Saturday due to the number of people shopping at these times.

Product Elements

The Total Product Concept

LO ② Marketers view products as having three different layers: the core product layer, the actual product layer, and the augmented product layer. The more complex and expensive the product, the more intricate the layers used to differentiate the product from the competition. Figure 7–2 shows how these layers work together.

The *core product* refers to the fundamental benefit that a consumer derives from having the product. In the case of a bicycle, the core benefit may be the transportation it provides, or the pleasure of participating in a leisurely sport. For a service such as a massage, the core benefit may be the relaxation it provides.

The *actual product* is the physical good or the service that a consumer purchases when buying a product. It includes the product's branding, design, and features. With a bicycle, a consumer purchases a piece of equipment, directly associated with a brand name, design, and features. With a massage, the actual product is the massage itself and the time spent having a trained and expert massage therapist relax a client's muscles. In this instance, one may think that branding has no role to play. On the contrary, in the case of a massage, the brand becomes either the name of the massage therapist or the organization providing massage-therapy services.

Finally, the *augmented product* refers to the additional features and attributes that accompany a product, such as a warranty, a service contract, delivery options, installation assistance, or a website used to distinguish the product from competitive offerings. For a bicycle, this may be a warranty, while for a massage there may in fact be no augmented product layer. Generally, augmented product layers exist for more expensive purchases such as cars, computers, or TVs, and are not part of a simple purchase such as a chocolate bar or a newspaper.

It is important to note that for online products it is more difficult to differentiate the core, actual, and augmented components of the product. Take, for example, the social network Facebook: What are the components of its core, actual, and augmented product? Refer to Figure 7–2 and determine these elements.

Packaging and Labelling

Marketers need to pay close attention to a product's packaging and labelling, which for many products is an integral part of the product and its design. Take, for example,

Packaging can differentiate a brand.

> *Marketers view products as having three different layers: the core product, the actual product, and the augmented product.*

Grolsch beer, which intentionally uses a traditional swing-top bottle cap to designate its heritage and differentiate the beer from competing products. The beer bottle is also purposefully made from thick, antiquated green glass with the brand name moulded into the glass to give it that authentic old-fashioned feel. Other products use packaging to differentiate themselves from the competition with items such as resealable bags for cookie manufacturers or reusable jars and bottles for organic milk and yogourt producers.

Packages and labels also provide many functional benefits, such as protection or facilitating product usage. In addition, they serve as platforms from which to communicate brand imagery, brand logos, detailed product information, and the occasional special offer. Packaging and labelling decisions are of paramount importance to a product's success, and marketers work hard to ensure that designs clearly reflect a product's positioning, its brand equity, and its image, which have all been nurtured over time. Changes to existing packaging and label designs need to be approached with caution to ensure that consumers are not confused and do not feel that their

Figure 7–2
The total product concept applied to a bicycle

THE TOTAL PRODUCT CONCEPT		
LAYER	**DESCRIPTION**	**EXAMPLE (BICYCLE)**
Core product	What the product does for the customer— the benefits derived from using the product	Provides transportation and leisure activity
Actual product	The physical good or service, including the branding, design, and features that the consumer receives	A branded product, with a metal frame, two wheels, and a seat
Augmented product	Additional features or benefits that accompany the product, such as a warranty, a service contract, delivery options, installation, or a website	Warranty or repair contract

favourite brands have been altered. Let's look at the recent redesign of the logo for the clothing retailer Gap to demonstrate this point. In 2010, Gap decided to redesign its logo to give it a more contemporary look and feel. However, the unveiling of the new logo prompted a barrage of negative comments on the Internet and in the media. Within a week, Gap swiftly changed its decision and reverted back to the old logo that people had come to love and respect. Interesting details on this incident are captured in the Marketing NewsFlash below.

Product Lines and Product Mixes

L③ Marketers often manage groups of products that are closely related under an umbrella product line and brand name. A **product line** is a group of similar products with the same product and brand name. It is directed to the same general target market and is marketed together as one line to retailers and consumers. A product line can be identified through its product name, brand name, and package design. Examples of a product line can be seen by examining Gatorade's new G Series that was launched in 2011 in Canada. The G Series consists of three related product lines: the Gatorade Prime line, designed for athletes prior to exercise; the Gatorade Perform line for consumption during exercise; and the Gatorade Recover line, which helps athletes recover after exercise. All three lines are marketed under the G Series flagship brand name. They are differentiated by the benefit of the specific line as well as its name and packaging. The Prime line comes in two flavours, Orange and Fruit Punch, which are formulated to be

> **product line**
> A group of similar products with the same product and brand name that is directed at the same general target market and is marketed together

marketing **NewsFlash**   Gap Logo Crisis Averted

On Monday, October 5, 2010, Gap announced a logo change that resulted in an immediate negative reaction from *Advertising Age*, shopping-activist sites such as The Consumerist, and Facebook and Twitter. Parody Twitter accounts such as @gaplogo, @oldgaplogo, and @craplogo mocked the new logo. A saucy website, www.craplogo.me, surfaced to mock the new logo with an online logo-creator. Visitors to this website entered up to 10 characters to have them instantly transformed into spoofs of the new Gap-style logo, complete with white background and a little blue square that demonstrated its amateurish feel.

Within a week, rethinking its approach and responding to consumers' indignation, Gap announced its decision to revert back to its old logo. The impetus: passionate comments supporting the old logo, a flood of over 1,500 Facebook comments on the retailer's Facebook page, and a flurry of negative comments on Twitter and in the mainstream press.

Gap's initial reaction to this negative press, to crowd-source the Gap logo by asking consumers to create their own version, was soon changed when Gap realized the importance of its logo. No surprise here: Logos represent brands—their quality, identity, and image—to the public. For Gap, its simple classic logo with white lettering on a dark blue background embodied its image as an icon of modern-day classic Americana. Its well-recognized logo not only adorned its shopping bags but also was featured in its ads and graced the front of all its clothing stores.

So what was Gap thinking? The purpose of the Gap logo redesign after 20 years of consistent communication was to capture a more modern brand image in line with store redesigns and new product introductions. Gap wanted to reflect a more modern brand and saw the logo as a way to communicate this change. The lesson: Be cautious when changing the insignia of iconic brands. Consumers are often emotionally attached to these brands and their logos can pull at special memories, such as a first pair of jeans, teenage friends, or a special shopping trip.

Kudos to Gap for looking beyond the logo redesign and taking a pause to see what all the fuss was really about. Take note: Logo changes of iconic brands need to be subtle, almost imperceptible to the public, a mere nudging in the right direction to reflect current times.[5]

Questions

1. Why do you think consumers and the media reacted so strongly to the change in the Gap logo?

2. What elements from the traditional Gap logo do you think should be maintained if considering a redesign?

used 15 minutes before an exercise session. The Perform line comes in several flavours and is designed to deliver hydration during exercise. The Recover line is created for use within 30 minutes after completing exercise and comes in mixed Berry and Lemon-Lime Orange flavours. These three product lines are clearly differentiated by their benefits and packaging as seen below.

Looking to the service industry, online or offline products in this sector can also be grouped into product lines. The services offered by the Hospital for Sick Children, for example, can be grouped into three main product lines based on usage: in-patient hospital care, outpatient physician services, and medical research. Looking to the digital arena, the product lines for a digital brand such as Google can also be grouped into product lines based on usage. For example, one of Google's product lines consists of advertising services for businesses that wish to reach consumers through online ads. This product line currently consists of products bucketed together under the Google brand name, including Google Adwords, Google AdSense, and Google Analytics.

Product lines are part of a company's product mix. **Product mix** refers to the array of product lines marketed by a company. While one can slice and analyze a company's product line in many different ways depending on the depth of analysis required, it is often helpful

to drill down into the product mix by looking at the product categories and product lines within these categories. An example can be seen in Figure 7–3 where a snapshot of BlackBerry's product mix is captured by separating the product mix into four main categories: smartphones, tablets, apps, and software. Under each category a number of different product lines are identified, such as the BlackBerry Torch smartphone, the BlackBerry PlayBook tablet, the BlackBerry business/finance/news apps, and the BlackBerry desktop software. A more in-depth analysis could then be conducted to pinpoint the specific products within each line, such as the ten different smartphones sold under the BlackBerry Curve product line or the numerous sports and recreational apps available through BlackBerry App World.

Figure 7–3 also shows BlackBerry's product width and product depth. The **width** of a company's product mix refers to the number of different categories offered by the company. The **depth** of a company's product mix refers to the variety of product lines and products sold within its product categories, groups, and lines.

Procter & Gamble uses this same concept of multiple product lines to market a wide selection of products to consumers. In the laundry and fabric care category, for instance, Procter & Gamble markets at least six different product lines: Tide, Ivory,

Figure 7–3
Reviewing BlackBerry's product mix

PRODUCT MIX AND PRODUCT DEPTH FOR BLACKBERRY

← Width of Product Mix →

↕ Depth of Product Mix

BLACKBERRY PRODUCT MIX

Product Category Smartphones	Product Category Tablets	Product Category Apps	Product Category Software
• BlackBerry Torch	• BlackBerry PlayBook	• Business, Finance, News Apps	• BlackBerry Desktop
• BlackBerry Style		• Education, Reference, eBooks Apps	• BlackBerry Device
• BlackBerry Curve		• Entertainment, Games, Photo, Video, Music, Audio Apps	• BlackBerry Business
• BlackBerry Pearl		• Health and Wellness, Productivity Apps	
• BlackBerry Bold		• IM, Social Networking Apps	
• BlackBerry Tour		• Shopping, Maps, Navigation Apps	
• BlackBerry Storm		• Sports and Recreation Apps	
		• Test Centre, Themes, Utilities Apps	
		• Travel, Weather Apps	

Gain, Era, Dreft, and Cheer. Each product line carries many different product sizes, varieties, and formats. The Tide website at www.tide.com illustrates the wide range of products offered under the umbrella Tide brand and the extensive product depth within most categories. Visit the Procter & Gamble website (www.pg.com) and examine its product mix, product width, and product depth.

ask yourself

1. Explain the difference between non-durable goods, durable goods, and services.
2. What elements make services unique?
3. What is included in the total product concept?

ask yourself

consumer products
Products purchased for their personal use by the ultimate consumer

business products
Products that are purchased either to run a business or to be used as a component in another product or service

convenience products
Items purchased frequently that are inexpensive and require minimum risk and shopping effort

shopping products
Items that require comparison-shopping between different brands and an investment of shopping time

The Classification of Consumer and Business Products

LO 4 Products are classified as either consumer or business products depending on their usage. **Consumer products** are purchased by the ultimate consumer for their personal use while **business products** (also called *industrial goods* or *organizational products*) are purchased either to run a business or to be used as a component in another product or service. In many instances, the differences are obvious: Oil of Olay face moisturizer and the Ontario Science Centre are examples of consumer products, while a cement mixing truck is primarily a business product. Some products, however, are both consumer and business products depending on their usage. A Canon printer can be classified as a consumer product when purchased as a final product for personal use, or it can be classified as a business product when purchased by an organization to help run a business. Consumer and business products consist of numerous types of products, as explained below.

Consumer Products

Convenience, shopping, specialty, and unsought products are the four different types of consumer goods that exist in the market. These items differ in terms of the amount of effort a consumer puts into making a purchase, and how often the items are purchased.

Convenience products are inexpensive items that a consumer purchases frequently with minimal shopping effort. If the product does not meet expectations, there is little risk because the product is inexpensive and easy to purchase. Examples of convenience products are bread, newspapers, or items purchased at a vending machine. **Shopping products** are items for which the consumer comparison-

The product mix for BlackBerry products consists of BlackBerry smartphones, BlackBerry apps, BlackBerry software, and BlackBerry tablet computers.

shops, assessing the attributes and prices of different products and brands. These types of products require a greater investment of shopping time, are more expensive than convenience products, and require a greater assurance of purchase satisfaction. Examples are jeans, books, and items such as TVs. **Specialty products** are items that require considerable time and effort to purchase. They tend to be more-expensive branded products that are needed for special occasions. They include specialty brands and require high purchase satisfaction. Examples of specialty products include a Rolex watch or taking a cruise with Norwegian Cruise Line. **Unsought products** are items that the consumer either does not know about or is not interested in purchasing. Examples of unsought products may be diapers for a person who does not have a baby or epilepsy medication for a person who does not suffer seizures.

The manner in which a consumer good is classified depends on the individual. One person may view a camera as a shopping product and quickly visit a couple of stores before deciding on a brand to purchase. A friend, however, may view a camera as a specialty good, looking for a high-end camera for their photography hobby. This may result in extensive shopping at high-end camera shops for a specific type of camera. It is important to understand that although many products are clearly separated into one category or another, people in varying stages of life will classify products differently. Figure 7–4 generally compares the different types of consumer products and how their marketing mixes may vary depending on the type of product.

Business Products

A major characteristic of business products is that their sales are often directly related to the sales of products with which they are associated. For example, if consumers' demand for Ford cars increases, the company's demand for industrial-grade paint and car stereo equipment, both business products,

> *PRODUCTS ARE CLASSIFIED AS EITHER CONSUMER OR BUSINESS PRODUCTS DEPENDING ON THEIR USAGE.*

Figure 7–4
Classification of consumer products

	TYPE OF CONSUMER PRODUCT			
	CONVENIENCE	**SHOPPING**	**SPECIALTY**	**UNSOUGHT**
Purchase behaviour of consumers	• Frequent purchases • Little time and effort spent shopping	• Occasional purchases • Needs to comparison-shop	• Infrequent purchases • Needs extensive time to search and purchase	• Very infrequent purchases • Some comparison shopping
Brand loyalty of consumers	• Aware of brand, but will accept substitutes	• Prefers specific brands, but will accept substitutes	• Very brand loyal • Will not accept substitutes	• Will accept substitutes
Product examples	• Newspapers, chocolate bars, soft drinks, bread	• Cameras, TVs, briefcases, clothing	• Wedding dresses, luxury items such as Rolex watches	• Insurance products, such as life and disability insurance
Price	• Inexpensive	• Fairly expensive	• Usually very expensive	• Varies
Place (distribution)	• Widespread; many outlets	• Large number of outlets	• Very limited distribution	• Often limited distribution
Promotion (communication)	• Emphasis on price, availability, and awareness	• Emphasis on differentiation from competitors	• Emphasis on uniqueness of brand and status	• Emphasis on awareness

will also increase. Business products may be classified as production goods and services, or support goods and services.

Production Goods and Services
Items used in the manufacturing process that become part of the final product are production goods and services. These can include raw materials, such as grain or lumber, or component parts, such as door hinges used by Ford in its car doors.

Support Goods and Services
The second class of business products is support goods and services, which are items used to assist in producing other goods and services. Support goods and services can include installations, accessory equipment, supplies, and the provision of services such as the delivery of component parts or the provision of training programs for new component parts.

● *Installations* consist of buildings and fixed equipment. Industrial buyers purchase these assets through sales representatives who often submit competitive bids.

Rolex watches are specialty goods.

• *Accessory equipment* includes tools and office equipment and is usually purchased in small-order sizes by buyers. As a result, sellers of industrial accessories use distributors to contact and deal directly with a large number of buyers.

• *Supplies* are the business equivalent of consumer convenience goods and consist of products that are used continually, such as stationery, paper clips, and brooms. These are purchased with little effort as price and delivery are the key considerations.

• *Services* are intangible activities needed to assist a business in its operations and in producing its goods and services. This category can include transportation services, maintenance and repair services, and advisory services such as tax or legal counsel. This may also include online analytics to monitor website traffic, the creation of a website to support the business, or the use of an e-mail database to send out newsletters.

Branding

L⑤ Selecting a memorable brand name is an important factor in the marketing of a product. A **brand** is a name or phrase uniquely given by a company to identify its product(s) and to distinguish the product(s) from the competition. These names are often created in tandem with associated brand-marks or logos, designed to visually represent the brand to consumers and to build brand recognition. Over the long term, the support that goes into marketing a brand results in strong brand associations for the brand and a certain degree of consumer loyalty to the product. This creates **brand equity**, which is formally described as the value of a brand that results from the favourable

> *"Brand equity is the result of considerable marketing investment and needs to be protected."*

exposure, interactions, associations, and experiences that consumers have with a brand over time. BlackBerry is an example of a global Canadian brand that enjoys strong brand equity in the smartphone category for Research in Motion (RIM). Realizing this strong brand equity, RIM leveraged this brand name with its new 2011 tablet, the BlackBerry PlayBook. The use of the BlackBerry brand name helped to launch this new product into the market. Launching new goods or services under an existing flagship brand name uses a **brand extension** approach, which results in the existence of many products under a family brand name.

Brands are classified as either individual brands or family brands depending on whether their name has been extended to cover more than one product category. An **individual brand** is when a company uses a brand name solely for a specific product category. Yop, the yogourt drink produced by Yoplait, Ultima Foods Inc., is an example of an individual brand that is currently used solely for this milk-based beverage. Twitter is another example of an individual brand with its name being used solely for the micro-blogging social networking site.

A **family brand** is when a company uses a brand name to cover a number of different product categories. The brand name Crest, although initially used only for toothpaste, is now used by Procter & Gamble for toothpaste, dental floss, mouthwash, and teeth-whitening products. Google is a similar example. When first introduced, and for a number of years, this individual brand was used solely to identify its search engine. Over the last few years, the Google brand has been extended into a family brand that encompasses not only its search engine but also Google Images, Google Video, Google Earth, Google Toolbar, Google Calendar, Google Chrome, and many other Google products.

▼

ask yourself

1. What is the difference between consumer products and business products?

2. What are the four main types of consumer goods?

3. What are the classifications of business products?

ask yourself

Top beauty editors think Crest 3D White is the best.
We think you'll agree.

Crest 3D White is the #1 whitening brand recognized by top beauty magazine editors. So transform your smile. And watch heads turn.

Visit 3DWhite.com/beautyawards to learn more.

life opens up when you do **Crest** 3D WHITE

A family branding approach from Crest

The advantage of using an established family brand name for new goods or services is that brand equity is quickly transferred from the flagship brand to the new product, thus saving the company the marketing funds needed to build this brand equity from scratch. A disadvantage of using a family branding approach is that if the new product does not live up to the image of the flagship brand, or share in its values, then the brand equity built up over time can be eroded for all products under this family brand name.

Brand equity is the result of considerable marketing investment and needs to be protected. Patents, copyrights, and trademarks are used to protect products,

brands, and processes from unethical infringement and illegal use. **Patents** are used to legally protect new technologies, unique processes, or specific formulations from other companies that may wish to benefit from their use. A patent is a right, granted by government, to exclude others from making, using, or selling an invention.[6] In Canada, patents currently protect owners for a period of 20 years, providing maintenance fees are paid during this time. After 20 years, this patent then becomes available to the market.

Copyrights are used to legally protect the written word, a sound-recording, or a form of communication from being copied by others. It covers music, literature, and performances, and can include slogans.

Trademarks are used by people or organizations to protect brands images, names, and designs from usage by others.[7] Trademarks are limited to a period of 15 years, but can be renewed by their owners to maintain their investment. A trademark legally protects a brand name and its related logo, colours, fonts, and various combinations that exist for use in a particular category, and in a part of the world. If trademarks are to be used in foreign countries, the owner is wise to register an application for that country. Companies hold separate trademarks for each version of a brand name and its associated graphics and logo.

For a brand to be trademarked, a company needs to first conduct a trademark search to ensure that the trademark is not already owned by another company. If the trademark is available and not challenged, then the brand and its associated design and logos can be legally registered in the company name. Care must be taken to renew these trademarks, as required, to ensure that they do not expire. Information on trademarks in Canada can be found at the Canadian Intellectual Property Office website at www.cipo.ic.gc.ca. Here you can easily conduct a search of the trademark database and its registered trademarks. The Canadian Intellectual Property Office provides information on which trademarks are registered, when they were registered, and who owns the trademark.

patents
Used to legally protect new technologies, unique processes, or formulations from usage by other companies

copyrights
Used to legally protect the written word, a sound-recording, or a form of communication from being copied by others

trademarks
Used to legally protect brand images, names, and designs from usage by others

> THE DEGREE OF ATTACHMENT THAT CONSUMERS HAVE TO A PARTICULAR BRAND TELLS A MARKETER ABOUT THEIR BRAND LOYALTY.

An interesting trademark infringement case in the online environment was recently resolved for the board game Scrabble, owned by Hasbro and Mattel since 1953. In 2006, two entrepreneurs, without consulting the owners of the Scrabble trademark, created an online version of the popular board game, complete with the same rules and visual components. It was titled Scrabulous and was soon enjoying over 50,000 daily users on the Internet. A legal battle ensued when the entrepreneurs ignored demands from the trademark owners to take down the game. (See the Focus on Ethics on page 158 for details on how this case was resolved.)

Brand Loyalty

Just how much do consumers like a particular brand? Will they choose another if their first choice is not available, or will they insist on finding their brand? These are brand loyalty decisions. The degree of attachment that consumers have to a particular brand tells a marketer about their **brand loyalty**. Consumers that readily switch brands depending on price generally have very little brand loyalty. Consumers with a stronger brand attachment may have some brand loyalty but may easily brand-switch if the brand is not available. A brand's most loyal consumers will insist on purchasing their brand of choice and will postpone a purchase if the brand is not available. Most people have different degrees of brand loyalty depending on the product, brand, or category. Consider the products you purchase, and determine where you have strong brand loyalty and where you have very little.

Many large, well-entrenched brands are often marketed around the world and have become **global**

Top Ten Global Brands

Ranking	Brand	Value ($ millions)
1	Coca-Cola	70,452
2	IBM	64,727
3	Microsoft	60,895
4	Google	43,557
5	GE	42,808
6	McDonald's	33,578
7	Intel	32,015
8	Nokia	29,495
9	Disney	28,731
10	Hewlett-Packard	26,867

Source: "Best Global Brands 2010," Interbrand, accessed January 2011, at www.interbrand.com/en/best-global-brands/Best-Global-Brands-2010.aspx.

brands. Global brands tend to enjoy strong brand equity due to their hefty marketing budgets and well-recognized trademarks. Interbrand recently identified Coca-Cola, IBM, Microsoft, and Google as the top four global brands in the world. (See box above).

Brand Personality

Marketers recognize that brands offer more than product recognition and identification. Successful brands take on a **brand personality** of their own—a set of human characteristics associated with the brand.[8] Research shows that consumers often associate particular personality traits with certain brands and prefer those whose personalities are most appealing. For example, Pepsi-Cola is seen as being youthful in spirit and exciting, while Dr Pepper is viewed as being unique and non-conformist. Through marketing practices, and particularly advertising campaigns, marketers work to associate brands with specific personality traits and to help consumers make emotional connections with their brands. Often marketers of highly recognized brands, realizing that consumers screen out advertising messages that try to make associations with brands, turn to product placement agencies to help integrate products and brands into movies and TV shows with similar associations. Movies such as *Iron Man 2*, for example, featured over 60 brands.

Brand Name

When we say Xbox, iPad, Virgin Mobile, Porsche, Pepsi, or Adidas, we typically do not think about how companies determined these brand names. Selecting a successful brand name can be an arduous and sometimes expensive process. Companies can spend thousands of dollars developing and testing a new brand name. Intel, for example, spent US$60,000 developing the Pentium brand name for its microchips.[9] Here are some key points to consider when determining a good brand name:

- **The name should suggest the product benefits.** This is demonstrated by brand names such as Easy-Off (oven cleaner) and *American Idol* (TV show), both of which clearly describe the product`s benefits. Care should be taken to review how the brand name translates into other languages to avoid future pitfalls. The 7Up brand name, for example, roughly translates into "death through drinking" in a local dialect in Shanghai, China, which clearly does not positively influence sales in this region.[10]

- **The name should be memorable, distinctive, and positive.** A number of new brands have been introduced over the last few

In sports marketing, brand loyalty is a primary marketing objective.

ask yourself

1. In what instances are patents, copyrights, and trademarks used?

2. Explain the concepts of brand equity and brand loyalty.

3. What are the components of a good brand name?

years with distinctive brand names such as iPad, Xbox, and Google. All these names are very distinctive and were entirely unique and unknown when first introduced. Today, these brand names have high awareness in Canada and enjoy very strong brand recognition.

- **The name should fit the company or product image.** The brand names iPad, Xbox, and Google all reflect the products they portray. iPad suggests something high-tech and flat; Xbox is a strong, crisp brand name associated with a video console (box) and the forbidden nature of something new and on the edge (X); and Google is a fun, casual word associated with creativity (doodle). Google is actually derived from the intentional misspelling of the word "googol," which refers to the digit "1" followed by 100 zeros, a representation of the amount of data the search engine manages.[11]

- **The name should have the ability to be legally protected.** A brand name must be "trademarkable" to protect a company's investment. If the brand name is too generic, or the trademark is owned by another company, the proposed brand name cannot be trademarked. For example, you cannot trademark the name "Bottled Water," as it is not unique

Number of Brands Featured in Movies

Iron Man 2
62 brands

The Social Network
49 brands

Inception
15 brands

Shrek Forever After
0 brands

marketing meter

Source: Brandchannel.com, "Ruling the Box Office This Week," Brandcameo – Films 2010, accessed January 2011 from www.brandchannel.com/brandcameo_films.asp?movie_year=2010.

enough to warrant a trademark. Increasingly, brand names also need a corresponding website address, which can complicate name selection.

An interesting example existed for a teenager in Victoria, British Columbia, named Mike Rowe who set up the website www.MikeRoweSoft.com to promote his web-design business. The software giant Microsoft demanded that Mike give up the domain name because it violated the Microsoft trademark. This generated negative publicity for Microsoft, which backed down and reached a settlement with Mike Rowe, who renamed his site www.MikeRoweForums.com.[12]

● **The name should be simple.** The brand names iPad, Xbox, and Google are all simple names to spell and remember. This makes them more memorable and helps build brand equity.

Types of Brands

LO 6 There are three types of brands: (1) manufacturer's brands, (2) private label brands, and (3) generic brands. This is easily understood by looking at the pharmaceutical industry and over-the-counter pain medications.

A **manufacturer's brand** is one that is owned and produced by the manufacturer. Tylenol is the manufacturer's

---

focus on *Ethics*

Scrabble® Wins Trademark Infringement

One of the best examples of trademark infringement in the digital age relates to Scrabble and the online game Scrabulous created illegally as a knock-off of the popular board game Scrabble. Scrabble was trademarked in 1948 with trademark ownership residing with Hasbro in Canada and the U.S. and with Mattel elsewhere. It is sold in 29 different languages.

Scrabulous, created by Rajat and Jayant Agarwalla and their software development company J Software, was made available in 2007 as a Facebook application with no prior discussions with the Scrabble owners. Enjoying over 500,000 online players per day, the game became one of Facebook's most popular applications.

Hasbro and Mattel soon sent cease-and-desist letters to Facebook and the Agarwalla brothers for copyright and trademark infringement of their Scrabble name and game. Facebook, staying neutral in the controversy, passed correspondence over to the developers of Scrabulous, who insisted Scrabulous did not infringe on the Scrabble® trademarks or copyrights. They claimed that Scrabble had become a generic term

for word games and that the Scrabble board, rules, and design were not protected under copyright protection law.

Unable to easily resolve the issue, Hasbro eventually launched its own Scrabble Facebook application and then filed a lawsuit against the two brothers and the J Software company. A few months later, facing the probable loss of the pending lawsuit, the Agarwalla brothers took down the Scrabulous application in Canada and the U.S., which caused an uproar among fans of the online game. Fans launched a Save Scrabulous Facebook page (with over 34,000 members), while blogs, chat rooms, and social networks buzzed about the loss of the online game.

Meanwhile, legally, the courts in Delhi, India, found the term Scrabulous was too close to the original Scrabble trademark and the brothers were told to cease using the Scrabulous name. In terms of copyright law, the initial ruling stated that technically the Scrabble copyrights were not being infringed. This ruling was under appeal when the Agarwalla

brothers signalled their agreement with the proceedings and the replacement of Scrabulous by launching a new Facebook application, Wordscraper, complete with new rules and a separate interface from the traditional Scrabble game. A few months later, Hasbro dropped the lawsuit.

At press time, Hasboro's new online Scrabble application enjoyed over 890,000 monthly active users compared to Wordscraper with just over 98,000 active monthly users—a far cry from the 500,000 users the Agarwalla brothers enjoyed with their Scrabulous game. These numbers alone speak to the strength of brand names, their ability to communicate an image to consumers, and why companies spend considerable time, effort, and money protecting them.[13] ●

Questions

1. Was it ethical for Scrabulous to create and launch an online application so similar to Scrabble?

2. Hasbro was criticized by Facebook fans for taking the Scrabulous developers to court. What are your views on this issue and what alternative approaches could they have taken?

brand created by Johnson & Johnson and sold to drugstores throughout Canada. In turn, drugstores display the product on their shelves and sell it at retail to consumers. Johnson & Johnson invested considerable time and effort into researching, creating, and marketing this brand. When initially launched, this product was protected by a patent, but as mentioned earlier, a patent is restricted to a limited number of years, currently 20 years in Canada. Once a patent expires—and this patent has—other manufacturers can produce a similar product. Regular Strength Tylenol is currently sold at drugstores at a cost of $9.49 for 100 tablets.

A **private label brand**, otherwise known as a store brand, is owned by a retailer that contracts its manufacturing to major suppliers and then sells the product at its own retail stores, under its own store brand name. Private label products are very popular in Canada with over 70 percent of people considering them a good alternative to a manufacturer's brands.[14] A private label brand provides a retailer with the opportunity to offer its customers a less expensive alternative to a manufacturer's brand. Private label products are generally sold at lower prices than a manufacturer's brands due to the absence of high fees to carry the products, and their lower marketing and product development costs.

An example of a private label product in the over-the-counter pain reliever category is Shoppers Drug Mart's Life Brand Acetaminophen. Life Brand is one of Shoppers Drug Mart's private label brands used to compete directly with

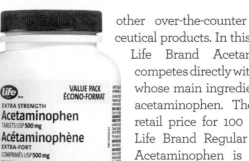

other over-the-counter pharmaceutical products. In this instance, Life Brand Acetaminophen competes directly with Tylenol, whose main ingredient is also acetaminophen. The current retail price for 100 tablets of Life Brand Regular Strength Acetaminophen is $5.99 for 100 tablets, considerably less than the comparable Tylenol product priced at $9.49.

One of the most successful private label brands in Canada is President's Choice. This brand was introduced by Loblaw Companies Ltd. (Loblaw, Real Canadian Superstore, No Frills, Fortinos, Provigo, etc.) as an upscale private label, selling a unique array of products that could not be found in other Canadian supermarkets. The brand is heavily promoted by Galen Weston Jr., Loblaw's executive chairman and latest TV spokesperson. (See the Marketing NewsFlash on page 161 for details on this brand's success.)

A **generic brand** has no branding at all and is sometimes produced as a cheap alternative to a manufacturer's brand and to a private label branded product. A generic brand typically highlights the main product ingredient as a means of selling the product, with its main point of difference being price.

Although a less expensive alternative to other branded products, a generic product lacks the brand equity and product recognition that is enjoyed by both a manufacturer's brand and branded private label products. In the pharmaceutical industry, many generic versions of prescription medications whose patents have expired are created and sold to pharmacies by generic drug manufacturer Apotex Inc., Canada's largest generic drug manufacturer, which exports to 115 countries around the world and has approximately 5,000 employees in Canada. When a prescription is filled, often these cheaper generic versions manufactured by Apotex are substituted by pharmacists for the branded medicines prescribed. This saves governments, insurance companies, and consumers substantial amounts of money.

In 2010, Apotex, which follows a socially responsible approach to business, contributed close to $2 million in earthquake relief medications to people in Haiti. It also recently addressed the ethical dilemma of third-world countries being unable to afford life-saving HIV/AIDS drugs. Apotex applied through the Canadian Access to Medicines Regime (CAMR) to sell cheaper generic versions of patented HIV/AIDS drugs to Rwanda. Apotex was awarded the contract

Private Label Products Canadian Fast Facts

Perception that private label products are a good alternative	71% of Canadians
Market size	$11.2 billion
Percentage of units purchased when shopping	45%
Percentage of dollars purchased when shopping	36%
Average price of private label products	30% lower than national brands

Source: News Release, "Private Label is Very Public," The Nielsen Company, October 14, 2009, accessed at http://ca.acnielsen.com/content/nielsen/en_ca/news/news_releases/2009/private_label_is_very.html.

and now sells Apo-TriAvir at cost to Rwanda where the medication is priced at 19.5 cents (US) per pill versus a comparable patented drug regime at $6.[15]

Outside of the pharmaceutical area, generic products can often be found at various retail outlets such as dollar stores where select products with no associated brand names are sold. Dollarama stores, for instance, sell plastic clogs for $2 per pair that are direct knock-offs of Crocs but have absolutely no branding at all.

A Practical Look at Marketing Products and Brands

So how are products and brands actually managed by marketers? A marketer is responsible for marketing products and brands in order to bring revenue or profits into an organization. To do this, marketers create annual marketing plans for the upcoming year to formally identify marketing activities and establish funding requirements and budget needs that will help generate profits and revenue streams for the company. These marketing plans review each element of the marketing mix and itemize when marketing programs will be in place, and their expected impact on sales, revenues, and profits. Any changes that relate to the product, its branding, and its product positioning will be clearly identified in the marketing plan, including elements such as new product launches, package redesigns, new sizes, or product research requirements.

Despite the existence of a marketing plan, the world of marketing is dynamic and ever-changing, and therefore, throughout the year, marketers constantly evaluate and assess product needs against marketing plan expectations. Marketers then recommend changes that are needed to help reach planned revenue and profit targets.

Managing a product requires a marketer to wear many hats. On an ongoing basis, a marketer needs to analyze daily sales numbers, review profit targets, be alerted to changes in product costs, be in contact with the sales force, and understand changes in the selling environment. A marketer must also be aware of market research insights, understand consumer interests, and work with a team to create meaningful marketing programs. Examples of how a marketer practically manages products are as follows: If a food-product marketer plans to introduce a new plastic container, but realizes that there is a consumer movement away from plastic due to health concerns, this marketer would most likely recommend against this planned program. Similarly, a marketer of an SUV may decide to delay the introduction of a new model due to the high price of gasoline and consumers' movement toward more fuel-efficient vehicles. In addition, if a product's profits are under pressure due to a sudden increase in the cost of manufacturing, then an expensive advertising campaign may be delayed or modified to reduce expenditures in an attempt to reach short-term profit targets. If a competitor unexpectedly reduces prices, then marketers will need to determine whether their product pricing needs to be adjusted and how this may impact profits.

In addition to managing these types of issues that arise as the year unfolds, a marketer must look to the future of the brand to ensure its relevancy to consumers. Product marketers manage the current competitive environment while also working on future programs and products for the upcoming years. In marketing, nothing remains static, and currently three main categories of interest are surfacing as areas where marketers need to be involved. First, we see marketers in Canada and around the world investing in "green" conservation programs

> *Marketing plans review each element of the marketing mix and itemize when marketing programs will be put in place, and their expected impact on sales, revenues, and profits.*

President's Choice Spokesperson Builds Business

Over the last few years, Galen Weston Jr., executive chairman of Loblaw Companies Ltd., has become the centrepiece of Loblaw's new advertising campaign, successfully focusing consumers on its President's Choice (PC) private label products. Today, with the same campaign approach that started six years ago, we see Galen Weston Jr. as the familiar, friendly, and credible spokesperson for PC products.

Facing its first annual financial loss in 2006, Loblaw Companies hastened to reconnect with consumers by reigniting their passion for PC products. Loblaw Companies was facing strong competition from Walmart's new grocery products and from other private label products in competing grocery stores. Loblaw needed to differentiate itself and to drive traffic and profitability back into its stores. It looked to its PC brand to help achieve this.

The PC brand was all about authenticity, a reflection of Loblaw's corporate platform of genuinely using socially responsible business practices. The two could work hand-in-hand to catapult the brand and company back into profitability. A national advertising campaign using Galen Weston Jr. as its spokesperson was created in 2007 to do just this and continues today in 2012. The campaign initially selected specific PC products to make a statement about Loblaw and its mission to be a leader in socially responsible business practices: PC's water filters reduced plastic bottle garbage; PC's organic baby food provided healthy food options; and Loblaw, by purchasing more Canadian produce than anyone else in Canada, supported Canadian farmers. Today, Galen Weston continues to emphasize Loblaw

Companies' socially responsible products by flaunting the healthy aspect of products such as its PC sparkling fruit juice beverages as well as many of the new PC products, such as mini-hamburger sliders.

The campaign, with its many different ads, was a resounding success. In its first two years Loblaw's downward spiral was turned around on many fronts: main store consideration increased 12 percentage points (from 31 to 43 percent, 2007–2009); the purchase of PC products at least once every two weeks increased by 10 percentage points (41 to 51 percent, 2007–2009); and net earnings went from a $219 million loss in 2006 to a $545 million gain by the start of 2009 and success continues today.[16]

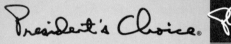

Questions

1. How is the PC brand differentiating itself from other private label store brands?

2. Should brand images stay static or evolve over time? Why or why not?

---

and new technologies that meet consumer demands in this area. A second category of interest for Canadian marketers is the increasingly multicultural composition of our society. This is demonstrated in the home language of people in Canada, which for 30 percent of the population is neither solely English nor French.[17] Marketers look to ensure that their products are relevant to these cultural groups and constantly examine the need to communicate their programs in a variety of languages. A third area of interest for marketers in Canada is the impact of the Internet on consumers' purchasing behaviour and the way it is changing how people communicate. Marketers look to how the music industry misread the impact of online music downloads, and are cautious to not overlook consumers' ability to control the market.

In practical terms, the managing of a product requires marketers to intimately understand the dynamics of the marketplace and to quickly assess the financial impact of recommendations that are needed to boost the business. Marketers must quickly react to market situations and recommend necessary changes to planned programs. Managing a product is not a static event but a process that is constantly changing and requires marketers to use their analytical skills, creativity, and strategic thinking to keep the business moving forward. In all instances, being true to a product's positioning, meeting consumer needs, and implementing competitive marketing programs helps ensure that products and brands are well-managed and have longevity.

> ## " A marketer is responsible for marketing products and brands to bring revenue into an organization. "

Summary...*just the facts*

- Product is a term used in marketing to designate non-durable goods, durable goods, and services that are marketed. Some products are a combination of both goods and services.

- There are four unique elements to services: intangibility, inconsistency, inseparability, and inventory. These four elements are referred to as the four Is of services.

- The total product concept includes the core product, the actual product, and the augmented product.

- Product mix is the combination of product lines managed by a company. The width of the product mix refers to the number of different categories offered by the company. The depth of the product mix refers to the number of product groups and product lines offered by a company within each category.

- Consumer products are classified into convenience products, shopping products, specialty products, and unsought products.

- Business products are classified into production or support goods. Production goods include raw materials and components parts, while support goods include installations, accessory equipment, supplies, and services.

- A brand is a name or phrase used to identify a product and to distinguish it from the competition. Brand equity is the result of the positive experiences consumers have with the brand over time and results in brand loyalty.

- Trademarks are used to legally protect brands, patents are used to protect unique processes, and copyrights are used to protect the written or spoken word.

- Brands are categorized as manufacturer's brands, private label brands, and generic brands.

- Companies may restrict a brand name for use with a single product line, thus using an individual brand, or may extend a brand name to encompass a number of different product categories, resulting in the creation of a family brand.

Key Terms and Concepts...*a refresher*

brand *p. 154*
brand equity *p. 154*
brand extension *p. 154*
brand loyalty *p. 156*
brand personality *p. 156*
business products *p. 151*
consumer products *p. 151*
convenience products *p. 151*
copyrights *p. 155*
durable good *p. 145*
family brand *p. 154*

generic brand *p. 159*
global brand *p. 156*
idle production capacity *p. 147*
individual brand *p. 154*
manufacturer's brand *p. 158*
non-durable good *p. 145*
patents *p. 155*
perishability *p. 147*
private label brand *p. 159*
product *p. 145*
product depth *p. 150*

product line *p. 149*
product mix *p. 150*
product width *p. 150*
service continuum *p. 146*
services *p. 145*
shopping products *p. 151*
specialty products *p. 152*
trademarks *p. 155*
unsought products *p. 152*
virtual services *p. 146*

Hands-on...*apply your knowledge*

Branding Assignment   The Virgin brand name became established in Canada with the launch and marketing of Virgin Mobile. In 2008, Virgin licensed its brand name to Astral Media for use with specific radio stations in Toronto, Calgary, Vancouver, Ottawa, and Montreal. In 2010, the Virgin brand name was also extended to encompass Virgin Games, an online destination for competitive gaming. Review the opening vignette on Virgin Mobile and outline the advantages and disadvantages of extending this brand name into radio stations and online gaming.

Reality Check...*reminder*

Refer back to this chapter's opening vignette and answer the Reality Check questions on page 144.

McGraw Hill connect *Practise and learn online with Connect*

Connect allows you to practise important concepts at your own pace and on your own schedule, with 24/7 online access to an eBook, practice quizzes, interactivities, video cases, study tools, and more.

Connect with classmates.

 connect™

New Product Development

This chapter looks at new products, how they are developed, and the importance of managing product life cycles. Ian Gordon, senior vice president at Loblaw Companies Ltd., manages product innovation for President's Choice and provides us with insight into this important aspect of marketing. He takes us into the world of product development at Loblaw Companies to explain how President's Choice (PC) Blue Menu became the success it is today and how it continues to evolve and develop in 2012.

Ian Gordon is a seasoned marketer with a passion for food. His extensive marketing background with Frito-Lay, Unilever, Robin Hood Multifoods, and the advertising agency ACLC gives him a realistic approach to product innovation. He tells us that for a new product to succeed, consumers must easily understand its benefit and relevancy. "Marketers must listen to what consumers tell them and make necessary changes to the marketing mix to help products become successful over time," states Gordon, reminding us that rarely do marketers get it entirely right the first time and that it is the journey down the road to product innovation that breeds success and profitability. He tells us that PC Blue Menu is the backbone of Loblaw Companies' healthy products, but that in 2012 it needed an infusion of newness to stay relevant and to move forward to the next level.

Listening to consumers, research flagged that most people saw PC Blue Menu as a low-calorie, low-sugar, low-fat, weight-management product line. In fact, in qualitative research the bulk of respondents confirmed this, with only hard-core label readers understanding that it stood for much more than just diet food. A product mix that skewed low-fat and low-calorie was partly to blame, but research also highlighted an opportunity to strengthen the brand's positioning and pointed out that marketing communications could play a more central role.

In 2005 PC Blue Menu was launched as a line of healthy products that contained new items and revamped offerings from the PC Too Good To Be True (TGTBT) line that was missing the mark. "Products had to either contain soy protein, be supplemented with Omega-3s, contain added fibre, be lower in calories, or have lower levels of sodium and fat," explains Gordon. "Today, although there are many successful Blue Menu items, we are moving the brand further down the nutrition path, looking at the latest in nutritional science to expand our offerings."

LEARNING OBJECTIVES

L1 Explain the concept of product life cycle and the elements involved in each stage

L2 Describe the ways product life cycles can be extended

L3 Differentiate between different types of new products

L4 Describe the adoption curve of new products

L5 Explain why new products succeed or fail

L6 Detail each step in the new product development process

In 2012 a revitalized PC Blue Menu brand addresses four key elements: (1) brand positioning, (2) product offerings, (3) brand communications, and (4) top-of-mind brand awareness with consumers and within the company itself. The PC Blue Menu team of chefs, nutrition researchers, registered dieticians, nutritionists, product developers, quality assurance specialists, regulatory affairs experts, and marketers all worked together to make this happen. This is what they did:

- **Clarified brand positioning:** The brand positioning was clarified as a well-priced line of nutritious and healthier foods. PC Blue Menu was reinforced as the brand that helps consumers make healthier eating choices without having to pay a premium— Blue Menu products will never be priced at a premium to regular PC products.

- **Expanded product offerings:** The brand platform was expanded to include the latest in nutritional science. PC Blue Menu items could now contain pre-and probiotics, plant sterols, and proteins, and could be fortified with vitamins and minerals—this in addition to the previous requirements of either containing soy protein, Omega-3s, added fibre, or be lower in calories, sodium, and fat. The line was expanded to include another 100 items so that a base of 500 healthy items better reflected this positioning. Items such as margarine with plant sterols, peanut butter with Omega-3, and frozen burgers with reduced fat and added Omega-3 were introduced to support this nutritional emphasis.

- **Redesigned packaging:** Packaging was redesigned to shout out PC Blue Menu's nutritional benefits. A large nutritional banner was boldly placed on the front of all PC Blue Menu products, flagging critical nutritional elements. It shouts out whether the item is high in fibre, contains prebiotics or plant sterols, is a good source of calcium, etc. These nutritional banners intentionally use symbols to highlight nutritional value, rather than rely on the text-heavy nutritional jargon that is traditionally placed on the back of packages. Loblaw understood that most consumers do not commonly read or understand this information.

- **Strengthened marketing communications:** Off-package marketing communications was strengthened with a solid 52-week plan to remind consumers of PC Blue Menu throughout the year. The plan was also designed to galvanize company employees behind the brand, from those working at head office to those on the front lines with con-

sumers. The tools of choice involved TV spots, high-profile inclusion in the *President's Choice Insider Report* flyers, in-store merchandising, and online communications through the PC website.

PC Blue Menu's success demonstrates how product innovation is about the journey and how product lines are crafted and perfected over time. The PC Blue Menu line started out as the TGTBT product line, which had no cohesive positioning; some products in the TGTBT line were healthy, while others were not. In 2005 Loblaw recognized an opportunity to re-launch the line in a more meaningful way under the PC Blue Menu banner with a simplified positioning. Less-healthy products were abandoned while new healthy snacks, pastas, cereals, soups, frozen entrees, and beverages were created to provide a critical mass for a line that was to become Loblaw's flagship banner for healthier eating. In 2012, listening to consumers and realizing the brand could reach greater heights, PC Blue Menu was revitalized with a stronger nutritional focus, healthier new products, and a package redesign to reflect this positioning. A more focused communications platform was also used to clarify PC Blue Menu as a brand concerned with healthier eating.

"New product marketing and innovation is all about understanding consumer insights and constantly moving products forward down the path to success," states Gordon. "It takes time, passion, and dedication to get it just right, and usually this takes a while. It is about learning and making changes along the way. Remember, innovation is about the journey, not the 'Eureka!'" states Ian Gordon, as he passionately talks about the next food item on his agenda.[1] 🍎

---

reality CHECK

As you read Chapter 8, refer back to this PC Blue Menu chapter-opening vignette to answer the following questions:

- In what stage of the product life cycle is the PC Blue Menu product line?

- What strategy or combination of strategies have been used to extend the product life cycle of the PC Blue Menu product line?

- Check the Loblaw President's Choice website at www.presidentschoice.ca to see how Blue Menu is supported online. Suggest additional online elements that could be used to help market the products.

> *The length of each stage in the product life cycle depends on the product, the category, and how it is being marketed.*

The Product Life Cycle

The concept of **product life cycle** describes the stages that a new product goes through, starting with its initial introduction into the marketplace and moving through to stages of growth, maturity, and decline. The concept of product life cycle is used by many marketers to help manage a product from its initial launch through to its eventual decline. Marketers try to manage products so that they do not reach the decline stage. Instead, products are revamped, retooled, and repositioned to meet evolving consumer needs and competitive challenges. This approach was clearly demonstrated with the PC TGTBT line that was re-launched under the PC Blue Menu line and which continues today to evolve under its even healthier premise.

Products in the online environment follow this same product life cycle approach, often experiencing shorter cycles that require frequent boosts to stay competitive. Blogger, for example, the free online blogging tool from Google, recently added new, customizable templates, an important development to compete with WordPress, which had become

increasingly popular. Twitter is another example of an online product that added new features to stay relevant to its users and compete with other social networks. In 2010, Twitter went from 50 million tweets per day to over 90 million, increasing its usage and popularity through new features. In 2011, it introduced official apps for iPhones, BlackBerrys, and iPads and added new elements such as geo-location features, suggested users, promoted Tweets, integration with LinkedIn, and a new consumer interface.[2] As this brand continues to grow and evolve, we can expect continued updates and changes to keep it in line with changing expectations and needs.

Figure 8–1 traces the curve of a product life cycle by plotting a product's sales and profits over time. The curves change in response to the competitive environment and to consumers' demand for the innovation.

Initially, during the introduction stage, a product enjoys minimal sales, profits, and competition, but then over time, propelled by marketing programs and product demand, a product moves into a period of rapid growth and profit increases. As the competition becomes more severe, consumers are presented with competitive products, which cause a product's sales and profits to flatten out and eventually, if not addressed by a marketer, decline. The length of each stage in the product life cycle depends on the product, the category, and how it is being marketed. An example of how marketers use the product life cycle can be seen with Sony and how, as an industry leader in consumer electronics, it first introduced the CD player (in conjunction with Philips) as the new digital format replacing record players. Before the product was launched, Sony had already mapped out the product life cycle for the innovation, looking at least five years into the future to identify what new product innovations would be needed at that time to stay ahead of the competition. Initially, during the introductory stage, Sony and Philips provided the technology free to the industry to facilitate its adoption as the new technology of choice. This was closely accompanied by the launch of CD players and CDs, followed sequentially by the portable CD Walkman, in-car stereos, and jukeboxes. The introduction of actual music CDs was also carefully orchestrated to gain consumer confidence and acceptance by the music industry.[3]

The Core: Chapter 8

New products can add vitality to a company.

New Products

Product life cycles need to be managed to meet evolving trends.

Figure 8–1
Product life cycle

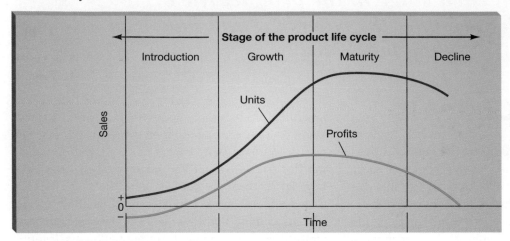

In November 2011, the Kindle replaced these eReaders with four new products that were faster, lighter, and more affordable. All products came with Wi-Fi and the ability to not only purchase books but also borrow them from the local public library and read them on these devices. The basic 6-inch Kindle, priced at $79, was 18 percent smaller and 10 percent faster than the previous model. The Kindle Touch, at $99, introduced touch technology to its eReaders and extra-long battery life. The Kindle Touch 3G, at $149, included free 3G access in over 100 countries. The Kindle Fire, a higher-end new product priced at $199, introduced full-colour screens, touch technology, and an entertainment device that allowed users to watch movies and TV shows, listen to music, download apps, play games, and read books, magazines, and newspapers.[5]

A more recent example of how products are marketed through their life cycles can be seen in the eReader category. Amazon.com launched their eReader, the Kindle, in 2007 and changed its features, pricing, and marketing over time (see Figure 8–2) to stay relevant and competitive against new category entries such as the iPad, the Nook (Barnes and Noble), and the Kobo (Indigo/Chapters). The first-generation Kindle hit the market in 2007 at $399 as a U.S.-only eReader with a 6-inch screen and capacity for 200 non-illustrated books. The product sold out within six hours. A few months later it was made available outside of the U.S. Fifteen months later, in February 2009, the product was replaced by a slimmer, second-generation Kindle that had a longer battery life and a capacity for 1,500 non-illustrated books. Its price at $359 was reduced versus the original $399, and it underwent a number of subsequent price reductions to compete with the Nook eReader from Barnes and Noble and in anticipation of the iPad's debut in mid-2010. Specifically, the Kindle's price fell from $359 in February 2009, to $299 in July 2009, to $259 in October 2009, and finally bottomed out at $189 in June 2010.

In July 2010, a new third-generation Kindle replaced previous versions, with the capacity to hold up to 3,500 non-illustrated books. It came in three versions: (1) a basic 6-inch version with Wi-Fi at $139, (2) a 3G/Wi-Fi 6-inch version at $189, and (3) a 9.7-inch 3G version at $379. The third-generation product was thinner, lighter, and easier-to-read and it had a longer battery life.[4]

Mass advertising for the Kindle was unheard of during its introductory stage in 2007. At this introductory point, online ads generated demand on the Amazon.com website and popularity spread through word of mouth. During the Kindle's 2010–2011 growth phase, the Kindle modified its approach and started to advertise on TV stations such as CNN to reach a wider audience of interested consumers. Competitive TV spots showed how the product could be used outdoors (unlike tablet computers) and emphasized its low price of $139. Its 2011 new product launch initially used public relations to gain traction with the media, complementing this with information and videos placed on the Amazon.com website to clearly communicate product benefits. It also used its affiliate marketing programs to spread the word through its database of customers. The 2011 eReader products also allowed customers to opt in to sponsored screensavers and special offers from sponsors to help reduce product pricing. Over time, Amazon.com carefully continues to adapt its Kindle eReader and marketing approaches to meet changing consumer needs in an increasingly competitive market.

In the following sections, we look at each stage of the product life cycle in more detail to appreciate how marketers use this concept to manage their products profitably (see Figure 8–3 on page 171). It is important to understand that this concept is widely used by marketers in many different ways. It is most often used to help manage products, but it can also be used to manage brands and, in some instances, to analyze an industry in general.

Introduction Stage

The introduction stage of the product life cycle occurs when a product is first introduced to its intended target market. During this period, sales grow slowly, and profits are minimal. Low profit levels are typically the result of three things: (1) slow sales growth, (2) high research and development costs to bring the product to market, and (3) high levels of marketing spending needed to launch the new product. The marketing objective during this stage is to create consumer awareness and stimulate trial for the new product.

This stage is characterized by little competition and a lack of consumer awareness about the product. Radical new categories or technological innovations also come with the added challenge of having to educate consumers on the existence and relevancy of the category itself. During this stage, companies often spend heavily on advertising and use other promotional tools to build awareness and trial among consumers. The other elements of the marketing mix are also carefully crafted to ensure that they are in step with the product launch and its consumers.

Figure 8–2
Kindle product life cycle

AMAZON.COM'S KINDLE — MANAGING THE PRODUCT LIFE CYCLE			
Product Overview	**Stage in Product Life Cycle**	**Date**	**Price (US$)**
Kindle 1st Generation - Up to 200 books - Basic model only (6-inch screen)	Introduction	Nov. 2007	$399
Kindle 2nd Generation - Up to 1,500 books - Basic model (6-inch screen), with two subsequent price reductions - DX model introduced (9.7-inch screen)	Introduction/growth	Feb. 2009–Oct. 2009	$359 $299 $259 $489
Kindle 3rd Generation - Up to 3,500 books - Includes Wi-Fi - Basic (6-inch screen) - 3G technology (6-inch screen) - 3G technology (9.7-inch screen)	Growth and entering maturity	July 2010	 $139 $189 $379
Kindle 4th Generation - Up to 3,000 books - Borrow books from libraries - Includes Wi-Fi - Kindle (6-inch screen) - Kindle Touch (6-inch screen) - Kindle Touch 3G (6-inch screen) - Kindle Fire (7-inch colour screen)	Early maturity	Nov. 2011	 $79 $99 $149 $199

Source: Kindle 3rd generation product information accessed from the Amazon.com Kindle Store, January 2011, at http://www.amazon.com/dp/B002Y27P3M/?tag=gocous-20&hvadid=5729120357&ref=pd_sl_cazfqv6ny_b; Kindle 4th generation product information accessed from Amazon.com, October 2011, at http://www.amazon.com/gp/product/B0051QVESA.

Chris Hughes, one of the initial founders of Facebook and the director of the online community for Barack Obama's 2008 U.S. presidential campaign, channels new technologies to make a difference. His 2010 start-up, Jumo, is a social network that connects non-profit organizations with people willing to lend support. In a little over 18 months, Jumo, a West African word for "together in concert," had successfully established itself in the non-profit world and had combined forces with GOOD, an established non-profit with more than 3 million monthly users. Jumo itself had over 1 million registered users and a database of more than 15,000 non-profit organizations. In its early days it welcomed well-known charities such as the Bill and Melinda Gates Foundation as well as many small and medium-size charities that could benefit from the social network. In an attempt to build the non-profit, Jumo was soon amalgamated into the already established GOOD media platform, which focuses on social causes. Chris Hughes became an advisor to the new amalgamated non-profit organization.

Jumo allowed people to easily find, follow, and support non-political charities. These charities had project pages within Jumo where information, updates, links, and newsfeeds could be seen. People could show support by following pages, or deciding to join conversations, spread the word, volunteer, or donate. "We expect people to be curious about a cause or an organization, and then over the course of a few weeks or a few months get to know that cause. Then at a point where they feel inspired or compelled or they feel that sense of responsibility, then we hope that they will take real action on behalf of those causes and for those organizations," states Hughes.

Interests spanned the arts, education, the environment, health, human rights, peace, and poverty. Projects encompassed a wide range of issues such as air quality, climate change, and HIV/AIDS. "Like" buttons allowed people to indicate support, post comments, and share comments on other social networks. You can check out Jumo updates at blog.jumo.com.[6]

Questions

1. Conduct a Google search for the Jumo website, Twitter account, and Facebook page. Review these sites and then discuss which stage of the product lifecycle Jumo is in.

2. What are the elements of the marketing mix—product, price, place, and promotion—for Jumo, and how do you expect these to change over the next few years?

During the introduction stage, pricing is typically high, but there are instances when a low pricing approach is used to encourage rapid acceptance of the product. A high initial price is called a *price skimming strategy* and is used by companies to help recover research and development costs. This approach takes advantage of the price insensitivity of early adopters. If a company uses a low price to enter the market, this is referred to as a *penetration pricing strategy* and is used to encourage rapid acceptance of an innovation or to combat a competitive threat.

Distribution can often be a challenge during the introduction stage of the product life cycle because channel members may be hesitant to carry a new product that is unproven. Listing fees may also present themselves as an expensive proposition for marketers who often experience retailers charging to recover the costs and risks of listing, shelving, and merchandising a new product in stores.

Looking at the Kindle product mentioned earlier, during its introductory stage it underwent a continuous trickle of innovative product updates and price changes to stay relevant to its users and to build on market momentum. Facebook, also riding the rapid growth stage of a popular product, has followed similar updates and changes to stay relevant. A recent development saw one member of its founding group, Chris Hughes, start an online social network, Jumo, designed for non-profits to connect with supporters. While still in its early introductory stage, this online product is rapidly gaining traction with consumers. (See the Marketing NewsFlash above.)

Growth Stage

The growth stage of the product life cycle sees an increase in competition and a rapid rise in sales and profits. The market is flooded with competing brands that thrust the category and its products into the forefront. This results in new consumers being enticed into the category and the resultant increase in sales and profits.

In this competitive arena, marketers focus their programs on differentiating products from competitive offerings. New features are added to original designs,

Figure 8–3
Managing the stages of the product life cycle

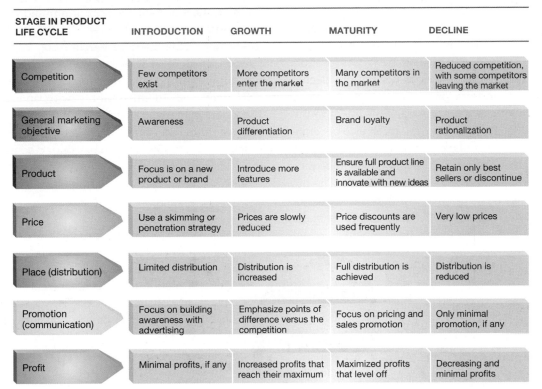

STAGE IN PRODUCT LIFE CYCLE	INTRODUCTION	GROWTH	MATURITY	DECLINE
Competition	Few competitors exist	More competitors enter the market	Many competitors in the market	Reduced competition, with some competitors leaving the market
General marketing objective	Awareness	Product differentiation	Brand loyalty	Product rationalization
Product	Focus is on a new product or brand	Introduce more features	Ensure full product line is available and innovate with new ideas	Retain only best sellers or discontinue
Price	Use a skimming or penetration strategy	Prices are slowly reduced	Price discounts are used frequently	Very low prices
Place (distribution)	Limited distribution	Distribution is increased	Full distribution is achieved	Distribution is reduced
Promotion (communication)	Focus on building awareness with advertising	Emphasize points of difference versus the competition	Focus on pricing and sales promotion	Only minimal promotion, if any
Profit	Minimal profits, if any	Increased profits that reach their maximum	Maximized profits that level off	Decreasing and minimal profits

and product proliferation often occurs. Pricing levels are generally lowered to become more competitive and distribution increases. Promotion at this stage becomes more product specific, with advertising playing a key role in focusing consumers toward particular brands.

The Kindle is a prime example of growth-stage marketing, but let's also look at the Apple iPad as an example of a product that quickly leapt into the growth stage of its product life cycle, limiting its introductory stage to months rather than years. The iPad was pre-announced to the world in a press conference in January 2010 and first sold only in the U.S. starting in April of that year. Using the hype created by its press conference that showcased the product, and by allowing people to pre-order the product, over 300,000 iPads were sold on its first day, reaching over 1 million units in its first month. Units were initially available only through the Apple retail store or its website.[7] Meanwhile, a carefully staged rollout released the iPad internationally: May 2010 saw the product roll out into Australia, Canada, France, Germany, Italy, Japan, Spain, Switzerland, and the U.K.; July 2010 saw the

iPad launched in Austria, Belgium, Hong Kong, Ireland, Luxembourg, Mexico, the Netherlands, New Zealand, and Singapore; and by the end of 2010 it was also available in China and Malaysia.

In its first year, the iPad successfully launched its first generation Wi-Fi and 3G versions, and hinted at the iPad 2, which was launched a year later in early 2011. This created further hype and momentum for the product and, no surprise, by the time the iPad 2 arrived on store shelves, the tablet market was now in its growth stage and flooded with competing gadgets such as tablet computers from HP, LG, Acer, Samsung, etc.. The iPad 2 is an example of a product that pushed itself into the growth stage of the product life cycle by creating hype for the category and satisfying pent-up product demand by including highly anticipated new features, such as video-chat, in its next generation of products. To stay competitive in this growth market, the iPad re-focused its advertising to be more feature-driven, and increased product availability through electronic retailers.

Maturity Stage

The maturity stage of the product life cycle is characterized by a slowdown of growth in both the sales and profit areas. Competitors are well-established and fewer new consumers enter the market. Marketing focuses on gaining market share and uses pricing as a key promotional

The maturity stage of the product life cycle is characterized by a slowdown of growth.

tool. This results in decreased profits for the market as a whole and also for individual products.

The maturity stage is generally the longest stage in the product life cycle with marketers focusing efforts on ensuring that the product does not go into decline. Marketers use short-term promotional tactics such as consumer promotions to encourage consumers to purchase the product. Product innovation can also become a priority at this stage as marketers try to reposition products in the market and revamp product lines to be more competitive and relevant to consumers' needs. The purpose of this renewed focus on innovation is to try to take the product back into the growth or early maturity stages of the product life cycle, as we have seen with products such as the Kindle eReader.

Numerous well-established products are in the maturity stage of their product life cycles; examples include Heinz Ketchup, Hellmann's Mayonnaise, and Kraft Dinner. What do marketers of these products do to maintain product relevancy in these categories and to stop them from going into decline? Packaging changes, product modifications, and extended-usage approaches are often used to keep them relevant.

Let's look at some less conventional products and examine how they manage their product life cycles. Television networks and individual TV shows are also products that need to be managed. Unlike products in the food industry, these services have relatively short product life cycles and go into decline when they no longer draw large audiences. At this point, a network typically replaces the show with a new program. The risk of managing these products is relatively high, with many new shows not lasting more than a single season and requiring the network to constantly monitor its program ratings. TSN is an example of a successful Canadian specialty network that continually brings new programming to its viewers. TSN periodically upgrades its studios, brings in new announcers, and adds new programming from around the world as needed. This keeps its product fresh and interesting. TSN uses research from Roper Reports Canada to monitor how viewers perceive its network and programming and then make required changes. TSN continues to rank highly with sports viewers.[8] Marketers in many industries use similar tracking studies to monitor changing consumer perceptions and attitudes. These studies need to be conducted periodically, often annually, for changes to be perceptible over time.

Decline Stage

The decline stage of the product life cycle occurs when sales and profits consistently decline over time. Frequently, a product enters this stage when products become obsolete due to technological innovation or changes in consumer needs. The word-processing capability of personal computers pushed typewriters into decline, CDs replaced records in the music industry, and DVDs replaced VHS tapes. In the TV broadcast industry, shows in the decline stage are generally discontinued, as seen with programs such as *Ugly Betty* and *Canadian Idol*, which had declining audiences. Other popular programs such as *Survivor* and *The Apprentice* manage to inject elements of newness into each season, thereby keeping the shows popular with viewers.

A company follows one of two strategies to deal with a declining product. It will either delete the product, as seen in the television entertainment industry, or harvest the product, as sometimes seen in the food industry. Deletion is when a product is discontinued, while **harvesting** is when a company keeps the product but reduces marketing support in an attempt to reap some minor profits at this stage in the life cycle.

Capacity of Kindle Touch eReaders—4th Generation

Capacity: **3,000** books

Fonts: **8** sizes

Download time: **60** seconds

Battery life: **2** months

marketing meter

Source: Amazon.com, accessed October 2011, http://www.amazon.com/gp/product/B005890G8O/ref=famstripe_kt3g.

Figure 8–4
Alternate product life cycles

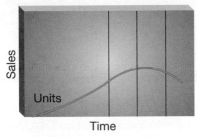

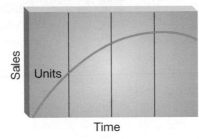

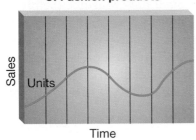

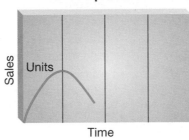

the advantages of the new technology, how to use it, and what to do with their VHS players and cassettes. It also required the entertainment industry to adopt this new technology for its movie releases instead of the traditional VHS format. It took considerable time for consumers and the industry to fully adopt this technology, resulting in an extended introductory period for DVDs.

In contrast, a **low-learning product** has a short introductory stage in the product life cycle. In these instances, the benefits of purchasing these products are self-evident and very little learning is required. An example of a successful low-learning product is the Apple iPad, which required little education on behalf of consumers. Consumers trusted the Apple brand, were often familiar with its touch-technology from use of the Apple iPhone, and found the interface intuitive and easy to use. Within 28 days, the iPad had sold more than a million units.[9]

The product life cycle for a **fashion product** is cyclical. The length of the cycle will vary, but it is relatively short, going from introduction to decline, generally within a two- to three-year period, only to resurface again a few years later. Life cycles for fashion products most often appear in men's and women's footware and apparel. UGG Australia boots is an interesting example of a fashion product that managed to extend its product life cycle well beyond the typical few years for a fashion product.

UGG boots, originally from rural Australia, were virtually unknown in North America until UGG Australia was purchased by Deckers Outdoor Corporation in 1995. The company repositioned the brand and started to market it in the early 2000s as a high-end, premium boot. In its introductory phase, the product was high-priced, not advertised, and only available at a few premium stores. The boots came in only a few colours and in

Shape of the Product Life Cycle

The length of a product life cycle varies according to the industry, the competition, technological innovation, and approaches to marketing the product. Television shows such as *The Apprentice* and products such as the Kindle may follow a consistent product life cycle curve as illustrated by the *generalized life cycle* shown in Figure 8–1 (see page 168). This consistent curve, however, does not always apply to all products. Products such as cellphones have very short product life cycles, moving from introduction to decline in only about 18 months. Other products, such as Heinz Ketchup, have extended product life cycles that have continued for years, driven by marketing approaches that keep the product relevant. Figure 8–4 shows four product life cycle curves that apply to different types of products. These products and their life cycles can be categorized into four main areas: (1) high-learning products, (2) low-learning products, (3) fashion products, and (4) fad products.

A **high-learning product** is one where there is an extended introductory period due to the significant efforts required to educate customers on the usage and benefits of the product. DVDs are examples of such a product. The DVD technology required consumers to understand

ask yourself

1. What are the four stages in the product life cycle? How do they differ in terms of sales and profits?

2. How do high-learning and low-learning products differ?

3. What is the shape of the product life cycle for a cellphone in today's marketplace?

fad
Novelty products with very short product life cycles that experience immediate rapid growth, followed by an equally rapid decline

line extension
The addition of a new item to an already existing product line

very limited quantities. In its early stages the company gave the boots to a few select celebrities who boosted demand—Pamela Anderson, Kate Hudson, and Jessica Simpson all wore the boots at highly publicized events. Oprah featured the boots on her show in 2000, 2003, and 2005, which immediately catapulted the boots into a rapid growth phase. By 2008 UGGs could be commonly found at regular shoe stores in a wide assortment of styles and colours. Now in their maturity stage, UGGs compete with similar sheepskin-type boots such as those found at Loblaw under its Joe Fresh Style banner.[10]

A **fad** refers to a product with a very short product life cycle. It typically experiences immediate rapid growth, followed by an equally rapid decline, with no real maturity stage at all. These products tend to be novelties. Children's toys often fall into this category.

Extending the Product Life Cycle

L② It is important for a firm to manage its products through their life cycles, profitably extending and prolonging their relevance in the market. Product life cycles can be extended in a number of ways, namely by (1) targeting current users with extended usage strategies, (2) targeting new consumers through new marketing approaches, (3) revitalizing a product with product improvements and line extensions, (4) repositioning a product, (5) introducing a new product, and (6) finding new uses for a product. It is important to realize that a combination of these approaches is most often used to keep products fresh and relevant.

Targeting Current Users with Extended Usage Strategies

This approach is typically used by marketers for products with strong brand equity and a loyal consumer

Kraft keeps its product lines fresh with new items and marketing campaigns.

> **Marketing ▶ tip**
>
> **"Innovation for the sake of innovation is worthless unless the consumer wants to buy the product at a price that will deliver profits."**
>
> *– Ian Gordon, senior vice president, Loblaw Companies Ltd.*

base. Current consumers are encouraged to consume more of the product in a variety of new ways. In the food industry, Knorr soup follows this approach by encouraging its users to not only consume the product as a soup but also to use it as an ingredient in main dish recipes. Another example is Rice Krispies, which often promotes its cereal usage as a baking ingredient for Rice Krispie Squares. Follow the links at www.kelloggs.ca to see the extended usage recipes used to market Rice Krispies.

Targeting New Consumers through New Marketing Approaches

Companies may decide that their current product is underrepresented with certain consumer groups and may see an opportunity to target these consumers. Marketers are often cautious and somewhat reluctant to follow this approach as it can be an expensive proposition that yields few results. This approach is currently being followed by Kraft with the 2010 introduction of its gourmet salad dressings, Pure Kraft Refrigerated Dressings. This new line of premium products is targeted to consumers looking for natural, higher-quality, gourmet salad dressings that contain top-quality, premium ingredients such as asiago cheese, extra virgin olive oil, and aged balsamic vinegars. These dressings, which can be found in the refrigerated section of the produce areas of supermarkets, have no artificial flavours, colours, or preservatives and are offered by Kraft as a new line of salad dressings. This line is in addition to Kraft's regular shelf-stable line of salad dressings, which are found in the regular salad dressing aisle. Time will tell whether this approach helps Kraft reach the premium, gourmet salad dressing market.

Revitalizing a Product with Product Improvements and Line Extensions

Product improvements and line extensions are often used by marketers to ensure that products remain competitive and address new trends in the market. Examples can be seen in the food industry where marketers are addressing consumers' demand for smaller portion sizes, healthier foods, and greener products. PC Blue Menu, for example, introduced products infused with Omega-3s, Knorr reformulated many of its Sidekick side dishes with 25 percent less sodium, and SunChips launched a 100 percent compostable bag. A line extension is the term used when a new item is added to an already existing product line, such as Cheerios adding its new Banana Nut

---

marketing NewsFlash

Did You Take a Samba Day Today?

What does a Brazilian samba dance have to do with a gift card at Shoppers Drug Mart? Not sure, unless of course you are Alex Barseghian, CEO and founder of Samba Days, a Canadian experiential gift card company, named after Brazilian samba dances that exude exuberance and passion. These gift cards capture this excitement and energy through an assortment of experiences that can be purchased as gift cards at retailers such as Shoppers Drug Mart, Sears, and Safeway. In fact, in just over three short years, 2,500 Canadian retailers now display Samba Days gift cards in store.

Samba Days gift cards are themed by interest into seven areas: Adventure, Body & Soul, Getaway, Gourmet, Golf, Wine, and Platinum (for the ultimate unique experience). Unlike other gift cards, these stand out in that recipients can choose among numerous experiences within each category (75 on average). The targeted demographic is looking for something different and unusual but without the hefty price tag.

Samba Days experiences are well priced at 10 to 30 percent below standard retail prices, providing value to Samba Days consumers. Prices start as low as $49, reaching to over $300 for Platinum

experiences. This is what Samba Days offers:

- **Adventure gift cards**—such as driving a Ferrari or taking a glass-blowing lesson
- **Body & Soul gift cards**—such as having a facial or taking yoga classes
- **Getaway gift cards**—such as a weekend gourmet getaway package
- **Gourmet gift cards**—such as dining at a local gourmet restaurant or a chef cooking for you at home
- **Golf gift cards**—such as a round of golf at Canada's premium courses
- **Wine gift cards**—such as a private wine tasting tour
- **Platinum gift cards**—such as a Porsche driving weekend or playing in a rock band

In three years, Samba Days has successfully sold thousands of experiences, partnering with heavy hitters such as Aeroplan and American Express. However, knowing the high failure rate of new products, and the required commitment and investment in pursuing this idea, Barseghian thoroughly researched the opportunity before he launched. He learned that 60 percent of people in Canada buy gift cards. He determined that experience gift cards are popular in Europe, and he discovered that people enjoy receiving gift experiences such

as weekend getaways. Importantly, he also determined that companies were interested in creating alliances with him to provide their experiences through Samba Days.

Samba Days was launched in 2008, first only online, then rolling out to 6 stores and then 400, now having distribution in 2,500 retail outlets across Canada. Online sales complement the retail offering with the gift cards also available at www.sambadays.com.

"Samba Days has been a passion for me," states Barseghian remembering the initial thrill of launching this new product in Canada. "It was both exhilarating and terrifying, knowing the risks involved and the uncertainty of launching a new product in a competitive marketplace. When I launched Samba Days, it was just me and my idea and now, 3 years later, 12 people work at making Samba Days a success." Barseghian cautions students to always do their homework first, to be inspired by new ideas, to follow their passions, but to also be cautious and realistic. You can see more on Samba Days at www.sambadays.com[11].

Questions

1. Why do you think Samba Days is a success when so many new products fail?

2. In what stage of the product life cycle is Samba Days? How can its product life cycle be extended?

Cheerios to the already well-established Cheerios product line.

Some of the most successful and long-lasting Canadian brands use a product-improvement and line-extension approach to extend their product life cycles and continue to be relevant to consumers. Interbrand's study, *Best Canadian Brands 2010*, points to the success of the Canadian BlackBerry brand with a brand value of $6 billion. BlackBerry smartphones successfully sell in 160 countries and have an estimated 20 percent market share. Subscribers have more than doubled since 2008.[12] The BlackBerry brand follows a strategy of continuous product improvement to extend its product life cycle and to extend its brand into the world of apps, software, and tablet computers.

An increased focus on the environment has prompted a surge in environmentally friendly products such as Sunlight Green Clean laundry detergent. This green product, designated as BrandSpark's best new laundry detergent of 2010,[13] is biodegradable, is made from plant-based ingredients, and has a highly concentrated formula that works in cold water. However, not all products live up to their environmental claims, giving rise to the term *greenwashing*. **Greenwashing** refers to the deceptive use of marketing practices to imply that a good, service, or organization is environmentally friendly. The Canadian Marketing Association provides a number of resources on green marketing to help reduce unethical business practices. Its website at www.the-cma.org includes green tips and information on best practices.

Repositioning a Product

Once a product has reached its maturity stage, it often needs an injection of newness to focus the market on the product and to provide it with a renewed competitive advantage. Many products appear tired at this stage and require a renewed focus. This can be achieved through new product development initiatives and/or repositioning the product to more readily meet changing consumer needs. Knorr is a well-known brand built on a tradition of powdered soup mixes and beef or chicken stock cubes. Many years ago, the product had become tired and needed to be associated with more contemporary approaches to cooking. The brand was revitalized with new products and new packaging to bring it into the forefront and position it as a modern brand that enhances the taste of cooking.

> *New products are the lifeblood of a company, helping to make products relevant and to bring future revenues into the company.*

Today the brand continues to evolve with a renewed focus on healthier eating: Knorr Sides Plus Veggies are promoted as a delicious way to include more vegetables in every meal; Knorr Sidekicks side dishes often have 25 percent less salt than before; and its new Knorr Homestyle Stock is positioned as an all-natural fat-free stock that is made from real chicken, beef, or vegetables, without artificial colours or ingredients. This revitalized image of healthier delicious eating is carried throughout Knorr's entire product mix of soups, sauces, seasonings, gravies, stocks, bouillon,

Knorr continues to revitalize its product mix with new products and line extensions.

frozen entrees, and side dishes. Check out the Knorr website at www.knorr.ca to see its latest offerings.

Introducing a New Product

Adding a new product can provide the focus that a mature product needs, bringing it back in the product life cycle to either the growth or early maturity stage. Apple has done this successfully by regularly introducing new versions of its iPads, iPods, and computers. Cellphone manufacturers similarly follow this approach, ensuring that these products remain fresh and relevant. In categories where technological change is not so prevalent, this approach is a little more difficult to manage. Kraft Canada's new Oreo Sippers product is a good example of a new product introduction that adds life to a traditional favourite. Oreo Sippers are hollow, straw-shaped, rolled-up adaptations of the traditional Oreo cookie that place renewed focus on this product line. Another example from Kraft is a cheesy-flavoured cracker that tastes like Kraft Dinner. Do you consider these two examples to be new products or simply line extensions? Check out the Kraft website at www.kraftcanada.com to determine your point of view.

Finding New Uses for a Product

Finding new uses for an existing product is not a simple task because many products do not lend themselves to this approach. Aspirin and Arm & Hammer are exceptions. Aspirin is mainly sold as a pain medication but it is also marketed as a heart and stroke preventative. Arm & Hammer baking soda is sold as a baking ingredient but it is also marketed as a product that eliminates odours, unblocks sinks, and cleans various household items.

New Product Innovation

L③ New products are the lifeblood of a company, helping to make products relevant and to bring future revenues into the company. There are many types of new products,

ranging from a slight product modification to a more radical innovation. How new products are categorized depends on the degree of newness involved, and how much time a consumer needs to learn to use the product. Based on these factors, we classify innovations as (1) minor innovations, (2) continuous innovations, and (3) radical innovations (see Figure 8–5).

Minor innovations refer to minor product modifications that require no adjustments on behalf of the consumer. Marketing a minor modification requires marketers to generate awareness for the innovation and to continue to market along current lines. Consumers do not need to be educated on how to use the product.

These types of innovations are relatively common and can be seen with new and improved detergents, diapers, and software that are frequently introduced by companies. An example is the Windows 7 operating system from Microsoft, which is an upgrade of its Windows Vista product, which is an upgrade of its Windows XP product, and so on.

Continuous innovations refer to new products that include more than just a minor product improvement but do not require radical changes in consumer behaviour. Continuous innovations are not common and require extensive

ask yourself

1. What approaches can be used to extend a product's life cycle?

2. If you were the marketer of a large SUV, what approach would you use today to extend its product life cycle?

3. Oreo Sippers was recently introduced by Kraft Canada. What approach is being used to extend the product life cycle of the traditional Oreo cookie?

product development by a company. Marketers must invest in marketing communications programs to launch these innovative products and to communicate their benefits to consumers. An example of a continuous innovation is the Rogers-on-Demand service that allows subscribers to select and play movies on their own TVs, in the comfort of their own homes, at their preferred time without having to visit a video store. Payment occurs on the customer's regular cable TV bill.

Radical innovations are the least common form of innovation. They involve the introduction of a product that is entirely new to the market. The success of these products is often dependent on the education of the consumer, usually through extensive advertising and public relations efforts. Public relations can add credibility to a radical innovation with the media encouraged through launch events, press kits, and press releases to discuss the product in its broadcasts or publications. This can result in considerable media coverage, which can boost sales by giving the public an objective and credible point of view. Examples of radical innovations are Crest Whitestrips and the BlackBerry smartphone, when they were first launched. Polaroid's recent introduction of

digital-camera-sunglasses is another example of a radical innovation. This product can be used as a regular pair of sunglasses or switched on to become a digital camera that can either store the images, send them to a wireless printer, or project them on the front of the sunglass lenses—a totally unique product in the market that requires considerable consumer education (see the Marketing NewsFlash on page 180).

The Adoption Curve

L4 The success of a new product and how quickly it is adopted by consumers is demonstrated in Figure 8–6, which shows the **adoption curve**. The adoption curve takes the point of view that some consumers are more ready than others to buy a product innovation. North American research (statistics vary across the world) shows that 2.5 percent of the population are innovators, risk takers who are the first to purchase innovative products; 13.5 percent are considered early adopters, another group that will accept a new offering sooner rather than later; and another 16 percent of the population are the laggards who are either reluctant or late purchasers of the innovation. In the middle of the pack are the early and late majority, each comprising approximately 34 percent of the population. Once accepted by the innovators and early adopters, the adoption of new products moves on to the early

Polaroid's' GL20 Camera Glasses protect the eyes from the sun and can be switched on to be used as a digital camera and image-display surface—a radical innovation.

Figure 8–5
Degree of product innovation

	MINOR INNOVATION	CONTINUOUS INNOVATION	RADICAL INNOVATION
Definition	Requires no new learning by consumers	Changes consumer's normal routine but does not require totally new learning	Requires new learning and consumption patterns by consumers
Examples	New and improved detergents or diapers	Electric toothbrushes or digital cameras	eReaders or GPS devices
Marketing emphasis	Gain consumer awareness and wide distribution	Advertise points of difference and benefits to consumers	Educate consumers through advertising, product trial, and personal selling; public relations can play a major role

majority and late majority who respond to the product being well-established in the market, and are influenced by the purchase habits of their peers. Finally, the product adoption moves onto the laggards of the population who are reluctant buyers of the product and may in fact never purchase it.

The relevancy of the adoption curve is that marketers try to move the product from the innovators through to the early majority so as to quickly reap the benefits of increased sales and profits as soon as possible. In this manner, marketers design marketing programs to target these specific groups in different ways and separately focus their marketing programs on the demographic and psychographic needs, interests, and drivers of these target groups.

An example of how the adoption curve applies to new product diffusion can be seen with Twitter and, separately, with 3-D TVs. In the social-media market, Twitter followed an interesting approach when introducing its updated interface in 2010, treading carefully so as to not alienate its current users—innovators and early adopters. Instead of migrating users immediately over to the new interface and its improved functionality, which may have resulted in a backlash, Twitter embedded a button on its homepage so that users could choose when to move over to the new interface. This button also allowed users to switch back to the old version if they wished. This flexible approach existed for many months until the new Twitter interface became a permanent fixture and its users were familiar with its new design.

A new product currently struggling to move along the adoption curve is 3-D TV. Introduced in 2010 after its successful adoption in movie theatres, 3-D TVs have gained little traction among the TV-buying public. Not innovative enough to attract the attention of innovators and early adopters, and lacking the substantial easy-to-recognize benefits that appeal to the early and late majority, the long-term viability of this product is questionable.

Why New Products Succeed or Fail

L⑤ This chapter's opening vignette spoke to the evolution of the PC Blue Menu line of products over time and how rarely new products succeed from day one. We are familiar with successful new products and brands such as Google, Xbox, and

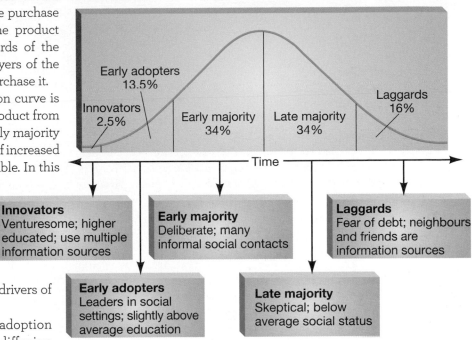

Figure 8–6
The adoption curve

iPad, yet only one in ten new products are successful over time.[14] It is important at this point to remember the insight that Ian Gordon from Loblaw Companies gives us on how to successfully craft new products. He reminds us that it is the *journey* of new product innovation that makes new products successful over time. He states that marketers are tasked to implement meaningful changes to the marketing mix based on listening and reacting to consumers, and not to be focused only on the innovation itself.

Reasons for New-Product Failures Using the research results from several studies on new product successes and failures, we can identify critical marketing factors that often spell failure for new product launches:[15]

1. **Insignificant point of difference:** Shown as one of the most important factors, a distinctive and meaningful point of difference is essential for a new product to compete in the market. In 2010, TV manufacturers introduced 3-D TVs to the market, expecting consumers to readily buy these units. Disappointing sales have pundits questioning the benefit of this technology, particularly when very little programming is available in 3-D. In an attempt to boost sales, manufacturers are joining forces with TV stations to provided 3-D programming. Sony is working with a TV station in Japan to create a 3D drama series, while Panasonic has created a 3-D music program for satellite TV.[16]

Whatever Happened to Polaroid?

In 2011 Lady Gaga and Polaroid launched Polaroid's new Grey Label line, showcasing three innovative new products: a new instant digital camera, an instant printer, and innovative sunglasses with a built-in digital camera. A year earlier, Polaroid had announced its surprising collaboration with Lady Gaga as their creative director, hired to bring the iconic Polaroid instant camera into the digital world.

The GL30 Instant Digital Camera, visually reminiscent of the old Polaroid camera, uses digital technology to make instant fun images. Photos can be taken, stored, displayed, and instantly printed on the device using filters and frames for innovative effects. The printed photos are 3-x-4-inch photo-lab quality, smudge-proof, tear-proof, and water resistant. They are printed using inkless ZINC technology, which does not require printer ribbons, toner, or print cartridges.

The GL10 Instant Mobile Printer is innovative in two ways: its handheld size makes it incredibly small for printing the high-quality, inkless photos mentioned above, and it uses wireless Bluetooth technology to print photos directly from cellphones.

The GL20 Camera Glasses protect the eyes from the sun and can be switched on to be used as a digital camera. Its images can be stored on a USB, wirelessly sent to a printer, or innovatively projected onto the front of the sunglasses, which are in fact LCD panels.

These new product introductions come on the heels of Polaroid's 2008 announcement of the closing of its instant film photography operations, effectively ending its instant camera line. The discontinuation, the result of changing technology, was surprisingly followed by attempts to revitalize the iconic brand. Will Mlacak, director of marketing for Polaroid Canada in the late 1990s, experienced the brand's demise firsthand but does not find the brand's latest announcements surprising. "This reminds me of Polaroid's iZone Camera introduced the mid-1990s as a fun, colourful instant camera with tiny photos for tweens and teens," states Mlacak. "But the product was a short-lived fad—it could not compete against digital technology. This new Grey Label line is another attempt by Polaroid to revive a brand that has incredible pull with consumers. Its success will depend on whether the products are truly relevant to consumers and whether they are marketed over time." Mlacak reminds us not to underestimate the power of this iconic brand, which has been around for over 70 years and is currently licensing its name for use with digital TVs, digital photo frames, digital HD camcorders, and waterproof digital cameras. Check out its latest products at http://polaroid.com.[17] ●

Questions

1. What type of innovation is Polaroid's GL10 Instant Mobile Printer?

2. Looking at the adoption curve, which consumer group(s) is Polaroid targeting with this cluster of new products?

2. **Incomplete new concept definition:** Ideally, before a new product is developed, it needs a well-defined, consumer-based reason for being. Its consumer insights must be clearly identified. If these areas are not clarified, the new products will have no meaningful positioning in the market. Coca-Cola Blak, a coffee-flavoured cola, is such as example. Introduced in Canada in August 2006, this new product took on both coffee shops and energy drinks with a beverage that had less caffeine than coffee and Red Bull, and more caffeine than Coca-Cola—clearly a confusing proposition. Its target market, according to Coca-Cola, was, "The adult that appreciates a good cup of coffee who is looking for something a little different, a little more premium."[18] However, the product missed its mark and was discontinued in Canada and the U.S. in 2007.

3. **Insufficient market attractiveness:** Market attractiveness refers to a product having strong

consumer appeal in a category with both growth and profit potential. Often, a target market can be too small or too competitive to result in a profitable entry. The Canadian theatre production *Lord of the Rings: The Musical* was a $27 million flop with poor sales that forced the production to be pulled after only five months. The three-and-a-half-hour production was deemed too lengthy for the traditional theatre-going audience and criticized for being neither a play nor a musical, which limited its appeal.[19]

4. **Inadequate marketing support:** Companies often launch products with little marketing support or a marketing mix that does not adequately support the innovation. The President's Choice TGTBT line of products (discussed in this chapter's opening vignette) points to a marketing mix that required revamping and more support for consumers to fully comprehend its benefits. The revamped PC Blue Menu line provided this needed support for product success and continues to thrive with continued marketing programs.

5. **Insensitivity to critical customer needs:** Ignoring a critical consumer insight can kill a product, even though the general concept may be well-accepted. For example, the Japanese, like the British, drive on the left side of the road, resulting in right-hand-drive vehicles on their roads. Until 1996, North American car makers continued to sell left-hand-drive options to Japan with little success. Contrast this with the German car manufacturers that successfully exported right-hand-drive models for a number of their brands to this market.[20]

6. **Bad timing:** A product can suffer negative consequences if it is introduced too soon, too late, or at a time when consumer tastes are shifting. An example exists in the aircraft industry. In March 2001, Boeing announced it would start the multibillion-dollar development of its Sonic Cruiser, designed to cross oceans with over 400 passengers at almost the speed of sound. However, the tragic attacks of September 11, 2001, caused such a decline in air travel that the project was postponed.[21]

7. **Limited access to buyers:** It is often difficult to obtain the

An unsuccessful new product from Coca-Cola

necessary distribution to reach a target market. Consumer products typically need a retailer to list and display their products in-store, but this distribution network is not always readily available. A new product may have tested well with consumers, but if a retailer does not carry the product, its distribution will be limited.

Cottonelle Fresh Rollwipes from Kimberly-Clark is an example of a product that suffered from poor distribution. This moist toilet-tissue on a roll was launched in the U.S. in 2001 in a plastic dispenser that clipped on to the side of a regular toilet-paper dispenser. Kimberly-Clark spent $100 million on research and development and protected the product with 30 patents. Within 10 months, sales had reached only a third of forecasts, and distribution was so sporadic that 18 months after launch, the product was available only in specific southern markets. Despite a national advertising campaign, the product could not be found at most retailers across the U.S.[22] Perhaps the journey of product development required more time and marketing adjustments to be successful.

ask yourself

1. Describe the three types of product innovation and explain which ones are most common.

2. How does the adoption curve apply to the diffusion of new products in the marketplace?

3. What are the main reasons that new products fail?

New Product Development

Developing and launching new products is an expensive undertaking with a high risk of failure. Research costs are high, as is the time and effort spent on developing prototypes and marketing materials. Product launches may also include expensive listing fees required to secure retail distribution. Product failure can result in expensive product write-offs and a lack of future credibility in the market. Hundreds of thousands of dollars are often at stake. In order to avoid expensive product failures, companies can use a number of different approaches to develop these new products. These range from providing clear strategic direction, to creating particular company structures, and to instituting rigorous product development processes. We look at these areas in more detail in the sections that follow.

Approaches to New Product Development

Strategic Direction   From a strategic point of view, companies can follow different approaches to innovation (see Figure 8–7). It is somewhat dependent on the degree of risk and investment that companies are willing to take. The most common forms of innovation take either a market penetration or product development slant, focusing on current consumers with promotional tactics (market penetration), or looking to develop a new product for these current consumers (product development). Higher risk considerations include either a market development or diversification

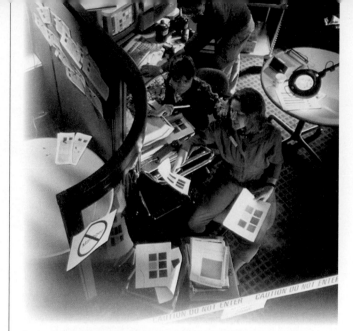

Cross-functional teams reduce new product development time.

strategy, taking the more expensive approach of either targeting new markets with current products (market development), or moving out into new arenas with totally new products (diversification).

Company Structure   Companies use different structures to encourage innovation. Some companies, such as Loblaw Companies, use teams to help marshal successful new products to Canadian consumers. They use a *team-based approach* that includes chefs, nutrition researchers, registered dieticians, nutritionists, product developers, quality assurance specialists, regulatory affairs experts, and marketers.

Other companies may follow a more individualized approach, appointing a new product development manager to concentrate entirely in this area. In other instances, full departments are tasked with this responsibility, or new product development is included in the role of the general marketer. In some instances, new venture teams are used to concentrate on all innovation projects for the company, which could include new products, new processes, or new business ventures.

Regardless of the formal structure, new product development success ultimately requires the expertise of people with different specializations and from varied backgrounds to ensure that the best product ideas are developed. These experts are either fully involved in the process from the start, or brought in along the way to contribute to the journey.

Figure 8–7
Strategic approaches to innovation

Markets	PRODUCTS	
	Current	New
	Market Penetration	**Product Development**
Current	Finding ways to make current products appeal to current customers	Reaching current customers with a new product
	Market Development	**Diversification**
New	Reaching new customers with a current product	Reaching new customers with a new product

new product
development
process
Sequence of steps
that a firm takes to
develop a new prod-
uct idea and take it
to market

new product
development
strategy
Setting the new
product strategic
direction for the
company as a whole,
and the precise
objectives for the
project at hand

idea generation
Focuses on brain-
storming sessions
to prompt new ideas

screening and
evaluation
Reduces the list of
brainstorming ideas
down to a list of
promising concepts

The New Product Development Process

L⑥ In order to avoid expensive product failures, companies use rigorous product develop-ment processes to minimize the risk. Each step in the process requires an individual or team to assess whether the project is still viable and should continue down the road to innovation. The **new prod-uct development process** includes the seven steps shown in Figure 8–8 and summarized in Figure 8–9, and starts with a clearly defined strategy. This is followed by a number of brainstorming, research, product-development, and business-analysis steps. A successful trip down this road faces many twists and turns and any new product development team needs to be flexible, creative, and responsive to the insights learned at each step.

Step 1: New Product Development Strategy

New product development success relies on many factors. Having a clear definition and understanding of what you are trying to achieve with the innova-tion is one of the most important building blocks in this process. A **new product development strategy** involves setting the new product strategic direction for the company as a whole, and the precise objec-tives for the project at hand. There must be consis-tency between the two.

An example can be seen with Procter & Gamble, which in 2000 refocused its new product development strategy from "new-to-the-world" products and brands, to evolving current brands such as Crest, Tide, and Pampers with new initiatives. The result was products such as Crest Whitestrips for teeth whitening and Crest SpinBrush for better dental care. These innovations helped boost global sales for the Crest brand by 50 percent within two years.[23]

Step 2: Idea Generation
Once the purpose and direction for the prod-uct development project is clarified, the second step of **idea generation** comes into play. This includes brainstorming sessions focused on participants com-ing up with new ideas for the project at hand. Ideas can come from inside or outside the company, depending on the organization's approach to new product development. It is important for these brainstorming sessions to include indi-viduals who are creative, have varied experiences, and have differing areas of expertise. This should stimulate a more varied and interesting pool of ideas.

Brainstorming sessions can result in a host of interesting ideas, but for this approach to work, par-ticipants must be willing to share their most ludicrous or boring ideas with the group. Participants need to be open-minded, energetic, flexible, and willing to build on each other's ideas. Often, companies hire an out-side moderator, skilled in these types of sessions, to promote creativity sessions that render results. As a rule of thumb, it takes at least 60 ideas to generate an inspired idea with some potential.

Step 3: Screening and Evaluation
The third stage of the new product development process, **screening and evaluation**, attempts to reduce the array of brainstorming ideas down to a manageable list of promising concepts. Ideas are initially screened internally by the new product development team, which eliminates ideas that do not meet the objectives, as well as those that are clearly not feasible. The short list of ideas is then developed by the team into concepts. A concept is a more detailed idea, couched in consumer terms, with more particulars for clarification. A concept is then presented to consumers for initial feedback in the form of a

Figure 8–8
Steps in the new product development process

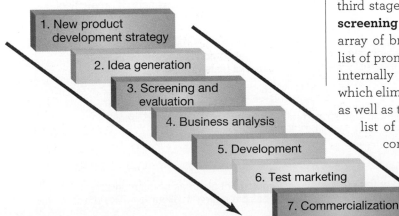

1. New product development strategy
2. Idea generation
3. Screening and evaluation
4. Business analysis
5. Development
6. Test marketing
7. Commercialization

concept tests External evaluations of a new product idea, rather than the actual product itself

business analysis Financial projections on the impact of bringing the new product to market and selling it in the future

concept test. This presents consumers with a short descriptive paragraph and an accompanying visual.

Concept tests are external evaluations of the new product idea, rather than the actual product itself. Several key issues are addressed during concept testing, such as how the customer perceives the product, who would use it, and how it would be used. The purpose of these evaluations is to get feedback on the strengths and weaknesses of the concepts and to understand what further modifications are required. Concept tests will result in some concepts being eliminated and others surfacing as more-promising opportunities that require further investigation. One may ask why product prototypes are not presented to consumers at this point. Product prototypes are typically expensive to develop, and a basic concept test avoids this unnecessary expense. It is also premature to develop a product prototype before a final concept is determined.

> *The business analysis stage results in profit projections.*

Once a clear concept has surfaced during this stage, further research is required to determine the specific elements of the marketing mix that will help the product succeed in the marketplace. Consumers need to be probed on elements such as pricing, brand names, and advertising ideas.

Step 4: Business Analysis After the concept tests have determined which product, or line of products, are strong new product candidates, the **business analysis** step is necessary. This involves determining financial projections on bringing the new product to market and selling it in the future. Typical financial projections for a new product cover a three-year period and often look five years into the future. Financial projections involve sales and revenue forecasts, cost projections, and budget requirements for marketing support. Marketers need to initially establish the

Figure 8–9
Elements in each stage of the new product development process

STAGE OF PROCESS	PURPOSE OF STAGE	MARKETING INFORMATION AND METHODS USED
New product development strategy	Identify new-product development focus that meets company objectives	Company objectives; SWOT analysis of company/product/brand
Idea generation	Brainstorm new ideas	Ideas from employees, co-workers, and consumers
Screening and evaluation	Evaluate product ideas and develop concepts	Internal evaluation of technical requirements, external concept tests
Business analysis	Identify the product's features and its marketing strategy, and make financial projections	Product's key features and anticipated marketing mix; assessment of production, legal, and profitability issues
Development	Create the prototype, and test it internally at the company and externally with consumers	Internal company assessments and external tests on product prototypes
Test marketing	Test the product and marketing strategy in the marketplace on a limited scale (if necessary)	Test marketing in defined areas
Commercialization	Launch and fully market the product in the marketplace	Implement all areas of the marketing mix; possible regional rollout

positioning of the product in the market and what marketing elements are needed for a successful launch. The new product is also studied to determine whether it can, and should, be protected with a patent, trademark, or copyright.

The business analysis step requires marketers to determine market share projections, price points, cost parameters, special discounts, distribution requirements, research needs, and all the marketing communications programs needed to ensure product success. Marketers also need to understand whether the product will require an investment in new machinery and whether it will cannibalize the sales of existing products. At this point in the new product development process, marketers are checking the commercial viability of the new product. This requires strong analytical skills and the ability to understand the dynamics of the market. A marketer must also be able to anticipate competitive reactions and foresee target market needs.

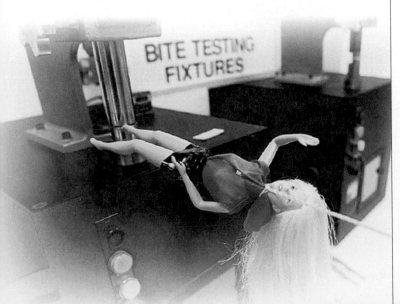

The business analysis stage results in profit projections. Marketers review these projections, taking a realistic view of the product and the market to decide whether the concept has real financial merit. Often at this stage, one can easily take an optimistic view, but it is important for marketers to be as realistic as possible and to consider severe competitive reactions to their launch. If the product can meet sales, profit, and market share targets, then the new product development process will continue to the next step. If not, marketers may reassess the concept, going back to consumers to conduct further research. It is important for marketers at this point to stop the process if the concept has little merit and weak profit forecasts. This is usually the last checkpoint before significant resources are invested in creating a *prototype*, a full-scale operating model of the product.

Step 5: Development New product ideas that survive the business analysis step proceed to actual **development**, turning the idea into a prototype for further consumer research and manufacturing tests. This step is considerably complex, involving laboratory and consumer tests to ensure that the product consistently meets legal and quality control requirements. Manufacturing trials are also conducted to eliminate manufacturing problems and to reduce costs.

This step can be time-consuming with some products requiring extensive testing before they can be safely brought to market. Pharmaceutical products, children's toys, cars, and food products that require shelf-life tests are examples that fall into this category. Mattel, for example, extensively tests its Barbie dolls to ensure that their heads cannot be detached from their bodies by small children biting on the head. Testing involves clamping the doll's head in steel jaws and pulling on the doll's head with a wire. Similarly, car manufacturers crash-test cars to determine safety standards.

The advantage of the development step is that it allows marketers to take actual product prototypes into consumer research. This may be needed to further probe elements of the marketing mix. In some instances, ambivalence may still exist on the subtleties of brand names, packaging, and pricing. Advertising campaigns may also require feedback on the clarity of the communication.

Step 6: Test Marketing **Test marketing** involves offering a product for sale on a limited basis in a defined geographic area. This test is done to

development
The new product idea is turned into a prototype for further consumer research and manufacturing tests

test marketing
Offering a new product for sale on a limited basis in a defined geographic area to assess its success

commercialization
When the new product is brought to market with full-scale production, sales, and marketing support

determine whether consumers will actually buy the product, and to what extent. Marketers may use this opportunity to test different marketing approaches to support the product.

In Canada, test markets are conducted in cities such as London, Edmonton, and Moncton. These cities are good candidates as their populations are representative of Canada in general. The media in these cities is also isolated, meaning that a company can advertise and test special promotions and be able to measure their success. Using tracking systems by firms such as Nielsen, marketers can correlate local advertising campaigns to in-store purchases by using data from store scanners.

The main drawbacks of test markets are that they are expensive to conduct and they immediately alert the competition. Competitors can easily sabotage test markets by altering their own pricing and marketing support to render the test market unsuccessful. These issues are so real that many marketers do not embark on test markets, relying on research to provide good direction for a full product launch.

Technology is assisting marketers by creating simulated test markets through a number of software programs. An emerging trend uses virtual reality testing to allow marketers to present consumers with a range of experiences such as simulated store environments. Elumens Corporation has developed VisionDome, which can accommodate up to 45 people at a time and provide them with an interactive 3-D experience.[24]

> *To minimize the risk of financial failure, many companies use regional rollouts.*

Step 7: Commercialization

Commercialization is the step when the new product is brought to market with full-scale production, sales, and marketing support. Companies proceed very carefully at the commercialization stage because this is the most expensive stage for most new products. To minimize the risk of financial failure, many companies use regional rollouts, introducing the product sequentially into geographic areas of the country to allow production levels and marketing activities to build gradually. Grocery product manufacturers and some telecommunication service providers are examples of firms that use this strategy.

Marketing plays a crucial role in the success of a new product, and marketers need to intimately understand their consumers and what is important to their purchase decisions. Each element of the marketing mix needs to be carefully crafted to help make a new product successful. The example of the PC Blue Menu line evolving from the TGTBT line of President's Choice products reminds us that all elements play a crucial role in new product success.

ask yourself

1. What occurs in the screening and evaluation step of the new product development process?

2. What is the purpose of the business analysis step in the new product development process?

3. What are the advantages and disadvantages of a test market?

Summary...*just the facts*

- Product life cycles are the stages that a new product goes through from its initial introduction through to growth, maturity, and decline.

- The shape of a product life cycle varies depending on the industry, the competition, technological innovation, and the marketing of the product.

- Product life cycles can be extended through various marketing techniques that encourage new and current users to keep purchasing the product and use it in new ways.

- There are many types of new products, ranging from slight product modifications, to more innovative changes, to the more radical innovations we see in the market.

- The adoption curve shows the sequential diffusion and acceptance of an innovation into the market by consumers.

- New products must have a distinct point of difference to enjoy long-term success in the market.

- From a strategic point of view, companies can follow a combination of approaches to innovation, including market penetration, product development, market development, and diversification.

- The new product development process follows seven steps: (1) new product development strategy, (2) idea generation, (3) screening and evaluation, (4) business analysis, (5) development, (6) test marketing, and (7) commercialization.

Key Terms and Concepts...*a refresher*

adoption curve *p. 178*
business analysis *p. 184*
commercialization *p. 186*
concept tests *p. 184*
continuous innovations *p. 177*
development *p. 185*
fad *p. 174*
fashion product *p. 173*

greenwashing *p. 176*
harvesting *p. 172*
high-learning product *p. 173*
idea generation *p. 183*
line extension *p. 174*
low-learning product *p. 173*
minor innovations *p. 177*
new product development process *p. 183*

new product development strategy *p. 183*
product life cycle *p. 167*
radical innovations *p. 178*
screening and evaluation *p. 183*
test marketing *p. 185*

Hands-on...*apply your knowledge*

New Product Development Assignment   PC Blue Menu is trying to reinforce the idea that its products are highly nutritious additions to consumers' food choices. Review this chapter's opening vignette on PC Blue Menu and brainstorm how the online environment can be used to emphasize this point with everyday consumers. As a starting point, be sure to review PC Blue Menu's support on the President's Choice website at www.presidentschoice.ca, examine its social media presence on websites such as Twitter and Facebook, and conduct a search-engine analysis on Google and Bing to find microsites and recent news.

Reality Check...*reminder*

Refer back to this chapter's opening vignette and answer the Reality Check questions on page 166.

McGraw Hill **connect** *Practise and learn online with Connect.*

Connect allows you to practise important concepts at your own pace and on your own schedule, with 24/7 online access to an eBook, practice quizzes, video cases, chapter application questions, discussion activities, Internet exercises, interactivities, study tools, and more.

Pricing

Pricing is a complex issue in marketing, requiring both analytical and strategic thinking. Marketers must have a clear understanding of what prices the market will bear, how competitors will react, and what their target market is willing to pay. Marketers need to have a tight grasp on their product costs so that accurate profit forecasts can be made.

Author Tina Powell writes children's books. Her popular picture books amuse and empower children, while celebrating the special view they have of the world. Through partnering with companies such as Canada Bread, Procter & Gamble, and Mars Canada, over 600,000 of Tina's books have reached children in North America. Her books have also been translated into French and Spanish. Here's an example of how her corporate programs work. Tina developed a custom children's activity book for Canada Bread and placed the Dempster's logo on the cover and on the interior pages. A Dempster's corporate message was also placed on the back cover. The promotional program had Tina's book *Samantha's Silly-icious Sandwiches* and the new Dempster's "silly icious" activity book distributed to 1,000 schools in the Greater Toronto Area. As part of a tour sponsored by Canada Bread, Tina personally visited over 100 Ontario schools encouraging children to read, write, and eat better.

L1 Identify the elements that make up a price

L2 Explain the approaches to pricing and the major factors considered in arriving at a final price

L3 Describe the demand curve and define price elasticity of demand

L4 Explain the role of revenues (sales) and costs in pricing decisions

L5 Discuss the value of break-even analysis and conduct break-even calculations

L6 Describe the price objectives a firm may have and the constraints under which they operate

L7 Outline the four steps in determining a final price

L8 Explain the adjustments made to price because of factors such as geography, discounts, and allowances

Through her initiatives in working with corporations, Tina's books have quickly become bestsellers. The success of her books and her growing understanding of the publishing industry prompted Tina to launch her own publishing company, Big Fat Pen Publishing Inc., in 2004.

When Tina determines the price to charge corporations for one of her customized children's books, she uses the cost-plus method. "I take the total cost of production per unit and then add a fair profit margin," explains Tina. "Since the print volumes for my corporate programs are usually quite high, it allows me to provide organizations with an excellent price per unit." The size of the promotional program can also influence Tina's unit price. Big Fat Pen's corporate book programs are often supported by author tours, website activity pages, and public relations programs—the larger the program, the lower the price per unit to the corporation.

Tina also sells her books in the traditional way through bookstores. In Canada, she uses a book distributor called Red Tuque Books that in turn sells her books to independent bookstores throughout Canada. Tina uses three methods to determine the retail selling price of her children's books. The first method considers a general guideline of the publishing industry, which is to multiply her costs for a book by five. The result is the suggested retail price. Tina includes the following in her costs: the cost to print the book; costs for illustrations, design, editing, and promotion; and her profit on a per unit basis.

The second method Tina uses to determine the retailer selling price is standard markup pricing. Tina starts with the total per unit cost to produce the book and then adds the markups that various channel members demand. Book retailers usually ask for a 40 percent markup on the retail selling price, while Tina's distributor, Red Tuque Books, receives 30 percent on its selling price to bookstores.

The third method is called target pricing. It begins with Tina estimating the price that the ultimate consumer would pay for her book at the bookstore. She does this by checking the prices of competitors' children's books at the bookstores and determines a reasonable price for her books, based on the market. She then works backward through the markups taken by the retailer and distributor to determine if the price she can charge the distributor for the book will cover her costs and provide a fair profit.

Tina's goal in using three different pricing methods is to not rely on any one method to determine a selling price. Ultimately, Tina looks at all three methods to help her derive a selling price for her books.

Tina says that the publishing industry is fraught with challenges and complexities that make pricing and distribution difficult for a publisher to manage. For example, almost all the books in a bookstore can be returned by the bookseller to the publisher for a full credit, even if the book is damaged. In addition to distribution fees, many book distributors also charge receiving fees, shipping fees, storage fees, and promotional fees. Big Fat Pen Publishing recently had an opportunity to distribute its books through a large U.S. book distributor. Once Tina calculated all the fees to be paid to the distributor, she discovered that each book would have to be sold at a loss. Needless to say, Tina did not proceed with the deal.

Tina's children's books retail for $9.95 each, plus sales tax, at independent bookstores. She sells these same books for an even $10 when making personal appearances. "This decision was strictly a matter of convenience," explains Tina. "It's much easier to deal with even numbers at an author event than to calculate tax for each purchase. Plus, because I am selling the books directly to consumers and I do not have to pay sales discounts to a distributor or retailer, I can pay the tax and still come out way ahead. Best of all, unlike booksellers, I have yet to have a consumer return a book and ask for their money back."

When asked about her thoughts on eBooks, Tina says that she is actively doing research to look at the feasibility of having her books available as eBooks. She feels, however, that children's books may be a little slower to convert to eBooks as kids still like the tactile feel of a paper book. 🍎

As you read Chapter 9, refer back to this opening vignette to answer the following questions:

- Although author Tina Powell is known for her children's books, she recently finished writing her first book for adults, *Picnic in Pisticci*. Which pricing objective(s) do you feel Tina should choose for marketing her book to bookstores? Why?

- Which pricing constraint(s) apply to Powell as she enters this new market? Why?

reality CHECK

Pricing has many implications for marketing.

Price

Marketers need to know how pricing impacts their target market and their competitors.

Chapter 9 introduces the all-important question of pricing and its many implications for marketing. This topic focuses on the price element of the 4Ps that make up the marketing mix.

Nature and Importance of Price

LO 1 The price paid for goods and services goes by many names. You pay *tuition* for your education, *rent* for an apartment, *interest* on a bank credit card, and a *premium* for car insurance. Your dentist or physician charges you a *fee*, a professional or social organization charges *dues*, and airlines charge a *fare*. And what you pay for clothes or a haircut is termed a *price*.

What Is a Price?

These examples highlight the many and varied ways that price plays a part in our daily lives. From a marketing viewpoint, **price** is the money or other considerations, including other goods and services, exchanged for the ownership or use of a product. Recently, Wilkinson Sword exchanged some of its knives for advertising used to promote its razor blades. This practice of exchanging goods and services for other goods and services rather than for money is called barter. These transactions account for billions of dollars annually in domestic and international trade.

For most products, money is exchanged. However, the amount paid is not always the same as the list, or quoted, price because of discounts, allowances, and extra fees. While discounts, allowances, and rebates make the effective price lower, other marketing tactics raise the real price. One new pricing tactic is to use "special fees" and "surcharges." This practice is driven by consumers' zeal for low prices combined with the ease of making price comparisons on the Internet. Buyers are more willing to pay extra fees than a higher list price, so sellers use add-on charges as a way of having the consumer pay more without raising the list price. Examples of such special fees include a Telus Mobility "system licensing charge" and "911 emergency service access charge" that increase the monthly cellphone bill, or an environmental surcharge on new tires and batteries for cars in some provinces. (See the Marketing NewsFlash on page 195 for a discussion of credit card fees.)

All these different factors that increase or decrease the price are put together in a "price equation," which is shown for several different products in Figure 9–1.

Suppose that you decide you want to buy a Bugatti Veyron, the world's fastest production car, which can move you from 0 to 100 km/h in 2.5 seconds with a top speed of 422 km/h. The Veyron has a list price of $1.5 million. However, if you put $500,000 down now and finance the balance over the next year, you will receive a rebate of $100,000 off the list price. For your 2000

Honda Civic DX 4-door sedan that has 100,000 kilometres and is in fair condition, you are given a trade-in allowance of $4,350.[1]

The finance fee on the $500,000 down is $41,974 and a $5,000 destination charge to ship the car from Europe.

Applying the price equation (as shown in Figure 9–1) to your purchase, your final price is:

$$\text{Final price} = \text{List price} - (\text{Incentives} + \text{Allowances}) + \text{Extra fees}$$

$$= \$1,500,000 - (\$100,000 + \$4,350) + (\$41,974 + \$5,000)$$

$$= \$1,442,624$$

Are you still interested in buying this car?

Price as an Indicator of Value

From a consumer's standpoint, price is often used to indicate value when it is compared with the perceived benefits such as quality, durability, and so on of a product or service. Specifically, **value** is the ratio of perceived benefits to price,[2] or

$$\text{Value} = \frac{\text{Perceived benefits}}{\text{Price}}$$

This relationship shows that for a given price, as perceived benefits increase, value increases. For example, if you're used to paying $13.99 for a medium pizza, wouldn't a large pizza at the same price be more valuable? Many marketers often engage in the practice of *value pricing*—increasing product or service benefits while maintaining or decreasing price.

> *Pricing decisions influence both total revenue (sales) and total cost, which makes pricing one of the most important decisions marketing executives face.*

Marketers must be careful when using price as an indicator of value. For example, for many consumers, a low price would imply poor quality, and ultimately poor perceived value. This is particularly true for services. For example, what would be your perception of a dentist who charges only $25 for a checkup and cleaning, when the average dentist charges between $10 and $150? This example illustrates that consumers make comparative value assessments.

In a survey of home-furnishing buyers, 84 percent agreed with the statement, "The higher the price, the higher the quality."[3] For example, Kohler introduced a walk-in bathtub that is safer for children and the elderly. Although priced higher than conventional step-in bathtubs, it has proven very successful because buyers are willing to pay more for what they perceive as the benefit of extra safety.

Price in the Marketing Mix

Pricing is a critical decision made by a marketing executive because price has a direct effect on a firm's profits. This is apparent from a firm's **profit equation**:

$$\text{Profit} = \text{Total revenue} - \text{Total cost}$$

$$= (\text{Unit price} \times \text{Quantity sold}) - \text{Total cost}$$

Figure 9–1
The price of three different purchases

ITEM PURCHASED	PRICE	= LIST PRICE	− INCENTIVES AND ALLOWANCES	+ EXTRA FEES
New car bought by an individual	Final price	= List price	− Rebate Cash discount Old car trade-in	+ Financing charges Special accessories Destination charges
Term in university bought by a student	Tuition	= Published tuition	− Scholarship Other financial aid	+ Special activity fees
Merchandise bought from a wholesaler by a retailer	Invoice price	= List price	− Quantity discount Cash discount Seasonal discount Functional or trade discount	+ Penalty for late payment

Figure 9–2
Four approaches for selecting an approximate price level

Demand-oriented approaches
- Skimming
- Penetration
- Prestige
- Odd-even
- Target
- Bundle
- Yield management

Cost-oriented approaches
- Standard markup
- Cost-plus

Profit-oriented approaches
- Target profit
- Target return on sales
- Target return on investment

Competition-oriented approaches
- Customary
- Above, at, or below market
- Loss leader

What makes this relationship even more complicated is that price affects the quantity sold, as illustrated with demand curves later in this chapter, because the quantity sold sometimes affects a firm's costs because of efficiency of production, price also indirectly affects costs. Thus, pricing decisions influence both total revenue (sales) and total cost, which makes pricing one of the most important decisions marketing executives face.

General Pricing Approaches

L❷ A key to a marketing manager's setting a final price for a product is to find an "approximate price level" to use as a reasonable starting point. Four common approaches to helping find this approximate price level are demand-oriented, cost-oriented, profit-oriented, and competition-oriented approaches (see Figure 9–2). Although these approaches are discussed separately below, some of them overlap, and an effective marketing manager will consider several in searching for an approximate price level.

Demand-Oriented Approaches

Demand-oriented approaches emphasize factors underlying expected customer tastes and preferences more than such factors as cost, profit, and competition when selecting a price level.

Skimming Pricing A firm introducing a new product can use *skimming pricing*, setting the highest initial price that those customers really desiring the product are willing to pay. These customers are not very price-sensitive because they weigh the new product's price, quality, and ability to satisfy their needs against the same characteristics of substitutes. As the demand of these customers is satisfied, the firm lowers the price to attract a more price-sensitive segment.

Thus, skimming pricing gets its name from skimming successive layers of "cream," or customer segments, as prices are lowered in a series of steps.

In early 2003, many manufacturers of flat-screen TVs were pricing them at about $5,000 and using skimming pricing because many prospective customers were willing to buy the product immediately at the high price. Over time, prices of flat-screen TVs have dropped considerably.

Penetration Pricing Setting a low initial price on a new product to appeal immediately to the mass market is *penetration pricing*, the exact opposite of skimming pricing. This strategy makes sense when consumers are price-sensitive; Nintendo consciously chose a penetration strategy when it introduced the Nintendo Wii, its popular video game console.

In addition to offering the potential to build sales, market share, and profits, penetration pricing discourages competitors from entering the market because the profit margin is relatively low. Furthermore, if the costs to produce drop because of the accumulated volume, competitors that enter the market will face higher unit costs, at least until their volume catches up with the early entrant. Walmart comes to mind when one thinks about penetration pricing. The same holds true for the very successful chain Dollarama, which is constantly increasing its number of stores in Canada

In some situations, penetration pricing may follow skimming pricing. A company might price a product

> *Creative marketers, aware that consumers often compare value between competing products, engage in value pricing.*

high in the early stages of the product life cycle to attract price-insensitive consumers. After the company has earned back the money spent on research and development and introductory promotions, it uses penetration pricing in the later stages of the product life cycle to appeal to a broader segment of the population and increase market share.[4]

Prestige Pricing Although consumers tend to buy more of a product when the price is lower, sometimes the reverse is true. If consumers are using price as a measure of the quality of an item, a company runs the risk of appearing to offer a low-quality product if it sets the price below a certain point. *Prestige pricing* involves setting a high price so that quality- or status-conscious consumers are attracted to the product and buy it. Rolls-Royce cars, Chanel perfume, and Cartier jewellery have an element of prestige pricing in them and may not sell as well at lower prices than at higher ones.[5]

The higher the price of a prestige product, the greater the status associated with it and the greater its exclusivity, because fewer people can afford to buy it. Unlike products such as flat-panel TVs, which have decreased in price over the product life cycle, prices of prestige products remain high throughout the product life cycle.

An example of prestige pricing is the All Day Heels® collection of women's high-heeled shoes developed by Canadian retailer Ron White. This fashionable line of women's shoes combines elegance as well as comfort. The All Day Heels collection is set at a high price that matches its superior quality. The shoes provide arch support, built-in cushioning materials, and thin lightweight insoles made of Poron, a flexible high-tech elastic polymer developed by NASA. Canadian entrepreneur Ron White is featured in this text in the opening vignette in Chapter 11.

Price Lining Often, a firm that is selling not just a single product but a line of products may price them at a number of different specific pricing points, which is called *price lining*. For example, a discount department store manager may price a line of women's dresses at $59, $79, and $99. In some instances, all the items may be purchased at the same cost and then marked up to different percentages to achieve these price points, based on colour, style, and expected demand. In other instances, manufacturers design products for different price points, and retailers apply approximately the same markup percentages to achieve the three price points offered to consumers.

Odd-Even Pricing Suppose that Sears offers a Craftsman radial saw for $599.99, and Zellers sells Windex glass cleaner on sale for 99 cents. Why not simply price these items at $600 and $1, respectively? These firms are using *odd-even pricing*, which involves setting prices a few dollars or cents under an even number. The presumption is that consumers see the radial saw as priced at

"something over $500" rather than "about $600." The effect this strategy has is psychological: $599.99 *feels* significantly lower than $600—even though there is only one cent difference. There is some evidence to suggest this does work. However, research suggests that overuse of odd-ending prices tends to mute its effect on demand.[6]

The Popularity of Private Label Brands

Canadian grocery shoppers who purchase private label brands such as President's Choice **80%**

Frequent private label buyers who say that the products are comparable, or better, in quality than national brand names **48%**

Private label buyers for whom the most popular category of food is canned **71%**

marketing meter

Source: "Private label brands transforming how Canadians shop," CNW Group, accessed at www.newswire.ca/en/releases/archive/July2010/07/c2795.html.

Target Pricing Manufacturers will sometimes estimate the price that the ultimate consumer would be willing to pay for a product. They then work backward through markups taken by retailers and wholesalers to determine what price they can charge for the product. This practice, called *target pricing*, results in the manufacturer deliberately adjusting the composition and features of a product to achieve the target price to consumers. Tina Powell, as described in this chapter's opening vignette, uses this pricing method to determine what price she can charge her distributor for each children's book.

Bundle Pricing A frequently used demand-oriented pricing practice is *bundle pricing*, which is the marketing of two or more products in a single "package" price. For example, Air Canada offers vacation packages that include airfare, car rental, and hotel. Bundle pricing is based on the idea that consumers value the package more than the individual items. This is due to benefits received from not having to make separate purchases as well as increased satisfaction from one item in the presence of another. Bundle pricing often provides a lower total cost to buyers and lower marketing costs to sellers.[7]

Yield Management Pricing Have you ever been on an airplane and discovered the person next to you paid a lower price for her ticket than you paid? Annoying, isn't it? But what you observed is *yield management pricing*, the charging of different prices to maximize revenue for a set amount of capacity at any given time.[8] Airlines, hotels, and car rental firms engage in capacity management by varying prices based on time, day, week, or season to match demand and supply.

▼

ask yourself

1. What is the profit equation?
2. What is the difference between skimming and penetration pricing?
3. What is odd-even pricing?

marketing NewsFlash — Retailers Lament High Credit Card Fees

Every time a merchant swipes a customer's credit card, it costs the retailer about 2 percent of the value of the purchase. That's $2 on every $100 worth of goods or services. To the customer, this little expense is invisible. It isn't added at the cash register. Instead, like heat and hydro and other costs of doing business, it's buried in the overall price of the merchandise, whether the consumer buys with a card or cash. It might not sound like a very high price to pay for all the convenience, rewards, and financial flexibility that credit cards offer both consumers and merchants. But some Canadian retailers say credit card fees now take $4.5 billion a year out of their pockets, and they're spiralling out of control.

Consumers argue it is they who are paying the $4.5 billion in hidden credit card fees because the retailers are passing on these hidden costs to the consumer in the price.

With two very large multinational companies, Visa and MasterCard, dominating the card market, retailers say it can only get worse unless government intervenes. Peter Woolford, vice-president of policy development and research at the Retail Council of Canada, says, "We don't disagree that credit cards are useful means of payment. Customers love them. They are a reasonably effective and efficient way of paying for goods. Our main concern is that they're exorbitantly expensive."

The fee that retailers pay is called *interchange*, the percentage of each transaction that Visa and MasterCard banks collect from merchants every time a credit card is used to pay for a purchase. The fee varies with type of card, size of merchant, and other factors, but as much as $2 of every $100 a consumer spends goes to card issuers. Interchange fees are higher in Canada, an average of 2 percent, compared with less than 1 percent in most other industrialized countries.[9]

Questions

1. Were you aware that retailers have to pay a fee every time you use a credit card?

2. What credit card do you use the most and why?

Cost-Oriented Approaches

With cost-oriented approaches, a price is more affected by the cost side of the pricing problem than the demand side. Price is set by looking at the production and marketing costs and then adding enough to cover direct expenses, overhead, and profit.

Standard Markup Pricing   In order to make a profit, firms sell their products at a price that exceeds their costs of producing or sourcing the items and the costs of marketing them. Conventionally, the difference between the selling price of an item and its cost is referred to as the **markup** and this is normally expressed as a percentage. Markup is also often referred to as gross margin.

Manufacturers commonly express markup as a percentage of cost, which is the difference between selling price and cost, divided by cost. This is also referred to as *standard markup*. Manufacturers use this approach because they are concerned most of the time with costs.

Parties who buy and resell products, for example wholesalers and retailers, are nearly always dealing with selling prices. They often express markup as a percentage of price, which is the difference between selling price and cost, divided by the selling price. Using the same markup percentage for both of the above approaches will result in a different selling price (see the example in Figure 9–3).

Figure 9–3
Markup examples

Markup table based on selling price		
	$	%
Selling price	$75.00	100%*
− (minus) Cost	$60.00	80%
= (equals) Markup	$15.00	20%

* Price is always 100% when markup is relative to price.

Markup table based on cost		
	$	%
Selling price	$72.00	120%
− (minus) Cost	$60.00	100%**
= (equals) Markup	$12.00	20%

** Cost is always 100% when markup is relative to cost.

Consider the example of a product that is produced by a manufacturer and sold to a wholesaler, who in turn sells it to a retailer, who then sells it to a consumer. The product will be subjected to a series of markups as shown below.

Manufacturer's cost:	**$50.00**
Markup % (based on manufacturer's cost):	40%
Markup $:	$20.00
Selling price to wholesaler:	$70.00
Wholesaler cost:	**$70.00**
Markup % (based on selling price to retailer):	15%
Markup $:	$12.35
Selling price to retailer:	**$82.35**
Retailer cost:	**$82.35**
Markup % (based on retailer selling price):	35%
Markup $:	$44.34
Retailer selling price:	**$126.69**

This may surprise you to find out that a product costing $50 to produce can end up costing a consumer more than twice that much when bought at a retailer, but this is not unusual. It is important to remember that markup is necessary at each stage so that companies involved can cover their costs of purchasing the item, can pay to market it to the next stage in the distribution channel, and can generate some profit. The markups shown would be representative of some items such as designer furniture.

This percentage markup varies depending on the type of retail store (such as furniture, clothing, or grocery) and on the product involved. High-volume products usually have smaller markups than do low-volume products. Supermarkets such as Loblaws and Safeway mark up staple items like sugar, flour, and dairy products 10 percent to 25 percent, whereas they mark up discretionary items like snack foods and candy 25 percent to 47 percent. These markups must cover all expenses of the store, pay for overhead costs, and contribute something to profits. For supermarkets, these markups, which may appear very large, can result in only a 1 percent profit on sales revenue.

Cost-Plus Pricing   Many manufacturers, professional services, and construction firms use a variation of standard markup pricing. *Cost-plus pricing* involves summing the total unit cost of providing a product or service and adding a specific amount to the cost to arrive at a price. In this chapter's opening vignette, we learned that Tina Powell determines the price to charge corporations for one of her customized children's books by using the cost-plus method. Cost-plus pricing is the most commonly used method to set prices for business products.[10] Increasingly, however, this method is finding favour among business-to-business marketers in the service sector. For example, the rising cost of legal fees has prompted some law firms to adopt a cost-plus pricing approach. Rather than billing business clients on an hourly basis, lawyers and their clients agree on a fixed fee based on expected costs plus a profit for the law firm. Many advertising agencies now use this approach. Here, the client agrees to pay the agency a fee based on the cost of its work plus some agreed-on profit.[11]

Profit-Oriented Approaches

A company may choose to balance both revenues and costs to set price using profit-oriented approaches. These might either involve setting a target of a specific dollar volume of profit or expressing this target profit as a percentage of sales or investment.

Target Profit Pricing   When a firm sets an annual target of a specific dollar amount of profit, this is called *target profit pricing*. For example, if you owned a picture frame store and wanted to achieve a target profit of $7,000 in the coming year, how much would you need to charge for each frame? Because profit depends on revenues and costs, you would have to know your costs and then estimate how many frames you would sell. Let's assume, based on sales in previous years, you expect to frame 1,000 pictures next year. The cost of your time and materials to frame an average picture is $22, while your overhead expenses (rent, manager salaries, and so on) are $26,000. Finally, your goal is to achieve a profit of $7,000. How do you calculate your price per picture?

$$\text{Profit} = \text{Total revenue} - \text{Total costs}$$
$$= (\text{Pictures sold} \times \text{Price/picture}) - [(\text{Cost/picture} \times \text{Pictures sold}) + \text{overhead cost}]$$

Solving for price per picture, the equation becomes:

$$\text{Price/picture} = \frac{\text{Profit} + [(\text{Cost/picture} \times \text{Pictures sold}) + \text{overhead cost}]}{\text{Pictures sold}}$$

$$= \frac{\$7,000 + [(\$22 \times 1,000) + \$26,000]}{1,000}$$

$$= \frac{\$7,000 + \$48,000}{1,000}$$

$$= \$55 \text{ per picture}$$

Clearly, this pricing method depends on an accurate estimate of demand. Because demand is often difficult to predict, this method has the potential for disaster if the estimate is too high. Generally, a target profit pricing strategy is best for firms offering new or unique products, without a lot of competition. What if other frame stores in your area were charging $40 per framed picture? As a marketing manager, you'd have to offer increased customer value with your more expensive frames, lower your costs, or settle for less profit.

Target Return-on-Sales Pricing   Firms such as supermarkets often use *target return-on-sales pricing* to set prices that will give them a profit that is a specified percentage—say, 1 percent—of the sales volume. This pricing method is often used because of the difficulty in establishing a benchmark of sales or investment to show how much of a firm's effort is needed to achieve the target.

Target Return-on-Investment Pricing

Firms such as General Motors and many public utilities use *target return-on-investment pricing* to set prices to achieve a return-on-investment (ROI) target, such as a percentage that is mandated by its board of directors or regulators. For example, a hydro utility may decide to seek 10 percent ROI. If its investment in plant and equipment is $50 million, it would need to set the price of hydro to its customers at a level that results in $5 million a year in profits.

Competition-Oriented Approaches

Rather than emphasize demand, cost, or profit factors, a company's approach may be based on an analysis of what competitors are doing.

Customary Pricing   For some products where tradition, a standardized channel of distribution, or other competitive factors dictate the price, *customary pricing* is used. Candy bars offered through standard vending machines have a customary price

marketing **NewsFlash**   Car Sharing Trend Is Growing

There are roughly 20,000 Toronto members of AutoShare and Zipcar, two car-sharing services in the city that have enjoyed rapid growth in recent years. In North America, membership in car-share services is expected to balloon more than eightfold between now and 2016, a trend that could trim the market for new auto sales by up to one million vehicles.

David Zhao, an automotive research analyst with Frost & Sullivan, says it's a wake-up call for the automakers. "Once that population of shared vehicles gets bigger, the impact on the car market will become more serious," says Zhao, who published a report on car-sharing. He predicts car-share membership in North America will reach 4.4 million by 2016, translating into a car-share fleet of more than 70,000 vehicles. There will be a million fewer cars on North American streets by 2016. "It's a trend that will happen and vehicle manufacturers need to carefully gauge the potential impact on their total sales," Zhao concludes.

Such predictions are no surprise for Kevin McLaughlin, founder and president of 12-year-old AutoShare. As big cities improve public transit, as the cost of car ownership rises, and as young people rely more on their iPhones and other technologies to connect and socialize, buying a car is becoming less of a priority, said McLaughlin.

McLaughlin says that in just four years, the number of Torontonians using car sharing services like AutoShare has gone from 2,000 to over 20,000. AutoShare, which operates only in Toronto, has roughly 10,000 members. The company has a fleet of about 210 cars representing 13 different models, from minivans to Mini Coopers to hybrids.

Cambridge, Mass.-based Zipcar has 350,000 members and a fleet of 6,500 vehicles operating in dozens of North American cities. Its Toronto fleet has grown to about 260 cars since 2006.

Promoting car-sharing also reduces air pollution and greenhouse-gas emissions. It is estimated that car-share members drive 31 percent less than they would if they owned their own vehicle. A consumer who owns a car wants to get as much use out of it as possible.

Faced with the option of driving a few blocks, walking, or taking transit, most people hop in the car. Paying by the hour from a car-sharing company means that a consumer makes every trip a financial calculation and forces consideration of other options. The pay-as-you-go model encourages conservation every time, whether it's applied to mobile phone minutes, hydro use, or water consumption.

A third player in the car-sharing market is Shelby Clark, a former Zipcar member. The 27-year-old Harvard MBA grad recently launched his own company called RelayRides, which is attempting to pioneer "peer-to-peer" car sharing. Here's how it works: A person who owns a car but doesn't use it very often signs up to RelayRides and offers to let other members drive his or her car for an hourly fee. The Boston-based RelayRides maintains an online reservation system, provides the insurance, does the background checks, confirms that a safety inspection has been done, and acts as a payment clearinghouse. In return, it takes a 15 percent cut of the action.[12]

Questions

1. Would you consider using a car-sharing service and why?

2. Do you feel car-sharing popularity will increase or decrease in the next few years? Give reasons.

> *Among watch manufacturers, Rolex takes pride in emphasizing that it makes one of the most expensive watches you can buy—a clear example of above-market pricing.*

of a dollar, and a significant departure from this price may result in a loss of sales for the manufacturer. Hershey typically has changed the amount of chocolate in its candy bars depending on the price of raw chocolate, rather than vary its customary retail price so that it can continue selling through vending machines.

Above-, at-, or below-Market Pricing The "market price" of a product is what customers are generally willing to pay, not necessarily the price that the firm sets. For most products, it is difficult to identify a specific market price for a product or product class. Still, marketing managers often have a subjective feel for the competitors' price or the market price. Using this benchmark, they then may deliberately choose a strategy of *above-*, *at-*, or *below-market pricing.*

Among watch manufacturers, Rolex takes pride in emphasizing that it makes one of the most expensive watches you can buy—a clear example of above-market pricing. Manufacturers of national brands of clothing such as Christian Dior and retailers such as Holt Renfrew deliberately set higher prices for their products than those seen at Sears.

Large mass-merchandise chains such as Sears and The Bay generally use at-market pricing. These chains often are seen as establishing the going market price in the minds of their competitors. They also provide a reference price for competitors that use above- and below-market pricing.

In contrast, a number of firms use below-market pricing. Zellers and Walmart are two retailers that position themselves this way. Manufacturers of generic products and retailers that offer their own private brands of products ranging from peanut butter to shampoo deliberately set prices for these products about 8 percent to 10 percent below the prices of nationally branded competitive products such as Skippy peanut butter or Pantene Pro-V shampoo.

Loss-Leader Pricing Retailers sometimes deliberately sell commonly used products, such as paper towels, soft drinks, and facial tissues, at very low prices to attract consumers who, the retailer hopes, will also buy other, regularly priced merchandise. The downside to loss-leader pricing is that some consumers move from store to store, making purchases only on those products that are loss leaders. This purchasing pattern, called cherry-picking, effectively foils the strategy underlying loss-leader pricing—to attract customers who will also buy products with healthier profit margins.

Estimating Demand and Revenue

L❸ Basic to setting a product's price is the extent of customer demand for it. Marketing executives must also translate this estimate of customer demand into estimates of revenues the firm expects to receive.

Fundamentals of Estimating Demand

Newsweek decided to conduct a pricing experiment at newsstands in 11 cities. In one city, newsstand buyers paid $2.25. In five other cities, newsstand buyers paid the regular $2.00 price. In another city, the price was $1.50, and in the remaining four cities it was only $1.00. By comparison, the regular newsstand price for a competing magazine, *Time*, was $1.95. Why did *Newsweek* conduct the experiment? According to a *Newsweek* executive, "We wanted to figure out what the demand curve for our magazine at the newsstand is."[13]

The Demand Curve A **demand curve** shows the number of products that will be sold at a given price. Demand curve D1 in Figure 9–4A shows the newsstand demand for *Newsweek* under the existing conditions. Note that as price falls, more people decide to buy and unit sales increase. But price is not the complete story in estimating demand. Economists emphasize three other key factors:

1. **Consumer tastes:** These depend on many factors such as demographics, culture, and technology. Because consumer tastes can change quickly, up-to-date marketing research is essential.

Tipping Etiquette

Restaurants	15% on the total bill before tax, 20% for exceptional service
Hairdressers, manicurists, aestheticians, and taxi drivers	10% minimum

Source: "Canada: Tipping & Etiquette," Trip Advisor, accessed at http://www.tripadvisor.com/Travel-g153339-s606/Canada:Tipping.And.Etiquette.html.

2. **Price and availability of similar products:** The laws of demand work for one's competitors, too. If the price of *Time* magazine falls, more people will buy it. That then means fewer people will buy *Newsweek*. *Time* is considered by economists to be a substitute for *Newsweek*. Online magazines are also a substitute—one for which availability has increased tremendously in recent years. The point to remember is that as the price of substitutes falls or their availability increases, the demand for a product (*Newsweek*, in this case) will fall.

3. **Consumer income:** In general, as real consumer income (allowing for inflation) increases, demand for a product also increases.

The first of these two factors influences what consumers *want* to buy, and the third affects what they *can* buy. Along with price, these are often called *demand factors*, or factors that determine consumers' willingness and ability to pay for goods and services. It is often very difficult to estimate demand for new products, especially because consumer likes and dislikes are often so difficult to read clearly. (See the Marketing NewsFlash on page 198 to find out how these factors are impacting demand for owning a car.)

Movement along versus Shift of a Demand
Curve Demand curve D1 in Figure 9–4A shows that as the price is lowered from $2.00 to $1.50, the quantity demanded increases from 3 million (Q1) to 4.5 million (Q2) units per year. This is an example of a *movement along a demand curve* and assumes that other factors (consumer tastes, price and availability of substitutes, and consumer income) remain unchanged.

What if some of these factors change? For example, if advertising causes more people to want *Newsweek*, newsstand distribution is increased, or if consumer incomes rise, then the demand increases. Now the original curve, D1 (the blue line in Figure 9–4B), no longer represents the demand; a new curve must be drawn (D2). Economists call this a *shift in the demand curve*—in this case, a shift to the right, from D1 to D2. This increased demand means that more *Newsweek* magazines are wanted for a given price: At a price of $2, the demand is 6 million units per year (Q3) on D2 rather than 3 million units per year (Q1) on D1.

What price did *Newsweek* select after conducting its experiment? It kept the price at $2.00. However, through expanded newsstand distribution and more aggressive advertising, *Newsweek* was later able to shift its demand curve to the right and charge a price of $2.50 without affecting its newsstand volume.

Price Elasticity of Demand
Marketing managers must also pay attention to *price elasticity*, a key consideration related to the product's demand curve. Price elasticity refers to how sensitive consumer demand and the firm's revenues are to changes in the product's price.

A product with *elastic demand* is one in which a slight decrease in price results in a relatively large increase in demand, or units sold. The reverse is also true: With elastic demand, a slight increase in price results in a relatively large decrease in demand. Marketing experiments on products that are price-sensitive, such as cola, coffee, and snack foods, show them often to have elastic demand. So marketing managers may cut price to increase the demand, the units sold, and total revenue for one of these products, depending on what competitors' prices are. The demand for many consumer products is elastic—think jeans, DVDs, and car stereos.

One major factor influencing the elasticity of demand is the availability of substitute products. If consumers can easily find close substitutes for a good or service, the product's demand tends to be elastic.

In contrast, a product with *inelastic demand* means that slight increases or decreases in price will not significantly affect the demand, or units sold, for the product. Products and services considered as necessities, such as hydro or going to the dentist, usually have inelastic demand. What about gasoline

Figure 9–4
Illustrative demand curves for *Newsweek*

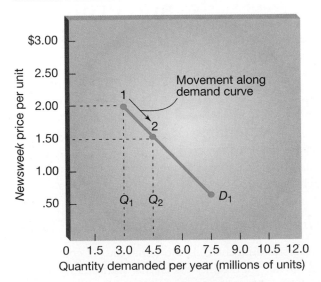

A Demand curve under initial conditions

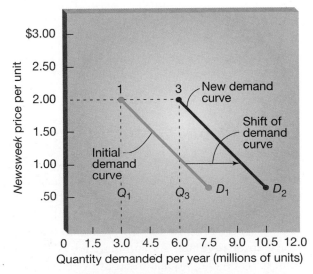

B Shift in the demand curve with different conditions

for your car? Will an increase of a few cents per litre cause you to drive fewer kilometres and buy less gasoline? No? Then you're like millions of other consumers, which is why gasoline has inelastic demand. This means that an increase of a few cents per litre may have a relatively minor impact on the number of litres sold, and may actually increase the total revenue of the gasoline producer. Inelastic demand is usually a relatively short-term phenomenon. Consumers, when they are faced with high prices for something they have to have, will seek out an alternative, and/or producers will see an opportunity to develop a new product. A hybrid car is, in some ways, a producer's response to high gas prices. Or maybe you could learn to love the bus!

Another example of inelastic demand is when buyers are less price-sensitive when the product they are buying is unique or is high in quality and prestige. In this case, consumers perceive that the high price means more quality and the demand for that product will not suffer very much. In some cases, a higher price may result in higher sales, which results in the demand curve actually sloping upwards.

The Internet has changed the elasticity of demand for some products. In the past, a consumer's choice when considering buying a product was limited to the number of bricks-and-mortar stores available. Now, with the Internet, there are many more choices of suppliers to choose from. The large number of suppliers competing with each other has led to lower prices on products that were once available only in stores. The availability of different suppliers on the Internet combines to create more products with elastic demand.

Fundamentals of Estimating Revenue

While economists may talk about "demand curves," marketing executives are more likely to speak in terms of "revenues generated." Demand curves lead directly to an essential revenue concept critical to pricing decisions: **total revenue**. As summarized in Figure 9–5, total revenue (TR) equals the unit price (P) times the quantity sold (Q). Using this equation, let's recall our picture frame shop and assume our annual demand

Figure 9–5
Total revenue concept

Total revenue (TR) is the total money received from the sale of a product. If

TR = Total revenue
P = Unit price of the product
Q = Quantity of the product sold

Then

TR = P × Q

has improved so that we can set a price of $100 per picture and sell 400 pictures per year. So,

$$TR = P \times Q$$
$$= \$100 \times 400$$
$$= \$40,000$$

This combination of price and quantity sold annually will give us a total revenue of $40,000 per year. Is that good? Are you making money, making a profit? Total revenue is only part of the profit equation that we saw earlier:

Total profit = Total revenue − Total cost

The next section covers the other part of the profit equation: cost.

ask yourself

1. What is loss-leader pricing?

2. What are three demand factors other than price that are used in estimating demand?

3. What is the difference between movement along a demand curve and a shift in a demand curve?

Determining Cost, Volume, and Profit Relationships

LO④ While revenues are the monies received by the firm from selling its products or services to customers, costs or expenses are the monies the firm pays out to its employees and suppliers. Marketing managers often use break-even analysis to relate revenues and costs, topics covered in this section.

The Importance of Controlling Costs

Understanding the role and behaviour of costs is critical for all marketing decisions, particularly pricing decisions. Many firms go bankrupt because their costs get out of control, causing their total costs to exceed

Figure 9–6
Total cost concept

Fixed cost (FC) is the sum of the expenses of the firm that are stable and do not change with the quantity of product that is produced and sold. Examples of fixed costs are rent on the building, executive salaries, and insurance.

Variable cost (VC) is the sum of the expenses of the firm that vary directly with the quantity of product that is produced and sold. Examples are the direct labour and direct materials used in producing the product. Variable cost expressed on a per unit basis is called *unit variable cost (UVC)*.

TC = FC + VC

Total cost (TC) is the total expense incurred by a firm in producing and marketing the product. Total cost is the sum of fixed cost and variable cost.

their total revenues over an extended period of time. This is why sophisticated marketing managers make pricing decisions that balance both their revenues and costs. Three cost concepts are important in pricing decisions: **total cost**, **fixed cost**, and **variable cost** (Figure 9–6).

Break-Even Analysis

LO 5 Marketing managers often employ an approach that considers cost, volume, and profit relationships, based on the profit equation. **Break-even analysis** is a technique that analyzes the relationship between total revenue and total cost to determine profitability at various levels of output. The *break-even point (BEP)* is the quantity at which total revenue and total cost are equal. Profit comes from any units sold after the BEP has been reached. In terms of the definitions in Figure 9–6,

$$BEP_{Quantity} = \frac{\text{Fixed cost}}{\text{Unit price} - \text{Unit variable cost}}$$

Calculating a Break-Even Point

Consider again your picture frame store. Suppose that you wish to identify how many pictures you must sell to cover your fixed cost at a given price. Let's assume demand for your framed pictures has increased, so the average price customers are willing to pay for each picture is $100. Also, suppose your fixed cost (*FC*) has grown to $28,000 (for real estate taxes, interest on a bank loan, and other fixed expenses) and unit variable cost (*UVC*) for a picture is now $30 (for labour, glass, frame, and matting). Your break-even quantity (BEPQuantity) is 400 pictures, as follows:

$$BEP_{Quantity} = \frac{\text{Fixed cost}}{\text{Unit price} - \text{Unit variable cost}}$$

$$= \frac{\$28{,}000}{\$100 - \$30}$$

$$= 400 \text{ pictures}$$

The row shaded in blue in Figure 9–7 shows that your break-even quantity at a price of $100 per picture is

total cost
Total expenses incurred by a firm in producing and marketing a product; total cost is the sum of fixed cost and variable costs

fixed cost
Firm's expenses that are stable and do not change with the quantity of product that is produced and sold

variable cost
Sum of the expenses of the firm that vary directly with the quantity of products that is produced and sold

break-even analysis
Examines the relationship between total revenue and total cost to determine profitability at different levels of output

Figure 9–7
Calculating a break-even point for a picture frame store

QUANTITY OF PICTURES SOLD (Q)	PRICE PER PICTURE (P)	TOTAL REVENUE (TR) = (P × Q)	UNIT VARIABLE COST (UVC)	TOTAL VARIABLE COST (TVC) = (UVC × Q)	FIXED COST (FC)	TOTAL COST (TC) = (FC + TVC)	PROFIT = (TR − TC)
0	$100	$0	$30	$0	$28,000	$28,000	−$28,000
200	100	20,000	30	6,000	28,000	34,000	−14,000
400	100	40,000	30	12,000	28,000	40,000	0
600	100	60,000	30	18,000	28,000	46,000	14,000
800	100	80,000	30	24,000	28,000	52,000	28,000
1,000	100	100,000	30	30,000	28,000	58,000	42,000
1,200	100	120,000	30	36,000	28,000	64,000	56,000

400 pictures. At less than 400 pictures your picture frame store incurs a
loss, and at more than 400 pictures it
makes a profit. Figure 9–7 also shows
that if you could double your annual
picture sales to 800, your store would make a profit of
$28,000—the row shaded in brown in the figure.

Figure 9–8 shows a graphic presentation of the
break-even analysis, called a *break-even chart*. It shows
that total revenue and total cost intersect and are equal
at a quantity of 400 pictures sold, which is the break-even
point at which profit is exactly $0. You want to
do better? If your frame store could double
the quantity sold annually to 800 pictures, the graph in Figure 9–8 shows
that you can earn an annual profit
of $28,000, as shown by the row
shaded in brown in Figure 9–7.

Applications of Break-Even Analysis
Because of
its simplicity, break-even analysis is used extensively in marketing, most frequently to study
the impact on profit of changes in
price, fixed cost, and variable cost.
The mechanics of break-even analysis
are the basis of the widely used electronic
spreadsheets offered by computer programs such as
Microsoft Excel that permit managers to answer hypothetical "what if" questions about the effect of changes
in price and cost on their profit.

Pricing Objectives and Constraints

LO6 With such a variety of alternative pricing strategies available, marketing managers must consider the pricing objectives and constraints that
will impact their decisions. While pricing objectives
frequently reflect corporate goals, pricing constraints
often relate to conditions existing in the marketplace.

Identifying Pricing Objectives

Pricing objectives specify the
role of price in an organization's
marketing and strategic plans.
To the extent possible, these
pricing objectives are carried
to lower levels in the organization, such as in setting objectives for marketing managers
responsible for an individual
brand. These objectives may
change, depending on the financial position of the company as a
whole, the success of its products, or the
segments in which it is doing business. H. J.
Heinz, for example, has specific pricing objectives for
its Heinz ketchup brand that vary by country.

Profit Three different objectives relate to a firm's
profit, which is often measured in terms of return on
investment (ROI). These objectives have different
implications for pricing strategy. One objective is *managing for long-run profits*, in which a company—such
as many Japanese car or TV set manufacturers—
gives up immediate profit in exchange for achieving
a higher market share. Products are priced relatively
low compared to their cost to develop, but the firm
expects to make greater profits later because of its
high market share.

A *maximizing current
profit* objective, such as for a
quarter or year, is common
in many firms because the
targets can be set and performance measured quickly.
North American firms are
sometimes criticized for this
short-run orientation.

A third profit objective
is a *target return* objective
that occurs when a firm sets

ask yourself

1. What is the difference between
fixed costs and variable costs?

2. What is a break-even point?

Figure 9–8
Break-even analysis for a picture frame store

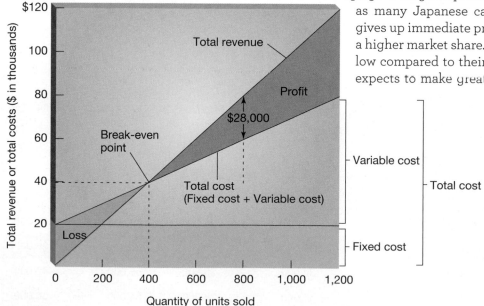

its price to achieve a profit goal (such as 20 percent for return on investment), usually determined by its board of directors. These three profit objectives have different implications for a firm's pricing objectives.

Another profit consideration for firms such as movie studios and manufacturers is to ensure that those firms in their channels of distribution make adequate profits. For example, Figure 9–9 shows where each dollar of your movie ticket goes. The 51 cents the movie studio gets must cover its profit plus the cost of making and marketing the movie. Although the studio would like more than 51 cents of your dollar, it settles for this amount to make sure theatres and distributors are satisfied and willing to handle its movies.

Sales

As long as a firm's profit is high enough for it to remain in business, an objective may be to increase sales revenue, which will in turn lead to increases in market share and profit. Cutting price on one product in a firm's line may increase its sales revenue but reduce those of related products. Objectives related to sales revenue or unit sales have the advantage of being translated easily into meaningful targets for marketing managers responsible for a product line or brand.

Market Share

Market share is the ratio of the firm's sales to those of the industry (competitors plus the firm itself). Companies often pursue a market share objective when industry sales are relatively flat or declining. For example, the cola market is declining, but Coke wants to keep its market share by retaining its piece of a dwindling pie. Although increased market share is a primary goal of some firms, others see it as a means to increasing sales and profits.

Adopting a market share objective does not always imply low price. The lowest-priced brand rarely has the highest market share. Tropicana orange juice, French's mustard, and Heinz ketchup are market share leaders and are all premium-priced. Brands such as these retain their market share positions because they offer value to consumers.

Volume

Many firms use volume, the quantity produced or sold, as a pricing objective. These firms often sell the same product at several different prices, at different times, or in different places in an attempt to match customer demand with the company's production capacity. Using volume as an objective can sometimes be misleading from a profit standpoint. Volume can be increased by using sales incentives (lowering prices, giving rebates, or offering lower interest rates). By doing this, the company chooses to lower profits in the short run to sell its product quickly. For example, a new health club might focus on getting a certain number of people to join by lowering its membership prices and accepting less profit, at first.

Survival

In some instances, profits, sales, and market share are less important objectives of the firm than mere survival. Air Canada has struggled to attract

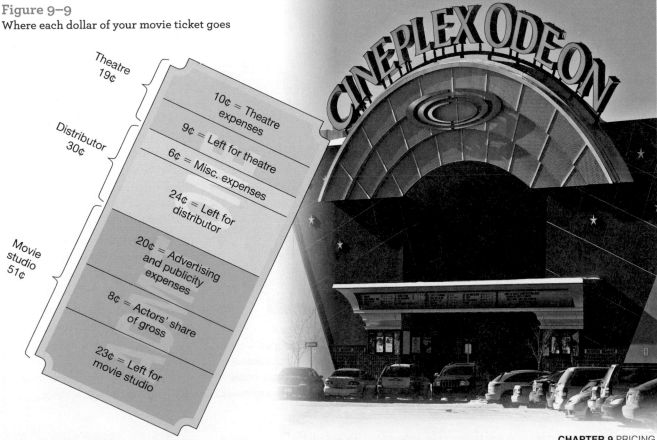

Figure 9–9
Where each dollar of your movie ticket goes

Theatre 19¢
Distributor 30¢
Movie studio 51¢

10¢ = Theatre expenses
9¢ = Left for theatre
6¢ = Misc. expenses
24¢ = Left for distributor
20¢ = Advertising and publicity expenses
8¢ = Actors' share of gross
23¢ = Left for movie studio

passengers with low fares and aggressive promotions to improve the firm's cash flow. This pricing objective has helped Air Canada to stay alive in the competitive airline industry.

Social Responsibility

A firm may forgo higher profit on sales and follow a pricing objective that recognizes its obligations to customers and society in general. Gerber supplies a specially formulated product free of charge to children who cannot tolerate foods based on cow's milk.

Identifying Pricing Constraints

Factors that limit the range of price a firm may set are **pricing constraints**. Consumer demand for the product clearly affects the price that can be charged. Other constraints on price vary from factors within the organization to competitive factors outside it.

Demand for the Product Class, Product, and Brand

The number of potential buyers for a product class (cars), product (sports cars), and brand (Bugatti Veyron) clearly affects the price a seller can charge. So does whether the item is a luxury, like a Bugatti Veyron, or a necessity, like bread and a roof over your head.

Newness of the Product: Stage in the Product Life Cycle

The newer the product and the earlier it is in its life cycle, the higher the price that can usually be charged. Consider the Apple iPad. With its new technology, Apple had no other direct competition at first, so it was possible to ask consumers to pay a high initial price for this innovative product.

Sometimes, such as when nostalgia or fad factors are present, prices may rise later in the product's life cycle. The legendary hockey jersey worn by Paul Henderson in the 1972 Summit Series was sold for over $1 million at an auction. Henderson was wearing the jersey when he scored the winning goal in Team Canada's emotional win over the Soviets.[14]

Cost of Producing and Marketing the Product

In the long run, a firm's price must cover all the costs of producing and marketing a product. If the price doesn't

Canadian hockey legend Paul Henderson, who scored the game-winning goal during the 1972 Summit Series against the Soviet Union, holds his original 1972 Team Canada sweater.

Breakdown of Gasoline Prices

Profit:	2%
Refining and marketing costs:	16%
Taxes:	35%*
Crude costs:	47%

* Federal and provincial governments receive over $14 billion per year in gasoline taxes.

Source: "The Facts on Gasoline Pricing," Canadian Automobile Association, accessed at www.caa.ca/mini%20sites/gasprice/pricing.html.

cover these costs, the firm will fail; so in the long run, a firm's costs set a floor under its price.

Competitors' Prices

When a firm sets its prices, an important consideration is the prices being charged by the competition. As we talked about previously, a firm has three choices: It can charge a higher price, the same price, or a lower price than its competitors. Each choice conveys a message to customers. For example, e-readers such as Amazon's Kindle and the Sony Reader were developed as single-function devices, meant solely for use as a reader. The iPad, on the other hand, is a multi-function appliance that allows the user to surf the Internet as well as use it as a reader. Because the e-readers made by Sony and Amazon have a limited use, they were forced to drop their prices dramatically when the iPad came on the scene.[15] Amazon has gone on to develop its own multi-function device, introducing the Kindle Fire in November 2011, which includes Internet, video, app, and gaming functionality to go along with its reader. Amazon's price for its Kindle Fire is dramatically lower than the iPad, a strategy to reach consumers who are price sensitive.

A high price signifies that the firm believes its offering represents a higher value in comparison to competing products—value being quality, brand image, benefits and unique features offering extra benefits, or something as simple as instant availability. Sony is known as a firm that typically prices higher than most of its competitors. Consumers wanting quality will pay a higher price.

Charging the same price as the competition means that the firm is relying on some aspect other than price to position and differentiate its products in the minds of customers—that differentiation may be a unique attribute, widespread availability, or an intensive marketing campaign. Thinking again of consumer electronics, Panasonic, JVC, and Sharp are examples of manufacturers whose prices are close for similar products. Consumers typically buy these brands on the basis of some unique attribute of the product, or because they prefer to deal with a specific retailer.

Lower prices can be a challenge, but many firms rely on this strategy. From the company standpoint, lower prices can mean lower profits on each sale, which may need to be offset by larger volume sales. In addition, larger volumes can result in production efficiencies and lower costs. Less well-known brands and some of the larger manufacturers such as RCA use this strategy. For consumers, the lower prices often mean forgoing some aspect such as quality or brand image.

The decision to charge a certain price is impacted by marketing and pricing objectives. If winning market share is an objective, lower prices may be the solution. If being perceived as the "best brand" is an objective, higher prices may be part of the answer. Being known as a *market leader* based on pricing is a title that could be ascribed to firms using either strategy.

Charging prices in line with the competition earns firms the title of *market follower*. This is a conscious choice of many smaller firms manufacturing and selling similar or often the same products. Emphasis is shifted away from price to some other aspect of the marketing mix.

There are occasions where other objectives override any consideration of competitor pricing, such as selling off discontinued models or time-sensitive items (summer-vacation packages, for example).

Legal and Ethical Considerations

Deciding on a final price is a complex process. In addition to the considerations we have just presented, there are laws and regulations that also play a role in the price decision. We will look at four of the most prominent considerations.

Price Fixing   When competitors collaborate and conspire to set prices, they agree to increase, decrease, or stabilize a price for their benefit. This is called *price fixing*, and it is illegal—the *Competition Act* prohibits this practice. The *Competition Act* consists of federal regulations governing most business conduct in Canada. Price fixing usually occurs where price is the most important factor in the marketing mix. Twelve global airlines that ran a cargo price-fixing cartel for years were hit with fines totalling $1.1 billion by European Union regulators. The European Commission slapped Air Canada with the third-smallest fine at $29.2 million.[16]

Price Discrimination   If different prices are charged to different customers for the same or very similar goods and the same terms, *price discrimination*

Figure 9–10
Most common deceptive pricing practices

DECEPTIVE PRACTICE	DESCRIPTION
Bait and switch	A firm offers a very low price for a product (the bait), and when consumers come to purchase it, they are persuaded to buy a more expensive product (the switch). Uses techniques such as downgrading the advertised item or not having it in stock.
Bargains conditional on other purchases	A firm advertises "buy one, get one free" or "get two for the price of one." If the first items are sold at the regular price, this is legal. If the price for the first items is inflated for the offer, it is not.
Price comparisons	Advertising "retail value $100—our price $85" is deceptive if a substantial number of stores in the area are not using the $100 price—in other words, if it is not the "going price." Advertising "below manufacturer's suggested list price" is deceptive if no sales occur at the manufacturer's list price. Advertising that the price is reduced 50% is deceptive if the item was not offered for sale at the higher price for a substantial previous period of time.
Double ticketing	When more than one price tag is placed on an item, it must be sold at the lower price; this practice is not illegal, but the law requires that the lower price be charged.

has occurred. The *Competition Act* prohibits this, but in order for a firm to be charged with the offence, there has to be evidence of a "practice" of price discrimination—that is, that it is not just a one time or occasional event.

Deceptive Pricing   Price offers that mislead the consumer are considered *deceptive pricing*, and this is prohibited under the *Competition Act*. Figure 9-10 shows the most common deceptive pricing practices. Many companies across the country have been accused of deceptive pricing, but it can be difficult to police and the laws are hard to enforce. Often regulators rely on the ethical standards of those making and publicizing pricing decisions. The Canadian Code of Advertising Standards provides guidelines for various aspects of promotion, and pricing is one of these; advertising industry members are expected to follow this Code and to self-regulate (ensure that they and their colleagues adhere to the Code).

An example of deceptive pricing is menswear retailer Grafton-Fraser Inc. The retailer agreed to pay a $1.2 million penalty to settle an advertising case regarding misleading sale prices. The Competition Bureau found that Grafton-Fraser had significantly inflated the regular price of certain garments sold in its stores, resulting in an overstatement of the savings to consumers when these garments were on sale. The retailer joins other merchants, including Suzy Shier, Sears Canada Ltd., and Forzani Group Ltd., that the Competition Bureau found were inflating an item's regular price and thereby overstating the savings of the sale price. Grafton-Fraser, the bureau found, was tagging garments with both a regular and a sale price; however, the items did not sell "in any significant quantity or for any reasonable period of time at the regular price," the Bureau said. Grafton-Fraser runs stores across the country that operate under several names, among them Tip Top Tailors, George Richards Big & Tall, and Grafton & Co.[17] Read the Marketing NewsFlash below for another example of misleading pricing.

Predatory Pricing   Charging a very low price for a product with the intent of undercutting competitors and

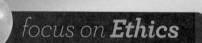 focus on **Ethics**

Zellers Rebuked for *Avatar* Promotion

Zellers Inc. agreed to change a promotion around the Hollywood blockbuster *Avatar* after Canada's competition watchdog, the Competition Bureau, ruled that the retailer's savings-card promotion misled consumers. Zellers was promoting the purchase of the movie *Avatar* on DVD or Blu-Ray by offering a card with the purchase. The card gave the customer $10 off purchases at Zellers, but one of the conditions was that the customer had to spend a minimum of $50 to redeem the $10 savings.

A review by the Competition Bureau suggested that the minimum purchase condition was not included in the store's advertising and was disclosed only after customers made their initial purchase. The Competition Bureau said that terms and conditions associated with these types of promotions that are not fully disclosed to consumers before the time of purchase raise concerns under the false or misleading representations provisions of the Competition Act. Misleading pricing representations remain a key concern for the Bureau. When making their purchasing decisions, consumers have the right to expect that information about pricing is truthful and accurate. Otherwise, consumers are hurt and rival businesses are put at an unfair competitive disadvantage.

Zellers agreed to take the following immediate steps to resolve the Bureau's concerns: Customers who presented a $10 savings card, or a sales receipt for the movie *Avatar* purchased within a certain period of time, received a $10 credit with no minimum purchase required. Zellers was also asked to bring these changes to the attention of consumers through in-store signage and a notice posted on their website. Two corrective notices were published in major Canadian newspapers, and Zellers advertised the details of the redemption in their flyers. The Bureau reminds retailers of the importance of clearly and conspicuously disclosing, prior to consumer purchases, all conditions, limitations, and exclusions as they relate to rebates and other types of promotions.[18] ●

Questions

1. Give an example from your own experience of encountering misleading price representations in stores.

2. Misleading pricing representations are a key concern for the Competition Bureau. Figure 9-10 (page 207) highlights four deceptive pricing practices. Which of the four do with you feel is the most unethical and unlawful? Give reasons.

possibly driving them out of the market is called *predatory pricing*. After the competitors have been driven out, the offending firm raises its prices. If a company can genuinely operate more efficiently than others, and this lets them offer its products at a lower price, should this be classified as predatory pricing? No! It's not easy to prove that the intent of the lower price is to eliminate a competitor, and that the prices set are unreasonably and artificially low, so there are many more charges of predatory pricing than there are convictions.

Global Pricing Strategy

Global companies face many challenges in determining a pricing strategy as part of their worldwide marketing effort. Individual countries, even those with free trade agreements, may place considerable competitive, political, and legal constraints on the pricing flexibility of global companies. For example, Walmart was told by German antitrust authorities that the prices in its stores were too low, relative to competitors, and faced a fine for violating the country's trade if the prices weren't raised![19]

Pricing too low or too high can have dire consequences. When prices appear too low in one country, companies can be charged with dumping, a practice subject to severe penalties and fines. **Dumping** occurs when a firm sells a product in a foreign country below its domestic price or below its actual cost. A recent trade dispute involving U.S. apple growers and Mexico is a case in point. Mexican trade officials claimed that U.S. growers were selling their red and golden delicious apples in Mexico below the actual cost of production. They imposed a 101 percent tariff on U.S. apples, and a severe drop in U.S. apple exports to Mexico resulted. Later negotiations set a price floor on the price of U.S. apples sold to Mexico.[20]

When companies price their products very high in

ask yourself

1. What is the difference between pricing objectives and pricing constraints?

2. Explain what bait and switch is and why it is an example of deceptive pricing.

some countries but competitively in others, they face a grey market problem. A **grey market**, also called *parallel importing*, is a situation where products are sold through unauthorized channels of distribution. A grey market comes about when individuals buy products in a lower-priced country from a manufacturer's authorized retailer, ship them to higher-priced countries, and then sell them below the manufacturer's suggested retail price through unauthorized retailers. Many well-known products have been sold through grey markets, including Olympus cameras, Seiko watches, and Mercedes-Benz cars. Parallel channels are not strictly illegal in Canada, but there are mounting legal challenges to them. Parallel importing is legal in the United States. It is illegal in the European Union.[21]

dumping
Occurs when a firm sells a product in a foreign country below its domestic prices or below its actual cost

grey market
Situations where products are sold through unauthorized channels of distribution

Setting a Final Price

L7 The final price set by the marketing manager serves many functions. It must be high enough to cover the cost of providing the product *and* meet the objectives of the company. Yet it must be low enough that customers are willing to pay it. But not too low, or customers may think they're purchasing an inferior product. Confused? Setting price is one of the most difficult tasks the marketing manager faces, but four generalized steps are useful to follow.

Step 1: Select an Approximate Price Level

Before setting a final price, the marketing manager must understand the market environment, the features and customer benefits of the particular product, and the goals of the firm. A balance must be struck between factors that might drive a price higher (such as a profit-oriented

No Ifs, Ands or Buts.

Truth is an essential part of any successful ad campaign. Smart advertisers have known this for years. That's why the advertising industry created the *Canadian Code of Advertising Standards* more than 40 years ago. Since then the *Code* has set the standards for acceptable advertising in Canada. It helps ensure that the ads you see and hear are truthful, fair and accurate. Check it out for yourself. Because the more you know about advertising, the more you get out of it.

Learn about the *Code* at:
www.adstandards.com

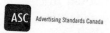 Advertising Standards Canada

approach) and other forces (such as increased competition from substitutes) that may drive a price down.

Marketing managers consider pricing objectives and constraints first, and then choose among the general pricing approaches—demand-, cost-, profit-, or competition-oriented—to arrive at an approximate price level. This price is then analyzed in terms of cost, volume, and profit relationships. Break-even analyses may be run at this point, and finally, if this approximate price level "works," it is time to take the next step: setting a specific list or quoted price.

Step 2: Set the List or Quoted Price

A seller must decide whether to follow a one-price or flexible-price policy.

One-Price Policy   A *one-price policy* involves setting one price for all buyers of a product or service. For example, when you buy a product at Walmart, you are offered the product at a single price. You can decide to buy it or not, but there is no variation of the price under the seller's one-price policy. Some retailers such as Dollarama have married this policy with a below-market approach and sell mostly everything in their stores for $1! Recently, Dollarama has added more products at $1.25, $1.50, and $2.

Flexible-Price Policy   In contrast, a *flexible-price policy* involves setting different prices for products and services depending on individual buyers and purchase situations in light of demand, cost, and competitive factors. Dell Computer adopted flexible pricing as it continually adjusts prices in response to changes in its own costs, competitive pressures, and demand from its various personal computer segments (home, small business, corporate, and so on). "Our flexibility allows us to be [priced] different even within a day," says a Dell spokesperson.[22]

Flexible pricing is not without its critics because of its discriminatory potential. For example, car dealers have traditionally used flexible pricing on the basis of buyer-seller negotiations to agree on a final price. Is it any wonder that 60 percent of prospective car buyers dread negotiating the price?

Step 3: Make Special Adjustments to the List or Quoted Price

When you pay $1 for a bag of M&Ms in a vending machine or receive a quoted price of $10,000 from a contractor to renovate a kitchen, the pricing sequence ends with the last step

just described: setting the list or quoted price. But when you are a manufacturer of M&M candies and sell your product to dozens or hundreds of wholesalers and retailers in your channel of distribution, you may need to make a variety of special adjustments to the list or quoted price. Wholesalers also must adjust list or quoted prices they set for retailers. Three special adjustments to the list or quoted price are discounts, allowances, and geographical adjustments.

Discounts   *Discounts* are reductions from list price that a seller gives a buyer as a reward for some activity of the buyer that is favourable to the seller. Four kinds of discounts are especially important in marketing strategy: quantity, seasonal, trade (functional), and cash.[23]

- **Quantity discounts:** To encourage customers to buy larger quantities of a product, firms at all levels in the channel of distribution offer quantity discounts, which are reductions in unit costs for a larger order. For example, an instant photocopying service might set a price of 10 cents a copy for 1 to 24 copies, 9 cents a copy for 25 to 99, and 8 cents a copy for 100 or more. Because the photocopying service gets more of the buyer's business and has longer production runs that reduce its order-handling costs, it is willing to pass on some of the cost savings in the form of quantity discounts to the buyer.

- **Seasonal discounts:** To encourage buyers to stock inventory earlier than their normal demand would require, manufacturers often use seasonal discounts. A firm such as Toro that manufactures lawn mowers and snow blowers offers seasonal discounts to encourage wholesalers and retailers to stock up on lawn mowers in January and February and on snow blowers in July and August—months before the seasonal demand by ultimate consumers. This enables

Is it any wonder that 60 percent of prospective car buyers dread negotiating the price?

Toro to smooth out seasonal manufacturing peaks and troughs, thereby contributing to more efficient production. It also rewards wholesalers and retailers for the risk they accept in assuming increased inventory carrying costs and gives them the benefit of having supplies in stock at the time they are wanted by customers.

- **Trade (functional) discounts:** To reward wholesalers and retailers for marketing functions they will perform in the future, a manufacturer often gives trade, or functional, discounts. These reductions off the list or base price are offered to resellers in the channel of distribution on the basis of where they are in the channel and the marketing activities they are expected to perform in the future.

Traditional trade discounts have been established in various product lines such as hardware, food, and pharmaceutical items. Although the manufacturer may suggest trade discounts, the sellers are free to alter the discount schedule depending on their competitive situation. Suppose that a manufacturer quotes prices in the following form:

List price – $100, less 30/10/5

The first number in the percentage sequence (in this example, 30/10/5) always refers to the retail end of the channel, and the last number always refers to the wholesaler or jobber closest to the manufacturer in the channel. The trade discounts are simply subtracted one at a time. This price quote shows that $100 is the manufacturer's suggested retail price:

- For the retailer, 30 percent of the suggested retail price ($100 × 0.3 = $30) is available to cover costs and provide a profit;
- Wholesalers closest to the retailer in the channel get 10 percent of their selling price ($70 × 0.1 = $7); and
- The final group of wholesalers in the channel (probably jobbers) that are closest to the manufacturer get 5 percent of their selling price ($63 × 0.05 = $3.15).

Toro uses seasonal discounts to stimulate consumer demand and smooth out seasonal manufacturing peaks and troughs.

Thus, starting with the manufacturer's retail price and subtracting the three trade discounts shows that the manufacturer's selling price to the wholesaler or jobber closest to the manufacturer is $59.85 (see Figure 9–11).

- **Cash discounts:** To encourage retailers to pay their bills quickly, manufacturers offer them cash discounts. Suppose that a retailer receives a bill quoted at $1,000, 2/10 net 30. This means that the bill for the product is $1,000, but the retailer can take a 2 percent discount ($1,000 × 0.02 = $20) if payment is made within 10 days and send a cheque for $980. If the payment cannot be made within 10 days, the total amount of $1,000 is due within 30 days. It is usually understood by the buyer that an interest charge will be added after the first 30 days of free credit.

Retailers provide cash discounts to consumers as well, to eliminate the cost of credit granted to consumers. These discounts take the form of discount-for-cash policies.

Allowances Allowances—like discounts—are reductions from list or quoted prices to buyers for performing some activity.

- **Trade-in allowances:** A new car dealer can offset the list price of that new Toyota Camry by offering you a trade-in allowance of $500 for your old Honda. A trade-in allowance is a price reduction given when a used product is part of the payment on a new product. Trade-ins are an effective way to lower the price a buyer has to pay without formally reducing the list price.

- **Promotional allowances:** Sellers in the channel of distribution can qualify for promotional allowances for undertaking certain advertising or selling activities to promote a product. Various types of allowances include an actual cash payment or an extra amount of "free goods" (as with a free case of pizzas to a retailer for every dozen cases purchased). Frequently, a portion of these savings is passed on to the consumer by retailers.

Figure 9–11
How trade discounts work

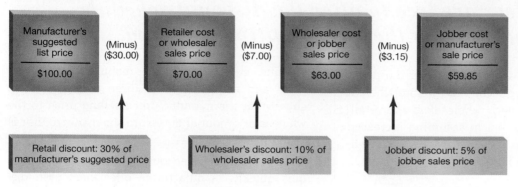

Geographical Adjustments Geographical adjustments are made by manufacturers or even wholesalers to list or quoted prices to reflect the cost of transportation of the products from seller to buyer. The two general methods for quoting prices related to transportation costs are FOB origin pricing and uniform delivered pricing.

- **FOB origin pricing:** FOB means "free on board" some vehicle at some location, which means the seller pays the cost of loading the product onto the vehicle that is used (such as a barge, railroad car, or truck). FOB origin pricing usually involves the seller's naming the location of this loading as the seller's factory or warehouse (such as "FOB Montreal" or "FOB factory"). The title and ownership to the goods passes to the buyer at the point of loading, so the buyer becomes responsible for picking the specific mode of transportation, for all the transportation costs, and for subsequent handling of the product. Buyers farthest

from the seller face the big disadvantage of paying the higher transportation costs.

- **Uniform delivered pricing:** When a uniform delivered pricing method is used, the price the seller quotes includes all transportation costs. It is quoted in a contract as "FOB buyer's location," and the seller selects the mode of transportation, pays the freight charges, and is responsible for any damage that may occur because the seller retains title to the goods until delivered to the buyer.

Step 4: Monitor and Adjust Prices

Rarely can a firm set a price and leave it at that. As you have learned, there are many constraints that affect setting prices, and the firm has objectives that it also takes into account. Things change both in the external business environment and within the firm itself; as a result, prices need to be reviewed and revised if necessary. A key activity is the monitoring of competitor activity, legislative changes, economic conditions, and—the ultimate measure—consumer demand! These factors, and their potential impact on the firm's ability to achieve its marketing goals, have to be examined and action taken when necessary.

ask yourself

1. Why would a seller choose a flexible-price policy over a one-price policy?

2. What is the purpose of (a) quantity discounts and (b) promotional allowances?

Summary...just the facts

- Price is the money or other considerations exchanged for the ownership or use of a product or service. Although price typically involves money, the amount exchanged is often different from the list or quoted price because of allowances and extra fees.

- Consumers use price as an indicator of value when it is paired with the perceived benefits of a good or service. Sometimes, price influences consumer perceptions of quality itself; at other times, consumers make value assessments by comparing the costs and benefits of substitute items.

- Four general approaches for finding an approximate price level for a product or service are demand-oriented, cost-oriented, profit-oriented, and competition-oriented pricing.

- Demand-oriented pricing approaches stress consumer demand and revenue implications of pricing and include seven types: skimming, penetration, prestige, price lining, odd-even, target, bundle, and yield management.

- Cost-oriented pricing approaches emphasize the cost aspects of pricing and include two types: standard and cost-plus pricing.

- Profit-oriented pricing approaches focus on a balance between revenues and costs to set a price and include three types: target profit, target return-on-sales, and target return-on-investment pricing.

- Competition-oriented pricing approaches emphasize what competitors or the marketplace are doing and include three types: customary; above-, at-, or below-market; and loss-leader pricing.

- A demand curve shows the maximum number of products consumers will buy at a given price and for a given set of (a) consumer tastes, (b) price and availability of other products, and (c) consumer income. When any of these change, there is a shift in the demand curve.

- It is necessary to consider cost behaviour when making pricing decisions. Important cost concepts include total cost, variable cost, and fixed cost. An essential revenue concept is total revenue.

- Break-even analysis shows the relationship between total revenue and total cost at various quantities of output for given conditions of price, fixed cost, and variable cost. The break-even point is where total revenue and total cost are equal.

- Pricing objectives, which specify the role of price in a firm's marketing strategy, may include pricing for profit, sales revenue, market share, unit sales, survival, or some socially responsible price level.

- Pricing constraints such as demand, product newness, costs, competitors, other products sold by the firm, and the type of competitive market restrict a firm's pricing range.

- Given an approximate price level for a product, a manager must set a list or quoted price by considering factors such as one-price versus a flexible-price policy.

- List or quoted price is often modified through discounts, allowances, and geographical adjustments. The pricing environment needs to be monitored continually.

Key Terms and Concepts...*a refresher*

break-even analysis p. 203
demand curve p. 200
dumping p. 209
fixed cost p. 203
grey market p. 209

markup p. 196
price p. 191
pricing constraints p. 206
pricing objectives p. 204
profit equation p. 192

total cost p. 203
total revenue p. 202
value p. 192
variable cost p. 203

Hands-on...*apply your knowledge*

Mathematical Pricing Assignment In this chapter's opening vignette, author Tina Powell determines her selling price using a method called target pricing. Tina first estimates the price that the ultimate consumer would pay for her book at the bookstore. She does this by checking the prices of competitors' children's books at the bookstores and determines a reasonable price for her books, based on the market. She then works backwards through the markups taken by the retailer and distributor to determine if the price she can charge the distributor for the book will cover her costs and provide a fair profit. Tina's children's books sell for $9.95 at the retail level.

Book retailers usually ask for a 40 percent markup on the retail selling price, while Tina's distributor, Red Tuque Books, receives 30 percent on its selling price to bookstores. Work backwards through the markups to determine the selling price that Tina charges the distributor.

Reality Check...*reminder*

Refer back to this chapter's opening vignette and answer the Reality Check questions on page 190.

Distribution
AND *Supply Chain*

The business of marketing touches on a wide range of elements that impact on consumers' willingness to buy a product and subsequently return to purchase another in the future. Although not top-of-mind with students, distribution and supply chain are key variables in the marketing mix that can impact on this decision. This chapter looks at this area, explaining its challenges and relevance to businesses today.

One part of a company's marketing plan shows the components of each of the marketing mix elements that are combined to provide a cohesive marketing program. In this chapter, we focus on the place component. We start by looking at the success of Freshii, a fast-food retail operation that is looking at franchising as a way to grow.

Matthew Corrin is the 28-year-old founder and CEO of Freshii, a restaurant chain that serves on-the-go customized salads, wraps, burritos, yogourts, soups, and rice bowls. The company's tag line is "Fresh food. Custom built. Fast." Matthew believes in thinking big. "Our goal for Freshii is to create the most convenient choice for fresh food, custom built, fast across the world," he says. The "custom-built" part of Freshii's goal refers to customers having the option to build their own meal consisting of salad or wrap, choice of cheese, fruits, veggies, nuts, protein, and dressings. The other option is to order right off the menu. Matthew is changing the way people eat by offering healthy choices instead of typically unhealthy fast food.

There are a growing number of Freshii locations in Canada and the United States. Some are corporate-owned, the rest are franchises. Approximately one new Freshii restaurant opens each week.

The inspiration for Freshii came to Matthew, who grew up in Winnipeg, while he was working in New York in publicity for fashion designer Oscar de la Renta. "Every day for lunch, I was eating at this mom-and-pop deli around the corner from Oscar's office. The quality was really great but the service was dull and the branding lacklustre," he says. "I thought if you could take this fresh-food concept and create a brand to it, you could potentially Starbucks the fresh-food business."

Matthew is looking to franchising for growth. He says that the franchising model of Freshii is an area-development model where a partner commits to a certain number of stores in one market and then hires store managers to run individual stores. Instead of bringing on board one franchisee at a time, Matthew is aiming for multi-unit deals with well-capitalized partners. Each partner could open anywhere from 3 to 40 stores in a particular city. So far, Freshii has signed franchise deals with 20 partners in 20 cities from Philadelphia to Calgary, New York to Dubai. Matthew plans to have 1,000 Freshii stores open by 2015.

Matthew had to learn about the legal aspects of franchising if he wanted to succeed, so he engaged one of the leading global law firms that specialized in franchise law. As far as training is concerned, new Freshii partners go through a hands-on ten-day course in Toronto. When asked whether Freshii franchisees have to purchase their supplies from the franchiser, Matthew says that they are encouraged to do so but they also have the right to source their own vendors if they wish.

In the field of franchising, some franchisers make it clear to their franchisees that they have to strictly follow the franchisers' rules in operating the business. Matthew, on the other hand, says that he encourages his partners' input, expertise, and entrepreneurial spirit. For example, if a franchisee comes up with an idea for something new on the menu or a better way of doing things, Matthew is very open to testing these suggestions. He gives the example of McDonald's where the Big Mac was created by a franchisee not the corporation. Open communication with the Freshii franchisees is encouraged. Matthew wants to "encourage the entrepreneurial spirit and creativity."

Matthew says that Freshii's goal is not to over-penetrate a market, which results in one store's sales being cannibalized by another Freshii store too close by. On the other hand, he says that under-penetration can lead to not realizing economies of scale that proper penetration can yield.

Matthew has received a lot of publicity about Freshii in magazines and newspapers. When asked how he obtained so much publicity, he said that his work in public relations with Oscar de la Renta provided him with the mechanics of obtaining PR.

Matthew is also concerned with the environment. He says that commercial-grade dishwashers create tremendous amounts of chemical and hydro waste. So Freshii replaced its food-prep dishes with biodegradable bags. Instead of using bowls and tongs, every single order at all locations is prepared in the bio bags instead. There's no longer a need for dishwashing machines, says Matthew, pointing out that they also don't have to hire and train often-transient human dishwashers.

Matthew says that greening his business model does not compromise profitability. The bags cost the company about a third of a cent each. Now that they don't have to buy a dishwasher, the company saves more than $10,000 in the initial build-out of each store, and annually saves more than $6,000 per store. The bags also maximize cleanliness. Each order is prepared in a fresh bag, so there's no risk of cross-contamination as with dishwashers. "Customers are served in takeout packaging, almost all of it biodegradable," says Matthew. 🍎

As you read Chapter 10, refer back to this Freshii vignette to answer the following questions:

- There are four categories of franchises described in this chapter. Which type of franchise arrangement does Freshii fall into?

- Go online to Freshii's home page at www.freshii.com and explore the site. Is Freshii's website transactional, promotional, or a combination of both?

reality CHECK

Chapter 10 focuses on the concept of distribution—getting the product to the customer—the place P of the 4Ps that make up the marketing mix.

Nature and Importance of Marketing Channels

Reaching potential buyers is obviously a critical part of successful marketing. Buyers benefit from well-structured and efficient distribution systems. The route to do this is direct in some cases and indirect in others.

What Is a Marketing Channel?

You see the results of distribution every day. You may have purchased Lay's Potato Chips at Mac's convenience store, a book through chapters.indigo.ca, or Levi's jeans at Sears. Each of these items was brought to you by a marketing channel of distribution, or simply a **marketing channel**, which consists of individuals and firms involved in the process of making a product or service available.

The concept of distribution is all about getting the product to the customer.

Distribution

Supply Chain

Marketers understand the value of the supply chain to perform activities required to deliver a good or service to customers.

Marketing channels can be compared with a pipeline through which water flows from a source to an endpoint. Marketing channels make possible the flow of goods from a producer, through **intermediaries**, to a buyer. There are several types of intermediaries—and specific names or terms for each type—and as shown in Figure 10–1, they perform various functions.[1] Some intermediaries actually purchase items from the producer, store them, and resell them to buyers. For example, Nestlé Canada produces Aero chocolate bars and sells it to wholesalers. The wholesalers then sell the bars to independent convenience and grocery stores, which in turn sell it to consumers. Other intermediaries, such as brokers and agents, represent sellers but do not actually ever own the products; their role is to bring a seller and buyer together. Real estate agents are examples of this type of intermediary.

Value Created by Intermediaries

Few consumers appreciate the value created by intermediaries. However, producers recognize that intermediaries make selling goods and services more efficient because the intermediaries minimize the number of sales contacts necessary to reach a target market.

Figure 10-2 shows a simple example of how this comes about in the flat-panel TV market. Without a retail intermediary (such as Future Shop), LG, Toshiba, Sharp, and Samsung would each have to make four contacts to reach the four consumers shown, who are in the target market. However, each producer has to make only one contact when Future Shop acts as an intermediary. Also, the number of industry transactions is reduced from 16 to 8, which reduces producer costs.

intermediaries
Individuals or firms performing a role in the marketing channel, involved in making a product available

Figure 10–1
Terms used for marketing intermediaries

TERM	DESCRIPTION
Middleman	Another name for intermediary
Agent or broker	Any intermediary with legal authority to act on behalf of another channel member (for example, a manufacturer)
Wholesaler	Any intermediary who sells to other intermediaries, usually to retailers—this term usually applies to intermediaries who deal in consumer goods
Retailer	An intermediary who sells to consumers
Distributor	A general term used to describe intermediaries who perform a variety of functions, including selling, maintaining inventories, extending credit, and others—usually used for those in business markets
Dealer	A general term that can mean the same as a distributor, a retailer, or a wholesaler

Figure 10–2
How intermediaries minimize transactions

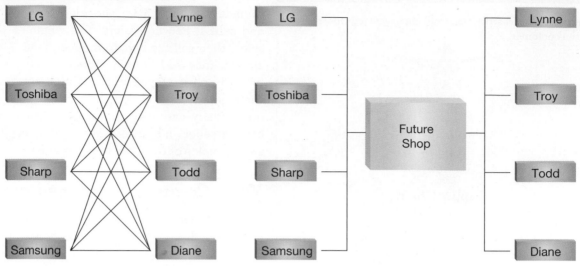

Contacts with no intermediary
4 producers × 4 buyers = 16 contacts

Contacts with one intermediary
4 producers + 4 buyers = 8 contacts

Functions Performed by Intermediaries

Intermediaries make possible the flow of products from producers to ultimate consumers by performing three basic functions (see Figure 10-3).

- **Transactional function:** Intermediaries perform a transactional function when they buy and sell goods or services. But an intermediary such as a wholesaler also performs the function of sharing risk with the producer when it stocks merchandise in anticipation of sales. If the stock is unsold for any reason, the intermediary—not the producer—suffers the loss.

- **Logistical function:** The logistics of a transaction (described at length later in this chapter) involve the details of preparing and getting a product to buyers. Gathering, sorting, and dispersing products are some of the logistical functions of the intermediary—imagine the various fruits and vegetables displayed at your local grocery store!

- **Facilitating function:** Finally, intermediaries perform facilitating functions that, by definition, make a transaction *easier* for buyers. For example, Sears issues credit cards to consumers so that they can buy now and pay later.

All three groups of functions must be performed in a marketing channel, even though each channel member may not participate in all three. Channel members often negotiate about which specific functions they will perform. Sometimes disagreements result, and a breakdown in relationships among channel members occurs. This happened when Pepsi-Cola's bottler in Venezuela switched to Coca-Cola. Given the intermediary's logistical role—storing and transporting Pepsi to Venezuelan customers in this case—Pepsi-Cola either had to set up its own bottling operation to perform these marketing channel functions, or find another bottler, which it did.[2]

Consumer Benefits from Intermediaries

Consumers also benefit from the actions of intermediaries. Having the goods and services you want, when you want them, where you want them, and in the form you want them is the ideal result of marketing channels. In more specific terms, marketing channels help create value for consumers through these five utilities: time, place, form, information, and possession.

- *Time utility* refers to having a product or service when you want it. For example, FedEx provides next-morning delivery.

Figure 10–3
Marketing channel functions performed by intermediaries

TYPE OF FUNCTION	ACTIVITIES RELATED TO FUNCTION
Transactional function	• *Buying*: Purchasing products for resale • *Selling*: Contacting potential customers, promoting products, and seeking orders • *Risk taking*: Assuming business risks in the ownership of inventory
Logistical function	• *Selection:* Putting together a selection of products from several different sources • *Storing*: Assembling and protecting products at a convenient location • *Sorting*: Purchasing in large quantities and dividing into smaller amounts • *Transporting*: Physically moving a product to customers
Facilitating function	• *Financing*: Extending credit to customers • *Marketing information and research*: Providing information to customers and suppliers, including competitive conditions and trends

- *Place utility* means having a product or service available where consumers want it, such as having a Petro-Canada gas station located on a long stretch of a provincial highway.

- *Form utility* involves enhancing a product or service to make it more appealing to buyers. For example, retail stores such as Harry Rosen and Roots provide appealing displays of their products and an environment that caters to their customers.

- *Information utility* means providing consumers with the information they need to make an informed choice; information-packed websites and user manuals provide this type of utility.

- *Possession utility* involves efforts by intermediaries to help buyers take possession of a product or service, such as providing various ways for payment to be made for a product—by credit card, debit card, cash, or cheque.

Channel Structure and Organization

LO② A product can take many routes on its journey from producer to buyer, and marketers search for the most efficient route from the many alternatives available. As you'll see, there are some important differences between the marketing channels for consumer goods and those for business goods.

ask yourself

1. What is meant by a marketing channel?

2. What are the three basic functions performed by intermediaries?

Marketing Channels for Consumer Goods and Services

Figure 10–4 shows the four most common marketing channel configurations for consumer goods and services. It also shows the number of levels in each marketing channel, that is, the number of intermediaries between a producer and ultimate buyers. As the number of intermediaries between a producer and buyer increases, the channel is viewed as increasing in length. The producer → wholesaler → retailer → consumer channel is longer than the producer → consumer channel.

Channel A in Figure 10–4 represents a *direct channel* because a producer and ultimate consumers deal directly with each other. Many products and services are distributed this way. A number of insurance companies sell their financial services using a direct channel and branch sales offices. The online store justwhiteshirts.com designs and produces high-quality men's shirts that are sold online and by catalogue to consumers around the world. Because there are no intermediaries with a direct channel, the producer must perform all channel functions.

The remaining three channel forms are *indirect channels* because intermediaries are inserted between the producer and consumers and perform numerous channel functions. Channel B, with a retailer added, is

Figure 10–4
Common marketing channels for consumer goods and services

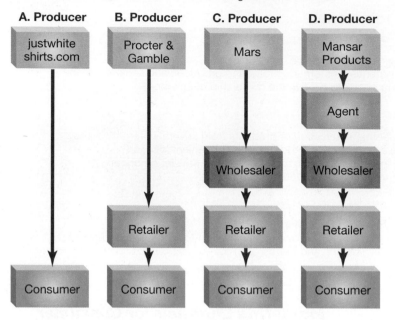

most common when the retailer is large and can buy in large quantities from a producer. Packaged goods companies such as Procter & Gamble use this channel with large retailers such as Loblaws and Sobeys. These retailers buy in sufficient quantities to make it cost-effective for a producer to deal with only a retail intermediary. Adding a wholesaler in channel C is most common when the wholesaler sells to small retailers, such as independent convenience stores and small grocery stores, that do not buy enough to warrant a producer selling to these retailers directly. Channel C is most common for low-cost, low-unit value items that are frequently purchased by consumers, such as candy, confectionary items, and magazines. For example, Mars sells its line of candies to wholesalers in case quantities; wholesalers can then break down (sort) the cases so that individual small retailers can order in boxes or much smaller quantities.

Channel D, the most indirect channel, is employed when there are many small manufacturers and many small retailers and an agent is used to help coordinate a large supply of the product. Mansar Products, Ltd., is a Belgian producer of specialty jewellery that uses agents to sell to wholesalers, which then sell to many small retailers.

Marketing Channels for Business Goods and Services

The four most common channels for business goods and services are shown in Figure 10–5. In contrast with channels for consumer products,

business channels typically are shorter and rely on one intermediary or none at all because business users are fewer in number, tend to be more concentrated geographically, and buy in larger quantities. For these reasons, business channels can be served directly or by a limited number of intermediaries.

Channel A, represented by IBM's large, mainframe computer business, is a direct channel. Firms using this kind of channel maintain their own sales force and perform all channel functions. This channel is employed when buyers are large and well-defined, the sales effort requires extensive negotiations, and the products are of high unit value and require hands-on expertise in terms of installation or use. Bombardier and Airbus Industries would be other examples.

Channels B, C, and D are indirect channels with one or more intermediaries to reach industrial users. In channel B an *industrial distributor* performs a variety of marketing channel functions, including selling, stocking, and delivering a full product assortment and financing. In many ways, industrial distributors are like wholesalers in consumer channels. Caterpillar relies on industrial distributors to sell and service its construction and mining equipment in almost 200 countries.

Channel C introduces another intermediary, an agent, who serves primarily as the independent selling arm of producers and represents a producer to industrial users. For example, Stake Fastener Company, a producer of industrial fasteners, has an agent call on industrial users rather than employing its own sales force.

Figure 10–5
Common marketing channels for business goods and service

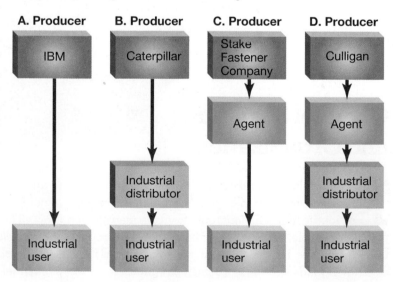

Channel D is the longest channel and includes both agents and distributors. For instance, Culligan, a producer of water treatment equipment, uses agents to call on distributors who sell to industrial users.

Electronic Marketing Channels

The marketing channels that we have just discussed for consumer and business goods and services are not the only routes to the marketplace. Advances in electronic commerce have opened new avenues for reaching buyers and creating customer value.

Interactive electronic technology has made possible **electronic marketing channels**, which employ the Internet to make goods and services available to consumers or business buyers. A unique feature of these channels is that they can combine electronic and traditional intermediaries to create time, place, form, and possession utility for buyers.[3]

Figure 10–6 shows the electronic marketing channels for books (Amazon.ca), travel reservation services (Travelocity.ca), and personal computers (Dell.ca). Are you surprised that they look a lot like common marketing channels? An important reason for the similarity resides in channel functions detailed in Figure 10–3 (see page 219). Electronic intermediaries can and do perform transactional and facilitating functions effectively and at a relatively lower cost than traditional intermediaries because of efficiencies made possible by information technology. However, electronic intermediaries are incapable of performing elements of the logistical function, particularly for products such as books and automobiles. This function remains with traditional intermediaries or with the producer, as seen with Dell and its direct channel.

Many services are distributed through electronic marketing channels, such as travel services marketed by Travelocity.ca, financial securities by Royal Bank, and insurance by Metropolitan Life. Software, too, can be marketed this way. However, many other services such as health care and auto repair still involve traditional intermediaries.

Multiple Channels and Strategic Alliances

In some situations producers use **dual distribution**, an arrangement whereby a firm reaches different buyers by employing two or more different types of channels for the same basic product. For instance, GE sells its large appliances directly to home and apartment builders but uses retail stores, including Walmart, to sell to consumers. In some instances, firms pair multiple channels with a multibrand strategy. This is done to minimize cannibalization of the firm's family brand and to differentiate the channels. For example, Hallmark sells its Hallmark greeting cards through Hallmark stores and select department stores, and its Ambassador brand of cards through discount and drugstore chains.

A recent development in marketing channels is the use of *strategic channel alliances*, whereby one firm's marketing channel is used to sell another firm's products.[4] An alliance between Canada Dry and Coke is a case in point. Coke distributes Canada Dry soft drinks to stores in Canada. Strategic alliances are popular in global marketing, where the creation of

Figure 10-6
Examples of electronic marketing channels

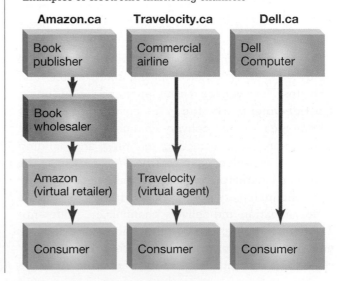

Amazon.ca	Travelocity.ca	Dell.ca
Book publisher	Commercial airline	Dell Computer
Book wholesaler		
Amazon (virtual retailer)	Travelocity (virtual agent)	
Consumer	Consumer	Consumer

marketing channel relationships is expensive and time consuming. For example, General Mills and Nestlé have an extensive alliance that spans 70 international markets from Brazil to Poland to Thailand.

Multichannel Marketing to the Online Consumer

L3 Consumers and companies populate two market environments today. One is the traditional marketplace, where buyers and sellers engage in face-to-face exchange relationships in an environment characterized by physical facilities (stores and offices) and mostly tangible objects. The other is the *marketspace*, an Internet/web-enabled digital environment characterized by "face-to-screen" exchange relationships and electronic images and offerings.

The existence of two market environments has benefited consumers tremendously. Today, consumers can shop for and purchase a wide variety of products and services in either market environment. Many consumers now browse and buy in both market environments, and more are expected to do so in the future. With so many consumers browsing and buying in two market environments, few companies limit their marketing programs exclusively to the traditional marketplace or to the online marketspace. Today, it is commonplace for companies to maintain a presence in both market environments. This dual presence is called *multichannel marketing*.

Integrating Multiple Channels with Multichannel Marketing Companies often employ multiple marketing channels for their products and services. Multichannel marketing bears some resemblance to dual distribution. For example, different communication and delivery channels are used, such as catalogues, kiosks, retail stores, and websites. However, the resemblance ends at this point. **Multichannel marketing** is the *blending* of different communication and delivery channels that are *mutually reinforcing* in attracting, retaining, and building relationships with consumers who shop and buy in the traditional marketplace and in the online marketspace. Multichannel marketing seeks to integrate a firm's communication and delivery channels, not differentiate them. In doing so, consumers can browse and buy anytime, anywhere, any way, expecting that the experience will be similar regardless of channel. At Eddie

> **The Gap generates more sales volume from its website than from any one of its stores, except for one.**

Bauer, for example, every effort is made to make the apparel shopping and purchase process for its customers the same in its retail stores, through its catalogues, and at its website. According to an Eddie Bauer marketing manager, "We don't distinguish between channels because it's all Eddie Bauer to our customers."[5] We will discuss the retail slant on this practice further in Chapter 11.

Multichannel marketing can also leverage the value-adding capabilities of different channels. For example, retail stores leverage their physical presence by allowing customers to pick up their online orders at a nearby store, or return or exchange non-store purchases at the store if they wish. For instance, a consumer can purchase a laptop computer on the Staples website and pick up the computer at any Staples store.

Another example of multichannel marketing is the **cross-channel shopper**, who researches products online and then purchases them at a retail store. These shoppers represent both genders equally. Cross-channel shoppers want the right product at the best price, and they don't want to wait several days for delivery. The top reasons these shoppers look online before buying in stores include (1) the desire to compare products among different retailers, (2) the need for more information than is available in stores, and (3) the ease of comparing options without having to trek to multiple retail locations.

Implementing Multichannel Marketing It should not be surprising to you that not all companies use websites for multichannel marketing the same way. Different companies apply the value-creation

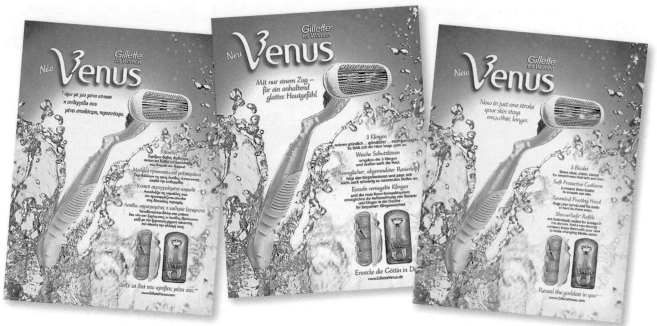

Gillette delivers the same global message whenever possible, as shown in the Gillette for Women Venus ads from Greece, Germany, and Canada.

capabilities of Internet/web technology differently depending on their overall marketing program. Websites can play multiple roles in multichannel marketing because they can serve as either a communication or delivery channel, or as both. There are two general types of websites, classified based on their intended purpose: transactional websites and promotional websites.

Transactional websites are essentially electronic storefronts. They focus mainly on converting an online browser into an online, catalogue, or in-store buyer using website design elements. Transactional websites are most common among store and catalogue retailers such as Lee Valley. The Gap, for instance, generates more sales volume from its website than from any one of its stores, except for one.[6]

Retailers and direct-selling firms have found that their websites, while cannibalizing sales volume from stores and catalogues, do attract new customers and influence sales. Consider Victoria's Secret, a specialty retailer of intimate apparel for women aged 18 to 45. Almost 60 percent of its website customers are men, most of whom generate new sales volume for the company.[7] Sears' website is estimated to account for millions of dollars worth of Sears in-store appliance sales. Why? Sears customers first research appliances online before visiting a store.[8]

Transactional websites are used less frequently by manufacturers of consumer products. A recurring issue for manufacturers is the threat of channel conflict by harming their relationships with their retailing intermediaries. The Bay, for instance, would not be very happy if a brand of jeans it carries is being sold online directly from the manufacturer to the consumer. Still, manufacturers do use transactional websites, often cooperating with retailers. For example, Ethan Allen, the furniture manufacturer, markets its product line at www.ethanallen.com whenever feasible. Ethan Allen retailers fill online orders and receive 25 percent of the sales price. For items shipped directly from the Ethan Allen factory, the store nearest the customer receives 10 percent of the sales price.[9]

In addition, Ethan Allen, like other manufacturers, typically lists its stores on its website where consumers can shop for and buy its merchandise. More often than not, however, manufacturers employ multichannel channels, using websites as advertising and promotional vehicles.

Promotional websites have a different purpose than transactional sites: No actual selling takes place on them, but they showcase products and services and provide information.

Global Channel Strategy

Distribution is of critical importance in global marketing. The availability and quality of retailers and wholesalers as well as transportation, communication, and warehousing facilities are often determined by a country's economic infrastructure. Figure 10–7 outlines the channel through which a product manufactured in one country must travel to reach its destination in another country.

The first step involves the seller; its headquarters is responsible for the successful distribution to the ultimate consumer.

The next step is the channel between two nations, moving the product from one country to another. Intermediaries that can handle this responsibility include resident buyers in a foreign country, independent merchant wholesalers who buy and sell the product, or agents who bring buyers and sellers together.

Once the product is in the foreign nation, that country's distribution channels take over. These channels can be very long or surprisingly short, depending on the product line. In Japan, fresh fish go through three intermediaries before getting to a retail outlet. Conversely, shoes go through only one intermediary. The sophistication of a country's distribution channels increases as its economic infrastructure develops. Supermarkets are helpful in selling products in many nations, but they are not popular or available in many others where culture and lack of refrigeration dictate shopping on a daily rather than a weekly basis. For example, when Coke and Pepsi entered China, both had to create direct distribution channels, investing in refrigerator units for small retailers.

Tiffany & Co. and H&R Block represent two different types of vertical marketing systems. Read the text to find out how they differ.

Vertical Marketing Systems

L4 The traditional marketing channels described so far represent a network of independent producers and intermediaries brought together to distribute goods and services. However, channel arrangements have emerged for the purpose of improving efficiency in performing channel functions and achieving greater marketing effectiveness. These arrangements are called vertical marketing systems. **Vertical marketing systems** are professionally managed and centrally coordinated marketing channels designed to achieve channel economies and maximum marketing impact.[10] Figure 10–8 depicts the major types of vertical marketing systems: corporate, contractual, and administered.

Corporate Systems Under a *corporate vertical marketing system*, a firm at one level of a channel owns the firm at the next level or owns the entire channel. For example, a producer might own the intermediary at the next level down in the channel. This practice, called *forward integration*, is exemplified by Polo/Ralph Lauren, which manufactures clothing and also owns apparel shops. Other examples of forward integration include Goodyear and Sherwin Williams. Alternatively, a retailer might own a manufacturing operation, a practice called *backward integration*. For example, Safeway supermarkets operate their own bakeries and have a subsidiary company, Lucerne Foods, that produces a wide variety of food products for their stores. Some of these products are sold as Safeway brand, and some under the Lucerne name. Another example of backwards integration is Tiffany & Co., the exclusive jewellery retailer, which manufactures about half of the fine jewellery items for sale through its 150 stores and boutiques worldwide.

Figure 10–7
Channels of distribution in global marketing

Figure 10–8
Types of vertical marketing systems

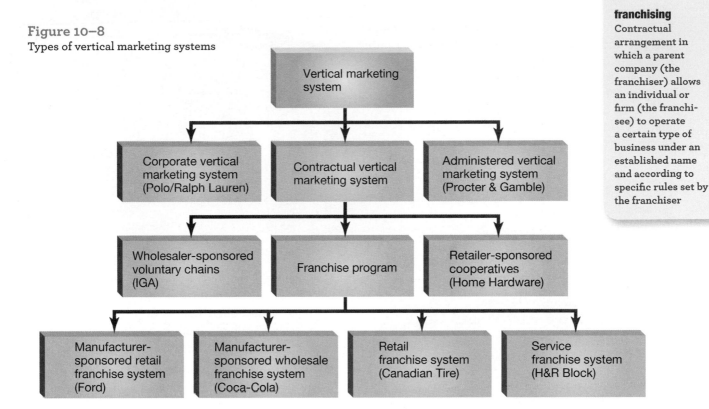

franchising
Contractual arrangement in which a parent company (the franchiser) allows an individual or firm (the franchisee) to operate a certain type of business under an established name and according to specific rules set by the franchiser

Companies seeking to reduce distribution costs and gain greater control over supply sources or resale of their products pursue forward and backward integration. Many companies favour contractual vertical marketing systems to achieve channel efficiencies and marketing effectiveness.

Contractual Systems Under a *contractual vertical marketing system*, independent production and distribution firms combine their efforts on a contractual basis to obtain greater functional economies and marketing impact than they could achieve alone. Contractual systems are the most popular among the three types of vertical marketing systems. They account for about 40 percent of all retail sales.

Three variations of contractual systems exist. *Wholesaler-sponsored voluntary chains* involve a wholesaler that develops a contractual relationship with small, independent retailers to standardize and coordinate buying practices, merchandising programs, and inventory management efforts. With the organization of a large number of independent retailers, economies of scale and volume discounts can be achieved to compete with chain stores. IGA is an example of a wholesaler-sponsored voluntary chain.

Retailer-sponsored cooperatives exist when small, independent retailers form an organization that operates a wholesale facility cooperatively. Member retailers then concentrate their buying power through the wholesaler and plan collaborative promotional and

pricing activities. Home Hardware is an example of a retailer-sponsored cooperative. The most visible variation of contractual systems is **franchising**, a contractual arrangement between a parent company (a franchiser) and an individual or firm (a franchisee) that allows the franchisee to operate a certain type of business under an established name and according to specific rules set by the franchiser.

Four types of franchise arrangements are most popular. *Manufacturer-sponsored retail franchise systems* are prominent in the automobile industry, where a manufacturer such as Ford licenses dealers to sell its cars subject to various sales and service conditions. *Manufacturer-sponsored wholesale franchise systems* appear in the soft-drink industry, where Pepsi-Cola licenses wholesalers (bottlers) that purchase concentrate from Pepsi-Cola and then carbonate, bottle, promote, and distribute its products to supermarkets and restaurants. *Retail franchise systems* are provided by firms that have designed a unique approach for selling merchandise to consumers. Canadian Tire and McDonald's represent this franchising approach.

Service franchise systems exist when franchisers license individuals or firms to dispense a service under a trade name and specific guidelines. An example is H&R Block tax services. Service franchise arrangements are the fastest-growing type of franchise.

Administered Systems By comparison, *administered vertical marketing systems* achieve coordination at successive stages of production and distribution by the size and influence of one channel member rather than through ownership. Procter & Gamble, given its broad product assortment ranging from disposable diapers to detergents, is able to obtain cooperation from supermarkets in displaying, promoting, and pricing its products. Walmart can obtain cooperation from manufacturers in terms of product specifications, price levels, and promotional support, given its position as the world's largest retailer.

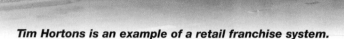

Tim Hortons is an example of a retail franchise system.

ask yourself

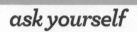

1. What is the difference between a direct and an indirect channel?

2. What is the major distinction between a corporate vertical marketing system and an administered vertical marketing system?

Channel Choice and Management

L5 Marketing channels not only link a producer to its buyers but also provide the means through which a firm executes various elements of its marketing strategy. Therefore, choosing a marketing channel is a critical decision.

Factors Affecting Channel Choice

The final choice of a marketing channel by a producer depends on a number of market, product, and company factors.

Market Factors

- **Geographic concentration of the market:** When most of a firm's customers are concentrated in a few geographic areas, a direct sale to customers is practical. When customers are geographically dispersed, a direct sale is likely to be impractical due to high

travel costs. Sellers may establish sales branches in densely populated markets and use intermediaries in less-concentrated markets.

- **Number of potential customers:** A manufacturer with few potential customers may use its own sales force to sell directly to ultimate consumers or business users. Bombardier uses this approach in selling its jet aircrafts and subway cars. For a large number of customers, the manufacturer would probably use intermediaries. For example, Tim Hortons relies on numerous franchisee outlets to reach the large number of consumers buying coffee.

- **Type of market:** Consumer products are made available through retailers while business products are sold either direct to customers or through intermediaries.

- **Order size:** Direct distribution makes sense when an order size is large. For example, Campbell's delivers its soups directly to large grocery chains. On the other hand, Campbell's uses wholesalers to reach small independent grocery and convenience stores, whose orders are usually too small to justify a direct sale.

Number of Restaurants in Canada

McDonald's	1,400
Tim Hortons	3,189

Source: Tim Hortons corporate website, "The History of Tim Hortons," accessed September 20, 2011, at www.timhortons.com/ca/en/about/2872.html; McDonald's Canada corporate website, "FAQs," accessed September 20, 2011, at www.mcdonalds.ca/en/aboutus/faq.aspx.

Product Factors

- **Technical factors:** In general, highly sophisticated products, such as custom-built machinery and scientific computers, are distributed direct to buyers. The producer's sales force must provide considerable pre-purchase and post-purchase service for these types of products, and typically wholesalers do not do these tasks.

- **Perishability:** Some goods such as milk and bread deteriorate fairly quickly. As a result, these types of products go directly from the producer to the retailer, no matter the size of the order.

- **Unit value:** The price attached to each unit of a product affects the amount of funds available for distribution. For example, a company like Bombardier can afford to use its own employees to sell aircrafts costing millions of dollars. But it would not make sense for Hershey Canada to call on households to sell an Oh Henry! chocolate bar. That's why intermediaries such as convenience stores, vending machines, and gasoline service stations carry low unit-value products.

- **Product life cycle:** Over time, some products such as the Apple iPod become very popular, easy to operate, and available in more mainstream channels such as Zellers and Costco.

Company Factors

- **Financial resources and ability of management:** A business with limited financial resources may be unable to employ its own salespeople, and thus resorts to using intermediaries such as selling agents or manufacturer's agents to reach customers. Also, businesses that have limited or no marketing know-how may elect to use intermediaries.

  A manufacturer of jams and marmalades may face limited markets for its products because it cannot afford the listing fees that supermarkets demand for the privilege of carrying the product. The manufacturer chooses instead to sell to small fruit and vegetable–type stores, who do not demand a listing fee and whose clientele enjoy buying products that are not available everywhere. The retailer may command a premium price for the jam because of its perceived quality and limited distribution.

- **Desire for channel control:** Some producers establish direct channels because they want to control their product's distribution, even though a direct channel may be more costly than an indirect channel.

For example, Gap Inc. employs designers to come up with the styles that consumers want. Instead of selling Gap products to independent retailers, Gap Inc. assures distribution with its more than 3,000 Gap stores. Having its own stores assures Gap that its products are marketed properly and merchandised prominently.

Channel Design Considerations

Marketing executives consider three questions when choosing a marketing channel and intermediaries:

1. Which channel and intermediaries will best reach the target market?

2. Which channel and intermediaries will best serve the needs of the target market?

3. Which channel and intermediaries will lead to the most cost-efficient and profitable results?

Target Market Coverage   Achieving the best coverage of the target market requires attention to the density—that is, the number of stores in a given geographical area—and type of intermediaries to be used at the retail level of distribution. Three degrees of distribution intensity exist: intensive, exclusive, and selective.

Intensive distribution means that a firm tries to place its products and services in as many outlets as possible. Intensive distribution is usually chosen for convenience products or services, such as candy, newspapers, and soft drinks. For example, Coca-Cola's retail distribution objective is to place its products "within an arm's reach of desire."

Exclusive distribution is the extreme opposite of intensive distribution because only one retail outlet in a specified geographical area carries the firm's products. Exclusive distribution is typically chosen for specialty products or services such as specialty automobiles, some women's fragrances, men's and women's apparel and accessories, and yachts. Sometimes retailers sign exclusive distribution agreements with manufacturers and suppliers.

Selective distribution lies between these two extremes and means that a firm selects a few retail outlets in a specific geographical area to carry its products. Selective distribution combines some of the market

> *It would not make sense for Hershey Canada to call on households to sell an Oh Henry! chocolate bar.*

intensive distribution
A firm tries to place its products or services in as many outlets as possible

exclusive distribution
Only one retail outlet in a specific geographical area carries the firm's products

selective distribution
A firm selects a few retail outlets in a specific geographical area to carry its products

coverage benefits of intensive distribution with the control measures possible with exclusive distribution. For this reason, selective distribution is the most common form of distribution intensity. It is usually associated with products such as Rolex watches, Levi's jeans, and Samsung flat-panel TVs.

Satisfying Buyer Requirements A second objective in channel design is gaining access to channels and intermediaries that satisfy at least some of the interests buyers might have when they purchase a firm's products or services. These requirements fall into four categories: information, convenience, variety, and pre- or post-sale services.

Information is an important requirement when buyers have limited knowledge or desire specific data about a product or service. Properly chosen intermediaries communicate with buyers through in-store displays, demonstrations, and personal selling. Electronics manufacturers such as Apple and Sony have opened their own retail outlets, with highly trained personnel to inform buyers about their products and how they can meet the buyers' needs.

Convenience has multiple meanings for buyers, such as proximity or driving time to a retail outlet or hours of operation. For example, Mac's convenience stores, with outlets nationwide, many of which are open 24 hours a day, satisfy this interest for buyers. Candy and snack food firms benefit by gaining display space in these stores.

For other consumers, convenience means a minimum of time and hassle. Jiffy Lube and Mr. Lube, which promise to change engine oil and filters quickly, appeal to this aspect of convenience. Another example of convenience is Tim Hortons, which has locations in Esso service stations across Canada.

Variety reflects buyers' interest in having numerous competing and complementary items from which to choose. Variety is seen in both the breadth and depth of products carried by intermediaries, which enhances their attractiveness to buyers. Thus, manufacturers of pet food and supplies seek distribution through pet stores such as PetSmart and PJ's Pets.

Services provided by intermediaries are an important buying requirement for products such as large household appliances that require delivery, installation, and credit. Therefore, Whirlpool seeks dealers that provide such services.

The late Steve Jobs, formerly Apple's CEO, was one person who believed that computer retailers have failed to satisfy the buying requirements of today's consumer. Believing that "buying a car is no longer the worst purchasing experience; buying a computer is number one," he launched Apple stores.[11]

Profitability The third consideration in designing a channel is profitability, which is determined by the revenues earned minus cost for each channel member and for the channel as a whole. Cost is the critical factor of channel profitability. These costs include distribution, advertising, and selling expenses. The extent to which channel members share these costs determines the profitability of each member and of the channel as a whole.

Channel Relationships: Conflict and Cooperation

Unfortunately, because channels consist of independent individuals and firms, there is always potential for disagreements concerning who performs which channel functions, how profits are distributed, which products and services will be provided by whom, and who makes critical channel-related decisions. These channel conflicts necessitate measures for dealing with them.

Percentage of Businesses That Have Acquired a Customer as a Result of Time Spent Blogging

Blogging daily **90%**

69% 2 to 3 times a week

Weekly **58%**

38% Monthly

marketing meter

Source: HubSpot, *The State of Inbound Marketing – 2010*, accessed September 20, 2011, at www.hubspot.com/Portals/53/docs/resellers/reports/state_of_inbound_marketing.pdf.

Conflict in Marketing Channels

Channel conflict arises when one channel member believes another channel member is engaged in behaviour that prevents it from achieving its goals. Two types of conflict occur in marketing channels: vertical conflict and horizontal conflict.[12]

Vertical conflict occurs between different levels in a marketing channel; for example, between a manufacturer and a wholesaler or between a manufacturer and a retailer. An example of vertical conflict is when Coke and Costco had a disagreement on price. Costco claimed that Coke's selling price to Costco was too high. As a result, Costco stopped carrying Coke products. It took a month for the two channel members to resolve their differences before Coke once again was made available at Costco.[13]

Another type of vertical conflict arises when a channel member bypasses another member and sells directly to consumers, a practice called **disintermediation**. Apple is an excellent example of how disintermediation works. Before Apple Stores existed, Apple products were sold through independent retailers. When Apple started opening their own stores, its retailers began to complain. In 2005, independent Apple retailers filed a lawsuit against Apple, accusing the company of giving preferential treatment to its own stores and harming their sales. The lawsuit claimed that Apple had favoured Apple Stores by providing significant discounts that were unavailable to independent retailers. It also claimed that Apple was holding back product from the independent retailers.

Horizontal conflict occurs between intermediaries at the same level in a marketing channel, such as between two or more retailers or two or more wholesalers that handle the same manufacturer's brands. For instance, one Toyota dealer might complain to Toyota that another Toyota dealer has located too close to its dealership and is affecting its business.

Cooperation in Marketing Channels

Conflict can have disruptive effects on the workings of a marketing channel, so it is necessary to secure cooperation among channel members. One means is through a *channel captain*, a dominant channel member that coordinates, directs, and supports other channel members. Channel captains can be producers, wholesalers, or retailers. Procter & Gamble assumes this role because it has a strong consumer following in brands such as Crest, Tide, and Pampers. Therefore, it can set policies or terms that supermarkets will follow. Walmart and Home Depot are retail channel captains because of their strong consumer image, number of outlets, and purchasing volume.

A firm becomes a channel captain because it is the channel member with the ability to influence the behaviour of other members.[14] Influence can take four forms. First, economic influence arises from the ability of a firm to reward other members because of its strong financial position. Microsoft Corporation and Toys "R" Us have such influence. Expertise is a second source of influence. Third, identification with a particular channel member creates influence for that channel member. For example, retailers may compete to carry the Ralph Lauren line, or clothing manufacturers may compete to be carried by The Bay or Holt Renfrew. In both instances, the desire to be associated with a channel member gives that firm influence over others. Finally, influence can arise from the legitimate right of one channel member to direct the behaviour of other members. This situation occurs under contractual vertical marketing systems where a franchiser can legitimately direct how a franchisee behaves.

Logistics and Supply Chain Management

L6 A marketing channel relies on logistics to make products available to consumers and industrial users. **Logistics** involves those activities that focus on getting the right amount of the right products to the right place at the right time at the lowest possible cost. The performance of these activities is *logistics management*, the practice of organizing the cost-effective flow of raw materials, in-process inventory, finished goods, and related information from point of origin to point of consumption to satisfy *customer requirements*.[15]

Three elements of this definition deserve emphasis. First, logistics deals with decisions from the source of raw materials to consumption of the final product—that is, the *flow* of the product. Second, those decisions have to be *cost-effective*. Third, while it is important to drive down logistics costs, there is a limit: A firm needs to drive down logistics costs as long as it can deliver expected *customer service*, while satisfying customer requirements. The role of management is to see that customer needs are satisfied in the most cost-effective manner. When properly done, the results can be spectacular. Procter & Gamble is a case in point. Beginning in the 1990s, the company set out to meet the needs of consumers more effectively by collaborating and partnering with its suppliers and retailers to ensure that the right products reached store shelves at the right time and at a lower cost. The effort was judged a success when, during an 18-month period, Procter & Gamble's retailers recorded a US$65 million savings in logistics costs while customer service increased.[16]

The Procter & Gamble experience is not an isolated incident. Companies now recognize that getting the right items needed for consumption or production to the right place at the right time in the right condition at the right cost is often beyond their individual capabilities and control. Instead, collaboration, coordination, and information sharing among manufacturers, suppliers, and distributors are necessary to create a seamless flow of goods and services to customers. This perspective is represented in the concept of a supply chain and the practice of supply chain management.

Supply Chains versus Marketing Channels

A **supply chain** is a series of firms that perform activities required to create and deliver a good or service to consumers or industrial users. It differs from a marketing channel in terms of the firms involved. A supply chain is longer and includes suppliers who provide raw material inputs to a manufacturer as well as the wholesalers and retailers who deliver finished goods to

ask yourself

1. What are the three degrees of distribution intensity?

2. What are the three questions marketing executives consider when choosing a marketing channel and intermediaries?

you. The management process is also different. **Supply chain management** is the integration and organization of information and logistics activities across firms in a supply chain for the purpose of creating and delivering goods and services that provide value to consumers. The relation among marketing channels, logistics management, and supply chain management is shown in Figure 10–9. An important feature of supply chain management is its use of sophisticated information technology that allows companies to share and operate systems for order processing, transportation scheduling, and inventory and facility management.

Sourcing, Assembling, and Delivering a New Car: The Automotive Supply Chain

All companies are members of one or more supply chains. A supply chain is essentially a series of linked suppliers and customers in which every customer is, in turn, a supplier to another customer until a finished product reaches the ultimate consumer. Even a simplified supply chain diagram for carmakers shown in Figure 10–10 illustrates how complex a supply chain can be.[17] A carmaker's supplier network includes thousands of firms that provide the 5,000 or so parts in a typical automobile. They provide items ranging from raw materials such as steel and rubber to components, including transmissions, tires, brakes, and seats, to complex subassemblies and assemblies such as in chassis and suspension systems that make for a smooth, stable ride. Coordinating and scheduling material and component flows for their assembly into actual automobiles by carmakers is heavily dependent on logistical activities, including transportation, order processing, inventory control, materials handling, and information technology. A central link is the carmaker

Figure 10–9

How distribution channels work: the relationships between supplier networks, marketing channels, logistics management, and supply chain management

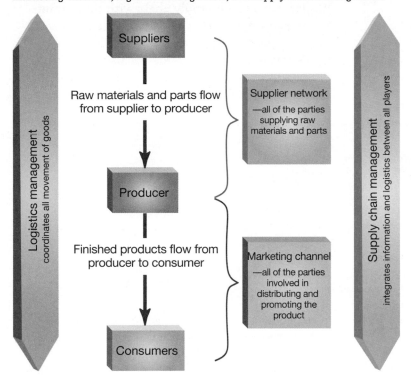

automobiles is delivered to each location. In addition, they make sure that spare and service parts are available so that dealers can meet the car maintenance and repair needs of consumers. All of this is done with the help of information technology that links the entire automotive supply chain. What does all of this cost? It is estimated that logistics costs represent 25 percent to 30 percent of the retail price of a typical new car.

Supply Chain Management and Marketing Strategy

The automotive supply chain illustration shows how logistics activities are interrelated and organized across firms to create and deliver a car for you. What's missing from this illustration is the linkage between a specific company's supply chain and its marketing strategy. Just as companies have different marketing strategies, they also manage supply chains differently. The goals to be achieved by a firm's marketing strategy determine whether its supply chain needs to focus on being more responsive or more efficient in meeting customer requirements.

Aligning a Supply Chain with Marketing Strategy

There are a variety of supply chain configurations, each of which is designed to perform different tasks well. Marketers today recognize that the choice of a supply chain follows from a clearly defined marketing strategy and involves three steps:[18]

1. **Understand the customer.** To understand the customer, a company must identify the needs of the customer segment being served. These needs, such as a desire for a low price or convenience

supply chain manager, who is responsible for translating customer requirements into actual orders and arranging for delivery dates and financial arrangements for automobile dealers.

Logistical aspects of the automobile marketing channel are also an important part of the supply chain. Major responsibilities include transportation (which involves the selection and management of external carriers—trucking, airline, railroad, and shipping companies—for cars and parts to dealers), the operation of distribution centres, the management of finished goods inventories, and order processing for sales. Supply chain managers also play an important role in the marketing channel. They work with extensive car dealer networks to ensure that the right mix of

Figure 10–10
The automotive supply chain

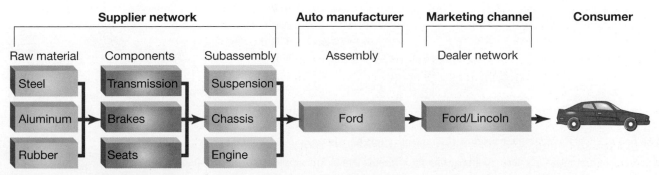

of purchase, help a company define the relative importance of efficiency and responsiveness in meeting customer requirements.

2. **Understand the supply chain.** Second, a company must understand what a supply chain is designed to do well. Supply chains range from those that emphasize being responsive to customer requirements and demand to those that emphasize efficiency with a goal of supplying products at the lowest possible delivered cost.

3. **Harmonize the supply chain with the marketing strategy.** Finally, a company needs to ensure that what the supply chain is capable of doing well is consistent with the targeted customer's needs and its marketing strategy. If a mismatch exists between what the supply chain does particularly

marketing NewsFlash — A Pioneer in Fast Fashion

The fashion industry is being transformed by retailers such as Zara that deliver fashion at lightning speeds to stores. Spanish retailer Zara, owned by retailer conglomerate Inditex, is extremely profitable. In Europe, Zara offers imitations of designer products at a low price, shortly after their release. In North America, Zara is positioned as a mid-priced retailer, reflecting the costs of exporting goods from Spain. Zara now has 1,341 stores in 73 countries.

Zara's production cycles are much faster than those of its rivals. An entirely new Zara garment takes about five weeks from design to delivery at the store level; a new version of an existing model can be in the shops within two weeks. In a typical year, Zara launches some 11,000 new items, compared with the 2,000 to 4,000 from companies such as H&M and Gap.

Zara has one of the most sophisticated supply chains of any apparel retailer. Zara's parent Inditex owns the dye and finishing plants, manufacturing plants, warehouse facilities, retail stores, and designer studios. Controlling notorious trouble spots along the supply chain is key to speed. Potential bottlenecks can be thwarted because Zara has a vertically integrated structure.

Dyeing and fit are critical processes within the supply chain. Zara is a large investor in a dye and finishing plant, allowing them to oversee the dyeing process—a notorious bottleneck. Although Zara uses sub-contractors for sewing, they do the vast majority of cutting themselves—a crucial process that determines fit. Fabric is cut in-house and then sent to a cluster of several hundred local co-operatives for sewing. When the finished product returns, it is ironed, carefully checked, and wrapped in plastic for transport on conveyor belts to a group of giant warehouses.

Under the Zara model, the retail store is the eyes and ears of the company. Instead of relying solely on electronically collected data, Zara utilizes word-of-mouth information to understand more about their customers. Empowered store managers report to head office what customers are saying. Products that are not selling well are quickly pulled off the shelf and hot items quickly replenished. Their quick turnaround on merchandise helps generate cash, which eliminates the need for significant debt.

This "fast fashion" system depends on a constant exchange of information throughout every part of Zara's supply chain—from customers to store managers, from store managers to market specialists and designers, from designers to production staff, from buyers to subcontractors, from warehouse managers to distributors, and so on. Most companies insert layers of bureaucracy that can bog down communication between departments. But Zara's organization, operational procedures, performance measures, and even its office layouts are all designed to make information transfer easy.

In Zara stores, customers can always find new products—but they're in limited supply. There is a sense of tantalizing exclusivity because only a few items are on display even though stores are spacious. A customer thinks, "This green shirt fits me, and there is one on the rack. If I don't buy it now, I'll lose my chance." Such a retail concept depends on the regular creation and rapid replenishment of small batches of new goods. Zara's designers create approximately 40,000 new designs annually, from which 11,000 are selected for production. Some of them resemble the latest couture creations. But Zara often beats the high-fashion houses to the market and offers almost the same products, made with less-expensive fabric, at much lower prices. Because most garments come in five to six colours and five to seven sizes, Zara's system has to deal with something in the realm of 300,000 new stock-keeping units (SKUs), on average, every year.[19]

Questions

1. Explain how Zara can get a product from design stage to in-store so quickly.

2. Compare Zara's supply chain to that of a traditional retailer of fashionable women's clothes.

well and a company's marketing strategy, the company will either need to redesign the supply chain to support the marketing strategy or change the marketing strategy. The bottom line is that a poorly designed supply chain can do serious damage to an otherwise brilliant marketing strategy. Read the Marketing NewsFlash (opposite) to find out how Zara has manipulated its supply chain strategy to position itself as a popular and profitable mid-priced fashion retailer.

How are these steps applied and how are efficiency and response considerations built into a supply chain? Let's briefly look at how two market leaders—Dell Computer Corporation and Walmart, Inc.—have harmonized their supply chain and marketing strategy.

Dell Computer Corporation: A Responsive Supply Chain   The

Dell marketing strategy targets customers who want to have the most up-to-date personal computer equipment customized to their needs. These customers are also willing to wait to have their customized personal computer delivered in a few days, rather than picking out a pre-packaged model at a retail store; and pay a reasonable, though not the lowest, price in the marketplace. Given Dell's market segments, the company has the option of choosing either an efficient or a responsive supply chain.

An efficient supply chain may use inexpensive but slower modes of transportation, emphasize economies of scale in its production process by reducing the variety of PC configurations offered, and limit its assembly and inventory storage facilities to a single location, say Austin, Texas, where the company is headquartered. If Dell opted only for efficiency in its supply chain, it would be difficult if not impossible to satisfy its target customer's desire for rapid delivery and a wide variety of customizable products. Dell instead has opted for a responsive supply chain. It relies on more expensive express transportation for receipt of components from suppliers and delivery of finished products to customers. The company achieves product variety and manufacturing efficiency by designing common platforms across several products and using common components. Dell also has invested heavily in information technology to link itself with suppliers and customers.

Walmart, Inc.: An Efficient Supply Chain   Now let's consider Walmart. Walmart's mar-

keting strategy is to be a reliable, lower-price retailer for a wide variety of mass consumption consumer goods. This strategy favours an efficient supply chain designed to deliver products to consumers at the lowest possible cost. Efficiency is achieved in a variety of ways. For instance, Walmart keeps relatively low inventory

levels, and most inventory is stocked in stores available for sale, not in warehouses gathering dust. The low inventory arises from Walmart's use of *cross-docking*—a practice that involves unloading products from suppliers, sorting products for individual stores, and quickly reloading products onto its trucks for a particular store. No warehousing or storing of products occurs, except for a few hours or, at most, a day. Cross-docking allows Walmart to operate only a small number of distribution centres to service its vast network of Walmart Stores and Supercentres, which contributes to efficiency. On the other hand, the company runs its own fleet of trucks to service its stores.

This does increase cost and investment, but the benefits in terms of responsiveness justify the cost in Walmart's case. Walmart has invested significantly more than its competitors in information technology to operate its supply chain. The company feeds information about customer requirements and demand from its stores back to its suppliers, which manufacture only what is being demanded. This large investment has improved the efficiency of Walmart's supply chain and made it responsive to customer needs.

RFID, which stands for *radio frequency identification*, is a tag that is incorporated in a product for tracking purposes. RFID improves the efficiency of inventory tracking and management. Walmart has already asked its suppliers to use RFID. Walmart says that RFID will result in a 30 percent reduction of out-of-stock items and less excess inventory in the supply chain.[20] Some suppliers have complied but many to date have not. The cost of using this new technology is the reason for them not going ahead. See the Marketing NewsFlash below for more information on RFID.

Three lessons can be learned from these two examples. First, there is no one best supply chain for every company. Second, the best supply chain is the one that is consistent with the needs of the customer

marketing **NewsFlash**   RFID: The Way of the Future

Scanning the bar code of every product is a way for retailers to keep track of what is sold. However, what inventory the retailer has in the store and where it actually is remains a blind spot for many businesses. Walmart discovered this some years back when trying to keep popular sales items on the shelves. Stock on the store floor would sell out and managers knew there was more stock in the back, but where it had been stored was a mystery. This resulted in lost sales. This kind of problem is easily resolved today with technology called *radio frequency identification (RFID)*. It works by attaching electronic tags to inventory that allows managers to know exactly where it is. Each RFID tag is composed of a chip and an antenna, which identifies that item and its location. The chips send data to readers using low-powered radio signals. The information is picked up by readers that identify the item and its location.

RFID allows 100 percent inventory visibility and tracking. RFID tags range in size from the large, label-like stickers sometimes found in books or on clothing to the nearly microscopic. The most miniature tags are the size of dust particles, and can be embedded in paper and attached to almost any surface.

Walmart was one of the first retailers to support this technology in 2003. It asked 100 of its largest suppliers to begin using RFID by 2005. Despite the reluctance of some manufacturers to take on the cost of tagging, the great majority complied, and Walmart continues to extend the list of suppliers who must either tag each pallet of goods or pay the costs for Walmart staff to do it themselves. Procter & Gamble was one of the first companies to use RFID technology. Procter & Gamble estimates that its use of RFID technology cuts inventory costs by $200 million a year.

The use of RFID technology has raised privacy concerns because the

tags are always emitting information. Most concerns revolve around the fact that RFID tags affixed to products remain functional even after the products have been purchased and taken home and thus can be used for surveillance and other purposes unrelated to their supply chain inventory functions. Walmart is demanding that suppliers add the tags to removable labels or packaging instead of embedding them in clothes so that the consumer can discard the chip before using the product. Walmart is hoping that this action will minimize fears that the tags can be used to track people's movements.[21]

Questions

1. What can RFID technology do that a bar code cannot do?

2. Explain privacy concerns that arise out of using RFID technology.

segment being served and complements a company's marketing strategy. And finally, supply chain managers are often called upon to make trade-offs between efficiency and responsiveness on various elements of a company's supply chain.

Key Logistics Functions in a Supply Chain

L⑦ The four key logistics functions in a supply chain are transportation, order processing, inventory management, and warehousing. These functions have become so complex that many companies are outsourcing them to third-party logistics providers. The four logistics functions are described next.

Transportation

There are five basic modes of transportation: railroads, motor carriers, air carriers, water carriers, pipelines, and combinations involving two or more modes, such as highway trailers on a rail flatcar. Although many manufacturers pay transportation expenses, some retailers negotiate with their vendors to absorb this expense. The transportation modes can be evaluated on six basic service criteria:

- **Cost:** Charges for transportation
- **Time:** Speed of transit
- **Capability:** What can be realistically carried with this mode, such as controlled temperatures and humidity levels
- **Dependability:** Reliability of service regarding time, loss, and damage
- **Accessibility:** Ability to move products over a specific route or network; e.g., some destinations such as remote areas in northern parts of Canada may be unavailable by truck or water
- **Frequency:** Refers to how often a marketer can ship products by a specific transportation mode. Pipelines provide continuous shipments whereas railways and water carriers follow specific schedules for moving products from one location to another.

Order Processing

Order processing is much more sophisticated these days with the use of **electronic data interchange (EDI)**. EDI is the computer-to-computer exchange of business documents from a retailer to a supplier and back. Purchase orders and invoices can be transmitted back and forth electronically, replacing manual processing. Walmart is a pioneer in using EDI. Now, many other retailers also use this system. The use of EDI increases the speed, accuracy, and streamlining of operations between retailer and supplier.

Inventory Management

Inventory management entails maintaining the delicate balance between keeping too little and too much inventory. For example, a retailer that carries too much inventory ends up with a lot of capital tied up in storing products in a warehouse. Too little inventory means that there is an increased risk for being out of stock and having unhappy customers.

A solution to this problem is a system called **just-in-time (JIT) inventory system**, which is designed to deliver less merchandise on a more frequent basis than traditional inventory systems. This system requires fast on-time delivery. The firm gets the merchandise "just-in-

electronic data interchange (EDI)
A computer-to-computer exchange of business documents from a retailer to a supplier and back

just-in-time (JIT) inventory system
A system designed to deliver less merchandise on a more frequent basis than traditional inventory systems

time" for it to be used in production of another product, or for sale when the customer wants it, in the case of consumer products.

Although firms achieve great benefits from a just-in-time system, it is not without its costs. The logistics function becomes more complicated with more frequent deliveries. Greater order frequencies result in smaller orders, which are more expensive to transport and more difficult to coordinate.

Warehousing

There are two types of warehouses: public and private. A private warehouse is used usually by large firms, whereas a public warehouse offers storage for small companies or individuals. Most storage warehouses are located in the outskirts of the city where rail and truck transportation are easily available. Warehouses are places to store products whereas distribution centres described below receive, store, and redistribute goods to customers.

Distribution centres can be divided into three types: traditional, cross-docking, and combination. In a traditional distribution centre, merchandise is unloaded from trucks and placed on shelves for storage. When the merchandise is required in stores, a worker goes to the shelf, picks up the item, and places it in a bin. A conveyer transports the merchandise to a staging area, where it is consolidated and made ready for shipment to stores.

The second type of distribution centre is called cross-docking, as was described earlier in the chapter. For example, Heinz ships ketchup pre-packaged in the quantity required for each Walmart store. It is then sent to a staging area rather than into storage. When all the merchandise going to a particular Walmart store has arrived in the staging area, it is loaded onto a Walmart truck that goes directly to the store.

The third type of distribution centre consists of a combination of the two types explained above. Most modern distribution centres are comprised of the third type. It is difficult for a company to operate without some storage facilities, even if merchandise is stored for only a few days.

Summary...*just the facts*

- A marketing channel consists of individuals and firms involved in the process of making a product or service available for use by consumers or business users.

- Intermediaries make possible the flow of products and services from producers to buyers by performing transactional, logistical, and facilitating functions. At the same time, intermediaries create time, place, form, and possession utility.

- In general, marketing channels for consumer products and services contain more intermediaries than do channels for business products and services. In some situations, producers use Internet, multiple channels and strategic channel alliances to reach buyers.

- The prevalence of consumer shopping online, as well as buying in retail stores, has made multichannel marketing popular. Multichannel marketing is the blending of different communication and delivery channels that are mutually reinforcing in attracting, retaining, and building relationships with consumers who shop and buy in the traditional marketplace as well as in the online marketspace.

- Not all companies approach multichannel marketing the same way. A major difference in approach is the use of transactional websites and promotional websites.

- Vertical marketing systems are channels designed to achieve channel function economies and marketing impact. A vertical marketing system may be one of three types: corporate, administered, or contractual.

- The final choice of a marketing channel by a producer depends on a number of factors. They are market factors, product factors, and company factors.

- Channel design considerations are based on the target market coverage sought by producers, the buyer requirements to be satisfied, and the profitability of the channel. Target market coverage comes about through one of three levels of distribution density: intensive, exclusive, and selective distribution. Buyer requirements are evident in the amount of information, convenience, variety, and service sought by consumers. Profitability—of each channel member and the channel as a whole—is largely affected by costs and whether or not costs can be shared by members.

- Conflicts in marketing channels are inevitable. Vertical conflict occurs between different levels in a channel. Horizontal conflict occurs between intermediaries at the same level in the channel.

- Logistics involves those activities that focus on getting the right amount of the right products to the right place at the right time at the lowest possible cost. Logistics management includes the coordination of the flows of both inbound and outbound goods, an emphasis on making these flows cost effective, and customer service.

- A supply chain is a sequence of firms that perform activities required to create and deliver a good or service to consumers or industrial users. Supply chain management is the integration and organization of information and logistics across firms for the purpose of creating value for consumers.

- The goals to be achieved by a firm's marketing strategy determine whether its supply chain needs to be more responsive or efficient in meeting customer requirements. Marketers today recognize that the choice of a supply chain involves three steps: (1) understand the customer, (2) understand the supply chain, and (3) harmonize the supply chain with the marketing strategy.

- The four key logistic functions in a supply chain are transportation, order processing, inventory management, and warehousing. These functions have become so complex that many companies are outsourcing them to third-party logistics providers.

Key Terms and Concepts...*a refresher*

channel conflict *p. 228*
cross-channel shopper *p. 222*
disintermediation *p. 229*
dual distribution *p. 221*
electronic marketing channels *p. 221*
electronic data interchange (EDI) *p. 235*

exclusive distribution *p. 227*
franchising *p. 225*
intensive distribution *p. 227*
intermediaries *p. 217*
just-in-time (JIT) inventory system *p. 235*
logistics *p. 229*

marketing channel *p. 216*
multichannel marketing *p. 222*
selective distribution *p. 227*
supply chain *p. 230*
supply chain management *p. 230*
vertical marketing systems *p. 224*

Hands-on...*apply your knowledge*

Online Franchise Assignment Explore the Freshii website at www.freshii.com and then answer the following questions:

- You are a health-conscious consumer who has not as yet been to a Freshii restaurant. Is the website appealing enough to make you want to visit Freshii? Why or why not?

- You are thinking of becoming a franchisee. Does Freshii seem like the type of franchise you would like to explore further? Why or why not?

Reality Check...*reminder*

Refer back to this chapter's opening vignette and answer the Reality Check questions on page 216.

Retailing
and Wholesaling

Ron White is the CEO and creative director of Ron White Shoes, a luxury shoe store with six locations in the Toronto area. Early in his career, Ron was an employee in an orthopedic shoe store where he learned a lot about orthotics, biomechanics, and how to analyze one's walking pattern and foot posture. Later in his career, when he was his own boss at Ron White Shoes, he put that knowledge to good use

by developing a line of women's shoes that combined elegance and comfort. The fashionable line, called All Day Heels®, provides arch support, built-in cushioning materials, and thin lightweight insoles made of Poron, a flexible high-tech elastic polymer developed by NASA. The All Day Heels line took three years of development, including prototypes and trials. Getting the name registered in the U.S. took just as long. Apparently, the trademark office had initially thought "all day heels" was an existing category of shoes like "cross-trainers" and therefore ineligible for trademarking.

Celebrities such as Kim Cattrall, from *Sex and the City*, and Sarah Ferguson, the Duchess of York, wear Ron's All Day Heels. What make Ron White stores unique is that All Day Heels are available only in his stores. This private-label brand differentiates Ron's stores from the other retail competitors in the same way that the President's Choice brand can be found only in stores such as Loblaws and No Frills.

Ron says that his All Day Heels collection bridges the gap between comfort and style by providing fashion that feels wonderful. According to Ron, the shoe market worldwide is split into two camps. The comfort camp stresses

retailing
All activities involved in selling, renting, and providing goods and services to ultimate consumers for personal, family, or household use

support, flexibility, and cushioning, but has a tired boring look. The fashion camp, on the other hand, stresses elegance but not comfort. Ron bridges the gap by getting the factories that produce Gucci and Chanel branded shoes to produce his All Day Heels to his specifications.

Ron White's All Day Heels is now the best-selling brand in his stores; the shoes do double the sales of his number-two brand of shoes. Ron breaks down his target market into three segments. There is the so-called "Audrey" segment, which is aged 55 plus; the "Andrea" segment, aged 35 to 55; and the "Amber" segment, which is under 35. Each of these segments exhibit different consumer behaviour patterns, but there is overlap within the three segments in the respect that they all appreciate the comfort of the All Day Heels technology. Ron says that he initially catered to the Audrey segment, until he introduced his All Day Heels, which attracted the Andrea segment. Ron also says that "the daughters" of the Andrea segment, who are found in the Amber segment, also shop at his stores.

Ron tries to find out as much as he can about the needs of his customers. He organizes such events as wine and cheese parties, where customers can share their comments in an informal setting. Ron's website started as most websites do, as a source of information for customers. It has evolved into a place where consumers can actually purchase online from his e-boutique. One of his challenges is to have customers order the correct size to minimize returns. Ron's site offers tips on ordering the right size, which results in a small return percentage, as opposed to Zappos, an online shoe retailer that gets a larger percentage of returns.

Ron's sales staff is a model for product knowledge and service. Every new hire goes through an extensive training program, which Ron calls "Ron White University," that allows them to graduate and become footwear specialists. The program includes a 65-page training guide, a number of tests, and a special designation for staff who complete the program. The staff's detailed knowledge of biomechanics and foot ailments ensures that the customer gets an extremely high level of product knowledge and customer service.

With Ron's unique knowledge in shoe construction, technology, and fashion, he has become the "go to" expert in Canada. Known as "Canada's Shoe-ru," Ron is regularly featured in Canada's national newspapers, magazines, and talk shows, and he provides ongoing commentary to a number of television programs including *Fashion Television*, *ET Canada*, *eTalk*, and CBC's *Steven and Chris*. Ron also pens a monthly shoe/style blog for the *National Post* and regularly appears on *Breakfast Television* as well as in international media.

Ron has been conducting annual fundraisers for many years. The stores raise funds for breast cancer every October and he conducts Canada's largest annual Shoe Drive for the Homeless, every winter, with the help of many national and international celebrities. These successful programs have led to the establishment of the Ron White Foundation, which focuses on raising funds, awareness, and education for human rights–based issues. 🍎

As you read Chapter 11, refer back to the Ron White Shoes vignette to answer the following questions:

- What is the form of ownership of Ron White Shoes?

- Describe the breadth and depth of product line as it applies to Ron White Shoes.

reality CHECK

Chapter 11 continues with the concept of distribution—creating a place where the customer can access the product—the place P of the 4Ps that make up the marketing mix.

The Value of Retailing

LO 1 **Retailing** includes all activities involved in selling, renting, and providing goods and services to ultimate customers for personal, family, or household use.

Retailing is an important marketing activity. Retailing engages the consumer; it provides a place for showcasing products and creates interest and excitement. Shopping is not only a way to acquire necessities but also a social activity and often an adventure—retailing makes this possible. Producers and consumers are brought together through retailing actions, and retailing also creates customer value and has a significant impact on the economy. Retailing's economic value is represented by the number of people employed in retailing as well as by the total amount of money exchanged in retail sales.

Consumer Utilities Offered by Retailing

The utilities provided by retailers create value for consumers. Time, place, form, information, and possession utilities are offered by most retailers in varying degrees, but one utility is often emphasized more than others. Look at Figure 11–1 to find out how well you can match the retailer with the utility being emphasized in the description.

Placing minibanks in supermarkets puts the bank's products and services close to the consumer, providing place utility.[1] The Bay makes the purchase easier by providing different ways to pay for the purchase and provides possession utility. Form utility—production or alteration of a product—is offered by Ralph Lauren through its online "Create Your Own" program, which offers shirts that meet each customer's specifications. Finding toy shelves well stocked year-round is the time utility dreamed about by every child (and many parents) who enters Toys "Я" Us. Many retailers offer a combination of the four basic utilities. Some supermarkets, for example, offer convenient locations (place utility) and are open 24 hours (time utility). In addition, consumers may seek additional utilities such as entertainment, recreation, or information.[2]

Retailing involves creating a place where the customer can access the product.

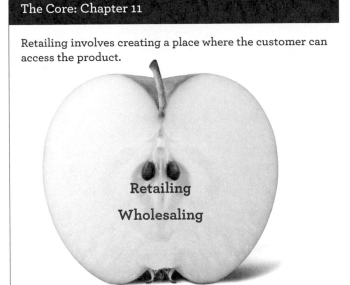

Marketers understand that retailers rely on wholesalers to provide selection and availability of product.

The Canadian Retail Scene

Maybe you have had a job in retail. Many students get their first taste of employment by working in a store or restaurant. Retail is a vibrant and important part of the Canadian economy. Retailers develop strong ties with Canadians by generating more than 2 million

Figure 11-1
Which company best represents which utilities?

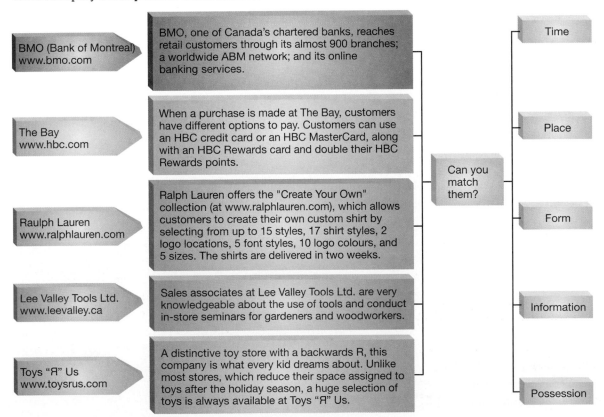

form of ownership
Distinguishes retail outlets on the basis of whether individuals, corporate chains, or contractual systems own the outlet

jobs. In fact, the retail trade represents Canada's second largest labour force.[3]

In 2010, $436 billion in retail sales were recorded in Canada.[4] The largest ten Canadian retailers, ranked in descending order, are Loblaw, Alimentation Couche-Tard, Empire Company Limited (Sobeys), Metro, Shoppers Drug Mart, Canadian Tire, Hudson's Bay Company, Katz Group, Jim Pattison Group, and Rona.[5]

Figure 11–2 tells us that $103.4 billion is spent on food per year. It follows logically that the three largest retailers in the country are predominantly in the food business.

There is a growing trend for American retailers to open locations in Canada. For example, HBC sold the bulk of its weakest chain Zellers Inc. to the U.S. retail giant Target. The chain assumed control of up to 220 Zellers stores. Target will spend more than $1 billion to convert 100 to 150 of them to its own banner within the next two years. The move, which comes after years of rumours and discussion about Target's desire to acquire space in Canada, will dramatically reshape the domestic retail landscape. It underscores the growing demand by foreign retailers for Canadian locations to take advantage of the country's relatively healthy economy.[6]

The Global Retail Picture

Retailing is also a very important factor in the global economy, and it is a difficult retail climate for store owners. In the past few years, the worldwide economy has been challenged by issues such as terrorism, economic downturn, reduced tourism, political crises, and low consumer confidence. All of these issues translate into lower sales for retail. At the same time, consumers are more savvy and empowered, and it is more difficult to gain and maintain their loyalty. Profits have to be worked at very diligently. Technology is making the industry more sophisticated and streamlined, and consolidation makes some competitors large and very powerful. It is a demanding and thorny business.

Not all countries have experienced the soft demand and market

ask yourself

1. When Ralph Lauren makes shirts to a customer's exact preferences, what utility is provided?

2. The customer has different ways to pay for a purchase at The Bay. What utility is provided?

challenges that have characterized the major industrialized nations. Some of the developing countries or emerging markets in Asia and Eastern Europe are experiencing solid growth and are developing modern types of retailing. China, India, and Russia are seen as some of the biggest growth opportunities for retail in the next few years.

On a global scale, who is biggest? Walmart! Walmart is number one, followed by Carrefour and Tesco. A study of the top 250 global retailers by the firm Deloitte Touche Tohmatsu ranks the world's biggest retailers (see Figure 11–3). Of the top 250 firms, 86 are American and 99 are located in Europe.

The chart accompanying Figure 11–3 tells an interesting story: Most of the top 10 global retailers have a presence in many parts of the globe.

Classifying Retail Outlets

For manufacturers, consumers, and the economy, retailing is an important component of marketing that has several variations. Because of the large number of alternative forms of retailing, it is easier to understand the differences among retail institutions by recognizing that outlets can be classified by ownership. **Form of ownership** distinguishes retail outlets on the basis of whether individuals, corporate chains, or contractual systems own or control the outlet.

Figure 11–2

Retail sales ($ millions) for 2010 in Canada by commodity group

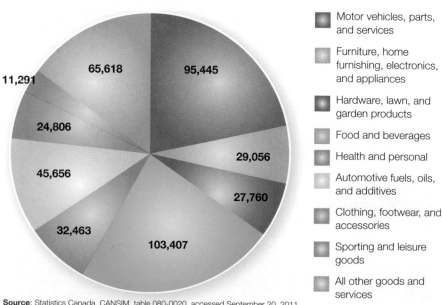

- Motor vehicles, parts, and services
- Furniture, home furnishing, electronics, and appliances
- Hardware, lawn, and garden products
- Food and beverages
- Health and personal
- Automotive fuels, oils, and additives
- Clothing, footwear, and accessories
- Sporting and leisure goods
- All other goods and services

Source: Statistics Canada, CANSIM, table 080-0020, accessed September 20, 2011, at http://www40.statcan.ca/l01/cst01/trad15a-eng.htm.

Figure 11–3

Where do we find the top retailers in the world? Who are they?

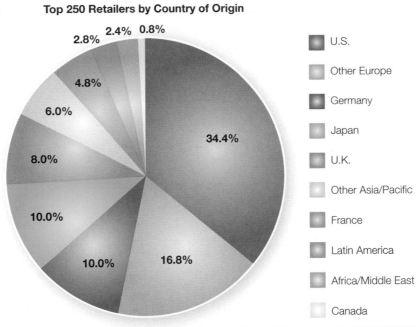

Top 250 Retailers by Country of Origin

- U.S. — 34.4%
- Other Europe — 16.8%
- Germany — 10.0%
- Japan — 10.0%
- U.K. — 8.0%
- Other Asia/Pacific — 6.0%
- France — 4.8%
- Latin America — 2.8%
- Africa/Middle East — 2.4%
- Canada — 0.8%

RANK	COUNTRY OF ORIGIN	NAME OF COMPANY	2007 SALES (US$ MILLIONS)	COUNTRIES OF OPERATION
1	U.S.	Walmart	$374,526	Argentina, Brazil, Canada, China, Costa Rica, El Salvador, Guatemala, Honduras, Nicaragua, Japan, Mexico, Puerto Rico, U.K., U.S.
2	France	Carrefour	$112,604	Algeria, Argentina, Belgium, Brazil, Chile, China, Colombia, Dominican Republic, Egypt, France, Guadeloupe, Greece, Indonesia, Italy, Japan, Malaysia, Martinique, Oman, Poland, Portugal, Qatar, Romania, Saudi Arabia, Singapore, Spain, Switzerland, Taiwan, Thailand, Tunisia, Turkey, UAE
3	U.K.	Tesco	$94,740	China, Czech Republic, Japan, Hungary, Republic of Ireland, Malaysia, Poland, Slovakia, South Korea, Taiwan, Thailand, Turkey, U.K., U.S.
4	Germany	Metro AG	$87,586	Austria, Belgium, Bulgaria, China, Croatia, Czech Republic, Denmark, France, Germany, Greece, Hungary, India, Italy, Japan, Luxembourg, Moldova, Morocco, Netherlands, Pakistan, Poland, Portugal, Romania, Russia, Serbia , Slovakia, Spain, Sweden, Switzerland, Turkey, Ukraine, U.K., Vietnam
5	U.S.	The Home Depot	$77,349	Canada, China, Guam, Mexico, Puerto Rico, U.S., Virgin Islands
6	U.S.	Kroger	$70,235	U.S.
7	Germany	Schwarz Unternehmens Treuhand KG	$69,346	Austria, Belgium, Bulgaria, Croatia, Cyprus, Czech Republic, Denmark, Finland, France, Germany, Greece, Hungary, Republic of Ireland, Italy, Luxembourg, Netherlands, Norway, Poland, Portugal, Romania, Slovakia, Spain, Sweden, U.K..
8	U.S.	Target	$63,367	U.S.
9	U.S.	Costco Wholesale Corp.	$63,088	Canada, Puerto Rico, U.S., Japan, Mexico, South Korea, Taiwan, U.K.
10	Germany	Aldi GmbH & Co. oHG	$58,487	Australia, Austria, Belgium, Denmark, France, Germany, Rep. of Ireland, Luxembourg, Netherlands, Portugal, Slovenia, Spain, Switzerland,

Source: 2009 Global Powers of Retailing. Accessed at http://public.deloitte.com/media/0460/2009GlobalPowersofRetail_FINAL2.pdf.

Form of Ownership

Independent Retailer One of the most common forms of retail ownership is the independent business, owned by an individual. Small independent retailers account for more than 60 percent of the total retail trade in Canada. They tend to be retailers such as bakeries, sporting goods stores, jewellery stores, or gift stores. Other types of small independent retailers include restaurants, automotive supply stores, bookstores, paint stores, flower shops, and women's accessories outlets. The advantage of this form of ownership for the owner is that he or she can be his or her own boss. For customers, the independent store can offer convenience, quality personal service, and lifestyle compatibility.[7]

Corporate Chain A second form of ownership, the corporate chain, involves multiple outlets under common ownership. If you've ever shopped at The Bay, Sears, or Real Canadian Superstore, you've shopped at a chain outlet.

marketing NewsFlash   Dollarama: A Success Story

Dollarama is the largest dollar-store chain in Canada with 594 stores across the country. Dollarama was founded in 1992 by third-generation retailer Larry Rossy. In 2004, private equity group Bain Capital L.P. purchased a majority stake in Dollarama. The chain intends to add 30 to 40 stores a year for the foreseeable future.

All stores are corporate-owned and provide customers with a consistent shopping experience. Dollarama's uncomplicated approach to its business involves operating clean stores, maintaining a consistent inventory of name brands and house brands, and dealing directly with suppliers. Under this no-frills strategy, the company has seen growth every year since it opened in 1992. The stores are accepting debit cards for the first time and toying with credit cards. Dollarama recently introduced multiple price points by selling $1.25, $1.50, and $2 items alongside its traditional $1 items.

Out of the roughly 4,400 items that line Dollarama's shelves at any given time, 700 are seasonal products. This ability to capitalize on seasonal demand is widely admired. "They run it like the U.S. Marines," says John Williams, a retail consultant.

"When Christmas is out, they go into Valentine's Day, and when that's out, they go into Easter."

Food, drinks, and other so-called consumables, which currently represent 37 percent of a Dollarama's store stock, occupy more and more shelf space. These items are not all obscure, low-quality brands being sold cheaply. Popular brands such as Perrier, Werther's candies, and Lay's chips are all prominently displayed.

Sometimes, rather than seeking out brand-name merchandise, Dollarama creates its own. Kids now seek out Studio notebooks, made for Dollarama, the same way they once sought out Hilroy for back-to-school. Dollarama sources many of its suppliers directly and gets involved with the product design, packaging, and labelling. Dollarama has 70 house brands, still a novel concept in the dollar-store world.

There is no denying that Dollarama dominates the Canadian dollar-store sector. There are thousands of "mom and pop" dollar stores, but only one other national dollar-store chain, Dollar Giant. It has just 75 stores. There are also four large franchise operations—Dollar Store with More, Great Canadian, Buck or Two, and Everything for a Dollar—but combined they operate less than 400 stores.

What percentage of Dollarama's customers fall into each of those two camps—rich and poor—is not entirely clear? In the United States, dollar stores undeniably rely on the lower class for business. But Canadian dollar stores seem to draw from a wider demographic. "There's a type of consumer who may drive a Mercedes but get their stationery from a dollar store," says retail consultant Wendy Evans. "You'll see them buying a no-name brand and driving luxury cars and wearing designer clothing. They care about brands for some things and not others."

Retail analyst John Williams argues the dollar-store industry is now in a "mature phase." Others contend there is still plenty of room for growth. In Canada, there is a dollar store for every 32,000 people, far less than the one per 15,500 people in the United States. Dollarama's current plans call for 900 stores across the country.[8]

Questions

1. If you have shopped in a Dollarama, describe the quality of the products.

2. How do you explain the success of Dollarama?

In a chain operation, centralization of decision-making and purchasing is common. Chain stores have advantages in dealing with manufacturers, particularly as the size of the chain grows. A large chain can bargain with a manufacturer to obtain good service or volume discounts on orders. Loblaws' large volume makes it a strong negotiator with manufacturers of most products. The buying power of chains is obvious to consumers who compare prices at chain stores with other types of stores. Consumers also benefit in dealing with chains because there are multiple outlets with similar merchandise and consistent management policies. See the Marketing NewsFlash opposite for one such example.

Retailing has become a high-tech business for many large chains. Walmart, for example, has developed a sophisticated inventory-management and cost-control system that allows rapid price changes for each product in every store. In addition, stores such as Walmart are implementing pioneering new technologies such as radio frequency identification (RFID) tags to improve the quality of information available about products. RFID is a tag that is incorporated in a product for tracking purposes and improves the efficiency of inventory tracking and management. A complete discussion on RFID can be found in Chapter 10.

Contractual System Contractual systems involve independently owned stores that band together to act like a chain. The three kinds described in Chapter 10 are retailer-sponsored cooperatives, wholesaler-sponsored voluntary chains, and franchises. One retailer-sponsored cooperative is Home Hardware, which is a collection of independent hardware and home-renovation stores across Canada. Home Hardware actually created its own wholesale operation to take full advantage of dealings with manufacturers and suppliers. As a cooperative, members can take advantage of volume discounts commonly available to chains and also give the impression of being a large chain, which may be viewed more favourably by some consumers. Wholesaler-sponsored voluntary chains such as Independent Grocers' Association (IGA) try to achieve similar benefits.

As noted in Chapter 10, in a franchise system, an individual or firm (the franchisee) contracts with a parent company (the franchiser) to set up a business or retail outlet. McDonald's, Holiday Inn, and Subway all offer franchising opportunities. The franchiser usually assists in selecting the store location, setting up the store, advertising, and training personnel. In addition, the franchiser provides step-by-step procedures for major aspects of the business and guidelines for the most likely decisions a franchisee will confront. The franchisee pays a one-time franchise fee and an annual royalty, usually tied to the store's sales.

Figure 11–4 shows five franchises that operate across Canada, and indicates the range of investment required and the number of units operating. By selling franchises, an organization reduces the cost of expansion, although they lose some control. A good franchiser concentrates on enhancing the image and reputation of the franchise name.[9]

Target Market Selection and Positioning

L3 Retailing involves many decisions and considerations. In this section, we look at the issues in selecting a target market and the concept of retail positioning.

Selecting a Target Market

The first task in developing a retail strategy is to define a target market, describing it in detail. In Chapter 6 we

Top Three Online Transaction Categories

Rank	Category
1	Online travel
2	Managing credit card account
3	Online banking

Source: Seeking Alpha, "Top 10 Online Retailers, Shopping Categories," accessed September 20, 2011, at http://seekingalpha.com/article/105889-top-10-online-retailers-shopping-categories.

discussed in detail how to segment a market and then how to choose the targets to focus on. Without customers, even the best-conceived retail concept is nothing, so focusing on customers is the guiding principle of successful retail businesses. This focus involves understanding wants and needs, knowing customer preferences, analyzing behaviour, and deciding how to craft all of the dimensions of the retail concept to appeal to the targeted customer. Look at any mall or shopping district, and you will see the varied selection of retail offerings the customer has to choose from. This provides a challenge to retailers. It is no longer enough to appeal to customers; now the retailer has to interest, delight, and wow customers so that they will become loyal customers.

How do we define target markets? The most common descriptors are geographics, demographics, psychographics, and behaviouristics. Retailers study these factors and adjust their retail mix accordingly. McDonald's and Subway look at demographics—population, family, and age characteristics—to determine where new restaurants should be located and what formats to offer. Retailers such as Zellers and Canadian Tire look at consumers' trends and tastes and adjust their product offerings

and store composition to match customer preferences. Office Depot and Shoppers Drug Mart have adjusted their store hours to respond to the behaviour of consumers; many now prefer to shop and do errands in the evening after working during the day.

Retail Positioning

We learned in Chapter 6 about the concept of positioning. Just as marketers of packaged goods position their products to differentiate themselves from competitors, so do retailers. For example, Harry Rosen is a high-end men's clothing retailer. It would be a mistake in times of recession for Harry Rosen to start carrying lower quality, low-priced suits. Larry Rosen, CEO and chairman, and son of founder Harry Rosen, of Harry Rosen Inc., says, "The customer who is used to the quality and calibre of our product is not looking for a cheaper product. Maybe he'll buy slightly less this year but it's not about reducing quality. It's about sticking to your guns, to who you are."[10]

> *McDonald's and Subway look at demographics— population, family, and age characteristics—to determine where new restaurants should be located and what formats to offer.*

Shopper Marketing

Shopper marketing is a hot trend in marketing today. It is a discipline designed to understand how consumers behave as shoppers in different channels and formats. Consequently, shopper marketing practices extend well outside of the store, to the place and time when a consumer first thinks about purchasing a product. That might be on a treadmill at the gym, at home reading a magazine, or in the car while driving to work. That means that shopper marketing is by necessity a multichannel

Figure 11–4
Selected franchises and key issues

FRANCHISE	TYPE OF BUSINESS	TOTAL # OF UNITS	# OF UNITS FRANCHISED	% OF UNITS FRANCHISED	# OF UNITS IN CANADA	INVESTMENT REQUIRED
McDonald's	Fast-food outlet	32,000	25,600	80%	1,400	$500,000
Harvey's	Fast-food outlet	236	189	80%	189	$450,000–$650,000
Tim Hortons	Fast-food outlet	3,750	3,750	100%	3,148	$430,000–$480,000
Second Cup	Coffee retailer	401	396	99%	350	$280,000–$400,000
Buck or Two Plus	Dollar store	70	70	100%	70	$260,000–$600,000

Source: McDonald's: http://www.aboutmcdonalds.com/mcd/our_company.html, http://www.mcdonalds.ca/en/aboutus/faq.aspx, http://www.mcdonalds.ca/en/careers/franchising_purchasing.aspx; Harvey's: http://www.cfa.ca/FranchiseDetail.aspx?item=Harvey's; Tim Horton's: http://www.timhortons.com/ca/en/about/profile.html; Second Cup: http://www.cfa.ca/franchisedetail.aspx?item=second+cup, http://www.secondcup.com/eng/franchising.php?section=4#m1; Buck or Two: http://www.cfa.ca/franchisedetail.aspx?item=buck+or+two+plus.

Harry Rosen, a high-end men's clothing retailer, provides a good example of retail positioning. Read the text for details.

practice that makes use of traditional media, new media, direct marketing, loyalty, trade promotion, and innumerable other marketing techniques.

Underneath it all is one area that is largely alien to traditional marketers, whose focus has been almost exclusively on understanding *consumers*—that is, the consumption of goods and services. What's been ignored is understanding *shoppers*—that is, consumers when they are in the shopping mode.[11]

Retailing Mix

LO 4 The marketing mix, or the 4 Ps (product, price, place, and promotion), are used in retail just as they are in other businesses, but with some unique considerations. In this section we look at the retailing mix, which includes product and service considerations, retail pricing, physical location factors, and communications, as shown in Figure 11–5. All of these components of the mix focus on the consumer. In retail it is often said that the consumer is king, and treating them that way is a winning idea for successful retailing.

The positioning of a retail store must be consistent with the store's **retailing mix**. The four elements must be coordinated so that they portray a clear position to consumers. For example, Winners is positioned as a store providing upscale designer clothing at a discount price. If prices suddenly rose and consumers came to the conclusion that they were not getting a bargain, Winners' positioning would not hold water anymore.

Products and Services

One of the first decisions that retailers make is what they are going to sell. Usually both services and products are offered. McDonald's offers a hambuger, which is the tangible product, but the smiles, thank yous, and clean washrooms make up some of the service components. A department store such as The Bay sells many products—from clothing to housewares—and also provide services such as bridal registries. Magicuts provides services such as haircuts, colouring, and styling, but also sells hair care products. The balance between products and services involves a trade-off between costs and customer satisfaction.

The product P of the marketing mix in retailing is expanded in this section to include level of service, merchandise mix, and store atmosphere.

Level of Service   Most customers perceive little variation in retail outlets by form of ownership. Rather, differences among retailers are more obvious in terms of level of service. **Level of service** is used to describe the degree of service provided to the customer. Three levels of service include self-, limited, and full-service retailers. In some department stores, such as Zellers, very few services are provided. Stores such as Costco do not offer bags. Other outlets, such as Holt Renfrew, provide a wide range of customer services from gift wrapping to wardrobe consultation.

Self-Service   Self-service is at the extreme end of the level-of-service continuum because the customer performs

retailing mix
The goods and services, pricing, physical distribution, and communications tactics chosen by a store

level of service
The degree of service provided to the customer by self-, limited-, and full-service retailers

Figure 11–5
The retailing mix

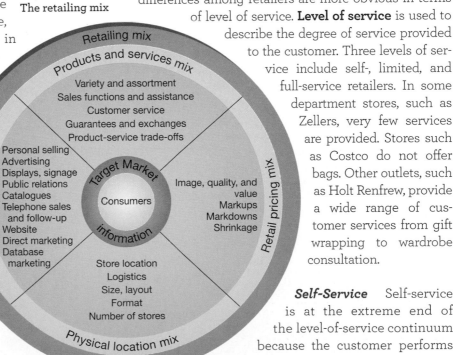

Retailing mix
Products and services mix
Variety and assortment
Sales functions and assistance
Customer service
Guarantees and exchanges
Product-service trade-offs

Communications mix
Personal selling
Advertising
Displays, signage
Public relations
Catalogues
Telephone sales and follow-up
Website
Direct marketing
Database marketing

Target Market
Consumers
information

Retail pricing mix
Image, quality, and value
Markups
Markdowns
Shrinkage

Store location
Logistics
Size, layout
Format
Number of stores

Physical location mix

many functions and little is provided by the outlet. Home building-supply outlets and gas stations are often self-service. Warehouse stores such as Costco, usually in buildings several times larger than a conventional store, are self-service with all nonessential customer services eliminated. Several new forms of self-service include FedEx's placement of self-service package shipping stations in retail stores and office buildings, and self-service scanning systems currently in use in Loblaw's, Home Depot, Walmart, and other retailers.

Limited Service   Limited-service outlets provide some services, such as credit and merchandise return, but not others, such as alterations to clothes. General merchandise stores such as Zellers, Shoppers Drug Mart, and Ikea are usually considered limited-service outlets. Customers are responsible for most shopping activities, although salespeople are available in departments such as cosmetics at Shoppers Drug Mart.

Full Service   Full-service retailers, which include most specialty stores and department stores, provide many services to their customers. Holt Renfrew, a Canadian specialty fashion retailer with nine stores across the country, is very committed to exemplary customer service (see the Marketing NewsFlash below). Its stores

marketing NewsFlash

Holt's Attempt to Make Customers Feel Welcome

Customers have long known the Toronto-based retailer Holt Renfrew & Co. Ltd. for providing luxury clothes, shoes, cosmetics, and accessories. The luxury retailer's president, Mark Derbyshire, is frustrated with recent customer complaints he is hearing about. Some customers feel intimidated by the store, overwhelmed by the high prices, or unable to find their sizes. Consumers also said that the sales clerks have a chilly attitude that intimidates them.

Derbyshire is determined to conquer this poor reputation. He is willing to improve Holt Renfrew's customer service to a level that makes every customer feel special. Taking a page from the Walmart playbook, he has hired greeters (also known as a "Holt's host") clad in upscale pink-tartan suits and pillbox hats to stand at the front of every store and genially engage customers in conversation as they walk in. He has also instructed his sales staff to move out from behind the counter and into the aisles to talk to shoppers. He's urging his sales staff to act as ambassadors,

smiling and engaging shoppers. For the first time, he's rewarding staff for positive feedback from their peers for customer service.

"The strength of our business is directly correlated to the strength of those relationships," Derbyshire says of the various service initiatives. "You won't be loyal when you don't get good service. It's all about creating a warm and inviting atmosphere—we want it to be a fun store." Derbyshire is rushing to make Holt's more accessible to win back apprehensive consumers. Some have fled to luxury online-shopping sites, while others are starting to head to the rejuvenated The Bay department store or crossing the border to shop.

Derbyshire is also making changes to the in-store restaurant. He has added burgers and new salads to its lineup. He's betting that adding hamburgers to the café menu rather than just open-faced *tartine*

sandwiches will draw more shoppers and get them into a buying mood.

The company, which sees 75 percent of its sales from the women's department, has also expanded the presence of more everyday wearable clothing, with a broader range of prices than in the past. While he's still stocking $8,000 Oscar de la Renta dresses, Derbyshire is featuring lower-priced lines such as Tory Burch, with tops starting at $100, and testing private-label items, including a $1,995 cashmere coat.

Holt Renfrew, which has estimated annual sales of $600 million, weathered the recession with steady but flat sales, a vast improvement over the performance of U.S. luxury retailers, many of which saw their volumes tumble about 20 percent as consumers cut back.[12]

Questions

1.   Describe the target market that Holt Renfrew is trying to reach.

2.   Do you think it's a good idea for Holt Renfrew to add lower-priced items to its line of products? Why?

feature more salespeople on the floor than other similarly sized stores, and Holt Renfrew offers a national concierge service, as well as personal shopping in each store. Employees are trained in customer follow-up, and many call their clients to advise them of new merchandise and send thank-you notes after purchase. With an eye kept fixed on customers and their evolving needs, Holt Renfrew is a leader in merchandise assortments and in innovations in customer services.[13]

Merchandise Mix Merchandise selection is one of the major attracting factors for customers, so choices and combinations must be made carefully and continually updated to reflect current trends and tastes. This involves finding sources of supply of the products, or having them manufactured, as well as managing inventory and warehousing. The **merchandise mix** describes how many different types of products a store carries and in what assortment.

Retail outlets vary by their merchandise mix, the key distinction being the breadth and depth of the items offered to customers (see Figure 11–6). **Depth of product line** means the assortment of products within each product line, such as a shoe store that

offers running shoes, dress shoes, and children's shoes. **Breadth of product line** refers to the variety of different lines a store carries, such as women's clothing, men's clothing, children's clothing, cosmetics, and housewares.

Depth of Line Stores that carry a large assortment (depth) of a related line of items are limited-line stores. Sport Chek sporting goods stores carry considerable depth in sports equipment ranging from golf accessories to running shoes. Stores that carry tremendous depth in one primary line of merchandise are single-line stores. La Senza, a nationwide chain, carries great depth in women's lingerie. Both limited- and single-line stores are often referred to as *specialty outlets*.

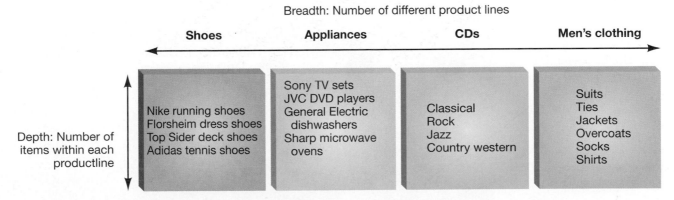

Brands That Have the Most Fans on Facebook

Rank	Brand
1	Coca-Cola
2	Starbucks
3	Oreo
4	Disney
5	Skittles

Source: TechCrunch, "TechCrunch Teardown: Top Facebook Brand Page Growth and Key Trends," accessed September 20, 2011, at http://techcrunch.com/2011/05/14/teardown-top-facebook-brand-page-growth.

Figure 11–6
Breadth versus depth of merchandise lines

Breadth: Number of different product lines

Shoes	Appliances	CDs	Men's clothing

Depth: Number of items within each product line

| Nike running shoes Florsheim dress shoes Top Sider deck shoes Adidas tennis shoes | Sony TV sets JVC DVD players General Electric dishwashers Sharp microwave ovens | Classical Rock Jazz Country western | Suits Ties Jackets Overcoats Socks Shirts |

Specialty outlets focus on one type of product, such as electronics (Future Shop), office supplies (Staples), or books (Indigo Books & Music) at very competitive prices. These outlets are referred to in the trade as category killers because they often dominate the market. Indigo Books & Music, for example, controls a large percentage of the retail book market in Canada.

!ndigo
Enrich your life

Indigo Books & Music is the largest book retailer in Canada and is a category killer.

Breadth of Line Stores that carry a variety of product lines, with limited depth, are referred to as *general merchandise stores*. For example, large department stores such as The Bay, Sears, and Zellers carry a wide range of different lines of products but not unusual sizes. The breadth and depth of merchandise lines are important decisions for a retailer. Traditionally, outlets carried related lines of goods. Today, however, **scrambled merchandising**, offering several unrelated product lines in a single store, is common. The modern drugstore carries food, cosmetics, camera equipment, magazines, paper products, toys, small hardware items, and pharmaceuticals. Supermarkets rent carpet-cleaning equipment, operate pharmacy departments, and sell flowers.

Scrambled merchandising makes it convenient for consumers because it eliminates the number of stops required in a shopping trip. However, for the retailer this merchandising policy means that there is competition between very dissimilar types of retail outlets, or **intertype competition**. A local bakery may compete with

a department store, discount outlet, or even a local gas station. Scrambled merchandising and intertype competition make retailing more challenging.

Planograms A planogram is a visual diagram, or drawing of fixtures and products, that illustrates how and where retail products should be placed on a store shelf. It also illustrates how many facings should be allocated for each stock-keeping unit (SKU). The planogram is arranged so that the fastest-moving high-margin products get the most space on the shelf. For example, Procter & Gamble works closely with Walmart by providing the retailer with planograms, which lead to higher profits than if products were placed indiscriminately on the shelf.

As competition increases, we're seeing suppliers and retailers becoming more aware of the importance of correctly merchandising their products. Some retailers produce their own planograms while others, such as Walmart, receive planograms from suppliers such as Procter & Gamble.

Store Atmosphere
Store atmosphere is related to the positioning of a store. For example, Costco has a warehouse appearance that is consistent with the low prices that it offers. Store atmosphere refers to the physical characteristics of a store that provide an overall impression to the consumer. These characteristics consist of the exterior and interior appearance and physical layout of the store. The Apple Store's customer-friendly layout encourages consumers to mingle and sample the products. Apple is trying to trademark its distinctive design and layout of its retail store. It has filed an application with the Canadian Intellectual Property Office.[14] If approved, competitors will not be able to copy the Apple layout for their retail stores.

The Apple Store is usually quite crowded. This frenetic atmosphere draws in even more people who

want to be part of the "event." Every Apple Store offers a range of services designed to help customers get the most out of their Apple products, including face-to-face support and advice at the Genius Bar, hands-on workshops, and special programs for kids. Apple recently announced a "Friend Bar," where Apple fans can go and discuss any topic or issues they have.[15]

Retail Pricing

In setting prices for merchandise, retailers must decide on the markup. The markup refers to how much should be added to the cost the retailer paid for a product to reach the final selling price. We discussed the calculation of markup in Chapter 9. The difference between the final selling price and retailer cost is called the gross margin.

Discounting a product, or taking a *markdown*, occurs when the product does not sell at the original price and an adjustment is necessary. Often, new models or styles force the price of existing models to be marked down. Discounts may also be used to increase demand for related products.[16] For example, retailers might take a markdown on DVD players to increase sales of DVDs or reduce the price of cake mix to generate frosting purchases. The *timing* of a markdown can be important. Many retailers take a markdown as soon as sales fall off, to free up valuable selling space and obtain cash. However, other stores delay markdowns to discourage bargain hunters and maintain an image of quality. There is no clear answer, but retailers must consider how the timing might affect future sales.

Although most retailers plan markdowns, many retailers use price discounts as a part of their regular merchandising policy. Walmart and Home Depot, for example, emphasize consistently low prices and eliminate most markdowns with a strategy often called *everyday low pricing*.[17] Consumers often use price as an indicator of product quality; however, the brand name of the product and the image of the store become important decision factors in these situations.[18]

A special issue for retailers trying to keep prices low is **shrinkage**, or breakage and theft of merchandise by customers and employees. What is surprising is that more than 50 percent of thefts are made not by consumers but by employees.

Off-price retailing is a retail pricing practice that is used by retailers such as Winners. **Off-price retailing** involves selling brand-name merchandise at lower than regular prices. The difference between the off-price retailer and a discount store is that off-price merchandise is bought by the retailer from manufacturers with excess inventory at prices below wholesale prices, whereas the discounter buys at full wholesale price but takes less of a markup than do traditional department stores. Because of this difference in the way merchandise is purchased by the retailer, selection at an off-price retailer is unpredictable, and searching for bargains has become a popular activity for many consumers. Savings to the consumer at off-price retailers are reported as high as 70 percent off the prices of a traditional department store.

Physical Location

Another aspect of the retailing mix involves deciding where to locate the store and how many stores to have. Department stores, which started downtown in most cities, have followed customers to the suburbs, and in recent years more stores have been opened in large regional malls. Most stores today are near several others in one of five settings: the central business district, the regional centre, the community shopping centre, the strip, or the power centre.

The **central business district** is the oldest retail setting, the community's downtown area. Until the regional outflow to suburbs, it was the major shopping area, but the suburban population has grown at the expense of the downtown shopping area.

---

ask yourself

1. What are the four components of the retailing mix?

2. What are some examples of stores with scrambled merchandising?

3. Would a shop for big men's clothes carrying pants in sizes 40 to 60 have a broad or deep product line?

---

shrinkage
Breakage and theft of merchandise by customers and employees

off-price retailing
Selling brand-name merchandise at lower than regular prices

central business district
The oldest retail setting, the community's downtown area

"*What is surprising is that more than 50 percent of thefts are made not by consumers but by employees.*"

Regional shopping centres consist of 50 to 150 stores that typically attract customers who live or work within a 5- to 15-kilometre range. These large shopping areas often contain two or three anchor stores, which are well-known national or regional stores such as Sears and The Bay. The largest variation of a regional centre is the West Edmonton Mall in Alberta. The shopping centre is a conglomerate of over 800 stores, seven amusement centres, 110 restaurants, and a 355-room Fantasyland hotel.[19]

A more limited approach to retail location is the **community shopping centre**, which typically has one primary store (usually a department store branch) and often about 20 to 40 smaller outlets. Generally, these centres serve a population of consumers who are within a 2- to 5-kilometre drive.

Not every suburban store is located in a shopping mall. Many neighbourhoods have clusters of stores, referred to as a **strip location**, to serve people who are within a 5- to 10-minute drive. Gas station, hardware, laundry, grocery, and pharmacy outlets are commonly found in a strip location. Unlike the larger shopping centres, the composition of these stores is usually unplanned. A variation of the strip shopping location is called the **power centre**, which is a large shopping strip with many national stores. Power centres are seen as having the convenient location found in many strip centres and the added power of national stores. These large strips often have two to five anchor stores plus a supermarket, which brings the shopper to the power centre on a weekly basis.[20]

Communications

The elements of the retailing communication mix described in Figure 11–5 (page 247) represent an exciting menu of choices for creating customer value in the marketplace. Each format allows retailers to offer unique benefits and meet particular needs of various customer groups. Today, retailers combine many of the formats to offer a broader spectrum of benefits and experiences. These **multichannel retailers** utilize and integrate a combination of traditional store and non-store formats such as catalogues and online retailing. Indigo Books & Music, for example, created chapters.indigo.ca to compete with Amazon.ca. Similarly, Office Depot has integrated its store, catalogue, and Internet operations.

Integrated channels can make shopping simpler and more convenient. A consumer can research choices online or in a catalogue and then make a purchase online, over the telephone, or at the closest store. In addition, the use of multiple channels allows retailers to reach a broader profile of customers. While online retailing may cannibalize catalogue business to some degree, a web transaction costs about half as much to process as a catalogue order. Multichannel retailers also benefit from the synergy of sharing information among the different channel operations.

ask yourself

1. Explain what shrinkage is.

2. A large shopping strip with multiple anchor stores is a _____ centre.

3. How do multichannel retailers make shopping simpler and more convenient?

Non-store Retailing

L⑤ Most of the retailing examples discussed earlier in the chapter, such as corporate chains, department stores, and limited- and single-line specialty stores, involve store retailing. Many retailing activities today, however, are not limited to sales in a store. Non-store retailing occurs outside a retail outlet through activities that involve varying levels of customer and retailer involvement. Forms of non-store retailing include automatic vending, television home shopping, and direct marketing (direct mail and catalogue retailing, telemarketing, direct selling, and online buying). Many traditional "bricks and mortar" stores are involved in non-store retailing, making them "click and mortar" concepts; for example, Indigo Books & Music has developed chaptersindigo.ca, its online store. Dell Computers, in contrast, relies mainly on non-store retailing for its consumer sales.

Automatic Vending

Non-store retailing includes vending machines, which make it possible to serve customers when and where stores cannot. Maintaining and operating vending machines is expensive, so product prices in vending machines tend to be higher than those in stores. Typically, small convenience products are available in vending machines. In Japan, products available in vending machines include dried squid, hair tonic, boxers, green tea, beer, CDs, books, clothing, and even music downloaded from a satellite transmission system. Sanyo Electric recently introduced a fully automated convenience store![21]

Improved technology will soon make vending machines easier to use by reducing the need for cash. In Europe, for example, Marconi Online Systems has installed 6,000 vending machines that allow consumers to pay for products using a cellphone. Similarly, the world's largest vending machine company, Canteen Services Inc., is testing a cashless system called FreedomPay, which allows consumers to wave a small wand in front of a sensor to make a purchase. Another improvement in vending machines—the use of wireless technology to notify retailers when their machines are empty—is one reason automatic merchandising sales are expected to increase in the future.[22]

Television Home Shopping

Television home shopping is possible when consumers watch a shopping channel on which products are displayed; orders are then placed over the telephone or the Internet. One popular network is The Shopping Channel, which has 24-hour programming and calls itself a broadcast retailer. A limitation of TV shopping has been the lack of buyer-seller interaction. New Internet technologies, however, now allow consumers to simultaneously shop, chat, and interact with their favourite show host while watching TV.[23]

Direct Marketing from a Retailing Perspective

We talk in detail about direct marketing in Chapter 12; here we introduce the idea, as it is an important form of retailing. In its simplest terms, direct marketing is an interactive process of marketing that uses advertising media or direct consumer contact to offer products or services. When a direct communication to a consumer or a business market is intended to generate a response from the recipient, direct marketing is the tactic being used.

Direct Mail and Catalogues Direct-mail and catalogue retailing is attractive because it eliminates the cost of a store and clerks. It costs a traditional retail store more than twice the amount to acquire a new customer than it costs a catalogue retailer. Why? Because catalogues improve marketing efficiency through segmentation and targeting. In addition, they create customer value by providing a fast and convenient means of making a purchase. In Canada, the amount spent on direct-mail catalogue merchandise continues to increase; internationally, spending is also increasing. IKEA delivers 130 million copies of its catalogue to 36 countries in 28 languages, including 5 million in Canada.[24]

telemarketing
Using the telephone
to interact with
and sell directly to
consumers

One reason for the growth in catalogue sales is that traditional retailers such as Office Depot are adding catalogue operations. Another reason is that many Internet retailers such as Amazon.com have also added catalogues. As consumers' direct-mail purchases have increased, the number of catalogues and the number of products sold through catalogues have increased. A typical Canadian household now receives dozens of catalogues every year, and there are billions circulated around the world. The competition, combined with recent increases in postal rates, however, have caused catalogue retailers to focus on proven customers rather than "prospects." Another successful new approach used by many catalogue retailers is to send specialty catalogues to market niches identified in their databases. L.L. Bean, a longstanding catalogue retailer, has developed an individual catalogue for fly-fishing enthusiasts. Lee Valley Tools Ltd. sends out specialized catalogues for hardware, woodworking, gardening, and Christmas.[25]

Telemarketing Another form of non-store retailing, called **telemarketing**, involves using the telephone to interact with and sell directly to consumers. Compared with direct mail, telemarketing is often viewed as a more efficient means of targeting consumers, although the two techniques are often used together. Sears Canada utilizes telemarketing to increase sales of extended warranty programs and other services. Communications companies such as Sprint and Bell Mobility telemarket new potential customers, and financial institutions such as HSBC and MBNA use telemarketing for customer follow-up and cross-selling. (Just in case you have not heard of these financial companies, here's a glimpse at who they are. HSBC, or the HSBC Group, is one of the largest banking and financial services organizations in the world, and over 100 years old, named from The Hongkong and Shanghai Banking Corporation Limited. MBNA is the largest independent credit-card issuer in the world; you may think that the letters MBNA should stand for some longer name, but apparently it does not.) Telemarketing has grown in popularity as companies search for ways to cut costs but still provide convenient access to their customers.

According to the American Teleservices Association, annual telemarketing sales exceed US$500 billion.[26]

As the use of telemarketing grows, consumer privacy has become a topic of discussion among consumers, governments, and businesses. Issues such as industry standards, ethical guidelines, and new privacy laws are evolving to provide a balance between the varying perspectives. In September 2008, the Canadian Radio-television and Telecommunications Commission (CRTC) instituted a National Do Not Call List (DNCL), which was created to enable Canadian consumers to reduce the number of unsolicited telemarketing calls they receive. Every year, thousands of Canadians raise concerns about receiving unwanted telemarketing calls, despite being on the DNCL list.

Direct Selling Direct selling, sometimes called door-to-door retailing, involves direct sales of goods and services to consumers through personal interactions and demonstrations in their home or office. A variety of companies, including familiar names such as Avon, Tupperware, and Mary Kay Cosmetics, have created an industry with billions in sales by providing consumers with personalized service and convenience. However, sales have been declining as retail chains begin to carry similar products at discount prices and as the increasing number of dual-career households reduces the number of potential buyers who can be found at home.

In response to change, many direct-selling retailers are expanding into other markets. Avon, for example, already has 5.8 million sales representatives in 100 countries.[27] Similarly, other retailers such as Amway (now also known as Quixtar), Herbalife, and Electrolux are rapidly expanding. More than 77 percent of Amway's US$10.7 billion in sales now comes from outside North America.[28]

Direct selling is likely to continue to grow in markets where the lack of effective distribution channels increases the importance of door-to-door convenience and where the lack of consumer knowledge about products and brands will increase the need for a person-to-person approach.[29]

Walmart.ca and ebay.ca are two examples of online retailing.

Online Retailing

L⑥ Online retailing allows customers to search for, evaluate, and order products through the Internet. For many consumers, the advantages of this form of retailing are the 24-hour access, the ability to comparison shop, and the in-home privacy. Four in ten Canadians aged 16 and over use the Internet to purchase products and services.[30]

Studies of online shoppers indicated that men were initially more likely than women to buy something online. As the number of online households increased to more than 50 percent, however, the profile of online shoppers changed to include all shoppers. In addition, the number of online retailers grew rapidly for several years but then declined as many stand-alone, Internet-only businesses failed or consolidated. Today, there has been a melding of traditional and online retailers—"bricks and clicks"—that are using experiences from both approaches to create better value and experiences for customers.

Online buying is getting a boost from the comments that consumers are leaving on social media sites such as Facebook and Twitter. These sites are having an influence on what consumers are buying online. Research shows that Facebook and Twitter influence up to 28 percent of online buying decisions.[31]

▼
ask yourself

1. Why are catalogue sales growing?

2. Where are direct-selling retail sales growing? Why?

Another related fact is that members of social networking sites also spend one-and-a-half times more online than the average Internet user.[32]

One of the biggest problems online retailers face is that nearly two-thirds of online shoppers make it to "checkout" and then leave the website to compare shipping costs and prices on other sites. Of the shoppers who leave, 70 percent do not return. One way online retailers are addressing this issue is to offer consumers a comparison of competitors' offerings. Online retailers are also trying to improve the online retailing experience by adding experiential, or interactive, activities to their websites, such as apparel stores' use of "virtual models" to involve consumers in the purchase process and help with product selection.[33] Car manufacturers such as BMW, Mercedes, and Jaguar encourage website visitors to "build" a vehicle by selecting interior and exterior colours, packages, and options and then view the customized virtual car.

There are indications of an increase in online customer satisfaction. A survey found that consumer satisfaction with the top 100 Web-based retailers is rising. According to the survey, several factors are contributing to a satisfied online customer: fair and competitive prices, variety and availability of products, usability of the retailer's website, and accuracy and quality of information on the site.[34]

IKEA DELIVERS 130 MILLION COPIES OF ITS CATALOGUE TO 36 COUNTRIES IN 28 LANGUAGES, INCLUDING 5 MILLION IN CANADA.

Figure 11–7
Why do consumers shop and buy online?

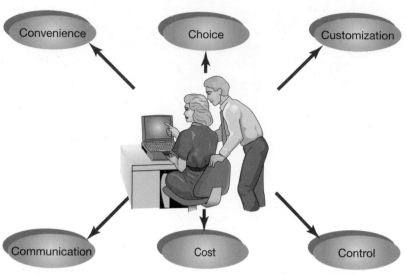

Read the text to learn how convenience, choice, customization, communication, cost, and control result in a favourable customer experience

Why Consumers Shop and Buy Online

Consumers typically offer six reasons why they shop and buy online: convenience, choice, customization, communication, cost, and control (see Figure 11–7).

- **Convenience:** Online shopping and buying is *convenient*, so websites must be easy to locate and navigate, and image downloads must be fast.

- **Choice:** There are two dimensions to choice: *selection*—numerous websites for almost anything consumers want—and *assistance*—interactive capabilities of Internet/web-enabled technologies assist customers to make informed choices.

- **Customization:** Internet/web-enabled capabilities make possible a highly interactive and individualized information and exchange environment for shoppers and buyers. Consumers get what they want and feel good about the experience. An

example is Dell, which allows consumers to choose the components of their computer rather than purchase a computer off the shelf at a bricks-and-mortar retailer.

- **Communication:** Communication can take three forms: marketer-to-consumer e-mail notification, consumer-to-marketer buying and service requests, and consumer-to-consumer chat rooms and instant messaging.[35]

- **Cost:** Many popular items bought online can be purchased at the same price or cheaper than in retail stores. Lower prices also result from Internet/web-enabled software that permits *dynamic pricing*, the practice of changing prices for products and services in real time in response to supply and demand conditions.

- **Control:** Online shoppers and buyers are empowered consumers. They readily use Internet/web-enabled technology to seek information, evaluate alternatives, and make purchase decisions on their own time, terms, and conditions.

When and Where Online Consumers Shop and Buy

Shopping and buying also happen at different times in the online marketspace than in the traditional marketplace.[36] About 80 percent of online retail sales occur Monday through Friday. The busiest shopping day is Wednesday. By comparison, 35 percent of retail store sales are registered on the weekend. Saturday is the most popular shopping day. Monday through Friday online shopping and buying often occurs during normal work hours—some 40 percent of online consumers say they visit websites from their place of work, which partially accounts for the

Social Media Influence on Online Purchases

Number of people who are influenced by social media to purchase online
28%

Number of consumers who visit an online store and make a purchase
7%

Number of consumers directed by social media to an online retailer and make a purchase
71%

marketing meter

Source: StartupMeme Technology Blog, "Facebook Twitter Influences up to 28% of Buying Decisions," accessed September 20, 2011, at http://startupmeme.com/facebook-twitter-influences-upto-28-of-online-buying-decisions; psfk, "Social Media Recommendations May Increase Online Purchases," accessed September 20, 2011, at www.psfk.com/2010/07/social-media-recommendations-may-increase-online-purchases.html.

sales level during the work-week. Favourite websites for workday shopping and buying include those featuring event tickets, flowers and gifts, consumer electronics, and travel.

Describing the Online Consumer

The average online Canadian now spends more time on the Internet than watching television, according to a survey from Ipsos Reid.[37]

Other research indicates that more than 80 percent of Canadians over the age of 16 are now connected to the Internet. Ninety-four percent of Canadians say they use the Internet to compare prices, and 60 percent go online to read or write reviews. As a result, consumers are becoming smarter, increasingly informed, and more demanding. This trend will continue as more and more Canadians are now embracing mobile technologies from smartphones to iPads.[38]

Many consumers are spending online time at social media sites such as Facebook and Twitter as well as purchasing products and services on company websites. The following points describe the effects of social media on the online consumer.

- Research suggests that social media recommendations tend to increase the chances of people buying products or services. For instance, a study found that 50 percent of people under 35 followed the recommendations of their social media friends, compared to only 17 percent who bought on celebrity endorsements.

- Another study reveals that while, on average, 7 percent of visitors to an online store make a purchase, if directed to the retailer via a social media site, the percentage of visitors who will make a purchase goes up to 71 percent. This means that people accessing an online retailer via social media are ten times more likely to buy something than other users.[39]

- Research has also shown that becoming a follower of a brand on Twitter or a fan on Facebook has a positive impact on the possibility to buy and to recommend a product or service.

Recommendations from personal acquaintances or opinions posted by consumers online are the most trusted forms of advertising, according to a Nielsen Global Online Consumer Survey of over 25,000 Internet consumers from 50 countries. Ninety percent of consumers surveyed noted that they trust recommendations from people they know, while 70 percent trusted consumer opinions posted online. The influence of word of mouth on consumer purchases is still strong, be it face to face or on social media sites.[40]

> *"The influence of word of mouth on consumer purchases is still strong, be it face to face or on social media sites."*

What Online Consumers Buy

There is a lot marketers have to learn about online consumer purchase behaviour. Although research has documented the most frequently purchased products and services bought online, marketers also need to know why these items are popular in the digital marketplace.

Figure 11–8 shows the estimated percentage of online retail sales by product/service category.

Retailer Usage of the Mobile Channel

L⑦ Retailers are becoming increasingly aware of the value of smartphone-equipped customers. Like they did with the emergence of the Internet, many retailers initially approached the mobile channel with a bit of trepidation. Today, retailers are looking at mobile as another important customer touchpoint. Cellphones, smartphones, and other handheld devices are a convenient way for customers to gather more information about a retailer's products or even conduct transactions on a mobile basis. In-store shoppers can research products and prices on their handsets using cameras, bar code scanners, QR codes, and other mobile applications.

Figure 11–8

Estimated percentage of online retail sales by product/service category: 2007 and 2012

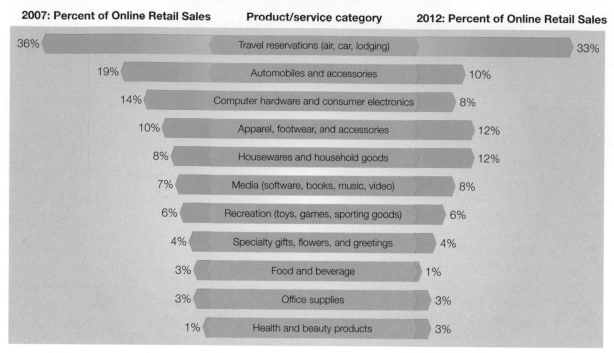

2007: Percent of Online Retail Sales	Product/service category	2012: Percent of Online Retail Sales
36%	Travel reservations (air, car, lodging)	33%
19%	Automobiles and accessories	10%
14%	Computer hardware and consumer electronics	8%
10%	Apparel, footwear, and accessories	12%
8%	Housewares and household goods	12%
7%	Media (software, books, music, video)	8%
6%	Recreation (toys, games, sporting goods)	6%
4%	Specialty gifts, flowers, and greetings	4%
3%	Food and beverage	1%
3%	Office supplies	3%
1%	Health and beauty products	3%

QR (quick response) codes are two-dimensional images that look like blobs of black on a white background. They are similar to standard bar codes but have much more functionality. QR codes are encoded with information ranging from text, to photos, to website addresses and are scanned by smartphones. They can be used to send consumers who scan the codes to places online and are very effective marketing tools.[41]

Retailers can provide immediate incentives by knowing the specific in-store location of the shopper via GPS technology. The customer can make the purchase in-store or over a mobile cellphone or smartphone. The key is to provide methods to retain customer interest and loyalty via a consistent shopping and branding experience across channels. Smartphones are being used to engage consumers and help them make better shopping choices.

The following scenarios demonstrate how mobile can be used:[42]

- Riding the chairlift of a major western ski resort, a customer of a ski apparel retailer pulls out a smartphone and clicks on the retailer's specialty application. The mobile software uses GPS technology to determine the skier's location, and the customer sees feedback on this specific mountain's terrain and recommendations on how to approach its trails.

- Walking through the pet food section of a major discount chain, a customer receives a text message with a digital coupon good for 20 percent off Iams dog food. The store has detected the shopper's presence in the pet food aisle, and knows that this particular shopper generally purchases the competitor's product, Purina. For the retailer's suppliers, this provides a chance to encourage a brand switch. For the retailer, it enhances loyalty from a customer who has opted in to participate in the mobile program.

- Two teenage girls rifle through the racks of tops in a major department store chain's juniors section. Stopping on one she likes, one girl takes out her phone and scans a QR code on the shelf next to the shirt. On the screen of her phone, she sees product reviews from other shoppers, and also gets a special offer on a pair of shoes to complete the outfit.

- As he jockeys to make his flight at Toronto's Pearson Airport, a Montreal-bound traveller realizes he's forgotten to pack his laptop's power cord. He turns to his cellphone and brings up Best Buy's wireless website. He orders a replacement cord, finds the store location closest to his hotel, and picks it up on his way to check in.

The above are examples of just a handful of customer interactions taking place today in the mobile commerce (*m-commerce*) channel. In each instance, a retailer uses mobile as a way to enhance customer engagement and loyalty. And it is the pervasiveness of cellphones, smartphones, and other mobile devices that is leading a growing number of retailers to explore what additional opportunities await in the mobile space.

Here's an example of how Sephora, the beauty products retailer, uses mobile strategy. It created a specific mobile website with thousands of product reviews intended to help shoppers evaluate and compare items on their smartphones when they are in the stores. All the shopper has to do to retrieve the reviews is type in the SKU number or the name of the product in their smartphone.

Retailers should take note that their websites might have to be adapted for smartphones. Regular websites are not configured for mobile, which may lead to frustration as a shopper, for example, tries to read words that are too tiny to read on a phone.[43]

The increasing number of shoppers arriving at stores with smartphones can also pose a threat for retailers. The threat comes from in-store shoppers using their phones to check prices at other retailers. Retailers that ignore the growing number of mobile Internet users will see their customers defect to competitors. A retailer's best defence for maintaining customer loyalty is to develop a mobile website, with information on the site that differentiates itself from competitors. This can take the form of such intangibles as product reviews, warranty information, customer service, product knowledge, and return policy. By providing mobile access to their extensive online product information, retailers can help customers feel more comfortable about making a purchase at that store as opposed to fleeing to another store solely for the low price.[44]

Wholesaling

L8 Many retailers rely on intermediaries to provide them with selection and availability of the products sold in their retail operations. Many other businesses also use intermediaries to provide them with selection and availability plus value-added services for products that they need to operate their businesses.

Those intermediaries are commonly called wholesalers and agents (described briefly in Chapter 10), according to the functions that they fulfill in the distribution process. In addition, there are manufacturers' sales offices operated by the original manufacturers of the products. All of these wholesaling intermediaries play an important role in the retailing process and in helping other businesses get the products they need.

Merchant Wholesalers

Merchant wholesalers are independently owned firms that take title to—that is, they buy—the merchandise they handle. They go by various names, described in detail below. About 83 percent of the firms engaged in wholesaling activities are merchant wholesalers.

Merchant wholesalers are classified as either full-service or limited-service wholesalers, depending on the number of functions performed. Two major types of full-service wholesalers exist. General merchandise (or full-line) wholesalers carry a broad assortment of merchandise and perform all channel functions. This type of wholesaler is most prevalent in the hardware, drug, and clothing industries. However, these wholesalers do not maintain much depth of assortment within specific product lines. Specialty merchandise (or limited-line) wholesalers offer a relatively narrow range of products but have an extensive assortment within the product lines carried. They perform all channel functions and are found in the health foods, automotive parts, and seafood industries.

Four major types of limited-service wholesalers exist. Rack jobbers furnish the racks or shelves that display merchandise in retail stores and perform all channel functions. They sell on consignment to retailers, which means they retain the title to the products displayed and bill retailers only for the merchandise sold. Familiar products such as hosiery, toys, housewares, and health and beauty aids are sold by rack jobbers. Cash and carry wholesalers take title to merchandise but sell only to buyers who call on them, pay cash for merchandise, and furnish their own transportation for merchandise. They carry a limited product assortment and do not make deliveries, extend credit, or supply market information. This wholesaler commonly deals in electric supplies, office supplies, hardware products, and groceries. Drop shippers, or desk jobbers, are wholesalers that own the merchandise they sell but do not physically handle, stock, or deliver it. They simply solicit orders from retailers and other wholesalers and have the

merchant wholesalers Independently owned firms that take title to the merchandise they handle

Sephora, the beauty products retailer, uses mobile strategy.

manufacturers' agents
Work for several producers and carry non-competitive, complementary merchandise in an exclusive territory

selling agents
Represent a single producer and are responsible for the entire marketing function of that producer

brokers
Independent firms or individuals whose main function is to bring buyers and sellers together to make sales

merchandise shipped directly from a producer to a buyer. Drop shippers are used for bulky products such as coal, lumber, and chemicals, which are sold in large quantities. Truck jobbers are small wholesalers that have a small warehouse from which they stock their trucks for distribution to retailers. They usually handle limited assortments of fast-moving or perishable items that are sold for cash directly from trucks in their original packages. Truck jobbers handle products such as bakery items, dairy products, and meat.

Agents and Brokers

Unlike merchant wholesalers, agents and brokers do not take title to merchandise and typically provide fewer channel functions. They make their profit from commissions or fees paid for their services, whereas merchant wholesalers make their profit from the sale of the merchandise they have bought and resold.

Manufacturers' agents and selling agents are the two major types of agents used by producers. **Manufacturers' agents**, or manufacturers' representatives, work for several producers and carry non-competitive, complementary merchandise in an exclusive territory. Manufacturers' agents act as a producer's sales arm in a territory and are principally responsible for the transactional channel functions, primarily selling. They are used extensively in the automotive supply, footwear,

and fabricated steel industries. By comparison, **selling agents** represent a single producer and are responsible for the entire marketing function of that producer. They design promotional plans, set prices, determine distribution policies, and make recommendations on product strategy. Selling agents are used by small producers in the textile, apparel, food, and home furnishing industries.

Brokers are independent firms or individuals whose main function is to bring buyers and sellers together to make sales. Brokers, unlike agents, usually have no continuous relationship with the buyer or seller but negotiate a contract between two parties and then move on to another task. Brokers are used extensively in the real estate industry.

A unique broker that acts in many ways like a manufacturer's agent is a food broker, representing buyers and sellers in the grocery industry. Food brokers differ from conventional brokers because they act on behalf of producers on a permanent basis and receive a commission for their services. For example, food giant Nabisco uses food brokers to sell its candies, margarine, and Planters peanuts, but it sells its line of cookies and crackers directly to retail stores.

Manufacturer's Branches and Offices

Unlike merchant wholesalers, agents, and brokers, manufacturer's branches and sales offices are wholly owned extensions of the producer that perform wholesaling activities. Producers assume wholesaling functions when there are no intermediaries to perform these activities, customers are few in number and geographically concentrated, orders are large or require significant attention, or they want to control the distribution of their products. A *manufacturer's branch office* carries a producer's inventory and performs the functions of a full-service wholesaler. A *manufacturer's sales office* does not carry inventory, typically performs only a sales function, and serves as an alternative to agents and brokers.

ask yourself

1. Describe how smartphones are being used by retailers to engage consumers and help them make better shopping choices.

2. What is the difference between merchant wholesalers and agents?

Summary...just the facts

- Retailing provides customer value in the form of various utilities: time, place, form, information, and possession. Economically, retailing is important in terms of the people employed and money exchanged in retail sales.

- Retailing outlets can be classified by forms of ownership, such as independent retailer, corporate chain, and contractual systems.

- The first task in developing a retail strategy is to define the target market and positioning of the retail store.
- The retailing mix consists of goods and services, retail pricing, physical location, and communications.
- The product P in retailing includes level of service, merchandise mix, and store atmosphere.
- Stores vary in the level of service they provide. Three levels are self-service, limited service, or full service.
- Retail outlets vary in terms of the breadth and depth of their merchandise lines. Breadth refers to the number of different items carried, and depth refers to the assortment of each item offered.
- In retail pricing, retailers must decide on the markup. Off-price retailers offer brand-name merchandise at lower than regular prices.
- Retail store location is an important retail mix decision. The common alternatives are the central business district, regional shopping centre, community shopping centre, or strip location. A variation of the strip location is the power centre, which is a strip location with multiple national anchor stores.
- Non-store retailing includes automatic vending, television home shopping, online retailing, and direct marketing (direct mail and catalogue retailing, telemarketing, and direct selling).
- Online retailing allows consumers to search for, evaluate, and purchase products and services online. The increasing sales and number of people purchasing online suggest that the profile of the online consumer is becoming more and more like the profile of the consumer of the traditional marketplace.
- Consumers refer to six reasons they shop and buy online: convenience, choice, customization, communication, cost, and control.
- Retailers are becoming increasingly aware of the value of smartphone-equipped customers. Retailers are looking at mobile as another important customer touchpoint. Cellphones, smartphones, and other handheld devices are a convenient way for customers to gather more information about a retailer's products or even conduct transactions on a mobile basis. Many retailers depend on the numerous types of intermediaries that engage in wholesaling activities.
- The main difference between the various types of wholesalers lies in whether or not they take title to the items they sell.

Key Terms and Concepts...*a refresher*

breadth of product line p. 249
brokers p. 260
central business district p. 251
community shopping centre p. 252
depth of product line p. 249
form of ownership p. 242
intertype competition p. 250
level of service p. 247

manufacturers' agents p. 260
merchandise mix p. 249
merchant wholesalers p. 259
multichannel retailers p. 252
off-price retailing p. 251
power centre p. 252
regional shopping centres p. 252
retailing p. 240

retailing mix p. 247
scrambled merchandising p. 250
selling agents p. 260
shrinkage p. 251
strip location p. 252
telemarketing p. 254

Hands-on...*apply your knowledge*

Online Retailing Assignment Explore Ron White's website at www.ronwhiteshoes.com/can, and then answer the following questions:

- Based on the appearance of the website and the information contained on the site, write a positioning statement for Ron White Shoes.

- Comment on the ease of purchasing shoes online from the website.
- Do you feel the website has an elegant look, consistent with Ron White's upscale line of shoes?
- Comment on the ease of navigating the website.

Reality Check...*reminder*

Refer back to this chapter's opening vignette and answer the Reality Check questions on page 240.

connect

Connect allows you to practise important concepts at your own pace and on your own schedule, with 24/7 online access to an eBook, practice quizzes, video cases, chapter application questions, discussion activities, Internet exercises, interactivities, study tools, and more.

chapter 12

Marketing Communications

The digital world brings a wealth of new tools and opportunities to marketing communications. This chapter looks at these new digital approaches as well as the traditional marketing communications tools used to communicate with target audiences, both online and offline.

We begin by looking to a non-profit organization, the Childhood Cancer Foundation, to understand how traditional time-tested fundraising techniques can be combined with new online approaches to reach contributors and people in need.

Mary Lye, director of marketing and communications for the Childhood Cancer Foundation of Canada (CCFC) starts by giving us a reality check and a good one at that. In 1987 when the CCFC first started, childhood cancer survival rates were only 10 percent and family support programs were sparse. Today, childhood cancer survival rates average 82 percent and institutions such as the CCFC provide support. The CCFC is a national charitable foundation run by a small group of staff and volunteers. It provides support programs for children

and their families facing cancer and raises childhood cancer medical research funds for the C17 Research Network of 17 children's hospitals in Canada.[1]

The CCFC relies on marketing communication programs to reach users of its services and to also communicate with volunteers and individuals who contribute time, money, and effort to the foundation. Mary Lye explains, "Gone are the letter-writing days of the 1980s. We now use online and offline approaches to communicate with individuals, communities, and companies. We embrace digital communications, realizing its ability to reach people quickly, easily, and at a low cost. Being able to do more with less is a blessing for us, but we do not turn our backs on the impact word-of-mouth and the old-fashioned pick-up-the-phone or 'Let's meet' approaches can have on our relationships."

The CCFC's online approaches involve a website, e-mail campaigns, e-newsletters, social media, and online fundraising tools. Its offline approaches veer away from placing ads in print and broadcast media, which is beyond its budget. Instead, it uses a multiplatform approach to reach individuals and companies on a personal level. This involves public relations, event marketing, direct response, and, on occasion, pro-bono print advertising to raise its profile. Mary Lye explains that, with the exception of a public relations company used periodically to spread information to the media, the CCFC runs its own marketing communications programs with a small office of four people who use creativity and determination to stretch budgets and

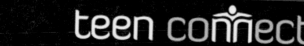

get results. Let's look at its marketing communications programs in more detail:

- **Public relations:** Grassroots public relations tools are used to drive support with educational groups, local communities, hospitals, corporations, and the media.
  - ◆ **Educational groups:** Mary Lye often visits educational institutions such as schools, universities, and colleges to speak to assemblies about its online fundraising tools. It creates mini-websites for individual fundraisers that facilitate online registration, provide tax receipts, and tally online contributions.

    The CCFC also provides school boards with online Educational Guides that explain how to best support children with childhood cancer. This guide is profiled on information postcards that are sent to school boards and made available through children's hospitals.
  - ◆ **Local communities:** Small Hands is an online tool used by the CCFC to support local community fundraisers that are often driven by families, friends, and communities impacted by childhood cancer. The fundraiser registers with the CCFC to receive a web page with its own link to be shared with others. This page can be personalized and allows for online donations, measures contributions, and provides donors with tax receipts.
  - ◆ **Hospitals:** The CCFC reaches out to families with Family Support Kits that contain pamphlets, information cards, books, answers to questions, and DVDs with inspiring stories. Links to the CCFC's Teen Connector social networking site are included for teens with cancer to realize they are not alone. Here teens can connect with other teens in similar situations on a private closed-access social network created specifically for them.
  - ◆ **Corporations:** The CCFC has strong ties with corporate supporters. An example is TEVA, a pharmaceutical company that funded an informational DVD and the Teen Connector social network. It now helps fund CCFC educational scholarships.
  - ◆ **Media:** Media relations are directly handled by the CCFC with interviews given to TV stations, radio broadcasters, and print journalists. The PR agency Strategic Objectives is occasionally used to seed articles with the mainstream media.

- **Event marketing:** Annual large fundraisers are organized by the CCFC throughout the year. It holds its annual spring Gala Dinner to raise funds through sponsorships, ticket sales, and silent auctions. Its summer fundraiser, Kick, Cut, Care, uses an outdoor BBQ event to raise funds through sponsorships, local vendors, and hair-cutting events, while its summer annual Golf Classic raises funds through sponsorships, participation fees, and auctions. Smaller events take place throughout the year at Toronto Marlies' hockey games.
- **Direct response:** CCFC events are promoted through direct response programs such as telemarketing, e-mail campaigns, and e-newsletters. E-newsletters and Twitter direct messages go out monthly with updates, while scheduled e-mails and reminder phone calls coincide with foundation events. Families can sign up to receive these informational updates.
- **Advertising:** While the CCFC does not run advertising campaigns, it has a print ad set aside for donated media that raises awareness for the CCFC. It was recently placed in *Motivated* magazine, courtesy of Incentive Travel Executives.

"We are never at a loss of ideas to help the CCFC," states Mary Lye, "We may be a small group of marketers but we have learned to stretch our dollars and use creativity to get successful results." This success can be measured in many ways. The positive feedback from families and hospitals speaks volumes, while the funds raised for the foundation points to the success of its programs. Annually, the CCFC contributes over $700,000 toward childhood cancer research, provides every child-applicant with $1,500 in educational scholarships, assists families in financial need with monetary funds, and supplies children's hospitals with support kits for families dealing with a diagnosis.[1] Only 10 percent of every dollar contributed goes into adminstration.[2] To learn more about the CCFC, visit its website at www.childhoodcancer.ca. 🍎

As you read Chapter 12, refer back to this Childhood Cancer Foundation vignette to answer the following questions:

- What role does word-of-mouth play in the CCFC's marketing communications efforts?
- What tools do not play a role in the CCFC's marketing communications efforts and why?
- How is event marketing used by the foundation?

Developments in Marketing Communications

LO 1 This chapter provides readers with a real view of marketing communications, bringing to the forefront the online and offline approaches used by marketers to reach consumers. We explain how the online digital world has changed marketing communications while also highlighting the traditional offline approaches needed to reach ever-elusive consumers. Frequently, online and offline marketing communications work together, hand-in-hand, to reach consumers in their worlds, relying on metrics to evaluate success and determine future direction.

Today, marketing communications is in a new phase: We call it the *Age of Selective Reception*, where social media keeps marketers and advertisers honest in 140-character bursts and where marketers increasingly interact in two-way conversations with consumers through digital formats such as blogs, social networks, podcasts, and online video. Whereas once marketers wholly controlled the messaging, today consumers are largely in control of whether they receive marketing communication messages, and if so, when, where, and on what device.

Uninhibited, and encouraged by easy-to-use social media platforms, consumers today readily scorn marketing messages that mislead or insult, instead choosing to forward messages that creatively engage and get people talking. As Arianna Huffington, co-founder of the *Huffington Post*, clearly explained at a recent *Advertising Week* event in Toronto, self-expression has become the new form of entertainment, with people posting comments, writing blogs, and creating video as forms of self-expression.[3] Marketers have taken note and realize that to yield results, they must weave creative components into campaigns to engage and interact with consumers.

We start by looking at how the consumer and the media have evolved in this digital world.

> *Self-expression has become the new form of entertainment.*

A Changing Consumer

In this Age of Selective Reception, consumers choose how, if, and when to listen to advertising messages. Initial concerns around baby boomers zapping TV ads and generation Xers changing channels during commercial breaks pale in comparison to the new reality: where young adults often catch the news online rather than in newspapers; where TV programs can be watched on laptops and tablet computers rather than on TVs; where music is listened to on iPods rather than radios; where magazines can be read on eReaders or accessed through apps on tablet computers; and where smartphones interact with marketing messages through text messages, quick response (QR) codes, and apps. Let's look at the facts.

Time Spent with the Media The amount of time consumers spend with the different forms of media has changed significantly over the last decade, prompting marketers to take note. Many

---

The Core: Chapter 12

Promotional tools include advertising, public relations, sales promotion, direct response, event marketing and sponsorship, and personal selling.

Promotional Tools

Promotional programs are created in line with target market interests.

consumers spend more time on the Internet than with other forms of media. While this varies by age, consumers 18 to 24 years of age spend most of their media time—39 percent—on the Internet, while TV, a previous top media choice, falls into second place, with significant time taken away from other choices such as radio and newspaper. The older age groups, while still favouring TV as their top media choice, are increasingly turning to the Internet to gather information, stay informed, and be entertained, again impacting other media choices.[4] Marketers tailor messages accordingly.

Use of Technology

Affordable Internet technology provides consumers with easy-to-use, portable communications that facilitate marketing communications. Free online services such as e-mail, search engines, and social media have democratized the media so that two-way communication now exists between marketers and consumers, and consumers and their friends.

Research studies tell us that consumers are very comfortable with new technology and frequently go online to communicate with others. Many multitask with the media, spending time on the Internet while watching TV.[5] When it comes to social media, Facebook

Figure 12–1

Top ten countries on Facebook (users, percent increases, and rank change)

Canada ranks in the world's top ten for Facebook users.

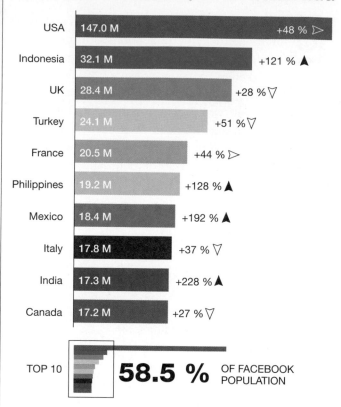

Source: Robin Wauters, "Facebook Averaged Almost 8 New Registrations Per Second In 2010," February 1, 2011, accessed at http://techcrunch.com/2011/02/01/facebook-averaged-almost-8-new-registrations-per-second-in-2010/?utm_source=feedburner&utm_medium=feed&utm_campaign=Feed:+Techcrunch+(TechCrunch). Originally sourced from Social Bakers (http://www.socialbakers.com/blog/109-facebook-in-2010-7-9-new-account-registrations-per-second/).

is the most popular social network in Canada with 17.2 million users. Founded in 2004, Facebook now boasts over 500 million users worldwide with Canada ranking in the top ten for country usage (see Figure 12–1). In 2010, its usage grew globally by 74 percent to 585 million users.[6] **Social media** refers to a form of online media that allows members to create a network of friends and contacts to share messages, comments, videos, and images as a form of self-expression.

In Canada, 66 percent of Internet users access Facebook to interact with friends, family, and marketers. It is the social media of choice, racking up 26 percent of daily connections, followed by YouTube and MySpace at 4 percent each, and Twitter at 3 percent. A high 75 percent of young people claim to access Facebook more than twice a day, averaging over 16 times per week.[7]

What is it that people do on Facebook? Most users in Canada—63 percent—prefer to look at what others have uploaded, while 13 percent contribute

Time Spent with the Canadian Media Varies by Age

Share of Weekly Time Spent with the Media
Weekly Minutes Per Capita

Age	18–24	25–34	35–54	55+
Internet	39%	27%	18%	8%
TV	34%	40%	45%	55%
Radio	24%	30%	33%	31%
Newspaper	2%	2%	3%	6%
Magazine	1%	1%	1%	1%
Total	100%	100%	100%	100%

Source: *2010 Canadian Media Usage Trend Study*, commissioned by the Interactive Advertising Bureau of Canada (March 2011). Uses 2009 data. (Note: Percentage figures are rounded.)

> **IN CANADA, 66 PERCENT OF INTERNET USERS ACCESS FACEBOOK TO INTERACT WITH FRIENDS, FAMILY, AND MARKETERS.**

material, and 30 percent react or share material they have accessed.

Twitter, while gaining in popularity in Canada, is still finding its user base. The *2010 Consumerology Report* highlights that it is most popular among 25- to 29-year-olds, followed by 18- to 24-year-olds, progressively dwindling in popularity with people over the age of 30 (see the Marketing Meter below).

An Evolving Media

The digital reality that sees consumers aggregate online is influencing traditional offline media organizations to create websites that attract people on the Internet. Magazines, newspapers, and TV news programs are blurring in their use of online video and articles to attract viewers. Major news organizations such as CNN, the BBC, and the CBC use YouTube channels to deliver content, despite having websites and TV channels of their own. In this new media universe we see newspapers such as the *Globe and Mail* undergo redesigns to compete, while news-blogs such

as the *Huffington Post,* launched as recently as 2005, become so reputable that six years after launch it was purchased for $315 million by AOL.[8]

The redesign of the *Globe and Mail* in 2010 addressed this Internet trend of crisp, easy-to-use, and readily accessible media by resizing its hard-copy format with smaller pages; adding many glossy, smudge-proof pages; and enhancing its colour. The front page was totally overhauled and reformatted as a type of "home page," pointing to interesting content within the publication. Online resources are continually tweaked at the *Globe and Mail*, which now spreads its content over eReaders, smartphones, computers, and tablet devices. Readers can also sign up to receive e-newsletters, e-mail alerts, Facebook applications, and RSS feeds (really simple syndication, which delivers content through an electronic reader accessed on a browser).

What percentage of people used Twitter the previous day?

18–24 years **30%**

25–29 years **44%**

30–34 years **18%**

Over 55 years **3%**

marketing meter

Source: *Consumerology Report – Technology and Canadian Consumers*, Bensimon Byrne, January 2010, accessed at www.consumerology.ca..pdf.

out-of-home
advertising

Casually referred to
as *outdoor*; reaches
consumers outside
the home in outdoor
locations, in transit,
or in commercial or
business locations

mobile marketing

The marketing on
mobile devices such
as cellphones and
tablet computers

Figure 12–2

Advertising expenditures — 2013 forecasted trends

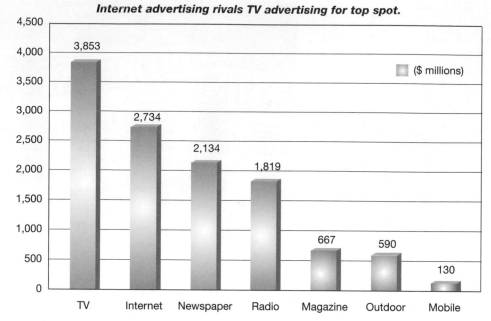

Internet advertising rivals TV advertising for top spot.

Source: ZenithOptimedia, "Advertising Expenditure Forecasts – July 2011"; Advertising data: 1999–2010: TVB, Statistics Canada, CRTC, CNA, LNA, NMR, Les Hebdos du Quebec, Magazines Canada, IAB Canada; 2011–2013: Agency forecasts.

A Changing Advertiser

Advertisers are following consumers to the digital arena, making adjustments to media plans to best serve clients. Spending on Internet advertising in 2012 ranks second to TV advertising in expenditures.

The Marketing Communications Industry

The marketing communications industry consists of five main areas that work together to form an industry that is ethical, trustworthy, cohesive, and measurable. These areas include the following: (1) the media, (2) marketing communication agencies, (3) research companies, (4) associations, and (5) regulatory bodies. These areas have all been impacted by the digital era. Let's look at these areas in more detail.

The Media

The main forms of media are TV, Internet, newspaper, magazine, radio, out-of-home, and mobile. **Out-of-home advertising**, casually referred to as *outdoor*, reaches consumers outside the home in outdoor locations, in transit, or in commercial or

business locations. It can take many forms such as billboards, posters, transit, electronic signage, closed-circuit TV, or street furniture. **Mobile marketing** refers to marketing that uses mobile devices such as cellphones and tablet computers to communicate with consumers through elements such as online mobile ads, apps, QR codes, text messaging, e-mail, mobile search, and web content repurposed for mobile devices.

Over the years, the media has evolved from a rudimentary word-of-mouth-dependent era to today's

Most Popular Online Activities

Reading news	65%
Facebook	51%
Reading printed news	51%
Instant messaging (computer/cellphone)	43%
Spending time online via smartphone	19%
Twitter	12%

Source: *Consumerology Report—Technology and Canadian Consumers,* Bensimon Byrne, January 2010, accessed at www.consumerology.ca.

Figure 12–3
Trends — advertising expenditures

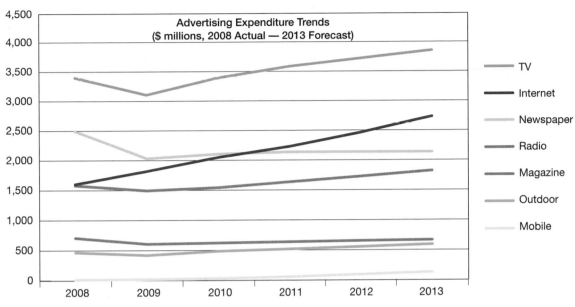

Source: ZenithOptimedia, "Advertising Expenditure Forecasts – July 2011"; Advertising data: 1999–2010: TVB, Statistics Canada, CRTC, CNA, LNA, NMR, Les Hebdos du Quebec, Magazines Canada, IAB Canada; 2011–2013: Agency forecasts

Internet era where social media spreads messages and allows for interactivity.

New media terms have surfaced in the Internet era: *paid media, owned media,* and *earned media.* **Paid media** is the media time that is purchased so that messages can be disseminated through channels that are controlled by others—TV advertising is an example. **Owned media** refers to the media channels that a company controls, either fully or partially, such as a website, microsite, or social media page that is used to directly communicate with consumers. **Earned media**, a term with origins in the public relations industry, refers to the free publicity secured through unpaid media mentions and consumers who spread the word through word-of-mouth or the Internet.

Successful campaigns use integrated approaches that creatively use paid and owned media as springboards into securing earned media. James Ready's award-winning "Share Our Billboard" campaign is such an example where an outdoor billboard campaign and a microsite created buzz about a local microbrewery placing consumer messages on its billboards—all you had

James Ready beer—user-generated content and outdoor ads increased sales by 55 percent.

James Ready's Share Our Billboard Campaign Sells More Beer

James Ready? Who is James Ready was the question asked when the Canadian beer brand won marketing and advertising awards for its innovative outdoor billboard campaign, "Share Our Billboard." So, for those unfamiliar with the microbrewing industry, James Ready is not a person but a brand of beer brewed since 1875 in Niagara Falls, Ontario. Its campaign, Share Our Billboard, created by Leo Burnett, won a 2009 Gold Lion at the Cannes Lions International Advertising Festival for its innovative outdoor advertising campaign and a 2010 Gold Cassie Award for Event and Seasonal on a small budget. This was followed by awards for its 2010 billboard campaign featuring local retailer coupons and a 2011 campaign. A 2011 campaign, run through Facebook, rectified a production error, which inadvertently shipped blank bottle caps on beer bottles instead of caps that normally contain lighthearted words on the inside. Consumers were asked to send back their bottle caps in return for humorous random gifts such as old hockey cards or plastic figurines.

The 2009 Share Our Billboard campaign stands out as the most creative, making a splash by asking people in southern Ontario to keep the price of James Ready beer at $1 per bottle by sharing in the cost of the billboard campaign. A billboard campaign spread the message, with the addition of classified ads that appeared in local Canadian newspapers. People were asked to "Help us keep James Ready a buck. Share our billboard." Billboard messages steered people to a website at www.jamesready.com where they could post their best offer (no actual cost was accepted), and upload messages and photos to include in their personal billboard.

The result was that submissions were posted on billboards placed outside local beer stores with a tagline from James Ready thanking them for keeping the price of the beer at $1!

James Ready spent approximately $140,000 on the campaign, used 106 billboards, and helped spread the word with their microsite at www.readyforless.com. The result was a sales increase of 55 percent versus the previous year and market share growth of 31 percent.

Judy John, CEO of the ad agency Leo Burnett Canada, explains that these lighthearted campaigns for James Ready beer continue to build business for the brand.[9]

Questions

1. What are the *paid, owned,* and *earned media* elements of this campaign?

2. How could you integrate Twitter and Facebook to boost this marketing program?

---

to do was enter your personal billboard request to be considered! The result was considerable buzz that helped boost sales by 55 percent. (See the Marketing NewsFlash above.)

Marketing Communication Agencies

Marketing communication agencies provide marketers with expertise on how best to communicate messages to their audiences. Agencies can be broad-spectrum and offer a variety of services to their clients, or they can be specialty agencies providing expertise in media, creative, public relations, event

ask yourself

1. How has social media changed marketing communications?

2. How are newspapers adapting to evolving media habits?

3. How much time do you spend weekly with each form of media?

marketing, product placement and branded integration, direct marketing, or sales promotion. These terms are discussed in more detail later in this chapter.

Research Companies

Metrics are central to the smooth functioning of the marketing communications industry. Data on audience measurement, readership, consumer trends, and the quality of communication messages is needed to provide transparent and reliable information to the media, agencies, and clients. Most major media sectors publish third-party data for the industry, which is used to determine advertising rates and trends. In addition, other research companies, such as Forrester Research and the Nielsen Company, provide data to keep the industry apprised on the latest developments.

Associations

The marketing communications industry has a number of active associations that provide research data and host informative events and educational workshops for the industry. Three top events are worth noting: Marketing Week, hosted by the Canadian Marketing Association (CMA) and *Marketing* magazine, is an annual event focused on media innovation; the MIXX Canada Conference Series, by the Interactive Advertising Bureau of Canada (IAB), presents full-day conferences on the digital and interactive industry, highlighting what is new and evolving; Advertising Week, created by the Institute of Communication Agencies (ICA), is a week-long series of presentations and events focused on the latest developments in the industry with a number of well-priced events available for students. The Out-of-Home Marketing Association is also worth noting for its informative website and top quality online webinars.

Regulations

Prior to embarking on a marketing communications program, marketers need to be well-versed on the limitations and restrictions placed upon them by regulatory bodies. Marketers are well-advised to become familiar with their specific industry associations and to stay up-to-date on marketing regulations, business

ASC helps protect Canadians from false messaging in advertising. Because among all the pretty words and pictures – truth matters.

ASC Advertising Standards Canada
adstandards.ca

This ASC ad encourages honest communications.

restrictions, and best practices. Chapter 2 provides details on these regulatory bodies and the regulations that guide marketing communications in Canada. It is advisable at this point for you to re-visit these pages to obtain details. The following is only a brief reminder.

In Canada there are four main regulatory groups that work toward limiting intentional, and unintentional, deceptive marketing practices. These are (1) Advertising Standards Canada (ASC), (2) the Competition Bureau, (3) the Canadian Radio-television and Telecommunications Commission (CRTC), and (4) the Canadian Marketing Association (CMA). Specialist areas and industry groups such as the public relations industry also have associations that provide codes of ethics and guidelines on best practices to assist its members.

1. **Advertising Standards Canada (ASC)** is a self-regulatory, non-government association that sets and regulates advertising. It uses a consumer-complaint process to review questionable ads that are withdrawn if they contravene its guidelines. The

Looking for Media Data?

Audit Bureau of Circulations (ABC)	www.accessabc.ca
BBM Media Research (BBM)	www.bbm.ca
Canadian Out-of-Home Measurement Bureau (COMB)	www.comb.org
comScore	www.comscore.com
Forrester Research	www.forrester.com
Interactive Advertising Bureau of Canada (IAB)	www.iabcanada.com
Media Digest	cmdc.ca
Newspaper Audience Databank (NADBank)	www.nadbank.com
Nielsen Company	ca.nielsen.com
Print Measurement Bureau (PMB)	www.pmb.ca
Television Bureau of Canada (TVB)	www.tvb.ca

ASC also provides advice and pre-clearance services for advertisers but has no legal jurisdiction and does not levy fines. Its guidelines discourage advertisers from misleading consumers with messages that are untrue, vague, fraudulent, or against the standards of public decency. Special care is taken to protect impressionable members of society from testimonials, claims, and images that misrepresent products. Detailed guidelines can be found at www.adstandards.com.

2. **The Competition Bureau** is an independent law-enforcement agency with jurisdiction in many areas. In the marketing communications area, it looks at fraudulent advertising and misleading representation to sell products, including price and warranty claims. Deceptive price claims and contests that do not publish the required terms and conditions are illegal and heavily scrutinized. Failure to comply with regulations can result in fines and jail time. To see more on the Competition Bureau, visit its website at competitionbureau.gc.ca.

3. **The Canadian Radio-television and Telecommunications Commission (CRTC)** is another government agency. It regulates the broadcast and telecommunications industry in Canada, including the licensing of stations. It also provides guidelines on Canadian content and sets limitations on the amount of advertising permitted during broadcasts. It oversees the advertising of alcoholic beverages and works with the ASC on advertising to children.

4. **The Canadian Marketing Association (CMA)** uses a *Code of Ethics and Standards of Practice* to guide the marketing industry in Canada on telemarketing, e-mail marketing, mobile marketing, Internet marketing, promotional contests, fundraising, database marketing, and marketing to children and teenagers. It also provides guidelines on privacy issues and anti-spam practices.

Failure to abide by marketing communication regulations can have dire consequences for marketers—campaigns may be forced off air, companies and individuals may be fined, and legal action can result in jail time. In 2010, after a two-month investigation, the Competition Bureau asked Rogers to pull its advertising campaign for its budget brand Chatr, which was claiming fewer dropped calls than competing brands. After Rogers refused to pull the ads, the Competition Bureau started legal proceedings to get the ads removed and to have Rogers served with a $10 million administrative penalty for misleading advertising. The lawsuit also asked for Rogers to compensate Chatr customers and issue corrective notices.[10] At press time, this issue had yet to be resolved.

Approaches to Marketing Communications

Outbound and Inbound Marketing Communications

There are two terms that we need to understand in marketing communications: outbound marketing and inbound marketing. **Outbound marketing** refers to the traditional marketing approach where marketers seek out consumers by widely broadcasting messages using advertising, direct mail, e-mail marketing, telemarketing, and personal selling approaches. It includes advertising methods that consumers are increasingly avoiding, such as ads on TV, radio, newspapers, and magazines, as well as Internet display ads. **Inbound marketing** is when interested consumers find the product and its messaging by using online techniques that marketers facilitate. It involves search engine optimization, pay-per-click ads, and the use of social media to connect with consumers through social networks, blogs, social bookmarks, social media releases, and microsites. It is the result of paid, earned, and owned media.

> *Deceptive price claims and contests that do not publish the required terms and conditions are illegal and heavily scrutinized.*

These two approaches are often used together to communicate with consumers in ways they prefer. Smaller businesses may rely more on inbound marketing, which is cheaper, while larger businesses, depending on the target market, may use a combination of both techniques.

Integrated Marketing Communications

The concept of designing a marketing communications program that coordinates all promotional activities to provide a consistent message to a target audience is referred to as **integrated marketing communications (IMC)**.

The key to developing successful IMC programs is to use a process that makes it easy to design and evaluate. In an integrated marketing communications program, each element has a distinct role as well as a purpose in the overall campaign. For example, TV advertising might be used to build awareness and drive consumers to a microsite, print advertising may be used to increase product usage, sales promotion might be needed to generate product trial, direct mail may be required to create a database of the target market, and personal selling might be needed to complete the transaction. Each tool is used for a different reason and needs to be evaluated against that purpose as well as its contribution to the overall success of the marketing communications program.

Maxwell House Coffee presents a leading-edge example of a fully integrated marketing communications program. From 2008 to 2012, the company ran

An online ad linked to www.brewsomegood.ca

Instead of making an expensive TV commercial, we're using the money to help fund good causes.

NOMINATE A WORTHY CAUSE

integrated marketing communications (IMC) A communications approach that coordinates all promotional activities to provide a consistent message to a target audience

its "Brew Some Good" campaign with an innovative approach that used multiple communication tools to deliver a simple message: We are doing good deeds and we want you too as well. This evolved into an uplifting message of optimism unified by common graphics and messaging spread through advertising, public relations, event marketing, and in-store elements.

It started with celebrity buskers creating buzz on street corners in Toronto and Montreal. Here Maxwell House gave subway riders free tokens and hot cups of coffee and alerted the media to the event. Carefully planned advertising rolled out over the following weeks with ads appearing on TV, in print, and on the Internet, all pointing to the campaign's microsite at www.brewsomegood.ca where consumers were asked to nominate charitable causes for the initiative.

TV ads showed a steaming cup of coffee and announced that the commercial cost only $19,000, a savings of over $200,000, which was earmarked for charitable donations, including $100,000 for Habitat for Humanity. Viewers were asked to recommend other worthy causes for $10,000 donations from Maxwell House. Subsequent TV spots encouraged consumers to do good deeds and focused on charities that received donations. The microsite showcased charities such as the Regent Park School of Music for inner-city youth and the Mira Foundation of guide dogs for the disabled.

Year two saw the launch of Brew Some Good Week, which used street teams to

Maxwell House's microsite at www. brewsomegood.ca

Free subway rides, concerts, and cups of coffee

reward Canadians for conducting random acts of kindness, while year three focused on optimism.

Campaign results outpaced business objectives with research showing consumers made emotional connections, and increased positive attitudes toward the brand. The media wrote over 200 stories on the topic, including 66 TV news segments that secured 1 million audience impressions. In addition, consumers submitted 4,500 charitable nominations and awarded the brand the Reader's Digest 2009 Most Trusted Award. The marketing industry also celebrated the campaign as a Cannes finalist with the Canadian Marketing Association presenting it with a silver award for Best Brand Advertising.[11]

Marketing Communication Tools

In this diverse media environment, a wide range of communication tools are available to reach consumers in the best possible way. Marketers look to advertising, public relations, sales promotion, direct response, event marketing and sponsorship, and personal selling as the tools that communicate to target markets either online or offline. The Childhood Cancer Foundation uses numerous online tools such as its website, fundraising microsites, and social media networks designed specifically for teenagers with cancer. Offline tools are evident through its gala event fundraisers and face-to-face communications in the hospitals, communities, and schools. Selecting appropriate communication tools is vital to the foundation's success.

Let's look at marketing communication tools in more detail and highlight when they are most useful.

Marketing communication tools consist of advertising, public relations, sales promotion, direct response, event marketing and sponsorship, and personal selling. Figure 12–4 summarizes the relative strengths and weaknesses of these six elements.

ask yourself

1. How is marketing communications regulated in Canada?
2. What is the role of the ASC?
3. What is IMC?

Advertising

L3 **Advertising** is a paid form of media used to communicate to consumers about an organization, good, service, or idea. The *paid* aspect of this definition is important because advertising space is normally purchased, with the exception of some public service announcements, which may use donated media.

Advertising can exist in many forms in Canada. In the broadcast media, there is TV and radio. In the print media, there is newspaper and magazine. In the out-of-home media, there are billboards, posters, bus shelter ads, transit ads, washroom ads, and a variety of non-conventional modes such as aerial advertising. In the digital media, there are websites, Internet ads, electronic newsletters, and permission-based e-mails.

Advertising can be very expensive. A one-time, national rate for a full-page, four-colour ad in *Maclean's* magazine, for example, costs $38,180.[12] This magazine also has an accompanying website where marketers can purchase various online advertising options. Television ads are even more expensive, with the average cost to produce a TV commercial running between $200,000 and $250,000. The cost of buying TV media varies, depending on when and where an advertiser wishes to run the spot. Costs can run as high as $100,000 to $150,000 to run a 30-second spot during a top, primetime, highly viewed TV show.

One of the latest forms of "advertising" that we see is the *webisode* with companies such as Ikea, Sara Lee, and Maybelline creating short online episodes with storylines that entertain and subtly weave in the product.[13] These advertising/branded-integration hybrids are still unproven in the marketplace and have yet to become mainstream.

Advertising Media Choices Marketers have a number of media options from which to choose. Selection is based on campaign objectives as well as the product, the target market, and budget constraints. Figure 12–5 on page 276 summarizes the advantages and disadvantages of the major forms of advertising: TV, Internet, newspaper, magazine, radio, and outdoor/transit. These media choices are described in more detail in the following pages.

Television Television is a valuable medium because it communicates with sight, sound, and motion and gets attention from large target audiences. When ads are well-designed and appropriately placed in the media, this tool can deliver very impactful and effective messages. Over the last few years, TV has experienced numerous changes with the launch of many new channels. There are now 148 commercial TV stations, which has resulted in audience fragmentation, making it more difficult for marketers to reach consumers.[14]

Marketers need to be aware that consumer behaviour is placing TV advertising effectiveness into question. TV viewers frequently change channels when ads appear during commercial breaks and often use

Figure 12–4
Strengths and weaknesses of communication tools

PROMOTIONAL TOOL	STRENGTHS	WEAKNESSES
Advertising	• An efficient means of reaching large numbers of people both online and offline • Many affordable online options exist for marketers with small budgets • Online and offline options can work together to enhance messaging • Advertisers control messaging	• High cost of offline approaches • Difficult to evaluate offline approaches • High clutter both online and offline • Low credibility of messaging • Viewers avoid both online and offline messaging
Public relations	• Highly credible messages when spread by the media • Inexpensive, particularly when using social media • New measurable tools available due to social media • Can be well-integrated into IMC programs	• Unable to control media messaging • Difficult to influence the number of messages spread through the media • Results can be difficult to evaluate
Sales promotion	• Effective at increasing short-term sales • Many options are available both online and offline • Social media provides an affordable way to disseminate offers • Results are measurable • Can be well-integrated into IMC programs	• Fraudulent involvement can occur • Can lead to promotional wars • Promotions can be easily duplicated by competitors • Consumers may wait for a sales promotion before purchasing • Legal regulations are complex
Direct response	• Messages can be targeted through online and offline approaches • Facilitates customer relationships • Results are measurable	• High cost of offline and online approaches • Negative customer reactions • Clutter • Requires a database to be done properly
Event marketing and sponsorship	• Small branded events can be used to create a buzz and spread viral messages • Major event sponsorships can reach large audiences and create positive associations • Can be integrated into IMC programs • Sponsorships can be carried into the online environment • Buzz can be affordably created through microsites and social media	• Large event-sponsorships can be limited to awareness-building messages • Sponsorships can be costly and difficult to evaluate • Results are difficult to measure
Personal selling	• Personal interactions can build lasting relationships with consumers • Online approaches can be used to enhance relationships • An important approach for expensive products • Can be used in large and small businesses • Can be a strong form of product differentiation	• Can become expensive when large sales forces are involved • Consistency in approach and messaging is difficult to achieve • People may not want to engage

Figure 12–5
Advertising options — advantages and disadvantages

MEDIUM	ADVANTAGES	DISADVANTAGES
Television	• Reaches a wide audience • Uses sight, sound, and motion • Can target specific audiences • Excellent for products requiring demonstration • Highly visible	• High cost to create ads • High cost to purchase media • Short exposure time • Perishable message • Difficult to convey complex information • High avoidance • Difficult to measure
Internet	• Video and audio capabilities • Animation and sound can get attention • Ads can be interactive • Ad can be placed on websites, web portals, search engines, or social networks • Detailed information can be conveyed • Many creative options • Easy to measure • Can be low cost	• Animation and interactivity require large files that can have long load-times • High avoidance • Short attention spans on the Internet
Newspapers	• Strong in local markets • Short lead-times for ad placement • Flexible ad sizes • Ads can be clipped and saved • Detailed information can be conveyed • Can be low cost for local placements	• Ads compete for attention with other newspaper features • Advertising clutter • Short lifespan • Poor colour reproduction • Relatively high cost for national ads
Magazines	• Can target specific audiences • High-quality colour • Pass-along readership • Ads can be clipped and saved • Complex information can be conveyed	• Long lead-times • Relatively high cost • Advertising clutter • Ads compete for attention with other magazine features
Radio	• Low cost of media and production • Good for local businesses • Short lead-times • Theatre of the mind gets attention	• No visual elements • Perishable message • Background media • Difficult to convey complex information • Difficult for national campaigns
Outdoor/Transit	• Relatively low cost • Local market focus • High visibility • Strong opportunity for repeat exposures • Good for building awareness in short time • Cannot be turned off	• Message must be short and simple • Low selectivity of audience • Visual pollution

personal video recorders (PVRs) such as TiVos to skip commercials. Sometimes people prefer to watch TV programs online where fewer ads exist, or catch a show at another time through on-demand digital programming that is now offered by cable providers.

Internet Marketing on the Internet provides marketers with numerous tools to reach online audiences. Many options exist such as online ads, search engine marketing, social networking, e-mail marketing, affiliate marketing, mobile marketing, and the use of promotional microsites, company websites, and intricate CRM sites such as iCoke.ca for redeeming points in exchange for rewards.

When it comes to online advertising, companies can use display ads and videos that are placed on major websites, e-mail platforms, and mobile devices. Pay-per-click ads can also appear on search engines, content networks, and social networks such as Facebook, LinkedIn, or YouTube, while online classified ads can be placed on Craigslist or Kijiji.

Dynamic ads can also be placed on gaming websites through companies such as Microsoft, which has a Gaming Solutions advertising platform that allows ads to be served through its MSN Games, Windows Live Messenger Games, Xbox, and in-game advertising platforms.

Display advertising refers to the use of online ads with graphics that are placed on websites. They can be placed on highly trafficked websites, web portals, social networks, e-mail service providers, or blogs that accept advertising messages. Display ads can be static or animated. They are commonly called **banner ads**, which come in a variety of shapes and sizes—leaderboards, rectangles, big boxes, or skyscrapers. **Leaderboards** stretch across the top of a web page, while rectangles and big boxes typically appear lower down, on the right-hand side of a webpage. A **skyscraper** is a tall, slim, vertical ad placed along the side of a web page.

Display ads can also be formatted as *home page takeovers* where an entire ad obscures the website home page. The most successful banner ads are interactive in nature and commonly link to an advertiser's promotional website. Gaming websites embed banner ads within their online games so that ads appear as billboards or posters within the games. This is called **advergaming**, an opportunity that allows marketers to dynamically rotate display ads as appropriate by time of day or day of the week. Ads can also be placed within offline games.

Online video advertising refers to the use of video ads on the Internet. These can be in the form of pre-roll TV-type ads that run before watching a TV show on the Internet, or display ads that include video and are placed on various websites. These types of ads are increasingly popular with marketers but have the disadvantage of being more expensive to produce than static or animated display ads.

Pay-per-click advertising (PPC) is an Internet marketing approach pioneered by the search engines and now also used by Facebook, LinkedIn, and YouTube in various instances. It is often referred to as *search advertising* because it primarily appears on search engines in the form of mini-text ads that are served during keyword searches on either the top or right-hand side of the search page. The search engine is paid by the PPC advertiser only when the ads are clicked. Facebook, LinkedIn, and YouTube follow similar approaches with text or image ads.

Newspapers Newspapers are an important advertising medium with excellent reach, particularly for local retailers. There are three types of newspapers: daily paid circulation newspapers, free

daily newspapers, and free community newspapers. The highest circulation of a paid daily newspaper in Canada is the *Toronto Star* followed in order by the *Globe and Mail*, the *National Post*, and the *Toronto Sun*. The two free daily newspapers, *Metro* and *24 Hours*, are enjoying high circulation numbers that rival the traditional paid circulation newspapers.[15] Community newspapers are published either weekly or monthly and are an excellent media choice for local retailers and for community events.

Magazines Magazines provide advertisers with a high-quality media environment. They have adapted well to the online environment by providing added online content such as searchable databases, blogs, contests, and polls. Magazines such *Canadian Living* and *Chatelaine* offer expansive recipe databases and in-depth coverage. News magazines such as *Maclean's* include added features such as blogs, polls, quizzes, and videos, and *Canadian Business* follows a similar approach.

The Canadian Print Measurement Bureau (PMB) issues topline reports detailing two-year data for circulation, readership, and target market information on many Canadian newspapers and magazines. The fall 2011 report shows that Canadian magazines with the highest readership are *Reader's Digest* and *Canadian Living*.[16] See the box on page 278 for a list of the top ten magazines, and navigate to the PMB website (www.pmb.ca) to review the latest data.

See the box on page 278 for a list of the top ten magazines

---

display advertising
The use of online ads with graphics or animation that are placed on websites

banner ads
Online ads that can stretch across the top of a web page or be formatted in various sizes, such as leaderboards, rectangles, big boxes, and skyscrapers

leaderboards
Banner ads that stretch across the top of a web page

skyscrapers
Banner ads that are tall, slim, and vertical and appear along the side of a web page

advergaming
Placing ads in online or offline video games

online video advertising
The use of video ads on the Internet

pay-per-click advertising (PPC)
Ads that appear on search engines and their networks, and on Facebook, LinkedIn, or YouTube in response to keyword triggers

Radio   Radio reaches 91 percent of Canadians over the age of 12 but listening continues to decline among teens that prefer to access music on a variety of devices.[17] The main characteristics of radio are that it is local and has a relatively low production cost. This makes it affordable for both small and large advertisers. There are 681 private commercial radio stations in Canada, many of which focus on specific listener interests, including news and talk, or music genres such as adult contemporary, country, contemporary hits, rock, classical, and the oldies. Stations also exist for specific ethnic groups, broadcasting their content in ethnic languages. Radio stations have responded to the Internet with simultaneous online broadcasts and downloadable podcasts. Satellite radio with its commercial-free programming is available through XM Canada and Sirius Canada, but its monthly fee of at least $12.99 per month limits its appeal.

Outdoor/Transit   Outdoor/transit advertising (often referred to as out-of-home) is an effective medium for quickly building awareness and interest in a product. It is also an excellent reminder for current products. Over the last few years, this media has experienced slight increases due to its participation in integrated marketing communications programs and the realization that this media cannot be turned off. New digital technology is widely used in this medium with outdoor digital billboards appearing in major cities across Canada. Clear Channel Media manages many of these digital billboards, sometimes using LED screens with full-motion video displays. Examples can be seen at Yonge-Dundas Square in Toronto where Canada's first media tower dominates with 20,000 square feet of advertising in the form of billboards and full-motion video or customized displays.

Digital media tower at Yonge-Dundas Square in Toronto

Top Magazines (Readership in Canada)

Ranking	Magazine
1	*Reader's Digest*
2	*Canadian Living*
3	*People*
4	*Chatelaine*
5	*What's Cooking*
6	*Canadian Geographic*
7	*Maclean's*
8	*Canadian House & Home*
9	*CAA Magazine*
10	*Canadian Gardening*

Source: *PMB 2011 Fall Topline Report,* Canadian Print Measurement Bureau, accessed at www.pmb.ca (rolling two-year data).

Outdoor advertising includes billboards, back-lit posters, superboards (large billboards), mall posters, digital signs, video signage/displays, wall banners, murals, and street-level columns. It also includes *place-based media* where messages are placed in out-of-home destinations such as shopping malls, airports, doctors' offices, health clubs, gas stations, elevators, and washrooms (in restaurants, bars, and post-secondary schools). Zoom media is an innovative company that manages washroom advertising, creating innovative designs that appeal to specific genders. Transit advertising refers to ads placed on the interior and exterior of buses, subway cars, and taxis as well as in subway stations and on transit shelters.

Washroom ads are becoming increasingly common in restaurants, bars, colleges, and universities.

Public Relations

LO ④ Public relations is an area increasingly used by marketers to deliver messages to consumers. While advertising may be viewed with suspicion, messages that come though a third party, such as the media, are often seen as more reliable and credible. In addition, for marketers with small budgets, public relations efforts can be a more affordable way to communicate with a wide audience. The Childhood Cancer Foundation, for example, discussed in this chapter's opening vignette, has a small budget and turns to public relations to help spread messages using direct contacts with the media, event marketing programs, social media, and community relations.

Public relations is a communications tool that seeks to influence the opinions and attitudes of target groups through the use of unpaid media exposure. Public relations professionals build relationships with the media and stakeholders and use tools such as press releases, social media releases, press kits, news conferences, and events to spread the word. Public relations specialists target the media in an attempt to generate

positive publicity for a company, product, or individual. While public relations specialists are paid to create public relations campaigns, the intent is to generate positive publicity that by far outweighs its cost. Public relations can also take the form of crisis management and image management.[18]

Crisis management can be an important aspect of public relations, as seen with the 2008 Maple Leaf Foods listeria food contamination issue linked to 20 deaths in Canada.[19] Issues that impact public health or the environment can have dire financial repercussions for a company and need to be handled professionally and with utmost care, keeping the public's best interest in mind. Maple Leaf Foods did just this. Its president, Michael McCain, immediately took full responsibility for the situation and personally addressed the media, with the message also being posted on YouTube. Before culpability had been established, all products from the suspected facilities were recalled, manufacturing plants were closed, and a spokesperson was appointed for media updates. Maple Leaf Foods also ran newspaper ads to advise consumers not to eat the products, posted updated lists of contaminated items on its website, and held ongoing press conferences to communicate with the media and the public. Its approach appeared genuine and heart-felt, with concern, regret, honesty, and openness underlying all communications. This helped temper the crisis and somewhat contained the fallout. Maple Leaf Foods paid $27 million in compensation to people impacted by the food-borne illness, and the company valuation was negatively impacted by the crisis.

It is important to understand that while public relations efforts can yield positive results, ultimately the media decides if, what, and when it may spread a message about a company, brand, or individual. The publicity is not controlled by the company itself and the company has no control over what is discussed.

public relations
A communications tool that seeks to influence the opinions and attitudes of target groups through the use of unpaid media exposure; targets the media in an attempt to generate positive publicity for a company, product, or individual

ask yourself

1. What types of advertising opportunities are available on the Internet?

2. Why is TV such a highly used media for advertisers?

3. What are some of the reasons newspaper advertising is so attractive to advertisers?

> *Crisis management can be an important aspect of public relations.*

Publicity is a non-personal form of communication that appears in the media and is not paid for directly by the organization.

The Best Job in the World campaign for Queensland Tourism in Australia is an example of how public relations can drum up positive publicity for a campaign. In 2009 it used a global public relations effort, the Best Job in the World campaign, to draw attention to the islands of the Great Barrier Reef as a tourist destination. It posted a classified ad for a job as an island caretaker of Hamilton Island in the Great Barrier Reef, complete with a job description that included writing a blog and feeding the fish! Video releases helped spread the world through the broadcast media that showcased the island, incredulous about this job posting. This secured media coverage that was valued at over $374 million. (See the Focus on Ethics box below.)

Public Relations Tools   Public relations activities need to be ethical and integrated into marketing communications efforts. Several tools and tactics are available for marketers, including press releases, press conferences, special events, and company reports. Social media releases and social media initiatives are relatively

focus on *Ethics*

Best Job Takes the World by Storm

In 2009, the Best Job in the World opportunity was everywhere—on the news, in magazines, and online—as people, captivated by the beauty of Hamilton Island in Queensland, Australia, spread the word about a job posting for an island caretaker. The job included feeding the fish, collecting mail, cleaning the pool, exploring the island, and capturing the adventure on a daily blog. Anyone could apply, with the winner receiving over $8,000 per month in salary and free luxury accommodation! Individuals had 6 weeks to submit a 60-second online video application at www.islandreefjob.com. The public voted on its top candidate, who, together with candidates selected by Queensland Tourism, attended a final interview on Hamilton Island itself. The winner was 34-year-old charity worker, Ben Southhall from the U.K.

The Best Job in the World was a public relations campaign orchestrated by Queensland Tourism in Australia to promote the islands of the Great Barrier Reef. While the job was real, the purpose of the campaign was to raise awareness among potential tourists from the U.K., U.S., Europe, Japan, New Zealand, India, China, and Korea, to boost tourism.

The campaign kicked off with Queensland Tourism courting the media with information that flaunted the beauty of Hamilton Island and the incredulity of the caretaker's job. The story was newsworthy and its stunning videos captivated the media, which broadcast the story during news programming. Meanwhile, small print ads were placed in the classified and employment sections of newspapers. Online ads were also posted on employment websites, and small banner ads were placed throughout the Internet. Branded pages on MySpace, Facebook, YouTube, and Twitter hyped the job opportunity and spread the word through social media. All elements pointed people to a microsite, www.islandreefjob.com, to submit their video job applications.

The campaign, priced at approximately $1.3 million, generated free publicity valued at more than $374 million, with more than 3 billion people exposed to its message. Highly watched TV stations such as the CBC, the BBC, and CNN carried the story, helping to boost job applications to 34,684 videos from 197 countries. Metrics show that the campaign microsite had 8,465,280 unique visitors and 55,002,415 page views, with an average time-on-site of 8.25 minutes per person. The general public cast 475,000 votes to select a winner.

The Best Job in the World campaign won numerous marketing awards, including a Direct Grand Prix, Public Relations Grand Prix, and Cyber Grand Prix for best website and interactive at the 2009 Cannes International Advertising Festival.[20] ●

Questions

1. Which elements do you think were the most important in making the Best Job in the World such a successful campaign?

2. A few people have criticized this campaign for not being transparent in its intent to raise awareness for the islands of the Great Barrier Reef. What ethical issues does this campaign raise?

new tools that can come under the guise of public relations. Let's look at the tools:

Press Releases One of the most frequently used public relations tools is the **press release**, an announcement written by the organization and sent to the media.

Press Conferences Another commonly used publicity tool is the **press conference**, when representatives of the media are invited to an informational meeting with the company. Advanced materials and press releases are often distributed ahead of time. This tool is often used during crisis management situations.

Special Events This growing area of public relations involves the creation, support, or sponsorship of special events such as company-sponsored seminars, conferences, and sporting or entertainment events. The goal of these events is to create a forum to disseminate company information and to create positive brand associations for participants or viewers.

Company Reports Formal company information that is published in annual reports, brochures, newsletters, or videos to the company's publics are also public relations tools that help spread positive messages.

Social Media This tool is seen as a hybrid of advertising and public relations and is often managed by public relations professionals to seed messages and spread the word. Public relations companies and advertising agencies often use social media specialists to manage these efforts.

A **social media release** is a relatively new tool available for marketers to efficiently and effectively communicate information to the media and the public. Unlike press releases, which exist online and offline with mainly text-based information, social media releases use online multimedia to communicate with recipients. Video, images, and text are included in online releases with comment areas and share-buttons where readers can easily share the release on blogs or social networks such as Twitter and Facebook.

Sales Promotion

LO⑤ **Sales promotion** is a communications tool that provides short-term incentives to generate interest in a product or cause and encourages purchase or support. Social media sites such as Facebook and Twitter are often used to deliver promotional offers to fans and followers while microsites provide online destinations where contests can be communicated and people can interact. While coupons, rebates, samples, and sweepstakes are some of the traditional sales promotion tools, the digital age has spawned new creative forms. We see agencies developing online promotions where consumers can create and share their own user-generated content, such as the video applications for the Best Job in the World campaign noted earlier. **User-generated content (UGC)** is consumer content that is created by participants. We see sales promotions directed at mobile devices with specific smartphone apps and text-message contests allowing for interaction. We see augmented reality chips embedded into magazines, postcards, and product labels so that when viewers hold the images up to a live webcam, it launches a website that interacts with the image. Such was the case with Coke Zero during the launch of the movie *Avatar* in the U.S., where augmented reality allowed people with the flagged product to interact with the movie's microsite. **Augmented reality (AR)** is when real-world images interact with computer-generated information to provide additional

▼

ask yourself

1. What are the advantages and disadvantages of using public relations?

2. What is a social media release?

3. What role do company reports play in public relations?

---

press release
An announcement written by an organization and sent to the media

press conference
A planned event where representatives of the media are invited to an informational meeting with the company

social media release
A multimedia online press release platform that includes video, text, and images, as well as social media buttons for sharing on social networks and comment areas where viewers can leave comments

sales promotion
A communications tool that provides short-term incentives to generate interest in a product or cause and encourages purchase or support

user-generated content (UGC)
Consumer content that is created by participants

augmented reality (AR)
When real-world images interact with computer-generated information to provide additional information

---

" FACEBOOK AND TWITTER ARE OFTEN USED TO DELIVER PROMOTIONAL OFFERS. "

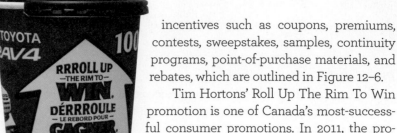

information to viewers. Another technological sales promotion tool is the use of *quick response (QR) codes*, black-and-white patterned squares that consumers may scan with an enabled smartphone in order to access online content (see page 258).

Jackson-Triggs Estate Wines, Sony Ericsson, and Doritos recently all used these new forms of sales promotion to engage consumers. Jackson-Triggs celebrated their status as the official wine supplier of the Vancouver 2010 Olympic Winter Games with a text-message contest for a trip for two to the Vancouver Games, all contestants winning a VIP wine-tasting voucher. Sony Ericsson created a global online Twitter campaign for the 2010 FIFA World Cup where fans had to tweet their favourite country for it to move on to the next round of an online contest. And in 2010, Doritos asked people to name a new chip flavour and create online videos about the product for a chance to win up to $250,000.

There are two basic types of sales promotion: (1) consumer promotions and (2) trade promotions. **Consumer promotions** are short-term marketing tools used to encourage immediate consumer purchase. They include

incentives such as coupons, premiums, contests, sweepstakes, samples, continuity programs, point-of-purchase materials, and rebates, which are outlined in Figure 12–6.

Tim Hortons' Roll Up The Rim To Win promotion is one of Canada's most-successful consumer promotions. In 2011, the promotion celebrated its 25th anniversary with 47 million prizes, including 40 Toyota Matrix cars, 100 Panasonic TVs, 1,000 Napoleon Gourmet Grills, 5,000 Raleigh mountain bikes, 25,000 $100 Tim Hortons gift cards, and numerous free coffee and free donut prizes.

The promotion's simplicity plays a major role in its success. Consumers just have to roll up the rim of their paper Tim Hortons coffee cups to reveal whether they have won a prize. The complexity of creating the program for Tim Hortons is another matter, with the program requiring detailed negotiations with the program partners, and complex dealings with cup manufacturers and agencies that pull together the communication elements, including the legal contest requirements, which in 2011 included over 4,000 words of contest rules and regulations that were available in restaurants and posted online![21]

Trade promotions are short-term promotional tools used to generate support with wholesalers, distributors, or retailers. Common approaches include trade shows, trade allowances and discounts, and cooperative advertising. (see Figure 12–7).

Figure 12–6
Consumer promotions

Consumer promotions are an effective way to increase short-term sales.

Consumer Promotions	Promotional Tools	Explanation
Short-term marketing tools used to encourage immediate consumer purchase	Coupons	Price reductions offered in exchange for tickets/documents. Can be distributed online, on-pack, through flyers, or on shelf.
	Premiums	Offers that provide merchandise in exchange for proof-of-purchase. Extra funds may also be required.
	Contests	Offers where participants require a skill to win a prize such as creative submissions or answering a skill-testing question.
	Sweepstakes	Offers which are pure games-of-chance and where consumers participate often by completing an entry form.
	Samples and free trials	The provision of free products or free trials to encourage consumers to try and purchase a product.
	Loyalty programs	Continuity programs that reward customers for ongoing purchases with points that can be redeemed for rewards.
	Rebates	A price reduction supplied via mail in exchange for proof-of-purchase.
	Bonus packs/special packs	The provision of oversized packs or bonus items attached to the original product. Special packs can also be created.
	Point-of sale materials	The use of in-store merchandising such as display materials, banners, floor decals, and posters to draw attention.

Offline approaches include face-to-face selling, direct mail, catalogues, telemarketing, and direct-response advertising on TV, radio, or print where telephone numbers or web addresses drive an immediate call to action. Online approaches look to the Internet to facilitate one-on-one interactions and use tools such as e-mail campaigns, online display ads, pay-per-click ads, and social media interactions to drive consumers to landing pages, websites, or microsites. In many instances, offline and online direct-response approaches work together to encourage consumers to go to a store or an e-commerce site to complete a transaction.

Direct response uses metrics to evaluate success such as business leads, traffic generation, and direct orders. **Lead generation** is the resultant request for additional information. **Traffic generation** is the resultant visit to a location or website.

A successful direct-marketing approach that uses a loyalty CRM (customer relationship marketing) database is the Shoppers Drug Mart Optimum program. The program collects purchase data from its Optimum card members and then tailors messages using print ads, flyers, direct mail, e-mail messages, and in-store signage to encourage retail purchases. The intent is to obtain a greater share of wallet from its customers.

direct response
A marketing communications tool designed to communicate with consumers one-on-one and elicit a direct action either online or offline

lead generation
The requests for additional information that result from direct response marketing

traffic generation
The visits to a location or website that result from direct response marketing

Direct Response

L⑥ **Direct response** is a marketing communications tool designed to communicate with consumers one-on-one and to elicit a direct action either online or offline. This action can be in the form of an order, a supportive gesture, a request for further information, or a visit to a retail outlet or website. In many instances, a direct marketing program is multi-faceted and designed with short-term blasts that ultimately build long-term relationships with the company that result in purchases over the long term. In this manner, short-term interactions such as e-mail newsletters, updates on points' programs, pre-recorded telephone messages, or letters received in the mail are designed as reminders that build relationships, product awareness, and business in the long run.

ask yourself

1. What types of consumer promotions are available to marketers?

2. How do trade promotions differ from consumer promotions?

3. What trade promotional tools are available to marketers?

Figure 12–7
Trade promotions

Trade promotions are often required to encourage retail support.

Trade Promotions	Promotional Tools	Explanation
Short-term promotional tools given to wholesalers, distributors, or retailers	Trade shows	Participation in industry events that showcase new products and initiatives.
	Off-invoice allowances	A price reduction taken off the invoice of a purchase that is made within a specific timeframe.
	Merchandising allowances	A price reduction taken off a purchase in return for displaying the product.
	Co-op advertising	The contribution of funds for inclusion in a wholesaler, distributor, or retailer advertising program such as a flyer.

iCoke.ca is another successful CRM direct-marketing approach that drives business for Coca-Cola in Canada by encouraging consumers to collect cap-tops from Coca-Cola products that are redeemed online at iCoke.ca.

While the CRM direct-response approach is one of the fastest-growing forms of promotion, it poses several challenges. First, it requires a comprehensive and up-to-date database of respondent information, including demographics, purchase habits, and offer responses. Second, developing and maintaining this database is expensive. And third, some consumers avoid participation due to privacy issues.

Event Marketing and Sponsorship

Event marketing refers to the creation or involvement of a brand in an experience or occasion that heightens its awareness, creates positive associations, and generates a desired response. Event marketing and sponsorship often go hand-in-hand with brands lending their names to established events. Companies often weave event marketing into integrated campaigns that use public relations, social media, and consumer promotions to make

A successful CRM program by Shoppers Drug Mart uses the Optimum card.

connections with consumers and create a buzz. Baskin-Robbins Canada is an example. They used all these elements to launch a new line of ice cream, BRight Choices, weaving it into a Toronto Fashion Week event that saw two lucky contest winners attend the event that showcased a spring collection inspired by the ice cream. Not only did Baskin-Robbins feature the products in-store and sample them with consumers, they also invited consumers to name outfits in the haute couture collection to win tickets—very creative! (See the Marketing NewsFlash opposite.)

Sponsorship involves a company paying a fee in exchange for inclusion in an event, involvement in its advertising opportunities, or exposure within the event itself. Sponsorship programs can encompass

Companies often weave event marketing into integrated campaigns.

An IMC campaign by Baskin-Robbins launched its new product line.

personal selling
The two-way flow of communication between a buyer and seller, often face-to-face, or facilitated through communication devices to influence an individual and group purchase decision

attracted sponsorship from 32 WTA Tour, tournament, and broadcast partners. This resulted in 91 advertising signs around centre court with platinum premium sponsors Acura, Desjardins, Dairy Farmers of Canada, Emirates, IRIS, and Lowe's receiving high-profile exposure with ads placed behind the baseline. Rogers, the event title sponsor, had a fully operating store on site while Rexall, the centre naming rights sponsor, handed out free branded bags and offered visitors a healthy ten-minute massage.[22]

Personal Selling

L7 **Personal selling** involves the two-way flow of communication between a buyer and seller, often face-to-face, or facilitated through communication devices, to influence an individual or group purchase-decision. Unlike advertising, personal selling is usually face-to-face communication, although telephone and electronic communication is also used.

In Canada, more than 4 million people are employed in sales- and service-related positions.[23] Included in this number are manufacturing sales

a multitude of approaches that range from simple ad mentions in brochures, to banner placement at events, to the naming of the event itself. An example of event marketing and sponsorship can be seen with the annual international tennis tournament hosted by Tennis Canada—the Rogers Cup. In 2009, the Rogers Cup women's tennis tournament, played at the Rexall Centre at the York University campus,

---

Baskin-Robbins Creates Buzz at Toronto Fashion Week

Fashion and ice cream—what's the connection? Just ask Baskin-Robbins, whose Indulgence That Fits campaign hit Toronto Fashion Week as the inspiration for celebrity designer Pat McDonagh's Spring Collection. Better known for designing clothes for the Beatles, Princess Diana, Veronica Tennant, and Grace Jones, McDonaugh's collection had the fashion industry buzzing about this whimsical, uplifting collection with hats that looked like ice cream cakes!

Social media, in-store posters, and press releases sent people to Baskin-Robbins' Facebook page to win VIP tickets to Toronto Fashion Week, including hotel and travel. Contestants had to submit name suggestions for two of the dresses in the Pat McDonagh 2010 Spring Collection. The winning names were Cherry Poppins and Decadent Diva! Social media was central to the campaign's

success with the Baskin-Robbins Facebook page announcing the contest to an already well-established fan base that today has over 33,000 fans. Periodically, online videos were posted that focused on the Pat McDonagh connection, showing a behind-the-scenes glimpse of the collection and subtly promoting the campaign and Baskin-Robbins. This created an interesting, newsworthy story for the brand, which helped create additional buzz with the media![24]

Questions

1. What was the objective of the Toronto Fashion Week connection for Baskin-Robbins?

2. Navigate to the Baskin-Robbins Facebook page in Canada. What recent consumer promotions are they running and how are they interacting with their fans?

relationship selling

The practice of building long-term loyalty from customers based on a salesperson's attention and commitment to customer needs over time

word-of-mouth marketing

The spread of positive messages about a product by listening to consumers, identifying influential individuals that can spread the word, and making it easier for them to do so

personnel, real estate brokers, stockbrokers, and salesclerks who work in retail stores. In reality, virtually every occupation that involves customer contact has an element of personal selling with the salespeople representing the company. **Relationship selling** is the practice of building long-term loyalty from customers based on a salesperson's attention and commitment to customer needs over time.

The personal selling process consists of six stages: prospecting, pre-approach, approach, presentation, close, and follow-up as detailed in Figure 12–8.

Alternative Marketing Communication Approaches

Marketing communications is often avoided by consumers who view it suspiciously and as a general annoyance. Marketers turn to alternative approaches to help deal with this avoidance, using word-of-mouth marketing techniques and product placement or branded entertainment initiatives to strengthen communications.

ask yourself

1. What are the differences between advertising and public relations?

2. Which promotional tools can generate immediate, short-term responses?

3. What are the stages in the personal selling process?

Word-of-Mouth Marketing Word-of-mouth communications is based on transparent and honest communication. It starts with organizations understanding where, when, and how opinions are being shared by listening and responding to supporters, detractors, and neutrals. **Word-of-mouth marketing** works by listening to consumers, identifying influential individuals, providing important information, and making it easier for them to spread the word.

Figure 12–8

Stages and objectives in the personal selling process

Stage	Objective	Comments
1. Prospecting	Search for and qualify prospects	Start of the selling process; prospects generated through advertising, referrals, and cold canvassing
2. Pre-approach	Gather information and decide how to approach the prospect	Information sources include personal observation, other customers, and company salespeople
3. Approach	Gain prospect's attention, stimulate interest, and make transition to the presentation	First impression is critical; gain attention and interest through references to common acquaintances, a referral, or product demonstration
4. Presentation	Begin converting a prospect into a customer by creating a desire for the product or service	Different presentation formats are possible; involving the customer is critical; responding to objections is key; a professional ethical approach is needed
5. Close	Obtain a purchase commitment from the prospect and secure a customer	Salesperson asks for the order; different approaches include the trial close and assumptive close; trial close can be used at any stage
6. Follow-up	Ensure that the customer is satisfied with the product or service	Resolve any problems faced by the customer to ensure customer satisfaction and future sales possibilities

Word-of-mouth communications typically works on three levels. On a *viral level*, it tries to create buzz through public relations events and social media that seed fun and interesting messages with influential people that spread the word. On a *grassroots level*, it identifies key communities, opinion leaders, and product advocates who get personally involved with the brand and have the ability to influence others. Online or offline community groups help in this regard. On a *professional level*, official referral programs may be put in place to reward satisfied customers who refer the brand to their friends and contacts.[25]

One of the best examples of successful word-of-mouth marketing is the group buying phenomenon pioneered by the company Groupon. Groupon, whose memorable name is a hybrid of the words *group* and *coupon*, started in 2008 in the U.S. Within a year, it had an e-mail database of over 1.5 million people and saved recipients $50 million. By 2010, the company was in 35 countries and its word-of-mouth tell-a-friend program reached more than 50 million subscribers. It recently brushed off a $6 billion takeover bid from Google and, as of press time, is expected to go public or look for future investors.

This is how it works. Instead of clipping coupons, subscribers receive daily a local deep-discounted deal from Groupon via e-mail or through their Twitter and Facebook feeds. Subscribers designate their location and the deals start rolling in.

Deals go live only when enough people have purchased the offer. Customers are encouraged to pass the deal onto others. For small businesses, Groupon helps reach local customers who may not be aware of their products. Deals are time-sensitive, come in limited quantities, and need to be redeemed within a few months.[26]

Product Placement and Branded Entertainment

The fact that consumers avoid TV ads by muting the sound, changing the channel, or leaving the room is encouraging marketers to include products in TV shows and movies. This can be done through **product placement**, the inclusion of a product such as a soft drink in a movie or TV program, or the creation of an entire TV episode around a brand, which is referred to as **branded entertainment**. When Coca-Cola pays *American Idol* to display its product on set in front of the judges, this is an example of product placement. When Embassy Suites hotels pays the reality series *The Apprentice* to create an episode focused on its hotels, this is branded entertainment.

Unique Online Tools

L⑧ While online advertising approaches were discussed earlier in this chapter, the Internet has a number of unique online tools that marketers use to engage individuals. These are namely search engine marketing, social network marketing, affiliate marketing, e-mail marketing, and mobile marketing.

Search engine marketing (SEM) is an Internet marketing approach that includes two areas: (1) search engine optimization and (2) pay-per-click advertising. **Search engine optimization (SEO)** looks at website design, technical coding, written content, incoming links, and website updates to ensure that websites are highly rated and properly indexed by search engines such as Google and Bing. Marketers often work with specialists to maximize search engine optimization. (For a pay-per-click refresher, see page 277.)

When it comes to websites, their design and content is central to successful ranking on the search engines and clear communications. Content needs to be fresh and frequently updated, thus the inclusion of blogs in many websites as a means of routinely adding fresh new content. Visual website appeal is also important. Consumers decide to click on a web page within seconds, therefore content and visual appeal needs to work together to present an appealing proposition.

Microsites are promotional websites created for short-term promotional purposes, often providing consumers with the ability to enter contests and access promotional offers. **Corporate websites** are important destination sites for consumers and the media that want to quickly access company and product information.

Social network marketing refers to the use of online communities or social networks to openly interact with the communities by sharing ideas, activities, events, and offers. Facebook, YouTube, and Twitter are examples of popular social networks, while numerous sports forums exist for fans to exchange ideas on players and teams. ShesConnected.com, shespeaks.com, and iVillage.com are examples of popular online communities where women share and exchange ideas. LinkedIn is a social network for business professionals.

Affiliate marketing is the term used when companies promote their businesses through a network of online associates (affiliates) to drive traffic, leads, and purchases. Affiliates are provided with ads and links to the business website and rewarded with

The Childhood Cancer Foundation uses websites, postcards, and word of mouth to communicate with educators.

commissions for resultant business. Amazon.com and Indigo Books & Music use this business model, providing affiliates with online ads and links to display on their own websites or blogs.

Mobile marketing refers to Internet marketing through mobile devices such as cellphones or tablet computers. It can use mobile apps, e-mail campaigns, text messaging, or quick response codes to communicate with consumers on a local level.

E-mail marketing includes the use of opt-in e-mail lists where consumers register and give permission to receive online communications. The Groupon phenomenon, mentioned earlier in this chapter, is such an example. The Canadian Marketing Association (CMA) strictly advises members not to use spam. **Permission-based e-mail** is when a recipient chooses to receive e-mail from a marketer, while **spam** is unsolicited e-mail that clutters the Internet.

Planning and Evaluation

Designing Marketing Communication Programs

L⑨ Marketing communications can be a fun yet daunting task for marketers. Its subjective nature and the ability of social media to make or break a campaign can make it daunting.

> **"***Microsites are promotional websites created for short-term promotional purposes.***"**

However, the creativity required to pull it together, and the ability of metrics to measure success, can make it rewarding.

Marketers turn to marketing communication experts to navigate this terrain. Communication agencies provide expertise on communication approaches with access to insights on new opportunities, consumer trends, and media research. They help guide strategy development, creative development, and media planning and buying, as well as program evaluation. Marketers shape the backdrop by providing company, product, and target market information, as well as insights into product positioning, previous campaigns, the competition, and budgetary constraints. They explain the balance between consumer and trade promotion, as well as how push and pull strategies are used. They are also involved in program creation and evaluation.

A **push strategy** is when marketers focus communication efforts on the distribution channel to gain support from retailers, distributors, and wholesalers through listings, sales, merchandising, featured pricing, and the inclusion in flyers. A **pull strategy** is when marketers focus communication efforts on ultimate consumers to build awareness, trial, and demand for a product. These approaches should work together (see Figure 12–9).

The Customer Advocacy Funnel

Marketers use integrated marketing communications approaches to ensure that all communication elements speak with the same messaging and use a shared visual platform. This approach involves developing, executing, and evaluating each element of a promotional program so that it encourages customers to

push strategy
When marketers focus communication on the distribution channel to gain support from retailers, distributors, and wholesalers

pull strategy
When marketers focus communication efforts on ultimate consumers to build awareness, trial, and demand for a product

Figure 12–9
Push and pull communication strategies

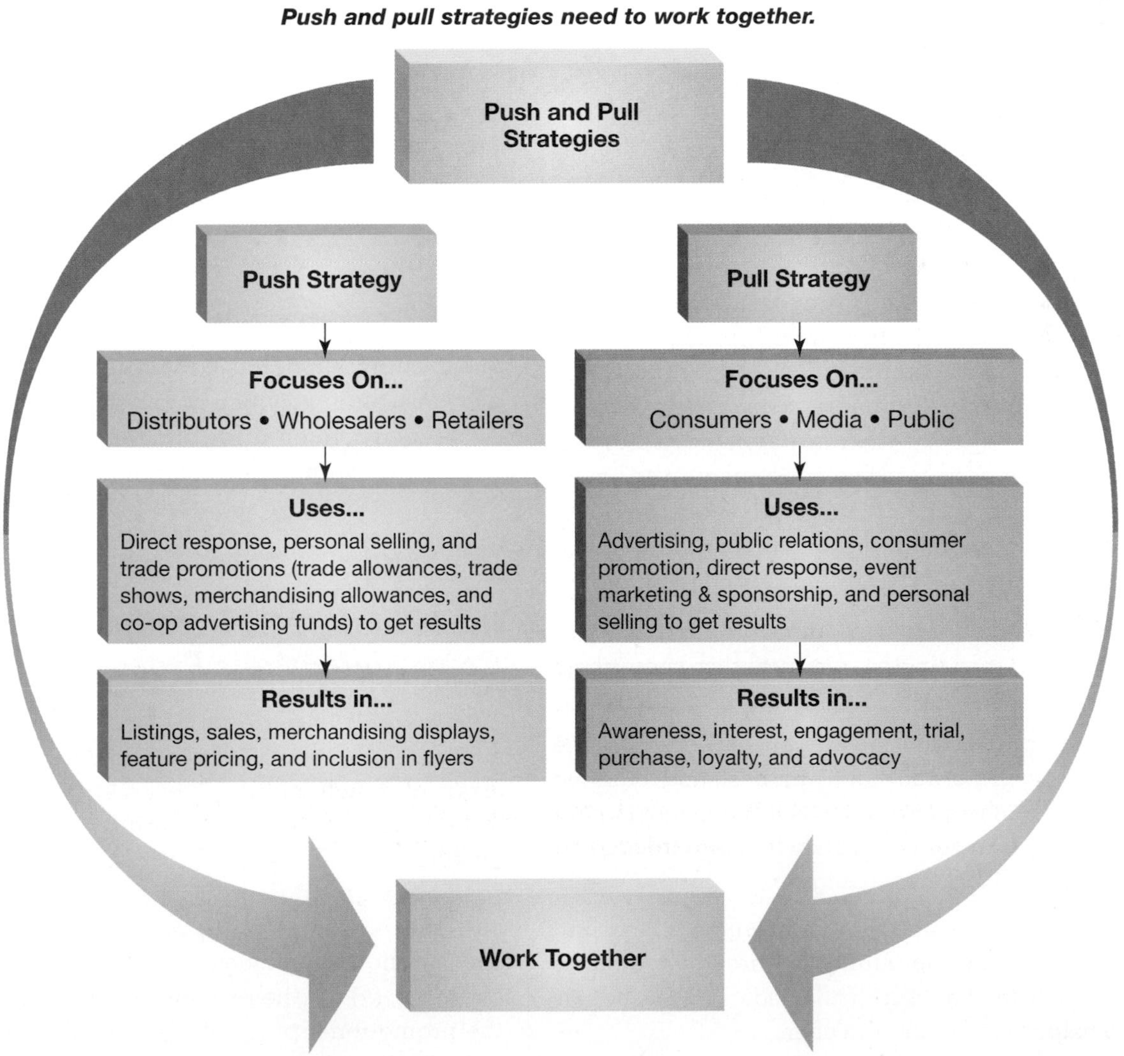

Push and pull strategies need to work together.

Push and Pull Strategies

Push Strategy

Focuses On...
Distributors • Wholesalers • Retailers

Uses...
Direct response, personal selling, and trade promotions (trade allowances, trade shows, merchandising allowances, and co-op advertising funds) to get results

Results in...
Listings, sales, merchandising displays, feature pricing, and inclusion in flyers

Pull Strategy

Focuses On...
Consumers • Media • Public

Uses...
Advertising, public relations, consumer promotion, direct response, event marketing & sponsorship, and personal selling to get results

Results in...
Awareness, interest, engagement, trial, purchase, loyalty, and advocacy

Work Together

Customer Advocacy Funnel
A communications approach that takes consumers down a path of initial product awareness through to brand advocacy

retargeted ads
Display ads that ad networks re-deliver to a computer's IP address when a consumer previously clicked on an ad but did not respond to its contents

Figure 12–10
The Customer Advocacy Funnel

- **Awareness**: A company trying to raise online product awareness may use a website, search engine optimization, online video, and display ads to drive consumers to an online destination.
- **Interest**: Interesting product attributes are highlighted to entice potential customers to learn more.
- **Engagement**: Potential customers are invited to participate in the product experience and interact with its marketing.
- **Trial**: Customers obtain free samples or purchase the product as a limited trial or download.
- **Purchase**: Positive product experiences lead to product purchase.
- **Loyalty**: Ongoing positive product experiences lead to repeat purchases.
- **Advocacy**: Loyal customers are rewarded with additional experiences and become advocates who recommend the product to others.

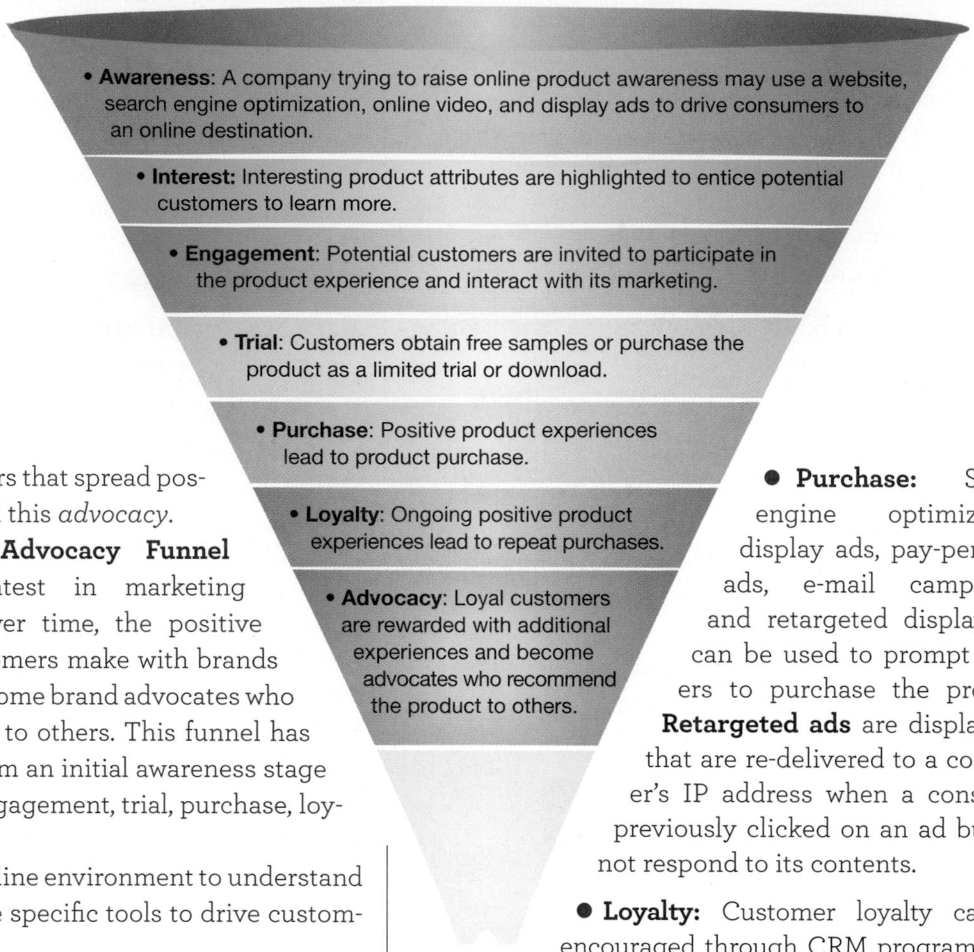

become loyal supporters that spread positive messages. We call this *advocacy*.

The **Customer Advocacy Funnel** encompasses the latest in marketing approaches where, over time, the positive connections that customers make with brands encourage them to become brand advocates who recommend the brand to others. This funnel has consumers moving from an initial awareness stage through to interest, engagement, trial, purchase, loyalty, and advocacy.

Let's look at the online environment to understand how marketers can use specific tools to drive customers through the funnel.

- **Awareness:** A company trying to raise online product awareness may use a website, search engine optimization, and online video within the website (recognizing that it is more likely to surface in a search engine result than text alone). Display ads may also be used to drive consumers to the website, research showing these ads boost product awareness, which often results in an online search at a later time.

- **Interest:** A company may turn to online video to increase interest in the product, this time using experts to demo the product and add credibility.

- **Engagement:** Social media can be added to the mix to generate additional interest and buzz on networks such as Facebook, YouTube, and Twitter. Microsites with contests can help integrate marketing communications messages.

- **Trial:** Contests, samples, free downloads, and limited trials can be communicated through microsites and social media with display ads and online ads also helping to feature the offers.

- **Purchase:** Search engine optimization, display ads, pay-per-click ads, e-mail campaigns, and retargeted display ads can be used to prompt viewers to purchase the product. **Retargeted ads** are display ads that are re-delivered to a computer's IP address when a consumer previously clicked on an ad but did not respond to its contents.

- **Loyalty:** Customer loyalty can be encouraged through CRM programs that reward continued purchases. Social media can help encourage interaction with the brand.

- **Advocacy:** Ongoing communications, often one-to-one, through e-mail newsletters, social networks, branded communities, and blogs can solidify connections with loyal customers, providing them with information and experiences they can share with others.

Steps in the Marketing Communications Process

Today, with the multitude of communication tools available, and consumers fragmented over a wide array of touch points, marketers follow an integrated approach to marketing communications, making sure all elements work together to reach specific target audiences. The steps in this process, outlined in Figure 12–11, require a marketer to (1) specify the IMC objectives, (2) identify the target audience, (3) set the promotional budget, (4) design the promotional program, (5) schedule and run the elements, and (6) evaluate the program and recommend changes. These steps are explained in further detail below.

Step 1: Specify the IMC Objectives

The first step formalizes the purpose of the promotional program, such as building brand awareness, creating customer engagement, or increasing brand loyalty. Specific numerical targets are often included at this point and used later to evaluate the program. The Customer Advocacy Funnel noted opposite may help determine these objectives.

Step 2: Identify the Target Audience

The second step pinpoints the audience that is to be targeted by the promotional program, identifying geographic, demographic, psychographic, and behavioural data. Media information is also provided, as well as insights on the consumer touch points. **Consumer touch points** are the points of interaction that can be used to connect with consumers, including personal time in the home, shopping time, workplace situations, social situations, travel time, and even face-to-face product time.

Step 3: Set the Promotional Budget

Determining the budget is no easy task, particularly since the program has yet to be recommended. Marketers generally allocate an initial amount based on prior years' spending and profit requirements. This is then adjusted once the promotional program is finalized and approved.

Step 4: Design the Promotional Program

The key component of a promotional program is its messaging. It needs to be visible, resonate with its target audience, and be memorable—no easy task! Media and creative teams work hand-in-hand at this point to share ideas to ensure that opportunities are not overlooked and that the best possible promotional mix is created. The creative team brainstorms on programs that engage the target market, while media experts conduct thorough analyses to bring forward ideas and communication platforms that will effectively and efficiently reach target audiences. The **promotional mix** refers to the selection of promotional tools used to communicate with a target market. It can encompass online and offline approaches and include advertising, public relations, sales promotion, direct response, event marketing and sponsorship, and personal selling.

consumer touch points
The points of interaction that can be used to connect with consumers, including personal time in the home, shopping time, workplace situations, social situations, travel time, and even face-to-face product time

promotional mix
The selection of promotional tools used to communicate with a target market

Figure 12–11
Steps in the marketing communications process

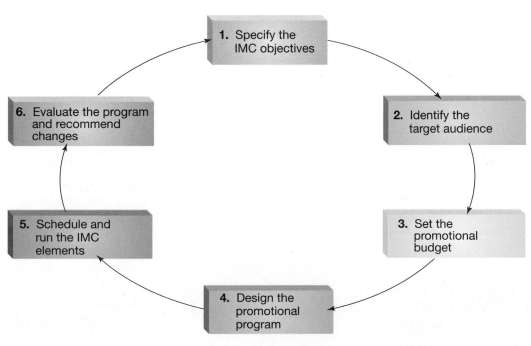

1. Specify the IMC objectives
2. Identify the target audience
3. Set the promotional budget
4. Design the promotional program
5. Schedule and run the IMC elements
6. Evaluate the program and recommend changes

Figure 12–12
Product life cycle considerations for promotional programs

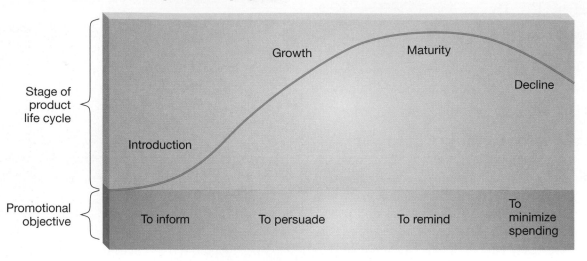

When determining the promotional program, marketers carefully consider their product's life cycle and the competitive nature of the market so that their programs are different, engaging, and meaningful to target markets (see Figure 12–12). Product life cycle considerations include the knowledge that during introductory stages, marketing communication builds awareness, provides information, and encourages trial. In the growth stage, promotional focus changes and starts to persuade and differentiate the brand from the competition. In the maturity stage, promotional efforts are designed as a reminder of the brand and to encourage repeat purchases through special offers. The decline stage often has little to no promotion at all.

Step 5: Schedule and Run the IMC Elements

The sequencing of promotional elements is carefully planned so that individual aspects seamlessly work together to communicate with target audiences. Awareness is the prime concern of any program, built during its early stages with the subsequent rollout of different elements to support and develop the program. Throughout the campaign, marketers carefully monitor developments, particularly in social media, to immediately answer questions, respond to comments, and carefully deal with negative feedback.

Step 6: Evaluate the Program and Recommend Changes

Promotional programs are evaluated on four levels. First, messaging is often evaluated before a program is fully developed to gauge responses so that adjustments can be made before launch.

Second, once the program is live, research may be fielded to measure campaign awareness and messaging elements such as *likeability*, *message comprehension*, and *attitude changes* toward the brand.

Third, upon completion, each individual element will be evaluated against expectations. Online aspects may look to click-throughs, unique visitors, page views, time-on-site, and return on investment (ROI). Social media campaigns may be evaluated on the basis of social mentions, buzz, sharing levels, and fans. Public relations efforts may be measured on publicity mentions and media equivalency values. Offline approaches may refer back to the *awareness*, *likeability*, *message comprehension*, and *attitude changes* mentioned earlier.

Fourth, the promotional program will be evaluated against its objectives. This will look at business results such as sales, profitability, market share, and return on investment (ROI).

All of these metrics will be used to determine campaign success and what elements can be strengthened in the future.

ask yourself

1. What are the stages in the Customer Advocacy Funnel?

2. What approaches are used to set the promotional budget?

3. How are marketing communications programs evaluated?

[*adAlyze*]

What is this ad trying to communicate?

This delicious snack will go straight to your bones.

Who is the target audience for this ad?

Check out the Mott's Fruitsations website at www.mottsfruitsations.ca and recommend an IMC campaign for its product line.

BONE HEALTH

NEW MOTT'S FRUITSATIONS.* ✚

WE'VE TAKEN OUR TASTY MOTT'S FRUITSATIONS MADE WITH REAL FRUIT AND FORTIFIED THEM WITH THE ESSENTIAL NUTRIENTS YOU NEED. CHOOSE FROM HARVEST APPLE WITH CALCIUM FOR STRONG BONES, OR APPLE POMEGRANATE WITH ANTIOXIDANTS FOR YOUR OVERALL HEALTH. IT'S A PERFECTLY DELICIOUS, PERFECTLY HEALTHY SNACK.

*TRADEMARK, USED UNDER LICENSE BY CANADA DRY MOTT'S INC.

Summary...just the facts

- The marketing communications industry consists of the media, marketing communications agencies, research companies, associations, and regulatory bodies.

- Media choices include TV, Internet, newspaper, magazine, radio, out-of-home/transit, and mobile marketing.

- The marketing communications industry is regulated by Advertising Standards Canada (ASC), the Competition Bureau, the Canadian Radio-television and Telecommunications Commission (CRTC), and the Canadian Marketing Association (CMA).

- Marketing communications approaches can include inbound and outbound approaches with marketers commonly using an integrated marketing communications approach (IMC).

- Marketing communication tools include advertising, public relations, sales promotion, direct response, event marketing and sponsorship, and personal selling.

- Public relations initiatives include press releases, press conferences, special events, company reports, and the use of social media.

- Consumer promotional tools include contests, sweepstakes, samples, free trials, loyalty programs, rebates, bonus packs, and point-of-sale materials.

- Trade promotions include trade shows, trade allowances, merchandising allowances, and co-op advertising.

- Direct-response marketing tools include face-to-face selling, direct mail, catalogues, telemarketing, and direct-response advertising on TV/radio/print, as well as e-mail marketing, online ads, and social media interactions.

- Event marketing and sponsorship refers to the involvement of a brand in an event through either an advertising package or on-site involvement.

- The personal selling process consists of six stages: prospecting, pre-approach, approach, presentation, close, and follow-up.

- Alternative marketing communication approaches include word-of-mouth marketing, product placement, and branded entertainment.

- Unique online approaches include the use of corporate websites, microsites, social networks, affiliate marketing, mobile marketing, and e-mail marketing, as well as search engine marketing (SEM) and search engine optimization (SEO).

- A push strategy directs promotional programs to distributors, wholesalers, or retailers. A pull strategy involves directs promotional efforts to ultimate consumers.

- The Consumer Advocacy Funnel is the path a consumer follows from awareness to interest, engagement, trial, purchase, loyalty, and advocacy.

- Creating promotional programs requires a marketer to (1) specify the IMC objectives, (2) identify the target audience, (3) set the promotional budget, (4) design the promotional program, (5) schedule and run the IMC elements, and (6) evaluate the program.

- Evaluation approaches look at the program in general as well as each individual element.

Key Terms and Concepts...a refresher

Hands-on...*apply your knowledge*

Promotion Assignment The Childhood Cancer Foundation (CCFC) is looking at the latest online approaches to determine whether it should be considering any opportunities. Review the opening vignette on the CCFC, navigate to its website at www.childhoodcancer.ca, and think about the approaches mentioned in this chapter. Brainstorm on ways to encourage increased participation in their gala fundraisers including new online approaches that may be appropriate. Outline the following factors: *IMC objectives, characteristics of the target market*, the *promotional idea*, the *promotional mix* you are recommending, and identify how the promotion will be *evaluated*. Assume you have very limited funds.

Reality Check...*reminder*

Refer back to this chapter's opening vignette and answer the Reality Check questions on page 264.

Mc Graw Hill connect

Connect allows you to practise important concepts at your own pace and on your own schedule, with 24/7 online access to an eBook, practice quizzes, video cases, chapter application questions, discussion activities, Internet exercises, interactivities, study tools, and more.

chapter 13

Customer Relationship *management*

Over the last few years, customer relationship management (CRM) has surfaced as a valuable tool rooted in database technology, allowing marketers to use specific information on individual customers in order to deliver superior customer value. Four Seasons Hotels and Resorts is an excellent example of an organization that has been delivering superior customer service and practising CRM successfully.

Four Seasons Hotels and Resorts is a luxury hotel chain consisting of 84 hotels that can be found in 34 countries around the world, with a staff of 35,000 employees. Founder Isadore Sharp has spent decades developing a culture in which all employees, right down to frontline staff, are empowered to take responsibility and make decisions, rather than exclusively relying on orders from management. Mr. Sharp says that culture has to start from the top, the person who really is able to control and make the decisions to reinforce the culture in a meaningful way. "That's not done by sending out a lot of memos and reading books about what people should be doing. It's really acting out how you expect people to behave. It's that old expression of 'walking the talk' or acting on core values." In dealing with employees and guests, Four Seasons is guided by the philosophy that is summed up in the golden rule, a version of which can be found in most world belief systems. The rule, "do unto others as you would have them do unto you," really boils down to treating people the way you would like to be treated. Mr. Sharp says that it's not difficult for employees to make decisions when they have that as their guideline.

Because people all over the world are familiar with the golden rule, it makes it easier for employees of Four Seasons in many countries to relate to.

One aspect of customer relationship management is to put information about the customer into a database so that is available for employees to refer to at any time. Mr. Sharp says that he wants to give the customer a memorable experience. Part of this experience means that the customers' preferences are recognized when they return to the hotel. Customers' likes, dislikes, or idiosyncrasies are put into the database so that they can be referred to in their next visit. For example, if a fruit basket is sent to a first-time guest's room and is not eaten, an employee will jot this down into the database so that the next time around, fruit will not be sent to the room. If that piece of information was not documented, and fruit was sent to the room again on the next visit, the guest may conclude that the hotel is wasting fruit by sending it to his or her room.

Four Seasons is a luxury hotel and guests expect and receive a high quality of personal service. Given their pressured lifestyles and a scarcity of time, nothing matters more to affluent guests and nothing is more difficult for hotels to deliver than personal service. Luxury hotel guests have high expectations.

LEARNING OBJECTIVES

LO 1 Define the concept of customer relationship management (CRM)

LO 2 Describe how CRM entails cultural changes

LO 3 Discuss the role of social media in CRM

LO 4 Describe customer retention and give examples of various loyalty programs

LO 5 Define data mining and customer lifetime value, and explain why each is important

LO 6 Explain the worth of retaining marginal customers and outline the process of customer reacquisition

They need 24-hour support: an assurance that whatever the hour or the request, it will be responded to quickly by someone who takes responsibility to carry through. They also expect exceptional promptness and accuracy: getting things right the first time and recovering well when mistakes occur. Four Seasons delivers on these benefits on a guest's timeline, not the organization's.

The following is one of many examples of Four Seasons' caring attitude and stellar customer service. A receptionist at Four Seasons Washington answered a telephone call from a woman who needed directions to get to the hotel. It was a rainy evening and the guest was late for an important meeting. The receptionist tried giving her directions but quickly realized that the guest was having trouble comprehending them. The receptionist then proceeded to guide the guest on the phone for the next 30 minutes, thus becoming her personal GPS system. This caring attitude runs throughout the organization.

When asked whether the hotel has loyalty programs such as Air Miles, Mr. Sharp said that giving a guest great personal service is the best loyalty program as opposed to giveaways. Personal service may be the single most-powerful weapon in a company's competitive arsenal because it is so important to consumers but it's so difficult to deliver. Superior personal service is where Four Seasons excels over its competition.

In the early years, it quickly became apparent to Mr. Sharp that offering a new level of service demanded methods of operation that were equally new and different, including how staff would be selected, trained, and provided with an environment that allowed them to excel. What Four Seasons calls its "unique service culture" is based on a series of insights and beliefs about the person who provides the act of service, and the one who receives it. The first insight is about the people themselves, namely that the desire to serve others with a positive attitude is innate, there to be discovered, and not taught by the hiring organization. As Mr. Sharp has observed, "Those few moments of service delivery are the company's make or break point when reputation is either confirmed or denied. And the outcome in our industry normally depends on frontline employees: doormen, bellmen, waiters, housekeepers—the lowest-paid people, and often in too many companies, the least motivated. Most companies hire for experience and appearance, how the applicants fit the company image. We hire for attitude. We want people who like other people and are, therefore, more motivated to serve them. Competence we can teach. Attitude is ingrained."

This thoughtful recruiting is a core aspect of Four Seasons' unique service culture, including multiple interviews for every position. In a hotel, the last interview is with the general manager or hotel manager. The goal is to find candidates with the personal qualities and values described above. Pride of association with the best, pride in the quality of one's work, and one's ability to contribute to a team are other key characteristics sought in this process.

For many years, Four Seasons has taken care to select employees who have these qualities. They are successful people serving successful people in a way that is genuine and unpretentious. Today's affluent travellers come in a wide variety of ages and backgrounds. Their definition of great service is personal—what feels appropriate and comfortable to them. They are less impressed by the trappings of traditional elegance, less likely to mistake formality or pretension for being well-served.

Why do Four Seasons employees go the extra mile for guests? Part of the reason is that they are in turn respected by their managers and thus have incentive to please the guests. Mr. Sharp says, "Supervisors need to be prepared to listen to their employees and give them an opportunity to participate in a meaningful way. You have to be sincere in the way you deal with people." Mr. Sharp saw a causal link between the way a hotel treated its employees and the way employees treated their guests. Rather than treating its employees as disposable, Four Seasons distinguished itself by hiring more for attitude than experience, by establishing career paths and promotion from within, and by paying as much attention to employee complaints as guests' complaints. Because employees are working in this positive environment, the turnover for Four Seasons' employees is a fraction of the industry rate. It's no secret that the Four Seasons Hotels and Resorts chain has been voted by its employees as one of *Fortune* magazine's "100 best companies to work for." Since the inception of the award, Four Seasons has been nominated 14 years in a row. 🍎

As you read Chapter 13, refer back to the Four Seasons vignette to answer the following questions:

- CRM entails cultural changes. Does Four Seasons have to institute cultural changes or is it fine as is? Explain.

- What customer retention strategies does Four Seasons use?

reality CHECK

This chapter's focus is on customer relationship management (CRM), and its three components: customer acquisition, customer retention, and customer reacquisition.

Customer Relationship Management

LO 1 **Customer relationship management (CRM)** is the overall process of building and maintaining profitable customer relationships by delivering superior customer value and satisfaction.[1]

The Core: Chapter 13

Marketers use customer relationship management tools to create marketing programs that satisfy customers.

Customer Relationship Management

Customer relationship management involves three stages: customer acquisition, customer retention, and customer reacquisition.

CRM focuses on using information about customers to create marketing programs that result in customer satisfaction. The heart of a CRM program is information technology and database systems. However, for CRM to be successful there must be attitude changes in the organization. This point will be covered in the next few pages. CRM originally started out as a tool to help the sales force keep track of customers and prospects.

A large corporation may spend tens of millions of dollars on a CRM system. Among the big suppliers are Oracle, SAP, and IBM; dozens of other companies specialize in components such as telephone call centre technology, database software, and Internet systems. The whole idea is to customize each system to a specific company's needs.

Call your local bank about your chequing account and you may discover that the person on the phone is looking at a screen that summarizes your previous calls and displays information about your mortgage and credit card as well. That's an example of CRM. Log on to Amazon.ca and you may find a personalized list of suggested books based on your previous purchases, as well as books that have appealed to readers who have bought the same books as you. That's another example of CRM.

amazon.ca

Generally, CRM is seen as a system for funnelling information to one place that otherwise would be dispersed in a big company. This allows all employees to access one customer profile instead of bits and pieces of information about the customer scattered throughout the company.

A concept similar to CRM is a process called **customer experience management (CEM)**. It's defined as managing customer interactions to build brand equity and improve long-term profitability.[2]

CEM's main focus is exclusively on customer interactions or touch points. **Touch points** are just another way to describe customer interactions with the brand or company.

Customer interactions include every point in which the customer interacts with a business, product, or service. For the Starbucks customer, it includes the anticipation of going to Starbucks, walking up to a shop, opening the door, ordering and paying for the coffee, talking to the

customer relationship management (CRM) The overall process of building and maintaining profitable customer relationships by delivering superior customer value and satisfaction

customer experience management (CEM) Managing customer interactions to build brand equity and improve long-term profitability

touch point Any situation in which a customer comes into contact with a brand or company

server, getting the coffee, and sitting down in the relaxed atmosphere of the shop to enjoy the coffee.

Apple knows that customers dislike the touch point that consists of impersonal technical support calls. Instead, Apple resolves this problem by creating "genius bars" that offer face-to-face help at the Apple Store.

Companies should measure and improve customer interactions on an ongoing basis. Levels of customer satisfaction at each touch point can be a better measure of customer loyalty than just measuring overall customer satisfaction. It starts by understanding and listing each individual interaction or touch point that influences customer satisfaction. Whether human (such as sales staff or a call centre), interactive (such as websites, e-mail, or Twitter), or static (such as radio or newspaper ads), each touch point is an opportunity to improve customer experience.[3]

It has been estimated that in a 200- to 300-room luxury hotel, there are as many as 5,000 interactions between guests and staff per day; in other words, thousands of opportunities for high performance or for mishaps. As the opening vignette shows, Four Seasons Hotels and Resorts excels in making its interactions with guests very positive.[4]

Here is an example of a company using CEM and touch points to maintain profitable relationships with its customers. Canadian Pacific Hotels (CP Hotels) was not well-regarded by business travellers, a notoriously demanding and diverse group to serve, but also very lucrative and much coveted by other hotel chains. By investing time and money in learning what would most satisfy this segment, the company discovered that customers wanted recognition of their individual preferences and lots of flexibility with check-ins and check-outs. CP Hotels mapped each step of customer interactions from check-in to check-out, and set a standard of performance for each activity. Along the way, the management structure was revamped so that each hotel had a champion with broad cross-functional ability to ensure that the hotel lived up to its ambitious goals.[5]

Ideally, CEM information is analyzed to gain insight into each customer's needs and behaviour, and then it is used to improve the customer's dealings with the company. This can be as simple as freeing the customer from having to repeat his mailing address every time he places an order, to something like being able to instantly tell the customer the status of a shipment. The analysis might guide promotion efforts so that the customer receives mailings, calls, e-mails, or website advertising tailored to his likes.

> *Listening to customers is as important as—if not more important than—talking to them.*

CRM Entails Cultural Changes

CRM databases allow companies to get closer to their customers to establish a mutually beneficial relationship. A company's failure with CRM is often the result of approaching CRM as a software project rather than an overall company strategy. A company may spend millions of dollars on software, but doesn't bother changing the cultural attitudes of the organization. A company may be looking for a quick fix for its problems. Companies feel that if they purchase CRM software, their problems will disappear. Take an example of a hotel that is suffering from poor employee customer service skills. No amount of CRM software by itself will solve the problem. CRM requires a top-down long-run commitment and attitude change by management. For example, if the hotel employees see that management treats them with little respect, there is no incentive for employees to treat customers with respect. One example of practising CRM in a hotel environment is having employees input information about a guest's preferences into a database, such as the number of the pillows that a guest wants. This information should be referred to by the employees the next time the guest returns to the hotel. This results in the guest feeling important and recognized. However, if the hotel employees are feeling unappreciated and have low morale, as a result of not being respected by their supervisors, they may not refer to the database when that guest returns, thus leaving the guest feeling unappreciated.

Apple knows that customers dislike the touch point that consists of impersonal technical support calls. Read the text for details.

Employees who take ownership in what they do have a heightened sense of customer service responsibility.

The cultural attitudes of the organization must change internally to what is called a CRM culture if the company is really interested in instituting positive customer service. Management must learn to "walk the talk." This means, for example, that it's one thing for management to say they appreciate their employees; it's another thing to actually show their appreciation by their actions. Four Seasons Hotels and Resorts, described in the opening vignette, practises CRM successfully because its unique service culture starts with top management and filters right down to the lowest-paid employees. All Four Seasons employees "walk the talk."

Another good example of a company that practises what it preaches is WestJet. Every employee takes ownership in what they do. They have a heightened sense of customer service responsibility uncharacteristic of many employees. WestJet has a series of ads that focuses on WestJet's theme of ownership.

The average business executive goes into CRM thinking it's about technology. If cultural attitudes don't change, employees won't use the system. Without employees using the system, the software becomes useless. The most senior levels of management need to embrace the business strategy of CRM and move the message and tactics of CRM throughout the organization. CEOs need to get the message out to their VPs and have them get it out to their managers, down to supervisors, and down to the front line.

A CRM culture does not come in a box of software. Before installing the tools of CRM, companies need to make sure that they are on their way to establishing a CRM culture. Here are some questions to assess how close the company is to developing a CRM culture.[6]

- Does the company's vision and mission statement reflect a customer-centric sentiment?
- What percentage of employees can state the company's vision or mission statement?
- Do employees complain about customers?
- To what degree do employees feel that they are rewarded (recognition, promotion, compensation) for behaving in a way that has the customer's interests at heart?
- Would the company feel comfortable talking to ten randomly chosen customers about their sales and aftercare experience?

The company should consider the answers to these questions to evaluate the state of the firm's cultural attitudes. The benefits of implementing CRM software are greater if the company adopts a CRM culture.

Customer Service Component of CRM at TD Canada Trust

Customer relationship management entails building and maintaining profitable customer relationships. According to a TD Canada Trust customer loyalty poll, more Canadians want customer service and more are getting it, even if it's just a friendly smile.[7]

But if they don't receive positive customer service, they may not be coming back. Businesses are constantly looking for ways to show customers that they care, such as through reward programs. Many customers appreciate the perks, but according to the findings of the TD Canada Trust loyalty poll, customers want to be treated well. When asked which form of appreciation they are most interested in, 49 percent ranked "just good customer service" as number one. This was followed by just 18 percent who cited reward programs. According to the results, respondents' definition of good service was friendly staff followed by quick and helpful service. For a discussion of another company that values quick and helpful customer service, turn to the Marketing NewsFlash about Zappos on page 309.

> "A CRM CULTURE DOES NOT COME IN A BOX OF SOFTWARE."

Social Media and CRM

L❸ A growing number of companies are keeping track of what's said about their brands on social media platforms such as Facebook and Twitter. This activity falls in line with the process of CRM, because it's an excellent way to build and maintain a relationship with customers. Dell, General Motors, H&R Block, Kodak, and Whole Foods Market are among a growing number of companies monitoring Twitter to see what people are saying about their brands as well as to provide solutions to customers' concerns. The attention to Twitter reflects the power of new social media tools in letting consumers shape public discussion over brands.[8]

A single Twitter message—known informally as a tweet—sent in frustration over a product or a service's performance, can be read by hundreds or thousands of people. Similarly, positive interaction with a representative of the company can help turn an unhappy customer into a more loyal one.

Some companies are also hiring social media analytics consultants to monitor social media sites such as Facebook and Twitter in order to digest and understand what consumers are saying about their brands. These consultants have developed specialized software for their clients to scour these sites in real time and provide actionable insights for smarter business decisions.

Airlines and Social Media

Hotels and airlines were among the first industries to recognize the value of social media platforms such as Twitter and Facebook, and monitor them to respond to angry customers. Increasingly, companies are taking the tactic to a new level, trying to listen in on every mention of their brands, for a real-time gauge of what people think of their offerings, competitors and industry trends.[9]

Airlines are increasingly using Twitter and other tools to deal with customer service issues. Consider this scenario, which actually took place at Porter Airlines. When an unhappy passenger found herself waiting in a check-in line that wasn't moving quickly enough, she tweeted her dissatisfaction from her smartphone. At the same time that this was occurring, Porter Airlines employees were scanning Twitter traffic and came across the woman's complaint. By the time that passenger got to the front of the line, Porter staff were on hand to directly deal with her complaint.[10]

Consumers are increasingly using tools such as Twitter to contact an airline as opposed to the old way of phoning the company. For flyers who have lost luggage or missed a flight, the immediacy of social media–based feedback could render toll-free numbers and website feedback forms obsolete in the near future. In an industry where every airline

---

Online Canadian households that use social networks such as Facebook and Twitter **68%**

Online Canadian households that access social networks weekly **74%**

Online Canadian households that spend six hours or more per week on social networks  **25%**

marketing meter

Source: "NM Incite, a Nielsen-McKinsey Joint Venture, Launches in Canada to Help Companies Use Social Media Intelligence for Superior Business Performance," NM Incite press release, September 8, 2010, accessed at http://ca.nielsen.com/content/dam/nielsen/en_ca/documents/pdf/news_releases/2010/NM%20Incite%20Launches%20in%20Canada.pdf.

Dave Carroll got his revenge when United Airlines broke his guitar. For the complete story, read the text

essentially sells the same commoditized service, airlines that use social media to turn disappointed customers into happy ones, or to simply enhance the travel experience, are already setting themselves apart and building loyalty.

Here's an example of how an airline neglected a customer's problem. United Airlines baggage handlers damaged Halifax songwriter David Carroll's $3,500 custom-made bass guitar on a flight from Halifax to Chicago. Carroll spent nine months seeking compensation by sending e-mails, writing letters, and calling airline representatives, all to no avail. Carroll, deeply frustrated and out of options, wrote a song entitled "United Breaks Guitars" and uploaded it to YouTube. The catchy song went viral, with 150,000 views the day it went live and nearly 10 million since then. United Airlines finally relented and, at Carroll's request, donated the $1,200 he paid for repairs to charity. It's interesting to note that within four days of the song going online, the bad PR caused United Airlines' stock price to suffer a plunge of 10 percent, costing shareholders $180 million.[11]

Credibility Issues of Social Media

One of the temptations for a company is to encourage consumers to say positive things about their brand on a social media platform. For example, Ford promoted its new Fiesta subcompact by letting 100 consumers drive the car for free for six months, gas included. All they had to do was blog, tweet, and post about the car. There exists the possibility that they were more likely to say good things about the car as a result of the freebie, instead of truly giving their unbiased opinions. Credibility can suffer as a result.[12]

Customer Acquisition

Part of the definition of CRM focuses on building customer relationships. Data-driven programs can examine the profiles of a company's most-popular customers and use these characteristics to find prospective customers. After a company has found commonalities among profitable customers, it can use this information to accurately target potential customers with the same profile.

Customer Retention

L④ The CRM definition includes maintaining profitable customer relationships. A company that builds strong relationships with customers will retain these customers, resulting in more sales and profits than the company would have if it focused only on getting new customers. It's important to note that making a sale to a current customer is way less expensive than making a sale to a new customer.

Listening to customers is as important as—if not more important than—talking to them. Some business-to-business (B2B) companies are now making a special effort to ask customers when and how they would like to be contacted by the company. This information is placed in a database so that it is readily available. This practice shows respect for loyal customers' time and allows companies to direct the brand communication in a way that is appropriate.

ask yourself

1. What is customer relationship management all about?

2. Describe how companies are using social media in their relationships with customers.

The increased profitability that is associated with customer retention is due to several factors that occur after a relationship has been established with a customer.[13]

- The cost of acquiring a customer occurs only at the beginning of a relationship, so the longer the relationship, the lower the amortized cost.

- Long-term customers tend to be less inclined to switch, and also tend to be less price-sensitive.

- Long-term customers may initiate word-of-mouth activity and referrals.

Loyalty Programs

One way to retain customers is through **loyalty programs**. It should be noted that all customers should be rewarded, but not all customers are the same. In most product categories, a small number of heavy users account for a large percentage of a brand's sales and profits. Heavy users are customers who buy an above-average amount of a given brand. According to **Pareto's Rule**, a marketing rule of thumb named after Italian economist Vilfredo Pareto, 80 percent of a brand's sales come from 20 percent of its customers. Heavy users should be rewarded differently than light users. The implication here is to take special care of

the 20 percent by offering them better rewards than the remaining 80 percent. Databases allow companies to do more than merely recognize their customers. Companies that surprise and delight their high-profit customers with reward programs are more likely to keep these customers in the long run.

The oldest and best-known loyalty program in Canada is Canadian Tire money. The Air Miles reward program is Canada's largest loyalty program; Air Miles can be earned through more than 100 different sponsors, and there are almost 1,000 different rewards that can be redeemed. BMO Bank of Montreal offers an Air Miles–sponsored program, and CIBC offers an Aeroplan program.

Another large Canadian loyalty program that has been around for a long time is HBC Rewards, first started by Zellers under the name Club Z. Loblaws offers the President's Choice Financial MasterCard, with which consumers can get PC points that can be redeemed for groceries. Finally, the Shoppers Drug Mart Optimum card is a very successful loyalty program. Loyalty programs have become a way for one company to differentiate itself from another.

An example of a loyalty program that recognizes Virgin Atlantic's best customers is its clubhouse in London's Heathrow Airport. Virgin's $21 million clubhouse is an expansive 27,000-square-feet lounge with an equally expansive range of ways for Virgin customers to indulge themselves. In the spa, the customer can get a manicure or pedicure as well as a facial, wet shave, and shoulder massage. With three dining options, refreshments are always at the ready. A customer can while away the time by playing retro video games, watching movies on a 16 × 5 foot screen in the cinema, or heading upstairs to the rooftop garden. The library offers quiet nooks, standard office supplies, and an antique refectory table that came straight from the home of Virgin Chairman Richard Branson.[14]

Another example of a loyalty program is Starwood Hotels & Resorts, which has such brands as Sheraton and Westin. The chain offers a different twist on personalizing a loyalty program. As well as the usual system of accumulating points that can be redeemed for free rooms, preferred-guest program members can use their points to bid for special experiences. The Moments program allows members to take part in online auctions to bid for "insider access" to red-carpet premieres, closed rehearsals with top musicians, private dinners with celebrity chefs, or rounds of golf with PGA Tour pros.[15]

Members of the Moments program can hone their golf skills with a hands-on clinic led by PGA TOUR Professional Jason Gore. Members learn golfing techniques from Gore and then test out their new skills with 18 holes of challenging play, where Jason joins the member for several holes and offers tips along the way.[16]

Canadians Love Their Loyalty Cards

Number of Canadians who have a Shoppers Optimum card	9.9 million
Number of Canadians who have a Cineplex Scene loyalty card	2.5 million
Percentage of Canadians who have at least one loyalty card	94 percent

Sources: Madhavi Acharya-Tom Yew, "With Canadians holding 114 million loyalty cards experts believe points have become a currency," *Toronto Star*, April 1, 2010, accessed at www.thestar.com/special/article/787462--rewarding-experiences; "Movie theatres lure viewers with loyalty programs," *National Post*, Sept. 29, 2010, accessed at http://nationalpost.specialsections.shoplocal.com/canwest/ss/index.aspx?webstoryid=15358211&area=SS&type=page&AdgroupID=133433&Locations=national post; Jacqueline Nunes, "Program is good medicine," *Toronto Star*, April 1, 2010, p. Y4, accessed at www.thestar.com/special/article/787464--program-is-good-medicine.

Another example of a unique loyalty program is HMV with its purehmv program. Over and above giving points to customers to redeem for merchandise, the HMV program offers rewards such as autographed memorabilia, limited-edition products, and celebrity meet-and-greets. One expensive reward recently on offer was a Disturbed-Autographed Schechter Diamond Series Guitar.[17]

In addition to rewarding customers, loyalty programs provide businesses with a wealth of information about their customers. This information is the raw material for data mining, which is discussed in the next section.

Data Mining

L5 How does a company use the reams of information in their databases? One answer is data mining. **Data mining** is an efficient way to sort through large amounts of data to find relationships between variables. It is a process of analyzing customer patterns and insights to make better marketing decisions. Data mining can spot trends and other nuggets of information that the company may not be aware of. Loyalty programs supply a lot of information that can then be used for data mining purposes. Information that customers supply when they apply for a loyalty program can then be tied to their purchase behaviour. Data mining can then be used to find patterns in consumer behaviour and also help marketers with customer segmentation. Read the Marketing NewsFlash opposite for examples of how data mining uncovered segments for Sobeys and Best Buy.

All the data about customers is stored in a central place, called the **data warehouse**. A data warehouse can be thought of as an electronics library where all the information is indexed. Once the data warehouse brings the data together, the company uses data mining techniques to find insights about customers.

Here's an example of data mining in the grocery industry. One grocery chain in the U.S. discovered through data mining that men who bought diapers on Thursday also tended to buy beer at the same time. Further analysis showed that these shoppers typically did their weekly grocery shopping on Saturdays. On Thursday they only bought a few items. The retailer concluded that they purchased the beer to have it available for the upcoming weekend. The grocery chain used this information to increase sales by moving the beer display closer to the diaper display.[18]

A second example is Canadian Tire. Data mining enabled the retailer's credit card division to create psychological profiles of its cardholders that were built upon alarmingly precise correlations. Data mining revealed that cardholders who purchased carbon-monoxide detectors, premium birdseed, and felt pads for the bottoms of their chair legs rarely missed a payment. On the other hand, those who bought cheap motor oil and visited a Montreal pool bar called "Sharx" were a higher risk. "If you show us what you buy, we can tell you who you are, maybe even better than you know yourself," a former Canadian Tire exec said.[19]

A third example of data mining involves Metro, a chain of supermarkets in Ontario and Quebec. Its bottled juices traditionally were placed on the shelves by brand. But data mining information showed that consumers preferred the juices to be shelved by flavour. Metro made the change and sales of juices increased.[20]

ask yourself

1. What is Pareto's Rule?
2. Give some examples of loyalty programs.
3. What is data mining?

Customer Lifetime Value

In customer relationship management, a company focuses on its relationship with customers with the ultimate goal of creating an unbreakable bond with its customers. Companies are starting to focus on the value of a customer if that customer remains loyal to the firm over the customer's lifetime. This is referred to as the **customer lifetime value**.

Carl Sewell, a successful car dealer-owner and author of a book called *Customers for Life*, looks at each customer as an investment. If he can provide

customer lifetime value
The potential sales that will be generated by a customer if the customer remains loyal to that company for a lifetime

marketing NewsFlash

Data Mining Uncovers Valuable Insights at Sobeys and Best Buy

Sobeys and Best Buy are examples of two retailers that are using data mining to better understand their customers. A recent study by market research firm Nielsen revealed that consumers regularly shop at multiple grocery stores. To make sure that Sobeys gets repeat customers in its store, the retailer has turned to highly specific e-mail targeting, sending out 1.4 million different combinations of loyalty offerings to customers who receive e-mail flyers from the retailer. The loyalty offerings can consist of coupons that are tailored to loyalty program information about consumer shopping habits.

Data mining has revealed that Sobeys' customers are divided into five segments, including price consciousness, life stage, lifestyle choices, tendency to entertain, and what kind of shopping trips they take—that is, quick convenience shops or buying the week's groceries. Knowing these customer segments has helped Sobeys avoid situations such as sending Pampers coupons to mothers who do not have a young child in diapers. The industry figure for direct-mail coupon redemption is about 2 percent or lower. Sobeys' targeted mailings have resulted in double-digit redemptions.

Best Buy has also done data mining that revealed five specific types of customers. They are as follows:

- **Barry:** The affluent professional who wants the best technology and entertainment, and who demands excellent service.

- **Jill:** The prototypical "soccer mom" who is a busy suburban mom who wants to enrich her children's lives with technology and entertainment.

- **Carrie and Buzz:** The "early adopter," active, younger customer who wants the latest technology and entertainment.

- **Ray:** The "practical adopter" who is a family man who wants technology that improves his life through technology and entertainment.

- **Mr. Storefront:** The customer who runs his or her own business and has specific needs relating to growing sales and increasing the profitability of the business.

Best Buy researchers then combed through reams of sales and demographic data to determine whether a particular location should be tailored to a specific segment. Nearly 40 percent of stores that were redone were aimed at the "Barry" segment. These stores have separate departments of home theatre systems, knowledgeable salespeople, and specialists in mobile electronics.

The "Jill" segment was eventually broadened to include all females. Research showed that women spend $68 billion on consumer electronics each year and influence 89 percent of all purchases. Unfortunately, females did not embrace the Best Buy experience, largely because its stores were male-oriented in merchandise, appearance, and staffing. "Men and women shop very differently," observed Joe Brandt, a store service manager at one of Best Buy's newest stores. Men "typically love the technology" and they like to "play with it" while women are "looking for a knowledgeable person who can answer their questions in a simple manner." To address this problem Best Buy began to implement many changes that would make Best Buy *the* place for women to shop.

"Jill" stores feature personal shopping assistants who accompany the customer through the store, demonstrate how the products function, and arrange for delivery and installation after the sale. Store layout has been changed to include larger aisles, softer colours, less noise, and reduced visibility of boxes and extra stock. Best Buy has also created rooms in the store that resemble a home to show customers exactly how the products will look when they are installed. According to Brandt, "We try to personalize the experience as much as possible, and we really try to build a relationship. Once we do that, we have the opportunity to really listen and answer questions that customers have."[21]

Questions

1. Have you ever received coupon offers in your e-mail from retailers as a result of you being a member of their loyalty programs? Was the coupon for a product that you were interested in purchasing?

2. Which of the Best Buy segments described above best describes you?

each customer with excellent customer service, that customer will likely remain loyal to Carl's dealership in the future. In a sense, that customer may have a lifetime value to Carl of hundreds of thousands of dollars. Knowing this, Carl keeps an insightful perspective in dealing with customers.[22]

For example, a customer came to pick up his car after servicing and noticed that his tennis racquet, which he had left in the car, was gone. Under normal circumstances, a dealer would say that it is not responsible for items left in a car. Carl Sewell, on the other hand, went over to the customer and apologized for the mishap. He then proceeded to write a cheque for replacement of the racquet. Carl surmised that it was not worth jeopardizing an investment of hundreds of thousands of dollars over the price of a tennis racquet.

A concept very close to customer lifetime value is **share of wallet**. CRM techniques can help marketers get a larger share of a customer's purchases from that company. Here's an example of how a bank can increase its share of wallet. The bank that holds a customer's mortgage and chequing account may learn at some point that the customer has children and may then try to sell the customer a registered education savings plan. Another example of a company increasing share of wallet is Shoppers Drug Mart. A customer with an Optimum card who purchases cosmetics may receive further mailings from Shoppers that offer coupons for related cosmetic products.

The Worth of Retaining Marginal Customers

LO₆ CRM allows firms to use information technology to quantify the value of individual customers in terms of sales and profits. High-value customers are provided with better privileges, discounts, or other inducements. CRM analysis shows that a small proportion

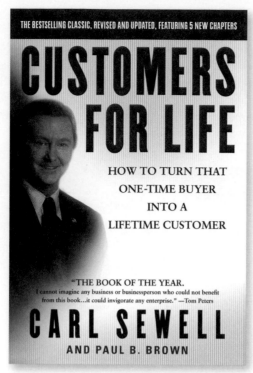

THE BESTSELLING CLASSIC, REVISED AND UPDATED, FEATURING 5 NEW CHAPTERS

CUSTOMERS FOR LIFE

HOW TO TURN THAT ONE-TIME BUYER INTO A LIFETIME CUSTOMER

"THE BOOK OF THE YEAR.
I cannot imagine any business or businessperson who could not benefit from this book...it could invigorate any enterprise." —Tom Peters

CARL SEWELL
AND PAUL B. BROWN

Carl Sewell is the author of the bestseller Customers For Life.

ask yourself

1. Why is customer lifetime value important for companies to calculate?

2. What does share of wallet mean?

of customers contribute to a large percentage of profits, and that many customers are unprofitable. Many firms are beginning to jettison or fire their low-value customers and are focusing their time on their high-valued customers. For example, in July 2007, CNN reported that Sprint had dropped about 1,000 customers who were calling the customer-care centre too frequently—40 to 50 times more than the average customer every month over an extended period.[23]

Firing low-value customers seems to be a commonsense approach, but in some cases there is a danger. If a company is left with only high-value customers, this leaves the company open to poaching by competitors if they are aware of its customer base.

CRM and Customer Reacquisition

Companies are realizing that losing a customer means more than losing a sale. It means losing the entire future stream of purchases that the customer would make over a lifetime of patronage. Customers stop

Survey of Retail Staff Shows Lack of Customer Service Skills

Staff who do not smile	25.9%
Staff who do not meet customers' needs	26.4%
Staff who fail to give a friendly comment once the transaction is complete	25.8%

Source: "Insight customer service: It helps to know the score," *Marketing Week*, January 5, 2006, p. 22.

Zappos — Customer Service at Its Best

Zappos is a well-known Las Vegas shoe retailer that was founded in 1999 to sell shoes online. In ten years, it has expanded to include other products such as handbags and sunglasses, and it has grown to be a $1-billion-per-year business. Customer service has always been a critical part of the Zappos brand. Early on in the history of the company, Zappos made the deliberate decision to divert its marketing budget to customer service.

According to Zappos CEO Tony Hsieh, the ultimate aim of the Zappos brand is to be the very best when it comes to customer service and consumer experience. "Our hope is in ten years people won't even realize we started out selling shoes online," he explains. "We sell clothing and handbags, accessories—even electronics and housewares." He also points out that it doesn't necessarily need to be online. "Twenty to thirty years from now, I wouldn't rule out Zappos Airlines," he said.

Great customer service is not something offered by the majority of companies, and Hsieh suspects a lot of people are frustrated by this. "In the long run, customer service is just good business," he says. "The problem, however, is that the payoff is usually two or three years down the line."

Hsieh is constantly building buzz by participating in social media. He has nearly two million followers on Twitter and he regales these fans with inspirational quotes and whatever else is on his mind.

The following list shows how Zappos differs from other retailers:

- The company provides free shipping both ways.
- Zappos has a 365-day return policy.
- Only products available in the warehouse are placed on the site.
- The warehouse is open 24 hours a day.
- The company is contactable 24 hours a day, 7 days a week.

- The toll-free phone number is prominently placed on every page of the site.
- The company trusts its reps; sales staff don't have scripts.
- If products are unavailable, sales staff direct customers to competitors.

Hsieh firmly believes that what makes Zappos so successful is creating a "wow" experience for the customer and investing in a corporate culture that allows employees freedom and space.[24] ●

Questions

1. Can you think of some Canadian retailers that provide excellent customer service?

2. What do you think are some of the reasons for poor customer service?

---

buying from a company for a variety of reasons. Very often, the reasons can be poor customer service as opposed to something inherently wrong with the brand. The first step in customer recovery is to find the customer who is in jeopardy of being lost to the company. The longer customers stay away from a business, the less likely they are to return. Because customer databases capture purchases, computers can be programmed to periodically examine transaction frequencies and create a list of

▼

ask yourself

1. What does firing a customer mean?

2. Describe the two steps in customer recovery.

all customers who have not made a purchase within a set period of time. Because each customer generally has a certain purchase frequency, software can determine when each customer's purchase frequency has been broken. After lapsed customers are identified, the next step is to contact them to determine why they have stopped buying.[25] If the problem is resolved, the lapsed customer may become a very loyal customer because the firm has shown interest in the customer.

[AdAlyze]

Describe the target market of the Becel ad.

try
BECEL BUTTERY TASTE

With a buttery taste you'll love, but 80% less saturated fat than butter, you can indulge your heart's desire.

Becel
LoVE YOUR HEART

Does this ad get your attention?

What is the benefit to the consumer in purchasing Becel, as explained in the headline?

Visit www.loveyourheart.ca

Becel
Buttery Taste
MARGARINE

A healthy diet low in saturated and trans fats may reduce the risk of heart disease. Becel Buttery Taste margarine is low in saturated fat and has no trans fat. Trade-mark owned or used under license by Unilever Canada, Toronto, Ontario M4W 3R2.

Summary...*just the facts*

- Customer relationship management (CRM) focuses on using information about customers to build and maintain profitable customer relationships.

- A company's failure with CRM is often the result of approaching CRM as a software project rather than as an overall company strategy.

- A growing number of companies are keeping track of what's said about their brands on social media platforms such as Facebook and Twitter. This activity falls in line with the process of CRM, because it's an excellent way to build a relationship with customers.

- One way to retain customers is through loyalty programs. It should be noted that all customers should be rewarded, but not all customers are the same. In most product categories, a small number of heavy users account for a large percentage of a brand's sales and profits.

- Data mining is an efficient way to sort through large amounts of data to find relationships between variables.

- Companies are starting to focus on the value of a customer if that customer remains loyal to the firm over the customer's lifetime.

- The customer service component of CRM is crucial to its success.

- Many firms are beginning to jettison or fire their low-value customers and are focusing their time on their high-valued customers.

- Companies are instituting customer reacquisition programs to prevent losing customers.

Key Terms and Concepts...*a refresher*

customer experience management (CEM) *p. 299*
customer lifetime value *p. 307*
customer relationship management (CRM) *p. 299*

data mining *p. 306*
data warehouse *p. 306*
loyalty programs *p. 304*
Pareto's Rule *p. 304*

share of wallet *p. 308*
touch point *p. 299*

Hands-on...*apply your knowledge*

Online CRM Assignment Visit the "About Us" section of the Four Seasons website at http://www.fourseasons.com/about_us/.

- On the left-hand navigation panel, click the "Service Culture" link. Summarize the unique service culture that is discussed on this page.

- Click the "Living Values" link. Four Seasons engages in sustainable practices that conserve natural resources and reduce environmental impact. Give some examples of these practices.

Reality Check...*reminder*

Refer back to this chapter's opening vignette and answer the Reality Check questions on page 298.

 *Practise and learn online with Connect.*

Connect allows you to practise important concepts at your own pace and on your own schedule, with 24/7 online access to an eBook, practice quizzes, video cases, chapter application questions, discussion activities, Internet exercises, interactivities, study tools, and more.

Marketing *and* Strategic Planning

Strategic planning is a continuous process used by large and small organizations to help ensure that they meet organizational objectives over a three- to five-year period. Both the profit and the not-for-profit industries use this approach to help achieve their long-term visions and to satisfy stakeholders' requirements. To better understand strategic planning, we look at its implementation in one not-for-profit organization: Georgian Bay General Hospital.

Strategic planning is a continuous process used by large and small companies to set direction and organizational objectives. Businesses and not-for-profit organizations use this approach to help set, and then work toward, achieving a long-term vision for an organization and to satisfy stakeholders' expectations. To better understand strategic planning, we look to the not-for profit health care industry to see how the North Simcoe Hospital Alliance (NSHA) used strategic planning to amalgamate two hospitals and continues today to use strategic planning to shape the Georgian Bay General Hospital.

First, a little background: Two neighbouring communities on Georgian Bay in Ontario, Midland and Penetanguishene, were serviced by two small hospitals with quality health care but with some overlap in medical services. The hospitals formed an alliance (the North Simcoe Hospital Alliance) to allow them to streamline medical services to minimize duplication and to reduce unnecessary spending in the wake of an Ontario Ministry of Health review of small hospitals. However, with two separate facilities remaining, some duplication existed. Two separate budgets, two individual boards, and two distinct CEOs ran the institutions. A decision was made to formally integrate the two hospitals under one corporation, and eventually one name ensuring top-quality care was still provided to the communities.

"The decision was not without its controversy," states Lucy Brun, partner at leading health care consulting firm Agnew Peckham, which facilitates strategic planning in the health care industry. "These two hospitals serviced very different cultural communities and there was an over-riding need to include the community in the decision-making process. The Penetanguishene General Hospital was a Catholic-sponsored hospital, while the Huronia District

Hospital had no religious affiliation." Agnew Peckham worked with the NSHA to create a unified vision for the new organization once the voluntary integration was complete. "The hospital wanted to create a platform that would be embraced by all stakeholders; it was important to be inclusive. We wanted the communities served by both hospitals, as well as hospital staff, medical staff, and administration, to help mould the vision for the new hospital and have it embraced by all—no small feat with so many different groups!" explains Brun.

In June 2009, the hospital engaged Agnew Peckham to facilitate their strategic planning process to create a vision, a mission, values, and strategic directions for the new amalgamated organization. The process was overseen by a steering committee of board members and senior hospital administrators, supported by Agnew Peckham consultants. A collaborative approach was put in motion to include staff, physicians, managers, board members, community stakeholders, and other health service providers in the process. It set guidelines to ensure that it would respond to issues and opportunities facing the hospital and be sensitive to unique cultural needs. As part of this process, the community became involved not only in setting direction for the new hospital but also later in its rebranding, name selection, and logo design.

Let's look at the strategic planning process in more detail to understand the steps that were taken by Agnew Peckham to create a unique partnership between a community and its hospital:

● **Step 1: External environmental scan:** Information was gathered in two key areas. First, factual information was collected from available studies on demographic data and local health care needs. Second, information was sourced on community expectations and stakeholder needs by speaking to hospital staff, physicians, health care partners, government representatives, seasonal residents, financial donors, and the community at large. More than 15 focus groups were engaged early in the process through their involvement in the groups or personal interviews where their opinions and ideas were solicited.

LEARNING OBJECTIVES

LO① Describe how strategy is developed at the corporate, business unit, and functional levels in an organization

LO② Define the concepts of business, mission, and goals, and explain why they are important in organizations

LO③ Explain why managers use marketing dashboards and marketing metrics

LO④ Discuss how organizations formulate strategies

LO⑤ Outline the strategic marketing process

Hôpital général de la **baie Georgienne**

GEORGIAN BAY
General Hospital

TANGUISHENE SITE

- **Step 2: Internal environment scan:** Future hospital priorities were assessed with input from senior professionals, such as board members, administrators, physicians, and front-line staff who were asked in personal interviews or focus groups to comment on issues and opportunities that faced the hospital.
- **Step 3: Strategic planning retreat:** Future strategic direction was established through offsite planning sessions held with senior executives, chief physicians, and board members. Key facts, strategic drivers, and focal points from the external and internal environmental scans were shared with the group. Workshops were then facilitated to develop a vision for the new hospital and to develop clear mission statements and core values. Strategic direction was then mapped-out for the next three years to help steer the hospital into achieving its goals.

"The results," states Jackie McLauchlin-Welch, director, communications & engagement at GBGH, "were tremendous and included support from all groups. Getting the community involved from the start made this *their* process, *their* hospital, *their* vision and of course they then went on to become involved in the hospital's next stage which was the branding process and selection of the new name." The strategic plan placed the community and its health care needs front and centre and it came out ahead with a hospital that is focused on its unique cultural identity and health care needs. The hospital's strategic direction is encompassed in its vision, mission, and value statements as follows:

- **Vision:** Exceptional Care, Every Person, Every Time.
- **Mission:** Our hospital is vibrant, progressive, and a partner in inspiring a healthier community.
- **Values:** Our values encompass caring, inclusiveness, dependability, and excellence.

The strategic planning process resulted in five *strategic directions* to move the hospital forward in achieving its new vision:

1. Provide exemplary hospital programs and services in selected areas of focus.
2. Excel in quality patient care and safety.
3. Be an employer of choice by providing a progressive and innovative workplace.
4. Build and strengthen relationships.
5. Achieve exceptional organizational performance.

The *community naming process* was launched by the hospital near the end of the strategic planning phase with a group of 20 representatives from among front-line hospital staff, physicians, volunteers, politicians, Francophones, and Aboriginal people.

Following a five-week process, the final stage was launched with fanfare at www.ourhospital.ca, hospital locations, and community sites, as well as through full-page local newspaper ads encouraging the community at large to vote. From a short list of three names; *Georgian Bay General Hospital*, *Georgian Bay Islands General Hospital*, and *The Hospital on Georgian Bay*, 1,100 people voted and selected *Georgian Bay General Hospital* as the name that best reflected the new hospital's identity. The hospital's new name and logo, and its new mission, vision, and value statements were revealed on December 16, 2009, at a public reception to which the entire community was invited.

Danielle Gibbons, designer of the winning name and logo, expressed her delight and excitement in being part of the Georgian Bay community and being able to take part in the re-branding project. Kelly Donaldson, runner-up designer, also echoed Danielle's sentiment, "I am truly honoured for the opportunity to contribute to my hospital's re-brand. The creative process reminded me of how much I appreciate the privilege of living in this community, surrounded by Georgian Bay's natural beauty."

Senior management developed an implementation plan to achieve the strategic directions, which is incorporated in the annual operating plan, and the board has a process for monitoring progress. Agnew Peckham continues to work with Georgian Bay General Hospital in developing clinical program plans to improve services and facility redesign to support the required infrastructure. The community's support for the hospital is evident in the record turnout at a recent Chamber of Commerce networking event. The hospital was also honoured with the Southern Georgian Bay Large Business of the Year Award in 2010 in recognition of its community contributions and new strategic direction.[1] 🍎

reality CHECK

As you read Chapter 14, refer back to the Georgian Bay General Hospital vignette to answer the following questions:

- The vignette states that senior management developed an implementation plan to achieve the strategic directions incorporated in the marketing plan and that the board had a process for monitoring the progress. Which phase of the marketing plan deals with monitoring the progress and comparing the results with the goals laid out in the marketing plan?

- What methods did the hospital use to conduct a SWOT analysis?

Chapter 14 describes how organizations set their mission and overall direction and link these activities to marketing strategies. As consumers become more concerned about a company's impact on society, marketing strategy may need to be linked to the social goals of the company's mission statement. Chapter 14 focuses on strategic planning and the role it plays in the marketing process.

Organizations and Their Levels of Strategy

L① Large organizations today are extremely complex. All of us deal in some way with huge organizations every day, so it is useful to understand the two basic kinds of organizations and the levels that exist in them and their link to marketing.

Today's organizations can be divided into business firms and not-for-profit organizations. A *business firm* is an organization that serves its customers in order to earn a profit. **Profit** is the excess of revenues over costs, the reward to a business for the risk it undertakes in offering a product for sale. In contrast to business firms, a *not-for-profit organization* is an organization that serves its customers but does not have profit as an organizational goal. For simplicity, however, we use the terms *firm, company, corporation,* and *organization* to cover both business and not-for-profit operations.

The Core: Chapter 14

Successful companies link corporate missions and goals to marketing strategies.

Strategic Marketing Process

The strategic marketing process helps marketers develop programs around a company's impact on society.

Levels in Organizations and How Marketing Links to Them

A **strategy** is a plan of action to achieve specific goals. All organizations should have a strategic direction—that is, they should have an idea of what they hope to achieve and how they plan to achieve it. Marketing not only helps set the direction but also helps the organization get there. Figure 14–1 illustrates the three levels of strategy in an optimal organization.

The *corporate level* is where top management directs overall strategy for the entire organization. Multimarket, multiproduct firms such as General Electric or Unilever really manage a group of different businesses, variously termed strategic business units (SBUs), strategic business segments, or product-market units (PMUs).[2] Each of these units markets a set of related products to a clearly defined group of customers. Management at the corporate level focuses on the interests of the shareholders of the firm, as measured by stock performance and profitability. The *business unit level* is where business unit managers set the direction for individual products and markets. Strategic direction is more specific at the business unit level of an organization. For less complex firms with a single business focus, the corporate and business unit strategies may merge.

At the *functional level*, each business unit has marketing and other specialized activities such as finance, manufacturing, or human resources. The name of a *department* generally refers to its specialized function, such as the marketing department or information systems department. At the functional level, the strategic direction becomes very specific and focused.

In a large corporation with multiple business units, marketing may be called on to assess consumer trends as an aid to corporate planning. At the business unit level, marketing may be asked to provide leadership in developing a new, integrated customer service program across all business units. At the functional level, marketing may implement an advertising campaign.

Strategy Issues in Organizations

L② Organizations need a reason for their existence—and a direction. This is where their business, mission, and goals converge. We'll discuss each below. As shown in Figure 14–1, business and mission apply to the corporate and business unit levels, while goals relate to all three levels.

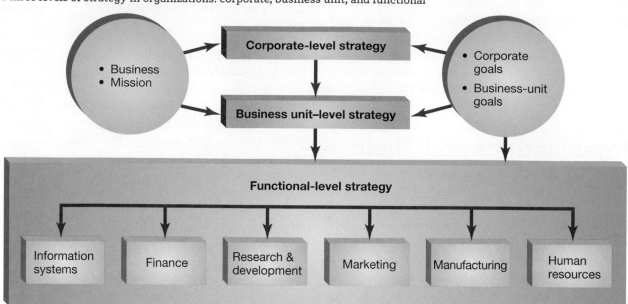

The three levels of strategy in organizations: corporate, business unit, and functional. Business • Mission → Corporate-level strategy ← Corporate goals • Business-unit goals → Business unit–level strategy → Functional-level strategy → Information systems, Finance, Research & development, Marketing, Manufacturing, Human resources

The Business Organizations like Canadian Blood Services and your college or university exist for a purpose—to accomplish something for someone. At the beginning, most organizations have clear ideas about what "something" and "someone" mean. But as the organization grows over time, often its purpose becomes fuzzy and continually unclear.

This is where the organization repeatedly asks some of the most difficult questions it ever faces: What business are we in? Who are our customers? What offerings should we provide to give these customers value? One guideline in defining the company's business is to try to understand the people served by the organization and the value they receive, which emphasizes the critical customer-driven focus that successful organizations have.

In a now-famous article, entitled "Marketing Myopia," Harvard professor Theodore Levitt cited railroads as organizations that had a narrow, production-oriented statement of their business: "We are in the railroad business!" This narrow

definition of their business lost sight of who their customers were and what their needs were. Railroads saw only other railroads as competitors and failed to design strategies to compete with airlines, barges, pipelines, trucks, bus lines, and cars. Railroads would probably have fared better over the past century by recognizing they are in "the transportation business."[3]

With this focus on the customer, Disney is *not* in the movie and theme park business, but rather it *is* in the business of entertainment, creating fun and fantasy for customers.

Ben & Jerry's, the maker of premium ice cream, has a mission statement consisting of three parts: social, product, and economic.

All Natural **BEN & JERRY'S** VERMONT'S FINEST

Ben & Jerry's Mission

Ben & Jerry's is founded on & dedicated to a sustainable corporate concept of linked prosperity. Our mission consists of 3 interrelated parts:

SOCIAL *mission*
To operate the Company in a way that actively recognizes the central role that business plays in society by initiating innovative ways to improve the quality of life locally, nationally and internationally.

PRODUCT *mission*
To make, distribute and sell the finest quality all natural ice cream and euphoric concoctions with a continued commitment to incorporating wholesome, natural ingredients and promoting business practices that respect the Earth and the Environment.

ECONOMIC *mission*
To operate the Company on a sustainable financial basis of profitable growth, increasing value for our stakeholders and expanding opportunities for development and career growth for our employees.

The Mission   By understanding its business, an organization can take steps to define its **mission**, a statement of the organization's scope, often identifying its customers, markets, products, technology, and values. Today, often used interchangeably with *vision*, the *mission statement* frequently has an inspirational theme—something that can ignite the loyalty of customers, employees, and others with whom the organization comes in contact.

To explore strange new worlds, to seek out new life and new civilizations, to boldly go where no one has gone before. This continuing mission for the starship *Enterprise*, as Gene Roddenberry wrote it for the *Star Trek* adventure series, is inspirational and focuses the advanced technology, strong leadership, and skilled crew of the *Enterprise* on what is to be accomplished.

Organizations must connect not just with their customers but with all their *stakeholders*. Stakeholders are the people who are affected by what the company does and how well it performs. This group includes employees, owners, and board members, as well as suppliers, distributors, unions, local communities, governments, society in general, and, of course, customers. Communicating the mission statement is an important corporate-level marketing function. Some companies publish their mission statement on their website or in their annual reports. One British Columbia company has its mission statement on a huge wall poster in its manufacturing facility, and every employee reads and signs it!

ask yourself

1. What are the three levels of organization in today's large corporations?

2. What is the purpose of an organization's mission?

3. What are stakeholders?

mission
Statement of the organization's purpose and direction

---

focus on **Ethics**

Loblaw Takes Corporate Social Responsibility Seriously

Galen G. Weston has become a familiar face to Canadians, touting cloth shopping bags rather than plastic ones in television ads for Loblaw Companies. Ltd. The executive chairman's pitch seems to be paying off. The grocer diverted 1.3 billion plastic bags from landfills in 2009, beating its goal of 1 billion.

The environmental initiative may frustrate some Loblaw customers who now have to shell out for plastic bags to line their garbage pails. But the chain's push to do the right thing in an array of corporate social responsibility (CSR) areas helped it snag the top score in a CSR survey of companies touting social responsibility as one of their goals. Mr. Weston says that a key part of implementing CSR is to set measurable goals and report on the results. His personal commitment to corporate responsibility has played its part in bolstering the chain's CSR rankings. Since taking the top job, the scion of the Weston family that controls Loblaw has focused on putting more discipline into the retailer's social-responsibility efforts. It now releases an annual CSR report.

Loblaw is not alone in blowing its CSR horn in a written report. According to a recent worldwide survey from consultants KPMG, about 60 percent of Canada's 100 largest companies now prepare CSR reports, up from 41 percent in 2005. Still, Canada lags behind many European countries where CSR reporting is much more widespread.

Reducing waste also makes good business sense. It helps the bottom line for Loblaw by saving millions of dollars annually.[4] ●

Questions

1. Give some examples of other companies practising corporate social responsibility.

2. Do you resent having to pay for plastic bags? Discuss.

Goals **Goals** or **objectives** take an organization's mission and translate it into targeted levels of performance to be achieved within a specific time frame. These goals measure how well the mission is being accomplished. As shown in Figure 14–1 on page 316, goals exist at the corporate, business unit, and functional levels. All lower-level goals must contribute to achieving goals at the next higher level.

Business firms can pursue several different types of goals:

- **Profit:** Most firms seek to maximize profits—to get as high a financial return on investment (ROI) as possible.

- **Sales:** A firm may elect to maintain or increase its sales level even though profitability may not be maximized.

- **Market share:** A firm may choose to maintain or increase its market share, sometimes at the expense of greater profits if industry status or prestige is a desired goal. **Market share** is the ratio of sales revenue of the firm to the total sales revenue of all firms in the industry, including the firm itself.

- **Quality:** A firm may target the highest quality, as Rolex does with its luxury wristwatches.

- **Customer satisfaction:** Customers are the key to an organization's success, so their perceptions and actions are of vital importance. Their satisfaction can be measured directly with surveys.

- **Employee welfare:** A firm may recognize the critical importance of its employees by having an explicit goal stating its commitment to good employment opportunities and working conditions.

- **Social responsibility:** A firm may seek to balance conflicting goals of stakeholders to promote overall welfare, even at the expense of profits. (See, for example, the discussion of the emphasis on corporate social responsibility at Loblaw Companies in the Focus on Ethics box on page 317.)

Many organizations (for example, museums, symphony orchestras, and private schools) do not seek profits as a primary goal. These organizations strive to serve consumers as efficiently as possible. Government

agencies also perform marketing activities in trying to achieve their goal of serving the public good.

Tracking Strategic Performance with Marketing Dashboards

Although marketing managers can set strategic directions for their organizations, how do they know if they are making progress in getting there? One answer is to measure performance by using marketing dashboards.

Car Dashboards and Marketing Dashboards

A **marketing dashboard** is the visual computer display of the essential information related to achieving a marketing objective. Often, it is a computer-based display with real-time information and active hyperlinks to provide further detail. An example is when a chief marketing officer (CMO) wants to see daily what the effect of a new TV advertising campaign is on a product's sales in order to allocate marketing resources effectively.

Figure 14–2

An effective marketing dashboard, like this one from Oracle, helps managers assess a business situation at a glance.

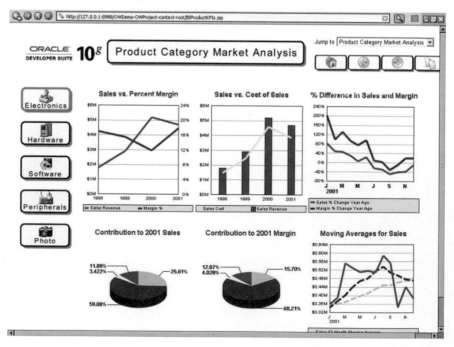

The idea of a marketing dashboard really comes from the display of information found on a car's dashboard. On a car's dashboard, we glance at the fuel gauge and take action when our gas is getting low. With a marketing dashboard, a marketing manager glances at a graph or table and makes a decision whether to take action or to analyze the problem further.

Dashboards and Metrics   The marketing dashboard of Oracle, a large software software firm, appears in Figure 14-2. It shows graphic displays of key performance measures of a product category, such as sales versus cost of sales. Each variable in a marketing dashboard is a **marketing metric**, which is a measure of the quantitative value or trend of a marketing activity or result. The choice of which marketing metrics to display is critical for a busy marketing manager, who can be overwhelmed with too much or inappropriate information.

Dashboard designers take great care to show graphs and tables in easy-to-understand formats to enable clear interpretation at a glance. The Oracle marketing dashboard in Figure 14-2 presents several marketing metrics on the computer screen.

> *With a marketing dashboard, a marketing manager glances at a graph or table and makes a decision whether to take action or to analyze the problem further*

Setting Strategic Directions

LO 4 Setting strategic directions involves answering challenging questions: Where are we now? Where do we want to go? How will we get there?

A Look Around: Where Are We Now?

Asking an organization where it is at the present time involves identifying its customers, competencies, and competitors. More detailed approaches of assessing "where are we now?" include SWOT analysis, discussed later in this chapter, and environmental scanning (Chapter 2). These may be done at each of the three levels in the organization.

marketing metric
A measure of the value or trend of a marketing activity or result

Customers   Tilley Endurables is a Canadian retailer that knows that its customers appreciate the fine hats and travel clothing that Tilley makes. Tilley provides an example of a clear focus on customers. Its stores and website give a remarkable statement about its commitments to customer relationships and the quality of its products. The Tilley guarantee for its legendary hats has always been an unconditional one: "Tilley Hats will be replaced free if they ever wear out, mildew, or shrink." The same guarantee applies to some of their shorts, vests, jackets, pants, and skirts. They are replaced free if they ever wear out.[5]

The crucial point: Strategic directions must be customer-focused and provide genuine value and benefits to existing and prospective customers.

Competencies   "What do we do best?" asks about an organization's competencies—an organization's special capabilities, including skills, technologies, and resources that distinguish it from other organizations. Exploiting these competencies can lead to success.[6] In Tilley's case, its competencies include an obsession with quality. To quote the founder Alex Tilley, "I'll make travel clothing! I'll make it the best in the world! And then I'll make it even better!" Tilley Endurables is one of the last remaining companies to manufacture all its products in Canada.[7]

Competitors   In today's global competition, the lines among competitive sectors are increasingly blurred. For example, Loblaws competes directly with other supermarkets such as Sobeys and Safeway. At the same time, it also competes against mass merchandisers such as Walmart Supercentres, which also carry groceries, and it competes with warehouse clubs such as Costco. Loblaws also carries many pharmacy items, which puts it into direct competition with pharmacies such as Shoppers Drug Mart and Pharma Plus. Shoppers Drug Mart carries many lines of cosmetics, which puts it into direct competition with department stores such as The Bay, which traditionally carries cosmetics.

Growth Strategies: Where Do We Want to Go?

Knowing where the organization is at the present time enables managers to set a direction for the firm and

commit resources to move in that direction. Two techniques to aid in these decisions are the business portfolio analysis and the market-product analysis.

Business Portfolio Analysis Developed by the Boston Consulting Group (BCG), *business portfolio analysis* uses quantified performance measures and market growth to analyze a firm's strategic business units as though they were a collection of separate investments.[8] While used at the business unit level here, the BCG analysis has also been applied at the product line or individual product or brand level. This kind of portfolio analysis is very popular; most large firms have used it in some form.

BCG, a leading management consulting firm, advises its clients to locate the position of each of its SBUs on a growth-share matrix (Figure 14–3). The vertical axis is the *market growth rate*, which is the annual rate of growth of the specific market or industry in which a given SBU is competing. The horizontal axis is the *relative market share*, defined as the sales of the SBU divided by the sales of the largest firm in the industry.

BCG has given specific names and descriptions to the four resulting quadrants in its growth-share matrix based on the amount of cash they generate for or require from the firm:

- *Cash cows* are SBUs that typically generate large amounts of cash, far more than they can invest profitably in their own product line. They have a dominant share of a slow-growth market and provide cash to pay large amounts of company overhead and to invest in other SBUs.

- *Stars* are SBUs with a high share of high-growth markets that may need extra cash to finance their own rapid future growth. When their growth slows, they are likely to become cash cows.

- *Question marks* or *problem children* are SBUs with a low share of high-growth markets. They require large injections of cash just to maintain their market share, and even more to increase it. Their name implies management's dilemma for these SBUs: choosing the right ones to invest in and phasing out the rest.

- *Dogs* are SBUs with a low share of low-growth markets. Although they may generate enough cash to sustain themselves, they do not hold the promise of ever becoming real winners for the firm. Dropping SBUs that are dogs may be required, except when relationships with other SBUs, competitive considerations, or potential strategic alliances exist.[9]

The circles in Figure 14–3 show the current SBUs in a strong, diversified firm. The area of each circle is proportional to the corresponding SBU's annual sales revenue.

Management often makes conscious decisions on what role each SBU should have in the future and either injects or removes cash from it. Four alternative strategies are available for each SBU. The firm can invest more in the SBU to *build* its share (SBU A in Figure 14–3). Or it can invest just enough to *hold* the SBU's share at about its current level (SBU B in Figure 14–3). Or it can *harvest* the SBU (SBU C in Figure 14–3), trying to milk its short-term cash flow even though it may lose share and become a dog in the longer run. Finally, the firm can *divest* the SBU (SBU D) by phasing it out or actually selling it to gain cash.

Figure 14–3
Boston Consulting Group growth-share matrix for a strong, diversified firm showing some strategic plans

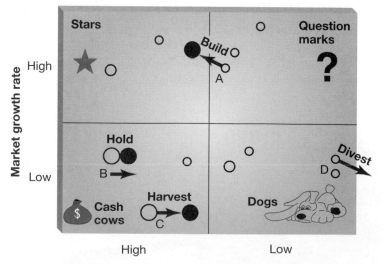

The digital revolution that resulted in plunging CD and DVD sales is pushing retailers such as HMV to diversify by exploring other options.

With over 90 years of music retailing history and 400+ stores worldwide, HMV, a British company, was the world's premier retailer of music, DVDs, videogames, books, and more. Its Canadian operation, HMV Canada, grew from a small retail music chain to become one of Canada's music market leaders with over 123 stores from Newfoundland to British Columbia. In 2011, Hilco UK, a British restructuring retail specialist, acquired HMV Canada for $3.23 million.

The digital revolution, together with other factors that have resulted in plunging CD and DVD sales, pushed retailers such as HMV to diversify into new product areas and services. In the U.K., three out of four independent record shops have closed in the past decade to leave HMV as the "last shop standing" in the music and entertainment retail business. The rise of Internet downloads has severely challenged the 90-year-old business that started life selling gramophones and sheet music.

HMV is now looking to transform itself to a broad-based entertainment brand as opposed to just a place to buy CDs, DVDS, or other physical products. Through the ownership of major concert venues and festivals, HMV is diversifying into live music and ticketing, while its stores are increasingly stocking personal technology products such as headphones, speakers, tablets, and accessories from such brands as Apple, Samsung, Monster Beats, Bose, and Skullcandy. HMV also has a downloads store at hmvdigital.com, which it runs with its partner 7digital, and is set to announce a video-on-demand site in association with FilmFlex. However, some analysts feel it may be too late for the company to make any major impact in this field given the huge dominance of the likes of iTunes.

HMV's award-winning loyalty scheme, purehmv, which enables customers to earn points that can be exchanged for "money can't buy" experiences, has attracted over 1.7 million members, and is proving to be a key way for the company to interact and engage with its customers.

In 2009, HMV began a trial putting cinemas above its stores in London, as part of a drive to diversify and create new revenue streams. In a partnership with "art-house" cinema chain Curzon Artificial Eye, HMV tested a 200-seat cinema above its Wimbledon store in South London. The site was rebranded into hmvcurzon, and also includes a café and bar with luxury seats and a merchandise area. The experiment has proved successful and may now create a template for other hmvcurzons in other parts of the country.[10] ●

Questions

1. Describe the new areas that HMV is pursuing in its effort to rebrand itself.

2. Do you feel that HMV will survive? Why?

Market-Product Analysis Firms can also view growth opportunities in terms of markets and products. Think of it this way: For any product there is both a current market (consisting of existing customers) and a new market (consisting of potential customers). And for any market, there is a current product (what they're now using) and a new product (something they might use if it were developed). Four possible market-product strategies are shown in Figure 14-4.

As Unilever attempts to increase sales revenues of its Ben & Jerry's business, it must consider all four of the alternative market-product strategies shown in Figure 14-4. For example, it can try to use a strategy of *market penetration*—increasing sales of present products in its existing markets, in this case by increasing sales of Ben & Jerry's present ice cream products to consumers. There is no change in either the basic product line or the market served, but increased sales are possible—either by selling more ice cream (through better promotion or distribution) or by selling the same amount of ice cream at a higher price to its existing customers.

Market development is a marketing strategy to sell current products to new markets. For Ben & Jerry's, Brazil is an attractive new market. There is good news and bad news for this strategy: As household incomes of Brazilians increase, consumers can buy more ice cream; however, the Ben & Jerry's brand may be unknown to Brazilian consumers.

An expansion strategy using *product development* involves selling a new product to existing markets. When Ben and Jerry's launched sorbet and frozen yogourt products, the firm was following a product development strategy. Figure 14-4 shows that the firm could try leveraging

Figure 14–4

Four market-product strategies: Alternative ways to expand sales revenues for Ben & Jerry's

| Markets | PRODUCTS | |
	Current	New
Current	**Market penetration** Selling more Ben & Jerry's super premium ice cream in North America	**Product development** Selling a new product such as frozen yogourt under the Ben & Jerry's brand in North America
New	**Market development** Selling Ben & Jerry's super premium ice cream in Brazil for the first time	**Diversification** Selling a new product such as breakfast cereal in China for the first time

the Ben & Jerry's brand by selling its own frozen yogourt in North America.

Diversification involves developing new products and selling them in new markets. This is a potentially high-risk strategy for Ben & Jerry's—and for most firms—because the company has neither previous production experience nor marketing experience on which to draw. For example, in trying to sell a Ben & Jerry's brand of breakfast cereal in China, the company has expertise neither in producing cereals nor in marketing to consumers in China.

Diversification can consist of a company getting into a completely new area of business, such as

Rogers purchasing the Toronto Blue Jays. Diversification can also consist of a company introducing a variation of a product to a new market. An example of this is Mike Leonetti, a Canadian author of many hockey books for adult hockey fans, who is now authoring children's books on hockey for kids aged six and up. The Marketing NewsFlash on page 321 describes how HMV is diversifying how it delivers its media products in the digital age.

ask yourself

1. What are competencies and why are they important?

2. What is business portfolio analysis?

3. What are the four market-product strategies?

The Strategic Marketing Process

L5 After an organization assesses where it's at and where it wants to go, it must work out how it will get there. Specifically, it must decide

- How to allocate resources

- How to convert plans into actions

- How results compare with plans, and whether deviations (results that differ from expectations) require new plans and actions

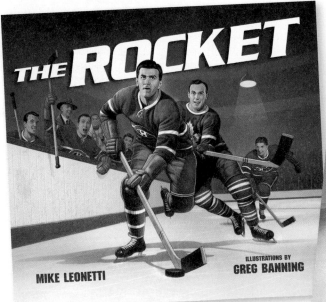
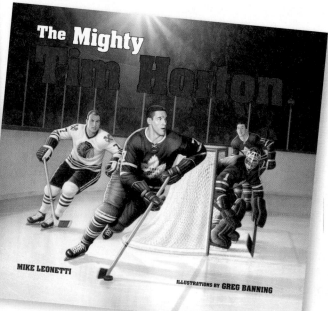

Two successful children's books on hockey by Canadian author Mike Leonetti are examples of diversification. Read the text for more details.

Figure 14–5
Outline of a marketing plan

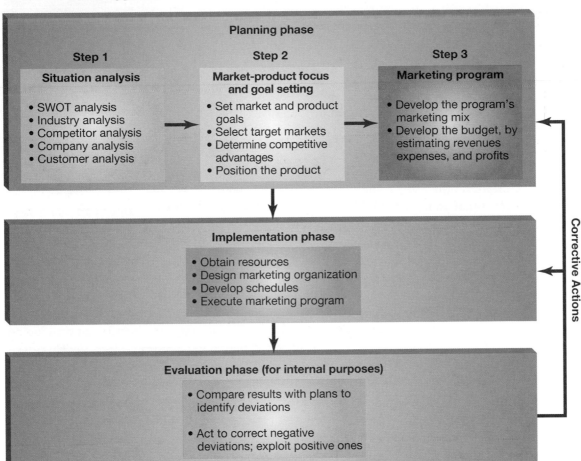

strategic marketing process
Approach whereby an organization allocates its marketing mix

marketing plan
Road map for the marketing activities of an organization for a specified future period of time

situation analysis
Taking stock of a firm or product's past performance, where it is now, and where it is headed

SWOT analysis
Organization's appraisal of its internal strengths and weaknesses and its external opportunities and threats

This approach is used in the **strategic marketing process**, whereby an organization allocates its marketing mix resources to reach its target markets and achieve its goals. The strategic marketing process is so central to the activities of most organizations that they formalize it as a **marketing plan**, which is a road map for the marketing activities of an organization for a specified future period of time, such as one year or five years. The marketing plan is divided into three phases: planning, implementation, and evaluation (Figure 14–5). See the Appendix, available in the connect Library, for an example of a complete marketing plan, which also includes an executive summary.

This chapter's opening vignette focuses on the strategic marketing process in a hospital. Both profit and not-for-profit industries use this approach to help achieve their long-term visions and to satisfy stakeholders' requirements.

The following sections give an overview of the marketing plan that puts Chapters 1 through 13 of this book in perspective.

The Planning Phase of the Marketing Plan

As shown in Figure 14–5, the planning phase of the marketing plan consists of the three steps shown at the top of the figure: situation analysis, market-product focus and goal setting, and the marketing program. Let's use the recent marketing planning experiences of several companies to look at each of these steps.

Step 1: Situation Analysis The essence of a **situation analysis** is taking stock of the firm or product's past performance, where it is now, and where it is headed in light of the organization's plans and the external factors and trends affecting it. The situation analysis box in Figure 14–5 is the first of the three steps in the planning phase.

Step 1 starts with a **SWOT analysis**, which describes an organization's appraisal of its internal **S**trengths and **W**eaknesses and its external **O**pportunities and **T**hreats. Both the situation and

market segmentation
Sorting potential buyers into groups that have common needs and will respond similarly to a marketing program

SWOT analyses can be done at the level of the entire organization, the business unit, the product line, or the specific product. As an analysis moves from the level of the entire organization to the specific product, it, of course, gets far more detailed. For small firms or those with basically a single product line, an analysis at the firm or product level is really the same thing.

Let's assume you are the Unilever vice president responsible for integrating Ben & Jerry's into Unilever's business. You might do the SWOT analysis shown in Figure 14–6. Note that your SWOT table has four cells formed by the combination of internal versus external factors (the rows) and favourable versus unfavourable factors (the columns) that summarize Ben & Jerry's strengths, weaknesses, opportunities, and threats.

A SWOT analysis helps a firm identify the strategy-related factors in these four cells that can have a major effect on the firm. The goal is not simply to develop the SWOT analysis but to translate the results of the analysis into specific actions to help the firm grow and succeed. The ultimate goal is to identify the critical factors affecting the firm and then build on vital strengths, correct glaring weaknesses, exploit significant opportunities, and avoid or prepare for disaster-laden threats. That is a big order.

The Ben and Jerry's SWOT analysis in Figure 14–6 can be the basis for these kinds of specific actions. An action in each of the four cells might be:

- **Build on a strength.** Find specific efficiencies in distribution with Unilever's existing ice cream brands.

- **Correct a weakness.** Recruit experienced managers from other consumer product firms to help stimulate growth.

- **Exploit an opportunity.** Develop a new line of low-fat yogourts to respond to consumer health concerns.

- **Avoid or prepare for a disaster-laden threat.** Focus on less risky international markets, such as Mexico.

The next areas to consider in step 1 are as follows:

- *Industry analysis* section focuses on the industry and trends.

- *Competitor analysis* section looks at the firm's competitors.

- *Company analysis* section provides details of the company itself.

- *Customer analysis* section addresses the question: Who are the customers of the firm's products?

One of 75 Ben & Jerry's flavours of ice cream.

Step 2: Market-Product Focus and Goal Setting Determining which products will be directed toward which customers (step 2 of the planning phase in Figure 14–5) is essential for developing an effective marketing program (step 3). This decision is often based on **market segmentation**, which involves considering prospective buyers in terms of groups, or segments. These groups have common needs and will respond similarly to a marketing program. Ideally, a firm can use market segmentation to identify the segments on which it will focus its

Figure 14–6
Ben & Jerry's: A SWOT analysis

Location of Factor	TYPE OF FACTOR	
	Favourable	**Unfavourable**
Internal	**Strengths** • Prestigious, well-known brand name among North American consumers • Major share of the super premium ice cream market • Can complement Unilever's existing ice cream brands • Widely recognized for its social responsibility actions	**Weaknesses** • Danger that B&J's social responsibility actions may add costs, reduce focus on core business • Need for experienced managers to help growth • Flat sales and profits in recent years
External	**Opportunities** • Growing demand for quality ice cream in overseas markets • Increasing demand for frozen yogourt and other low-fat desserts • Success of many firms in extending successful brand in one product category to others	**Threats** • Consumer concern with fatty desserts; B&J customers are the type who read new government-ordered nutritional labels • Competes with Haagen-Dazs brand • Increased competition in international markets

> **A SWOT ANALYSIS HELPS A FIRM IDENTIFY THE STRATEGY-RELATED FACTORS IN THESE FOUR CELLS THAT CAN HAVE A MAJOR EFFECT ON THE FIRM.**

efforts—its target market segments—and develop one or more marketing programs to reach them.

Goal setting involves setting measurable marketing objectives to be achieved. For a specific market, the goal may be to introduce a new product—such as General Motors' launch of its electric car, the Chevrolet Volt. For a specific brand or product, the goal may be to create a promotional campaign or pricing strategy that will get more consumers to purchase. (Think of all those commercials touting the auto industry's popular zero percent financing?) For an entire marketing program, the objective is often a series of actions to be implemented over several years.

Using the marketing plan outline shown in Figure 14-5 (see page 323), let's examine step 2 by way of using Sleep Country Canada as an example:

- **Set marketing and product goals.** Based on listening to what is important to customers, Sleep Country Canada offers lots of choice in mattresses. It also makes each experience before, during, and after the sale an enjoyable one for the customer. One of its marketing goals may be to increase its market share by a certain percentage in the retailing mattress business in Canada. It's important to quantify the percentage so that the company can measure whether it successfully meets its goals.

- **Select target markets.** Sleep Country Canada targets consumers who want a quality mattress as well as a positive customer service experience.

- **Determine competitive advantages. Competitive advantages** are those characteristics of a product that make it superior to competing substitutes. Sleep Country Canada offers the mattress purchaser an enjoyable customer service experience unparalleled in this market. It offers clean, bright stores; sleep experts who put the customer's comfort and budget needs first; and courteous delivery people.

- **Position the product.** Sleep Country Canada is positioned as a mattress specialist that offers quality products with the added benefit of courteous and knowledgeable staff, an attractive in-store setting, and a convenient delivery service.

Details in these four elements of step 2 provide a solid foundation to use in developing the marketing program—the next step in the planning phase of the marketing plan.

Step 3: Marketing Program Activities in step 2 tell the marketing manager which customers to target and which customer needs the firm's product offerings can satisfy— the *who* and *what* aspects of the marketing plan. The *how* aspect—step 3 in the marketing plan—involves developing the program's marketing mix and its budget.

Figure 14-7 shows components of each marketing mix element that are combined to provide a cohesive

Ben & Jerry's Contest for Canadian Ice Cream Flavour

Ben & Jerry's had a contest to give a Canadian name to their newest creation, a combination of vanilla ice cream, fudge covered waffle cone pieces and a fudge swirl. Some contest submissions:

1. Le Leonard Cone
2. Laid Back and Lovin' It
3. It's Good, Eh!
4. Oh, Cone-ada!
5. Canucks Deluxe
6. Canadian Rocky Road

Winner: Oh, Cone-ada!

Source: Judy Creighton, "Burlington woman scoops ice cream naming contest," *Toronto Star*, July 26, 2010, accessed at www.thestar.com/news/gta/article/840310--gta-woman-wins-ben-jerry-s-contest-with-flavour-name-oh-cone-ada.

ask yourself

1. What is the difference between a strength and an opportunity in a SWOT analysis?

2. What is market segmentation?

3. What are competitive advantages and why are they important?

Figure 14–7

Elements of the marketing mix that comprise a cohesive marketing program

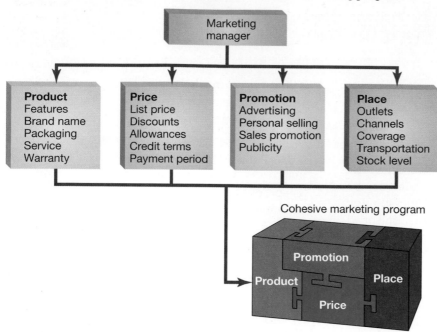

management. In the sample marketing plan in the Appendix, available in the ▨ **connect** Library, this is referred to as financial data and projections.

The Implementation Phase of the Marketing Plan

A firm's marketing plan is the result of the many hours spent in the planning phase of the strategic marketing process. Implementation, the second phase of the marketing plan, involves implementing the marketing program that emerges from the planning phase. If the firm cannot put the marketing program into effect—in the implementation phase—the planning phase was a waste of time. Figure 14–5 (see page 323) shows the four components of the implementation phase: obtaining resources, designing the marketing organization, developing schedules, and actually executing the marketing program designed in the planning phase.

Obtaining Resources Most companies have numerous options for growth. But such growth requires an investment. Corporate leadership within an organization determines the best options for growth and how they should be funded.

Designing the Marketing Organization A marketing program needs marketing staff to implement it. Figure 14–8 shows the organization chart of a typical manufacturing firm, giving some details of the marketing department's structure. Four managers of marketing activities are shown to report to the vice president of marketing. Several regional sales managers and an international sales manager may report to the manager of sales. This marketing organization is responsible for converting marketing plans to reality.

marketing program. For Sleep Country Canada, the marketing mix activities can include the following:

- **Product strategy:** Offer consumers one of the largest selections of top, name-brand mattresses.

- **Price strategy:** Offer consumers a low-price guarantee. If consumers find a comparable product at a competitor that is equal to or lower than Sleep Country Canada's price, the company will beat that figure by 5 percent.

- **Promotion strategy:** Sleep Country Canada uses mass media advertising to communicate its unique retail experience to prospective and current customers.

- **Place (distribution) strategy:** Sleep Country Canada is conveniently located in five Canadian provinces with 148 stores in total.

Putting a marketing program into effect requires that the firm commit time and money to it, prepare a sales forecast, and establish a budget that must be approved by top

Top 3 Brands in *Interbrand's* Annual Ranking of the 100 Best Global Brands

Source: "Best Global Brands: 2010 Rankings," accessed at www.interbrand.com/en/best-global-brands/best-global-brands-2008/best-global-brands-2010.aspx.

Figure 14–8
Organization of a typical manufacturing firm, showing a breakdown of the marketing department

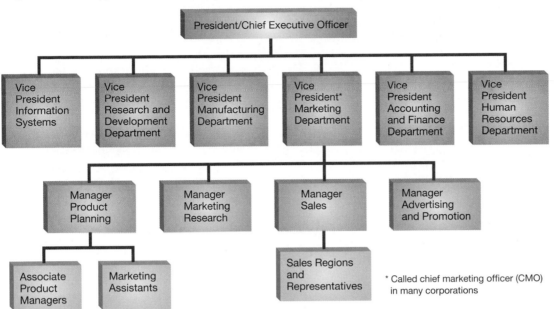

Developing Schedules Effective implementation requires developing appropriate schedules and determining specific deadlines for the creation and execution of marketing activities. For example, if a company wants to place an ad in *Time* magazine, it must reserve space a month prior to the date that the ad appears in the magazine. Also, the company must allow time for creating and producing the ad.

Executing the Marketing Program Marketing plans are meaningless unless they are put into action. This requires attention to detail to both marketing strategies and marketing tactics. A **marketing strategy** is the means by which a marketing goal is to be achieved, usually characterized by a specified target market and a marketing program to reach it. Although the term strategy is often used loosely, it implies both the end sought (target market) and the means to achieve it (marketing program).

To implement a marketing program successfully, hundreds of detailed decisions are often required, such as writing ads or setting prices. These decisions, called **marketing tactics**, are detailed day-to-day operational decisions essential to the overall success of marketing strategies.

ask yourself

1. How would you distinguish a marketing strategy from a marketing tactic?

2. Describe the four components of the implementation phase of the marketing plan.

The Evaluation Phase of the Marketing Plan (for Internal Purposes)

The evaluation phase of the marketing plan is used for a company's internal purposes. The marketing manager compares the results of the marketing activities with the goals laid out in the marketing plan to identify deviations and to act on these deviations—correcting negative deviations and exploiting positive ones.

Comparing Results with Plans When a company sets goals and then compares them to actual results, it needs to research the reasons for the differences. Where plans are exceeded, the company determines the drivers of this success and identifies ways to build on them as it moves forward. When there is a shortfall (actual results less than planned—often referred to as the *planning gap*), the company has to "fill in" this planning gap with a revised marketing program and possibly new goals.

Acting on Deviations Sometimes, the marketing program falls short of its goals. When this occurs, managers need to take corrective action. This is called correcting a negative deviation. But when actual results are far better than the plan called for, creative managers find ways to exploit the situation. This is called exploiting a positive deviation.

Summary...*just the facts*

- Today's large organizations, both business firms and not-for-profit organizations, are often divided into three levels: the corporate, business unit, and functional levels.

- Marketing has a role in all three levels by keeping a focus on customers and finding ways to add genuine customer value. At the lowest level, marketing serves as part of a team of functional specialists whose day-to-day actions actually involve customers and create customer value.

- Organizations exist to accomplish something for someone. To give itself focus, an organization continuously assesses its business, mission, and goals.

- One way marketing managers can measure its performance is by using marketing dashboards.

- Setting strategic directions for an organization involves asking "Where are we now?" to assess the organization's customers, competencies, and competitors. It also involves asking "Where do we want to go?" and using techniques like portfolio analysis and market-product analysis, and asking questions like "How will we get there?" that uses marketing plans.

- The strategic marketing process involves an organization allocating its marketing mix resources to reach its target markets using three phases: planning, implementation, and evaluation.

- The planning phase of the marketing plan has three steps, each with more specific elements: situation (SWOT) analysis, market-product focus and goal setting, and marketing program.

- The implementation phase of the marketing plan has four key elements: obtaining resources, designing the marketing organization, developing schedules, and executing the marketing program.

- The evaluation phase of the marketing plan is used for internal purposes and involves comparing results with the planned targets to identify deviations and taking actions to correct negative deviations and exploit positive ones.

Key Terms and Concepts...*a refresher*

competitive advantages *p. 325*
goals *p. 318*
market segmentation *p. 324*
market share *p. 318*
marketing dashboard *p. 318*
marketing metric *p. 319*

marketing plan *p. 323*
marketing strategy *p. 327*
marketing tactics *p. 327*
mission *p. 317*
objectives *p. 318*
profit *p. 315*

situation analysis *p. 323*
strategic marketing process *p. 323*
strategy *p. 315*
SWOT analysis *p. 323*

Hands-on...*apply your knowledge*

Strategic Planning Assignment The opening vignette on Georgian Bay General Hospital outlines the steps in strategic planning. Go to the Canadian Blood Services' website at www.bloodservices.ca and navigate to the "About Us" section. Explore the links on this page and list points that indicate that Canadian Blood Services has engaged in strategic planning.

Reality Check...*reminder*

Refer back to this chapter's opening vignette and answer the Reality Check questions on page 314.

McGraw Hill **connect** *Practise and learn online with Connect.*

Connect allows you to practise important concepts at your own pace and on your own schedule, with 24/7 online access to an eBook, practice quizzes, video cases, chapter application questions, discussion activities, Internet exercises, interactivities, study tools, and more.

Glossary

Numbers following the definitions indicate pages where the terms were identified. Consult the index for further page references.

adoption curve The sequential diffusion and acceptance of an innovation into the market by consumers (178)

advergaming Placing ads in online or offline video games (277)

advertising A paid form of media used to communicate to consumers; includes broadcast, print, out-of-home, and digital media (274)

affiliate marketing When companies promote their businesses through a network of online associates (affiliates) to drive traffic, leads, and purchases; affiliates are provided with ads and links to business websites and rewarded with commissions for resultant business (288)

attitude Tendency to respond to something in a consistently favourable or unfavourable way (65)

augmented reality (AR) When real-world images interact with computer-generated information to provide additional information (281)

baby boomers Generation of people born between 1946 and 1964 (33)

back translation Retranslating a word or phrase back into the original language by a different interpreter to catch errors (75)

banner ads Online ads that can stretch across the top of a web page or be formatted in various sizes, such as leaderboards, rectangles, big boxes, and skyscrapers (277)

behaviouristics Why consumers buy a product, the product benefit, how they use it, and whether they are brand loyal in their purchase behaviour (132)

beliefs Consumer's perceptions of how a product or brand performs (65)

brand A name or phrase uniquely given by a company to a product to distinguish it from the competition (154)

brand equity The value of a brand that results from the favourable exposure, interactions, associations, and experiences that consumers have with a brand over time (154)

brand extension When new goods or services are introduced under an existing flagship brand name (154)

brand loyalty Favourable attitude toward and consistent purchase of a single brand over time; the degree of consumer attachment to a particular brand (65, 156)

brand personality A set of human characteristics associated with a brand (156)

branded entertainment The creation of an entertainment program, such as a TV episode, that is highly focused on a brand in exchange for payment (287)

breadth of product line The variety of different items a store carries (249)

break-even analysis Examines the relationship between total revenue and total cost to determine profitability at different levels of output (203)

brokers Independent firms or individuals whose main function is to bring buyers and sellers together to make sales (260)

business analysis Financial projections on the impact of bringing the new product to market and selling it in the future (184)

business market Products that are purchased either to run a business or to be used as a component in another product or service (123)

business marketing Marketing to firms, governments, or non-profit organizations (103)

business products Products that are purchased either to run a business or to be used as a component in another product or service (123, 151)

buy classes Three types of organizational buying situations: straight rebuy, modified rebuy, or new buy (114)

buying centre Group of people in an organization who participate in the buying process (113)

causal research Research designed to identify cause-and-effect relationships among variables (84)

central business district The oldest retail setting, the community's downtown area (251)

channel conflict Arises when one channel member believes another channel member is engaged in behaviour that prevents it from achieving its goals (228)

commercialization When the new product is brought to market with full-scale production, sales, and marketing support (186)

community shopping centre Retail location that typically has one primary store and 20 to 40 smaller outlets, serving a population of consumers within a 2- to 5-kilometre drive (252)

competitive advantages Those characteristics of a product or service that make it superior to competing substitutes (325)

competitive forces Alternative products that can satisfy a specific market's needs (45)

concept tests External evaluations of a new product idea, rather than the actual product itself (184)

consumer behaviour Actions a person takes when purchasing and using products and services (56)

consumer market Consists of products, ideas, and services that a person can purchase or support for personal use (123)

consumer products Products purchased for their own personal use by the ultimate consumer (151)

consumer promotions Short-term marketing tools used to encourage immediate consumer purchase (282)

consumer touch points The points of interaction that can be used to connect with consumers, including personal time in the home, shopping time, workplace situations, social situations, travel time, and even face-to-face product time (291)

continuous innovations New products with more than just a minor product improvement, but that do not require radical changes by the consumer (177)

convenience products Items purchased frequently that are inexpensive and require minimum risk and shopping effort (151)

copyrights Used to legally protect the written word, a sound-recording, or a form of communication from being copied by others (155)

corporate social responsibility (CSR) When organizations voluntarily consider the well-being of society by taking responsibility for how their businesses impact consumers, customers, suppliers, employees, shareholders, communities, the environment, and society in general (16)

corporate websites Websites that provide corporate and brand information to consumers and the media (288)

cross-channel shopper An online consumer who researches products online and then purchases them at a retail store (222)

cross-cultural analysis Study of similarities and differences among consumers in two or more societies (74)

cultural symbols Objects, ideas, or processes that represent a particular group of people or society (74)

culture A set of values, ideas, and attitudes that are learned and shared among the members of a group (70)

Customer Advocacy Funnel A communications approach that takes consumers down a path of initial product awareness through to brand advocacy (290)

customer experience management (CEM) Managing customer interactions to build brand equity and improve long-term profitability (299)

customer lifetime value The potential sales that will be generated by a customer if that customer remains loyal to that company for a lifetime (307)

customer relationship management (CRM) The overall process of building and maintaining profitable customer relationships by delivering superior customer value and satisfaction (16, 299)

customer value The unique combination of benefits received by targeted buyers that includes quality, price, convenience, delivery, and both before-sale and after-sale service (6)

customs Norms and expectations about the way people do things in a specific country or culture (74)

data mining A process of analyzing customer patterns and insights to make better marketing decisions (306)

data warehouse A central repository of an organization's electronically stored data (306)

demand curve Graph relating quantity sold and price, which shows how many units will be sold at a given price (200)

demographics The statistical data on a population according to characteristics such as gender, age, ethnicity, income, education, and occupation (32, 130)

depth of product line Assortment of products within each product line that a store carries (249)

derived demand Demand for industrial products and services driven by demand for consumer products and services (107)

descriptive research Research designed to describe basic characteristics of a given population or to clarify its usage and attitudes (83)

development The new product idea is turned into a prototype for further consumer research and manufacturing tests (185)

direct competitors Similar products sold in the same category (45)

direct response A marketing communications tool designed to communicate with consumers one-on-one and elicit a direct action either online or offline (283)

discretionary income Money that consumers have left after paying taxes and buying necessities (43)

disintermediation Vertical channel conflict that arises when a channel member bypasses another member and sells directly to consumers (229)

display advertising The use of online ads with graphics or animation that are placed on websites (277)

disposable income Balance of income left after paying taxes; income that is used for spending and savings (42)

Do Not Call List (DNCL) Gives customers the ability to not receive telemarketing calls on cellphones, landline phones, and fax machines by registering the numbers of their communication devices (48)

dual distribution Arrangement whereby a firm reaches buyers by using two or more different types of channels for the same basic product (221)

dumping Occurs when a firm sells a product in a foreign country below its domestic prices or below its actual cost (209)

durable good An item that lasts over an extended number of uses (145)

earned media The free publicity secured through unpaid media mentions and consumers who spread the word through word-of-mouth or the Internet (269)

economy   The collective income, expenditures, and resources that affect the cost of running a business or a household (41)

electronic data interchange (EDI)   A computer-to-computer exchange of business documents from a retailer to a supplier and back (235)

electronic marketing channels   Channels that use the Internet to make goods and services available to consumers or business buyers (221)

e-mail marketing   The use of opt-in e-mail lists where consumers register and give permission to receive online communications (288)

e-marketplaces   Online trading communities that bring together buyers and supplier organizations (116)

event marketing   The creation or involvement of a brand in an experience or occasion that will heighten its awareness, create positive associations, and generate a desired response (284)

exchange   The trade of things of value between buyers and sellers so that each benefits (10)

exclusive distribution   Only one retail outlet in a specific geographical area carries the firm's products (227)

experiential marketing   Creating opportunities for consumers to directly interact with brands (19)

experiment   In marketing, changing a variable involved in a customer purchase to find out what happens (95)

exploratory research   Preliminary research conducted to clarify the scope and nature of the marketing problem (83)

fad   Novelty products with very short product life cycles that experience immediate rapid growth, followed by an equally rapid decline (174)

family brand   When a company uses a brand name to cover a number of different product categories (154)

family life cycle   A family's progression from formation to retirement, with each phase bringing distinct needs and purchasing behaviours (69)

fashion product   The life cycle for fashion is relatively short and cyclical, going from introduction to decline within two to three years, only to resurface again a few years later (173)

fixed cost   Firm's expenses that are stable and do not change with the quantity of product that is produced and sold (203)

fluctuating demand   Demand for business products and services fluctuates more than demand for consumer products and services (108)

focus group   A research technique where a small group of people (usually six to ten) meet for a few hours with a trained moderator to discuss predetermined areas (90)

form of ownership   Distinguishes retail outlets on the basis of whether individuals, corporate chains, or contractual systems own the outlet (242)

franchising   Contractual arrangement in which a parent company (the franchiser) allows an individual or firm (the franchisee) to operate a certain type of business under an established name and according to specific rules set by the franchiser (225)

Generation X   People born between 1965 and 1974 (34)

Generation Y   Also known as the millenials, people born between 1975 and 1991 (34)

Generation Z   Also known as the net generation, people born after 1992 (34)

generic brand   A product that has no branding and is produced as a cheap alternative to a manufacturer's brand and to branded private label products (159)

geographics   Where a target market lives using variables such as country, region, province, city size, and types of location such as urban, suburban, or rural (130)

global brand   Brand that is sold in a variety of international markets and enjoys wide recognition in these markets (156)

goals (objectives)   Targets of performance to be achieved within a specific time frame (318)

good   A product you can touch and own (10)

greenwashing   The deceptive use of marketing practices to give the impression that a good, service, or organization is environmentally friendly (176)

grey market   Situations where products are sold through unauthorized channels of distribution (209)

gross income   Total amount of money made in one year by a person, household, or family unit, including taxes (42)

harvesting   When a company keeps a product but reduces marketing support in an attempt to reap minor profits (172)

high-learning product   Significant consumer education is required for these products, which have an extended introductory period (173)

idea   A concept that typically looks for support (11)

idea generation   Focuses on brainstorming sessions to prompt new ideas (183)

idle production capacity   When the supply of a service exceeds its demand (147)

inbound marketing   When interested consumers find the product and its messaging by using online techniques that marketers facilitate, including search engine optimization, pay-per-click ads, and the use of social media to connect with consumers (272)

in-depth interview   A detailed interview where a researcher questions an individual at length in a free-flowing conversational style in order to discover information that may help solve a marketing problem (90)

indirect competitors   Products competing for the same buying dollar in a slightly different, but related category (45)

individual brand   When a company uses a brand name solely for a specific product category (154)

individualized marketing   Involves customizing offers and, in some cases, products to fit individual needs (127)

inelastic demand Demand for products does not change because of increases or decreases in price (108)

inflation A period when the cost to produce and buy products and services gets higher as prices rise (42)

integrated marketing communications (IMC) A communications approach that coordinates all promotional activities to provide a consistent message to a target audience (273)

intensive distribution A firm tries to place its products or services in as many outlets as possible (227)

intermediaries Individuals or firms performing a role in the marketing channel, involved in making a product available (217)

intertype competition Competition between very dissimilar types of retail outlets (250)

involvement Personal, social, and economic significance of a purchase to the consumer (59)

just-in-time (JIT) inventory system A system designed to deliver less merchandise on a more frequent basis than traditional inventory systems (235)

lead generation The requests for additional information that result from direct response marketing (283)

leaderboards Banner ads that stretch across the top of a web page (277)

learning Behaviours that result from repeated experience or reasoning (64)

level of service The degree of service provided to the customer by self-, limited-, and full-service retailers (247)

line extension The addition of a new item to an already existing product line (174)

logistics Activities that focus on getting the right amount of the right products to the right place at the right time at the lowest possible cost (229)

low-learning product Little consumer education is required, resulting in a short introductory stage for the product (173)

loyalty programs Programs specifically designed for customer retention (304)

macroeconomic forces The state of a country's economy as a whole as indicated by its growth rates, inflation rates, unemployment rates, and consumer confidence indexes (42)

manufacturers' agents Work for several producers and carry non-competitive, complementary merchandise in an exclusive territory (260)

manufacturer's brand A brand owned and produced by the manufacturer (158)

market Potential consumers with both the willingness and ability to buy (12)

market research The process of planning, collecting, and analyzing information in order to recommend actions to improve marketing activities (82)

market segmentation The aggregation of prospective buyers into groups that have common needs and respond similarly to marketing programs (123, 324)

market share Ratio of a firm's sales to the total sales of all firms in the industry (318)

marketing The process of planning and managing goods, services, or ideas to meet consumer needs and organizational objectives. It includes the conception of these products and the pricing, promotion, and distribution programs designed to make a profit and generate revenue or support for an organization. (10)

marketing channel The set of individuals or firms involved in the process of making a product available (216)

marketing communication agencies Broad-spectrum integrated agencies or specialist agencies that provide marketers with expertise on how best to communicate messages to their audiences (270)

marketing communication tools Advertising, public relations, sales promotion, direct response, event marketing and sponsorship, and personal selling (274)

marketing concept The idea that an organization should strive to satisfy the needs of consumers while also trying to achieve organizational goals (14)

marketing dashboard A visual computer display of essential marketing information (318)

marketing environmental scan The process of continually acquiring information on events occurring outside an organization to identify trends, opportunities, and threats to your business (31)

marketing information system (MIS) A set of procedures and processes for collecting, sorting, analyzing, and summarizing information on an ongoing basis (82)

marketing metric A measure of the value or trend of a marketing activity or result (319)

marketing mix The 4 Ps—product, price, place, and promotion (7)

marketing orientation Focusing organizational efforts to collect and use information about customers' needs to create customer value (14)

marketing plan Road map for the marketing activities of an organization for a specified future period of time (323)

marketing process The process of (1) identifying consumer needs, (2) managing the marketing mix to meet these needs, and (3) realizing profits (9)

marketing strategy Means by which a marketing goal is to be achieved (327)

marketing tactics Detailed day-to-day operational decisions essential to the overall success of marketing strategies (327)

markup The difference between selling price and cost, usually expressed as a percentage of cost (196)

mass marketing The marketing of a product to the entire market with no differentiation at all (124)

merchandise mix How many different types of products a store carries and in what assortment (249)

merchant wholesalers Independently owned firms that take title to the merchandise they handle (259)

metrics Measures and monitors business performance through the collection and usage of data used to evaluate marketing programs (21)

microeconomic forces The supply and demand of goods and services and how this is impacted by individual, household, and company decisions to purchase (42)

microsites Promotional websites created for short-term promotional purposes, often allowing consumers to enter contests and access promotional information (288)

minor innovations Minor product modifications that require no adjustments on behalf of the consumer (177)

mission Statement of the organization's purpose and direction (317)

mobile marketing The marketing on mobile devices such as cellphones and tablet computers to communicate with consumers through elements such as apps, quick response codes, text messaging, e-mail, mobile search, and web content repurposed for mobile devices (268)

monopolistic competition Type of competition where a large number of sellers compete with each other, offering customers similar or substitute products (46)

monopoly When only one company sells in a particular market (46)

motivation Energizing force that stimulates behaviour to satisfy a need (62)

multichannel marketing Blending of different communication and delivery channels that are mutually reinforcing in attracting, retaining, and building relationships with customers (222)

multichannel retailers Use a combination of traditional store formats and non-store formats such as catalogues and online retailing (252)

new product development process Sequence of steps that a firm takes to develop a new product idea and take it to market (183)

new product development strategy Setting the new product strategic direction for the company as a whole, and the precise objectives for the project at hand (183)

niche marketing Allows a company to focus its efforts on a limited segment in the market (126)

non-durable good An item that does not last and is consumed only once, or for a limited number of times (145)

non-probability sampling Selecting a sample so that the chance of selecting a particular element of a population is either unknown or zero (87)

North American Industry Classification System (NAICS) Provides common industry definitions for Canada, Mexico, and the United States (106)

objectives Specific, measurable goals (85, 318)

observational research Obtained by watching how people behave either in person or by using a machine to record the event (94)

off-price retailing Selling brand-name merchandise at lower than regular prices (251)

oligopoly Type of competition that occurs when a few companies control a market (46)

omnibus survey The voluntary participation of respondents in routine research surveys that allow marketers to add a small number of questions to an existing survey to receive cost-effective data (95)

online research bulletin boards Private online static forums, without real-time dialogue and engaging conversations, where respondents can post their responses to questions posed by researchers (91)

online research communities The use of consumer groups, brought together privately in an online environment, to answer questions, respond to ideas, and collaborate with researchers in real time (91)

online video advertising The use of video ads on the Internet (277)

opinion leaders Individuals who have social influence over others (68)

organizational buyers Manufacturers, wholesalers, retailers, and government agencies that buy goods and services for their own use or for resale (103)

organizational buying behaviour Process by which organizations determine the need for goods and then choose among alternative suppliers (112)

outbound marketing Marketers seek out consumers by widely broadcasting messages using advertising, direct mail, e-mail marketing, telemarketing, and personal selling approaches (272)

out-of-home advertising Casually referred to as outdoor; reaches consumers outside the home in outdoor locations, in transit, or in commercial or business locations (268)

owned media The media channels that a company controls, either fully or partially, such as a website, microsite, or social media page that is used to directly communicate with consumers (269)

paid media The media time purchased so that messages can be disseminated through channels that are controlled by others (269)

panel A large sample of respondents that voluntarily complete questionnaires on a regular basis so that researchers can assess changes in behaviour and attitudes (94)

Pareto's Rule The concept that 80 percent of a brand's sales come from 20 percent of its customers (304)

partnership marketing The creation of formal associations between brands that will result in incremental business for both brands that could not have been achieved separately (20)

patents Used to legally protect new technologies, unique processes, or formulations from usage by other companies (155)

pay-per-click advertising (PPC) Ads that appear on search engines and their networks, and on Facebook, LinkedIn, or YouTube in response to keyword triggers (277)

perceived risk   Anxiety felt when a consumer cannot anticipate possible negative outcomes of a purchase (64)

perception   Process by which someone selects, organizes, and interprets information to create a meaningful picture of the world (63)

perfect competition   Type of competition where there are many sellers with nearly identical products and little differentiation (46)

perishability   When products cannot be stored for long periods of time to use at a later date (147)

permission-based e-mail   When a recipient chooses to receive e-mail from an advertiser (288)

personal selling   The two-way flow of communication between a buyer and seller, often face-to-face, or facilitated through communication devices to influence an individual and group purchase decision (285, 270)

personality   A person's character traits that influence behavioural responses (63)

place   Distribution channels, retail formats, and merchandising used to sell a product (8)

positioning maps   Visual representations of how products are positioned in a category to consumers (136)

positioning statement   A tool that identifies the main reasons the target market buys a product and what sets it apart in the market (134)

power centre   Large shopping strip with multiple anchor stores, a convenient location, and a supermarket (252)

press conference   A planned event where representatives of the media are invited to an informational meeting with the company (281)

press release   An announcement written by an organization and sent to the media (281)

price   Expected retail or sale price of a product; money or other considerations exchanged for the ownership or use of a good or service (8, 191)

pricing constraints   Factors that limit the range of price a firm may set (206)

pricing objectives   Expectations that specify the role of price in an organization's marketing and strategic plans (204)

primary data   Data that is original and specifically collected for a project (90)

private label brand   Otherwise known as a store brand, a brand owned by a retailer that contracts its manufacturing to major suppliers, and then sells the product at its own retail stores (159)

probability sampling   Selecting a sample so that each element of a population has a specific known chance of being selected (87)

product   A good, a service, or an idea made up of tangible and intangible features, including product design, features, colour, packaging, warranty, and service levels (8, 10, 145)

product depth   The variety of product lines and products sold within a company's product categories, groups, or lines (150)

product differentiation   Involves positioning a product apart from the competition in the eyes of consumers (123)

product life cycle   The stages that a new product goes through starting with introduction and evolving into growth, maturity, and decline (167)

product line   A group of similar products with the same product and brand name that is directed at the same general target market and is marketed together (149)

product mix   The combination of product lines offered by a company (150)

product placement   The inclusion of a product in a movie or TV program in return for payment (287)

product positioning   The impression of the product you want to establish in consumers' minds relative to their needs and the competition (133)

product width   The number of different categories offered by the company (150)

production orientation   Focusing organizational efforts on the manufacture of goods (13)

profit   The excess of revenues over costs, the reward to a business for the risk it undertakes in offering a product for sale (315)

profit equation   Profit = Total revenue − Total cost (192)

promotion   Communication tools needed to inform consumers about a product, including advertising, public relations, sales promotion, direct response, event marketing and sponsorship, and personal selling (8, 230)

promotional mix   The selection of promotional tools used to communicate with a target market (291)

promotional partnerships   Simple short-term promotional offers between brands (20)

psychographics   Understanding consumers' attitudes to life, their personalities, general interests, opinions, and activities (131)

public relations   A communications tool that seeks to influence the opinions and attitudes of target groups through the use of unpaid media exposure; targets the media in an attempt to generate positive publicity for a company, product, or individual (279)

publicity   A non-personal form of communication that appears in the media and is and not paid for directly by the organization (280)

pull strategy   When marketers focus communication efforts on ultimate consumers to build awareness, trial, and demand for a product (289)

purchase decision process   Stages that a buyer passes through when making choices about which products or services to buy (56)

push strategy   When marketers focus communication on the distribution channel to gain support from retailers, distributors, and wholesalers through listings, sales, merchandising, or the inclusion in flyers (289)

qualitative research   A form of research that uses approaches such as focus groups, in-depth interviews, online communities, online bulletin boards, and social listening to provide insightful and directional information (88)

quantitative research Statistically reliable information that uses observational and/or questioning techniques such as observations, surveys, and experiments (93)

questionnaire Obtaining information by posing standardized questions through surveys that can be conducted in person, through the mail, on the telephone, or through the Internet (94)

radical innovations New products that involve the introduction of a product that is entirely new and innovative to the market (178)

recession A time of slow economic activity with two consecutive periods of negative growth (42)

reference groups Groups of people that influence a person's attitudes, values, and behaviour (68)

regional shopping centres Consist of 50 to 150 stores that typically attract customers who live within a 5- to 15-kilometre range; often containing two or three anchor stores (252)

regulations Restrictions placed on marketing practices by government and industry associations (47)

relationship marketing When organizations create long-term links with customers, employees, suppliers, and other partners to increase loyalty and customer retention (14)

relationship selling The practice of building long-term loyalty from customers based on a salesperson's attention and commitment to customer needs over time (286)

repositioning A revamping of a product and its marketing mix to more accurately meet consumer needs (135)

retailing All activities involved in selling, renting, and providing goods and services to ultimate consumers for personal, family, or household use (240)

retailing mix The goods and services, pricing, physical distribution, and communications tactics chosen by a store (247)

retargeted ads Display ads that ad networks re-deliver to a computer's IP address when a consumer previously clicked on an ad but did not respond to the offer (290)

reverse auction Occurs when a buyer communicates a need for something and would-be suppliers bid in competition with each other (118)

sales orientation Focusing organizational efforts on selling as many products as possible (13)

sales promotion A communications tool that provides short-term incentives to generate interest in a product or cause and encourages purchase or support (281)

sampling The process of gathering data from a subset of the total population rather than from all members of that particular group (87)

scrambled merchandising Offering several unrelated product lines in a single retail store (250)

screening and evaluation Reduces the list of brainstorming ideas down to a list of promising concepts (183)

search engine marketing (SEM) Includes the use of search engine optimization and pay-per-click advertising to market on search engines (287)

search engine optimization (SEO) Ensuring that websites are written, indexed, and coded so that they are highly rated and ranked by the search engines (287)

secondary data Facts and figures that have already been recorded by a third party (89)

segment marketing Designing different products and services to meet the needs of different target groups (124)

selective distribution A firm selects a few retail outlets in a specific geographical area to carry its products (227)

selling agent Represent a single producer and are responsible for the entire marketing function of that producer (260)

service A product that is intangible; an activity, benefit, or satisfaction offered for sale that you cannot touch (11, 145)

service continuum A range from tangible goods to intangible services (146)

share of wallet The percentage of a customer's purchases that a company has in a specific product category (308)

shopping products Items that require comparison-shopping between different brands and an investment of shopping time (151)

shrinkage Breakage and theft of merchandise by customers and employees (251)

situation analysis Taking stock of a firm or product's past performance, where it is now, and where it is headed (323)

skyscrapers Banner ads that are tall, slim, and vertical and appear along the side of a web page (277)

social listening Research that monitors public online consumer conversations on social media sites such as social networks, blogs, and forums (92)

social media A form of online media that allows members to create their own network of friends and contacts to share comments, videos, and images as a form of self-expression (15, 266)

social media release A multimedia online press release platform that includes video, text, and images, as well as social media buttons for sharing on social networks and comment areas where viewers can leave comments (281)

social network marketing The use of online communities or social networks to openly interact with the communities by sharing ideas, activities, events, and offers (288)

societal marketing concept Marketing programs that focus on the consumer and the well-being of society (18)

socio-cultural forces Cultural values, ideas, and attitudes, as well as society's morals and beliefs (37)

spam The dissemination of unsolicited electronic messages to recipients that have not requested them (50, 288)

specialty products Items for special occasions that require a specific product or brand and require considerable time and effort to purchase (152)

sponsorship When an advertiser pays a fee in exchange for inclusion in an event, involvement in its advertising opportunities, or exposure within the event itself (284)

strategic alliances Long-term strategic alliances between companies with similar values and marketing objectives that extend beyond short-term promotional offers into long-term formal business agreements (21)

strategic marketing process Approach whereby an organization allocates its marketing mix (323)

strategy A plan of action to achieve specific goals (315)

strip location A cluster of stores serving people who live within a 5- to 10-minute drive (252)

subcultures Subgroups within a larger culture that have unique values, ideas, and attitudes (71)

supply chain Sequence of firms that perform activities required to create and deliver a product to consumers or industrial users (230)

supply chain management Integration and organization of information and logistics activities across firms in a supply chain for the purpose of creating and delivering goods and services that provide value to consumers (230)

supply partnership Relationship between a buyer and supplier that adopt mutually beneficial objectives, policies, and procedures (111)

SWOT analysis Process by which a company can assess its internal strengths and weaknesses, as well as its external opportunities and threats, to identify opportunities and whether it has the strength to compete in a segment that may already

be well-served by the competition (32, 128, 323)

syndicated studies A hybrid of primary and secondary research whereby the cost of a research study is shared among clients and made available at a price to interested parties (94)

target market The specific group of existing and potential consumers to which marketers direct their marketing efforts (7)

technological forces Inventions from science or engineering research (43)

telemarketing Using the telephone to interact with and sell directly to consumers (254)

test market An in-market localized regional approach, or short-term online destination, used to test the success of promotional offers, new services, or new-product launches (95)

test marketing Offering a new product for sale on a limited basis in a defined geographic area to assess its success (185)

total cost Total expenses incurred by a firm in producing and marketing a product; total cost is the sum of fixed cost and variable costs (203)

total revenue Total money received from the sale of a product (202)

touch point Any situation in which a customer comes into contact with a brand or company (299)

trademarks Used to legally protect brand images, names, and designs from usage by others (155)

trade promotions Short-term promotional tools used to generate support with wholesalers, distributors, or retailers (282)

traditional auction Occurs when a seller puts an item up for sale and would-be buyers bid in competition with each other (118)

traffic generation The visits to a location or website that result from direct response marketing (283)

unsought products Unknown items or those of no interest to the purchaser (152)

user-generated content (UGC) Consumer content that is created by participants (281)

value The ratio of perceived benefits to price (192)

values Socially preferable modes of conduct or states of existence that tend to persist over time (74)

variable cost Sum of the expenses of the firm that vary directly with the quantity of products that is produced and sold (203)

vertical marketing systems Professionally managed and centrally coordinated marketing channels designed to achieve channel economies and maximum marketing impact (224)

virtual services Services that exist only online and have no person-to-person interaction (146)

word of mouth People influencing each other in personal conversations (68)

word-of-mouth marketing The spread of positive messages about a product by listening to consumers, identifying influential individuals that can spread the word, and making it easier for them to do so (286)

Chapter Notes

Chapter 1

1. iTunes apps, accessed at http://itunes.apple.com/app/snaptell/id291920403?mt=8#; SnapTell website, accessed at www.snaptell.com/apps.

2. Personal interview with Rob Morash, managing director Suunto Canada, May 2010.

3. "More Marketers Move Toward Engagement on Social Media," *eMarketer*, March 10, 2011, accessed at www.emarketer.com/Article.aspx?R=1008274.

4. ComScore press release, June 11, 2010, accessed at www.comscore.com/Press_Events/Press_Releases/2010/6/comScore_Releases_May_2010_U.S._Search_Engine_Rankings.

5. Mark Brohan, "The Top 500 Guide 2010," *Internet Retailer*, May 27, 2010, accessed at www.internetretailer.com/2010/05/27/top-500-guide?p=1.

6. Adapted from "Marketing," Business Dictionary website, 2010, accessed at www.businessdictionary.com/definition/marketing.html.

7. "Earth Hour," WWF-Canada website, 20110, accessed at www.wwf.ca/earthhour; Earth Hour newsletter, March 26, 2011, accessed at http://mail.panda.org/inxmail5/html_mail.jsp?params=336645+christina.clements%40humber.ca+0+mwj0i00e0000bnf3; "Canadians go dark with world for Earth Hour," CBC News, March 29, 2008, accessed at www.cbc.ca/world/story/2008/03/29/earth-hour.html; Jennifer MacMillan,"Canadians embrace Earth Hour," *The Globe and Mail*, March 27, 2008, accessed at www.theglobeandmail.com/news/national/article675949.ece; "Canada douses lights for Earth Hour," CBC News, March 27, 2010, accessed at www.cbc.ca/world/story/2010/03/27/earth-hour.html; Sara Falconer, "Earth Hour results are in!" WWF-Canada blog, April 1, 2010, accessed at http://blog.wwf.ca/blog/2010/04/01/earth-hour-results-are-in/2010.

8. "Scene adds Milestones Grill + Bar to its Points Program Menu," Marketwire, March 30, 2010, accessed at www.marketwire.com/press-release/SCENE-Adds-Milestones-Grill-Bar-to-its-Points-Program-Menu-1139906.htm.

9. WWF-Canada website, April 2011, accessed at http://wwf.ca/earthhour.

10. "Smart for two electric car," May 2011, accessed at www.thesmart.ca/information-service-electric-drive/e46d8929-c110-5337-8f7f-9a8c3549a788;sid=OxyBsPbp1hiGsLuSnZ9PvOZFjd_1kBISYJu7A9XR3-faN_2yArlUo7fzAa-iiIWNcbIddN5ljd_1kK-KLR4=; Toronto Hydro Smart Experience website, March 2011, accessed at www.smartexperience.ca; Smart Facebook page, March 2011, accessed at www.facebook.com/smartCanada; Club Smart car website, March 2011, accessed at www.clubsmartcar.ca; Jonathan Jenkins, "Dawn of the electric Smart Car era," *Toronto Sun*, November 29, 2010, accessed at www.torontosun.com/news/torontoandgta/2010/11/29/16365711.html; Nick Krewen, "Smart Horns in on Auto Show Action," *Strategy* magazine, February 17, 2010, accessed at www.strategyonline.ca/articles/news/20100217/smart.html; Emily Wexler, "AOY Honourable Mention: BBDO Winning Insights," *Strategy* magazine, November 1, 2010, accessed at www.strategyonline.ca/articles/magazine/20101101/aoyhonourable.html?page=3.

11. American Marketing Association, Marketing Power Resource Library, Dictionary, June 2010, accessed at www.marketingpower.com/_layouts/dictionary.aspx?dLetter=M.

12. Philip Kotler, Gary Armstrong, and Peggy H. Cunningham, *Principles of Marketing*, Seventh Canadian Edition (Toronto: Pearson, 2008).

13. "Good For Business: Corporate Social Responsibility Report 2010," *Maclean's* magazine, June 4, 2010, accessed at www2.macleans.ca/2010/06/14/jantzi-macleans-csr-report-2010.

14. "Sustainability & Responsibility Summary," Tim Hortons website, June 2010, accessed at www.timhortons.com/ca/pdf/2009CSR.pdf.

15. "CIBC Run for the Cure," CIBC website, May 2011, accessed at www.cibc.com/ca/inside-cibc/community-matters/cibc-run-for-the-cure.html.

16. "2008 Corporate Social Responsibility Update," HBC website, 2009, accessed at www.hbc.com/hbc/hbc_csr_eng_08/CSR08.pdf; "Social Responsibility," HBC website, 2009, accessed at www.hbc.com/hbc/socialresponsibility/environment/consumption; "Media Centre," HBC website, February 8, 2010, accessed at www.hbc.com/hbc/mediacentre/press/hbc/press.asp?prId=376.

17. "Doing Good 101," Pepsi Refresh Project website, May 2011, accessed at www.refresheverything.ca/docs/idea-toolkit.pdf; Pepsi Refresh Project, "Funded Ideas," May 2011, accessed at www.refresheverything.ca/grant-recipients; "Pepsi to Give away over $1 million Dollars to Fund Positive Ideas as the Pepsi Refresh Project Comes to Canada," CNW Group, April 16, 2010, accessed at http://smr.newswire.ca/en/pepsico-beverages-canada/pepsi-to-give-away-over-1-million-dollars-to-fund; Matt Semansky, "Pepsi enlists musicians to help refresh Canadian communities," *Marketing*, May 20, 2010, accessed at www.marketingmag.ca/english/news/marketer/article.jsp?content=20100520_144834_1620.

18. Interactive Advertising Bureau of Canada, *2010 Canadian Media Usage Trend Study*, March 2011.

19. comScore, *Canada Digital Year in Review 2010*, March 2011, accessed at www.comscore.com/Press_Events/Presentations_Whitepapers/2011/2010_Canada_Digital_Year_in_Review; "Canadians' Internet usage nearly double the worldwide average," *The Globe and Mail*, March 9, 2011, accessed at http://m.theglobeandmail.com/news/technology/canadians-internet-usage-nearly-double-the-worldwide-average/article1934508/?service=mobile; Matt Hartley, "Canada maintains title as world's most engaged Web nation," *National Post*, March 11, 2011, accessed at http://business.financialpost.com/2011/03/08/canada-maintains-title-as-worlds-most-engaged-web-nation.

20. The Shops at Don Mills website, June 2010, accessed at www.shopsatdonmills.ca/en/Pages/default.aspx; "Media Advisory—Shops at Don Mills—Ontario's first outdoor urban village—Celebrates opening weekend with family fun-filled Festival in the Square," CNW Group, April 24, 2009, accessed at www.newswire.ca/en/releases/archive/April2009/24/c4721.html; Jonathan Paul, "Extreme Group bags the Shops at Don Mills," *Strategy* magazine, June 3, 2010, accessed at www.strategyonline.ca/articles/news/20100603/extreme.html?__b=yes.

21. Kristen Laird, "John Freida highlights blonde hair care at special event," *Marketing*, June 21, 2010, accessed at www.marketingmag.ca/english/news/marketer/article.jsp?content=20100621_145726_1448; John Freida Facebook event page, June 2010, accessed at www.facebook.com/event.php?eid=115752068452420&index=1; John Freida Facebook page, June 2010, accessed at www.facebook.com/SheerBlondeCanada; John Freida website, June 2010, accessed at www.johnfrieda.ca/en.

22. "Partnership Marketing Seminar - Part 1," CMA website, June 2010, accessed at www.the-cma.org/?WCE=C=47|K=229840; Rod Kurtz, "Effective Affinity Marketing Programs," *Bloomberg Business Week*, October 8, 2007, accessed at www.businessweek.com/smallbiz/tips/archives/2007/10/effective_affinity_marketing_programs.html.

23. Sean B. Pasternak, "Scotiabank Adds 100,000 New Accounts in SCENE Loyalty Program," *Bloomberg*, July 24, 2008, accessed at www.bloomberg.com/apps/news?pid=newsarchive&sid=az7BZ9e5b5CE.

24. "Telus Case Study," Ontario Science Centre website, June 2010, accessed at www.ontariosciencecentre.ca/sponsor/partners/telus.asp.

25. Peter Nowak, "Copyright law could result in police state: critics," CBC News, June 12, 2008, accessed at www.cbc.ca/technology/story/2008/06/12/tech-copyright.html; Bill C-61, June 2010, accessed at www2.parl.gc.ca/housepublications/publication.aspx?docid=3570473&language=e&mode=1; "Copyright bill would bam breaking digital locks," CBC News, June 3, 2010, accessed at www.cbc.ca/technology/story/2010/06/02/copyright-bill-clement-montreal.html.

26. "Tougher consumer protection bill lauded," CBC News, June 10, 2010, accessed at www.cbc.ca/consumer/story/2010/06/10/con-consumer-bill-reax.html; "Federal consumer protection bill unveiled," CBC News, June 9, 2010, accessed at www.cbc.ca/consumer/story/2010/06/09/con-consumer-legislation.html; Tony Van Alphern and Dana Flavelle, "Toyota's troubles an example of consumer safety power," *Toronto Star*, February 20, 2010, accessed at www.thestar.com/news/insight/article/767771--toyota-s-troubles-an-example-of-consumer-safety-power.

27. "Simon Creet on social marketing," *Globe and Mail Report on Business*, June 4, 2009, accessed at www.theglobeandmail.com/report-on-business/article1133378.ece; "Cadbury Inspires Canadians to Make the World a Better Place, One Bicycle at a Time," Marketwire, April 16, 2009, accessed at www.marketwire.com/press-release/Cadbury-Inspires-Canadians-to-Make-the-World-a-Better-Place-One-Bicycle-at-a-Time-975667.htm; The Bicycle Factory website, June 2010, April 2011 accessed at www.thebicyclefactory.ca/Landing.aspx; Katherine Dorell, "Hope, Survival, Freedom," *Canadian Living*, May 2010, pp. 93–96; The Bicycle Factory Facebook page, April 2011, accessed at www.facebook.com/BicycleFactory.

Chapter 2

1. Personal interview with Andrew Pollock, senior VP marketing, Canada Bread, May 2010.

2. "2006 Census of Canada," Statistics Canada, www12.statcan.ca/census-recensement/index-eng.cfm.

3. "2006 Census: Age and sex," *The Daily*, Statistics Canada, July 17, 2007, accessed at www.statcan.gc.ca/daily-quotidien/070717/dq070717a-eng.htm.

4. "Money and the Canadian Family," The Vanier Institute, www.vifamily.ca.

5. "Births: 2006," Statistics Canada Catalogue no. 84F0210X, September 2008, accessed at www.statcan.gc.ca/pub/84f0210x/84f0210x2006000-eng.pdf.

6. Statistics Canada, Market Research Handbook, 63-224.

7. Lisa E. Philips, "Boomers and Social Media," *eMarketer*, January 2010, accessed at www.emarketer.com/Report.aspx?code=emarketer_2000649.

8. David K. Foot, *Boom, Bust & Echo: How to Profit from the Coming Demographic Shift* (Toronto: Macfarlane Walter & Ross, 1996).

9. "Getting Inside Gen Y," *American Demographics*, September 2001, p. 44.

10. "Portrait of the Canadian Population in 2006, by Age and Sex, 2006 Census," Statistics Canada Catalogue no. 97-551-XIE, July 2007, p. 13, accessed at www12.statcan.gc.ca/english/census06/analysis/agesex/pdf/97-551-XIE2006001.pdf.

11. "Population and dwelling counts," *The Daily*, Statistics Canada, March 13, 2007, accessed at www.statcan.gc.ca/daily-quotidien/070313/dq070313a-eng.htm.

12. Terry Poulton, "Boomers ready to spend: Ipsos Reid," *Media in Canada*, May 9, 2008, accessed at www.mediaincanada.com/articles/mic/20080509/boomers.html; Chris Powell, "Marketers missing boomer boat: CNA study," *Marketing* magazine, May 09, 2008, accessed at www.marketingmag.ca/english/news/media/article.jsp?content=20080509_777333_2521; Lisa E. Philips, "Boomers and Social Media"; Jennifer Van Grove, "Baby Boomers and Seniors Are Flocking to Facebook [STATS]," *Mashable*, January 2010, accessed at http://mashable.com/2010/01/28/baby-boomers-social-media; Anderson Analytics, "Social Network Service (SNS) A&U Profiler," July 13, 2009, cited by Lisa E. Philips in "Boomers and Social Media."

13. "Portrait of the Canadian Population in 2006, 2006 Census," Statistics Canada Catalogue no. 97-550-XIE, March 2007, p. 24, www12.statcan.ca/census-recensement/2006/as-sa/97-550/pdf/97-550-XIE2006001.pdf.

14. "2006 Census: Immigration, citizenship, language, mobility and migration," *The Daily*, Statistics Canada, December 4, 2007, accessed at www.statcan.gc.ca/daily-quotidien/071204/dq071204a-eng.htm.

15. Ibid.

16. U.S. Census Bureau, International Data Base, December 15, 2008, accessed at www.census.gov/cgi-bin/ipc/idbrank.pl.

17. Various Olympic Game websites, including www.cineplex.com/Promos/CTVOlympicGamesBroadcastAtCineplex/FAQ.aspx, accessed February 1, 2010; www.facebook.com/ctvolympics, accessed March 1, 2010; http://twitter.com/W_Olympics_2010, accessed March 1, 2010; www.fark.com/farq, accessed March 1, 2010; http://ctvmedia.ca/olympics, accessed March 1, 2010.

18. "Canadian Food Trends to 2020," *Agriculture and Agri-Food Canada*, February 24, 2009, accessed at www4.agr.gc.ca/AAFC-AAC/display-afficher.do?id=1170944121865&lang=eng.

19. SupperWorks website, June 2010, accessed at www.supperworks.com.

20. "Many buy green products for status," CBC News, March 16, 2010, accessed at www.cbc.ca/consumer/story/2010/03/16/green-products-status.html.

21. Paul Brent, "Changing Lanes," *CAA Magazine*, Spring 2010, pp. 28–29.

22. "About the RBC Blue Water Project," RBC Blue Water Project website, June 2010, accessed at http://bluewater.rbc.com/about.php; Jeromy Lloyd, "RBC makes a splash for Blue Water Project," *Marketing*, June 14, 2010, accessed at www.marketingmag.ca/english/news/marketer/article.jsp?content=20100611_170416_13320; "RBC announces first wave of 2010 RBC Blue Water Project Leadership Grant recipients," CNW, June 10, 2010, accessed at www.newswire.ca/en/releases/archive/June2010/10/c3708.html.

23. "Ottawa boosts Canada's GDP forecast," CBC News, April 26, 2010, accessed at www.cbc.ca/money/story/2010/04/26/ottawa-forecast-private-sector.html.

24. *The Bensimon Byrne Consumerology Report: Technology and Canadian Consumers*, January 2010, accessed at www.consumerology.ca.

25. Press release, "comScore Introduces Device Essentials™ for Measuring Digital Traffic from All Devices, Enabling Optimization of Marketing Strategies and Customer Experience," ComScore, June 23, 2011, accessed at www.comscore.com/Press_Events/Press_Releases/2011/6/comScore_Introduces_Device_Essentials.

26. "Deloitte predicts 2010 technology trends," *The Globe and Mail*, January 19, 2010, accessed at www.theglobeandmail.com/news/technology/deloitte-predicts-2010-technology-trends/article1436466; "The TMT Predictions 2010 edition," Deloitte Canada YouTube channel, December 19, 2009, accessed at www.youtube.

com/watch?v=l-6ZAIBpO84&feature=player_embedded; Matthew Knell, "This Cloud Computing Has No Silver Lining," *Advertising Age*, June 15, 2009, accessed at http://adage.com/digitalnext/article?article_id=137286.

27. "False or Misleading Representations," Ensuring Truth in Advertising, Competition Bureau, February 18, 2010, accessed at http://competitionbureau.gc.ca/eic/site/cb-bc.nsf/eng/00513.html; news release, "Jail Sentence for Deceptive Telemarketer," Competition Bureau, April 29, 2008, accessed at www.competitionbureau.gc.ca/eic/site/cb-bc.nsf/eng/02666.html; news release, "Deceptive Telemarketer Receives Jail Time," Competition Bureau, July 27, 2009, accessed at www.competitionbureau.gc.ca/eic/site/cb-bc.nsf/eng/03112.html; news release, "Toronto Company Receives Record $15 Million Fine," Competition Bureau, December 18, 2009, accessed at www.competitionbureau.gc.ca/eic/site/cb-bc.nsf/eng/03175.html.

28. News release, "CRTC announces that Bell Canada has paid a $1.3 million penalty for violating the National Do Not Call List Rules," Canadian Radio-television and Telecommunications Commission, December 20, 2010, accessed at www.crtc.gc.ca/eng/com100/2010/r101220.htm.

29. "Broadcast Advertising Basics: Revenue, Limits and Content," Consumers-Radio and Television—Advertising, Canadian Radio-television and Telecommunications Commission, February 18, 2010, accessed at www.crtc.gc.ca/eng/info_sht/b300.htm.

30. "Canadian Children's Food and Beverage Advertising," Advertising Standards Canada, accessed July 2010 at www.adstandards.com/en/childrensinitiative/default.htm; news release, "Canada's Food and Beverage Industry Unveils Integrated Children-Focused Initiatives: New Social Marketing Campaign and Advertising Commitment Focused on Healthy Active Living," Food and Consumer Products of Canada, April 16, 2007, accessed at www.fcpmc.com/mediaroom/releases/2007/ca041607-eng.pdf; Elaine D. Kolish, "Progress In Action: Children's Food & Beverage Advertising Self Regulation: A Report From the BBB FTC/HHS Forum," July 18, 2007, accessed at www.ftc.gov/bcp/workshops/childobesity/presentations/kolish.pdf; Canadian Marketing Association website, July 2010, accessed at www.the-cma.org.

31. "CMA Privacy Compliance Guide," Canadian Marketing Association, May 2010, accessed from www.the-cma.org/PublicUploads/225771PCG2006.pdf.

32. "Canadian Marketing Association Guide to Promotional Contests," Canadian Marketing Association, May 2010, accessed from www.the-cma.org/?WCE=C=47|K=225856.

Chapter 3

1. Personal interview with Gordon Woit, June 2010.

2. James F. Engel, Roger D. Blackwell, and Paul Miniard, *Consumer Behavior*, 9th ed. (Fort Worth, TX: Dryden Press, 1998).

3. For thorough descriptions of consumer expertise, see Joseph W. Alba and J. Wesley Hutchinson, "Knowledge Calibration: What Consumers Know and What They Think They Know," *Journal of Consumer Research*, September 2000, pp. 123–56.

4. For in-depth studies on external information search patterns, see Sridhar Moorthy, Brian T. Ratchford, and Debabrata Tulukdar, "Consumer Information Search Revisited: Theory and Empirical Analysis," *Journal of Consumer Research*, March 1997, pp. 263–77; and Joel E. Urbany, Peter R. Dickson, and William L. Wilkie, "Buyer Uncertainty and Information Search," *Journal of Consumer Research*, March 1992, pp. 452–63.

5. For an extended discussion on evaluative criteria, see Del J. Hawkins, Roger J. Best, and Kenneth A. Coney, *Consumer Behavior*, 8th ed. (New York: Irwin/McGraw-Hill, 2001), pp. 566–83.

6. John A. Howard, *Buyer Behavior in Marketing Strategy*, 2nd ed. (Englewood Cliffs, NJ: Prentice Hall, 1994), pp. 101, 128–89.

7. Jagdish N. Sheth, Banwari Mitral, and Bruce Newman, *Consumer Behavior* (Fort Worth, TX: Dryden Press, 1999), p. 22.

8. For an overview of research on involvement, see John C. Mowen and Michael Minor, *Consumer Behavior*, 6th ed. (Upper Saddle River, NJ: Prentice Hall, 2001), pp. 64–68; and Frank R. Kardes, *Consumer Behavior* (Reading, MA: Addison-Wesley, 1999), pp. 256–58.

9. For an overview on the three problem-solving variations, see Hawkins, Best, and Coney, *Consumer Behavior*, pp. 506–7; and Howard, *Buyer Behavior*, pp. 69–162.

10. Hollie Shaw, "Fast Food Makes You Think Fast," *National Post*, April 23, 2010, page FP10; "Importance of Brand Recognition," accessed June 2010 at www.syncrat.com/articles/importance-of-brand-recognition; "Fast food makes you think fast," *The Trucker's Report*, April 26, 2010, accessed at www.thetruckersreport.com/truckingindustryforum/financial-news-and-stocks/108907-fast-food-makes-you-think-fast.html.

11. Russell Belk, "Situational Variables and Consumer Behavior," *Journal of Consumer Research*, December 1975, pp. 157–63.

12. "Shopping As Therapy: Good Health Comes In Small Packages," *Discover Fit & Health*, accessed June 2011 at http://health.howstuffworks.com/wellness/women/general/shopping-as-therapy.htm.

13. A. H. Maslow, *Motivation and Personality* (New York: Harper & Row, 1970).

14. Arthur Koponen, "The Personality Characteristics of Purchasers," *Journal of Advertising Research*, September 1960, pp. 89–92; Joel B. Cohen, "An Interpersonal Orientation to the Study of Consumer Behavior," *Journal of Marketing Research*, August 1967, pp. 270–78; and Rena Bartos, *Marketing to Women Around the World* (Cambridge, MA: Harvard Business School, 1989).

15. Michael R. Solomon, *Consumer Behavior*, 5th ed. (Upper Saddle River, NJ: Prentice Hall, 2002), p. 61.

16. BMW website, www.bmw.com/generic/com/en/services/service/index.html?content=service_overview.html.

17. Martin Fishbein and I. Aizen, *Belief, Attitude, Intention and Behavior: An Introduction to Theory and Research* (Reading, MA: Addison-Wesley, 1975), p. 6.

18. Richard J. Lutz, "Changing Brand Attitudes through Modification of Cognitive Structure," *Journal of Consumer Research*, March 1975, pp. 49–59; "Pepsi's Gamble Hits Freshness Dating Jackpot," *Advertising Age*, September 19, 1994, p. 50; and "Every Which Way to Color, Whiten, Brighten," *Brandweek*, June 17, 2002, p. 558.

19. "How many hours of sleep are enough?" Mayo Clinic website, accessed at www.mayoclinic.com/health/how-many-hours-of-sleep-are-enough/AN01487.

20. See, for example, Lawrence F. Feick and Linda Price, "The Market Maven: A Diffuser of Marketplace Information," *Journal of Marketing*, January 1987, pp. 83–97.

21. "Maximizing the Market with Influentials," *American Demographics*, July 1995, p. 42; also see, "I'll Have What He's Having," *American Demographics*, July 2000, p. 22.

22. Representative recent work on positive and negative word of mouth can be found in Robert E. Smith and Christine A. Vogt, "The Effects of Integrating Advertising and Negative Word-of-Mouth Communications on Message Processing and Response," *Journal of Consumer Psychology* 4 (1995), pp. 133-51; Paula Bone, "Word-of-Mouth Effects on Short-Term and Long-Term Product Judgments," *Journal of Business Research* 32 (1995), pp. 213-23; Chip Walker, "Word of Mouth," *American Demographics*, July 1995, pp. 38-45; and Dale F. Duhan, Scott D. Johnson, James B. Wilcox, and Gilbert D. Harrell, "Influences on Consumer Use of Word-of-Mouth Recommendation Sources," *Journal of the Academy of Marketing Science*, Fall 1997, pp. 283-95.

23. For an extended discussion on reference groups, see Wayne D. Hoyer and Deborah J. MacInnis, *Consumer Behavior*, 2nd ed. (Boston: Houghton Miffin, 2001), chap. 15.

24. For an extensive review on consumer socialization of children, see Deborah Roedder John, "Consumer Socialization of Children: A Retrospective Look at Twenty-Five Years of Research," *Journal of Consumer Research*, December 1999, pp. 183-213.

25. This discussion is based on "The American Family in the 21st Century," *American Demographics*, August 2001, p. 20; and J. Paul Peter and Jerry C. Olson, *Consumer Behavior and Marketing Strategy*, 5th ed. (New York: Irwin/McGraw-Hill, 1999), pp. 341-43.

26. "Household Type, in Private Households, 2001 Counts, for Canada, Provinces and Territories," Statistics Canada, www12.statcan.ca/english/census01/products/highlight/PrivateHouseholds/Page.cfm?Lang=E&Geo=PR&Code=0&View=1a&Table=1&StartRec=1&Sort=2&B1=Counts.

27. Diane Crispell, "Dual-Earner Diversity," *American Demographics*, July 1995, pp. 32–37.

28. "There She Is . . . ." *American Demographics*, August 2001, p. 6; "Wearing the Pants," *Brandweek*, October 20, 1997, pp. 20, 22; and "Look Who's Shopping," *Progressive Grocer*, January 1998, p. 18.

29. "Call It 'Kid-fluence,'" *U.S. News & World Report*, July 30, 2001, pp. 32–33; "Special Report: Superstars of Spending," *Advertising Age*, February 20, 2001, pp. S1, S10; and Teen Research Unlimited, www.teenresearch.com, downloaded September 4, 2001.

30. Word of Mouth Marketing Association (WoMMA), www.womma.org.

31. Statistics Canada Catalogue # 97F0007XCB1007.

32. Danny Kucharsky, "French Lessons," *Marketing* magazine, March 27, 2006, p. 8.

33. Ed Crain, "Say 'Oui' to the Quebec Market," *Electronic Retailer*, August 2010, accessed at www.electronicretailermag.com/er0810_quebec.

34. Rebecca Harris, "Embrace and Prosper," *Marketing* magazine, January 23, 2006.

35. Joel Kurtzman, "Toyota's Problems Start at the Top," *Harvard Business Review*, March 11, 2010, accessed at http://blogs.hbr.org/cs/2010/03/toyotas_problems_start_at_the_1.html; Chauncey Zalkin, "Made in Japan: The Culture Behind the Brand," Brandchannel.com, April 13, 2009, accessed at www.brandchannel.com/features_effect.asp?pf_id=473; Jean-Claude Saade, "Fall from Grace", Brandchannel.com, March, 2010, accessed at www.brandchannel.com/images/papers/497_Fall_From_Grace.pdf; "Toyota Vindicated by U.S. Investigation," Macleans.ca, February 10, 2011, accessed at www2.macleans.ca/2011/02/10/toyota-vindicated-by-u-s-investigation.

36. For comprehensive references on cross-cultural aspects of marketing, see Paul A. Herbig, *Handbook of Cross-Cultural Marketing* (New York: Halworth Press, 1998); and Jean-Claude Usunier, *Marketing across Cultures*, 2nd ed. (London: Prentice Hall Europe, 1996). Unless otherwise indicated, examples found in this section appear in these excellent sources.

37. "McDonald's Adapts Mac Attack to Foreign Tastes with Expansion," *Dallas Morning News*, December 7, 1997, p. 3H; and "Taking Credit," *The Economist*, November 2, 1996, p. 75.

38. Patricia Adams, "Foreign aid corruption case puts Canada on trial," *National Post*, August 20, 1999.

39. These examples appear in Del I. Hawkins, Roger J. Best, and Kenneth A. Coney, *Consumer Behavior*, 8th ed. (Burr Ridge, IL: McGraw-Hill/Irwin, 2001), chap. 2.

40. "Greeks Protest Coke's Use of Parthenon," *Dallas Morning News*, August 17, 1992, p. D4.

41. Valentina Vescovi and Aixa Rocca, "In Argentina, Pepsi Becomes 'Pecsi,'" *Advertising Age*, July 15, 2009, accessed at http://adage.com/globalnews/article?article_id=137946.

42. "Global Thinking Paces Computer Biz," *Advertising Age*, March 6, 1995, p. 10.

43. "If only Krispy Kreme makes you smarter," *Business 2.0*, August 2005, p. 108.

Chapter 4

1. Interview and discussions with Luke Sklar, partner and founder of SW&A, August 2010 and April 2011.

2. Gandalf Group, *The Bensymon Byrne Consumerology Report Segmentation*, January 2011, accessed at http://consumerology.ca.

3. For an expanded definition, consult the American Marketing Association's website at www.marketingpower.com; for a researcher's comments on this and other definitions of marketing research, see Lawrence D. Gibson, "Quo Vadis, Marketing Research?" *Marketing Research*, Spring 2000, pp. 36–41.

4. Syncapse Corporation in association with Hotspex, "The Value of a Facebook Fan: An Empirical Review, June 2010," accessed at www.syncapse.com/media/syncapse-value-of-a-facebook-fan.pdf; Syncapse Corporation, "Powerful New Research Reveals Value of Facebook for Marketers," Marketwire, Jun 11, 2010, accessed at www.marketwire.com/press-release/Powerful-New-Research-Reveals-Value-of-Facebook-for-Marketers-1274905.htm.

5. "Focus on Consumers," *General Mills Midyear Report* (Minneapolis, MN: General Mills, January 8, 1998), pp. 2–3.

6. Jessica Hogue, "Building a Better Burger? Try Listening for Product Development," Nielsenwire, April 2010, accessed at http://blog.nielsen.com/nielsenwire/online_mobile/building-a-better-burger-try-social-listening-for-product-development; Paul M. Banas, "Social Listening: Focusing on Insights," *Insight Buzz*, January 2010, accessed at www.insightbuzz.com/2010/01/18/social-listening-focusing-on-insights; Suresh Vittal, "Listening Metrics that Matter. Avoid Data Overload by Targeting Metrics that Support Specific Listening Goals," Forrester Research, May 29, 2009, accessed at www.forrester.com/rb/Research/listening_metrics_that_matter/q/id/54700/t/2.

7. BBM Canada, "The PPM System," accessed August 2010 at http://bbm.ca/index.php?option=com_content&task=view&id=16&Itemid=89.

8. Conversation with John Vavrik, director of the B.C. Centre for Strategic Management of Risk in Transportation, n.d.

9. Leger Marketing, "Online Surveys," accessed August 2010 at www.legermarketing.com/eng/webstudies.asp.

10. Interview with Paula Gignac, president, IAB Canada, March 2011.

Chapter 5

1. Peter LaPlaca, "From the Editor," *Journal of Business and Industrial Marketing*, Summer 1992, p. 3.

2. This figure is based on Statistical Abstract of the United States: 2002, 122nd ed. (Washington, DC: U.S. Census Bureau, 2002).

3. Umberto Milletti, "B2B Companies Must Keep Pace with the Customer 2.0," *Social Media B2B*, June 7, 2010, accessed at http://socialmediab2b.com/2010/06/b2b-company-customer; Danny Brown, "B2B Marketing and Social Media—Close, But No Cigar. Yet..." blog, June 1, 2010, accessed at http://dannybrown.me/2010/06/01/bb-marketing-social-media-close-but-no-cigar-yet.

4. "Canada's Manley Says Government Spending C$5 Bln Under Budget," Bloomberg.com, September 29, 2003.

5. "List of Canadian registered charities," Canada Revenue Agency website, www.cra-arc.gc.ca/tax/charities/online_listings/can-reg_interim-e.html.

6. *2002 NAICS United States Manual* (Washington, DC: Office of Management and Budget, January 2002).

7. This listing and portions of the following discussion are based on F. Robert Dwyer and John F. Tanner, Jr., *Business Marketing*, 2nd ed. (Burr Ridge, IL: McGraw-Hill/Irwin, 2002); and Edward G. Brierty, Robert W. Eckles, and Robert R. Reeder, *Business Marketing*, 3rd ed. (Upper Saddle River, NJ: Prentice Hall, 1998).

8. John T. Connelly, "Bombardier: 186 Subway Cars Ordered for Toronto Transit," *Business Review Canada*, May 13, 2010, accessed at www.businessreviewcanada.ca/news/transportation/bombardier-186-subway-cars-ordered-toronto-transit.

9. Gord Hotchkiss, "The Buyer Sphere Project," *Enquiro*, accessed at www.enquiro.com/b2bresearch.

10. Joe Castaldo, "Those Emotional Canadians!" *Canadian Business*, April 27–May 10, 2010, Vol. 83, Iss. 7, p. 32; Jason Buckland, "Top 10 places to work in Canada," *MSN Money*, accessed at http://money.ca.msn.com/savings-debt/gallery/gallery.aspx?cp-documentid=23864240.

11. These definitions are adapted from Frederick E. Webster, Jr., and Yoram Wind, *Organizational Buying Behavior* (Englewood Cliffs, NJ: Prentice Hall, 1972), p. 6.

12. Thomas V. Bonoma, "Major Sales: Who Really Does the Buying?" *Harvard Business Review*, May–June 1982, pp. 11–19.

13. Ibid.

14. These definitions are adapted from Frederick E. Webster, Jr., and Yoram Wind, *Organizational Buying Behavior* (Englewood Cliffs, NJ: Prentice Hall, 1972), p. 6.

15. "Can Corning Find Its Optic Nerve?" *Fortune*, March 19, 2001, pp. 148–50.

16. Representative studies on the buy-class framework that document its usefulness include Erin Anderson, Wujin Chu, and Barton Weitz, "Industrial Purchasing: An Empirical Exploration of the Buy-Class Framework," *Journal of Marketing*, July 1987, pp. 71–86; Morry Ghingold, "Testing the 'Buy-Grid' Buying Process Model," *Journal of Purchasing and Materials Management*, Winter 1986, pp. 30–36; P. Matthyssens and W. Faes, "OEM Buying Process for New Components: Purchasing and Marketing Implications," *Industrial Marketing Management*, August 1985, pp. 147–57; and Thomas W. Leigh and Arno J. Ethans, "A Script-Theoretic Analysis of Industrial Purchasing Behavior," *Journal of Marketing*, Fall 1984, pp. 22–32. Studies not supporting the buy-class framework include Joseph A. Bellizi and Philip McVey, "How Valid Is the Buy-Grid Model?" *Industrial Marketing Management*, February 1983, pp. 57–62; and Donald W. Jackson, Janet E. Keith, and Richard K. Burdick, "Purchasing Agents' Perceptions of Industrial Buying Center Influences: A Situational Approach," *Journal of Marketing*, Fall 1984, pp. 75–83.

17. "Evolution, Not Revolution," *Forbes*, May 21, 2001, pp. 38–39; "Business Connections: The Wired Way We Work," *Newsweek*, April 30, 2001, p. 59; and "Behind the Crystal Ball," *The Industry Standard*, March 26, 2001, pp. 81–83.

18. This discussion is based on Mark Roberti, "General Electric's Spin Machine," *The Industry Standard*, January 22–29, 2001, pp. 74–83; "Smart Business 50," *Smart Business*, November 2000, pp. 121–50; and "Grainger Lightens Its Digital Load," *Industrial Distribution*, March 2001, pp. 77–79.

19. "Internet Trading Exchanges: E-Marketplaces Come of Age," *Fortune*, April 15, 2001, special section; "Private Exchanges May Allow B-to-B Commerce to Thrive after All," *The Wall Street Journal*, March 16, 2001, pp. B1, B4; and Steven Kaplan and Mohanbir Sawhney, "E-Hubs: The New B2B Marketplaces," *Harvard Business Review*, May–June, 2000, pp. 97–103.

20. "Doing Business in Japan," accessed at www.kwintessential.co.uk/etiquette/doing-business-japan.html; "Doing Business in Japan," accessed at http://eurotechnology.com/doing-business-in-japan/06_japanese_business_etiquette.shtml; "Business Card & Travel Etiquette Guide: For Japan", accessed at www.asianbusinesscards.com/japanese-business-card-culture-tips-japan.html.

21. Quadrem website, www.quadrem.com.

22. A major portion of this discussion is based on Robert J. Dolan and Youngme Moon, "Pricing and Market Making on the Internet," *Journal of Interactive Marketing*, Spring 2000, pp. 56–73; and "Auctions Have Taken the Internet by Storm," *Dallas Morning News*, January 25, 2001, pp. 1F, 9F.

23. Bob Tedeschi, "GE Has a Bright Idea," *Smart Business*, June 2001, pp. 86–91.

24. Sandy Jap, "Going, Going, Going," *Harvard Business Review*, November–December, 2000, p. 30.

Chapter 6

1. Personal interview with Kyle McCarthy, director Atomic Skis, May 2010.

2. Cassies 2009 Cases, "Brand/Case: Koodo Mobile Reshapes the Category," accessed at http://cassies.ca/caselibrary/winners/2009pdfs/9_C09_Koodo_BL_Web_inc_credits.pdf; Koodo website, accessed September 2010 at www.koodomobile.com; Koodo YouTube channel, accessed September 2010 at www.youtube.com/user/Koodo; press release, "INQ Chat 3G Available Now at Koodo. Koodo Helps Bring Affordable Social Phones to Canada," Marketwire, July 28, 2010, accessed at www.marketwire.com/press-release/INQ-Chat-3G-Available-Now-at-Koodo-1296609.htm; Melita Kuburas, "Koodo Mobile throws an all-ages party," *Media in Canada*, August 11, 2009, accessed at www.mediaincanada.com/articles/mic/20090811/koodo.html; Katie Bailey, "Koodo invites fans into the ring with El Tabador," *Media in Canada*, April 5, 2010, accessed at www.mediaincanada.com/

articles/mic/20100405/koodo_game.html; Melita Kuburas, "Koodo rings bell for Last Mask Standing competition," *Media in Canada*, August 6, 2010, accessed at www.mediaincanada.com/articles/mic/20100806/koodo.html; David Brown, "Koodo is working out," *Marketing* magazine, March 31, 2008, accessed at http://marketingblog.blogspot.com/2008/03/koodo-is-working-out.html; David George-Cosh, "Telus' Koodo Mobile brand launched," *Financial Post*, March 18, 2008, accessed at http://network.nationalpost.com/np/blogs/fpposted/archive/2008/03/18/telus-koodo-mobile-brand-launched.aspx; Lisa Hannam, "Is Koodo campaign a good fit?" Marketing magazine, April 4, 2008, accessed at http://marketingblog.blogspot.com/2008/04/is-koodo-campaign-good-fit.html; Roberto Rocha, "Koodos to Telus," *The Gazette*, April 3, 2008, accessed at www.canada.com/montrealgazette/news/business/story.html?id=0b384d47-a6bd-442d-919c-38a37abf094b.

3. Press release, "Kellogg Company Acquires Kashi Company," PR Newswire, June 29, 2000, accessed at www.highbeam.com/doc/1G1-63041175.html.

4. Kashi website, accessed September 2010, at www.kashi.ca/AboutUs.

5. "Method introduces new laundry detergent in pump bottle. Package is designed to dispense detergent directly into washer, reduce waste," *Packaging Digest*, January 14, 2010, accessed at www.packagingdigest.com/article/444345-Method_introduces_new_laundry_detergent_in_pump_bottle.php; press release, "Method Revolutionizes Laundry Detergent with New Technology and Design," Businesswire, January 14, 2010, accessed at www.businesswire.com/news/home/20100114005315/en/Method-Revolutionizes-Laundry-Detergent-Technology-Design; Method website, accessed September 2010 at www.methodhome.com; Method Facebook page, accessed September 2010 at www.facebook.com/method?v=info.

6. National Consumer Survey Choices 3 Cross tabulation Report: Fast-Food Restaurants (New York: Simmons Market Research Bureau, Spring, 2001).

7. John Intini, "Joe's Fresh Take. How Loblaws became the new king of Canadian fashion," *Maclean's*, January 25, 2010, accessed at www2.macleans.ca/2010/01/25/joes-fresh-take; press release, "Canadian Children's Fashion 'Grows with Joe' as Joe Fresh Style Launches Kids Collection for Back-to-School Season," CNW Group, July 25, 2007, accessed at www.newswire.ca/en/releases/archive/July2007/25/c9169.html; press release, "Loblaws & Joe Fresh Style launch cosmetics collection," CNW Group, March 17, 2009, accessed at www.newswire.ca/en/releases/archive/March2009/17/c9286.html; press release, "Joe Fresh Beauty & Loblaws launch Bath collection," CNW Group, October, 2009, accessed at www.newswire.ca/en/releases/archive/October2009/20/c8079.html; press release, "Kim Cattrall Is Announced as the Face of This Year's Fashion Targets Breast Cancer Campaign. Rethink Breast Cancer and the Joe Fresh Style brand launch new product and exciting contest to help beat breast cancer," Marketwire, April 15, 2010, accessed at www.marketwire.com/press-release/Kim-Cattrall-Is-Announced-as-Face-This-Years-Fashion-Targets-Breast-Cancer-Campaign-1148149.htm; Carey Toane," Manufacturing Chic," *Strategy*, February 1, 2010, accessed at www.strategyonline.ca/articles/magazine/20100201/bizfashion.html; press release, "Walmart redesigns 300+ stores to welcome restyled George," CNW Group, August 2010, accessed at www.newswire.ca/en/releases/archive/August2010/31/c6021.html; Kristin Laird, "Walmart Counts on George in a Big Way," *Marketing* magazine, September 02, 2010, accessed at www.marketingmag.ca/english/news/marketer/article.jsp?content=20100902_143918_5736; Hollie Shaw, "Wal-Mart pits its George vs. Joe Fresh," *National Post*, August 31, 2010, accessed at www.nationalpost.com/Mart+pits+George+Fresh/3462627/story.html#ixzz10SGYnVky.

8. Press release, "PepsiCo Canada Leads with First Nationally Available Beverage Innovation Containing Pure Stevia Extract. Introducing Aquafina Plus Vitamins 10 CalTM Vitamin-enhanced Water With PureViaTM All Natural Sweetener," Marketwire, October 14, 2009, accessed at www.marketwire.com/press-release/PepsiCo-Canada-Leads-With-First-Nationally-Available-Beverage-Innovation-Containing-1059529.htm.

9. "Fact Sheet: Starbucks VIA™ Ready Brew Fact Sheet – Canada," Starbucks Newsroom, August 31, 2009, accessed at http://news.starbucks.com/article_display.cfm?article_id=257.

10. "McDonald's wins back breakfast," Cassies 2010, accessed at http://cassies.ca/winners/2010Winners/winners_mcdonalds.html; Kristin Laird, "McDonald's Serves Up Fresh, Free Coffee for All," *Marketing* magazine, April 20, 2009, accessed at www.marketingmag.ca/english/news/marketer/article.jsp?content=20090417_172002_8608; Rob Roberts, "McDonald's goes all Starbucks on us," *National Post*, September 13, 2007, accessed at http://network.nationalpost.com/np/blogs/toronto/archive/2007/09/13/mcdonald-s-goes-all-starbucks-on-us.aspx; Thulasi Srikanthan, "McDonald's outlets getting comfy look," *Toronto Star*, September 13, 2007, accessed at www.thestar.com/Business/article/256023.

Chapter 7

1. Richard E. Brown, *Superbrands Canada: An Insight into Many of Canada's Strongest and Most Trusted Brands*, Volume II, Superbrands Canada Inc.: 2008.

2. "Virgin Mobile Canada Uses Rewards to Inspire Volunteers," Ad-Age blog, June 9, 2011.

3. Personal interview with Peter Furnish, director of retail experience, Virgin Mobile, June 2010.

4. Statistics Canada, "Gross Domestic Product (GDP) by Industry Sector: 2001-2009," Canadian Industry Statistics, accessed January 2011 from Industry Canada at www.ic.gc.ca/eic/site/cis-sic.nsf/eng/h_00016.html#gdp2c.

5. Christina Clements, "Gap Logo Redesign—A Look Back," *Mktg-Cliks* blog, December 12, 2010, accessed January 2011 at http://mktgcliks.blogspot.com/2010/12/gap-logo-redesign-look-back.html (adapted with permission); Juli Weiner, "New Gap Logo, Despised Symbol of Corporate Banality, Dead at One Week," *Vanity Fair*, October 12, 2010, accessed January 2011 at www.vanityfair.com/online/daily/2010/10/new-gap-logo-despised-symbol-of-corporate-banality-dead-at-one-week.html; Armin, "Don't Mind the Gap, or the Square," *Brand New* blog, October 6, 2010, accessed January 2011 from www.underconsideration.com/brandnew/archives/dont_mind_the_gap_or_the_square.php; Jennifer Van Grove, "Gap Asks Facebook Fans for Alternative Designs to Derided New Logo," *Mashable* blog, October 7, 2010, accessed January 2011 at http://mashable.com/2010/10/07/gap-logo-redesign; Marka Hansen, "The Gap's New Logo," *The Huffington Post*, October 7, 2010, accessed January 20111 at www.huffingtonpost.com/marka-hansen/the-gaps-new-logo_b_754981.html; Melissa Bell, "After Internet hazing, Gap logo goes away," *The Washington Post*, October 12, 2010, accessed January 2011 at http://voices.washingtonpost.com/blog-post/2010/10/gap_logo_gets_internet_hazed_a.html; Press release, "Gap Listens to Customers and will Keep Classic Blue Box Logo," Gap website, October 11, 2010, accessed January 2011 at www.gapinc.com/public/Media/Press_Releases/med_pr_GapLogoStatement10112010.shtml.

6. "What is a Patent?" Canadian Intellectual Property Office, accessed January 2011 from www.cipo.ic.gc.ca/eic/site/cipointernetinternetopic.nsf/eng/Home.

7. "What is a Trade-mark?" Canadian Intellectual Property Office, accessed January 2011 from www.cipo.ic.gc.ca/eic/site/cipointernet-internetopic.nsf/eng/Home.

8. "Branding, Advertising, and Marketing Dictionary," Brandchannel.com, accessed January 2011 from www.brandchannel.com/education_glossary.asp#B.

9. Rob Osler, "The Name Game: Tips on How to Get It Right," *Marketing News*, September 14, 1998, p. 50; and Keller, *Strategic Brand Management*. See also Pamela W. Henderson and Joseph A. Cote, "Guidelines for Selecting or Modifying Logos," *Journal of Marketing*, April 1998, pp. 14–30; and Chiranjeev Kohli and Douglas W. LaBahn, "Creating Effective Brand Names: A Study of the Naming Process," *Journal of Advertising Research*, January–February 1997, pp. 67–75.

10. "A Survey of Multinationals," *The Economist*, June 24, 1995, p. 8.

11. Rachel Hanley, "From Googol to Google," *The Stanford Daily*, February 12, 2003, accessed January 2011 at www.stanforddaily.com/2003/02/12/from-googol-to-google.

12. Paul Thurrott, "The Fun Never Stops: Microsoft vs. MikeRowe-Soft," *Windows IT Pro*, January 20, 2004, www.winnetmag.com/Article/ArticleID/41510/41510.html.

13. Facebook application "Wordscraper," accessed January 2011 at www.facebook.com/apps/application.php?id=2521910901; Facebook application "Scrabble," accessed January 2011 at www.facebook.com/Theofficialscrabble; Facebook group "Save Scrabulous," accessed January 2011 at www.facebook.com/group.php?gid=4772916593; Nick Parrish, "Hasbro Moves Beyond Uproar to Create a New Web 'Monopoly,'" *Advertising Age*, February 22, 2010, accessed at http://adage.com/digitalalist10/article?article_id=142172; "Scrabble loses copyright claim but wins trademark," KNS Partners website, accessed January 2011 at www.knspartners.com/files/Scrabble_loses_copyright_claim_but.pdf; "Facebook asked to pull Scrabulous game," CBC News, January 16, 2008, accessed at www.cbc.ca/technology/story/2008/01/16/tech-scrabulous.html; Mathew Ingram, "Viral marketing or trademark theft?" *The Globe and Mail*, January 16, 2008, accessed, at www.theglobeandmail.com/servlet/story/RTGAM.20080116.WBmingram20080116132835/WBstory/WBmingram/?page=rss&; Matt Semansky, "How Do You Spell 'D-I-L-E-M-M-A'?" *Marketing* magazine, April 14, 2008, accessed at www.marketingmag.ca/english/news/marketer/article.jsp?content=20080414_71238_71238; Chris Sorensen, "Scrabble makers want Scrabulous scrapped," *Toronto Star*, January 16, 2008, accessed at www.thestar.com/Business/article/294676; "Scrabble knockoff returns," Associated Press, July 31, 2008, accessed at www.theglobeandmail.com/servlet/story/RTGAM.20080731.wgtscrabulous0731/BNstory/Technology/home.

14. News release, "Private Label is Very Public," The Nielsen Company, October 14, 2009, accessed at http://ca.acnielsen.com/content/nielsen/en_ca/news/news_releases/2009/private_label_is_very.html.

15. "Canadian Company Receives Final Tender Approval from Rwanda for Vital AIDS Drug," Apotex press release, May 7, 2008, accessed at www.apotex.com/PressReleases/20080507-01.asp?flash=Yes; press release, "Second Shipment Of Life-Saving Aids Drug Leaving for Africa," Apotex, September 18, 2009, accessed from www.apotex.com/global/about/press/20090918.asp.

16. Cassies 2009 Cases, "Brand/Case: President's Choice Winner: Retail–Silver," Cassies Case Library, accessed January 2010 from http://cassies.ca/content/caselibrary/winners/2009pdfs/18_C09_PChoice_Web.pdf; Katie Bailey, "PC Financial Galen-ifies its marketing," *Media in Canada*, September 16, 2010, accessed from www.mediaincanada.com/articles/mic/20100916/pcfinancial.html.

17. *Canadian Media Directors' Council Media Digest 2008/2009*, p. 6, accessed at www.cmdc.ca/pdf/2008_09_media_digest.pdf.

Chapter 8

1. Personal interview with Ian Gordon, January 2011.

2. Ethan Bloch, "A Year of Twitter," *Flowtown* blog, December 13, 2010, accessed at www.flowtown.com/blog/a-year-of-twitter?; site analytics of Twitter, accessed at Compete.com.

3. C. Phocas, *The management of innovations with specific reference to the compact disc.* M.B.A. Dissertation, University of Bradford Management Centre, 1983.

4. "Book Club Gadgets," *Chatelaine*, December 2010, p. 178; Amazon.com Kindle Store, accessed January 2011 at www.amazon.com/dp/B002Y27P3M/?tag=gocous-20-&hvadid=5729120357&ref=pd_sl_cazfqv6ny_b.

5. Press release, "Introducing the All-New Kindle Family: Four New Kindles, Four Amazing Price Points," Amazon.com, September 28, 2011, accessed at http://phx.corporate-ir.net/phoenix.zhtml?ID=1610968&p=irol-newsArticle&c=176060.

6. Raymund Flandez, "Small Charities Could Get Big Lift From New Social Network," *The Chronicle of Philanthropy*, November 16, 2010, accessed at http://philanthropy.com/blogs/social-philanthropy/small-charities-could-get-big-lift-from-new-social-network/27716; Brenna Ehrich, "Facebook Co-founder Launches Non-profit Platform Called Jumo," *Mashable* blog, March 18, 2010, accessed at http://mashable.com/2010/03/18/jumo; "Facebook Meets Charity: Talk to Chris Hughes, Founder of Jumo," *The Chronicle of Philanthropy*, December 7, 2010, accessed at http://philanthropy.com/article/Facebook-Meets-Charity/125; Jumo website, www.jumo.com; Adrianne Jeffries and Ben Popper, "Jumo 'Acquired' for $0 and a Graceful Exit," *BetaBeat*, August 17, 2011, accessed at www.betabeat.com/2011/08/17/0-acquisition-of-jumo-gets-chris-hughes-a-graceful-exit-great-pr-for-good; Ellen McGirt, "Chris Hughes' Jumo and GOOD Join Forces," *Fast Company*, August 16, 2011, accessed at www.fastcompany.com/1774012/jumo-and-good-join-forces-for-even-more-good.

7. Gabriel Madway, "Jobs Blast Rivals as iPad Sales Disappoint," Reuters, October 19, 2010, accessed at www.reuters.com/article/idUSTRE69H4UX20101019; Ben Patterson, "iPad Sales Cross Million Mark Twice as Fast as Original iPhone," Yahoo News, May 3, 2010, accessed at http://news.yahoo.com/s/ytech_gadg/20100503/tc_ytech_gadg/ytech_gadg_tc1901.

8. "TSN is No. 1 with Canadian Sports Fans, According to National Audience Survey," CNW Group, April 16, 2008, accessed at www.newswire.ca/en/releases/archive/April2008/16/c6088.html.

9. Patterson, "iPad Sales Cross Million Mark Twice as Fast as Original iPhone."

10. Barry Silverstein, "UGG Australia the Good, the Bad, and the UGGly," *Brandchannel*, December 10, 2007, accessed at www.brandchannel.com/features_profile.asp?pr_id=365; Barry Silverstein, "New Counterfeit Gambit; Knock off Cheaper brands," *Brandchannel*, August 3, 2010; accessed at www.brandchannel.com/home/post/2010/08/03/New-Counterfeit-Gambit-Knock-Off-Cheaper-Brands.aspx#continue.

11. Product information sheet, "Samba Days Gift-experiences Cadeaud'activites, Canada's Leading Gift Experience Provider," accessed November 2011; Sanam Islam, "Partners leverage gift card idea 'Experience' boxes," *Financial Post*, December 8, 2010; interview with Alex Barseghian, CEO Samba Days, November 2011.

12. Press release, "Interbrand Announces Canada's 201 Best brands by Value," Interbrand, May 17, 2010, accessed at www.interbrand.com/en/news-room/press-releases/2010-05-17.aspx; "Best Canadian Brands 2010 The Definitive Guide to Canada's Most Valuable Brands," Interbrand, May 2010, accessed at www.interbrand.com/Libraries/Branding_Studies/Best_Canadian_Brands_2010.sflb.ashx.

13. Press release, "2010 Best New Product Award Winners Announced," BrandSpark International, January 19, 2010, accessed at www.bestnewproductawards.biz/canada/pdf/2010-BNPA-Winners-19-JAN-10.pdf.

14. Kevin J. Clancy, Peter C. Krieg, and Marianne McGarry Wolf, *Market New Products Successfully: Using Simulated Test Market Technology*, Lexington Books, page 5, The Rowan and Littlefield Publishing Company, 2006.

15. Lisa C. Troy, Tanawat Hirunyawipada, and Audhesh K. Paswan, "Cross-functional I and New Product Success: An Empirical Investigation of the Findings," *Journal of Marketing*, November 2011; Calvin Hodock, "Winning the New Products Game; Know What Kills and Innovation Ahead of Time and Dodge Failures," *Advertising Age*, November 12, 2007, accessed at http://adage.com/print?article_id=121912; Clancy, et al, *Market New Products Successfully: Using Simulated Test Market Technology*; Copernicus Market Consulting, "10 Reasons Why New Products and Services Fail," Copernicum University, accessed at www.copernicusmarketing.com/univers/reasons_for_product_failure.shtml; Eugene Sivadas and F. Robert Dwyer, "An Examination of Organizational Factors Influencing New Product Success in Internal and Alliance-Based Processes," *The Journal of Marketing*, Vol. 64, No. 1 (Jan., 2000), pp. 31-49, American Marketing Association, accessed at www.jstor.org/pss/3203389; J.C. Narver, S.F. Slater, and D. L MacLachlan, "Responsive and Proactive Market Orientation and New-Product Success," *Journal of Product Innovation Management*, Vol. 21, pp. 334–347, September 2004; Lane Anderson, "Ten Keys to New Consumer Products," Prospecta Marketing, accessed January 2011 at www.prospectamarketing.com/ArticlesAndCaseStudies/tenkeys.htm; R. G. Cooper and E. J. Kleinschmidt, "New Products—What Separates Winners from Losers?" Journal of Product Innovation Management, September 1987, pp. 169–84; Robert G. Cooper, *Winning at New Products*, 2nd ed. (Reading, MA: Addison-Wesley, 1993), pp. 49–66; and Thomas D. Kuczmarski, "Measuring Your Return on Innovation," *Marketing Management*, Spring 2000, pp. 25–32.

16. Chris Sorensen, "Bright Idea: Drama for 3-D TVs," *Maclean's*, January 31, 2011, p. 45.

17. Press release, "Polaroid and Lady Gaga Announce Grey Label," Polaroid, Jan 6, 2011, accessed at http://polaroid.com/en/press/2011/1/6/polaroid-and-lady-gaga-announce-grey-label; Shirley Brady, "Lady Gaga Unveils Polaroid Grey Label Collaboration at CES," *Brandchannel*, January 6, 2011, accessed at www.brandchannel.com/home/post/2011/01/06/Lady-Gaga-Unveils-Polaroid-Grey-Label-at-CES.aspx; Barry Silverstein, "Polaroid Touched up," *Brandchannel*, May 4, 2009, accessed at www.brandchannel.com/features_profile.asp?pr_id=437; Don Clarke, "Lady Gaga at CES: Camera Glasses anyone?" *Wall Street Journal*, January 6, 2011, accessed at http://blogs.wsj.com/digits/2011/01/06/lady-gaga-returns-to-ces-with-new-products; personal interview with Will Mlacak, January 2011.

18. "Coca-Cola Blak Enters Canada," Canwest News Service, August 31, 2006, accessed at www.canada.com/topics/finance/story.html?id=9b4cd2d7-344b-4095-ba60-31b1bbf2166d&k=4816.

19. "Mixed Reviews for 'Lord of the Rings' Musical," CBC News, March 25, 2006, accessed at www.cbc.ca/arts/story/2006/03/24/lordoftherings-reviews.html; Jordan Timm, "With This Ring, They Thee Mock. A New Production Sends up Toronto's Disastrous 'Lord of the Rings: The Musical," Macleans.ca, accessed at www.macleans.ca/article.jsp?content=20070709_107127_107127.

20. John Gilbert, "To Sell Cars in Japan, U.S. Needs to Offer More Right-Drive Models," *Star Tribune*, May 27, 1995, p. M1.

21. "Sonic Sinker," *The Economist*, November 23, 2002, p. 58.

22. Kevin J. Clancy and Peter C. Krieg, "Surviving Innovation: Common Testing Mistakes Can Derail a Promising New product Launch," *Marketing Management*, March/April 2003, pp.14–20.

23. Robert Berner, "Why P&G's Smile Is So Bright," *Business Week*, August 12, 2002, pp. 58–60.

24. Christopher Ryan, "Virtual reality in marketing," *Direct Marketing*, April 2001, p. 57.

Chapter 9

1. Sue Zesiger Callaway, "Bachelor Meets Bugatti," *Fortune*, March 19, 2007, pp. 214–15; and www.bugatti.com.

2. Adapted from Kent B. Monroe, *Pricing: Making Profitable Decisions*, 3rd ed. (New York: McGraw-Hill, 2003).

3. Roger A. Kerin and Robert A. Peterson, "Throckmorten Furniture (A)," *Strategic Marketing Problems: Cases and Comments*, 9th ed. (Englewood Cliffs, NJ: Prentice Hall, 1998), pp. 235–45.

4. For the classic description of skimming and penetration pricing, see Joel Dean, "Pricing Policies for New Products," *Harvard Business Review*, November–December 1976, pp. 141–53. See also, Reed K. Holden and Thomas T. Nagle, "Kamikaze Pricing," *Marketing Management*, Summer 1998, pp. 31–39.

5. Jean-Noel Kapferer, "Managing Luxury Brands," *Journal of Brand Management*, July 1997, pp. 251–60.

6. "Why That Deal Is Only $9.99," *Business Week*, January 10, 2000, p. 36. For further reading on odd-even pricing, see Robert M. Schindler and Thomas M. Kilbarian, "Increased Consumer Sales Response through Use of 99-Ending Prices," *Journal of Retailing*, Summer 1996, pp. 187–99; Mark Stiving and Russell S. Winer, "An Empirical Analysis of Price Endings with Scanner Data," *Journal*

of *Consumer Research*, June 1997, pp. 57–67; and Robert M. Schindler, "Patterns of Rightmost Digits Used in Advertised Prices: Implications for Nine-Ending Effects," *Journal of Consumer Research*, September 1997, pp. 192–201.

7. Thomas T. Nagle and Reed K. Holden, *The Strategy and Tactics of Pricing*, 3rd ed. (Englewood Cliffs, NJ: Prentice Hall, 2002), pp. 243–49.

8. Ibid., pp. 237–39.

9. "Credit card fee battle in the cards?" *Toronto Star*, November 29, 2008, accessed at www.thestar.com/article/545726; "What Are These Fees?" accessed at http://stopstickingittous.com/about.

10. Peter M. Noble and Thomas S. Gruca, "Industrial Pricing: Theory and Managerial Practice," *Marketing Science* 18, no. 3 (1999), pp. 435–54.

11. George E. Belch and Michael A. Belch, *Introduction to Advertising and Promotion*, 5th ed. (New York: Irwin/McGraw-Hill, 2001), p. 93.

12. Tyler Hamilton, "Sharing the Road," *Toronto Star*, February 20, 2010, accessed at www.thestar.com/business/article/768531; "Taking Car-sharing to the Max," *Toronto Star*, February 20, 2010, accessed at www.thestar.com/business/article/768533.

13. Frank Bruni, "Price of Newsweek? It Depends," *Dallas Times Herald*, August 14, 1986, pp. S1, S20.

14. "Henderson jersey coming back to Canada: Buyer," CBC News, June 23, 2010, accessed at www.cbc.ca/canada/story/2010/06/23/henderson-hockey-canada.html.

15. "Will Tablets Close the Book on e-Readers?" Knowledge @ Wharton, July 7, 2010, accessed at http://knowledge.wharton.upenn.edu/printer_friendly.cfm?articleid=2539.

16. Brent Jang, "Airlines fined $1.1-billion over price-fixing," *The Globe and Mail*, November 9, 2010, accessed at www.theglobeandmail.com/globe-investor/air-canada-others-fined-for-price-fixing/article1791755.

17. Marina Strauss, "Grafton-Fraser fined for misleading sale prices," *The Globe and Mail*, July 28, 2006. p. B8.

18. News release, "Zellers Agrees to Take Action to Correct Misleading Promotion," Competition Bureau, June 29, 2010, accessed at www.competitionbureau.gc.ca/eic/site/cb-bc.nsf/eng/03255.html; "Zellers rebuked for Avatar promotion," CBC News, June 29, 2010, accessed at www.cbc.ca/consumer/story/2010/06/29/zellers-competition.html.

19. "Stores Told to Lift Prices in Germany," *The Wall Street Journal*, September 11, 2000, pp. A27, .

20. "Rotten Apples," *Dallas Morning News*, April 7, 1998, p. 14A.

21. "When Grey Is Good," *The Economist*, August 22, 1998, p. 17; and Neil Belmore, "Parallel Imports and Grey Market Issues," The Canadian Institute, December 5–6, 2001.

22. "How Dell Fine-Tunes Its PC Pricing to Gain Edge in a Slow Market," *The Wall Street Journal*, June 8, 2001, pp. A1, A8.

23. For an extensive discussion on discounts, see Kent B. Monroe, *Pricing: Making Profitable Decisions*, 2nd ed. (New York: McGraw Hill, 1990), chaps. 14 and 15.

Chapter 10

1. See Peter D. Bennett, ed., *Dictionary of Marketing Terms*, 2nd ed. (Chicago: American Marketing Association, 1995).

2. PepsiCo, Inc., Annual Report 1997.

3. This discussion is based on Bert Rosenbloom, *Marketing Channels: A Management View*, 6th ed. (Fort Worth: Dryden Press, 1999), pp. 452–58.

4. Johny K. Johansson, "International Alliances: Why Now?" *Journal of the Academy of Marketing Science*, Fall 1995, pp. 301–4.

5. "Eddie Bauer's Banner Time of Year," *Advertising Age*, October 1, 2001, p. 55.

6. Michael Krantz, "Click Till You Drop," *Time*, July 20, 1998, pp. 34–39.

7. *Multi-Channel Integration — The New Retail Battleground* (Columbus, OH: PricewaterhouseCoopers, March 2001).

8. "Don't Cut Back Now," *Business Week e-biz*, October 1, 2001, p. EB34.

9. *Fighting Fire with Water — From Channel Conflict to Confluence* (Cambridge, MA: Bain & Company, July 1, 2000).

10. For an overview of vertical marketing systems, see Lou Pelton, David Strutton, and James R. Lumpkin, *Marketing Channels*, 2nd ed. (Burr Ridge, IL: McGraw-Hill/Irwin, 2003), chap. 14.

11. "5 Down 95 to Go," www.apple.com, downloaded August 1, 2001; Apple Computer, press release, May 21, 2001; "Apple to Open Its First Retail Store in New York City," www.apple.com, downloaded July 20, 2002.

12. For an extensive discussion on channel conflict, see Anne T. Coughlan, Erin Anderson, Louis W. Stern, and Adel I. El-Ansary, *Marketing Channels*, 6th ed. (Upper Saddle River, NJ: Prentice Hall, 2001).

13. "Coke Returns to Costco with its Dignity Intact," *Brandchannel*, Dec. 11, 2009, accessed at www.brandchannel.com/home/post/2009/12/11/Coke-Returns-To-Costco-With-Its-Dignity-Intact.aspx.

14. For an extensive discussion on power and influence in marketing channels, see Coughlan et al., *Marketing Channels*.

15. *What's It All About?* (Oakbrook, IL: Council of Logistics Management, 1993).

16. This example is described in David Sinchi-Levi, Philip Kaminsky, and Edith Sinchi-Levi, *Designing and Managing the Supply Chain* (Burr Ridge, IL: McGraw-Hill/Irwin, 2000), p. 5.

17. This discussion is based on Robyn Meredith, "Harder than the Hype," *Forbes*, April 16, 2001, pp. 188–94; Robert M. Monczka and Jim Morgan, "Supply Chain Management Strategies," *Purchasing*, January 15, 1998, pp. 78–85; and Robert B. Handfield and Earnest Z. Nichols, *Introduction to Supply Chain Management* (Upper Saddle River, NJ: Prentice Hall, 1998), chap. 1.

18. Major portions of this discussion are based on Sunil Chopra and Peter Meindl, *Supply Chain Management: Strategy, Planning, and Operations* (Upper Saddle River, NJ: Prentice Hall, 2001), chaps. 1–3; and Marshall L. Fisher, "What Is the Right Supply Chain for Your Product?" *Harvard Business Review*, March–April 1997, pp. 105–17.

19. Kasra Ferdows, Michael A. Lewis and Jose A.D. Machuca, "Rapid-Fire Fulfillment," *Harvard Business Review*, Vol. 82, No. 11, November 2004, accessed at http://hbswk.hbs.edu/archive/4652.html; "The future of fast fashion; Inditex," *The Economist*, Vol. 375, Iss. 8431, June 18, 2005, p. 63; Richard D'Aveni, "Fashion Conscious: Lessons in Commoditization from the Fashion Industry," *Ivey Business Journal*, March/April 2010, accessed at www.iveybusinessjournal.com/article.asp?intArticle_ID=889; Kim Anderson and Jim Lovejoy, "The Speeding Bullet: Zara's Apparel Supply Chain," accessed at www.techexchange.com/thelibrary/speeding.html.

20. "Wal-Mart Expands Commitment to RFID," *Material Handling Management*, May 2007, Vol. 62, Iss. 5, pg. 8.

21. Rebecca Walberg, "Never Lose Inventory Again," *Financial Post*, July 6, 2010, accessed at www.financialpost.com/Never+lose+inventory+again/3239772/story.html; Miguel Bustillo "Wal-Mart Radio Tags to Track Clothing," *Business Technology*, July 23, 2010, accessed at http://bx.businessweek.com/rfid/view?url=http%3A%2F%2Fonline.wsj.com%2Farticle%2FSB10001424052748704421304575383213061198090.html.

Chapter 11

1. Kenneth Cline, "The Devil in the Details," *Banking Strategies*, November–December 1997, p. 24; and Roger Trap, "Design Your Own Jeans," *The Independent*, October 18, 1998, p. 22.

2. Bank of Montreal website, www.bmo.com.

3. Retail Council of Canada website, www.retailcouncil.org/news/media/profile.

4. "Retail trade, by industry," Statistics Canada, accessed at www40.statcan.ca/l01/cst01/trad15a-eng.htm; "Yukon Retail Sales," Yukon Bureau of Statistics, December 2010, accessed at www.eco.gov.yk.ca/stats/pdf/retail_dec10.pdf.

5. "Feeling the squeeze: Global Powers of Retailing 2009," Deloitte Touche Tohmatsu, accessed at http://public.deloitte.com/media/0460/2009GlobalPowersofRetail_FINAL2.pdf.

6. Marina Strauss and Jacquie McNish, "With Target, Canada's retail landscape set for massive makeover", *The Globe and Mail*, January 13, 2011, accessed at www.theglobeandmail.com/globe-investor/with-target-canadas-retail-landscape-set-for-massive-makeover/article1868308.

7. "Retail Trade-Establishments, Employees, and Payroll," *Statistical Abstract of the United States*, 120th ed. (Washington, DC: U.S. Department of Commerce, Bureau of the Census, October 2000); and Gene Koretz, "Those Plucky Corner Stores," *Business Week*, December 5, 1994, p. 26.

8. James Cowan, "Retail: The genius of Dollarama," *Canadian Business*, February 15, 2010, accessed at www.canadianbusiness.com/managing/strategy/article.jsp?content=20100113_10020_10020; Sean Silcoff, "How Does Dollarama Make a Profit? One Buck at a Time," *Canadian Business*, January 9, 2009, accessed at www.citytv.com/toronto/citynews/life/money/article/7834--how-does-dollarama-make-a-profit-one-buck-at-a-time; Marina Strauss, "Dollarama Aims to Keep it Simple", *The Globe and Mail*, August 10, 2010, accessed at www.theglobeandmail.com/globe-investor/dollarama-aims-to-keep-it-simple/article1668621.

9. "Franchise 500," *Entrepreneur*, January 2001; and Scott Shane and Chester Spell, "Factors for New Franchise Success," *Sloan Management Review*, Spring 1998, pp. 43–50.

10. Alexandra Lopez-Pacheco, "Customers expect quality even in recession," *National Post*, January 27, 2008, p. FP7.

11. Tim Manners, "Shopper Marketing," *Fast Company*, June 14, 2008, accessed at www.fastcompany.com/blog/tim-manners/shop-talk/shopper-marketing.

12. Marina Strauss, "Holt's Opens Doors a Little More Widely," *The Globe and Mail*, September 2, 2010, accessed at www.theglobeandmail.com/report-on-business/holts-opens-doors-a-little-more-widely/article1693204/?cmpid=tgc; Hollie Shaw, "Holt Renfrew Wants to Make You Feel Welcome," *National Post*, September 2, 2010, accessed at www.canada.com/nationalpost/financialpost/story.html?id=fe06d3f5-9230-47b5-bf90-23674d0559d3.

13. "Holt Renfrew... One of the World's Leading Fashion and Lifestyle Shopping Experiences Benchmarked against the Best," Holt Renfrew website, accessed at www.holtrenfrew.com/english/history.

14. "Canadian Trade-Mark Data," Canadian Intellectual Property Office, accessed at www.cipo.ic.gc.ca/app/opic-cipo/trdmrks/srch/vwTrdmrk.do;jsessionid=0001aVzIlRWXB-TRtDf81OHAa5I:3UAPV7CT3?lang=eng&status=OK&fileNumber=1503650&extension=0&startingDocumentIndexOnPage=1.

15. "Media Advisory - Apple to Open Retail Store at Southgate Centre in Edmonton on Friday, May 28," CNW Group, May 28, 2010, accessed at www.newswire.ca/en/releases/archive/May2010/26/c6729.html.

16. Francis J. Mulhern and Robert P. Leon, "Implicit Price Bundling of Retail Products: A Multiproduct Approach to Maximizing Store Profitability," *Journal of Marketing*, October 1991, pp. 63–76.

17. Gwen Ortmeyer, John A. Quelch, and Walter Salmon, "Restoring Credibility to Retail Pricing," *Sloan Management Review*, Fall 1991, pp. 55–66.

18. William B. Dodds, "In Search of Value: How Price and Store Name Information Influence Buyers' Product Perceptions," *Journal of Consumer Marketing*, Spring 1991, pp. 15–24.

19. Barry Brown, "Edmonton Makes Size Pay Off in Down Market," *Advertising Age*, January 27, 1992, pp. 4–5.

20. James R. Lowry, "The Life Cycle of Shopping Centers," *Business Horizons*, January–February 1997, pp. 77–86; Eric Peterson, "Power Centers! Now!" *Stores*, March 1989, pp. 61–66; and "Power Centers Flex Their Muscle," *Chain Store Age Executive*, February 1989, pp. 3A, 4A.

21. Ginny Parker, "Vending the Rules," *Time*, May 7, 2001, p. 24.

22. Julie Mitchell, "Electronic Payment Services Move beyond Tollbooths," *Investor's Business Daily*, August 30, 2001, p. 10; and Steve Scrupski, "Tiny 'Brains' Seen for Vending Machines," *Electronic Design*, December 1, 1998, p. 64F.

23. "Joe Namath, Franco Harris, Boomer Esiason, and Tim Brown Appear on Home Shopping Network during Super Bowl Week," PR Newswire, January 23, 2001; "Cover Girls Queen Latifah and Molly Sims Brush Up on Youth Volunteerism," PR Newswire, August 22, 2001; Carole Nicksin, "QVC Opens Up in Mall Space," *HFN*, August 20, 2001, p. 6; and Chris Wynn and Tim Adler, "Battle for UK Home-Shopping Viewers Hots Up as QVC Gets Heavyweight Rival," *New Media Markets*, May 11, 2001.

24. Vito Pilieci, "The IKEA Catalog: It's Bigger than the Bible," *Ottawa Citizen*, August 27, 2003, p. A1.

25. Lee Valley website, www.leevalley.com.

26. Donna Bursey, "Targeting Small Businesses for Telemarketing and Mail Order Sales," *Direct Marketing*, September 1995, pp. 18–20; "Inbound, Outbound Telemarketing Keeps Ryder Sales in Fast Lane," *Direct Marketing*, July 1995, pp. 34–36; "Despite Hangups, Telemarketing a Success," *Marketing News*, March 27, 1995, p. 19; Kelly Shermach, "Outsourcing Seen as a Way to Cut Costs, Retain Service," *Marketing News*, June 19, 1995, pp. 5, 8; and Greg Gattuso, "Marketing Vision," *Direct Marketing*, February 1994, pp. 24–26.

27. Nanette Byrnes, "The New Calling," *Business Week*, September 18, 2000, pp. 137–48.

28. Betsy Verckey, "Avon Products Boosts Restructuring, Freezes Hiring," The Associated Press, Feb. 19, 2009.

29. Mathew Schifrin, "Okay, Big Mouth," *Forbes*, October 9, 1995, pp. 47–48; Veronica Byrd and Wendy Zellner, "The Avon Lady of the Amazon," *Business Week*, October 24, 1994, pp. 93–96; and Ann Marsh "Avon Is Calling on Eastern Europe," *Advertising Age*, June 20, 1994, p. 116.

30. Tavia Grant, "More Canadians Shopping on Net," *The Globe and Mail*, September 28, 2010, accessed at www.theglobeandmail.com/report-on-business/more-canadians-shopping-on-net/article1727434.

31. Bilal Hameed, "Facebook, Twitter Influences up to 28% of Online Buying Decisions," StartupMeme Technology Blog, December 14, 2009, accessed at http://startupmeme.com/facebook-twitter-influences-upto-28-of-online-buying-decisions.

32. Brian Solis, "Facebook and Twitter Users Spend 1.5x More Online than the Average Internet User," @BrianSolis blog, June 25, 2010, accessed at www.briansolis.com/2010/06/e-commerce-report-facebook-and-twitter-users-make-it-rain.

33. "My Virtual Model Inc. Acquires EZsize," PR Newswire, June 21, 2001; Steve Casimiro, "Shop Till You Crash," *Fortune*, December 21, 1998, pp. 267–70; and De' Ann Weimer, "Can I Try (Click) That Blouse (Drag) in Blue?" *Business Week*, November 9, 1998, p. 86.

34. Gary Beerman, "The effect of Web performance on online shopper satisfaction," SmartBear Software blog, May 13, 2010, accessed at http://bx.businessweek.com/online-retail/view?url=http%3A%2F%2Fblog.alertsite.com%2F2010%2F05%2Fthe-effect-of-web-performance-on-online-shopper-satisfaction%2F.

35. "What's so new about the 'New Economy'? Glad you asked," *Business 2.0*, August–September 2001, p. 84.

36. This discussion is based on "By the Numbers: Buying Breakdown," *The Wall Street Journal*, September 24, 2001, p. R4; "Factoids," *Research Alert*, November 17, 2000, p. 4; and Weiss, "Online America."

37. Iain Marlow, "Canadians' Internet Use Exceeds TV Time," *The Globe and Mail*, March 22, 2010, accessed at www.theglobeandmail.com/news/technology/canadians-internet-use-exceeds-tv-time/article1508091.

38. Alexandra Lopez-Pacheco, "Welcome the New Consumer," *Financial Post*, September 21, 2010, accessed at www.financialpost.com/news/technology/Welcome+consumer/3553503/story.html.

39. Naresh Kumar, "Social Media Recommendations May Increase Online Purchases," psfk.com, July 1, 2010, accessed at www.psfk.com/2010/07/social-media-recommendations-may-increase-online-purchases.html.

40. "Global Advertising: Consumers Trust Real Friends and Virtual Strangers the Most," NielsenWire blog, July 7, 2009, accessed at http://blog.nielsen.com/nielsenwire/consumer/global-advertising-consumers-trust-real-friends-and-virtual-strangers-the-most.

41. Jeff Weidauer, "QR codes: Building a mobile loyalty program beyond key tags," Retail Customer Experience.com, April 20, 2010, accessed at www.retailcustomerexperience.com/article/21622/QR-codes-Building-a-mobile-loyalty-program-beyond-key-tags.

42. "Retail's Mobility Imperative: A Measured Approach to the Emerging Channel," *Forbes Insight*, July 2010, accessed at www.forbes.com/forbesinsights/retailmobility/index.html.

43. Tobi Elkin, "Case Study: Sephora Offers Ratings and Reviews via Mobile," *eMarketer*, May 28, 2010, accessed at www.emarketer.com/blog/index.php/case-study-sephora-offers-ratings-reviews-mobile/#more-2854.

44. Ibid.

Chapter 12

1. Personal interview with Mary Lye, director marketing and communications, Childhood Cancer Foundation of Canada, May 2010.

2. *Report to the Community 2005–2007*, Childhood Cancer Foundation—Candlelighters Canada, p. 13.

3. Arianna Huffington, "The Brave New World of the 'New Media,'" *Advertising Week 2010*, January 26, 2010.

4. *2010 Canadian Media Usage Trend Study*, commissioned by the Interactive Advertising Bureau of Canada, March 2011.

5. *Consumerology Report: Technology and the Consumer*, Bensimon Byrne, January 2010, accessed at www.consumerology.ca.

6. Robin Wauters, "Facebook Averaged Almost 8 New Registrations per Second in 2010," *TechCrunch*, February 1, 2011, accessed at http://techcrunch.com/2011/02/01/facebook-averaged-almost-8-new-registrations-per-second-in-2010.

7. Nick Krewen, "Social Media More Than Just a Fad: Studies," *Media in Canada*, December 16, 2009, accessed at www.mediaincanada.com/articles/mic/20091216/socialmediastudies.html.

8. Press release, "AOL Agrees to Acquire The Huffington Post," AOL and *The Huffington Post*, accessed at www.huffingtonpost.com/2011/02/07/aol-huffington-post_n_819375.html.

9. Adapted with permission from the MktgCliks blog at http://MktgCliks.blogspot.com; campaign credits for Share Our Billboard go to James Ready Brewing Company and Leo Burnett Canada as follows: James Ready Brewing Company: Matt Johnston, director, North American Markets; Chris Waldock, brand manager. Leo Burnett Canada: Judy John, SVP, chief creative officer; David Buckspan, group account director; Natasha Dagenais, account director; Sean Barlow / Paul Giannetta, creative directors; Shirley Ward-Taggart, digital creative director; Steve Persico, copywriter; Anthony Chelvanathan, art director; Ross Butcher, digital art director; Emily Zamir, digital copywriter; STARCOM MEDIAVEST GROUP, media planning and buying; "James Ready Wins Gold at Cannes," MktgCliks Blog, June 4, 2009, accessed at http://mktgcliks.blogspot.com/2009/06/james-ready-wins-gold-at-cannes.html; "James Ready Wins Friends and Share," 2010 Cassie Winners, accessed at http://cassies.ca/winners/2010Winners/winners_jamesReady.html; David Brown, "Leo Burnett And James Ready Win Gold At One Show," Marketingmag.ca, May 13, 2011, accessed at www.marketingmag.ca/news/awards/leo-burnett-and-james-ready-win-gold-at-one-show-27380; Drew Wehrle, "James Ready Beer—Billboard Coupon," Leo Burnett blog, April 30, 2010, accessed at www.blog.leoburnett.com/index.php/2010/04/30/james-ready-beer-billboard-coupon.

10. News release, "Competition Bureau Takes Action Against Rogers Over Misleading Advertising," Competition Bureau, November 19, 2010, accessed at www.competitionbureau.gc.ca/eic/site/cb-bc.nsf/eng/03316.html; Sharon Oosthoek, "Rogers faces $10M fine over dropped-call ads," CBC News, November 19, 2010, accessed at www.cbc.ca/news/technology/story/2010/11/19/consumer-chatr-rogers-competition-bureau.html; Canadian Press, "Rogers faces $10 million penalty on ads," *Toronto Star*, November 19, 2010, accessed at www.thestar.com/business/companies/rogers/article/893883--rogers-faces-10-million-penalty-on-ads.

11. Brew Some Good website, http://brewsomegood.ca; David

Ogilvy Awards, "Beverages Gold Winner Kraft Canada Maxwell House 'Brew Some Good,'" *Advertising Research Foundation*, accessed at https://thearf-org-aux-assets.s3.amazonaws.com/ogilvy/cs2010/Maxwell%20House_Case%20Study.pdf; Emily Wexler, "Maxwell House Brews Some Good," *Strategy*, May 1, 2010, accessed at www.strategyonline.ca/articles/magazine/20100501/causemaxwell.html.

12. *Maclean's* 2011 advertising rates, accessed at www.rogersconnect.com/files/Macleans_MediaKit.pdf.

13. Stephanie Startz, "Webisodes Offer Brands Like Ikea, Sara Lee And Maybelline A New Outlet," *Brandchannel*, November 25, 2009, accessed at www.brandchannel.com/home/post/2009/11/25/Webisodes-Offer-Brands-Like-Ikea-Sara-Lee-And-Maybelline-A-New-Outlet.aspx.

14. *Canadian Media Directors' Council Media Digest 10/11*, *Marketing* magazine, accessed at www.cmdc.ca/pdf/MediaDigest_1010.pdf.

15. Ibid.

16. *PMB 2011 Fall Topline Report*, Print Measurement Bureau, accessed at www.pmb.ca.

17. *Canadian Media Directors' Council Media Digest 10/11*.

18. Adapted from *American Marketing Association Marketing Power Resource Library Dictionary*, February 19, 2010, accessed at www.marketingpower.com/_layouts/Dictionary.aspx?dLetter=P.

19. Sarah Schmidt, "CFIA allows non-accredited labs to do some listeria work," *National Post*, April 29, 2009, accessed at www.nationalpost.com/CFIA+allows+accredited+labs+some+listeria+work/1547167/story.html; news release, "Maple Leaf Foods Media Statement," CNW Group, March 4, 2009, accessed at www.newswire.ca/en/releases/archive/March2009/04/c5969.html; news release "Maple Leaf Listeriosis Settlement Headed to Courts for Approval," CNW Group, February 2, 2009, accessed at www.newswire.ca/en/releases/archive/March2009/04/c5969.html; "CFIA still moving on Listeria recommendations," CBC News, October 24, 2010, accessed at www.cbc.ca/health/story/2010/10/22/con-listeria-report.html; "Maple Leaf settles class action listeriosis lawsuits for $27M," December 18, 2008, CBC News, accessed at www.cbc.ca/canada/story/2008/12/18/listeriosis-settlement.html#ixzz1EQB5fskP.

20. Adapted with permission from the MktgCliks blog at http://mktgCliks.blogspot.com. Campaign credits go to Tourism Queensland and CumminsNitro agency as follows: Tourism Queensland, Best Job In The World: Tourism Queensland, Advertiser; Islands Of The Great Barrier Reef, Product. Agency: CumminsNitro, Brisbane, Australia, 2009: Merrin Mccormick, copywriter; Ralph Barnett / Cristian Staal / Adam Ford, art directors; Darren Mccoll, national strategy / planning director; Anne-Maree Wilson / Edwina Gilmour, account directors; Nancy Hartley / James Burchill, creative directors; Jason Kibsgaard / Matt Farrugia, senior digital producers, Horia Traian, head of technology; Glen Peterson / Anton Ward, senior developers. Best Job in the World Award entry website, February 21, 2010, accessed at www.ourawardentry.com.au/bestjob/index.html; "Best Job in the World Wins Big and Cannes," MktgCliks blog, June 23, 2009, accessed at http://mktgcliks.blogspot.com/2009/06/best-job-in-world-wins-big-at-cannes.html.

21. Tim Hortons ROLL UP THE RIM TO WIN®CONTEST—2011, accessed at www.rolluptherimtowin.com/en/rules.php and www.rolluptherimtowin.com/pdf/2011_Rules-Regulations_RUTR_EN_.pdf; Chris Powell, "The Roll Up The Rim Marketing Phenomenon," *Marketing* magazine, February 25, 2011, accessed at www.marketingmag.ca/news/marketer-news/the-roll-up-the-rim-marketing-phenomenon-23355.

22. "Retail at the Rogers Cup," *The Sponsorship Report*, September 2009 (The Sponsorship Marketing Council of Canada).

23. "Labour force survey estimates (LFS), by full- and part-time students during school months, sex and age group, annual," Statistics Canada, Table 282-0095, May 2003.

24. Personal interview with Livia Grulich, co-founder and managing director On-Q Communications, and Gene Swinton, national marketing manager Baskin-Robbins.

25. Adapted from the Word of Mouth Marketing Association, "WOM—COMM 101," accessed at http://womma.org/wom101.

26. Reuters, "Online advertising business Groupon's IPO expected to sell at US$31.59 a share," *National Post*, January 3, 2011, accessed at www.nationalpost.com/todays-paper/Online+advertising+busine ss+Groupon+expected+sell+share/4051382/story.html; *NBC Today Show*, aired December 4, 2009, accessed at www.youtube.com/watch?v=54WKCfjLinU; Michael Hickins "The Groupon Frodo Memo," *Wall Street Journal* blog, February 25, 2011, accessed at http://blogs.wsj.com/digits/2011/02/25/the-groupon-frodo-memo; Groupon website, accessed February 26, 2011, at www.groupon.com/learn.

Chapter 13

1. Kotler et al., *Principles of Marketing*, 7th Canadian edition (Toronto: Pearson, 2008).

2. Bob Thompson, "Customer Experience Management: The Value of 'Moments of Truth,'" CRMGuru.com, May 2006, accessed at http://aaabrandcentral.com/pdfs/communications/customer-experience/customer-experienceCEM_CRMGuru_Pt_1.pdf?PHP SESSID=ac71ec743ee651de8a16b90c63fa5d64.

3. Michael Hinshaw, "Customer Satisfaction is Not Enough - Why High Satisfaction Scores May Actually Spell Danger for Your Brand," *Brandchannel*, November 19, 2010. Accessed at www.brandchannel.com/brand_speak.asp?bs_id=259&utm_source=feedburner&utm_medium=feed&utm_campaign=Feed%3 A+Brandchannel+%28brandchannel.com%29.

4. Barbara Talbot, "The Power of Personal Service," The Centre for Hospitality Research, Cornell University, September 2006, accessed at www.fourseasons.com/cgi-bin/pdf-we.exe//pdfs/about_us/service_culture/PersonalService.pdf.

5. "Why Some Companies Succeed at CRM (and Many Fail)," Knowledge@Wharton, January 15, 2003, accessed at http://knowledge.wharton.upenn.edu/article.cfm?articleid=699.

6. The Ultimate CRM Guide.com website, www.ultimatecrmguide.com/crm-strategy/culture.

7. Eric Beauchesne, "Customers Want Friendly Service Most," *Star Phoenix*, June 20, 2008.

8. Rachel King, "How Companies Use Twitter to Bolster Their Brands," *Bloomberg Business Week*, September 6, 2008, accessed at www.businessweek.com/technology/content/sep2008/tc2008095_320491.htm.

9. Colin Campbell, "Tuning into Twitter," *Maclean's*, October 7, 2010, accessed at www2.macleans.ca/2010/10/07/tuning-in-to-twitter.

10. Carmi Levy, "Airlines use Twitter, other social tools to revolutionize customer service," *Toronto Star*, October 10, 2010, accessed at www.thestar.com/business/companies/porter/article/871979--airlines-use-twitter-other-social-tools-to-revolutionize-customer-service.

11. Ravi Sawhney, "Broken Guitar Has United Playing the Blues to the Tune of $180 Million," *Fast Company*, July 28, 2009, accessed at www.fastcompany.com/blog/ravi-sawhney/design-reach/youtube-serves-180-million-heartbreak.

12. Keith Barry, "Ford Bets the Fiesta on Social Networking," *Wired*, April 17, 2009, accessed at www.wired.com/autopia/2009/04/how-the-fiesta/all/1.

13. R. Buchanan and C. Gillies, "Value Managed Relationship: The Key to Customer Retention and Profitability," *European Management Journal*, Vol. 8, No. 4, 1990.

14. Lindsay Blakely, "Lounging in Style," *Business 2.0*, August 2007, p. 92.

15. "Hotels Encourage Loyalty with Perks," *National Post*, April 10, 2008, p.1, s5

16. Starwoods Hotel website, accessed at http://auction.starwoodhotels.com/cgi-bin/ncommerce3/ProductDisplay?prrfnbr=13884647 6&prmenbr=67280009&aunbr=139193186&topcat=Y.

17. "HMV Rewards Top Cool Category," *The Globe and Mail*, November 24, 2010, p. RR3.

18. Hokey Min, "Developing the Profile of Supermarket Customers through Data Mining," *Service Industries Journal*, October 2006.

19. Nicholas Ciarelli, "How MasterCard Predicts Divorce," *The Daily Beast*, April 6, 2010, accessed at www.thedailybeast.com/blogs-and-stories/2010-04-06/how-mastercard-predicts-divorce.

20. Peter Hadekel, "Loyalty Programs Start to Pay Off for Grocer Metro," *The Gazette*, November 24, 2010, accessed at www.montrealgazette.com/columnists/Loyalty+program+starts+grocer+Met ro/3875329/story.html.

21. Hollie Shaw, "Battle for grocery shoppers heats up; Sobeys has you in its sights with new strategy," *Calgary Herald*, July 23, 2010, p. E6; Matthew Boyle, "Best Buy's Giant Gamble," *Fortune*, March 29, 2006, accessed at http://money.cnn.com/magazines/fortune/fortune_archive/2006/04/03/8373034/index.htm.

22. Carl Sewell and Paul Brown, *Customers For Life*, Doubleday Publishing, 2002.

23. Knowledge @Wharton website, www.knowledge.wharton.upenn.edu.

24. Matt Rhodes, "Extending the Customer Experience - the Zappos Story," *FutureLab*, April 12, 2009, accessed at www.futurelab.net/blogs/marketing-strategy-innovation/2009/04/extending_the_customer_experie.html; Lidija Davis, "Zappos CEO Talks Culture Fit and the Importance of Creating a 'Wow' Experience," *Read Write Web*, February 8, 2009, accessed at www.readwriteweb.com/archives/zappos_ceo_talks_culture_fit_a.php; Christopher Palmeri, "Zappos Retails Its Culture," *Bloomberg Business Week*, December 30, 2009, accessed at www.businessweek.com/magazine/content/10_02/b4162057120453.htm.

25. Tom Duncan, *Principles of Advertising + IMC*, 2nd Edition (New York: McGraw-Hill/Irwin, 2005), p. 266.

Chapter 14

1. www.ourhospital.ca/Our_Hospital_LogoBrand.cfm.

2. Roger A. Kerin, Vijay Mahajan, and P. Rajan Varadarajan, *Contemporary Perspectives on Strategic Marketing Planning* (Boston: Allyn & Bacon, 1990), chap. 1; and Orville C. Walker, Jr., Harper W. Boyd, Jr., and Jean-Claude Larreche, *Marketing Strategy* (Burr Ridge, IL: Richard D. Irwin, 1992), chaps. 1 and 2.

3. Theodore Levitt, "Marketing Myopia," *Harvard Business Review*, July - August 1960, pp. 45–56.

4. Marina Strauss, "Why Loblaw takes top honours for corporate social responsibility," *The Globe and Mail*, June 21, 2010, accessed at www.theglobeandmail.com/report-on-business/managing/report-on-corporate-responsibil/why-loblaw-takes-top-honours-for-corporate-social-responsibility/article1605337; Richard Blackwell, "The double-edged sword of corporate altruism," *The Globe and Mail*, November 10, 2008, accessed at http://v1.theglobeandmail.com/servlet/story/RTGAM.20081110.wrbgcsr10/BNStory/boardgames2008/home.

5. Tilley Endurables website, accessed at www.tilley.com/home.asp.

6. George Stalk, Phillip Evans, and Lawrence E. Shulman, "Competing on Capabilities. The New Rules of Corporate Strategy," *Harvard Business Review*, March–April 1992, pp. 57–69.

7. Tilley Endurables website, accessed at www.tilley.com/home.asp.

8. Adapted from "The Experience Curve Reviewed, IV. The Growth Share Matrix of the Product Portfolio" (Boston: The Boston Consulting Group, 1973).

9. Kerin, Mahajan, and Vardarajan, *Contemporary Perspectives*, p. 52.

10. Alexandra Topping "HMV reinvents itself to survive declining market," Guardian News & Media Ltd., October 26, 2010, accessed at http://gulfnews.com/business/retail/hmv-reinvents-itself-to-survive-declining-market-1.701596; Geoffrey Macnab, "HMV, Curzon Artificial Eye to create in-store cinema venues," *Screen Daily*, April 26, 2009, accessed at www.screendaily.com/news/corporate/hmv-curzon-artificial-eye-to-create-in-store-cinema-venues/5000273.article; Andrew Moran, "British retail specialist acquires HMV Canada for $3.23 million," *Digital Journal*, June 27, 2011, accessed at http://digitaljournal.com/article/308444.

Credits

Chapter 7

pp. 140–141: James Jagger/getstock.com

p. 144: With permission of the Royal Ontario Museum, © 2011

p. 146: Martin Lee/Alamy/getstock.com

p. 147: Used with permission from GAP

p. 148: Used with permission from PepsiCo Beverages Canada

p. 150 (top): BlackBerry®, RIM®, Research In Motion®, SureType®, SurePress™ and related trademarks, names and logos are the property of Research In Motion Limited and are registered and/or used in the U.S. and countries around the world.

p. 150 (bottom): BlackBerry®, RIM®, Research In Motion®, SureType®, SurePress™ and related trademarks, names and logos are the property of Research In Motion Limited and are registered and/or used in the U.S. and countries around the world.

p. 151: Norman Price/GetStock.com

p. 153: Courtesy of Procter & Gamble

p. 154: © The McGraw-Hill Companies, Inc./ Jill Braaten, photographer

p. 155: © BMO Financial Group

p. 156: © Tracy Leonard

p. 157: © 2008 Shoppers Drug Mart Inc. Shoppers Drug Mart and Life Brand are trade-marks of 911979 Alberta Ltd., used under license.

p. 159: Photo courtesy of Loblaw Companies Limited

p. 160: © Yield Branding

Chapter 8

pp. 164–165: Photo courtesy of Loblaw Companies Limited

p. 168: © Amazon.com

p. 170: Used with permission of Jumo

p. 172: © Ken Reid/Getty Images

p. 174: Photo taken on behalf of McGraw-Hill Ryerson

p. 175: Courtesy of Samba Days

p. 176: Used by permission of Unilever Canada Inc.

p. 177 (left): Ian Dagnall/getstock.com

p. 177 (right): Photo taken on behalf of McGraw-Hill Ryerson

p. 178: The Canadian Press/Mark Lennihan/ AP Photo

p. 180: Getty Images

p. 181: Photo courtesy of Wikipedia.org

p. 182: Courtesy of Hewlett-Packard Company

p. 185: Jose Azel/Aurora

p. 186 (top): Royalty-Free/CORBIS

p. 186 (bottom): Toronto Star/GetStock.com

Chapter 9

pp. 188–189: Used with permission from Tina Powell

p. 191: Hans Dieter Seufert/GetStock.com

p. 193: © The McGraw-Hill Companies, Inc./ Jill Braaten, photographer

p. 194: © Reuters 2001

p. 195: © Anykeen/Dreamstime.com/get-stock.com

p. 196: © AFP/Getty Images

p. 197: © Chuck Savage/CORBIS

p. 198: Getty Images

p. 199 (top): © Time & Life Pictures/Getty Images

p. 199 (bottom): © Tracy Leonard

p. 200: © M. Hruby

p. 205: The Canadian Press/Francis Vachon

p. 206: The Canadian Press/Nathan Denette

p. 208: Archives du 7eme Art/Alamy/get-stock.com

p. 209: Reprinted with permission from Advertising Standards Canada

p. 210: © Tracy Leonard

p. 211: Courtesy of The Toro Company

Chapter 10

pp. 214–215: Used with permission of Matthew Corrin

p. 218: © The McGraw-Hill Companies, Inc./ Jill Braaten, photographer

p. 221: © Helen Sessions/Alamy/getstock.com

p. 222: © McGraw-Hill Ryerson

p. 223: Courtesy of the Gillette Company

p. 224 (left): The Canadian Press/Steve White

p. 224 (right): © Tracy Leonard

p. 226: © Tracy Leonard

p. 228: © Tracy Leonard

p. 229: © John Lee/Aurora Photos/getstock.com

p. 232: © Rex Features [2005] all rights reserved/The Canadian Press

p. 233 (top): © The McGraw-Hill Companies, Inc./Jill Braaten, photographer

p. 233 (bottom): AP Images/Morry Gash

p. 234: © Baloncici/Dreamstime.com/Get-Stock.com

p. 235: © David Frazier/Corbis

p. 236: Used with permission from Sobeys

Chapter 11

p. 238 (inset): Used with permission from Ron White Shoes

pp. 238–239: Used with permission from Ron White Shoes

p. 244: © Tracy Leonard

p. 245: The Canadian Press/Eugene Hoshiko/ AP Photo

p. 247: Used with permission from Harry Rosen Inc.

p. 248: © McGraw-Hill Ryerson

p. 249: © Helen Sessions/Alamy/getstock.com

p. 250 (top): Used with permission from Indigo

p. 250 (bottom): Copyright (c) 2011 Antonio Vernon/Wikipedia

p. 252: © Tracy Leonard

p. 253: Courtesy of Marconi Commerce Systems

p. 254 (top): © Tracy Leonard

p. 254 (bottom): Used with permission from Lee Valley Tools Ltd.

p. 255 (left): Used by permission of Wal-Mart Stores, Inc.

p. 255 (right): Used by permission of eBay Inc.

p. 257 (top): © itravel2000.com

p. 257 (bottom): © Alex Segre/Alamy/get-stock.com

p. 259: Jeremy Stone/Getty Images

p. 260: © Digital Vision/Punchstock

Chapter 12

pp. 262–263: Used with permission of Childhood Cancer Foundation Canada

p. 266 (top left): Bloomberg via Getty Images

p. 267 (top): Courtesy of The Globe and Mail Inc.

p. 267 (bottom): The Twitter name, logo, Twitter T, Tweet, and Twitter blue bird are trademarks of Twitter, Inc.

p. 269: Used by permission of Moosehead Breweries Limited

p. 270: © Tracy Leonard

p. 271: Reprinted with permission from Advertising Standards Canada

p. 272: Alisonh29/Dreamstime.com/getstock.com

p. 273 (top): © KRAFT

p. 273 (bottom left): © KRAFT

p. 273 (bottom right): © KRAFT

p. 274: macleans.ca is owned by and used with permission of Rogers Publishing Limited. All Rights Reserved.

p. 277: © Tracy Leonard

p. 278: Jean Heguy/Getty Images

p. 279: Zoom Media, Classic Display, Evian Campaign

p. 280: Panoramic Images/Getty Images

p. 282: The Canadian Press Images/Charles-Antoine Auger

p. 283: © Darren Hick

p. 284 (top): © Tracy Leonard

p. 284 (bottom): Used with permission of Baskin-Robbins

p. 285 (top): © Rob Melnychuk/Getty Images

p. 285 (bottom): Used with permission of Baskin Robbins

p. 287: Courtesy Groupon, Inc.

p. 288: Used with permission of Childhood Cancer Foundation Canada

p. 293: Courtesy of Canada Dry Mott's Inc.

Chapter 13

pp. 296–297: Used with permission of Four Seasons Hotels

p. 299 (top left): © Digital Vision/Punchstock

p. 299 (right): Amazon, Amazon.com and the Amazon.com logo are registered trademarks of Amazon.com, Inc. or its affiliates.

p. 300: Bloomberg via Getty Images

p. 301: © Sean Locke/istockphoto.com

p. 302 (top): Used with permission from Porter Airlines Inc.

p. 302 (bottom): The Twitter name, logo, Twitter T, Tweet, and Twitter blue bird are trademarks of Twitter, Inc.

p. 303 (top): Used with permission from Dave Carroll

p. 303 (bottom): The Canadian Press/Carlos Osorio

p. 304: C Squared Studios/Getty Images

p. 305: © Tracy Leonard

p. 306 (top): Redferns/Getty Images

p. 306 (bottom): © Tracy Leonard

p. 307: Jonathon Evans/Getty Images

p. 308: Used with permission from Random House

p. 309: Jared McMillen/getstock.com

p. 310: Used by permission of Unilever Canada Inc.

Chapter 14

pp. 312–313: © Jackie McLauchlin and Paul Heinrich

p. 316: Courtesy of Ben & Jerry's Homemade, Inc.

p. 317: Photo courtesy of Loblaw Companies Limited

p. 318: Courtesy of Oracle Corporation

p. 319: © Tilley Endurables

p. 321: Used with permission from HMV

p. 322 (bottom left): Used with permission of Scholastic Canada Ltd.

p. 322 (bottom right): Used with permission of Scholastic Canada Ltd.

p. 324: Courtesy of Ben & Jerry's Homemade, Inc.

Name Index

Company/Product Index

Subject Index